READINGS IN
AMERICAN
POLITICS

READINGS IN AMERICAN POLITICS

Analysis and Perspectives

Ken Kollman

UNIVERSITY OF MICHIGAN

W. W. Norton & Company ■ New York ■ London

W. W. Norton & Company has been independent since its founding in 1923, when William Warder Norton and Mary D. Herter Norton first published lectures delivered at the People's Institute, the adult education division of New York City's Cooper Union. The firm soon expanded its program beyond the Institute, publishing books by celebrated academics from America and abroad. By mid-century, the two major pillars of Norton's publishing program—trade books and college texts—were firmly established. In the 1950s, the Norton family transferred control of the company to its employees, and today—with a staff of four hundred and a comparable number of trade, college, and professional titles published each year—W. W. Norton & Company stands as the largest and oldest publishing house owned wholly by its employees.

Editor: Ann Shin
Editorial assistant: Jake Schindel
Production manager: Christine D'Antonio
Project supervised by Westchester Book Group/Debbie Masi
Composition by Westchester Book Group
Manufacturing by Courier Companies—Westford

Library of Congress Cataloging-in-Publication Data

Kollman, Ken, 1966–
Readings in American politics : analysis and perspectives / Ken Kollman.—1st ed.
p. cm.
Includes bibliographical references.
ISBN 978-0-393-93508-0 (pbk.)
1. United States—Politics and government. I. Title.
JK21.K65 2010
320.473—dc22

2009054276

W. W. Norton & Company, Inc., 500 Fifth Avenue, New York, N.Y. 10110-0017

www.wwnorton.com

W. W. Norton & Company Ltd., Castle House, 75/76 Wells Street, London W1T 3QT

1 2 3 4 5 6 7 8 9 0

CONTENTS

17 FOREIGN POLICY

PREFACE

This reader makes some of the most important work in political science and the subfield of American politics easily accessible to students in introductory courses.

The selections included here have been chosen to help accomplish several things in a college classroom: introduce students to fundamental concepts in political science and the study of American politics, such as collective action problems, agenda-setting power, ideologies, and the median voter; provide specific insights into the workings of the major institutions and processes of American government; spur discussion on controversial topics, such as affirmative action, gay rights, abortion, and contemporary American foreign policy; and improve students' abilities to digest official government documents like Supreme Court cases and presidential signing statements.

The first chapter, "Fundamentals," introduces students to three crucial problems for understanding politics:

1. *collective action problems* among groups of people and how organizers and leaders of institutions can try to overcome such problems
2. *common resource problems,* which are variants of the standard collective action problem but refer specifically to allocating scarce resources
3. *delegation (or principal-agent) problems* that are ubiquitous in modern, democratic government and that require contract-like arrangements to solve

The material in Chapter 1 is a good foundation for students approaching the rest of the readings. Students reading the classic selections can approach them fresh with knowledge of the "problems." One can read Madison's *Federalist* 10, for instance, with an eye toward common resource problems. Madison was concerned that an overpowering majority interest would oppress other groups, and he favored having many different groups represented in a single government. It is worth discussing the question: Was Madison naïve about collective action problems inherent when many groups compete for common resources? The selection from Jenna Bednar in Chapter 3 offers insights into Madison's views on federalism and specifically about how the state governments might provide the checks needed to prevent an over-reaching national government.

Many of the contemporary selections also have one or more of the "problems" from Chapter 1 as backdrop. To take an example from Chapter 5 on Congress, the delegation problem is at the root of the arguments by Cox and McCubbins on how (and why) partisan majorities grant agenda control to party leaders in Congress. And Strolovitch's arguments in Chapter 11 focus attention on the ways leaders of political advocacy groups must appeal to specific types of activists in order to sustain collective action. Students benefit greatly from seeing these theoretical threads in contemporary political science scholarship.

Quite a few of the readings provide grist for lively discussion of current events and policy controversies. Students will gain knowledge of legal arguments about gay marriage and abortion, and will confront arguments about the sustainability of recent trends in American foreign policy.

I use these readings when I teach. I hope you find these readings as useful as I do in understanding politics, and specifically the American political system.

Three people were very helpful to me in assembling this reader. Special thanks to Erin Ackerman, Jake Schindel, and Ann Shin for making it possible for me to pull it all together.

KEN KOLLMAN

ABOUT THE EDITOR

KEN KOLLMAN is professor in the Department of Political Science and research professor in the Center for Political Studies in the Institute for Social Research at the University of Michigan, Ann Arbor. His research and teaching focus on political parties, elections, lobbying, and federal systems. He also regularly teaches the introductory American politics course at the University of Michigan. In addition to numerous articles, he has written *The Formation of National Party Systems: Federalism and Party Competition in Canada, Great Britain, India, and the United States* (with Pradeep Chhibber, 2004) and *Outside Lobbying: Public Opinion and Interest Group Strategies* (1998). Professor Kollman is currently at work on a book on centralization in federated systems and a new American government textbook to be published by W. W. Norton.

1

FUNDAMENTALS

1.1

MANCUR OLSON, JR.

From *The Logic of Collective Action: Public Goods and the Theory of Groups*

Olson introduces us to the concept of the collective action problem. This "problem" arises when individuals have incentives to free-ride off the contributions of others, reaping the benefits of some action without paying any of the costs. In describing the collective action problem and how groups or organizations can overcome it, Olson strongly challenges the widely held notion that having common interests is a sufficient condition for a political group to form.

I. A THEORY OF GROUPS AND ORGANIZATIONS

A. The Purpose of Organization

Since most (though by no means all) of the action taken by or on behalf of groups of individuals is taken through organizations, it will be helpful to consider organizations in a general or theoretical way.[1] The logical place to begin any systematic study of organizations is with their purpose. But there are all types and shapes and sizes of organizations, even of economic organizations, and there is then some question whether there is any single purpose that would be characteristic of organizations generally. One purpose that is nonetheless characteristic of most organizations, and surely of practically all organizations with an important economic aspect, is the furtherance of the interests of their members. That would seem obvious, at least from the economist's perspective. To be sure, some organizations may out of ignorance fail to further their

1

members' interests, and others may be enticed into serving only the ends of the leadership.[2] But organizations often perish if they do nothing to further the interests of their members, and this factor must severely limit the number of organizations that fail to serve their members.

The idea that organizations or associations exist to further the interests of their members is hardly novel, nor peculiar to economics; it goes back at least to Aristotle, who wrote, "Men journey together with a view to particular advantage, and by way of providing some particular thing needed for the purposes of life, and similarly the political association seems to have come together originally, and to continue in existence, for the sake of the *general* advantages it brings."[3] More recently Professor Leon Festinger, a social psychologist, pointed out that "the attraction of group membership is not so much in sheer belonging, but rather in attaining something by means of this membership."[4] The late Harold Laski, a political scientist, took it for granted that "associations exist to fulfill purposes which a group of men have in common."[5]

The kinds of organizations that are the focus of this study are *expected* to further the interests of their members.[6] Labor unions are expected to strive for higher wages and better working conditions for their members; farm organizations are expected to strive for favorable legislation for their members; cartels are expected to strive for higher prices for participating firms; the corporation is expected to further the interests of its stockholders;[7] and the state is expected to further the common interests of its citizens (though in this nationalistic age the state often has interests and ambitions apart from those of its citizens).

Notice that the interests that all of these diverse types of organizations are expected to further are for the most part *common* interests: the union members' common interest in higher wages, the farmers' common interest in favorable legislation, the cartel members' common interest in higher prices, the stockholders' common interest in higher dividends and stock prices, the citizens' common interest in good government. It is not an accident that the diverse types of organizations listed are all supposed to work primarily for the *common* interests of their members. Purely personal or individual interests can be advanced, and usually advanced most efficiently, by individual, unorganized action. There is obviously no purpose in having an organization when individual, unorganized action can serve the interests of the individual as well as or better than an organization; there would, for example, be no point in forming an organization simply to play solitaire. But when a number of individuals have a common or collective interest—when they share a single purpose or objective—individual, unorganized action (as we shall soon see) will either not be able to advance that common interest at all, or will not be able to advance that interest adequately. Organizations can therefore perform a function when there are common or group interests, and though organizations often also serve purely personal, individual interests, their characteristic and primary function is to advance the common interests of groups of individuals.

The assumption that organizations typically exist to further the common interests of groups of people is implicit in most of the literature about organizations, and two of the writers already cited make this assumption explicit: Harold Laski emphasized that organizations exist to achieve purposes or interests which "a group of men have in common," and Aristotle apparently had a similar notion in mind when he argued that political associations are created and maintained because of the "general advantages" they bring. R. M. MacIver also made this point explicitly when he said that "every organization presupposes an interest which its members all share."[8]

Even when unorganized groups are discussed, at least in treatments of "pressure groups" and "group theory," the word "group" is used in such a way that it means "a number of individuals with a common interest." It would of course be reasonable to label even a number of people selected at random (and thus without any common interest or unifying characteristic) as a "group"; but most discussions of group behavior seem to deal mainly with groups that do have common interests. As Arthur Bentley, the founder of the "group theory" of modern political science, put it, "there is no group without its interest."[9] The social psychologist Raymond Cattell was equally explicit, and stated that "every group has its interest."[10] This is also the way the word "group" will be used here.

Just as those who belong to an organization or a group can be presumed to have a common interest,[11] so they obviously also have purely individual interests, different from those of the others in the organization or group. All of the members of a labor union, for example, have a common interest in higher wages, but at the same time each worker has a unique interest in his personal income, which depends not only on the rate of wages but also on the length of time that he works.

B. Public Goods and Large Groups

The combination of individual interests and common interests in an organization suggests an analogy with a competitive market. The firms in a perfectly competitive industry, for example, have a common interest in a higher price for the industry's product. Since a uniform price must prevail in such a market, a firm cannot expect a higher price for itself unless all of the other firms in the industry also have this higher price. But a firm in a competitive market also has an interest in selling as much as it can, until the cost of producing another unit exceeds the price of that unit. In this there is no common interest; each firm's interest is directly opposed to that of every other firm, for the more other firms sell, the lower the price and income for any given firm. In short, while all firms have a common interest in a higher price, they have antagonistic interests where output is concerned. This can be illustrated with a simple supply-and-demand model. For the sake of a simple argument, assume that a perfectly competitive industry is momentarily in a disequilibrium position, with price exceeding marginal cost for all firms at their present output. Suppose, too, that all of the adjustments will be made by the firms already in the industry rather than by new entrants, and that the industry is on an inelastic portion of its demand curve. Since price exceeds marginal cost for all firms, output will increase. But as all firms increase production, the price falls; indeed, since the industry demand curve is by assumption inelastic, the total revenue of the industry will decline. Apparently each firm finds that with price exceeding marginal cost, it pays to increase its output, but the result is that each firm gets a smaller profit. Some economists in an earlier day may have questioned this result,[12] but the fact that profit-maximizing firms in a perfectly competitive industry can act contrary to their interests as a group is now widely understood and accepted.[13] A group of profit-maximizing firms can act to reduce their aggregate profits because in perfect competition each firm is, by definition, so small that it can ignore the effect of its output on price. Each firm finds it to its advantage to increase output to the point where marginal cost equals price and to ignore the effects of its extra output on the position of the industry. It is true that the net result is that all firms are worse off, but this does not mean that every firm has not maximized its profits. If a firm, foreseeing the fall in price resulting from the increase in industry output, were to restrict its own output, it would lose more than ever, for its price would fall quite as much in any case and it would have a smaller output as well. A firm in a perfectly competitive market gets only a small part of the benefit (of a small share of the industry's extra revenue) resulting from a reduction in that firm's output.

For these reasons it is now generally understood that if the firms in an industry are maximizing profits, the profits for the industry as a whole will be less than they might otherwise be.[14] And almost everyone would agree that this theoretical conclusion fits the facts for markets characterized by pure competition. The important point is that this is true because, though all the firms have a common interest in a higher price for the industry's product, it is in the interest of each firm that the other firms pay the cost—in terms of the necessary reduction in output—needed to obtain a higher price.

About the only thing that keeps prices from falling in accordance with the process just described in perfectly competitive markets is outside intervention. Government price supports, tariffs, cartel agreements, and the like may keep the firms in a competitive market from acting contrary to their interests. Such aid or intervention is quite common. It is then important to ask how it comes about. How does a competitive industry obtain government assistance in maintaining the price of its product?

Consider a hypothetical, competitive industry, and suppose that most of the producers in that industry desire a tariff, a price-support program, or some other government intervention to increase the price for their product. To obtain any such assistance from the government the producers in this industry will presumably have to organize a lobbying organization; they will have to become an active pressure group.[15] This lobbying organization may have to conduct a considerable campaign. If significant resistance is encountered, a great amount of money will be required.[16] Public relations experts will be needed to influence the newspapers, and some advertising may be necessary. Professional organizers will probably be needed to organize "spontaneous grass roots" meetings among the distressed producers in the industry, and to get those in the industry to write letters to their congressmen.[17] The campaign for the government assistance will take the time of some of the producers in the industry, as well as their money.

There is a striking parallel between the problem the perfectly competitive industry faces as it strives to obtain government assistance, and the problem it faces in the marketplace when the firms increase output and bring about a fall in price. *Just as it was not rational for a particular producer to restrict his output in order that there might be a higher price for the product of his industry, so it would not be rational for him to sacrifice his time and money to support a lobbying organization to obtain government assistance for the industry. In neither case would it be in the interest of the individual producer to assume any of the costs himself. A lobbying organization, or indeed a labor union or any other organization, working in the interest of a large group of firms or workers in some industry, would get no assistance from the rational, self-interested individuals in that industry.* This would be true even if everyone in the industry were absolutely convinced that the proposed program was in their interest (though in fact some might think otherwise and make the organization's task yet more difficult).[18]

Although the lobbying organization is only one example of the logical analogy between the organization and the market, it is of some practical importance. There are many powerful and well-financed lobbies with mass support in existence now, but these lobbying organizations do not get that support because of their legislative achievements. The most powerful lobbying organizations now obtain their funds and their following for other reasons.

Some critics may argue that the rational person will, indeed support a large organization, like a lobbying organization, that works in his interest, because he knows that if he does not, others will not do so either, and then the organization will fail, and he will be without the benefit that the organization could have provided. This argument shows the need for the analogy with the perfectly competitive market. For it would be quite as reasonable to argue that prices will never fall below the levels a monopoly would have charged in a perfectly competitive market, because if one firm increased its output, other firms would also, and the price would fall; but each firm could foresee this, so it would not start a chain of price-destroying increases in output. In fact, it does not work out this way in a competitive market; nor in a large organization. When the number of firms involved is large, no one will notice the effect on price if one firm increases its output, and so no one will change his plans because of it. Similarly, in a large organization, the loss of one dues payer will not noticeably increase the burden for any other one dues payer, and so a rational person would not believe that if he were to withdraw from an organization he would drive others to do so.

The foregoing argument must at the least have some relevance to economic organizations that are mainly means through which individuals attempt to obtain the same things they obtain through their activities in the market. Labor unions, for example, are organizations through which workers strive to get the same things they get with their individual efforts in the market— higher wages, better working conditions, and the like. It would be strange indeed if the workers did not confront some of the same problems in the union that they meet in the market, since their efforts in both places have some of the same purposes.

However similar the purposes may be, critics may object that attitudes in organizations are not at all like those in markets. In organizations, an emotional or ideological element is often also involved. Does this make the argument offered here practically irrelevant?

A most important type of organization—the national state—will serve to test this objection. Patriotism is probably the strongest non-economic motive for organizational allegiance in modern times. This age is sometimes called the age of nationalism. Many nations draw additional strength and unity from some powerful ideology, such as democracy or communism, as well as from a common religion, language, or cultural inheritance. The state not only has many such powerful sources of support; it also is very important economically. Almost any government is economically beneficial to its citizens, in that the law and order it provides is a prerequisite of all civilized economic activity. But despite the force of patriotism, the appeal of the national ideology, the bond of a common culture, and the indispensability of the system of law and order, no major state in modern history has been able to support itself through voluntary dues or contributions. Philanthropic contributions are not even a significant source of revenue for most countries. Taxes, *compulsory* payments by definition, are needed. Indeed, as the old saying indicates, their necessity is as certain as death itself.

If the state, with all of the emotional resources at its command, cannot finance its most basic and vital activities without resort to compulsion, it would seem that large private organizations might also have difficulty in getting the individuals in the groups whose interests they attempt to advance to make the necessary contributions voluntarily.[19]

The reason the state cannot survive on voluntary dues or payments, but must rely on taxation, is that the most fundamental services a nation-state provides are, in one important respect, like the higher price in a competitive market: they must be available to everyone if they are available to anyone. The basic and most elementary goods or services provided by government, like defense and police protection, and the system of law and order generally, are such that they go to everyone or practically everyone in the nation. It would obviously not be feasible, if indeed it were possible, to deny the protection provided by the military services, the police, and the courts to those who did not voluntarily pay their share of the costs of government, and taxation is accordingly necessary. The common or collective benefits provided by governments are usually called "public goods" by economists, and the concept of public goods is one of the oldest and most important ideas in the study of public finance. A common, collective, or public good is here defined as any good such that, if any person X_i in a group $X_1, \ldots, X_i, \ldots, X_n$ consumes if, it cannot feasibly be withheld from the others in that group.[20] In other words, those who do not purchase or pay for any of the public or collective good cannot be excluded or kept from sharing in the consumption of the good, as they can where noncollective goods are concerned.

Students of public finance have, however, neglected the fact that *the achievement of any common goal or the satisfaction of any common interest means that a public or collective good has been provided for that group.*[21] The very fact that a goal or purpose is *common* to a group means that no one in the group is excluded from the benefit or satisfaction brought about by its achievement. As the opening paragraphs of this chapter indicated, almost all groups and organizations have the purpose of serving the common interests of their members. As R. M. MacIver puts it, "Persons . . . have common interests in the degree to which they participate in a cause . . . which indivisibly embraces them all."[22] It is of the essence of an organization that it provides an inseparable, generalized benefit. It follows that the provision of public or collective goods is the fundamental function of organizations generally. A state is first of all an organization that provides public goods for its members, the citizens; and other types of organizations similarly provide collective goods for their members.

And just as a state cannot support itself by voluntary contributions, or by selling its basic services on the market, neither can other large organizations support themselves without providing some sanction, or some attraction distinct from the public good itself, that will lead individuals to help bear the burdens of maintaining the organization. The individual member of the typical large organization is in a position analogous to that of the firm in a perfectly competitive market, or the taxpayer in the state: his own efforts will not have a noticeable effect on the situation of his organization, and he can enjoy any improvements brought about by others whether or not he has worked in support of his organization.

There is no suggestion here that states or other organizations provide *only* public or collective goods. Governments often provide noncollective goods like electric power, for example, and they usually sell such goods on the market much as private firms would do. Moreover, as later parts of this study will argue, large organizations that are not able to make membership compulsory *must also* provide some noncollective goods in order to give potential members an incentive to join. Still, collective goods are the characteristic organizational goods, for ordinary noncollective goods can always be provided by individual action, and only where common purposes of collective goods are concerned is organization or group action ever indispensable.[23]

▪   ▪   ▪

Nontechnical summary of section D

The technical part of this section has shown that certain small groups can provide themselves with collective goods without relying on coercion or any positive inducements apart from the collective good itself.[24] This is because in some small groups each of the members, or at least one of them, will find that his personal gain from having the collective good exceeds the total cost of providing some amount of that collective good; there are members who would be better off if the collective good were provided, even if they had to pay the entire cost of providing it themselves, than they would be if it were not provided. In such situations there is a presumption that the collective good will be provided. Such a situation will exist only when the benefit to the group from having the collective good exceeds the total cost by more than it exceeds the gain to one or more individuals in the group. Thus, in a very small group, where each member gets a substantial proportion of the total gain simply because there are few others in the group, a collective good can often be provided by the voluntary, self-interested action of the members of the group. In smaller groups marked by considerable degrees of inequality—that is, in groups of members of unequal "size" or extent of interest in the collective good—there is the greatest likelihood that a collective good will be provided; for the greater the interest in the collective good of any single member, the greater the likelihood that that member will get such a significant proportion of the total benefit from the collective good that he will gain from seeing that the good is provided, even if he has to pay all of the cost himself.

Even in the smallest groups, however, the collective good will not ordinarily be provided on an optimal scale. That is to say, the members of the group will not provide as much of the good as it would be in their common interest to provide. Only certain special institutional arrangements will give the individual members an incentive to purchase the amounts of the collective good that would add up to the amount that would be in the best interest of the group as a whole. This tendency toward suboptimality is due to the fact that a collective good is, by definition, such that other individuals in the group cannot be kept from consuming it once any individual in the group has provided it for himself. Since an individual member thus gets only part of the benefit of any expenditure he makes to obtain more of the collective good, he will discontinue his purchase of the collective good before the optimal amount for the group as a whole has been obtained. In addition, the amounts of the collective good that a member of the group receives free from other members will further reduce his incentive to provide more of that good at his own expense. Accordingly, *the larger the group, the farther it will fall short of providing an optimal amount of a collective good.*

This suboptimality or inefficiency will be somewhat less serious in groups composed of members of greatly different size or interest in the collective good. In such unequal groups, on the other hand, there is a tendency toward an arbitrary sharing of the burden of providing the collective good. The largest member, the member who would on his own provide the largest amount of the collective good, bears a disproportionate share of the burden of providing the collective good. The smaller member by definition gets a smaller fraction of the benefit of any amount of the collective good he provides than a larger member, and therefore has less incentive to provide additional amounts of the collective good. Once a smaller member has the amount of the collective good he gets free from the largest member, he has more than he would have purchased for himself, and has no incentive to obtain any of the collective good at his own expense. In small groups with common interests there is accordingly *a surprising tendency for the "exploitation" of the great by the small.*

The argument that small groups providing themselves with collective goods tend to provide suboptimal quantities of these goods, and that the burdens of providing them are borne in an arbitrary and disproportionate way, does not hold in all logically possible situations. Certain institutional or procedural arrangements can lead to different outcomes. The subject cannot be analyzed adequately in any brief discussion. For this reason, and because the main focus of this reading is on large groups, many of the complexities of small-group behavior have been neglected in this study. An argument of the kind just outlined could, however, fit some important practical situations rather well, and may serve the purpose of suggesting that a more detailed analysis of the kind outlined above could help to explain the apparent tendency for large countries to bear disproportionate shares of the burdens of multinational organizations, like the United Nations and NATO, and could help to explain some of the popularity of neutralism among smaller countries. Such an analysis would also tend to explain the continual complaints that international organizations and alliances are not given adequate (optimal) amounts of resources.[25] It would also suggest that neighboring local governments in metropolitan areas that provide collective goods (like commuter roads and education) that benefit individuals in two or more local government jurisdictions would tend to provide inadequate amounts of these services, and that the largest local government (e.g., the one representing the central city) would bear disproportionate shares of the burdens of providing them.[26] An analysis of the foregoing type might, finally, provide some additional insight into the phenomenon of price leadership, and particularly the possible disadvantages involved in being the largest firm in an industry.

The most important single point about small groups in the present context, however, is that they may very well be able to provide themselves with a collective good simply because of the attraction of the collective good to the individual members. In this, small groups differ from larger ones. The larger a group is, the farther it will fall short of obtaining an optimal supply of any collective good, and the less likely that it will act to obtain even a minimal amount of such a good. In short, the larger the group, the less it will further its common interests.

▪   ▪   ▪

F. A Taxonomy of Groups

To be sure, there can also be many instances in inclusive or non-market groups in which individual members do take into account the reactions of other members to their actions when they decide what action to take—that is, instances in which there is the strategic interaction among members characteristic of oligopolistic industries in which mutual dependence is recognized. In groups of one size range at least, such strategic interaction must be relatively important. That is the size range where the group is not so small that one individual would find it profitable to purchase some of the collective good himself, but where the number in the group is nonetheless sufficiently small that each member's attempts or lack of attempts to obtain the collective good would bring about noticeable differences in the welfare of some, or all, of the others in the group. This can best be understood by assuming for a moment that an inclusive collective good is already being provided in such a group through a formal organization, and then asking what would happen if one member of the group were to cease paying his share of the cost of the good. If, in a reasonably small organization, a particular person stops paying for the collective good he enjoys, the costs will rise noticeably for each of the others in the group; accordingly, they may then refuse to continue making their contributions, and the collective good may no longer be provided. However, the first person could realize that this might be the result of his refusal to pay anything for the collective good, and that he would be worse off when the collective good is not provided than when it was provided and he met part of the cost. Accordingly he might continue making a contribution toward the purchase of the collective good. He might; or he might not. As in oligopoly in a market situation, the result is indeterminate. The rational member of such a group faces a strategic problem and while the Theory of Games and other types of analyses might prove very helpful, there seems to be no way at present of getting a general, valid, and determinate solution at the level of abstraction of this chapter.[27]

What is the range of this indeterminateness? In a small group in which a member gets such a large fraction of the total benefit that he would be better off if he paid the entire cost himself, rather than go without the good, there is some presumption that the collective good will be provided. In a group in which no one member got such a large benefit from the collective good that he had an interest in providing it even if he had to pay all of the cost, but in which the individual was still so important in terms of the whole group that his contribution or lack of contribution to the group objective had a noticeable effect on the costs or benefits of others in the group, the result is indeterminate.[28] By contrast, in a large group in which no single individual's contribution makes a perceptible difference to the group as a whole, or the burden or benefit of any single member of the group, it is certain that a collective good will *not* be provided unless there is coercion or some outside inducements that will lead the members of the large group to act in their common interest.[29]

The last distinction, between the group so large it definitely cannot provide itself with a collective good, and the oligopoly-sized group which may provide itself with a collective good, is particularly important. It depends upon whether any two or more members of the group have a perceptible interdependence, that is, on whether the contribution or lack of contribution of any one individual in the group will have a perceptible effect on the burden or benefit of any other individual or individuals in the group. Whether a group will have the possibility of providing itself with a collective good without coercion or outside inducements therefore depends to a striking degree upon the number of individuals in the group, since the larger the group, the less the likelihood that the contribution of any one will be perceptible. It is not, however, strictly accurate to say that it depends solely on the number of individuals in the group. The relation between the size of the group and the significance of an individual member cannot be defined quite that simply. A group which has members with highly unequal degrees of interest in a collective good, and which wants a collective good that is (at some level of provision) extremely valuable in relation to its cost, will be more apt to provide itself with a collective good than other groups with the same number of members. The same situation prevails in the study of market structure, where again the number of firms an industry can have and still remain oligopolistic (and have the possibility of supracompetitive returns) varies somewhat from case to case. The standard for determining whether a group will have the capacity to act, without coercion or outside inducements, in its group interest is (as it should be) the same for market and non-market groups: it depends on whether the individual actions of any one or more members in a group are noticeable to any other individuals in the group.[30] This is most obviously, but not exclusively, a function of the number in the group.

It is now possible to specify when either informal coordination or formal organization will be necessary to obtain a collective good. The smallest type of group—the group in which one or more members get such a large fraction of the total benefit that they find it worthwhile to see that the collective good is provided, even if they have to pay the entire cost—may get along without any group agreement or organization. A group agreement might be set up to spread the costs more widely or to step up the level of provision of the collective good. But since there is an incentive for unilateral and individual action to obtain the collective good, neither a formal organization nor even an informal group agreement is indispensable to obtain a collective good. In any group larger than this, on the other hand, no collective good can be obtained without some group agreement, coordination, or organization. In the intermediate or oligopoly-sized group, where two or more members must act simultaneously before a collective good can be obtained, there must be at least tacit coordination or organization. Moreover, the larger a group is, the more agreement and organization it will need. The larger the group, the greater the number that will usually have to be included in the group agreement or organization. It may not be necessary that the entire group be organized, since some subset of the whole group may be able to provide the collective good. But to establish a group agreement or organization will nonetheless always tend to be more difficult the larger the size of the group, for the larger the group the more difficult it will be to locate and organize even a subset of the group, and those in the subset will have an incentive to continue bargaining with the others in the group until the burden is widely shared, thereby adding to the expense of bargaining. In short, costs of organization are an increasing function of the number of individuals in the group. (Though the more members in the group the greater the total costs of organization, the costs of organization per person need not rise, for there are surely economies of scale in organization.) In certain cases a group will already be organized for some other purpose, and then these costs of organization are already being met. In such a case a group's capacity to provide itself with a collective good will be explained in part by whatever it was that originally enabled it to organize and maintain itself. This brings attention back again to the costs of organization and shows that these costs cannot be left out of the model, except for the smallest type of group in which unilateral action can provide a collective good. The costs of organization must be clearly distinguished from the type of cost that has previously been considered. The cost functions considered before involved only the direct resource costs of obtaining various levels of provision of a collective good. When there is no pre-existing organization of a group, and when the direct resource costs of a collective good it wants are more than any single individual could profitably bear, additional costs must be incurred to obtain an agreement about how the burden will be shared and to coordinate or organize the effort to obtain the collective good. These are the costs of communication among group members, the costs of any bargaining among them, and the costs of creating, staffing, and maintaining any formal group organization.

A group cannot get infinitesimally small quantities of a formal organization, or even of an informal group agreement; a group with a given number of members must have a certain minimal amount of organization or agreement if it is to have any at all. Thus there are significant initial or minimal costs of organization for each group. Any group that must organize to obtain a collective good, then, will find that it has a certain minimum organization cost that must be met, however little of the collective good it obtains. The greater the number in the group, the greater these minimal costs will be. When this minimal organizational cost is added to the other initial or minimal costs of a collective good, which arise from its previously mentioned technical characteristics, it is evident that the cost of the first unit of a collective good will be quite high in relation to the cost of some subsequent units. However immense the benefits of a collective good, the higher the absolute total costs of getting any amount of that good, the less likely it is that even a minimal amount of that good could be obtained without coercion or separate, outside incentives.

This means that there are now three separate but cumulative factors that keep larger groups from furthering their own interest. First, the larger the group, the smaller the fraction of the total group benefit any person acting in the group interest receives, and the less adequate the reward for any group-oriented action, and the farther the group falls short of getting an optimal supply of the collective good, even if it should get some. Second, since the larger the group, the smaller the share of the total benefit going to any individual, or to any (absolutely) small subset of members of the group, the less the likelihood that any small subset of the group, much less any single individual, will gain enough from getting the collective good to bear the burden of providing even a small amount of it; in other words, the larger the group the smaller the likelihood of oligopolistic interaction that might help obtain the good. Third, the larger the number of members in the group the greater the organization costs, and thus the higher the hurdle that must be jumped before any of the collective good at all can be obtained. For these reasons, the larger the group the farther it will fall short of providing an optimal supply of a collective good, and very large groups normally will not, in the absence of coercion or separate, outside incentives, provide themselves with even minimal amounts of a collective good.[31]

■   ■   ■

NOTES

1. Economists have for the most part neglected to develop theories of organizations, but there are a few works from an economic point of view on the subject. See, for example, three papers by Jacob Marschak, "Elements for a Theory of Teams," *Management Science*, I (January 1955), 127–137, "Towards an Economic Theory of Organization and Information," in *Decision Processes*, ed. R. M. Thrall, C. H. Combs, and R. L. Davis (New York: John Wiley, 1954), pp. 187–220, and "Efficient and Viable Organization Forms," in *Modern Organization Theory*, ed. Mason Haire (New York: John Wiley, 1959), pp. 307–320; two papers by R. Radner, "Application of Linear Programming to Team Decision Problems," *Management Science*, V (January 1959), 143–150, and "Team Decision Problems," *Annals of Mathematical Statistics*, XXXIII (September 1962), 857–881; C. B. McGuire, "Some Team Models of a Sales Organization," *Management Science*, VII (January 1961), 101–130; Oskar Morgenstern, *Prolegomena to a Theory of Organization* (Santa Monica, Calif.: RAND Research Memorandum 734, 1951); James

G. March and Herbert A. Simon, *Organizations* (New York: John Wiley, 1958); Kenneth Boulding, *The Organizational Revolution* (New York: Harper, 1953).

2. Max Weber called attention to the case where an organization continues to exist for some time after it has become meaningless because some official is making a living out of it. See his *Theory of Social and Economic Organization,* trans. Talcott Parsons and A. M. Henderson (New York: Oxford University Press, 1947), p. 318.

3. Aristotle, *Ethics* viii.9.1160a.

4. Leon Festinger, "Group Attraction and Membership," in *Group Dynamics,* ed. Dorwin Cartwright and Alvin Zander (Evanston, Ill.: Row, Peterson, 1953), p. 93.

5. *A Grammar of Politics,* 4th ed. (London: George Allen & Unwin, 1939), p. 67.

6. Philanthropic and religious organizations are not necessarily expected to serve only the interests of their members; such organizations have other purposes that are considered more important, however much their members "need" to belong, or are improved or helped by belonging. But the complexity of such organizations need not be debated at length here, because this study will focus on organizations with a significant economic aspect. The emphasis here will have something in common with what Max Weber called the "associative group"; he called a group associative if "the orientation of social action with it rests on a rationally motivated agreement." Weber contrasted his "associative group" with the "communal group" which was centered on personal affection, erotic relationships, etc., like the family. (See Weber, pp. 136–139, and Grace Coyle, *Social Process in Organized Groups,* New York: Richard Smith, Inc., 1930, pp. 7–9.) The logic of the theory developed here can be extended to cover communal, religious, and philanthropic organizations, but the theory is not particularly useful in studying such groups.

7. That is, its members. This study does not follow the terminological usage of those organization theorists who describe employees as "members" of the organization for which they work. Here it is more convenient to follow the language of everyday usage instead, and to distinguish the members of, say, a union from the employees of that union. Similarly, the members of the union will be considered employees of the corporation for which they work, whereas the members of the corporation are the common stockholders.

8. R. M. MacIver, "Interests," *Encyclopaedia of the Social Sciences,* VII (New York: Macmillan, 1932), p. 147.

9. Arthur Bentley, *The Process of Government* (Evanston, Ill.: Principia Press, 1949), p. 211. David B. Truman takes a similar approach; see his *The Governmental Process* (New York: Alfred A. Knopf, 1958), pp. 33–35. See also Sidney Verba, *Small Groups and Political Behavior* (Princeton, N.J.: Princeton University Press, 1961), pp. 12–13.

10. Raymond Cattell, "Concepts and Methods in the Measurement of Group Syntality," in *Small Groups,* ed. A. Paul Hare, Edgard F. Borgatta, and Robert F. Bales (New York: Alfred A. Knopf, 1955), p. 115.

11. Any organization or group will of course usually be divided into subgroups or factions that are opposed to one another. This fact does not weaken the assumption made here that organizations exist to serve the common interests of members, for the assumption does not imply that intragroup conflict is neglected. The opposing groups within an organization ordinarily have some interest in common (if not, why would they maintain the organization?), and the members of any subgroup or faction also have a separate common interest of their own. They will indeed often have a common purpose in defeating some other subgroup or faction. The approach used here does not neglect the conflict within groups and organizations, then, because it considers each

organization as a unit only to the extent that it does in fact attempt to serve a common interest, and considers the various subgroups as the relevant units with common interests to analyze the factional strife.

12. See J. M. Clark, *The Economics of Overhead Costs* (Chicago: University of Chicago Press, 1923), p. 417, and Frank H. Knight, *Risk, Uncertainty and Profit* (Boston: Houghton Mifflin, 1921), p. 193.

13. Edward H. Chamberlin, *Monopolistic Competition*, 6th ed. (Cambridge, Mass.: Harvard University Press, 1950), p. 4.

14. For a fuller discussion of this question see Mancur Olson, Jr., and David McFarland, "The Restoration of Pure Monopoly and the Concept of the Industry, *Quarterly Journal of Economics*, LXXVI (November 1962), 613–631.

15. Robert Michels contends in his classic study that "democracy is inconceivable without organization," and that "the principle of organization is an absolutely essential condition for the political struggle of the masses." See his *Political Parties*, trans. Eden and Cedar Paul (New York: Dover Publications, 1959), pp. 21–22. See also Robert A. Brady, *Business as a System of Power* (New York: Columbia University Press, 1943), p. 193.

16. Alexander Heard, *The Costs of Democracy* (Chapel Hill: University of North Carolina Press, 1960), especially note 1, pp. 95–96. For example, in 1947 the National Association of Manufacturers spent over $4.6 million, and over a somewhat longer period the American Medical Association spent as much on a campaign against compulsory health insurance.

17. "If the full truth were ever known . . . lobbying, in all its ramifications, would prove to be a billion dollar industry." U.S. Congress, House, Select Committee on Lobbying Activities, *Report*, 81st Cong., 2nd Sess. (1950), as quoted in the *Congressional Quarterly Almanac*, 81st Cong., 2nd Sess., VI, 764–765.

18. For a logically possible but practically meaningless exception to the conclusion of this paragraph.

19. Sociologists as well as economists have observed that ideological motives alone are not sufficient to bring forth the continuing effort of large masses of people. Max Weber provides a notable example:

"All economic activity in a market economy is undertaken and carried through by individuals for their own ideal or material interests. This is naturally just as true when economic activity is oriented to the patterns of order of corporate groups . . .

"Even if an economic system were organized on a socialistic basis, there would be no fundamental difference in this respect . . . The structure of interests and the relevant situation might change; there would be other means of pursuing interests, but this fundamental factor would remain just as relevant as before. It is of course true that economic action which is oriented on purely ideological grounds to the interest of others does exist. But it is even more certain that the mass of men do not act in this way, and it is an induction from experience that they cannot do so and never will . . .

"In a market economy the interest in the maximization of income is necessarily the driving force of all economic activity." (Weber, pp. 319–320.)

Talcott Parsons and Neil Smelser go even further in postulating that "performance" throughout society is proportional to the "rewards" and "sanctions" involved. See their *Economy and Society* (Glencoe, Ill.: Free Press, 1954), pp. 50–69.

20. This simple definition focuses upon two points that are important in the present context. The first point is that most collective goods can only be defined with respect to some specific group. One collective good goes to one group of people, another collective

good to another group; one may benefit the whole world, another only two specific people. Moreover, some goods are collective goods to those in one group and at the same time private goods to those in another, because some individuals can be kept from consuming them and others can't. Take for example the parade that is a collective good to all those who live in tall buildings overlooking the parade route, but which appears to be a private good to those who can see it only by buying ticket, for a seat in the stands along the way. The second point is that once the relevant group has been defined, the definition used here, like Musgrave's, distinguishes collective good in terms of infeasibility of excluding potential consumers of the good. This approach is used because collective goods produced by organizations of all kinds seem to be such that exclusion is normally not feasible. To be sure, for some collective goods it is physically possible to practice exclusion. But, as Head has shown, it is not necessary that exclusion be technically impossible; it is only necessary that it be infeasible or uneconomic. Head has also shown most clearly that nonexcludability is only one of two basic elements in the traditional understanding of public goods. The other, he points out, is "jointness of supply." A good has "jointness" if making it available to one individual means that it can be easily or freely supplied to others as well. The polar case of jointness would be Samuelson's pure public good, which is a good such that additional consumption of it by one individual does not diminish the amount available to others. By the definition used here, jointness is not a necessary attribute of a public good. At least one type of collective good considered here exhibits no jointness whatever, and few if any would have the degree of jointness needed to qualify as pure public goods. Nonetheless, most of the collective goods to be studied here do display a large measure of jointness. On the definition and importance of public goods, see John G. Head, "Public Goods and Public Policy," *Public Finance*, vol. XVII, no. 3 (1962), 197–219; Richard Musgrave, *The Theory of Public Finance* (New York: McGraw-Hill, 1959); Paul A. Samuelson, "The Pure Theory of Public Expenditure," "Diagrammatic Exposition of A Theory of Public Expenditure," and "Aspects of Public Expenditure Theories," in *Review of Economics and Statistics*, XXXVI (November 1954), 387–390, XXXVII (November 1955), 350–356, and XL (November 1958), 332–338. For somewhat different opinions about the usefulness of the concept of public goods, see Julius Margolis, "A Comment on the Pure Theory of Public Expenditure," *Review of Economics and Statistics*, XXXVII (November 1955), 347–349, and Gerhard Colm, "Theory of Public Expenditures," *Annals of the American Academy of Political and Social Science*, CLXXXIII (January 1936), 1–11.

21. There is no necessity that a public good to one group in a society is necessarily in the interest of the society as a whole. Just as a tariff could be a public good to the industry that sought it, so the removal of the tariff could be a public good to those who consumed the industry's product. This is equally true when the public-good concept is applied only to governments; for a military expenditure, or a tariff, or an immigration restriction that is a public good to one country could be a "public bad" to another country, and harmful to world society as a whole.

22. R. M. MacIver in *Encyclopaedia of the Social Sciences*, VII, 147.

23. It does not, however, follow that organized or coordinated group action is *always* necessary to obtain a collective good.

24. I am indebted to Professor John Rawls of the Department of Philosophy at Harvard University for reminding me of the fact that the philosopher David Hume sensed that small groups could achieve common purposes but large groups could not. Hume's argument is however somewhat different from my own. In A *Treatise of Human Nature*, Everyman edition (London: J. M. Dent, 1952), II, 239, Hume wrote: "There is no quality

in human nature which causes more fatal errors in our conduct, than that which leads us to prefer whatever is present to the distant and remote, and makes us desire objects more according to their situation than their intrinsic value. Two neighbours may agree to drain a meadow, which they possess in common: because it is easy for them to know each other's mind; and each must perceive, that the immediate consequence of his failing in his part, is the abandoning of the whole project. But it is very difficult, and indeed impossible, that a thousand persons should agree in any such action; it being difficult for them to concert so complicated a design, and still more difficult for them to execute it; while each seeks a pretext to free himself of the trouble and expense, and would lay the whole burden on others. Political society easily remedies both these inconveniences. Magistrates find an immediate interest in the interest of any considerable part of their subjects. They need consult nobody but themselves to form any scheme for promoting that interest. And as the failure of any one piece in the execution is connected, though not immediately, with the failure of the whole, they prevent that failure, because they find no interest in it, either immediate or remote. Thus, bridges are built, harbours opened, ramparts raised, canals formed, fleets equipped, and armies disciplined everywhere, by the care of government, which, though composed of men subject to all human infirmities, becomes, by one of the finest and most subtle inventions imaginable, a composition which is in some measure exempted from all these infirmities."

25. Some of the complexities of behavior in small groups are treated in Mancur Olson, Jr., and Richard Zeckhauser, "An Economic Theory of Alliances," *Review of Economics and Statistics*, XLVIII (August 1966), 266–279, and in "Collective Goods, Comparative Advantage, and Alliance Efficiency," in *Issues of Defense Economics* (A Conference of the Universities-National Bureau-Committee for Economics Research), ed. Roland McKean (New York: National Bureau of Economic Research, 1967), pp. 25–48. [Footnote added in 1970.]

26. I am indebted to Alan Williams of York University in England, whose study of local government brought the importance of these sorts of spillovers among local govenments to my attention.

27. It is of incidental interest here to note also that oligopoly in the marketplace is in some respects akin to logrolling in the organization. If the "majority" that various interests in a legislature need is viewed as a collective good—something that a particular interest cannot obtain unless other interests also share it—then the parallel is quite close. The cost each special-interest legislator would like to avoid is the passage of the legislation desired by the other special-interest legislators, for if these interests gain from their legislation, often others, including his own constituents, may lose. But unless he is willing to vote for the legislation desired by the others, the particular special-interest legislator in question will not be able to get his own legislation passed. So his goal would be to work out a coalition with other special-interest legislators in which they would vote for exactly the legislation he wanted, and he in turn would give them as little in return as possible, by insisting that they moderate their legislative demands. But since every potential logroller has this same strategy, the result is indeterminate: the logs may be rolled or they may not. Every one of the interests will be better off if the logrolling is done than if it is not, but as individual interests strive for better legislative bargains the result of the competing strategies may be that no agreement is reached. This is quite similar to the situation oligopolistic groups are in, as they all desire a higher price and will all gain if they restrict output to get it, but they may not be able to agree on market shares.

28. The result is clearly indeterminate when F_4 is less than C/V_g at every point and it is also true that the group is not so large that no one member's actions have a noticeable effect.

29. One friendly critic has suggested that even a large pre-existing organization could continue providing a collective good simply by conducting a kind of plebiscite among its members, with the understanding that if there were not a unanimous or nearly unanimous pledge to contribute toward providing the collective good, this good would no longer be provided. This argument, if I understand it correctly, is mistaken. In such a situation, an individual would know that if others provided the collective good he would get the benefits whether he made any contribution or not. He would therefore have no incentive to make a pledge unless a completely unanimous set of pledges was required, or for some other reason his one pledge would decide whether or not the good would be provided. But if a pledge were required of every single member, or if for any other reason any one member could decide whether or not the group would get a collective good, this one member could deprive all of the others in the group of great gains. He would therefore be in a position to bargain for bribes. But since any other members of the group might gain just as much from the same holdout strategy, there is no likelihood that the collective good would be provided. See Buchanan and Tullock, pp. 96–116.

30. The noticeability of the actions of a single member of a group may be influenced by the arrangements the group itself sets up. A previously organized group, for example, might ensure that the contributions or lack of contributions of any member of the group, and the effect of each such member's course on the burden and benefit for others, would be advertised, thus ensuring that the group effort would not collapse from imperfect knowledge. I therefore define "noticeability" in terms of the degree of knowledge, and the institutional arrangements, that actually exist in any given group, instead of assuming a "natural noticeability" unaffected by any group advertising or other arrangements. This point, along with many other valuable comments, has been brought to my attention by Professor Jerome Rothenberg, who does, however, make much more of a group's assumed capacity to create "artificial noticeability" than I would want to do. I know of no practical example of a group or organization that has done much of anything, apart from improve information, to enhance the noticeability of an individual's actions in striving for a collective good.

31. There is one logically conceivable, but surely empirically trivial, case in which a large group could be provided with a very small amount of a collective good without coercion or outside incentives. If some very small group enjoyed a collective good so inexpensive that any one of the members would benefit by making sure that it was provided, even if he had to pay all of the cost, and if millions of people then entered the group, with the cost of the good nonetheless remaining constant, the large group could be provided with a little of this collective good. This is because by hypothesis in this example the costs have remained unchanged, so that one person still has an incentive to see that the good is provided. Even in such a case as this, however, it would still not be quite right to say that the large group was acting in its group interest, since the output of the collective good would be incredibly suboptimal. The optimal level of provision of the public good would increase each time an individual entered the group, since the unit cost of the collective good by hypothesis is constant, while the benefit from an additional unit of it increases with every entrant. Yet the original provider would have no incentive to provide more as the group expanded, unless he formed an organization to share costs with the others in this (now large) group. But that would

entail incurring the considerable costs of a large organization, and there would be no way these costs could be covered through the voluntary and rational action of the individuals in the group. Thus, if the total benefit from a collective good exceeded its costs by the thousandfold or millionfold, it is logically possible that a large group could provide itself with some amount of that collective good, but the level of provision of the collective good in such a case would be only a minute fraction of the optimal level. It is not easy to think of practical examples of groups that would fit this description, but one possible example is discussed on page 161, note 94. It would be easy to rule out even any such exceptional cases, however, simply by defining *all* groups that could provide themselves with some amount of a collective good as "small groups" (or by giving them other names), while putting all groups that could not provide themselves with a collective good in another class. But this easy route must be rejected, for that would make this part of the theory tautologous and thus incapable of refutation. Therefore the approach here has been to make the (surely reasonable) empirical hypothesis that the total costs of the collective goods wanted by large groups are large enough to exceed the value of the small fraction of the total benefit that an individual in a large group would get, so that he will not provide the good. There may be exceptions to this, as to any other empirical statement, and thus there may be instances in which large groups could provide themselves with (at most minute amounts of) collective goods through the voluntary and rational action of one of their members.

1.2

GARRETT HARDIN

"The Tragedy of the Commons"

In this powerful reading, Hardin builds on Olson's ideas to show the negative consequences that may ensue when people are not constrained in their acquisition of food, energy, land, water, minerals, and other natural resources. People pursuing their own interests can overdraw publicly owned resources, leading to a depletion of those resources. This argument is significant in the study of politics because many governmental institutions not only prevent the overdrawing of fixed resources, but also determine who has access to those resources.

The population problem has no technical solution; it requires a fundamental extension in morality.

At the end of a thoughtful article on the future of nuclear war, Wiesner and York[1] concluded that: "Both sides in the arms race are . . . confronted by the dilemma of steadily increasing military power and steadily decreasing national security. *It is our considered professional judgment that this dilemma has no technical solution.* If the great powers continue to look for solutions in the area of science and technology only, the result will be to worsen the situation."

I would like to focus your attention not on the subject of the article (national security in a nuclear world) but on the kind of conclusion they reached, namely that there is no technical solution to the problem. An implicit and almost universal assumption of discussions published in professional and semipopular scientific journals is that the problem under discussion has a technical solution. A technical solution may be defined as one that requires a change only in the techniques of the natural sciences, demanding little or nothing in the way of change in human values or ideas of morality.

In our day (though not in earlier times) technical solutions are always welcome. Because of previous failures in prophecy, it takes courage to assert that a desired technical solution is not possible. Wiesner and York exhibited this courage; publishing in a science journal, they insisted that the solution to the problem was not to be found in the natural sciences. They cautiously qualified their statement with the phrase, "It is our considered professional judgment. . . ." Whether they were right or not is not the concern of the present article. Rather, the concern here is with the important concept of a class of human problems which can be called "no technical solution problems," and, more specifically, with the identification and discussion of one of these.

It is easy to show that the class is not a null class. Recall the game of tick-tack-toe. Consider the problem, "How can I win the game of tick-tack-toe?" It is well known that I cannot, if I assume (in keeping with the conventions of game theory) that my opponent understands the game perfectly. Put another way, there is no "technical solution" to the problem. I can win only by giving a radical meaning to the word "win." I can hit my opponent over the head; or I can drug him; or I can falsify the records. Every way in which I "win" involves, in some sense, an abandonment of the game, as we intuitively understand it. (I can also, of course, openly abandon the game—refuse to play it. This is what most adults do.)

The class of "No technical solution problems" has members. My thesis is that the "population problem," as conventionally conceived, is a member of this class. How it is conventionally conceived needs some comment. It is fair to say that most people who anguish over the population problem are trying to find a way to avoid the evils of overpopulation without relinquishing any of the privileges they now enjoy. They think that farming the seas or developing new strains of wheat will solve the problem—technologically. I try to show here that the solution they seek cannot be found. The population problem cannot be solved in a technical way, any more than can the problem of winning the game of tick-tack-toe.

WHAT SHALL WE MAXIMIZE?

Population, as Malthus said, naturally tends to grow "geometrically," or, as we would now say, exponentially. In a finite world this means that the per capita share of the world's goods must steadily decrease. Is ours a finite world?

A fair defense can be put forward for the view that the world is infinite; or that we do not know that it is not. But, in terms of the practical problems that we must face in the next few generations with the foreseeable technology, it is clear that we will greatly increase human misery if we do not, during the immediate future, assume that the world available to the terrestrial human population is finite. "Space" is no escape.[2]

A finite world can support only a finite population; therefore, population growth must eventually equal zero. (The case of perpetual wide fluctuations above and below zero is a trivial variant that need not be discussed.) When this condition is met, what will be the situation of mankind? Specifically, can Bentham's goal of "the greatest good for the greatest number" be realized?

No—for two reasons, each sufficient by itself. The first is a theoretical one. It is not mathematically possible to maximize for two (or more) variables at the same time. This was clearly stated by von Neumann and Morgenstern,[3] but the principle is implicit in the theory of partial differential equations, dating back at least to D'Alembert (1717–1783).

The second reason springs directly from biological facts. To live, any organism must have a source of energy (for example, food). This energy is utilized for two purposes: mere maintenance and work. For man, maintenance of life requires about 1600 kilocalories a day ("maintenance calories"). Anything that he does over and above merely staying alive will be defined as work, and is supported by "work calories" which he takes in. Work calories are used not only for what we call work in common speech; they are also required for all forms of enjoyment, from swimming and automobile racing to playing music and writing poetry. If our goal is to maximize population it is obvious what we must do: We must make the work calories per person approach as close to zero as possible. No gourmet meals, no vacations, no sports, no music, no literature, no art. . . . I think that everyone will grant, without argument or proof, that maximizing population does not maximize goods. Bentham's goal is impossible.

In reaching this conclusion I have made the usual assumption that it is the acquisition of energy that is the problem. The appearance of atomic energy has led some to question this assumption. However, given an infinite source of energy, population growth still produces an inescapable problem. The problem of the acquisition of energy is replaced by the problem of its dissipation, as J. H. Fremlin has so wittily shown.[4] The arithmetic signs in the analysis are, as it were, reversed; but Bentham's goal is still unobtainable.

The optimum population is, then, less than the maximum. The difficulty of defining the optimum is enormous; so far as I know, no one has seriously tackled this problem. Reaching an acceptable and stable solution will surely require more than one generation of hard analytical work—and much persuasion.

We want the maximum good per person; but what is good? To one person it is wilderness, to another it is ski lodges for thousands. To one it is estuaries to nourish ducks for hunters to shoot; to another it is factory land. Comparing one good with another is, we usually say, impossible because goods are incommensurable. Incommensurables cannot be compared.

Theoretically this may be true; but in real life incommensurables *are* commensurable. Only a criterion of judgment and a system of weighting are needed. In nature the criterion is survival. Is it better for a species to be small and hideable, or large and powerful? Natural selection commensurates the incommensurables. The compromise achieved depends on a natural weighting of the values of the variables.

Man must imitate this process. There is no doubt that in fact he already does, but unconsciously. It is when the hidden decisions are made explicit that the arguments begin. The problem for the years ahead is to work out an acceptable theory of weighting. Synergistic effects, nonlinear variation, and difficulties in discounting the future make the intellectual problem difficult, but not (in principle) insoluble.

Has any cultural group solved this practical problem at the present time, even on an intuitive level? One simple fact proves that none has: there is no prosperous population in the world today that has, and has had for some time, a growth rate of zero. Any people that has intuitively identified its optimum point will soon reach it, after which its growth rate becomes and remains zero.

Of course, a positive growth rate might be taken as evidence that a population is below its optimum. However, by any reasonable standards, the most rapidly growing populations on earth today are (in general) the most miserable. This association (which need not be invariable) casts doubt on the optimistic assumption that the positive growth rate of a population is evidence that it has yet to reach its optimum.

We can make little progress in working toward optimum population size until we explicitly exorcize the spirit of Adam Smith in the field of practical demography. In economic affairs, *The Wealth of Nations* (1776) popularized the "invisible hand," the idea that an individual who "intends only his own gain," is, as it were, "led by an invisible hand to promote . . . the public interest."[5] Adam Smith did not assert that this was invariably true, and perhaps neither did any of his followers. But he contributed to a dominant tendency of thought that has ever since interfered with positive action based on rational analysis, namely, the tendency to assume that decisions reached individually will, in fact, be the best decisions for an entire society. If this assumption is correct it justifies the continuance of our present policy of laissez-faire in reproduction. If it is correct we can assume that men will control their individual fecundity so as to produce the optimum population. If the assumption is not correct, we need to reexamine our individual freedoms to see which ones are defensible.

TRAGEDY OF FREEDOM IN A COMMONS

The rebuttal to the invisible hand in population control is to be found in a scenario first sketched in a little-known pamphlet[6] in 1833 by a mathematical amateur named William Forster Lloyd (1794–1852). We may well call it "the tragedy of the commons," using the word "tragedy" as the philosopher Whitehead used it:[7] "The essence of dramatic tragedy is not unhappiness. It resides in the solemnity of the remorseless working of things." He then goes on to say, "This inevitableness of destiny can only be illustrated in terms of human life by incidents which in fact involve unhappiness. For it is only by them that the futility of escape can be made evident in the drama."

The tragedy of the commons develops in this way. Picture a pasture open to all. It is to be expected that each herdsman will try to keep as many cattle as possible on the commons. Such an arrangement may work reasonably satisfactorily for centuries because tribal wars, poaching, and disease keep the numbers of both man and beast well below the carrying capacity of the land. Finally, however, comes the day of reckoning, that is, the day when the long-desired goal of social stability becomes a reality. At this point, the inherent logic of the commons remorselessly generates tragedy.

As a rational being, each herdsman seeks to maximize his gain. Explicitly or implicitly, more or less consciously, he asks, "What is the utility *to me* of adding one more animal to my herd?" This utility has one negative and one positive component.

1. The positive component is a function of the increment of one animal. Since the herdsman receives all the proceeds from the sale of the additional animal, the positive utility is nearly +1.
2. The negative component is a function of the additional overgrazing created by one more animal. Since, however, the effects of overgrazing are shared by all the herdsmen, the negative utility for any particular decision-making herdsman is only a fraction of –1.

Adding together the component partial utilities, the rational herdsman concludes that the only sensible course for him to pursue is to add another animal to his herd. And another; and another. . . . But this is the conclusion reached by each and every rational herdsman sharing a commons. Therein is the tragedy. Each man is locked into a system that compels him to increase his herd without limit—in a world that is limited. Ruin is the destination toward which all men rush, each pursuing his own best interest in a society that believes in the freedom of the commons. Freedom in a commons brings ruin to all.

Some would say that this is a platitude. Would that it were! In a sense, it was learned thousands of years ago, but natural selection favors the forces of psychological denial.[8] The individual benefits as an individual from his ability to deny the truth even though society as a whole, of which he is a part, suffers. Education can counteract the natural tendency to do the wrong thing, but the inexorable succession of generations requires that the basis for this knowledge be constantly refreshed.

A simple incident that occurred a few years ago in Leominster, Massachusetts, shows how perishable the knowledge is. During the Christmas shopping season the parking meters downtown were covered with plastic bags that bore tags reading: "Do not open until after Christmas. Free parking courtesy of the mayor and city council." In other words, facing the prospect of an increased demand for already scarce space, the city fathers reinstituted the system of the commons. (Cynically, we suspect that they gained more votes than they lost by this retrogressive act.)

In an approximate way, the logic of the commons has been understood for a long time, perhaps since the discovery of agriculture or the invention of private property in real estate. But it is understood mostly only in special cases which are not sufficiently generalized. Even at this late date, cattlemen leasing national land on the western ranges demonstrate no more than an ambivalent understanding, in constantly pressuring federal authorities to increase the head count to the point where overgrazing produces erosion and weed-dominance. Likewise, the oceans of the world continue to suffer from the survival of the philosophy of the commons. Maritime nations still respond automatically to the shibboleth of the "freedom of the seas." Professing to believe in the "inexhaustible resources of the oceans," they bring species after species of fish and whales closer to extinction.[9]

The National Parks present another instance of the working out of the tragedy of the commons. At present, they are open to all, without limit. The parks themselves are limited in extent—there is only one Yosemite Valley—whereas population seems to grow without limit. The values that visitors seek in the parks are steadily eroded. Plainly, we must soon cease to treat the parks as commons or they will be of no value to anyone.

What shall we do? We have several options. We might sell them off as private property. We might keep them as public property, but allocate the right to enter them. The allocation might be on the basis of wealth, by the use of an auction system. It might be on the basis of merit, as defined by some agreed-upon standards. It might be by lottery. Or it might be on a first-come, first-served basis, administered to long queues. These, I think, are all the reasonable possibilities. They are all objectionable. But we must choose—or acquiesce in the destruction of the commons that we call our National Parks.

POLLUTION

In a reverse way, the tragedy of the commons reappears in problems of pollution. Here it is not a question of taking something out of the commons, but of putting something in—sewage, or chemical, radioactive, and heat wastes into water; noxious and dangerous fumes into the air; and distracting and unpleasant advertising signs into the line of sight. The calculations of utility are much the same as before. The rational man finds that his share of the cost of the wastes he discharges into the commons is less than the cost of purifying his wastes before releasing them. Since this is true for everyone, we are locked into a system of "fouling our own nest," so long as we behave only as independent, rational, free-enterprisers.

The tragedy of the commons as a food basket is averted by private property, or something formally like it. But the air and waters surrounding us cannot readily be fenced, and so the tragedy of the commons as a cesspool must be prevented by different means, by coercive laws or taxing devices that make it cheaper for the polluter to treat his pollutants than to discharge them untreated. We have not progressed as far with the solution of this problem as we have with the first. Indeed, our particular concept of private property, which deters us from exhausting the positive resources of the earth, favors pollution. The owner of a factory on the bank of a stream—whose property extends to the middle of the stream—often has difficulty seeing why it is not his natural right to muddy the waters flowing past his door. The law, always behind the times, requires elaborate stitching and fitting to adapt it to this newly perceived aspect of the commons.

The pollution problem is a consequence of population. It did not much matter how a lonely American frontiersman disposed of his waste. "Flowing water purifies itself every 10 miles," my grandfather used to say, and the myth was near enough to the truth when he was a boy, for there were not too many people. But as population became denser, the natural chemical and biological recycling processes became overloaded, calling for a redefinition of property rights.

HOW TO LEGISLATE TEMPERANCE?

Analysis of the pollution problem as a function of population density uncovers a not generally recognized principle of morality, namely: *the morality of an act is a function of the state of the system at the time it is performed*.[10] Using the commons as a cesspool does not harm the general public under frontier conditions, because there is no public; the same behavior in a metropolis is unbearable. A hundred and fifty years ago a plainsman could kill an American bison, cut out only the tongue for his dinner, and discard the rest of the animal. He was not in any important sense being wasteful. Today, with only a few thousand bison left, we would be appalled at such behavior.

In passing, it is worth noting that the morality of an act cannot be determined from a photograph. One does not know whether a man killing an elephant or setting fire to the grassland is harming others until one knows the total system in which his act appears. "One picture is worth a thousand words," said an ancient Chinese; but it may take 10,000 words to validate it. It is as tempting to ecologists as it is to reformers in general to try to persuade others by way of the photographic shortcut. But the essense of an argument cannot be photographed: it must be presented rationally—in words.

That morality is system-sensitive escaped the attention of most codifiers of ethics in the past. "Thou shalt not . . ." is the form of traditional ethical directives which make no allowance for particular circumstances. The laws of our society follow the pattern of ancient ethics, and therefore are poorly suited to governing a complex, crowded, changeable world. Our epicyclic solution is to augment statutory law with administrative law. Since it is practically impossible to spell out all the conditions under which it is safe to burn trash in the back yard or to run an automobile without smog-control, by law we delegate the details to bureaus. The result is administrative law, which is rightly feared for an ancient reason—*Quis custodiet ipsos custodes?*—"Who shall watch the watchers themselves?" John Adams said that we must have "a government of laws and not men." Bureau administrators, trying to evaluate the morality of acts in the total system, are singularly liable to corruption, producing a government by men, not laws.

Prohibition is easy to legislate (though not necessarily to enforce); but how do we legislate temperance? Experience indicates that it can be accomplished best through the mediation of administrative law. We limit possibilities unnecessarily if we suppose that the sentiment of *Quis custodiet* denies us the use of administrative law. We should rather retain the phrase as a perpetual reminder of fearful dangers we cannot avoid. The great challenge facing us now is to invent the corrective feedbacks that are needed to keep custodians honest. We must find ways to legitimate the needed authority of both the custodians and the corrective feedbacks.

FREEDOM TO BREED IS INTOLERABLE

The tragedy of the commons is involved in population problems in another way. In a world governed solely by the principle of "dog eat dog"—if indeed there ever was such a world—how many children a family had would not be a matter of public concern. Parents who bred too exuberantly would leave fewer descendants, not more, because they would be unable to care adequately for their children. David Lack and others have found that such a negative feedback demonstrably controls the fecundity of birds.[11] But men are not birds, and have not acted like them for millenniums, at least.

If each human family were dependent only on its own resources; *if* the children of improvident parents starved to death; *if*, thus, overbreeding brought its own "punishment" to the germ line—*then* there would be no public interest in controlling the breeding of families. But our society is deeply committed to the welfare state,[12] and hence is confronted with another aspect of the tragedy of the commons.

In a welfare state, how shall we deal with the family, the religion, the race, or the class (or indeed any distinguishable and cohesive group) that adopts overbreeding as a policy to secure its own aggrandizement?[13] To couple the concept of freedom to breed with the belief that everyone born has an equal right to the commons is to lock the world into a tragic course of action.

Unfortunately this is just the course of action that is being pursued by the United Nations. In late 1967, some 30 nations agreed to the following:[14]

> The Universal Declaration of Human Rights describes the family as the natural and fundamental unit of society. It follows that any choice and decision with regard to the size of the family must irrevocably rest with the family itself, and cannot be made by anyone else.

It is painful to have to deny categorically the validity of this right; denying it, one feels as uncomfortable as a resident of Salem, Massachusetts, who denied the reality of witches in the 17th century. At the present time, in liberal quarters, something like a taboo acts to inhibit criticism of the United Nations. There is a feeling that the United Nations is "our last and best hope," that we shouldn't find fault with it; we shouldn't play into the hands of the archconservatives. However, let us not forget what Robert Louis Stevenson said: "The truth that is suppressed by friends is the readiest weapon of the enemy." If we love the truth we must openly deny the validity of the Universal Declaration of Human Rights, even though it is promoted by the United Nations. We should also join with Kingsley Davis [15] in attempting to get Planned Parenthood-World Population to see the error of its ways in embracing the same tragic ideal.

CONSCIENCE IS SELF-ELIMINATING

It is a mistake to think that we can control the breeding of mankind in the long run by an appeal to conscience. Charles Galton Darwin made this point when he spoke on the centennial of the publication of his grandfather's great book. The argument is straightforward and Darwinian.

People vary. Confronted with appeals to limit breeding, some people will undoubtedly respond to the plea more than others. Those who have more children will produce a larger fraction of the next generation than those with more susceptible consciences. The difference will be accentuated, generation by generation.

In C. G. Darwin's words: "It may well be that it would take hundreds of generations for the progenitive instinct to develop in this way, but if it should do so, nature would have taken her revenge, and the variety *Homo contra-cipiens* would become extinct and would be replaced by the variety *Homo progenitivus*." [16]

The argument assumes that conscience or the desire for children (no matter which) is hereditary—but hereditary only in the most general formal sense. The result will be the same whether the attitude is transmitted through germ cells, or exosomatically, to use A. J. Lotka's term. (If one denies the latter possibility as well as the former, then what's the point of education?) The argument has here been stated in the context of the population problem, but it applies equally well to any instance in which society appeals to an individual exploiting a commons to restrain himself for the general good—by means of his conscience. To make such an appeal is to set up a selective system that works toward the elimination of conscience from the race.

PATHOGENIC EFFECTS OF CONSCIENCE

The long-term disadvantage of an appeal to conscience should be enough to condemn it; but has serious short-term disadvantages as well. If we ask a man who is exploiting a commons to desist "in the name of conscience," what are we saying to him? What does he hear?—not only at the moment but also in the wee small hours of the night when, half asleep, he remembers not merely the words we used but also the nonverbal communication cues we gave him unawares? Sooner or later, consciously or subconsciously, he senses that he has received two communications, and that they are contradictory: (i) (intended communication) "If you don't do as we ask, we will openly condemn you for not acting like a responsible citizen"; (ii) (the unintended communication) "If you *do* behave as we ask, we will secretly condemn you for a simpleton who can be shamed into standing aside while the rest of us exploit the commons."

Everyman then is caught in what Bateson has called a "double bind." Bateson and his co-workers have made a plausible case for viewing the double bind as an important causative factor in the genesis of schizophrenia.[17] The double bind may not always be so damaging, but it always endangers the mental health of anyone to whom it is applied. "A bad conscience," said Nietzsche, "is a kind of illness."

To conjure up a conscience in others is tempting to anyone who wishes to extend his control beyond the legal limits. Leaders at the highest level succumb to this temptation. Has any President during the past generation failed to call on labor unions to moderate voluntarily their demands for higher wages, or to steel companies to honor voluntary guidelines on prices? I can recall none. The rhetoric used on such occasions is designed to produce feelings of guilt in non-cooperators.

For centuries it was assumed without proof that guilt was a valuable, perhaps even an indispensable, ingredient of the civilized life. Now, in this post-Freudian world, we doubt it.

Paul Goodman speaks from the modern point of view when he says: "No good has ever come from feeling guilty, neither intelligence, policy, nor compassion. The guilty do not pay attention to the object but only to themselves, and not even to their own interests, which might make sense, but to their anxieties."[18]

One does not have to be a professional psychiatrist to see the consequences of anxiety. We in the Western world are just emerging from a dreadful two-centuries-long Dark Ages of Eros that was sustained partly by prohibition laws, but perhaps more effectively by the anxiety–generating mechanisms of education. Alex Comfort has told the story well in *The Anxiety Makers*;[19] it is not a pretty one.

Since proof is difficult, we may even concede that the results of anxiety may sometimes, from certain points of view, be desirable. The larger question we should ask is whether, as a matter of policy, we should ever encourage the use of a technique the tendency (if not the intention) of which is psychologically pathogenic. We hear much talk these days of responsible parenthood; the coupled words are incorporated into the titles of some organizations devoted to birth control. Some people have proposed massive propaganda campaigns to instill responsibility into the nation's (or the world's) breeders.

But what is the meaning of the word responsibility in this context? Is it not merely a synonym for the word conscience? When we use the word responsibility in the absence of substantial sanctions are we not trying to browbeat a free man in a commons into acting against his own interest? Responsibility is a verbal counterfeit for a substantial *quid pro quo*. It is an attempt to get something for nothing.

If the word responsibility is to be used at all, I suggest that it be in the sense Charles Frankel uses it.[20] "Responsibility," says this philosopher, "is the product of definite social arrangements." Notice that Frankel calls for social arrangements—not propaganda.

MUTUAL COERCION MUTUALLY AGREED UPON

The social arrangements that produce responsibility are arrangements that create coercion, of some sort. Consider bank-robbing. The man who takes money from a bank acts as if the bank were a commons. How do we prevent such action? Certainly not by trying to control his behavior solely by a verbal appeal to his sense of responsibility. Rather than rely on propaganda we follow Frankel's lead and insist that a bank is not a commons; we seek the definite social arrangements that will keep it from becoming a commons. That we thereby infringe on the freedom of would-be robbers we neither deny nor regret.

The morality of bank-robbing is particularly easy to understand because we accept complete prohibition of this activity. We are willing to say "Thou shalt not rob banks," without providing for exceptions. But temperance also can be created by coercion. Taxing is a good coercive device. To keep downtown shoppers temperate in their use of parking space we introduce parking meters for short periods, and traffic fines for longer ones. We need not actually forbid a citizen to park as long as he wants to; we need merely make it increasingly expensive for him to do so. Not prohibition, but carefully biased options are what we offer him. A Madison Avenue man might call this persuasion; I prefer the greater candor of the word coercion.

Coercion is a dirty word to most liberals now, but it need not forever be so. As with the four-letter words, its dirtiness can be cleansed away by exposure to the light, by saying it over and over without apology or embarrassment. To many, the word coercion implies arbitrary decisions of distant and irresponsible bureaucrats; but this is not a necessary part of its meaning. The only kind of coercion I recommend is mutual coercion, mutually agreed upon by the majority of the people affected.

To say that we mutually agree to coercion is not to say that we are required to enjoy it, or even to pretend we enjoy it. Who enjoys taxes? We all grumble about them. But we accept compulsory taxes because we recognize that voluntary taxes would favor the conscienceless. We institute and (grumblingly) support taxes and other coercive devices to escape the horror of the commons.

An alternative to the commons need not be perfectly just to be preferable. With real estate and other material goods, the alternative we have chosen is the institution of private property coupled with legal inheritance. Is this system perfectly just? As a genetically trained biologist I deny that it is. It seems to me that, if there are to be differences in individual inheritance, legal possession should be perfectly correlated with biological inheritance—that those who are biologically more fit to be the custodians of property and power should legally inherit more. But genetic recombination continually makes a mockery of the doctrine of "like father, like son" implicit in our laws of legal inheritance. An idiot can inherit millions, and a trust fund can keep his estate intact. We must admit that our legal system of private property plus inheritance is unjust—but we put up with it because we are not convinced, at the moment, that anyone has invented a better system. The alternative of the commons is too horrifying to contemplate. Injustice is preferable to total ruin.

It is one of the peculiarities of the warfare between reform and the status quo that it is thoughtlessly governed by a double standard. Whenever a reform measure is proposed it is often defeated when its opponents triumphantly discover a flaw in it. As Kingsley Davis has pointed out,[21] worshippers of the status quo sometimes imply that no reform is possible without unanimous agreement, an implication contrary to historical fact. As nearly as I can make out, automatic rejection of proposed reforms is based on one of two unconscious assumptions: (i) that the status quo is perfect; or (ii) that the choice we face is between reform and no action; if the proposed reform is imperfect, we presumably should take no action at all, while we wait for a perfect proposal.

But we can never do nothing. That which we have done for thousands of years is also action. It also produces evils. Once we are aware that the status quo is action, we can then compare its discoverable advantages and disadvantages with the predicted advantages and disadvantages of the proposed reform, discounting as best we can for our lack of experience. On the basis of such a comparison, we can make a rational decision which will not involve the unworkable assumption that only perfect systems are tolerable.

RECOGNITION OF NECESSITY

Perhaps the simplest summary of this analysis of man's population problems is this: the commons, if justifiable at all, is justifiable only under conditions of low-population density. As the human population has increased, the commons has had to be abandoned in one aspect after another.

First we abandoned the commons in food gathering, enclosing farm land and restricting pastures and hunting and fishing areas. These restrictions are still not complete throughout the world.

Somewhat later we saw that the commons as a place for waste disposal would also have to be abandoned. Restrictions on the disposal of domestic sewage are widely accepted in the Western world; we are still struggling to close the commons to pollution by automobiles, factories, insecticide spray-ers, fertilizing operations, and atomic energy installations.

In a still more embryonic state is our recognition of the evils of the com-mons in matters of pleasure. There is almost no restriction on the propaga-tion of sound waves in the public medium. The shopping public is assaulted with mindless music, without its consent. Our government is paying out bil-lions of dollars to create supersonic transport which will disturb 50,000 people for every one person who is whisked from coast to coast 3 hours faster. Advertisers muddy the airwaves of radio and television and pollute the view of travelers. We are a long way from outlawing the commons in matters of pleasure. Is this because our Puritan inheritance makes us view pleasure as something of a sin, and plain (that is, the pollution of advertising) as the sign of virtue?

Every new enclosure of the commons involves the infringement of some-body's personal liberty. Infringements made in the distant past are accepted because no contemporary complains of a loss. It is the newly proposed infringements that we vigorously oppose; cries of "rights" and "freedom" fill the air. But what does "freedom" mean? When men mutually agreed to pass laws against robbing, mankind became more free, not less so. Individuals locked into the logic of the commons are free only to bring on universal ruin; once they see the necessity of mutual coercion, they become free to pursue other goals. I believe it was Hegel who said, "Freedom is the recognition of necessity."

The most important aspect of necessity that we must now recognize, is the necessity of abandoning the commons in breeding. No technical solution can rescue us from the misery of overpopulation. Freedom to breed will bring ruin to all. At the moment, to avoid hard decisions many of us are tempted to propagandize for conscience and responsible parenthood. The temptation must be resisted, because an appeal to independently acting consciences selects for the disappearance of all conscience in the long run, and an increase in anxiety in the short.

The only way we can preserve and nurture other and more precious free-doms is by relinquishing the freedom to breed, and that very soon. "Freedom is the recognition of necessity"—and it is the role of education to reveal to all the necessity of abandoning the freedom to breed. Only so, can we put an end to this aspect of the tragedy of the commons.

NOTES

1. J. B. Wiesner and H. F. York. *Sci. Amer.* 211 (No. 4), 27 (1964).

2. G. Hardin, *J. Hered.* 50, 68 (1959); S. von Hoernor, *Science* 137, 18 (1962).

3. J. von Neumann and O. Morgenstern, *Theory of Games and Economic Behavior* (Princeton Univ. Press, Princeton, N.J., 1947), p. 11.

4. J. H. Fremlin, *New Sci.*, No. 415 (1964), p. 285.

5. A. Smith, *The Wealth of Nations* (Modern Library, New York, 1937), p. 423.

6. W. F. Lloyd, *Two Lectures on the Checks to Population* (Oxford Univ. Press, Oxford, England, 1833), reprinted (in part) in *Population, Evolution, and Birth Control*, G. Hardin, Ed. (Freeman, San Francisco, 1964), p. 37.

7. A. N. Whitehead, *Science and the Modern World* (Mentor, New York, 1948), p. 17.

8. G. Hardin, Ed. *Population, Evolution, and Birth Control* (Freeman, San Francisco, 1964), p. 56.

9. S. McVay, *Sci. Amer.* 216 (No. 8), 13 (1966).

10. J. Fletcher, *Situation Ethics* (Westminster, Philadelphia, 1966).

11. D. Lack, *The Natural Regulation of Animal Numbers* (Clarendon Press, Oxford, 1954).

12. H. Girvetz, *From Wealth to Welfare* (Stanford Univ. Press, Stanford, Calif., 1950).

13. G. Hardin, *Perspec. Biol. Med.* 6, 366 (1963).

14. U. Thant, *Int. Planned Parenthood News*, No. 168 (February 1968), p. 3.

15. K. Davis, *Science* 158, 730 (1967).

16. S. Tax, Ed., *Evolution after Darwin* (Univ. of Chicago Press, Chicago, 1960), vol. 2, p. 469.

17. G. Bateson, D. D. Jackson, J. Haley, J. Weakland, *Behav. Sci.* 1, 251 (1956).

18. P. Goodman, *New York Rev. Books* 10 (No. 8), 22 (23 May 1968).

19. A. Comfort, *The Anxiety Makers* (Nelson, London, 1967).

20. C. Frankel, *The Case for Modern Man* (Harper, New York, 1955), p. 203.

21. J. D. Roslansky, *Genetics and the Future of Man* (Appleton-Century-Crofts, New York, 1966), p. 177.

1.3

D. RODERICK KIEWIET AND MATHEW McCUBBINS

From *The Logic of Delegation*

Kiewiet and McCubbins describe the pervasive problem of delegation, sometimes called the principal-agent problem. This common "problem" occurs when there is a conflict of interest between the people who make decisions (principals) and the people hired by principals to carry out the decisions (agents). A key task of modern representative government is to ensure that decision makers have the means to manage the behavior of those implementing policies. For example, elected representatives rely on government agencies and bureaucrats to implement policies. How do elected officials control what government bureaucrats do?

COLLECTIVE ACTION AND DELEGATION

. . . The most familiar collective action problem is the prisoner's dilemma. It takes its name from the simple two-person game, but the social contexts in which most human interaction takes place tend to make *n*-person prisoners' dilemmas the more pervasive phenomenon. The crux of the dilemma is that individuals, in seeking to maximize their self-interest, have incentives to behave in ways that are inimical to the interests of the community as a whole (Hardin 1968). A good example of the dilemma is that of public goods (Olson 1965). The community would on net benefit from such a good, but those who do not contribute to its provision cannot be excluded from enjoying it. Everyone therefore has an incentive to free ride on the contributions of others. Even though the community may unanimously favor acquisition of the public good, little or no effort is expended to supply it. Rational individual choices produce irrational collective outcomes.

Collective action may also be stymied by a lack of coordination. In contrast to the prisoner's dilemma, where dominant strategies yield an inefficient equilibrium, other situations confront the community with multiple efficient equilibria. Members of the community are uncertain as to which strategies other members will pursue, and coordination may never be achieved. A simple coordination problem occurs when two cars enter an intersection simultaneously. Neither driver cares particularly who goes first; both are far more concerned about avoiding a collision. What frequently occurs, however, is a nerve-wracking *pas de deux* of false starts and sudden stops as the drivers make their way through the crossing. Even if everyone in the community would benefit from all alternatives under consideration, problems of coordination are exacerbated when different alternatives benefit some members relative to others.

■ ■ ■

According to property rights theorists, the best response to collective action problems is to minimize their occurrence, something that is accomplished by relegating as much human activity as possible to the realm of the marketplace. Adam Smith argued long ago that the well-being of a community is better realized through individual market transactions than through the schemes of even the most benevolent planner. Much social benefit can also be derived from simple patterns of reciprocity. But there are limits to what can be achieved through voluntary trade and cooperation; uncoordinated, unorganized activity will get a community only so far. In most cases, the benefits of collective action are realized through organizations. It is in the context of organizations that collective action is most effectively coordinated, that prisoners' dilemmas are most readily overcome, and that stable social decisions are most likely to be reached.

The organizational bases of collective action are many—firms, bureaucracies, associations, committees, leagues, representative assemblies, to name a few. What the most prominent forms of organization have in common, however, is the delegation of authority to take action from the individual or individuals to whom it was originally endowed—the principal—to one or more agents. One major organizational theorist, in fact, defines organizations as "networks of overlapping or nested principal/agent relationships" (Tirole 1986, p. 181). Delegation from principals to agents is the key to the division of labor and development of specialization; tremendous gains accrue if tasks are delegated to those with the talent, training, and inclination to do them. This, when all is said and done, is what allows firms to profit, economies to grow, and governments to govern.

The underlings in an organization are obviously agents of their superiors, but the heads of organizations, such as coaches, firm managers, party leaders, are agents, too. Indeed, it is the delegation of authority to a central agent to lead or manage the organization that is the key to overcoming problems of collective action. Agents performing as leaders or managers must be endowed with the resources they need to discharge their duties effectively. In the case of congressional parties, leaders can exploit the prominence of their position to identify a focal point, thus solving problems of coordination by rallying support around one of possibly many acceptable alternatives. Their ability to structure the voting agenda, moreover, can overcome social choice instability.

In such a relationship the agent seeks to maximize his or her return subject to the constraints and incentives offered by the principal. The principal, conversely, seeks to structure the relationship with the agent so that the outcomes produced through the agent's efforts are the best the principal can achieve, given the choice to delegate in the first place. There is, then, a natural conflict of interest between the two. In economic settings this conflict is often over the amount of effort expended by the agent. In political settings it is more likely to be over the course of action the agent is to pursue. The policy agenda of agency bureaucrats, for example, can be quite at odds with the preferences of the elected officials who oversee them. As a consequence of this conflict of interest, the principal always experiences some reduction in welfare. First, he suffers agency losses that result from the agent behaving in ways other than those that best serve his interests. Second, the principal incurs agency costs in undertaking efforts to mitigate agency losses. Agency problems may be so great that they exceed the benefits to be derived from collection action, in which case the delegation should not occur.

The opportunistic behavior that is at the root of agency problems is by no means confined to principal/agent relationships. Individuals involved in market transactions have similar incentives to behave in a less than noble manner. Certain conditions that are generally present in principal/agent relationships, however, make it a particularly congenial environment for opportunism. These are the conditions of hidden action, hidden information, and a form of strategic vulnerability on the part of the principal that we refer to as Madison's dilemma.

Hidden Action and Hidden Information

In a wide variety of agency relationships, the agent possesses or acquires information that is either unavailable to the principal or prohibitively costly to obtain. The agent has incentives to use this information strategically or to simply keep it hidden—a situation referred to variously as the problem of truthful revelation or incentive incompatibility. In a firm, workers have information that is not available to management, such as how fast the assembly line can run before quality is compromised. They would prefer not to reveal this information, however, because they would rather not work at a breakneck pace. Another type of information that agents often have and principals do not is the agent's type (for example, knowledge of whether the agent is hardworking or lazy, talented or untalented, risk-averse or risk-acceptant). This variation on the hidden information problem is referred to as adverse selection.

Situations in which agents acquire information that is unavailable to the principal pervade public policy-making. The basis of Niskanen's (1971) argument as to how bureaus maximize the size of their budgets is that bureaucrats are privy to information about service delivery costs that is not available to elected politicians. Through their investigations, congressional committees uncover information that is not available to other members of the chamber. Individual members, similarly, have better information than do congressional party leaders as to whether or not supporting the party's position might cause them trouble back home.

The second problem, that of hidden action, manifests itself in a variety of situations. Stockholders cannot observe whether the actions that firm managers take are in their best interest. Voters cannot observe whether the actions of elected representatives—their agents—are in their best interest. Hidden action is especially problematic when the agent's actions only partially determine outcomes, as in the case of team production or committee decisions, or when outcomes are partially determined by chance. In such cases, the principal is unable to infer the appropriateness of the agent's actions even from observed results.

Madison's Dilemma

Arguing for the separation of powers specified under the new Constitution, Madison wrote in *Federalist 51*, "In framing a government to be administered by men over men, the great difficulty lies in this: you must first enable the government to control the governed; and in the next place oblige it to control itself." Whatever their views about the document that was ultimately produced, members of the Constitutional Convention were keenly appreciative of Madison's observation. They had seen that under the Articles of Confederation the federal government had not been delegated enough authority to accomplish much of anything. Yet they feared that a government powerful enough to govern effectively would necessarily be powerful enough to oppress them.

In addition to problems of hidden action and hidden information, this third problem, one we call Madison's dilemma, is a potential pitfall in all institutions that rely upon delegation. The essence of the problem is that resources or authority granted to an agent for the purpose of advancing the interests of the principal can be turned against the principal. Although the problem is a general one of agency, it has long been recognized in liberal political theory as being of paramount importance when the agents involved are those in a position of leadership. Madison's dilemma is not a consequence of agents taking hidden action or acquiring hidden information, although these conditions can certainly make matters worse. Rather, it arises from agents exploiting the favorable strategic situation in which they have been placed.

In seeking to solve collective action problems, members of the community must be prescient in their delegation of authority to a central agent. If not, they may find that that they would have been better off continuing to endure their problems than they are living with the solution their agent has achieved.

Collective Principals and Collective Agents

Problems of hidden action, hidden information, and Madison's dilemma are endemic to all agency relationships. There are additional hazards to delegation, however, when either collective principals or collective agents are involved. Specifically, the very same collective action problems that delegation is intended to overcome—prisoners' dilemmas, lack of coordination, and social choice instability—can reemerge to afflict either the collective agent or a collective principal. A collective principal may be unable to announce a single preference over its agent's actions or to offer a single contract governing compensation for the agent. A subset of the membership may strategically manipulate the decision-making process of the collective principal. Similarly, agents who are delegated management or leadership roles may use their agenda powers to do the same thing, thus leaving the collective principal vulnerable to a form of Madison's dilemma. A related consideration is that in appointing a new individual to a collective agent, such as a production team or a committee, that person's abilities and preferences cannot be evaluated in isolation. The principal must consider instead how the new agent will interact with existing members of the team or committee.

Distinct from the problems of collective principals and agents are problems specific to multiple principals and agents. An agent attempting to serve multiple principals often finds that any action he or she might take to benefit one principal injures another. Federal agencies are buffeted by conflicting pressures from their departments, the president, the courts, their interest group clients, as well as several congressional committees and subcommittees. Second, when there are multiple agents it is possible that they will collude against the principal. This can occur in a number of ways. Workers who break the curve, for example, are likely to be castigated by their fellow workers. The essence of "iron triangle" or "subgovernment" theories of public policy formation is that collusion between two sets of agents—federal agencies and the congressional committees that ostensibly oversee them—serves to undermine the welfare of the general public (their ultimate principal) rather than to promote it.

OVERCOMING AGENCY PROBLEMS

Agency losses can be contained, but only by undertaking measures that are themselves costly. There are are four major classes of such measures: (1) contract design, (2) screening and selection mechanisms, (3) monitoring and reporting requirements, and (4) institutional checks.

Contract Design

Any contract between a principal and agent must satisfy the participation constraint. The agent's compensation must be at least as great as his or her opportunity costs, but less than the marginal benefit the principal derives from the actions of the agent. If this condition is not met, one side or the other will not be made better off by entering into the relationship and will decline to do so. Assuming that the participation constraint is satisfied, the principal's goal is to delegate tasks and responsibilities and to specify a corresponding schedule of compensation in such a way that the agent is motivated to best serve the principal's interests. Such contracts may specify negative rewards, or sanctions, particularly when the agent is capable of taking actions that are very harmful to the principal. In some situations, particularly when noncompliance with the principal's directives is hard to detect, the sanctions required to effect compliance are far greater in magnitude than the benefits that the principal derives from compliance.

Under conditions that usually exist in principal/agent relationships—hidden information and hidden action—designing compensation schedules is a tricky business. Examples abound of compensation schemes that create incentives for agent behavior other than that intended by the principal. If not otherwise constrained, brokers receiving a commission on trades churn through their clients' portfolios. Ford factory managers, no less creative than their celebrated Soviet counterparts, often met their quotas by surreptitiously building large numbers of automobiles prior to the official start of the production run (Halberstam 1986). Governmental agencies have an especially difficult time designing appropriate compensation schedules. Medicare administrators, for example, came to realize that simply reimbursing hospitals for all "reasonable" costs incurred in treating patients contributed to rapidly escalating claims. In 1982 they won congressional approval for a new system under which hospitals receive a fixed fee for treatment based upon the diagnosis related group (DRG) to which the patient has been assigned. In short order the system began to experience "DRG creep"; elderly Americans were succumbing to increasingly expensive diseases that often could be diagnosed only with the most advanced (and expensive) medical technology.

The problem of inappropriate incentives in compensation schemes can be mitigated by giving agents a residual claim on output. The compensation received by corporate executives, for example, is often in the form of profit sharing or other bonuses linked to the performance of the firm. Another example of this arrangement is sharecropping. Instead of charging a fixed rent, the landlord leases land to a tenant in return for a percentage of the crop. Compensation contracts of this form can be used in the public sector as well. In previous centuries, the king of France and other European monarchs garnered much of their revenue from "tax farmers," that is, individuals who were given the right to collect taxes in a particular geographic area so long as they surrendered an agreed-upon amount of the proceeds to the crown. The state of Ohio actually implemented this method for garnering revenue at the end of the Civil War; counties and cities were permitted to engage "tax inquisitors" who were empowered to find concealed taxable holdings (usually stocks and bank deposits) in return for a percentage of the proceeds.

Although such profit-sharing arrangements can help mitigate agency losses, they are hardly a panacea. They can be very expensive to the principal and do not necessarily remove all inappropriate incentives. In the realm of public policy, awarding agents a residual claim on output can have particularly obnoxious consequences; the interested student should be able to surmise why the institution of tax farming fell out of favor. Even if it were desirable to motivate public servants with a piece of the action, most important policy outputs are impossible to measure. How, for example, could the military establishment be awarded an incentive bonus that hinged upon whether or not they had had a good year?

Given the difficulties involved in designing optimal contracts prior to the establishment of an agency relationship, an alternative strategy for the principal may be to simply offer a compensation contract and, conditioned on the agent accepting it, to see how well he or she works out. There is, after all, no better information about how well an agent performs than his or her actual performance. Most employment contracts specify an initial probationary period (ranging from three or four days for waiters to three or four years for professors) and provide for periodic reviews after that. The principal can minimize the risk associated with this strategy by initially assigning an agent a modest set of tasks and responsibilities at a modest level of compensation. Those who perform well are rewarded by increasing the range of their authority and responsibility and, concommitantly, the level of their compensation. Agents who perform poorly will not similarly advance, or may even be demoted or dismissed. Like other strategies available to the principal, this one works best when agents can be induced to compete with each other. One of the major rationales for hierarchy in organizations is that it means there are more people seeking promotion to the next level than there are opportunities available.

Screening and Selection Mechanisms

A policy of hiring first and adjusting compensation later does nothing to address the problem of adverse selection discussed earlier; the offer of a given level of compensation attracts only those applicants whose opportunity costs are lower than the offer. This is not a damaging critique, however, because there is little that can be done about adverse selection simply by altering the terms of the compensation contract. The more telling problem is that information revealed by the agent's on-the-job performance, as valuable as it is, can be exceedingly expensive to obtain. Spence (1974) details several reasons why it can be so costly to sort out good agents from bad after they have been hired and why it pays both principals and agents to invest time and effort into avoiding bad matches in the first place:

> One might ask why the employer would not simply hire the person, determine his productivity, and then either fire him or adjust his wage or salary accordingly. There are several reasons why he will not do this. Frequently, he cannot. It may take time (even a long time) for the individual's real capabilities to become apparent. There may be a specific training required before the individual can handle certain kinds of jobs. There may be a contract and a contract period within which the individual cannot be fired and his salary cannot be adjusted. All of these factors tend to make the hiring decision an investment decision for the employer. Certain costs incurred in hiring and in the early

period of employment are sunk and cannot be recovered if the investment turns out badly. (p. 14)

To the extent they share in the benefits of minimizing agency losses and
agency costs, both sides are better off if principals are able to identify those
individuals who possess the appropriate talents, skills, and other personal
characteristics prior to the establishment of the principal/agent relationship.
The greater the investment entailed in the hiring decision, the more critical
screening and selection mechanisms become. Thus Spence's arguments apply
with even more force in the public sector than in the private. Congressional
members appointed to committees do not serve a probationary period to see
how well they work out. Civil Service employees, for all practical purposes,
cannot be fired. And as incumbent presidents typically point out when running for reelection, the Oval Office is no place for on-the-job training.

But how are principals and agents able to find suitable matches when they
lack the requisite information? Principals cannot observe agents' actual performance until after the commitment to hire them has been made. Potential
agents, similarly, cannot know exactly what the job is like until they start doing
it. This problem is compounded by the fact that both potential principals and
potential agents frequently have an incentive to misrepresent their abilities and
preferences. According to Spence, this informational gap is bridged by observing properties of each other that are reliable signals of the underlying qualities
of interest. Many signals that employers attend to in the labor market are
beyond the applicants' control, such as race, age, or gender, and for that reason
can be illegitimate sources of discrimination. Other signals, however, the applicant has at least partial control over, such as appearing on time for the job
interview, presenting a neat personal appearance, and expressing enthusiasm
for the job.

Signaling is an important phenomenon in the political world as well. Congressional candidates who have served in an elected office before are far more
likely to get elected than those who have not. A major reason for this is that
their previous success signals to potential contributors that they are high-
quality candidates. Congressional parties also tend not to name freshmen to
the House Appropriations Committee. This is because freshmen have not been
around long enough to demonstrate that they are the type of *homme sérieux*
who has traditionally served on the committee—hardworking, respectful,
and, whatever their ideological predilections, responsive to the needs of the
party.

Monitoring and Reporting Requirements

Once a principal and agent have entered into a relationship, the most straightforward way to eliminate the conditions of hidden action and information
would seem to be to institute procedures requiring agents to report whatever
relevant information they have obtained and whatever actions they have

taken. After all, hidden information is no longer hidden if you make the agent reveal it. On the basis of information provided by the agent, the principal can presumably tie the agent's compensation more directly to his or her actual conduct. As before, to the extent both sides share in a reduction in agency losses and agency costs, both principal and agent can be made better off.

In fact, reporting requirements are ubiquitous in both the private and public sectors. Employees fill out weekly progress reports for their supervisors, who in turn report to their supervisors on the status of their operations. Every year congressional committees, regulatory agencies, and executive departments report millions of pages of material on their hearings, investigations, and policy recommendations.

There are, however, costs entailed both in the agent's provision and in the principal's consumption of information. If nothing else, the transfer of information deflects time and attention away from tasks that they would otherwise be performing. Rather than require agents to report all relevant information, their reports should be at an optimal level of "coarsification." Unfortunately, this is difficult to modulate; a principal can either be starving for information or, more often, drowning in a sea of it. That hundreds of millions of dollars are invested annually in the design of management information systems attests to the difficulty of this problem.

The more serious drawback to reporting requirements, however, has already been broached, and that is the problem of truthful revelation or incentive incompatibility. The agent has incentives to shade things, to make reports that reflect favorably upon himself, or to reveal information in some other strategic manner. Employees may discover that energy, skill, and creativity applied to their weekly progress reports pays off much more handsomely than actually doing the job. Even if agents can somehow be constrained to be truthful in their reports, the principal will still not know what they are not reporting. For that reason principals typically supplement these requirements with what McCubbins and Schwartz (1984) have dubbed "police patrol" oversight—audits, investigations, and other direct methods of monitoring. To be effective, monitoring policies should be applied stochastically so as to preserve the element of surprise. Direct monitoring can cost the principal a great deal of time and effort. Anyone who has ever worked on a factory floor can attest to the fact that constant supervision is also demeaning and corrosive to the morale of both supervisor and supervisee.

Frequently an agent's actions affect individuals who are not a party to the original principal/agent contract. These individuals may be the intended beneficiaries of the agent's actions, as when an employee supplies a service to a customer on behalf of the firm's owners, or when bureaucrats deliver benefits to constituents on behalf of members of Congress or the president. Because affected third parties have an incentive to observe and to influence the actions of the agent, opportunities arise for oversight that is potentially less costly and more reliable than "police patrols." Instead of examining a sample of the agent's activities (or, more typically, the agent's reports about his or her activities), looking for inappropriate actions or improper use of information, the principal instead obtains information from the affected third parties. This McCubbins and Schwartz refer to as "fire alarm" oversight.

Fire alarm oversight offers several advantages. First, it allows the principal to gather information at lower cost; even when it is as costly as police patrol oversight, much of the cost is borne by the affected third parties. Second, it can yield better information. Under a realistic police patrol policy the principal examines only a small sample of the agent's actions and is therefore likely to miss violations. Under a well-designed fire alarm system, third parties can bring to the principal's attention any serious violation by the agent. More important, the affected third parties have incentives that are in accord with the principal's interests and not, as in the case of the agent, in conflict with them. Third, it is usually difficult to specify a priori a contract with the agent that unambiguously covers all contingencies, and consequently it is hard to tell whether an agent has violated the contract. In this situation, complaints by the affected third parties give principals the opportunity to spell out their goals more clearly.

Often it is no easier for affected third parties to oversee the agent's actions than it is for the principal. In such cases the principal can provide third parties with the means and the incentive to gather information and to report it to him. One common example is that of companies who post on the rear of their trucks an 800 number that motorists can call to report reckless driving by the vehicle's operator. Until 1874 the federal government awarded 25 percent of the fines and forfeiture collected to those who informed on fraudulent valuations by customs officers (Studenski and Krooss 1952, p. 170). Today several agencies of the federal government, including the Department of Defense, the Internal Revenue Service, and the Security and Exchange Commission, have taken similar measures by setting up fraud "hotlines" and advertising rewards for whistle-blowers. Although such programs have a number of operational problems, their deterrent effect may be substantial.

Alternatively, principals can set up a fire alarm system by requiring agents to notify third parties of any actions that affect them. According to McCubbins, Noll, and Weingast (1987), this requirement is a key feature of the Administrative Procedures Act of 1946. To comply with this legislation, an administrative agency must announce its intention to consider an issue well in advance of any decision. It must solicit comments and allow all interested parties to communicate their views. The agency must explicitly address any and all evidence presented and provide a rationalizable link between the evidence and its decisions. Such procedures, of course, do not necessarily remove inherent biases in agency decision making. But the mandated sequence of notice, comment, collection of evidence, and deliberation affords numerous opportunities for members of Congress to respond when an agency seeks to move in a direction that a key constituency group finds objectionable. This makes it very difficult for agencies to strategically manipulate congressional decisions by presenting a fait accompli, that is, a new policy with already mobilized supporters.

Institutional Checks

Most applications of the principal/agent framework in economics characterize the principal's problem as one of seeking to induce the agent to expend more effort. The assumption is that the harder they work, the more they produce. But agents are often in a position to do more harm to the principal than to simply withhold effort; embezzlement, insider trading, official corruption, abuse of authority, and coups d'etat are all testaments to this fact. Whenever an agent can take actions that might seriously jeopardize the principal's interests, the principal needs to thwart the agent's ability to pursue such courses of action unilaterally.

We refer to various countermeasures the principal may take in this regard as institutional checks. Operationally, institutional checks require that when authority has been delegated to an agent, there is at least one other agent with the authority to veto or to block the actions of that agent. The framers of the Constitution established many interlocking checks with the intention of constraining the more powerful central government they had created. Most firms also employ systems of checks. Large expenditures, for example, typically require the approval of both management and the comptroller. Some of the most check-laden institutions are universities. Granting tenure usually requires an overwhelmingly favorable vote in the department, the approval of the dean, the acquiescence of a university-wide ad hoc committee, and ratification by the trustees.

As Madison observed, ambition is best checked by ambition—agents positioned against each other should have countervailing interests. This is most readily accomplished by making the agents' compensation contingent on different standards, such as rewarding managers for increasing production but rewarding comptrollers for cutting costs. Checks can also be applied in information acquisition. Rather than striving for an unbiased source of information, a principal may do better obtaining biased reports from different agents who have conflicting incentives. The view that legal proceedings should be adversarial rather than administrative is based on the same logic. Conversely, checks are disabled when agents' incentives cease to be in conflict.

Checks are equivalent to what social choice theorists refer to as the presence of veto subgroups. The major theoretical results concerning the effects of veto subgroups are generally intuitive. First, the more veto subgroups (checks) there are, the harder it is to change the status quo. The status quo also becomes more difficult to change as preferences within veto subgroups become more homogeneous and as preferences between veto subgroups become more diverse. Checks, then, inhibit the ability of agents to take actions that the principal considers undesirable, but necessarily retard agents from taking desirable actions as well; security comes at the price of flexibility. The desirability of imposing checks on delegated authority thus increases with the utility the principal derives from the status quo and with the amount of danger posed by inappropriate agency actions.

REFERENCES

Halberstam, David. 1986. *The Reckoning.* New York, NY: William Morrow and Company.

Hardin, Garrett. 1968. "The Tragedy of the Commons." *Science* 162:1243–48.

McCubbins, Mathew, Roger Noll, and Barry Weingast. 1987. "Administrative Procedures as an Instrument of Political Control." *Journal of Law, Economics, and Organization* 3:243–77.

———, and Thomas Schwartz. 1984. "Congressional Oversight Overlooked: Police Patrols versus Fire Alarms." *American Journal of Political Science* 28:165–79.

Niskanen, William A. 1971. *Bureaucracy and Representative Government.* Chicago, IL: Aldine-Atherton.

Olson, Mancur, 1965. *The Logic of Collective Action.* Cambridge, MA: Harvard University Press.

Spence, A. Michael. 1974. *Market Signalling: Informational Transfer in Hiring and Related Screening Processes.* Cambridge, MA: Harvard University Press.

Studenski, Paul, and Herman Krooss. 1952. *Financial History of the United States.* New York, NY: McGraw-Hill.

Tirole, Jean. 1986. "Hierarchies and Bureaucracies: On the Role of Coercion in Organizations." *Journal of Law, Economics, and Organization* 2:181–214.

2

THE CONSTITUTION
AND THE FOUNDING

2.1

JAMES MADISON

The Federalist, No. 10

In this famous reading first published in 1787, James Madison promotes the view that a large republic will be better than a small republic. He argues that a large republic will have multiple, competing interest groups, none of which will be able to form a majority on its own. A small republic would likely be dominated by powerful interests.

Among the numerous advantages promised by a well constructed Union, none deserves to be more accurately developed than its tendency to break and control the violence of faction. The friend of popular governments never finds himself so much alarmed for their character and fate, as when he contemplates their propensity to this dangerous vice. He will not fail, therefore, to set a due value on any plan which, without violating the principles to which he is attached, provides a proper cure for it. The instability, injustice, and confusion introduced into the public councils, have, in truth, been the mortal diseases under which popular governments have everywhere perished; as they continue to be the favorite and fruitful topics from which the adversaries to liberty derive their most specious declamations. The valuable improvements made by the American constitutions on the popular models, both ancient and modern, cannot certainly be too much admired; but it would be an unwarrantable partiality, to contend that they have as effectually obviated the danger on this side, as was wished and expected. Complaints are everywhere heard from our most considerate and virtuous citizens, equally the friends of public and private faith, and of public and personal liberty, that our governments are too unstable, that the public good is disregarded in the conflicts of rival parties, and that measures are too often decided, not according to the rules of justice and the rights of the minor party, but by the superior force of an interested and overbearing majority. However anxiously we may wish that these complaints had no foundation, the evidence, of known facts will not permit us to deny that they are in some degree true. It will be found, indeed, on a candid review of our situation, that some of the distresses under which we labor have been erroneously charged on the operation of our governments; but it will be found, at the same time, that other causes will not alone account for many of our heaviest misfortunes; and, particularly, for that prevailing and increasing distrust of public engagements, and alarm for private rights, which are echoed from one end of the continent to the other. These must be chiefly, if not wholly, effects of the unsteadiness and injustice with which a factious spirit has tainted our public administrations.

By a faction, I understand a number of citizens, whether amounting to a majority or a minority of the whole, who are united and actuated by some common impulse of passion, or of interest, adversed to the rights of other citizens, or to the permanent and aggregate interests of the community.

There are two methods of curing the mischiefs of faction: the one, by removing its causes; the other, by controlling its effects.

There are again two methods of removing the causes of faction: the one, by destroying the liberty which is essential to its existence; the other, by giving to every citizen the same opinions, the same passions, and the same interests.

It could never be more truly said than of the first remedy, that it was worse than the disease. Liberty is to faction what air is to fire, an aliment without which it instantly expires. But it could not be less folly to abolish liberty, which is essential to political life, because it nourishes faction, than it would be to wish the annihilation of air, which is essential to animal life, because it imparts to fire its destructive agency.

The second expedient is as impracticable as the first would be unwise. As long as the reason of man continues fallible, and he is at liberty to exercise it, different opinions will be formed. As long as the connection subsists between his reason and his self-love, his opinions and his passions will have a reciprocal influence on each other; and the former will be objects to which the latter will attach themselves. The diversity in the faculties of men, from which the rights of property originate, is not less an insuperable obstacle to a uniformity of interests. The protection of these faculties is the first object of government. From the protection of different and unequal faculties of acquiring property, the possession of different degrees and kinds of property immediately results; and from the influence of these on the sentiments and views of the respective proprietors, ensues a division of the society into different interests and parties.

The latent causes of faction are thus sown in the nature of man; and we see them everywhere brought into different degrees of activity, according to the different circumstances of civil society. A zeal for different opinions concerning religion, concerning government, and many other points, as well of speculation as of practice; an attachment to different leaders ambitiously contending for pre-eminence and power; or to persons of other descriptions whose fortunes have been interesting to the human passions, have, in turn, divided mankind into parties, inflamed them with mutual animosity, and rendered them much more disposed to vex and oppress each other than to co-operate for their common good. So strong is this propensity of mankind to fall into mutual animosities, that where no substantial occasion presents itself, the most frivolous and fanciful distinctions have been sufficient to kindle their unfriendly passions and excite their most violent conflicts. But the most common and durable source of factions has been the various and unequal distribution of property. Those who hold and those who are without property have ever formed distinct interests in society. Those who are creditors, and those who are debtors, fall under a like discrimination. A landed interest, a manufacturing interest, a mercantile interest, a moneyed interest, with many lesser interests, grow up of necessity in civilized nations, and divide them into different classes, actuated by different sentiments and views. The regulation of these various and interfering interests forms the principal task of modern legislation, and involves the spirit of party and faction in the necessary and ordinary operations of the government.

No man is allowed to be a judge in his own cause, because his interest would certainly bias his judgment, and, not improbably, corrupt his integrity. With equal, nay with greater reason, a body of men are unfit to be both judges and parties at the same time; yet what are many of the most important acts of legislation, but so many judicial determinations, not indeed concerning the rights of single persons, but concerning the rights of large bodies of citizens? And what are the different classes of legislators but advocates and parties to the causes which they determine? Is a law proposed concerning private debts? It is a question to which the creditors are parties on one side and the debtors on the other. Justice ought to hold the balance between them. Yet the parties are, and must be, themselves the judges; and the most numerous party, or, in other words, the most powerful faction must be expected to prevail. Shall domestic manufactures be encouraged, and in what degree, by restrictions on foreign manufactures? are questions which would be differently decided by the landed and the manufacturing classes, and probably by neither with a sole regard to justice and the public good. The apportionment of taxes on the various descriptions of property is an act which seems to require the most exact impartiality; yet there is, perhaps, no legislative act in which greater opportunity and temptation are given to a predominant party to trample on the rules of justice. Every shilling with which they overburden the inferior number, is a shilling saved to their own pockets.

It is in vain to say that enlightened statesmen will be able to adjust these clashing interests, and render them all subservient to the public good. Enlightened statesmen will not always be at the helm. Nor, in many cases, can such an adjustment be made at all without taking into view indirect and remote considerations, which will rarely prevail over the immediate interest which one party may find in disregarding the rights of another or the good of the whole.

The inference to which we are brought is, that the *causes* of faction cannot be removed, and that relief is only to be sought in the means of controlling its *effects*.

If a faction consists of less than a majority, relief is supplied by the republican principle, which enables the majority to defeat its sinister views by regular vote. It may clog the administration, it may convulse the society; but it will be unable to execute and mask its violence under the forms of the Constitution. When a majority is included in a faction, the form of popular government, on the other hand, enables it to sacrifice to its ruling passion or interest both the public good and the rights of other citizens. To secure the public good and private rights against the danger of such a faction, and at the same time to preserve the spirit and the form of popular government, is then the great object to which our inquiries are directed. Let me add that it is the great desideratum by which this form of government can be rescued from the opprobrium under which it has so long labored, and be recommended to the esteem and adoption of mankind.

By what means is this object attainable? Evidently by one of two only. Either the existence of the same passion or interest in a majority at the same time must be prevented, or the majority, having such coexistent passion or interest, must be rendered, by their number and local situation, unable to concert and carry into effect schemes of oppression. If the impulse and the opportunity be suffered to coincide, we well know that neither moral nor religious motives can be relied on as an adequate control. They are not found to be such on the injustice and violence of individuals, and lose their efficacy in proportion to the number combined together, that is, in proportion as their efficacy becomes needful.

From this view of the subject it may be concluded that a pure democracy, by which I mean a society consisting of a small number of citizens, who assemble and administer the government in person, can admit of no cure for the mischiefs of faction. A common passion or interest will, in almost every case, be felt by a majority of the whole; a communication and concert result from the form of government itself; and there is nothing to check the inducements to sacrifice the weaker party or an obnoxious individual. Hence it is that such democracies have ever been spectacles of turbulence and contention; have ever been found incompatible with personal security or the rights of property; and have in general been as short in their lives as they have been violent in their deaths. Theoretic politicians, who have patronized this species of government, have erroneously supposed that by reducing mankind to a perfect equality in their political rights, they would, at the same time, be perfectly equalized and assimilated in their possessions, their opinions, and their passions.

A republic, by which I mean a government in which the scheme of representation takes place, opens a different prospect, and promises the cure for which we are seeking. Let us examine the points in which it varies from pure democracy, and we shall comprehend both the nature of the cure and the efficacy which it must derive from the Union.

The two great points of difference between a democracy and a republic are: first, the delegation of the government, in the latter, to a small number of citizens elected by the rest; secondly, the greater number of citizens, and greater sphere of country, over which the latter may be extended.

The effect of the first difference is, on the one hand, to refine and enlarge the public views, by passing them through the medium of a chosen body of citizens, whose wisdom may best discern the true interest of their country, and whose patriotism and love of justice will be least likely to sacrifice it to temporary or partial considerations. Under such a regulation, it may well happen that the public voice, pronounced by the representatives of the people, will be more consonant to the public good than if pronounced by the people themselves, convened for the purpose. On the other hand, the effect may be inverted. Men of factious tempers, of local prejudices, or of sinister designs, may, by intrigue, by corruption, or by other means, first obtain the suffrages, and then betray the interests, of the people. The question resulting is, whether small or extensive republics are more favorable to the election of proper guardians of the public weal; and it is clearly decided in favor of the latter by two obvious considerations:

In the first place, it is to be remarked that, however small the republic may be, the representatives must be raised to a certain number, in order to guard against the cabals of a few; and that, however large it may be, they must be limited to a certain number, in order to guard against the confusion of a multitude. Hence, the number of representatives in the two cases not being in proportion to that of the two constituents, and being proportionally greater in the small republic, it follows that, if the proportion of fit characters be not less in the large than in the small republic, the former will present a greater option, and consequently a greater probability of a fit choice.

In the next place, as each representative will be chosen by a greater number of citizens in the large than in the small republic, it will be more difficult for unworthy candidates to practice with success the vicious arts by which elections are too often carried; and the suffrages of the people being more free, will be more likely to centre in men who possess the most attractive merit and the most diffusive and established characters.

It must be confessed that in this, as in most other cases, there is a mean, on both sides of which inconveniences will be found to lie. By enlarging too much the number of electors, you render the representatives too little acquainted with all their local circumstances and lesser interests; as by reducing it too much, you render him unduly attached to these, and too little fit to comprehend and pursue great and national objects. The federal Constitution forms a happy combination in this respect; the great and aggregate interests being referred to the national, the local and particular to the State legislatures.

The other point of difference is, the greater number of citizens and extent of territory which may be brought within the compass of republican than of democratic government; and it is this circumstance principally which renders factious combinations less to be dreaded in the former than in the latter. The smaller the society, the fewer probably will be the distinct parties and interests composing it; the fewer the distinct parties and interests, the more frequently will a majority be found of the same party; and the smaller the number of individuals composing a majority, and the smaller the compass within which they are placed, the more easily will they concert and execute their plans of oppression. Extend the sphere, and you take in a greater variety of parties and interests; you make it less probable that a majority of the whole will have a common motive to invade the rights of other citizens; or if such a common motive exists, it will be more difficult for all who feel it to discover their own strength, and to act in unison with each other. Besides other impediments, it may be remarked that, where there is a consciousness of unjust or dishonorable purposes, communication is always checked by distrust in proportion to the number whose concurrence is necessary.

Hence, it clearly appears, that the same advantage which a republic has over a democracy, in controlling the effects of faction, is enjoyed by a large over a small republic,—is enjoyed by the Union over the States composing it. Does the advantage consist in the substitution of representatives whose enlightened views and virtuous sentiments render them superior to local prejudices and schemes of injustice? It will not be denied that the representation of the Union will be most likely to possess these requisite endowments. Does it consist in the greater security afforded by a greater variety of parties, against the event of any one party being able to outnumber and oppress the rest? In an equal degree does the increased variety of parties comprised within the Union, increase this security. Does it, in fine, consist in the greater obstacles opposed to the concert and accomplishment of the secret wishes of an unjust and interested majority? Here, again, the extent of the Union gives it the most palpable advantage.

The influence of factious leaders may kindle a flame within their particular States, but will be unable to spread a general conflagration through the other States. A religious sect may degenerate into a political faction in a part of the Confederacy; but the variety of sects dispersed over the entire face of it must secure the national councils against any danger from that source. A rage for paper money, for an abolition of debts, for an equal division of property, or for any other improper or wicked project, will be less apt to pervade the whole body of the Union than a particular member of it; in the same proportion as such a malady is more likely to taint a particular county or district, than an entire State.

In the extent and proper structure of the Union, therefore, we behold a republican remedy for the diseases most incident to republican government. And according to the degree of pleasure and pride we feel in being republicans, ought to be our zeal in cherishing the spirit and supporting the character of Federalists.

PUBLIUS

2.2

JAMES MADISON

The Federalist, No. 51

Here, James Madison offers a clear justification for having a form of government that fragments power among different branches and across different levels of government, arguing, "Ambition must be made to counteract ambition." This famous reading lays out the theoretical basis for three core features of the U.S. Constitution: separation of powers, checks and balances, and federalism.

To what expedient, then, shall we finally resort, for maintaining in practice the necessary partition of power among the several departments, as laid down in the Constitution? The only answer that can be given is, that as all these exterior provisions are found to be inadequate, the defect must be supplied, by so contriving the interior structure of the government as that its several constituent parts may, by their mutual relations, be the means of keeping each other in their proper places. Without presuming to undertake a full development of this important idea, I will hazard a few general observations, which may perhaps place it in a clearer light, and enable us to form a more correct judgment of the principles and structure of the government planned by the convention.

In order to lay a due foundation for that separate and distinct exercise of the different powers of government, which to a certain extent is admitted on all hands to be essential to the preservation of liberty, it is evident that each department should have a will of its own; and consequently should be so constituted that the members of each should have as little agency as possible in the appointment of the members of the others. Were this principle rigorously adhered to, it would require that all the appointments for the supreme executive, legislative, and judiciary magistracies should be drawn from the same fountain of authority, the people, through channels having no communication whatever with one another. Perhaps such a plan of constructing the several departments would be less difficult in practice than it may in contemplation appear. Some difficulties, however, and some additional expense would attend the execution of it. Some deviations, therefore, from the principle must be admitted. In the constitution of the judiciary department in particular, it might be inexpedient to insist rigorously on the principle: first, because peculiar qualifications being essential in the members, the primary consideration ought to be to select that mode of choice which best secures these qualifications; secondly, because the permanent tenure by which the appointments are held in that department, must soon destroy all sense of dependence on the authority conferring them.

It is equally evident, that the members of each department should be as little dependent as possible on those of the others, for the emoluments annexed to their offices. Were the executive magistrate, or the judges, not independent of the legislature in this particular, their independence in every other would be merely nominal. But the great security against a gradual concentration of the several powers in the same department, consists in giving to those who administer each department the necessary constitutional means and personal motives to resist encroachments of the others. The provision for defense must in this, as in all other cases, be made commensurate to the danger of attack. Ambition must be made to counteract ambition. The interest of the man must be connected with the constitutional rights of the place. It may be a reflection on human nature, that such devices should be necessary to control the abuses of government. But what is government itself, but the greatest of all reflections on human nature? If men were angels, no government would be necessary. If angels were to govern men, neither external nor internal controls on government would be necessary. In framing a government which is to be administered by men over men, the great difficulty lies in this: you must first enable the government to control the governed; and in the next place oblige it to control itself.

A dependence on the people is, no doubt, the primary control on the government; but experience has taught mankind the necessity of auxiliary precautions. This policy of supplying, by opposite and rival interests, the defect of better motives, might be traced through the whole system of human affairs, private as well as public. We see it particularly displayed in all the subordinate distributions of power, where the constant aim is to divide and arrange the several offices in such a manner as that each may be a check on the other that the private interest of every individual may be a sentinel over the public rights. These inventions of prudence cannot be less requisite in the distribution of the supreme powers of the State. But it is not possible to give to each department an equal power of self-defense. In republican government, the legislative authority necessarily predominates. The remedy for this inconveniency is to divide the legislature into different branches; and to render them, by different modes of election and different principles of action, as little connected with each other as the nature of their common functions and their common dependence on the society will admit. It may even be necessary to guard against dangerous encroachments by still further precautions. As the weight of the legislative authority requires that it should be thus divided, the weakness of the executive may require, on the other hand, that it should be fortified.

An absolute negative on the legislature appears, at first view, to be the natural defense with which the executive magistrate should be armed. But perhaps it would be neither altogether safe nor alone sufficient. On ordinary occasions it might not be exerted with the requisite firmness, and on extraordinary occasions it might be perfidiously abused. May not this defect of an absolute negative be supplied by some qualified connection between this weaker department and the weaker branch of the stronger department, by which the latter may be led to support the constitutional rights of the former, without being too much detached from the rights of its own department? If the principles on which these observations are founded be just, as I persuade myself they are, and they be applied as a criterion to the several State constitutions, and to the federal Constitution it will be found that if the latter does not perfectly correspond with them, the former are infinitely less able to bear such a test.

There are, moreover, two considerations particularly applicable to the federal system of America, which place that system in a very interesting point of view. First. In a single republic, all the power surrendered by the people is submitted to the administration of a single government; and the usurpations are guarded against by a division of the government into distinct and separate departments. In the compound republic of America, the power surrendered by the people is first divided between two distinct governments, and then the portion allotted to each subdivided among distinct and separate departments. Hence a double security arises to the rights of the people. The different governments will control each other, at the same time that each will be controlled by itself. Second. It is of great importance in a republic not only to guard the society against the oppression of its rulers, but to guard one part of the society against the injustice of the other part. Different interests necessarily exist in different classes of citizens. If a majority be united by a common interest, the rights of the minority will be insecure.

There are but two methods of providing against this evil: the one by creating a will in the community independent of the majority that is, of the society itself; the other, by comprehending in the society so many separate descriptions of citizens as will render an unjust combination of a majority of the whole very improbable, if not impracticable. The first method prevails in all governments possessing an hereditary or self-appointed authority. This, at best, is but a precarious security; because a power independent of the society may as well espouse the unjust views of the major, as the rightful interests of the minor party, and may possibly be turned against both parties. The second method will be exemplified in the federal republic of the United States. Whilst all authority in it will be derived from and dependent on the society, the society itself will be broken into so many parts, interests, and classes of citizens, that the rights of individuals, or of the minority, will be in little danger from interested combinations of the majority.

In a free government the security for civil rights must be the same as that for religious rights. It consists in the one case in the multiplicity of interests, and in the other in the multiplicity of sects. The degree of security in both cases will depend on the number of interests and sects; and this may be presumed to depend on the extent of country and number of people comprehended under the same government. This view of the subject must particularly recommend a proper federal system to all the sincere and considerate friends of republican government, since it shows that in exact proportion as the territory of the Union may be formed into more circumscribed Confederacies, or States oppressive combinations of a majority will be facilitated: the best security, under the republican forms, for the rights of every class of citizens, will be diminished: and consequently the stability and independence of some member of the government, the only other security, must be proportionately increased. Justice is the end of government. It is the end of civil society. It ever has been and ever will be pursued until it be obtained, or until liberty be lost in the pursuit. In a society under the forms of which the stronger faction can readily unite and oppress the weaker, anarchy may as truly be said to reign as in a state of nature, where the weaker individual is not secured against the violence of the stronger; and as, in the latter state, even the stronger individuals are prompted, by the uncertainty of their condition, to submit to a government which may protect the weak as well as themselves; so, in the former state, will the more powerful factions or parties be gradually induced, by a like motive, to wish for a government which will protect all parties, the weaker as well as the more powerful.

It can be little doubted that if the State of Rhode Island was separated from the Confederacy and left to itself, the insecurity of rights under the popular form of government within such narrow limits would be displayed by such reiterated oppressions of factious majorities that some power altogether independent of the people would soon be called for by the voice of the very factions whose misrule had proved the necessity of it. In the extended republic of the United States, and among the great variety of interests, parties, and sects which it embraces, a coalition of a majority of the whole society could seldom take place on any other principles than those of justice and the general good; whilst there being thus less danger to a minor from the will of a major party, there must be less pretext, also, to provide for the security of the former, by introducing into the government a will not dependent on the latter, or, in other words, a will independent of the society itself. It is no less certain than it is important, notwithstanding the contrary opinions which have been entertained, that the larger the society, provided it lie within a practical sphere, the more duly capable it will be of self-government. And happily for the REPUBLICAN CAUSE, the practicable sphere may be carried to a very great extent, by a judicious modification and mixture of the FEDERAL PRINCIPLE.

PUBLIUS

2.3

ANONYMOUS

Letters from the Federal Farmer, No. 2

Writing under the pseudonym the Federal Farmer, the Antifederalist author of this 1787 reading argues against the Constitution, saying that it will grant too much power to the central, national government. If granted the powers as described in the Constitution, the author claims, the national government will eventually come to dominate the states and oppress the people.

Dear Sir,

The essential parts of a free and good government are a full and equal representation of the people in the legislature, and the jury trial of the vicinage in the administration of justice—a full and equal representation, is that which possesses the same interests, feelings, opinions, and views the people themselves would were they all assembled—a fair representation, therefore, should be so regulated, that every order of men in the community, according to the common course of elections, can have a share in it—in order to allow professional men, merchants, traders, farmers, mechanics, etc. to bring a just proportion of their best informed men respectively into the legislature, the representation must be considerably numerous—We have about 200 state senators in the United States, and a less number than that of federal representatives cannot, clearly, be a full representation of this people, in the affairs of internal taxation and police, were there but one legislature for the whole union. The representation cannot be equal, or the situation of the people proper for one government only—if the extreme parts of the society cannot be represented as fully as the central—It is apparently impracticable that this should be the case in this extensive country—it would be impossible to collect a representation of the parts of the country five, six, and seven hundred miles from the seat of government.

Under one general government alone, there could be but one judiciary, one supreme and a proper number of inferior courts. I think it would be totally impracticable in this case to preserve a due administration of justice, and the real benefits of the jury trial of the vicinage,—there are now supreme courts in each state in the union; and a great number of county and other courts subordinate to each supreme court—most of these supreme and inferior courts are itinerant, and hold their sessions in different parts every year of their respective states, counties and districts—with all these moving courts, our citizens, from the vast extent of the country must travel very considerable distances from home to find the place where justice is administered. I am not for bringing justice so near to individuals as to afford them any temptation to engage in law suits; though I think it one of the greatest benefits in a good government, that each citizen should find a court of justice within a reasonable distance, perhaps, within a day's travel of his home; so that, without great inconveniences and enormous expences, he may have the advantages of his witnesses and jury—it would be impracticable to derive these advantages from one judiciary—the one supreme court at most could only set in the centre of the union, and move once a year into the centre of the eastern and southern extremes of it—and, in this case, each citizen, on an average, would travel 150 or 200 miles to find this court—that, however, inferior courts might be properly placed in the different counties, and districts of the union, the appellate jurisdiction would be intolerable and expensive.

If it were possible to consolidate the states, and preserve the features of a free government, still it is evident that the middle states, the parts of the union, about the seat of government, would enjoy great advantages, while the remote states would experience the many inconveniences of remote provinces. Wealth, offices, and the benefits of government would collect in the centre: and the extreme states and their principal towns, become much less important.

There are other considerations which tend to prove that the idea of one consolidated whole, on free principles, is ill-founded—the laws of a free government rest on the confidence of the people, and operate gently—and never can extend their influence very far—if they are executed on free principles, about the centre, where the benefits of the government induce the people to support it voluntarily; yet they must be executed on the principles of fear and force in the extremes—This has been the case with every extensive republic of which we have any accurate account.

There are certain unalienable and fundamental rights, which in forming the social compact, ought to be explicitly ascertained and fixed—a free and enlightened people, in forming this compact, will not resign all their rights to those who govern, and they will fix limits to their legislators and rulers, which will soon be plainly seen by those who are governed, as well as by those who govern: and the latter will know they cannot be passed unperceived by the former, and without giving a general alarm—These rights should be made the basis of every constitution: and if a people be so situated, or have such different opinions that they cannot agree in ascertaining and fixing them, it is a very strong argument against their attempting to form one entire society, to live under one system of laws only.—I confess, I never thought the people of these states differed essentially in these respects; they having derived all these rights from one common source, the British systems; and having in the formation of their state constitutions, discovered that their ideas relative to these rights are very similar. However, it is now said that the states differ so essentially in these respects, and even in the important article of the trial by jury, that when assembled in convention, they can agree to no words by which to establish that trial, or by which to ascertain and establish many other of these rights, as fundamental articles in the social compact. If so, we proceed to consolidate the states on no solid basis whatever.

But I do not pay much regard to the reasons given for not bottoming the new constitution on a better bill of rights. I still believe a complete federal bill of rights to be very practicable. Nevertheless I acknowledge the proceedings of the convention furnish my mind with many new and strong reasons, against a complete consolidation of the states. They tend to convince me, that it cannot be carried with propriety very far—that the convention have gone much farther in one respect than they found it practicable to go in another; that is, they propose to lodge in the general government very extensive powers—*powers* nearly, if not altogether, complete and unlimited, over the purse and the sword. But, in its organization, they furnish the strongest proof that the proper limbs, or parts of a government, to support and execute those powers on proper principles (or in which they can be safely lodged) cannot be formed. These powers must be lodged somewhere in every society; but then they should be lodged where the strength and guardians of the people are collected. They can be wielded, or safely used, in a free country only by an able executive and judiciary, a respectable senate, and a secure, full, and equal representation of the people. I think the principles I have premised or brought into view, are well founded—I think they will not be denied by any fair reasoner. It is in connection with these, and other solid principles, we are to examine the constitution. It is not a few democratic phrases, or a few well formed features, that will prove its merits; or a few small omissions that will produce its rejection among men of sense; they will enquire what are the essential powers in a community, and what are nominal ones; where and how the essential powers shall be lodged to secure government, and to secure true liberty.

In examining the proposed constitution carefully, we must clearly perceive an unnatural separation of these powers from the substantial representation of the people. The state governments will exist, with all their governors, senators, representatives, officers and expences; in these will be nineteen-twentieths of the representatives of the people; they will have a near connection, and their members an immediate intercourse with the people; and the probability is, that the state governments will possess the confidence of the people, and be considered generally as their immediate guardians.

The general government will consist of a new species of executive, a small senate, and a very small house of representatives. As many citizens will be more than three hundred miles from the seat of this government as will be nearer to it, its judges and officers cannot be very numerous, without making our governments very expensive. Thus will stand the state and the general governments, should the constitution be adopted without any alterations in their organization; but as to powers, the general government will possess all essential ones, at least on paper, and those of the states a mere shadow of power. And therefore, unless the people shall make some great exertions to restore to the state governments their powers in matters of internal police; as the powers to lay and collect, exclusively, internal taxes, to govern the militia, and to hold the decisions of their own judicial courts upon their own laws final, the balance cannot possibly continue long; but the state governments must be annihilated, or continue to exist for no purpose.

It is however to be observed, that many of the essential powers given the national government are not exclusively given; and the general government may have prudence enough to forbear the exercise of those which may still be exercised by the respective states. But this cannot justify the impropriety of giving powers, the exercise of which prudent men will not attempt, and imprudent men will, or probably can, exercise only in a manner destructive of free government. The general government, organized as it is, may be adequate to many valuable objects, and be able to carry its laws into execution on proper principles in several cases; but I think its wannest friends will not contend, that it can carry all the powers proposed to be lodged in it into effect, without calling to its aid a military force, which must very soon destroy all elective governments in the country, produce anarchy, or establish despotism. Though we cannot have now a complete idea of what will be the operations of the proposed system, we may, allowing things to have their common course, have a very tolerable one. The powers lodged in the general government, if exercised by it, must intimately effect the internal police of the states, as well as external concerns; and there is no reason to expect the numerous state governments, and their connections, will be very friendly to the execution of federal laws in those internal affairs, which hitherto have been under their own immediate management. There is more reason to believe, that the general government, far removed from the people, and none of its members elected oftener than once in two years, will be forgot or neglected, and its laws in many cases disregarded, unless a multitude of officers and military force be continually kept in view, and employed to enforce the execution of the laws, and to make the government feared and respected. No position can be truer than this, that in this country either neglected laws, or a military execution of them, must lead to a revolution, and to the destruction of freedom. Neglected laws must first lead to anarchy and confusion; and a military execution of laws is only a shorter way to the same point—despotic government.

YOUR'S, & C.
THE FEDERAL FARMER

2.4

Senate Judiciary Committee Hearings, Sonia Sotomayor, Supreme Court Nominee, July 2009

The Supreme Court is the final interpreter of the Constitution and how it should be applied to real-life situations. The Senate must approve Supreme Court appointments. Sonia Sotomayor, President Obama's nominee for the Supreme Court, faced questions from senators on the Judiciary Committee during hearings in summer 2009. These excerpts from those hearings highlight controversies over constitutional interpretation. How much does specific language in the Constitution matter today? How does our understanding of the Constitution evolve through court decisions? What role do courts play in the separation of powers system?

SENATOR HERB KOHL (D-Wisconsin): Is there a general constitutional right to privacy? And where is the right to privacy, in your opinion, found in the Constitution?

SOTOMAYOR: There is a right of privacy. The court has found it in various places in the Constitution, has recognized rights under those various provisions of the Constitution.

It's found it in the Fourth Amendment's right and prohibition against unreasonable search and seizures.

Most commonly, it's considered—I shouldn't say most commonly, because search and seizure cases are quite frequent before the court, but it's also found in the Fourteenth Amendment of the Constitution when it is considered in the context of the liberty interests protected by the due process clause of the Constitution.

KOHL: All right. Judge, the court's ruling about the right to privacy in Griswold[1] laid the foundation for *Roe v. Wade.*[2] In your opinion, is Roe settled law?

SOTOMAYOR: The court's decision in *Planned Parenthood v. Casey* reaffirmed the court holding of *Roe.* That is the precedent of the court and settled, in terms of the holding of the court.

SENATOR TOM COBURN (R-Oklahoma): In the Constitution, we have the right to bear arms. Whether it's incorporated or not, it's stated there. I'm having trouble understanding how we got to a point where a right to privacy, which is not explicitly spelled out but is spelled out to some degree in the Fourth Amendment, which has settled law and is fixed, and something such as the Second Amendment, which is spelled out in the Constitution, is not settled law and settled fixed.

I don't want you to answer that specifically. What I would like to hear you say is, how did we get there? How did we get to the point where something that's spelled out in our Constitution and guaranteed to us, but something that isn't spelled out specifically in our Constitution is? Would you give me your philosophical answer?

I don't want to tie you down on any future decisions, but how'd we get there when we can read this book, and it says certain things, and those aren't guaranteed, but the things that it doesn't say are?

SOTOMAYOR: One of the frustrations with judges and their decisions by citizens is that . . . what we do is different than the conversation that the public has about what it wants the law to do.

We don't, judges, make law. What we do is, we get a particular set of facts presented to us. We look at what those facts are, what in the case of different constitutional amendments is, what states are deciding to do or not do, and then look at the Constitution, and see what it says, and attempt to take its words and its—the principles and the precedents that have described those principles, and apply them to the facts before you.

In discussing the Second Amendment as it applies to the federal government, Justice Scalia noted that there have been long regulation by many states on a variety of different issues related to possession of guns. And he wasn't suggesting that all regulation was unconstitutional; he was holding in that case that D.C.'s particular regulation was illegal.

As you know, there are many states that prohibit felons from possessing guns. So does the federal government.

And so it's not that we make a broad policy choice and say, "This is what we want—what judges do." What we look at is what other actors in the system are doing, what their interest in doing it is, and how that fits to whatever situation they think they have to fix, what Congress or state legislature has to fix.

All of that is the court's function, so I can't explain it philosophically. I can only explain it by its setting and what—what the function of judging is about.

SENATOR AL FRANKEN (D-Minnesota): Yesterday, a member of this committee asked you a few times whether the word "abortion" appears in the Constitution, and you agreed that, no, the word "abortion" is not in the Constitution. Are the words "birth control" in the Constitution?

SOTOMAYOR: No, sir.

FRANKEN: Are—are you sure?

SOTOMAYOR: Yes.

FRANKEN: OK. (LAUGHTER) Are the words "privacy" in the Constitution or the word?

SOTOMAYOR: The word "privacy" is not.

FRANKEN: Senators Kohl, Feinstein, and Cardin all raised the issue of privacy, but I want to hit this head on. Do you believe that the Constitution contains a fundamental right to privacy?

SOTOMAYOR: It contains, as has been recognized by the courts for over 90 years, certain rights under the liberty provision of the due process clause that extend to the right to privacy in certain situations.

This line of cases started with a recognition that parents have a right to direct the education of their children and that the state could not force parents to send their children to public schools or to bar their children from being educated in ways a state found objectionable.

Obviously, states do regulate the content of education, at least in terms of requiring certain things with respect to education that I don't think the Supreme Court has considered, but the basic—that basic right to privacy has been recognized and was recognized. And there have been other decisions.

FRANKEN: So the issue of whether a word actually appears in the Constitution is not really relevant, is it?

SOTOMAYOR: Certainly, there are very specific words in the Constitution that have to be given direct application. There are some direct commands by the Constitution. You know, senators have to be a certain age to be senators. And so you've got to do what those words say.

But the Constitution is written in broad terms. And what a court does is then look at how those terms apply to a particular factual setting before it.

FRANKEN: OK. In *Roe v. Wade*, the Supreme Court found that the fundamental right to privacy included the right to decide whether or not to have an abortion. And as Senator Specter said, that's been upheld or ruled on many times. Do you believe that this right to privacy includes the right to have an abortion?

SOTOMAYOR: The court has said in many cases—and as I think has been repeated in the court's jurisprudence in *Casey*—that there is a right to privacy that women have with respect to the termination of their pregnancies in certain situations.

■　　■　　■

SENATOR BENJAMIN CARDIN (D-Maryland): The freedom of religion is one of the basic principles in our Constitution, as I said in my opening comments. It was one of the reasons why my grandparents came to America. The freedom of religion, expression is truly a fundamental American right.

Please share with us your philosophy as to—maybe it's a wrong use of terms—but the importance of that provision in the Constitution and how you would go about dealing with cases that could affect that fundamental right in our Constitution.

SOTOMAYOR: I don't mean to be funny, but the court has held that it's fundamental in the sense of incorporation against the state. But it is a very important and central part of our democratic society that we do give freedom of religion, the practice of religion, that the Constitution restricts the—the state from establishing a religion, and that we have freedom of expression in speech, as well.

Those freedoms are central to our Constitution. The Ford case,[3] as others that I had rendered in this area, recognize the importance of that in terms of one's consideration of actions that are being taken to restrict it in a particular circumstance.

Speaking further is difficult to do. Again, because of the role of a judge, to say it's important, that it's fundamental, and it's legal and common meaning is always looked at in the context of a particular case. What's the state doing?

In the Ford case that you just mentioned, the question there before the court was, did the district court err in considering whether or not the religious belief that this prisoner had was consistent with the established traditional interpretation of a meal at issue, OK?

And what I was doing was applying very important Supreme Court precedent that said, it's the subjective belief of the individual. Is it really motivated by a religious belief?

It's one of the reasons we recognize conscientious objectors, because we're asking a court not to look at whether this is orthodox or not, but to look at the sincerity of the individual's religious belief and then look at what the state is doing in light of that. So that was what the issue was in Ford.

■　　■　　■

SENATOR ORRIN HATCH (R-Utah): But one constituent asked whether you see the courts, especially the Supreme Court, as an institution for resolving perceived social injustices, inequities and disadvantages. Now, please address this both in terms of the justices' intention and the effect of their decisions. That was the question. And I thought it was an interesting question.

SOTOMAYOR: No, that's not the role of the courts. The role of the courts is to interpret the law as Congress writes it. It may be the effect in a particular situation that, in the court doing that, in giving effect to Congress's intent, it has that outcome, but it's not the role of the judge to create that outcome. It's to interpret what Congress is doing and do what Congress wants.

NOTES

1. In the *Griswold* (1965) decision the Supreme Court struck down all laws banning the use of contraceptives, basing the decision on the idea that privacy, especially between married persons in their sexual relations, is a right implied by the Constitution [*Editor*].

2. See Chapter 4 on *Roe v. Wade* [*Editor*].

3. When she was on the 2nd Circuit Court, Sotomayor in a case known as *Ford* ruled in favor of a Muslim prison inmate who sued to be able to participate in Islamic feasts [*Editor*].

3

FEDERALISM

3.1

JAMES MADISON

The Federalist, No. 39

James Madison portrays the American government as having a dual nature. He uses the terminology of national *versus* federal *to describe the underlying tensions in the constitutional design. Some institutional features (national) represent the entire people, while others (federal) represent the states.*

The last paper having concluded the observations which were meant to introduce a candid survey of the plan of government reported by the convention, we now proceed to the execution of that part of our undertaking.

The first question that offers itself is, whether the general form and aspect of the government be strictly republican. It is evident that no other form would be reconcilable with the genius of the people of America; with the fundamental principles of the Revolution; or with that honorable determination which animates every votary of freedom, to rest all our political experiments on the capacity of mankind for self-government. If the plan of the convention, therefore, be found to depart from the republican character, its advocates must abandon it as no longer defensible.

What, then, are the distinctive characters of the republican form? Were an answer to this question to be sought, not by recurring to principles, but in the application of the term by political writers, to the constitution of different States, no satisfactory one would ever be found. Holland, in which no particle of the supreme authority is derived from the people, has passed almost universally under the denomination of a republic. The same title has been bestowed on Venice, where absolute power over the great body of the people is exercised, in the most absolute manner, by a small body of hereditary nobles. Poland, which is a mixture of aristocracy and of monarchy in their worst forms, has been dignified with the same appellation. The government of England, which has one republican branch only, combined with an hereditary aristocracy and monarchy, has, with equal impropriety, been frequently placed on the list of republics. These examples, which are nearly as dissimilar to each other as to a genuine republic, show the extreme inaccuracy with which the term has been used in political disquisitions.

If we resort for a criterion to the different principles on which different forms of government are established, we may define a republic to be, or at least may bestow that name on, a government which derives all its powers directly or indirectly from the great body of the people, and is administered by persons holding their offices during pleasure, for a limited period, or during good behavior. It is ESSENTIAL to such a government that it be derived from the great body of the society, not from an inconsiderable proportion, or a favored class of it; otherwise a handful of tyrannical nobles, exercising their oppressions by a delegation of their powers, might aspire to the rank of republicans, and claim for their government the honorable title of republic. It is SUFFICIENT for such a government that the persons administering it be appointed, either directly or indirectly, by the people; and that they hold their appointments by either of the tenures just specified; otherwise every government in the United States, as well as every other popular government that has been or can be well organized or well executed, would be degraded from the republican character. According to the constitution of every State in the Union, some or other of the officers of government are appointed indirectly only by the people. According to most of them, the chief magistrate himself is so appointed. And according to one, this mode of appointment is extended to one of the co-ordinate branches of the legislature. According to all the constitutions, also, the tenure of the highest offices is extended to a definite period, and in many instances, both within the legislative and executive departments, to a period of years. According to the provisions of most of the constitutions, again, as well as according to the most respectable and received opinions on the subject, the members of the judiciary department are to retain their offices by the firm tenure of good behavior.

On comparing the Constitution planned by the convention with the standard here fixed, we perceive at once that it is, in the most rigid sense, conformable to it. The House of Representatives, like that of one branch at least of all the State legislatures, is elected immediately by the great body of the people. The Senate, like the present Congress, and the Senate of Maryland, derives its appointment indirectly from the people. The President is indirectly derived from the choice of the people, according to the example in most of the States. Even the judges, with all other officers of the Union, will, as in the several States, be the choice, though a remote choice, of the people themselves, the duration of the appointments is equally conformable to the republican standard, and to the model of State constitutions The House of Representatives is periodically elective, as in all the States; and for the period of two years, as in the State of South Carolina. The Senate is elective, for the period of six years; which is but one year more than the period of the Senate of Maryland, and but two more than that of the Senates of New York and Virginia. The President is to continue in office for the period of four years; as in New York and Delaware, the chief magistrate is elected for three years, and in South Carolina for two years. In the other States the election is annual. In several of the States, however, no constitutional provision is made for the impeachment of the chief magistrate. And in Delaware and Virginia he is not impeachable till out of office. The President of the United States is impeachable at any time during his continuance in office. The tenure by which the judges are to hold their places, is, as it unquestionably ought to be, that of good behavior. The tenure of the ministerial offices generally, will be a subject of legal regulation, conformably to the reason of the case and the example of the State constitutions.

Could any further proof be required of the republican complexion of this system, the most decisive one might be found in its absolute prohibition of titles of nobility, both under the federal and the State governments; and in its express guaranty of the republican form to each of the latter.

"But it was not sufficient," say the adversaries of the proposed Constitution, "for the convention to adhere to the republican form. They ought, with equal care, to have preserved the FEDERAL form, which regards the Union as a CONFEDERACY of sovereign states; instead of which, they have framed a NATIONAL government, which regards the Union as a CONSOLIDATION of the States." And it is asked by what authority this bold and radical innovation was undertaken? The handle which has been made of this objection requires that it should be examined with some precision.

Without inquiring into the accuracy of the distinction on which the objection is founded, it will be necessary to a just estimate of its force, first, to ascertain the real character of the government in question; secondly, to inquire how far the convention were authorized to propose such a government; and thirdly, how far the duty they owed to their country could supply any defect of regular authority.

First. In order to ascertain the real character of the government, it may be considered in relation to the foundation on which it is to be established; to the sources from which its ordinary powers are to be drawn; to the operation of those powers; to the extent of them; and to the authority by which future changes in the government are to be introduced.

On examining the first relation, it appears, on one hand, that the Constitution is to be founded on the assent and ratification of the people of America, given by deputies elected for the special purpose; but, on the other, that this assent and ratification is to be given by the people, not as individuals composing one entire nation, but as composing the distinct and independent States to which they respectively belong. It is to be the assent and ratification of the several States, derived from the supreme authority in each State, the authority of the people themselves. The act, therefore, establishing the Constitution, will not be a NATIONAL, but a FEDERAL act.

That it will be a federal and not a national act, as these terms are understood by the objectors; the act of the people, as forming so many independent States, not as forming one aggregate nation, is obvious from this single consideration, that it is to result neither from the decision of a MAJORITY of the people of the Union, nor from that of a MAJORITY of the States. It must result from the UNANIMOUS assent of the several States that are parties to it, differing no otherwise from their ordinary assent than in its being expressed, not by the legislative authority, but by that of the people themselves. Were the people regarded in this transaction as forming one nation, the will of the majority of the whole people of the United States would bind the minority, in the same manner as the majority in each State must bind the minority; and the will of the majority must be determined either by a comparison of the individual votes, or by considering the will of the majority of the States as evidence of the will of a majority of the people of the United States. Neither of these rules have been adopted. Each State, in ratifying the Constitution, is considered as a sovereign body, independent of all others, and only to be bound by its own voluntary act. In this relation, then, the new Constitution will, if established, be a FEDERAL, and not a NATIONAL constitution.

The next relation is, to the sources from which the ordinary powers of government are to be derived. The House of Representatives will derive its powers from the people of America; and the people will be represented in the same proportion, and on the same principle, as they are in the legislature of a particular State. So far the government is NATIONAL, not FEDERAL. The Senate, on the other hand, will derive its powers from the States, as political and coequal societies; and these will be represented on the principle of equality in the Senate, as they now are in the existing Congress. So far the government is FEDERAL, not NATIONAL. The executive power will be derived from a very compound source. The immediate election of the President is to be made by the States in their political characters. The votes allotted to them are in a compound ratio, which considers them partly as distinct and coequal societies, partly as unequal members of the same society. The eventual election, again, is to be made by that branch of the legislature which consists of the national representatives; but in this particular act they are to be thrown into the form of individual delegations, from so many distinct and coequal bodies politic. From this aspect of the government it appears to be of a mixed character, presenting at least as many FEDERAL as NATIONAL features.

The difference between a federal and national government, as it relates to the OPERATION OF THE GOVERNMENT, is supposed to consist in this, that in the former the powers operate on the political bodies composing the Confederacy, in their political capacities; in the latter, on the individual citizens composing the nation, in their individual capacities. On trying the

Constitution by this criterion, it falls under the NATIONAL, not the FEDERAL character; though perhaps not so completely as has been understood. In several cases, and particularly in the trial of controversies to which States may be parties, they must be viewed and proceeded against in their collective and political capacities only. So far the national countenance of the government on this side seems to be disfigured by a few federal features. But this blemish is perhaps unavoidable in any plan; and the operation of the government on the people, in their individual capacities, in its ordinary and most essential proceedings, may, on the whole, designate it, in this relation, a NATIONAL government.

But if the government be national with regard to the OPERATION of its powers, it changes its aspect again when we contemplate it in relation to the EXTENT of its powers. The idea of a national government involves in it, not only an authority over the individual citizens, but an indefinite supremacy over all persons and things, so far as they are objects of lawful government. Among a people consolidated into one nation, this supremacy is completely vested in the national legislature. Among communities united for particular purposes, it is vested partly in the general and partly in the municipal legislatures. In the former case, all local authorities are subordinate to the supreme; and may be controlled, directed, or abolished by it at pleasure. In the latter, the local or municipal authorities form distinct and independent portions of the supremacy, no more subject, within their respective spheres, to the general authority, than the general authority is subject to them, within its own sphere. In this relation, then, the proposed government cannot be deemed a NATIONAL one; since its jurisdiction extends to certain enumerated objects only, and leaves to the several States a residuary and inviolable sovereignty over all other objects. It is true that in controversies relating to the boundary between the two jurisdictions, the tribunal which is ultimately to decide, is to be established under the general government. But this does not change the principle of the case. The decision is to be impartially made, according to the rules of the Constitution; and all the usual and most effectual precautions are taken to secure this impartiality. Some such tribunal is clearly essential to prevent an appeal to the sword and a dissolution of the compact; and that it ought to be established under the general rather than under the local governments, or, to speak more properly, that it could be safely established under the first alone, is a position not likely to be combated.

If we try the Constitution by its last relation to the authority by which amendments are to be made, we find it neither wholly NATIONAL nor wholly FEDERAL. Were it wholly national, the supreme and ultimate authority would reside in the MAJORITY of the people of the Union; and this authority would be competent at all times, like that of a majority of every national society, to alter or abolish its established government. Were it wholly federal, on the other hand, the concurrence of each State in the Union would be essential to every alteration that would be binding on all. The mode provided by the plan of the convention is not founded on either of these principles. In requiring more than a majority, and principles. In requiring more than a majority, and particularly in computing the proportion by STATES, not by CITIZENS, it departs from the NATIONAL and advances towards the FEDERAL character; in rendering the concurrence of less than the whole number of States sufficient, it loses again the FEDERAL and partakes of the NATIONAL character.

The proposed Constitution, therefore, is, in strictness, neither a national nor a federal Constitution, but a composition of both. In its foundation it is federal, not national; in the sources from which the ordinary powers of the government are drawn, it is partly federal and partly national; in the operation of these powers, it is national, not federal; in the extent of them, again, it is federal, not national; and, finally, in the authoritative mode of introducing amendments, it is neither wholly federal nor wholly national.

PUBLIUS

3.2

WILLIAM H. RIKER

From *Federalism: Origin, Operation, Significance*

*In this selection from his classic book on federalism, Riker offers a largely nega-
tive view of American federalism. While the benefits of federalism can be identified in theory, the costs have been steep in actual practice: through the 1960s the
protection of privileged, wealthy minorities by state governments resulted in the
oppression of poor, previously enslaved minorities.*

6. IS THE FEDERAL BARGAIN WORTH KEEPING?

Up to this point this interpretation of federalism has been as simply descriptive as I have been able to keep it. The questions of whether or not federalism
is superior to its contemporary alternative, unitary government, or its previous alternative, imperialism; of whether or not federalism makes for good
government or the good life; of whether or not federalism is an effective
instrument of political integration—all these I have tried to keep out of the
discussion in order to concentrate on the descriptive questions: What occasions federalism and what maintains it?

But most of the interest in federalism, both academic and popular, is about
the further question: Is federalism worth keeping? And so in this final chapter we shall consider this moral question, not attempting to answer it but
rather attempting to indicate some of the considerations that may properly
enter into the answer.

Please note that I put the question "Is federalism worth keeping?" not "Is
federalism worth starting?" If the argument has any validity at all, the latter
question is trivial. In the drive for territorial expansion at the breakup of
empire, one either needs to use the federal device to expand or one does not.
Normative considerations presumably do not enter into calculation, once the
decision to expand has been made. (Of course, that decision is itself normative; but, once it is made, the decision on the procedure of expansion is
purely technical. Since the normative question is usually settled by unconscious consensus, the salient question at the beginning of federalisms is
typically the technical one.) But even if the original question of adopting
federalism is purely technical, still, once federalism has been established
and once a federalism has reached that degree of centralization previously

described as category B, the question of whether or not it ought to be maintained is open. Presumably a society with a federal government in category B has attained sufficient unity that it is no longer necessary to use the federal device to keep the expanded society viable. So at that point a normative judgment can be made about whether or not to keep the institutions that originally permitted the expansion.

Of course, the question of whether or not federalism is worth keeping seldom arises as a matter of complete constitutional revision (e.g., in Austria and Germany after each of the world wars). More frequently, the question arises in a partial form; i.e., "What attitude ought one to adopt on this measure that will tend to reinforce (or break down) the guarantees of federalism?" In mature and stable federalisms such as the United States or Australia, where complete constitutional revision seems unlikely in the foreseeable future, there is nevertheless a frequent opportunity to decide constitutional questions on the basis of an attitude toward federalism and this is where the partial form of the question arises.[1] Whether the question arises in its partial form or in a proposal for full-scale constitutional revision is, however, irrelevant to the considerations involved in the answer. Hence, the evaluation of whether or not federalism is worth keeping need not be restrained by the infrequency of constitutional conventions. Rather it is a question that politicians in a mature federalism, especially politicians in a category B federalism, must think about almost every day.

The considerations that commonly enter into decisions on these questions are the arguments advanced in favor of maintaining (or abrogating) the guarantees to constituent units. In the following sections, we shall therefore examine these arguments and some of the evidence adduced in support of them.

I. Federalism and Freedom—The Theoretical Argument for Retention

Probably the commonest argument in public debate for support of the guarantees to constituent units is the assertion that federalism is a guarantee of freedom, followed by the prescription that, in order to preserve freedom, one must preserve federalism. Assuming, as most of us would, that freedom (whatever it is) is worth preserving, the prescription nevertheless depends on a purportedly descriptive assertion, which may or may not be true. In what way is federalism related to freedom?

The political traditions of most federally governed societies predispose most of their citizens to believe that their constitutional form (i.e., federalism) encourages a state of affairs (i.e., freedom) that is almost universally approved. And in the traditions of both Anglo-American and Latin-American federalisms this predisposition has been reinforced by the identification of the spirit of federalism with the notion of local self-government, which in turn is often identified with freedom.

But despite these predispositions of the tradition, there are also some *a priori* reasons to be sceptical about the truth of the assertion that federalism encourages freedom. There are, for example, a number of societies that keep a high degree of freedom without the use of federalism and, on the other hand, a number of federalisms simultaneously have been dictatorships. Local self-government and personal freedom both coexist with a highly centralized unitary government in Great Britain and the Vargas dictatorship in Brazil managed to coexist with federalism.

In the United States, moreover, we have even more reasons to be sceptical about the truth of the assertion when we observe that the most persistent exponents of "states' rights"—a doctrine that makes much of the freedom-encouraging features of federalism—have been those who use the doctrine as a veiled defense first of slavery, then of civil tyranny. Here it seems that federalism may have more to do with destroying freedom than with encouraging it.

Clearly the relationship, if any, between federalism and freedom is not immediately clear and deserves further investigation.

The traditional argument, which derives from *The Federalist* papers and which has been reiterated continually by advocates of states' rights in all federal systems, is the assertion that concentrated power is dangerous, a position best expressed in Acton's aphorism that power tends to corrupt and absolute power corrupts absolutely. Federalism is said to be a device to prevent absolute power and therefore to prevent tyranny. I do not think we need to take this argument very seriously. It is based on a wise saw that has the same standing in the study of politics that weather wisdom has in the study of meteorology. The aphorism is not true—indeed, sometimes its opposite is.[2] And indeed, even if it were true, there is no assurance that separating power is the appropriate way to prevent tyranny. The separation may actually promote tyranny by its constant frustration of majorities which, in their frustration, come to behave tyrannically.[3] So let us leave aside the traditional argument, which is at best folk wisdom, and examine the relationship between federalism and freedom *de novo*.

Of course, though we know fairly well what "federalism" means, we have at best a confused notion of what "freedom" means. So before we can go further, the word "freedom" must be defined. And many volumes have been written on this subject without conspicuous success in reaching agreement. Owing to the tradition of controversy over the meaning of this word, we do know, however, that one of the variables involved in the notion is the specific reference to persons. That is, one elementary question about freedom is: "freedom for whom?"

The question arises in this way: Given a society with a multiplicity of goals (and surely all societies with federal governments satisfy this assumption) and given the possibility that the achievement of goal A renders the achievement of another goal, B, unlikely or impossible. Then, when one speaks of freedom, one must specify whether one means freedom for the supporters of goal A or for those of goal B. If political life were conveniently arranged so that all feasible goals were compatible with one another, then this question could not arise. But usually we do not find such neat dovetailing of aspirations. And so in the presence of conflicting goals, a definition of freedom must always specify freedom for whom.

One convenient answer that some theories of freedom have offered is "the majority," which is unfortunately a highly artificial creation of rules of voting. Owing to this artificiality, therefore, other theories of freedom have suggested that freedom involves liberty for minorities to achieve their goals. The first kind of answer solves the problem in a somewhat arbitrary fashion, whereas the second kind begs the question completely.

But since this reading has no space to pursue the problem of the meaning of freedom, we shall merely assume the existence of two kinds, majoritarian and minoritarian, and then inquire whether or not it is theoretically true that federalism is a guarantee of either kind.

Considering, first, majoritarian freedom, it seems fairly obvious that federalism cannot at all be a guarantee of this kind of freedom; but rather can actually be an impediment. The effect of allowing ultimate decision at two different levels of government (which is the essence of the federal relationship) is that the losers at the national level may reverse the decision at the constituent level. Thus, the losers nationally may become the winners locally which of course negates the national decision in at least portions of the federal nation. Thereby, of course, the freedom of the national majority is infringed upon by local majorities.

A notorious example of such negation is the reversal of decision on civil rights for Negroes in the Southern and border states. The original national decision, taken by a narrow majority in the Civil War era, was soon reversed by local decisions in the South and along the border—where, of course, most Negroes lived. As a consequence, the Civil War decisions were thoroughly negated for most Negroes until sufficient numbers migrated northward and reawakened interest in again enforcing the old and, in recent years, frequently reaffirmed national decision.

To one who believes in the majoritarian notion of freedom, it is impossible to interpret federalism as other than a device for minority tyranny. At the present time in the United States (*i.e.*, from roughly 1954 to that future time, if it ever comes, when most Negroes have full citizen rights) the chief question of public morals is whether or not the national decision will be enforced. To those who wish to enforce it, the plea for states' rights or for maintaining the guarantees of federalism is simply a hypocritical plea for the special privilege to disregard the national majority and, of course, to permit one minority, segregationist Southern whites, to tyrannize over another minority, the Southern Negroes. When freedom is defined as the right of self-direction for majorities, then the assertion that federalism promotes freedom is simply a hypocritical falsehood.

Considering, in the second place, minoritarian freedom, which is usually presented as the freedom of a minority to preserve its civil rights against a tyrannical majority, it is apparent, I shall argue, that for this kind of freedom federalism is, if not an impediment, still quite irrelevant.

Minoritarian freedom can be interpreted either as (1) the right of minorities to have a chance to become majorities and thus to make policy or (2) the right of minorities to make policy without becoming majorities. The first interpretation; *i.e.*, the right to the chance to make policy, is in practice the maintenance of civil liberties so that prospective majorities will not be destroyed before they become such. The latter interpretation, though often set forth as the abstract ideal of freedom, is of course simply a rationale of confusion. Given, as previously, the existence of conflicting social goals, then the guarantee of the right of minorities to make policy merely assures the simultaneous existence of contradictory policies.

If minoritarian freedom is the right to have a chance to make policy, then federalism is undoubtedly an impediment to freedom in many circumstances and irrelevant to it in others. Federalism is a guarantee to constituent units of the *right* to make policy, not of the *chance* to make policy. Thus it grants far more than is necessary for freedom. The analysis works out as follows: Suppose the constituent unit granted the right to make policy agrees for the most part with the kind of policy that would be made by the national officials. Then the right to make policy means relatively little and in general federalism is irrelevant to the maintenance of freedom. Suppose, however, that the constituent unit does not so agree; then the right to make policy allows it to impinge on the right of local minorities to become majorities. This is exactly what has happened in the American South where, under its freedom to make policy, the local majority (which is a minority nationally) has deprived the local minority of its civil rights (even though that local minority has close links with the national majority). In short, federalism that grants *more* local autonomy than is necessary for freedom and civil liberty encourages local tyranny, even when freedom is narrowly interpreted as the grant of the right to minorities to have a chance to become majorities.

If, on the other hand, minoritarian freedom is the right to make policy; *i.e.*, to allow minorities to create confusion, then federalism is again irrelevant to freedom in some circumstances and a positive hindrance to freedom in others. One may distinguish the circumstances according to whether or not it costs the society more to obtain uniformity than uniformity is worth. Consider an instance in which the cost of uniformity is greater than the reward: women's clothing. At numerous times in many societies sumptuary laws and laws against nudity have been passed and frequently they have been enforced only briefly. Presumably in such instances of laxity the cost of enforcement against numerous minorities of one is greater than the reward of uniformity. When enforcement costs more than the reward, federalism is irrelevant to freedom. If freedom is the grant to minorities of one of the right to decide, *e.g.*, on physical decoration, then the right of constituent units to make policy they probably will not care to enforce against minorities is a meaningless grant. In such an instance, federalism has nothing to do with freedom, although it may guarantee tyranny.

But when national uniformity is worth more than confusion, then federalism is an impediment to freedom because it deprives the national majority of the chance to eliminate the excess costs of confusion. Consider, for example, the matter of civil rights for Negroes in the United States. The grant to constituent units to make policy on this question has meant at least the following consequences: For the last century approximately 10 percent of the people have been denied civil rights. Those so denied have been a kind of *lumpenproletariat* and hence a drain on the whole society. In short, the grant of autonomy to local majorities to create confused policies has resulted in a cost to the whole society that is probably greater than the cost of uniformity. At least, so the present restiveness of the national majority toward Southern whites' practices of tyranny so indicates. In such an instance, we may infer that, when the costs of the consequences of federalism are greater than the costs of enforcing uniformity, local tyrannies are also national tyrannies because they prevent national majorities from reducing costs. For example, the national costs of putting up with the consequences of Southern bigotry are so great that the permission to enforce bigotry locally constitutes a cost on the whole nation, a cost which is presumably greater than the cost of enforcing desegregation. In this instance, therefore, federalism is an impediment to the freedom of everybody except segregationist whites in the South.

In summary, the abstract assertion that federalism is a guarantee of freedom is undoubtedly false. If this assertion is intended as a description of nature, then it is manifestly false, as shown by counterinstances of the coexistence of federalism and dictatorship. If it is, however, intended as a theoretical assertion about an abstract relationship undisturbed by other institutional arrangements, then it is still false. If freedom is interpreted in a majoritarian way, then the assertion is invariably false, for federalism is an impediment to freedom. If freedom is interpreted in a minoritarian way, then either federalism has nothing to do with freedom or federalism is again an impediment to freedom.

II. The High Cost of Uniformity—The Practical Argument for Retention

The most frequently presented practical argument for the maintenance of the federal guarantees to the constituent units is that the cost of national decision making is greater than the reward that might be obtained from it. This argument is usually presented as a defense of expediency (*e.g.*, that it would cost more in prospective civil disturbance to integrate the schools of Mississippi than can presently be gained from this action). But sometimes it is also presented as a moral good (*e.g.*, that a positive value is obtained from diversity of culture). (The latter was a favorite argument of Justice Holmes, who interpreted the states as laboratories for solving public problems.) In either form, however, this argument is essentially an economic one involving a kind of cost analysis of constitutional forms.[4]

National decision making is in the abstract more efficient than local decision making on every issue. That is, assuming uniformity is itself costless, it is cheaper on any subject of legislation to have a uniform rule, which is made by a majority, than not to have uniformity. There are at least two strong theoretical reasons for this circumstance. For one thing there is some saving in uniformity; and for another, there is less likelihood of a minority imposing high external costs on the majority. Considering the first and lesser reason, it is apparent that there is some saving in personal learning to have something like nationally uniform rules of the road. If a red light meant different things in different localities it is highly likely that the cost of enforcement of road rules would increase enormously. But the more important saving through uniformity is the minimization of the external costs imposed on individuals when minorities are allowed to legislate a minority policy. These costs are, of course, very high when two minority policies are in direct conflict. But even when they do not seem to be in direct conflict, external costs may still be inordinately high. Consider the sum of the costs to individuals when there are different minimum wages in different localities. There is then much likelihood of capital flow from the high-wage localities to the low-wage localities for all those industries in which labor represents a high proportion of the cost. Aside from the imposition of a nationally uniform minimum wage, the only way that high-wage localities may counter this capital flow is by reducing the minimum wage level. Thus the localities with the low minimum wage are permitted to set this wage nationally. For all the localities that would like to have the high wage, the imposition of the low wage is, of course, a high external cost. Since only the lowest-wage locality will be satisfied, all other localities will suffer these external costs. The obvious way to reduce this cost is to impose a national policy. It is this possibility that accounts for the greater efficiency of uniform rules. The only circumstances in which the uniform policy would not reduce external costs over local policies would be when the low-wage locality constituted a national majority. But in this case, the supposedly local policy is in fact imposed by a national majority and is thus a uniform policy. Hence in all cases a uniform policy is cheaper from the point of view of external costs than a non-uniform policy.

Or consider the savings from uniformity in the regulation of morality rather than the regulation of the economy. Given the possibility of variation in divorce codes among constituent units, divorce may be easier to obtain in one jurisdiction than in another. Then, so long as some provision like the full faith and credit clause of the United States Constitution exists—and all federalisms have something like it—it follows that the code that will in fact regulate is the one with easiest divorce. We have an excellent example of this in the United States, where the national scandal of excessively large numbers of divorces and the concomitant scandal of ill-considered marriages are both the consequences of a variation in divorce codes. The existence of a few jurisdictions that grant divorces on the most trivial grounds and after only the briefest periods of residence are sufficient to render nugatory the more restrictive grounds and longer residence requirements of most other states. Thus the different moral standards of a few states, the codes of which seem to have been motivated more by a concern for tourist business than by any convictions one way or another about family stability, have the effect of imposing easy divorce on all jurisdictions. The external costs of the existence of what most citizens of most states regard as low moral standards are thus very high for the probably overwhelming majority that opposes easy divorce. Uniformity of divorce laws could materially lighten these costs for the majority, although it might raise costs for Nevada lawyers.

It seems clear on the basis of both theory and example that uniform national decision making is invariably more efficient, *i.e.*, less costly in undesired impositions on other people, than is local decision making. This is simply to say that decisions made by a majority hurt fewer people than do decisions made by minorities. Since constituent governments are invariably minorities in the nation, the maintenance of federal guarantees to constituent units assures that the whole society must bear some extra and unnecessary external costs.

So far, however, we have considered the cost of decision making only in a vacuum. Even if national decision making is clearly more efficient in decreasing external costs, it still may be more expensive than local decision making because of (1) costs of decision making and (2) costs of enforcement.

Costs of decision making are those incurred in the process of assembling a coalition of the size necessary to make a decision. As the requirements increase from minorities (*e.g.*, majorities in a constituent unit) to majorities (*i.e.*, a national majority), the cost of making side-payments to reluctant members (*i.e.*, logrolling) and of negotiating with all prospective members increases greatly. The cost of national decision making may well be greater than the rewards obtained from eliminating anarchy. Consider, for example, standards of beach clothing for females. Possibly a majority of people in the United States are offended by the appearance of bikinis and, were the decision costless, they would be glad to prohibit them. But, in fact, the decision is not costless. Some effort must be expended on defining what is offensive and what is not; more effort must be expended on finding the people who make up this majority; and finally additional effort must be expended on bringing them together in a group for action. In this imaginary example, the cost of decision is clearly very high, whereas the sum of the rewards to the majority is probably relatively low. Quite possibly the decision costs exceed the rewards.

Costs of enforcement are those incurred in the process of enforcing a majority decision against a recalcitrant minority. These costs vary with (1) the relative size of the minority, (2) the intensity of feeling of the minority, and (3) the ability of the minority to resist enforcement. It makes a difference for the existence of a national policy of prohibition, for example, whether or not most of the people are convinced teetotalers. In the United States during the prohibition era, the minority of regular users of alcohol was almost as large as the group of teetotalers, if indeed not larger. Hence enforcement was exceptionally costly. In India, on the other hand, where a much larger proportion of the population consists of teetotalers and where the indigenous pharmacopoeia includes a variety of drugs with physiological and social effects similar to those of alcohol, the enforcement of prohibition is relatively less costly. Again it makes a difference for the existence of a national policy of assessing an income tax whether or not the prosperous and the rich believe deeply that they should not be taxed. Thus, in the United States, the prosperous and the rich accept the basic notion of the tax and hence usually obey the exact letter of the law. The existence of this attitude means that enforcement officers are freed to pursue the minority of dishonest taxpayers. Hence the income tax works pretty well as the basic tax of the nation. In India, on the other hand, the justice of the tax is not as widely acknowledged by the prosperous and rich. Hence enforcement agents must spend most of their efforts on what would elsewhere be regarded as ordinary collection. As a consequence, enforcement is costly and the income tax cannot be used as the basic tax system. Finally, it makes a difference for the existence of a national policy of civil rights for depressed classes whether or not those who oppress them can successfully defend the oppression both practically and philosophically. Again compare India and the United States, in both of which national decisions have repeatedly condemned the oppression of in one case the Scheduled Castes and in the other case Negroes. In both cases there are good practical devices to avoid enforcement; *e.g.*, the relative unanimity of the rural upper classes on the desirability of resistance. In both cases there are also good philosophical grounds to resist enforcement; *e.g.*, the doctrine of states' rights in the United States and the doctrines of Hinduism in India. But the outlook for enforcement of the national policy is much better in the United States than in India simply because (1) the unanimity of the rural upper classes is nationwide in India whereas in the United States it is breaking down and indeed is limited to two or three very recalcitrant states and (2) the doctrine of states' rights is increasingly regarded as a sham for oppression whereas, owing to the new nationalism, the doctrines of Hinduism are held to even more tenaciously than before. Negroes are likely to obtain civil rights sooner than untouchables simply because the ability of their oppressors to resist enforcement is less.

In this analysis of the costs of national decision making in relation to decision making by constituent units, we have thus identified three kinds of charges:

1. the profits of uniformity, symbolized by "U"; which are invariably positive in sign because majority decision is always better than anarchy;
2. the costs of making decisions, symbolized by "D", which are invariably negative in sign because it is more costly to assemble a majority than a minority; and
3. the costs of enforcement of decisions, symbolized by "E" which are also invariably negative in sign because the existence of a majority implies the existence of a minority that must be coerced.

The practical argument in favor of maintaining the federal guarantees to the constituent units is that $U + D + E \leq 0$. Of course, this argument cannot be uttered generally for it would mean the desirability of the dissolution of the federalism. Rather, it must be uttered in particular instances and where it is asserted after a rough assessment of the values of U, D, and E. Since the argument cannot be asserted generally except as a proposal for civil war, one wonders about what kind of instances it seems reasonable in. In short, what kinds of circumstances minimize the sum of U, D, and E?

It is impossible, of course, to offer an exhaustive list; but one can specify some typical circumstances. As for minimizing U, which of course increases the likelihood that the inequation $U + D + E \leq 0$ will hold, the most important circumstance probably is that the policy field will be fairly low on the preference schedules of most of the members of the prospective majority. If most people don't care much whether or not policy in a specific area (*e.g.*, women's beachwear) is anarchic, then the positive value of U will be low. The issue of whether or not to maintain the federal guarantee to constituent units does not, however, arise when U is low, for to say U is low is to say it concerns something to which most people are close to indifferent. So the problem is: In what circumstances, when U is high, is—$(D + E)$ higher?

What minimizes D is the existence of numerous territorial minorities, each of whose schedules of preference is quite different from others. The fact that these minorities are territorially based gives them some strength to insist on obtaining their preferences and the fact that their preference schedules are different renders the bargaining process expensive. India is a federalism in which, *a priori*, one might expect D to be very low in many areas of public policy.

What minimizes E is the intensity of feeling of a minority, a defensive sense that their separateness is both under attack and worth preserving. Coupled with this sense of separateness must also be a large territorial and population base so that the minority actually has some strength to resist enforcement.

Canada is a federalism in which, *a priori*, one might expect E to be very low in many areas of public policy.

The practical argument for the maintenance of the federal guarantees to the constituent units, *viz.*, that $U + D + E \leq 0$, is clearly dependent upon the calculations of politicians and citizens about the magnitudes of U, D, and E in particular sets of circumstances. In general, if there are numerous areas *of importance* in which it is agreed that the inequation $U + D + E \leq 0$ holds, then the argument in favor of maintaining the guarantees is good. If not, then the argument fails. For me, the argument is reasonable and impressive with respect to such federalisms as Canada and India, but it is specious and unreasonable with respect to such federalisms as the United States, Germany, Austria, and Australia.

III. Abrogating the Guarantees

The main theoretical argument in favor of abrogating the federal guarantees to constituent units has already been developed in connection with arguments for maintaining them: Decisions made by constituent units are invariably minority decisions that impose high external costs on the national majority. This assertion is wholly irrefutable on the level of theory, although it may be shown, as I have also indicated, that in particular instances it may cost more to remove the external costs than is saved with uniformity. But even though the assertion is theoretically irrefutable some effort has been expended in showing that it is not necessarily true in all circumstances. Cohen and Grodzins, for example, have attempted to show that state fiscal policies in the United States do not always conflict with national policies.[5] And they did indeed show that the state policies are less sharply in conflict with national policy than had previously been believed.[6] But to show that the anarchy of numerous minority decisions does not impose external costs as high as Hansen and Perloff believed is also to admit that external costs do exist. Indeed, the chief significance of Cohen and Grodzins' work is that they found a way to measure them. The existence of external costs is an invitation to eliminate them, which is the chief theoretical argument in favor of abrogating the guarantees.

Unfortunately the theoretical arguments, though theoretically decisive, are practically uncertain because of the uncertainty surrounding the magnitudes of U, D, and E. Hence, to decide in particular instances whether or not to abrogate the guarantees it is necessary to examine the cultural and institutional setting of the constitution. The appropriate questions are: Who benefits by the imposition of external costs on others? or, What minority is allowed by the federal device to impose its rules on the majority? According as one disapproves or approves of the values and purposes of these minorities, one favors or opposes the abrogation of the guarantees. One does not decide on the merits of federalism by an examination of federalism in the abstract, but rather on its actual meaning for particular societies.

What minorities benefit from the grant to make policy in:

The United States?

The main beneficiary throughout American history has been the Southern whites, who have been given the freedom to oppress Negroes, first as slaves and later as a depressed caste. Other minorities have from time to time also managed to obtain some of these benefits; *e.g.*, special business interests have been allowed to regulate themselves, especially in the era from about 1890 to 1936, by means of the judicial doctrine of dual federalism, which eliminated both state and national regulation of such matters as wage rates and hours of labor. But the significance of federal benefits to economic interests pales beside the significance of benefits to the Southern segregationist whites. The judgment to be passed on federalism in the United States is therefore a judgment on the values of segregation and racial oppression.

Canada?

The main beneficiary in Canada from the beginning has been the French-speaking minority, whose dissidence was the original occasion for adopting federalism and is the justification for retaining it today. Secondarily, as in the United States, commercial interests have also benefited by escaping regulation. But since the French Canadians have no particular alliance with business, economic conservatives have benefited less in Canada than in the United States (where Southern segregationists have a tacit alliance with economic conservatives). That is, the French speakers have seen less reason to rig the competitive market to the advantage of owners (as against workers or consumers) because very few French Canadians have been owners.

Brazil?

The most significant minority benefiting from Brazilian federalism is the class of large landowners, especially in the relatively underdeveloped north and east. Although Brazilian federalism lacks the tone of racism associated with federalism in the United States, the social consequences are the same: the maintenance of a class of poor and inefficient farm laborers for the presumed benefit of agrarian landlords.

India?

Indian federalism is probably too youthful to identify the main beneficiaries of the privilege of minority decision making. But two kinds of minorities have tended to emphasize states' rights: non-Hindi-speaking groups (who, together, are of course a majority) and landlords in the least-developed agricultural areas.

Australia?

Since no single minority has been able to exploit the advantages of minority decision exclusively or for long periods of time, it is difficult to identify the main beneficiary. Nevertheless, it seems that commercial interests have been granted freedom from regulation more than any other group.

Germany?

Originally, federalism was intended to grant the right of minority decision to the non-Prussian southwest. But the significance of this minority has declined in the successive transformations of German federalism so that today it is difficult to specify who, if anyone, benefits most.

The foregoing survey of several federal systems suggests the wide variety of kinds of minorities that may benefit especially from the privilege to legislate. The kind of minorities that appears most frequently on this list is business and agricultural owners. It is not difficult to understand why. In capitalistic nations conflicting economic interests are engaged constantly in an effort to rig the competitive system in their favor. Those groups which constitute national majorities, *e.g.*, workers, farm laborers, consumers, etc., are those which might be expected to benefit most from majoritarian decision processes. To allow minoritarian processes is, therefore, to deprive the very large groups of their chance to influence outcomes. Of course, the minority most likely to benefit from the chance to manipulate the market is that of the owners, business or agricultural according to whether the nation is primarily industrial or agrarian.

But it is not always or only the owners who benefit, for, as the brief survey indicates, linguistic or racist minorities may also thrive on federalism. One possible classification of federalism, especially appropriate for passing judgment on the desirability of retaining federalism, is by the main beneficiaries of the chance of minorities to legislate for the whole. A moral judgment must be passed in each instance and for comparative purposes I submit a list (Table 1) of the main characteristics of the main federalisms. It is notable that the federalism of the United States is unique in fostering racism.

TABLE 1 Main Beneficiaries of Federalism

	Capitalists	*Landlords*	*Linguistic minorities*	*Racists*
United States	X	X		X
Canada	X		X	
Mexico		X		
Brazil	X	X		
Argentina	X	X		
Australia	X			
India		X	X	
Switzerland	X		X	
Germany	X			
Yugoslavia			X	
Soviet Union			X	

IV. Is Federalism Worth Keeping?

One seldom has the opportunity to rewrite whole constitutions so the question of keeping or abandoning federalism can seldom arise. But a related question does frequently arise: What ought to be one's posture toward federalism? Should one always attempt to maintain or abrogate the guarantees to the constituent units?

In pure theory, the answer is that what one ought to seek to abrogate for federalism is a system of minority decision that imposes high external costs on everybody other than the minority. But practically the answer is not so clear, for the costs of decision and enforcement may outweigh the advantages of majoritarianism when the minority favored by federalism is passionate in its convictions.

Since the actual calculation of rewards and costs from abrogating federal guarantees is simply a rough "more or less" necessarily calculated by interested parties, one probably cannot even use a cost analysis in judging actual federalisms. Rather one must look to what they do and determine what minorities they favor. If one approves the goals and values of the privileged minority, one should approve the federalism. Thus, if in the United States one approves of Southern white racists, then one should approve of American federalism. If, on the other hand, one disapproves of the values of the privileged minority, one should disapprove of federalism. Thus, if in the United States one disapproves of racism, one should disapprove of federalism.

NOTES

1. For a concrete example of such an occasion, consider the creation (in 1935) of the unemployment insurance system as an adjunct to the social security system. President Roosevelt, apparently out of a concern for federalism, personally decided to assign the unemployment insurance and employment service to the states, at least so his advisor Tugwell tells us. (Rexford Tugwell, "The Experimental Roosevelt," *The Political Quarterly*, Vol. 21 (1950) pp. 239–62, at p. 241.) In turning down the advice of experts, Roosevelt personally preserved, at least in a small way, the constitutional guarantees of federalism. Whether or not he was wise to do so is, of course, another matter. Since the federal part of this system has been quietly and selectively administered, whereas the state part has been the center of much political turbulence and has often been charged with inefficiency, the experts were probably right from an administrative point of view. But constitutional considerations may be more important than administrative ones. What concerns us here, however, is not the correctness or incorrectness of Roosevelt's action, but simply the opportunity he had to decide a policy question on the basis of an interpretation of federalism.

2. See Arnold Rogow and Harold Lasswell, *Power, Corruption and Rectitude* (New York: Prentice-Hall, 1963).

3. See William H. Riker, *Democracy in the United States* (New York: Macmillan, 1953) Chapter 4.

4. An earlier attempt to apply a quasi-economic analysis to the costs of federalism is: J. Roland Pennock, "Federal and Unitary Government—Disharmony and Frustra-

tion," *Behavioral Science*, Vol. 4 (1959) pp. 147–57. This article contains an *ad hoc* and tendentious model from which calculations are made of the "harmony (or lessened frustration) which it is the peculiar genius of federalism to achieve." By conveniently ignoring what are here called external costs, *e.g.*, those imposed on the majority when the minority is permitted to make rules, the author finds that federalism lessens the frustrations of a minority, which, of course, no one has ever denied. The unanswered question is: At whose expense is the frustration relieved?

5. Jacob Cohen and Morton Grodzins, "How Much Economic Sharing in American Federalism," *American Political Science Review*, Vol. 57 (1963) pp. 5–23.

6. Alvin Hansen and Harvey Perloff, *State and Local Finance in the National Economy* (New York: Norton, 1944).

3.3

United States v. Lopez (1995)

In a relatively rare rebuke of the national government, the U.S. Supreme Court in this case decided in favor of state authority and against national authority in a case involving guns near schools. This decision is representative of the Court under Chief Justice William Rehnquist; in the Rehnquist era the Court limited the reach of national government regulation.

Chief Justice Rehnquist delivered the opinion of the Court.

In the Gun-Free School Zones Act of 1990, Congress made it a federal offense "for any individual knowingly to possess a firearm at a place that the individual knows, or has reasonable cause to believe, is a school zone." 18 U.S.C. 922(q). The Act neither regulates a commercial activity nor contains a requirement that the possession be connected in any way to interstate commerce. We hold that the Act exceeds the authority of Congress "[t]o regulate Commerce . . . among the several States. . . ." U.S. Const., Art. I, 8, cl. 3.

On March 10, 1992, respondent, who was then a 12th-grade student, arrived at Edison High School in San Antonio, Texas, carrying a concealed .38 caliber handgun and five bullets. Acting upon an anonymous tip, school authorities confronted respondent, who admitted that he was carrying the weapon. He was arrested and charged under Texas law with firearm possession on school premises. The next day, the state charges were dismissed after federal agents charged respondent by complaint with violating the Gun-Free School Zones Act of 1990.

A federal grand jury indicted respondent on one count of knowing possession of a firearm at a school zone, in violation of 922(q). Respondent moved to dismiss his federal indictment on the ground that 922(q) "is unconstitutional as it is beyond the power of Congress to legislate control over our public schools." The District Court denied the motion, concluding that 922(q) "is a constitutional exercise of Congress' well-defined power to regulate activities in and affecting commerce, and the 'business' of elementary, middle and high schools . . . affects interstate commerce." Respondent waived his right to a jury trial. The District Court conducted a bench trial, found him guilty of violating 922(q), and sentenced him to six months' imprisonment and two years' supervised release.

On appeal, respondent challenged his conviction based on his claim that 922(q) exceeded Congress' power to legislate under the Commerce Clause. The Court of Appeals for the Fifth Circuit agreed and reversed respondent's conviction. It held that, in light of what it characterized as insufficient congressional findings and legislative history, "section 922(q), in the full reach of its terms, is invalid as beyond the power of Congress under the Commerce Clause." Because of the importance of the issue, we granted certiorari, and we now affirm.

We start with first principles. The Constitution creates a Federal Government of enumerated powers. As James Madison wrote, "[t]he powers delegated by the proposed Constitution to the federal government are few and defined. Those which are to remain in the State governments are numerous and indefinite." The Federalist No. 45. This constitutionally mandated division of authority "was adopted by the Framers to ensure protection of our fundamental liberties." *Gregory v. Ashcroft* (1991). "Just as the separation and independence of the coordinate branches of the Federal Government serves to prevent the accumulation of excessive power in any one branch, a healthy balance of power between the States and the Federal Government will reduce the risk of tyranny and abuse from either front."

The Constitution delegates to Congress the power "[t]o regulate Commerce with foreign Nations, and among the several States, and with the Indian Tribes." The Court, through Chief Justice Marshall, first defined the nature of Congress' commerce power in *Gibbons v. Ogden* (1824):

Commerce, undoubtedly, is traffic, but it is something more: it is intercourse. It describes the commercial intercourse between nations, and parts of nations, in all its branches, and is regulated by prescribing rules for carrying on that intercourse.

The commerce power "is the power to regulate; that is, to prescribe the rule by which commerce is to be governed. This power, like all others vested in Congress, is complete in itself, may be exercised to its utmost extent, and acknowledges no limitations, other than are prescribed in the constitution." The *Gibbons* Court, however, acknowledged that limitations on the commerce power are inherent in the very language of the Commerce Clause.

It is not intended to say that these words comprehend that commerce, which is completely internal, which is carried on between man and man in a State, or between different parts of the same State, and which does not extend to or affect other States. Such a power would be inconvenient, and is certainly unnecessary.

Comprehensive as the word "among" is, it may very properly be restricted to that commerce which concerns more States than one. . . . The enumeration presupposes something not enumerated; and that something, if we regard the language or the subject of the sentence, must be the exclusively internal commerce of a State.

For nearly a century thereafter, the Court's Commerce Clause decisions dealt but rarely with the extent of Congress' power, and almost entirely with the Commerce Clause as a limit on state legislation that discriminated against interstate commerce. Under this line of precedent, the Court held that certain categories of activity such as "production," "manufacturing," and "mining" were within the province of state governments, and thus were beyond the power of Congress under the Commerce Clause.

In 1887, Congress enacted the Interstate Commerce Act, and in 1890, Congress enacted the Sherman Antitrust Act. These laws ushered in a new era of federal regulation under the commerce power. When cases involving these laws first reached this Court, we imported from our negative Commerce Clause cases the approach that Congress could not regulate activities such as "production," "manufacturing," and "mining." Simultaneously, however, the Court held that, where the interstate and intrastate aspects of commerce were so mingled together that full regulation of interstate commerce required incidental regulation of intrastate commerce, the Commerce Clause authorized such regulation.

In *A. L. A. Schecter Poultry Corp. v. United States* (1935), the Court struck down regulations that fixed the hours and wages of individuals employed by an intrastate business because the activity being regulated related to interstate commerce only indirectly. In doing so, the Court characterized the distinction between direct and indirect effects of intrastate transactions upon interstate commerce as "a fundamental one, essential to the maintenance of our constitutional system." Activities that affected interstate commerce directly were within Congress' power; activities that affected interstate commerce indirectly were beyond Congress' reach. The justification for this formal distinction was rooted in the fear that otherwise "there would be virtually no limit to the federal power and for all practical purposes we should have a completely centralized government."

Two years later, in the watershed case of *NLRB v. Jones & Laughlin Steel Corp.*, (1937), the Court upheld the National Labor Relations Act against a Commerce Clause challenge, and in the process, departed from the distinction between "direct" and "indirect" effects on interstate commerce. ("The question [of the scope of Congress' power] is necessarily one of degree"). The Court held that intrastate activities that "have such a close and substantial relation to interstate commerce that their control is essential or appropriate to protect that commerce from burdens and obstructions" are within Congress' power to regulate.

In *United States v. Darby* (1941), the Court upheld the Fair Labor Standards Act, stating:

The power of Congress over interstate commerce is not confined to the regulation of commerce among the states. It extends to those activities intrastate which so affect interstate commerce or the exercise of the power of Congress over it as to make regulation of them appropriate means to the attainment of a legitimate end, the exercise of the granted power of Congress to regulate interstate commerce.

In *Wickard v. Filburn*, the Court upheld the application of amendments to the Agricultural Adjustment Act of 1938 to the production and consumption of home-grown wheat. The *Wickard* Court explicitly rejected earlier distinctions between direct and indirect effects on interstate commerce, stating:

[E]ven if appellee's activity be local and though it may not be regarded as commerce, it may still, whatever its nature, be reached by Congress if it exerts a substantial economic effect on interstate commerce, and this irrespective of whether such effect is what might at some earlier time have been defined as "direct" or "indirect."

The *Wickard* Court emphasized that although Filburn's own contribution to the demand for wheat may have been trivial by itself, that was not "enough to remove him from the scope of federal regulation where, as here, his contribution, taken together with that of many others similarly situated, is far from trivial."

Jones & Laughlin Steel, *Darby*, and *Wickard* ushered in an era of Commerce Clause jurisprudence that greatly expanded the previously defined authority of Congress under that Clause. In part, this was a recognition of the great changes that had occurred in the way business was carried on in this country. Enterprises that had once been local or at most regional in nature had become national in scope. But the doctrinal change also reflected a view that earlier Commerce Clause cases artificially had constrained the authority of Congress to regulate interstate commerce.

But even these modern-era precedents which have expanded congressional power under the Commerce Clause confirm that this power is subject to outer limits. In *Jones & Laughlin Steel*, the Court warned that the scope of the interstate commerce power "must be considered in the light of our dual system of government and may not be extended so as to embrace effects upon interstate commerce so indirect and remote that to embrace them, in view of our complex society, would effectually obliterate the distinction between what is national and what is local and create a completely centralized government." Since that time, the Court has heeded that warning and undertaken to decide whether a rational basis existed for concluding that a regulated activity sufficiently affected interstate commerce.

Similarly, in *Maryland v. Wirtz* (1968), the Court reaffirmed that "the power to regulate commerce, though broad indeed, has limits" that "[t]he Court has ample power" to enforce. In response to the dissent's warnings that the Court was powerless to enforce the limitations on Congress' commerce powers because "[a]ll activities affecting commerce, even in the minutest degree, [*Wickard*], may be regulated and controlled by Congress," (Douglas, J., dissenting), the *Wirtz* Court replied that the dissent had misread precedent as "[n] either here nor in *Wickard* has the Court declared that Congress may use a relatively trivial impact on commerce as an excuse for broad general regulation of state or private activities." Rather, "[t]he Court has said only that where a general regulatory statute bears a substantial relation to commerce, the de minimis character of individual instances arising under that statute is of no consequence."

Consistent with this structure, we have identified three broad categories of activity that Congress may regulate under its commerce power. First, Congress may regulate the use of the channels of interstate commerce. Second, Congress is empowered to regulate and protect the instrumentalities of interstate commerce, or persons or things in interstate commerce, even though the threat may come only from intrastate activities. Finally, Congress' commerce authority includes the power to regulate those activities having a substantial relation to interstate commerce, *Jones & Laughlin Steel*, i.e., those activities that substantially affect interstate commerce.

Within this final category, admittedly, our case law has not been clear whether an activity must "affect" or "substantially affect" interstate commerce in order to be within Congress' power to regulate it under the Commerce Clause. We conclude, consistent with the great weight of our case law, that the proper test requires an analysis of whether the regulated activity "substantially affects" interstate commerce.

We now turn to consider the power of Congress, in the light of this framework, to enact 922(q). The first two categories of authority may be quickly disposed of: 922(q) is not a regulation of the use of the channels of interstate commerce, nor is it an attempt to prohibit the interstate transportation of a commodity through the channels of commerce; nor can 922(q) be justified as a regulation by which Congress has sought to protect an instrumentality of interstate commerce or a thing in interstate commerce. Thus, if 922(q) is to be sustained, it must be under the third category as a regulation of an activity that substantially affects interstate commerce.

First, we have upheld a wide variety of congressional Acts regulating intrastate economic activity where we have concluded that the activity substantially affected interstate commerce. Examples include the regulation of intrastate coal mining, intrastate extortionate credit transactions, restaurants utilizing substantial interstate supplies, inns and hotels catering to interstate guests, and production and consumption of home-grown wheat. These examples are by no means exhaustive, but the pattern is clear. Where economic activity substantially affects interstate commerce, legislation regulating that activity will be sustained.

Even [*Wickard v. Filburn* (1942)], which is perhaps the most far reaching example of Commerce Clause authority over intrastate activity, involved economic activity in a way that the possession of a gun in a school zone does not. Roscoe Filburn operated a small farm in Ohio, on which, in the year involved, he raised 23 acres of wheat. It was his practice to sow winter wheat in the fall, and after harvesting it in July to sell a portion of the crop, to feed part of it to poultry and livestock on the farm, to use some in making flour for home consumption, and to keep the remainder for seeding future crops. The Secretary of Agriculture assessed a penalty against him under the Agricultural Adjustment Act of 1938 because he harvested about 12 acres more wheat than his allotment under the Act permitted. The Act was designed to regulate the volume of wheat moving in interstate and foreign commerce in order to avoid surpluses and shortages, and concomitant fluctuation in wheat prices, which had previously obtained. The Court said, in an opinion sustaining the application of the Act to Filburn's activity:

> One of the primary purposes of the Act in question was to increase the market price of wheat and to that end to limit the volume thereof that could affect the market. It can hardly be denied that a factor of such volume and variability as home-consumed wheat would have a substantial influence on price and market conditions. This may arise because being in marketable condition such wheat overhangs the market and, if induced by rising prices, tends to flow into the market and check price increases. But if we assume that it is never marketed, it supplies a need of the man who grew it which would otherwise be reflected by purchases in the open market. Home-grown wheat in this sense competes with wheat in commerce.

Section 922(q) is a criminal statute that by its terms has nothing to do with "commerce" or any sort of economic enterprise, however broadly one might define those terms. Section 922(q) is not an essential part of a larger regulation of economic activity, in which the regulatory scheme could be undercut unless the intrastate activity were regulated. It cannot, therefore, be sustained under our cases upholding regulations of activities that arise out of or are connected with a commercial transaction, which viewed in the aggregate, substantially affects interstate commerce.

Second, 922(q) contains no jurisdictional element which would ensure, through case-by-case inquiry, that the firearm possession in question affects interstate commerce. For example, in *United States v. Bass* (1971), the Court interpreted former 18 U.S.C. 1202(a), which made it a crime for a felon to "receiv[e], posses[s], or transpor[t] in commerce or affecting commerce . . . any firearm." The Court interpreted the possession component of 1202(a) to require an additional nexus to interstate commerce both because the statute was ambiguous and because "unless Congress conveys its purpose clearly, it will not be deemed to have significantly changed the federal-state balance." The *Bass* Court set aside the conviction because although the Government had demonstrated that Bass had possessed a firearm, it had failed "to show the requisite nexus with interstate commerce." The Court thus interpreted the statute to reserve the constitutional question whether Congress could regulate, without more, the "mere possession" of firearms. Unlike the statute in *Bass*, 922(q) has no express jurisdictional element which might limit its reach to a discrete set of firearm possessions that additionally have an explicit connection with or effect on interstate commerce.

Although as part of our independent evaluation of constitutionality under the Commerce Clause we of course consider legislative findings, and indeed even congressional committee findings, regarding effect on interstate commerce, the Government concedes that "[n]either the statute nor its legislative history contain[s] express congressional findings regarding the effects upon interstate commerce of gun possession in a school zone." We agree with the Government that Congress normally is not required to make formal findings as to the substantial burdens that an activity has on interstate commerce. But to the extent that congressional findings would enable us to evaluate the legislative judgment that the activity in question substantially affected interstate commerce, even though no such substantial effect was visible to the naked eye, they are lacking here.

The Government argues that Congress has accumulated institutional expertise regarding the regulation of firearms through previous enactments. We agree, however, with the Fifth Circuit that importation of previous findings to justify 922(q) is especially inappropriate here because the "prior federal enactments or Congressional findings [do not] speak to the subject matter of section 922(q) or its relationship to interstate commerce. Indeed, section 922(q) plows thoroughly new ground and represents a sharp break with the long-standing pattern of federal firearms legislation."

The Government's essential contention, in fine, is that we may determine here that 922(q) is valid because possession of a firearm in a local school zone does indeed substantially affect interstate commerce. The Government argues that possession of a firearm in a school zone may result in violent crime and that violent crime can be expected to affect the functioning of the national economy in two ways. First, the costs of violent crime are substantial, and, through the mechanism of insurance, those costs are spread throughout the population. Second, violent crime reduces the willingness of individuals to travel to areas within the country that are perceived to be unsafe. The Government also argues that the presence of guns in schools poses a substantial threat to the educational process by threatening the learning environment. A handicapped educational process, in turn, will result in a less productive citizenry. That, in turn, would have an adverse effect on the Nation's economic well-being. As a result, the Government argues that Congress could rationally have concluded that 922(q) substantially affects interstate commerce.

We pause to consider the implications of the Government's arguments. The Government admits, under its "costs of crime" reasoning, that Congress could regulate not only all violent crime, but all activities that might lead to violent crime, regardless of how tenuously they relate to interstate commerce. Similarly, under the Government's "national productivity" reasoning, Congress could regulate any activity that it found was related to the economic productivity of individual citizens: family law (including marriage, divorce, and child custody), for example. Under the theories that the Government presents in support of 922(q), it is difficult to perceive any limitation on federal power, even in areas such as criminal law enforcement or education where States historically have been sovereign. Thus, if we were to accept the Government's arguments, we are hard-pressed to posit any activity by an individual that Congress is without power to regulate.

Although Justice Breyer argues that acceptance of the Government's rationales would not authorize a general federal police power, he is unable to identify any activity that the States may regulate but Congress may not. Justice Breyer posits that there might be some limitations on Congress' commerce power such as family law or certain aspects of education. These suggested limitations, when viewed in light of the dissent's expansive analysis, are devoid of substance.

Justice Breyer focuses, for the most part, on the threat that firearm possession in and near schools poses to the educational process and the potential economic consequences flowing from that threat. Specifically, the dissent reasons that (1) gun-related violence is a serious problem; (2) that problem, in turn, has an adverse effect on classroom learning; and (3) that adverse effect on classroom learning, in turn, represents a substantial threat to trade and commerce. This analysis would be equally applicable, if not more so, to subjects such as family law and direct regulation of education.

For instance, if Congress can, pursuant to its Commerce Clause power, regulate activities that adversely affect the learning environment, then, a fortiori, it also can regulate the educational process directly. Congress could determine that a school's curriculum has a "significant" effect on the extent of classroom learning. As a result, Congress could mandate a federal curriculum for local elementary and secondary schools because what is taught in local schools has a significant "effect on classroom learning," and that, in turn, has a substantial effect on interstate commerce.

Justice Breyer rejects our reading of precedent and argues that "Congress . . . could rationally conclude that schools fall on the commercial side of the line." Again, Justice Breyer's rationale lacks any real limits because, depending on the level of generality, any activity can be looked upon as commercial. Under the dissent's rationale, Congress could just as easily look at child rearing as "fall[ing] on the commercial side of the line" because it provides a "valuable service—namely, to equip [children] with the skills they need to survive in life and, more specifically, in the workplace." We do not doubt that Congress has authority under the Commerce Clause to regulate numerous commercial activities that substantially affect interstate commerce and also affect the educational process. That authority, though broad, does not include the authority to regulate each and every aspect of local schools.

Admittedly, a determination whether an intrastate activity is commercial or noncommercial may in some cases result in legal uncertainty. But, so long as Congress' authority is limited to those powers enumerated in the Constitution, and so long as those enumerated powers are interpreted as having judicially enforceable outer limits, congressional legislation under the Commerce Clause always will engender "legal uncertainty." As Chief Justice Marshall stated in *McCulloch v. Maryland* (1819):

> The [federal] government is acknowledged by all to be one of enumerated powers. The principle, that it can exercise only the powers granted to it . . . is now universally admitted. But the question respecting the extent of the powers actually granted, is perpetually arising, and will probably continue to arise, as long as our system shall exist.

The Constitution mandates this uncertainty by withholding from Congress a plenary police power that would authorize enactment of every type of legislation. Congress has operated within this framework of legal uncertainty ever since this Court determined that it was the judiciary's duty "to say what the law is." *Marbury v. Madison* (1803). Any possible benefit from eliminating this "legal uncertainty" would be at the expense of the Constitution's system of enumerated powers.

In *Jones & Laughlin Steel*, we held that the question of congressional power under the Commerce Clause "is necessarily one of degree." To the same effect is the concurring opinion of Justice Cardozo in *Schecter Poultry*:

> There is a view of causation that would obliterate the distinction of what is national and what is local in the activities of commerce. Motion at the outer rim is communicated perceptibly, though minutely, to recording instruments at the center. A society such as ours "is an elastic medium which transmits all tremors throughout its territory; the only question is of their size."

These are not precise formulations, and in the nature of things they cannot be. But we think they point the way to a correct decision of this case. The possession of a gun in a local school zone is in no sense an economic activity that might, through repetition elsewhere, substantially affect any sort of interstate commerce. Respondent was a local student at a local school; there is no indication that he had recently moved in interstate commerce, and there is no requirement that his possession of the firearm have any concrete tie to interstate commerce.

To uphold the Government's contentions here, we would have to pile infer-ence upon inference in a manner that would bid fair to convert congressional authority under the Commerce Clause to a general police power of the sort retained by the States. Admittedly, some of our prior cases have taken long steps down that road, giving great deference to congressional action. See supra, at 8. The broad language in these opinions has suggested the possibil-ity of additional expansion, but we decline here to proceed any further. To do so would require us to conclude that the Constitution's enumeration of pow-ers does not presuppose something not enumerated, and that there never will be a distinction between what is truly national and what is truly local. This we are unwilling to do.

For the foregoing reasons the judgment of the Court of Appeals is Affirmed.

3.4

JENNA BEDNAR

"The Madisonian Scheme to Control the National Government"

Madison believed that "vigorous federalism was necessary for a healthy democracy," according to Bednar. Just like his contemporaries among both Federalists and Antifederalists, Madison worried about vesting too much power in any one part of the government, including Congress or the presidency. Yet Madison was ardently a Federalist, favoring a strong national government (but not too strong). As Bednar explains, he pushed to design the American federation so that the states would be able to check national power.

MADISON'S TESTAMENT ON THE VICES OF THE UNITED STATES AND ADVICE FOR ITS SALVATION

The title of this reading might be surprising. Certainly, Madison set out to control the *state* governments by *expanding* the powers of the national government. But no theory of federalism is complete without a provision to draw and maintain the boundaries on all governments, including the national government. Most likely, the proposed government would have failed ratification had the Constitution's opponents continued to believe that the state governments would be diminished to administrative subunits, as the political Madison well understood. Therefore, he devoted much thought to controlling the national government, and the resulting theory, especially the separation of powers component, has been his greatest contribution to the study of political institutions.

Madison's scheme for controlling the national government is inseparable from his understanding of what was wrong with the state governments. After an extensive study of classical confederacies, Madison observed that in all unions where the states retained their sovereignty, the union eventually collapsed from interstate rivalry. He then recorded his thoughts on the problems with the American government under the Articles of Confederation. Famously labeling the problems "vices," his notes are a laundry list of the intransigence of the state governments, in their trespasses on one another, in their wildly divergent laws, and in their encroachments on the national government. It was imperative that any new government reduce the ability of the states to harm the union.

Madison's concerns extended beyond making federalism work: he was worried that state governmental opportunism would forever tarnish republican democracy.[1] Several state legislatures had shown tendencies to ignore the rights of their citizens and otherwise lean toward tyrannical behavior unbridled by their constitution or bills of rights to such an extent that some called for an end to the experiment with republican governance. While for Hamilton (and others) the solution was to establish a monarchical system similar to Britain's, Madison was reluctant to give up hope for representative democracy. If the institutions of aggregation could be perfected, he reasoned, then republican government would succeed.

To Madison, the solution to both problems, federal and democratic, was clear: a strengthened national government would overcome the vices of the present system, thereby serving as double-cure, both by stabilizing the union and relegitimizing republican government. A strong national government, with direct powers over the people, would be necessary to patrol conflict between the states. It would also field better politicians and reduce the problems of faction. Republics can be too small, Madison reasoned in *Federalist* 10 and 51.[2] The larger union would have two advantages: it could draw its candidates from a larger pool, increasing the chance of getting an excellent public servant, and the larger union would dilute the potency of factions.

Madison's primary point seems vindicated: the subordination of state governments to a strong national government does appear to reduce interstate conflict. And the experiment in republican government has long proven successful. But the two prongs of Madison's solution—a decentralized, layered system with a strong center—each create problems of their own. At the same time that it created a new interest—the national government—for the citizens to control, Madison's federal solution erected obstacles for effective republican government. Institutional mechanisms stitched onto electoral control as "auxiliary precautions" (*Federalist* 51) do not make a seamless federal fabric; flaws remain that can doom the union.

▪   ▪   ▪

Interinstitutional Oversight

In Madison's scheme of harnessing conflict to invoke obedience, separation of powers is without question the crown jewel—Madison's most enduring contribution to the theory of political institutions. Breaking with the parliamentary model, Madison advocated the fragmentation of executive, legislative, and judicial power at the national level. In so doing, Madison implicitly acknowledged that federalism, in its rawest form as decentralized government, is not self-regulating but needs institutional support.

Institutions create incentive environments; rules and organizational structures affect individual behavior by changing the means to achieve desired ends. One theory of human motivation posits that we are all essentially selfish. We would be unlikely to deny ourselves opportunities and therefore are incapable of self-restraint, but our jealousy prompts us to monitor one another's actions closely. Madison applies this theory of human nature to government; governments are groups of selfish men and therefore also likely to act selfishly. Brilliantly, he transforms vice into virtue by manipulating the institutions of government to mimic the forces of selfishness in society: "[A]mbition must be able to counteract ambition." Madison's theoretical trick is to fragment government, while leaving the components partially dependent on one another through checks and balances. The antagonism within governmental parts induces a self-regulating whole.

To Madison, separation of powers was necessary for "preservation of liberty" and the prevention of tyrannical laws.[3] Madison fused protection of the people with maintenance of federalism, and separation of powers could help achieve both ends, by providing a "double security" (*Federalist* 51): "[So] it is to be hoped . . . the two governments possess each the means of preventing or correcting unconstitutional encroachments of the other" (*The Papers of James Madison* [hereafter MP] 14, 218). While separation of powers might contribute to governmental efficiency because of task specialization, it seems far more likely to stall government action as the distinct interests bargain. For this reason, stagnation is evidence that separation of powers is working according to theory, because gridlock means that no one interest is able to overwhelm another. By frustrating attempts to dominate, separation of powers preserves federalism and protects people from tyranny.

In Madison's theory, separation of powers has two necessary ingredients: distinct but partially overlapping power, and independence. Overlapping power allows one branch to oversee the actions of another. In a 1785 reply to questions asked by his friend Caleb Wallace, in the course of agreeing with Wallace that amendment was necessary, he slipped in a comment about the importance of having some remedy available to one branch that believes another has superseded its powers (MP 8, 355): interbranch conflict was on his mind, and rather than promote a unified government, he sought an institutional outlet for internal disagreement. The cousin to separate powers, bicameralism, further unravels the monolith of parliamentary government by fragmenting power within the legislature. In the same letter to Wallace, Madison denigrated the design of the existing Senate, but "bad as it is, it is often a usefull bitt in the mouth of the house of Delegates" (MP 8, 351). In the Constitutional Convention, speaking on the proposed Senate, Madison argued: "[A]ll business liable to abuses is made to pass thro' separate hands, the one being a check on the other" (ibid. 10, 76).

Separation of powers can work only if the institutions have a motivation to cry foul. Task specialization is not enough to break the team mentality of the government. Their objectives and incentives must be independent as well. "Each department should have a will of its own," writes Madison in *Federalist* 51. His appreciation for the difficulties in achieving independence grew. The Virginia Plan called for the lower legislative house to appoint an upper, and the two chambers together would appoint the other branches. Staggered terms would "ensure" independence. Following the Convention, he was much more support-ive of fragmenting the elections and the constituencies of the separate branches and the two legislative houses. Electoral separation prevents the coagulation of interests, thereby exploiting institutional self-interest by inducing the branches to be watchful of one another's actions. In a unified government, whistle-blowers lose their jobs when their party is punished at the polls. With separa-tion of powers, constituents are not restricted to such a blunt instrument; they may retain their district's representative while rejecting their president.

Even when the prudence of independence and overlapping powers is seen, it is still difficult to work out in practice a combination of institutions that can carry it off. Certainly Madison's vision of the government evolved with experience: he seems to have grown more convinced of the necessity to disen-tangle the branches and put them on much more equal footing. If the mecha-nisms to provide independence are functioning correctly, a consequence is conflicting interests that need to be aired and reconciled. One feature that the remainder of this section will highlight is different mechanisms proposed to mediate intergovernmental disputes.

While separation of powers promotes contest and compromise, if it is at all imbalanced, it alone does not provide a means to halt interbranch encroach-ment, nor does it guarantee the Constitution. A complete institutional recipe must include some method of binding government action through constitu-tional review. Instinctively, the judiciary seems a likely candidate, but Madi-son and his colleagues were wary of vesting so much power in an unelected body,[4] and Madison doubted that the judiciary alone would be strong enough to counter the other two branches.

■ ■ ■

Madison and his contemporaries viewed the court as the natural arbiter in interstate disputes and also thought the court could monitor state transgres-sions on federal jurisdictions, although in this latter capacity Madison was dubious about the judiciary's ability to enforce its rulings, without force to back up its words. If Madison had had his way, of course, the national legisla-ture would have had the bite of the negative on state legislation, so judiciary weakness wouldn't matter.[5] Despite his expression of confidence in *Federalist* 39,[6] Madison worried that the judiciary still would not have enough influence to control the state governments.[7]

■ ■ ■

Madison's confidence in the judiciary did seem to grow over time, as did this sense of the urgency of having effective checks on the legislature.

■ ■ ■

In sum, interinstitutional oversight works through a combination of inde-pendence and dependence. Institutions should have distinct wills but need one another to act. When this balance is achieved, the federal government is less likely to behave opportunistically, whether by encroaching on the state governments or by tyrannizing its citizens.

State Supervision

Madison's skepticism of the abilities of state governments is well known, and so we must unravel his theory here with care. Without a doubt, much of his writing is rhetoric to gain support for the Constitution. However, the theory is consistent with interinstitutional oversight because it works through a combination of independence and dependence, and while it is the least elaborated component of Madison's system of constraints on the federal government, it is one of the most cited today.

Although we remember *Federalist* 51 as a defense of separation of powers, in it Madison describes a parallel system for maintaining the power balance between state and federal governments: "the different governments will control each other, at the same time that each will be controlled by itself" (*Federalist* 51). States supervise federal action both from within and without the federal apparatus because the Constitution has made the national government dependent upon them to act. In correspondence with Thomas Jefferson, Madison wrote: "This dependence of the General, on the local authorities, seems effectually to guard the latter against any dangerous encroachments of the former" (MP 10, 211). The entanglement of state and federal interests in the national legislature makes it unlikely that a federal interest will evolve. Reminiscent of his earlier assurances that the national government will have no desire to encroach on the states, he submitted in later correspondence that: "encroachments of [state sovereignty] are more to be apprehended from impulses given to it by a majority of the States seduced by expected advantages, than from the love of Power in the Body itself, controuled as it *now* is by its responsibility to the Constituent Body" (Hunt 9, 58). Federal encroachment, if it occurs, is likely to be from state capture of the federal government. The federal government itself has no desire to increase its power.

Within the government, states have many avenues to express their interests. In *Federalist* 39, Madison describes how the Constitution is both federal and national: by federal he means that the states are involved in the central level decision-making, and he cites the Senate, the electoral college, and state ratification of the Constitution, as well as the "natural attachment" (*Federalist* 46) that citizens have to their own state, as evidence. The American formulation of bicameralism protected state interests in two ways: it provided for equal representation of the states, and until the 17th Amendment, state legislatures appointed the senators.

Madison blamed the state legislatures for the anemic performance of the union under the Articles; if he had had his druthers, the last thing he would have advocated was perpetuating their power in the new federal union.[8] Yet we remember him (disguised as Publius) as one of equal representation's more eloquent advocates, and state representation in the federal decision-making structure is considered by many to be an integral part of the Madisonian vision for governmental reform.

The resolution of this inconsistency is to be found in Madison's practicality and political skills: he believed that the institutional structure would minimize the danger posed by state intervention in the federal government, and he knew that equal representation was very popular and would increase the Constitution's chance for ratification. So we find him writing persuasive passages in the *Federalist* in support of the institutionalization of state input in the federal government. In *Federalist* 62 he alludes to the compromise that brought about equal representation and praises it for maintaining state autonomy, and especially that it is a useful mechanism for incorporating state input in national decision-making: "In this spirit it may be remarked, that the equal vote allowed to each state, is at once a constitutional recognition of the portion of sovereignty remaining in the individual states, and an instrument for preserving that residuary sovereignty."

Ever the statesman, he continues the thought by criticizing the position he had held prior to the vote on July 16: "So far the equality ought to be no less acceptable to the large than to the small states; since they are not less solicitous to guard by every possible expedient against an improper consolidation of the states into one simple republic. . . . No law or resolution can now be passed without the concurrence . . . of a majority of the states" (*Federalist* 62). Equal representation in the Senate will help to stabilize the union by ensuring the balance of power between state and federal governments.

Several other institutions incorporate state input in federal decision-making, as Madison delineates in *Federalist* 45. Not only will states be represented in the Senate, but the president cannot be elected without the states, and the House members, although directly elected by the people, will likely have state legislative experience.[9]

Structural political safeguards were just the first stage in the system of state protection as envisaged by the Founders. The states could also work outside of the formal structure by protesting when the federal government overstepped its bounds. James Wilson, delegate of Pennsylvania, describes the following chain reaction:

> The States having in general a similar interest, in case of any proposition in the National Legislature to encroach on the State Legislatures, he conceived a general alarm wd. take place in the National Legislature itself, that it would communicate itself to the State Legislatures, and wd. finally spread among the people at large. The Genl. Govt. will be as ready to preserve the rights of the States as the latter are to preserve the rights of individuals; all the members of the former, having a common interest, as

representatives of all the people of the latter, to leave the State Govts. in possession of what the people wish them to retain. (Farrand 1966, 1, 356)

Wilson refers to the state legislatures responding to the cry of alarm from the U.S. senators. Madison echoes this argument in *Federalist* 45: "But ambitious encroachments of the federal government, on the authority of the State governments, would not excite the opposition of the single State, or of a few States only. They would be signals of general alarm. Every government would espouse the common cause." Ignoring any collective action problem,[10] much less the possibility that the federal government's encroachment may be welcomed by some of the states, Madison argued that the states would watch federal action closely and jointly protest any violation.

When the Adams administration's passage of the Alien and Sedition Acts infuriated Madison for its encroachments on civil liberties, he federalized a political issue by enlisting the Virginia assembly (along with his colleague Thomas Jefferson, in Kentucky) to challenge the administration's moves (MP 17, 189–90, 303–51). States not only had the right to protest unconstitutional federal activity; it was their duty as an obedient member of the union to protect the union and maintain the constitutional covenant with the people.

Later in life he continued to support his position and the decision to write the Virginia Resolutions, although he regretted South Carolina's reference to the Resolutions while it attempted to nullify congressional legislation (Hunt 383–403). While it seems that Madison believed in the protective force of political safeguards, particularly state involvement, on balance it is a poorly worked out component of his theory. Its greatest impact was no doubt as the rhetoric expressed to win over the states' rights constituency.

■   ■   ■

In *Federalist* 49, Madison describes a characteristic he would like to see in any body that would regulate intergovernmental dispute: "[It] is the reason, alone, of the public that ought to control and regulate the government. The passions ought to be controlled and regulated by the government."[11] The judiciary alone stands removed from public passion. Madison says so himself not two paragraphs earlier: "[T]he [judiciary], by the mode of their appointment, as well as by the nature and permanency of it, are too far removed from the people to share much in their prepossessions."

The judiciary is a viable solution for both of the problems created by Madison's federalism. It is not subject to electoral approval, so is freed from the motivation shared by the legislature and executive to encroach. While it cannot—and should not—decide the people's will for them, it is the guardian of the Constitution, which is the only expression we have of what we as a people want our federalism to look like. It can recover the second form of failure by promising a coherent practice of federalism according to our Constitution, offering the possibility that time and perspective might do what an instant's decision cannot: we can tinker (but not frivolously!) with our Constitution as we gain experience with its effects. Therefore, the judiciary has much to offer to federal stability.

■   ■   ■

Madison knew that the federal government would have an incentive to embellish its power, but at the time of Founding he believed that the destructive motivation was sufficiently constrained by institutional design. He quickly learned otherwise, and when his backup plan of state protest backfired with the nullification crisis, he began to have more faith in judicial review. But it remained underappreciated by him and definitely by Madisonian scholars.

Madison was a nationalist and a populist, albeit perhaps not according to today's standards. He wanted a stronger national government and qualified democratic control significantly, but all with the aim of making republican democracy work. He pragmatically accepted the faults of men and designed a government to transform those flaws into virtues. When transformation was impossible, his mechanisms suppressed them. Madison believed that a vigorous federalism was necessary for a healthy democracy.

NOTES

1. Hobson (1979) describes this crisis as more important to Madison than the problems of controlling the state legislatures. He writes: "Madison regarded the crisis of the Confederation in the 1780s as foremost a crisis of republican government. The question at stake for him was whether a government that derived its authority from the people and was administered by persons who were directly or indirectly appointed by the people would prove to be more than a vain hope or merely theoretical ideal" (pp. 218–19). This reading agrees with Hobson that Madison most wanted to create a government of manageable popular sovereignty.

2. Madison first developed the size of states argument in his notes on the "Vices." Note 8 blames the poor quality of the laws on two factors: the representatives and the people themselves. Politicians seek office for three motives, Madison reasoned: ambition, personal interest, and public good, and he feared that the first two reasons outweigh the third, often causing the "honest but unenlightened representative [to] be the dupe of a favorite leader, veiling his selfish views under the professions of public good." *Federalist* to famously elaborates his position on faction, but Note 8 contains his early thoughts: the wider the sphere, the more difficult it is for factions to influence outcomes.

3. See, for example, "Remarks in the Federal Convention on Electing the Executive," July 17, 1787 (MP 10, 103), and *Federalist* 51. Note, however, the contributions of Kernell and McLean in this volume, arguing that Madison was much less committed to separation of powers than we assume today.

4. For the modern edition of this concern, see Ely 1980 and Friedman 1993.

5. The supremacy clause was added to the Constitution as a weak compromise once the negative was lost.

6. Here I refer especially to the third-to-last paragraph of *Federalist* 39, regarding the necessity of a federal-level tribunal to resolve disputes between the levels of government. Although much later, in an 1830 letter to Edward Everett, Madison refers to this essay as early support for judicial intervention (discussed below), I think that when writing *Federalist* 39 he had in mind only state encroachment on federal power, and not the inverse; I do not consider it to be a recommendation of judicial involvement in federal encroachment claims.

7. See the discussion in Rakove 1996, 171–77; and Rakove 2002.

8. As a large state delegate, and moreover because of his suspicions of the state governments, Madison fought against equal representation in the Senate. He searched in vain for some principle other than state representation to guide Senate membership once his Virginia Plan proposal, in which the second chamber would be elected by members of the first chamber (who were themselves directly elected by the people), was rejected by the Convention. In the weeks preceding the "Great Compromise" (the July 16 vote for equal representation in the Senate), Madison's arguments against equal representation accelerate in bitterness and desperation. On June 7, Madison complained in debates that rather than serve as a useful check on inexpedient governmental practices in the national legislature, state appointment of senators might *promote* it, as the states had proven themselves to be prone to incompetent government (MP 10, 40); on June 21, he wrote that state governments are maintained, not to serve as checks on the national government, but instead because they are needed to attend to all the minutiae of local government that they can do more efficiently than a purely national one (ibid. 10, 68). His desperation showed on June 30, when in an attempt to frighten his compatriots into agreement, he spoke the unspeakable (and implicitly burst a hole in his theory of faction). He said that while equal representation might do no harm, it wouldn't help either, as "the Majority of the States might still injure the majority of the people" (ibid. 10, 90), and he introduced the possibility of sectional conflict, as a more important cleavage than the large state-small state division. As late as July 5, he was still protesting the proposed compromise, calling it "unjust" and saying further that he did not think it necessary to achieve ratification:

> Harmony in the Convention was no doubt much to be desired. Satisfaction to all the States, in the first instance still more so. But if the principal States comprehending a majority of the people of the U.S. should concur in a just & judicious Plan, he had the firmest hopes, that all the other States would by degrees accede to it. (Ibid., 120–21)

On July 14 he made his final attempt to persuade his colleagues. He hotly delineated the fault with equal representation. With remarkable prescience, his closing argument reiterated his June 30 concern regarding the North–South division over slavery: "[T]he perpetuity it would give to the preponderance of the Northn. agst. the Southn. Scale was a serious consideration" (ibid. 10, 102).

9. Whether or not we should take seriously Madison's proclamation that because of the institutional incorporation of state interests the federal government would be politically dependent upon the state governments is unclear. We know how opposed he was to equal representation in the Senate and how disdainful he was of the competence of state representation. The connection between the Electoral College and state interests is weak, and his argument about the House contradicts his theory of enlarged republics.

10. Madison's logical slip here is worth noting because he well understood the collective action problem in state financing of war debt. We must assume that he believed protest was costless—that it was in each individual state's interest to protest—thereby skirting the collective action problem, or that he still did not believe that the federal government would encroach, so given the irrelevance of counterstrategies, he did not devote much thought to the protest mechanism.

11. Madison supplies a curious bit of food for thought regarding the legitimacy of unanimous decisions: he implies that they are an indication that the decision was governed by passion, not reason. "When men exercise their reason coolly and freely on a variety of distinct questions, they inevitably fall into different opinions on some of them. When they are governed by a common passion, their opinions, if they are so to be called, will be the same" (*Federalist* 50).

WORKS CITED

Ely, John Hart. 1980. *Democracy and Distrust: A Theory of Judicial Review*. Cambridge, MA: Harvard University Press.

Farrand, Max, ed. 1966. *The Records of the Federal Convention of 1787*. 4 vols. New Haven, Conn.: Yale University Press.

Friedman, Barry. 1993. "Dialogue and Judicial Review." *Michigan Law Review* 91: 577–682.

Hobson, Charles F. 1979. "The Negative on State Laws: James Madison, the Constitution, and the Crisis of Republican Government." *William and Mary Quarterly* 36, no. 2: 215–35.

Hunt, Galliard. 1900. *The Writings of James Madison*. New York: G.P. Putnam's Sons.

Madison, James. 1966. *Notes of debates in the Federal Convention of 1787, reported by James Madison*. (Originally published in 1840 in *The Papers of James Madison*.) Athens: Ohio University Press.

———. 1969–85. *The Papers of James Madison*. 15 vols. Various eds. (William M. E. Rachel, Robert A. Rutland, Charles F. Hobson, and others). Chicago: University of Chicago Press; Charlottesville: University Press of Virginia.

Rakove, Jack. 1996. *Original Meanings: Politics and Ideas in the Making of the Constitution*. New York: Alfred A. Knopf.

———. 2002. "Judicial Power in the Constitutional Theory of James Madison." *William and Mary Law Review* 43, no. 4: 1513–47.

4

CIVIL RIGHTS AND CIVIL LIBERTIES

4.1

MICHAEL DAWSON

From *Behind the Mule*

Dawson reminds us of what other scholars have found: that many individual African Americans believe that their fate is linked to the status of others who are similar. But similarity can mean different things. Do African Americans believe they have common political interests with others of similar economic class? Or do they believe they have common political interests with others of the same race? Using survey data, Dawson shows that race is more important than class in explaining African American political behavior.

... This reading examines the tension—highlighted by these two images—between racial interests and class interests as factors shaping African-American politics. The tension arises from the historical legacy of racial and economic oppression that forged racial identity of African Americans. As bluesman Booker White suggests, the key to the historical origins of African-American social identity can be found "behind the mule." It is this legacy of a social identity in which racial and economic oppression have been intertwined for generations that has been the critical component in understanding not only the cultural basis of African-American politics, as Henry (1990) has argued, but also the material roots of black politics. As blues analyst Samuel Charters suggests, only when one "stripped away the misconception that the black society in the United States was simply a poor, discouraged version of the white" could one understand African-American society (Baker 1984).

Although Charters was referring to the blues, his point is equally applicable to black politics. African-American politics, including political behavior, is *different*. It has been shaped by historical forces that produced a different pattern of political behavior from the pattern found among white citizens.[1]

■   ■   ■

THE PROBLEM: RACE AND CLASS AS COMPETING THEORIES OF AFRICAN-AMERICAN POLITICS

This study was motivated by a set of questions that have captured the attention of scholars such as W.E.B. Du Bois, Robert Dahl, and William Wilson. The central question, simply stated, is whether race or class is more important in shaping African-American politics. This question has been central both to the study of African-American society and to the study of ethnic politics. Both traditions have investigated when social scientists should expect racial and ethnic loyalties to decline, and when that decline is accompanied by a parallel decline in racially or ethnically oriented politics.

These questions are of general interest for two reasons. First, America is becoming racially and ethnically more diverse, and the effects of that diversity are being felt politically: rapidly growing Asian and Latino populations are reshaping politics in politically important states such as Florida and California, and, in addition, the increasing racial tensions that accompany increased diversity are sometimes played out in the political arena. Examples of the salience of racial tensions in the political arena during the 1980s and early 1990s include the 1983 mayoral races in Chicago and Philadelphia (won by Harold Washington and W. Wilson Goode, respectively), the strong showing among white voters in David Duke's 1991 gubernatorial race in Louisiana, and the English-only referenda in several states. Jesse Helms's 1990 Senate campaign, already mentioned, was a model of how to exploit racial fears, tensions, and outright racism.

Second, racial politics presents analysts of the American party system with several puzzles. One is the lack of diversity in African-American politics. Many scholars and political activists ask, Where are the black Republicans? Another puzzle is why the study of black politics has not become more central to the study of American political parties and other major American political institutions, despite the recognized importance of racial politics. Carmines and Stimson (1989) have argued that the party system has been transformed by racial politics, whereas Huckfeldt and Kohfeld (1989) argue that class politics has been submerged by racial politics.

■   ■   ■

Race

Most students of black politics generally, and of black political behavior specifically, argue that one should expect continued political homogeneity among African Americans. This position is based on the belief that the primary imperative in black politics is to advance the political interests of African Americans as a racial group (Barker 1988; Pinderhughes 1987; Walters 1988).

This belief, in turn, is based on studies by numerous observers showing that race is still a major social, economic, and political force in American society and a major shaper of African-American lives. Socially, scholars of this school argue, residential segregation is still a fact of American life and has major ramifications. Residential segregation, they argue, determines the quality of schooling available to African Americans; it means that the property of the black middle and working classes appreciates more slowly than the property of the white middle and working classes, contributing to the enormous gap in wealth between black and white Americans; and by concentrating poverty in black neighborhoods, it negatively affects the neighborhoods even of the black middle class, which is less able to escape neighborhoods with significant concentrations of poverty than it would be if residential segregation did not exist. These scholars also point to the apparent increase in violent racial incidents during the 1980s in cities and suburbs and on college campuses as a social factor that affects African Americans regardless of their class.

Within the economic sphere, adherents of this view argue, the entire class structure of black America is distorted by the legacy of racism. A black capitalist class does not fully exist. Further, the black middle class is economically vulnerable because of its extreme reliance on public sector and quasi-public sector employment. In addition, middle-class blacks own less wealth per family than poor whites. The median and mean levels of household wealth are less for black families that earn over $50,000 a year than for white families that earn under $10,000 a year.

Wealth is an often ignored but important indicator of life chances because it signifies the ability to transmit resources from one generation to the next, to produce income from resources, and to survive financial setbacks. Thus, the lack of wealth in the black middle class means that even affluent black families often find it difficult to pass resources to their children, that a pool of capital (often necessary for the survival of small businesses) is not available, and that many black middle-class families are, in Landry's words, "one paycheck from disaster" (Landry 1987). Glass ceilings (unspoken barriers to the promotion of minorities and women to partnership in firms and top managerial ranks) and other forms of inequity have also harmed the financial stability of the black middle and working classes.

Politically, these same scholars argue, race remains a major force in the lives of African Americans. The lack of competition between the two parties for the black vote, in combination with the recent shift to the right in American politics, reinforces the need for African-American political unity to continue. Whether one is talking about the cutback of means-tested programs of vital importance to the black poor or about the massive attack on the affirmative action programs that benefit the more affluent African Americans, these scholars conclude that the political interests of all African Americans are still bound by race.

According to this line of reasoning, because the social, economic, and political realities of whites and blacks differ substantially *because of race,* racial interests continue to override class interests (whether individual or family). And as long as this is true—as long as the political interests of African Americans are bound by race—one should expect high levels of political unity among African Americans *regardless of economic status.*

Class

There is, however, increasing support for the competing hypothesis that race is no longer the most salient factor in African-American lives because economic polarization within the black community is accelerating. University of Chicago sociologist William Wilson has been the most forceful proponent of the thesis that class has become the most salient social determinant of African Americans' life chances. In *The Declining Significance of Race* (1980) he makes three important claims. The first (the one that has given the book so much notoriety) is that discrimination is now less important in determining a person's life chances than social status or economic class. His second claim (which several scholars and politicians have embraced) is that the civil rights movement benefited mostly middle-class, well-trained, younger African Americans. Wilson's third claim is that to some degree the civil rights movement was consciously led by the black middle class mainly to benefit their own class interests.

Wilson's claims taken as a whole have profound implications for African-American politics. If it is true that in the 1960s American society changed so much that race ceased to be the overwhelming or even the major determinant of the fate of individual African Americans, one would expect African-American political behavior to reflect increasing diversity. As Dawson and Wilson (1991) have detailed, most major social science theories would predict that increased economic heterogeneity in a population would lead to increasing diversity in political behavior. Social theorist Robert Dahl, for example, in *Who Governs?* (1961), a sophisticated presentation of ethnic political development, certainly predicted this growing political diversity.

Some empirical evidence exists to support Wilson and like-minded scholars. Economic polarization among African Americans has indeed been increasing over the past twenty years. Both the black middle class and the group of economically marginalized African Americans have grown.

From 1960 to 1991, the black middle class more than doubled in size. Approximately one third of employed blacks now have middle-class occupations. (But when the unemployed and discouraged workers are added to the pool, the relative size of the black middle class shrinks to approximately 15 percent.) So on the one hand, there is a growing, if vulnerable, black middle class. Moreover, those such as Wilson would argue, despite glass ceilings, job and social segregation, residential segregation, and the like, this class has more opportunities than any group of African Americans in history. This is held to be particularly true of the new black middle class, which has grown as a result of advances in black civil rights—blacks whose economic status is based on employment in sectors not traditionally tied to the black community, such as multinational corporations, the media, predominantly white universities, and businesses that sell to predominantly white markets or to the government (Boston 1988; Landry 1987). In the future, the new black middle class may not identify as strongly with the black community, the Democratic party, or liberal causes.

On the other hand, the number of African Americans without stable employment is also growing. In the 1980s, black unemployment rates in states such as Illinois and Michigan were significantly higher than 20 percent. Among key age cohorts of black men—those who should be at the beginning or in the middle of their prime earning years—labor force participation rates have been decreasing. The result is that African Americans—adults and children alike—are three times more likely to live below the poverty line than whites. And when we look at families as opposed to individuals, as late as 1987, 30 percent of black families, containing 45 percent of black children, were below the poverty line. Nearly 70 percent of these poor families are headed by women. The lives of economically marginalized African Americans are dominated by the struggle for economic survival.

Many would argue that economic polarization within the black community will continue to increase throughout the 1990s and will bring in its wake increasing political polarization. African Americans already display an unusually high degree of class consciousness when compared with other Americans. Such consciousness is likely to grow, particularly among less affluent African Americans; as the objective importance of race in the lives of African Americans declines interests diverge. According to the proponents of the class thesis, the dire *economic* status of large numbers of African Americans, especially in contrast to the improved economic status of large numbers of other African Americans, dictates that class will supersede race as the most politically salient factor for African Americans.

A SOLUTION: A GROUP-INTERESTS PERSPECTIVE ON AFRICAN-AMERICAN POLITICS

This reading develops a framework for analyzing African-American political choice by testing whether race or class is the primary determinant of contemporary African-American political behavior and public opinion. This framework draws in recent work in the psychology of social groups to help explain how psychological processes are critical for the formation of social identity. Particularly the work of Turner (1987) is used to help develop a theory of African-American group interests that explains the continued political homogeneity of African Americans and describes the conditions under which African Americans will begin to display political diversity.

My framework is based on two assumptions. First, it is quite clear that, until the mid-1960s, race was the decisive factor in determining the opportunities and life chances available to virtually all African Americans, regardless of their own or their family's social and economic status. Consequently, it was much more efficient for African Americans to determine what was good for the racial group than to determine what was good for themselves individually, and more efficient for them to use the status of the group, both relative and absolute, as a proxy for individual utility. I call this phenomenon the *black utility heuristic*.[2] The black utility heuristic is the basis for my framework for analyzing micro black politics. It was more efficient to use group status as a proxy not only because a piece of legislation or a public policy could be analyzed relatively easily for its effect on the race but also because the information sources available in the black community—the media outlets, kinship networks, community and civil rights organizations, and especially the preeminent institution in the black community, the black church—would all reinforce the political salience of racial interests and would provide information about racial group status.

Second, I assume that cognitive psychological processes are critical in shaping perceptions of racial group status. Psychological theories of attribution and self-categorization suggest that psychological processes on the individual level would reinforce the salience of racial politics for African Americans. Information that either minimized intragroup differences or exaggerated intergroup differences would be accepted more easily than information that contradicted current images of the importance of race in politics. Errors in information processing and biases in decision making would tend to favor racial explanations of the social world. The salience of one's racial identity, or of any other group identity, is a function of the cognitive accessibility of information pertinent to that identity, and the fit of that identity with social reality. This fact suggests two ways in which racial identity can become less salient for African Americans. One way is if information about the political, economic, and social world of black America becomes less accessible, either because individual blacks do not live in the black community (some members of the black middle class are in fact moving out of black communities) or because social networks in the black community are breaking down, as has happened in some of the most economically devastated inner-city neighborhoods (Marable 1983; Wilson 1980, 1987). The other way, particularly for the new black middle class, is if race becomes less salient in individuals' own lives. This is essentially the process described by Wilson and Dahl.

If neither of those developments takes place—that is, if information does not become less accessible and race does not become less personally salient—we should expect the combination of the cognitive phenomenon of accessibility and fit to slow the growth of political diversity in the African

American community. And, in fact, exiting from their community is much harder for black Americans than it was for European ethnic groups earlier in the nation's history or for Asians or Latinos today. In addition, to the degree to which the political and social climate is still perceived to be racially hostile, economic information is counteracted, with the result that racial group politics remains salient for African Americans. It is upon these assumptions that my framework for analyzing African-American political choice is based.

■ ■ ■

4. INTRODUCTION

Political and economic concerns have been at the forefront of African-American activism throughout American history. While either economic or political concerns may be more prominent during any given period in African-American history, politics and economics have been constant arenas for black struggle. Several scholars have documented the historical interplay between African Americans' efforts to achieve both racial and economic justice. . . .[3] The fierce Booker T. Washington-W.E.B. Du Bois debate was partly over the relative importance of economic and political strategies for black advancement. However, most African Americans, and Du Bois himself later in his career, have believed that advancement on both fronts is necessary and that the two types of progress are intertwined. The New Deal policies of Franklin D. Roosevelt confirmed the importance of the link between politics and economics for African Americans. As numerous scholars have shown for the white electorate, evaluations of the status of the American economy itself structure African-American individual-level as well as aggregate-level political choices and evaluations. Not surprisingly, however, *how* economic evaluations structure political decision making for blacks differs from how it does for whites. These interest-based evaluations of the economy powerfully structure African Americans' political behavior. Economic group interests directly and indirectly influence such basic political phenomena as African-American party identification, candidate evaluations, and voting behavior.

MEASURES OF CLASS AND THE AFRICAN-AMERICAN CLASS STRUCTURE

Wilson in *The Declining Significance of Race* (1980), calls class a "slippery concept." For African Americans the concept of class is even more problematic than usual because of the severe distortion of the African-American class structure due to the historical legacy of racism and exploitation. Several students of the American class structure have noted the extreme attenuation of the African-American class structure as compared with that of whites. Wright and colleagues (1982), working from a neo-Marxist framework, state that the black middle class is much smaller and the black working class is much larger than those of whites. According to Wright, for example, the black working class comprises 64 percent of the black population while the white working class comprises only 44 percent of the white population. Black managers are only 7 percent of the black population while white managers are 14 percent of the white population. Small-business owners (the Marxist petty bourgeoisie) and capitalists/employers combined only make up 3 percent of the black population as compared to 25 percent of whites. Boston (1988) finds similar divergence in his work on black social classes. He also argues that a black capitalist class with any social influence within the black community does not exist. He finds that the black middle class, when adjusted for the high rate of black unemployment, comprises 11 percent of the black population as opposed to an unemployment-adjusted white percentage of 27 percent.

This distortion of the African-American class structure is apparent whether one looks at various occupational structures, or looks at income and employment patterns. . . . Wilson (1980, ix) defines class as "any group of people who have more or less similar goods, services, or skills to offer for income in a given economic order and do therefore receive similar remuneration in the marketplace." This is the definition adopted here.

Several reasons—some theoretical, others pragmatic—support the adoption of Wilson's admittedly broad definition. First, it is flexible enough to accommodate both changes in the structure of the American political economy and changes in the African-American political economy. For many observers of African-American society, the stunning change in the African-American class structure that has occurred in the second half of the twentieth century is the creation of a new black middle class at the same time that many African-American workers became economically marginalized. This definition allows for the possibility that as the structure of the economy changes, new segments within classes may develop, or over time new classes may develop. Certainly, new structural opportunities have led to a situation in which a new segment has developed consisting of people whose income is less dependent on the black community and more dependent on traditionally white enterprises, both in the government and in the private sector. For Wilson, higher class means, among other things, greater life chances and higher income. Although Landry rejects a notion of class based on income or education, he argues that education is an enabling factor for higher class position while income is a reward for higher class position. Indeed, Boston argues that the new black middle class, in particular, is distinguished both by its members' possession of "scarce skills" and by their resulting relatively high salaries.

Boston and Wilson explicitly argue that different classes within the African-American population have different political interests. Of course, Wilson argues that race is declining in importance as a factor for determining African-American life chances and that class is an increasingly important factor. Boston, who directly challenges Wilson, still argues that within each class there are strata of African Americans who share similar class-based interests and political beliefs, even though for virtually all classes of African Americans, class positions have been influenced by racism. Consequently, he argues that if there is a social basis for the media pronouncements of a new black conservatism that were frequent during the Reagan administration, it is to be found in the new black middle class. This is because the financial well-being of the new black middle class is separate from that of the African-American community as a whole. Wilson (1987) would add that this class has also physically separated itself from the black community in a new suburban exodus from the inner city.

However, as Boston and others have pointed out, this class is so small as to be almost undetectable using social surveys. Research strategies such as participant observation or analysis of the social organizations of this new, up-and-coming black economic elite may be more fruitful in understanding the political beliefs of all classes of African Americans. Surveys, however, do provide tools with which to test the basic *political* proposition that as African Americans' station in life has improved in the late twentieth century, their political beliefs have become increasingly divergent from those of less affluent blacks. Most of the arguments advanced by scholars such as Boston and Wilson restate fairly directly the somewhat simplistic phrase "being determines consciousness." In other words, as *objective status* improves, African Americans become more conservative.

Jackman and Jackman (1983), however, argue that while individuals' perceptions of social class are highly correlated with income, education, and occupation, cultural beliefs are also important in all Americans' perceptions of class; for African Americans, they further contend that cultural beliefs are more important than objective criteria. They do argue that simple white collar-blue collar schemes of class, which ignore, for example, the routinized work of those such as secretaries, are inadequate for understanding even objective perceptions of class.[4] When exploring the "class consciousness" of African Americans, Jackman and Jackman found that working-class and middle-class blacks, unlike whites, exhibit higher degrees of racial identity than class identity. Those who are in a subordinate position seem to feel that they share a common fate, according to the Jackmans. Thus, racial identity cuts across class lines. However, because I am concerned in this reading to test Wilson's and others' thesis that *objective changes in the African-American class structure should lead to political divergence,* the objective measures of economic status are the ones that will be utilized here.

I also considered measures of occupation, income, and education. As previously mentioned, the new black middle class possess unprecedented educational opportunities and subsequent remuneration that allegedly follows their investment in "human capital." I also considered occupation, but the lack of variation among African Americans in their occupational attainment captured in social surveys limits the utility of occupation as a measure of class in this analysis. On the other hand, even those such as Landry who strongly prefer occupational measures state that one's education and income are closely related to one's class position. Further, the type of complex analysis of occupation and job content preferred by those influenced by the Marxist tradition such as Wright and colleagues (1982) is unsuitable for this analysis for two reasons. First, as Wright himself reports, the small number of African Americans falling into the petty bourgeois and employer categories makes any systematic analysis of how African-American political behavior and public opinion vary with class extremely difficult. Second, political surveys of African Americans do not contain the instrumentation necessary to probe the complex class positions suggested by Wright. Third, the concept of occupation itself becomes fuzzy when one examines a population such as African Americans in which a significant portion is either temporarily out of the labor force or has never been in the labor force.

More fundamentally, the concept of occupation imperfectly captures the shifts in the African-American class structure. Consider two black lawyers. One is a recent graduate from an elite law school who is working at a major corporation or law firm. She is earning an excellent salary that is at least somewhat on par with those of her white classmates. The other is an older lawyer who was not allowed to go to an elite law school and has a practice based in the black community. This lawyer's income hardly matches the salary of the other lawyer, but both share the same occupation. In this case, income better captures the disparities between class segments than does occupation. Income and education are the primary class measures used in this study.

COMPONENTS OF GROUP INTERESTS: MEASURES AND DATA

The central assumption of the black utility heuristic is that the more one believes one's own life chances are linked to those of blacks as a group, the more one will consider racial group interests in evaluating alternative political choices. This evaluation includes choosing between different public policies and evaluating candidates and parties, as well as engaging in other forms of political action. Such consideration of racial group interests contrasts with the use of other criteria for evaluating self-interest, particularly individual economic status. It has been argued that economic domination has been (and, many would argue, continues to be) an important aspect of African-American *political* reality over the past three centuries. Hence, a belief about the economic subordination of blacks is a component of racial group interests.

This theory is based to a significant degree on the self-categorization and social identity theories of Turner (1987). Individuals form their concepts of self at least in part by judging their similarities with and differences from others. This social identity theory allows for multiple self-concepts, prompted by different contexts, but the key to understanding the self-categorization process for African Americans is the fact that *the social category "black" in American society cuts across multiple boundaries.* African Americans and whites pray, play, and get paid differently.

Crucial to the formation of social identity is the active process of comparing in-group and out-group members. The more differences that are perceived between the in-group and the out-group on the salient social dimensions, the stronger the group identity of in-group members. A salient contrast between blacks and whites is the difference between black and white economic status. As a consequence of the process of comparison, black economic status shapes evaluations of the national economy. In the political domain, black evaluation of the political parties is based on African Americans' perceptions of how well the political parties serve black interests.

This approach is different from that of scholars who analyze social identity from the standpoint of group consciousness. While the concept of linked fate is similar to Conover's concept of interdependence and very close to Gurin's and colleagues' concept of common fate, it differs in that it explicitly links perceptions of self-interest to perceptions of racial group interests. Gurin's concept of group consciousness incorporates discontent with illegitimate social inequities, social comparisons, social identity, and collective action (Gurin, Hatchett, and Jackson 1989). Conover's definition also incorporates social identification, causal attributions concerning in-groups' and out-groups' status, and cognitive structures that incorporate affect as well as the other psychological attributes. While these definitions of group consciousness provide a useful measure of available psychological resources, the heuristic introduced here is intended to suggest a simpler mechanism by which the proposition that African-American political solidarity breaks down as economic polarization increases can be directly tested. Conover (1984) suggests that one's perceptions of group interests can become "personally relevant," but not "synonymous" with self-interest. My claim is somewhat different: the historical experiences of African Americans have resulted in a situation in which group interests have served as a useful proxy for self-interest.

MEASURES OF AFRICAN-AMERICAN RACIAL INTERESTS

Two components of group interests are critical to the political process for African Americans. For group interests to affect the political process, a significant number of African Americans must believe that what happens to the group as a whole affects their own lives. A construct of *linked fate* is needed to measure the degree to which African Americans believe that their own self-interests are linked to the interests of the race. Second, evaluations of relative group status, particularly economic status, are essential for understanding African-American perceptions of racial group interests.

The National Black Election Panel Study (NBES) of 1984–1988 demonstrates both the basic underpinnings of black group interests and the role they played in shaping African-American political behavior and political beliefs in 1984 and 1988. The study consisted of a national telephone survey in which 1,150 interviews were conducted with members of the adult African-American population. The NBES is one of the most extensive political surveys of the African-American population that has been conducted. . . .

The 1988 NBES survey provides both economic and general measures of absolute and relative group status. These measures allow us to compare the different hypotheses according to which the most important determinants of political choice are based on class, individual utility, evaluations of what is good for society, or racial group utility, respectively. Further, measures are provided that allow us to test the relative salience of both current and retrospective evaluations.

The concept of linked fate was measured in both 1984 and 1988. Survey participants were asked, "Do you think that what happens generally to the black people in this country will have something to do with what happens in your life?" Figure 1 shows the distribution of responses to this question. In 1984, 63 percent of the NBES sample responded affirmatively, and in 1988, the figure was 64 percent. Perceptions of economic subordination of blacks were also measured. The question was asked, "On the whole, would you say that the economic position of blacks is better, about the same, or worse than

FIGURE 1 Perceptions of linked fate, 1984 and 1988: "Do you think that what happens generally to the black people in this country will have something to do with what happens in your life?" Category values represent percentage of respondents responding in that category.

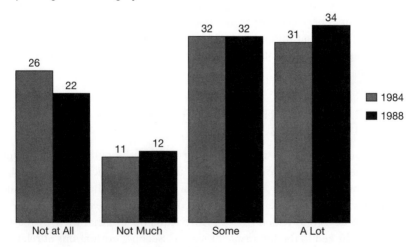

SOURCE: 1984–1988 National Black Election Panel Study.

FIGURE 2   Perceptions of economic subordination, 1984 and 1988: "On the whole, would you say that the economic position of blacks is better, about the same, or worse than that of whites?" Category values represent percentage of respondents responding in that category.

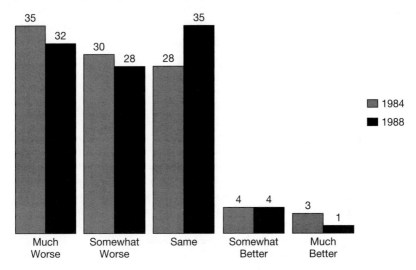

SOURCE: 1984–1988 National Black Election Panel Study.

that of whites?" As shown in Figure 2, 65 percent of African Americans in both years of the sampling responded that blacks are in a worse economic position than whites.

Do perceptions of either linked fate or economic subordination vary with one's class position? To answer this question I look first at the ... relationships between perceptions of linked fate and education. ... Linked fate varies very slightly with socioeconomic variables. Variables associated with linked fate in 1984 were not associated with linked fate in 1988. ...

A parallel analysis was conducted for perceptions of economic subordination. ... There appears to be very little covariation between the socioeconomic measures and the measure of perceptions of economic subordination. Furthermore, occupation seems to add little information to that provided by education and income. Clearly, there is a relationship between socioeconomic status and perceptions of economic subordination. ... This preliminary analysis suggests that those with more education and status are more likely than their less affluent cousins to believe that blacks as a group are in a poor economic state absolutely and relatively.

■   ■   ■

CONCLUSION

. . . Socioeconomic status only weakly influences perceptions of linked fate. The economic and political components of group interest have a major role in shaping perceptions of both economic well-being and relative group influence. . . . Throughout the 1980s, individual beliefs and perceptions constituted a firm basis for relatively unified group political behavior.

NOTES

1. By extension, the degree to which the politics of Latinos and Asian-Americans deviates from standard American politics also warrants an investigation.

2. This heuristic should in principle be applicable to other groups; the particular way it is manifest would depend on the historical context. For example, in many periods and places, a Jewish person's religious identity might well have dominated all other social identities; in the France of the 1980s, North Africans' identity and political struggles with other French were tied to the North Africans' belief in Islam. For African Americans, I shall argue, identity has been tied to subordinate economic status.

3. Marable's political economy approach to black politics is based partly on the political economy approach of Poulantzas (see Poulantzas 1974).

4. Thus, they argue, secretarial work is misclassified as white collar both because of the way the work has changed with the coming of large office pools, and because of the relatively low prestige ranking of secretarial, clerical, and related occupations that employ a significant percentage of women.

REFERENCES

Baker, Houston A., Jr. 1984. *Blues, ideology, and Afro-American literature: A vernacular theory.* Chicago: University of Chicago Press.

Barker, Lucius J. 1988. *Our time has come: A delegate's diary of Jesse Jackson's 1984 presidential campaign.* Urbana: University of Illinois Press.

Boston, Thomas D. 1988. *Race, class, and conservatism.* London: Unwin Hyman.

Carmines, Edward G., and James A. Stimson. 1989. *Issue evolution: Race and the transformation of American Politics.* Princeton: Princeton University Press.

Conover, Pamela Johnston. 1984. The influence of group identification on political perception and evaluation. *Journal of Politics* 46: 760–85.

Dahl, Robert A. 1961. *Who governs?* New Haven: Yale University Press.

Dawson, Michael C., and Ernest J. Wilson III. 1991. Paradigms and paradoxes: Political science and African American politics. In *Political science: Looking to the future,* ed. William Crotty, 1: 189–234.

Gurin, Patricia, Shirley Hatchett, and James S. Jackson. 1989. *Hope and independence: Blacks' response to electoral and party politics.* New York: Russell Sage Foundation.

Henry, Charles P. 1990. *Culture and African American politics.* Bloomington: Indiana University Press.

Huckfeldt, Robert R., and Carol Weitzel Kohfeld. 1989. *Race and the decline of class in American politics.* Urbana: University of Illinois Press.

Jackman, Mary R., and Robert W. Jackman. 1983. *Class awareness in the United States.* Berkeley: University of California Press.

Landry, Bart. 1987. *The new black middle class.* Berkeley: University of California Press.

Marable, Manning. 1983. *How capitalism underdeveloped black America: Problems in race, political economy, and society.* Boston: South End Press.

Pinderhughes, Dianne. 1987. *Race and ethnicity in Chicago politics.* Urbana: University of Illinois Press.

Poulantzas, Nicos. 1974. *Political power and social classes.* London: New Left Books.

Turner, John C. 1987. *Rediscovering the social group: A self-categorization theory.* Oxford: Basil Blackwell.

Walters, Ronald W. 1988. *Black presidential politics in America: A strategic approach.* Albany: State University of New York Press.

Wilson, William J. 1980. *The declining significance of race.* 2d ed. Chicago: University of Chicago Press.

———. 1987. *The truly disadvantaged: The inner city, the underclass, and public policy.* Chicago: University of Chicago Press.

Wright, Erik Olin, David Hachen, Cynthia Costello, and Joey Sprague. 1982. The American class structure. *American Sociological Review* 47: 709–26.

4.2

Brown v. Board of Education (1954)

In one of the most important Supreme Court cases in American history, the justices unanimously and emphatically overturned the precedent from Plessy v. Ferguson (1896), *which had upheld the right of local communities and states to maintain separate public facilities for the races. "[I]n the field of public education," the Court declared, "the doctrine of 'separate but equal' has no place." This 1954 decision started the American legal system down a new path of active intervention in the racial policies of government at all levels.*

Mr. Chief Justice Warren delivered the opinion of the Court.

These cases come to us from the States of Kansas, South Carolina, Virginia, and Delaware. They are premised on different facts and different local conditions, but a common legal question justifies their consideration together in this consolidated opinion.

In each of the cases, minors of the Negro race, through their legal representatives, seek the aid of the courts in obtaining admission to the public schools of their community on a nonsegregated basis. In each instance, they had been denied admission to schools attended by white children under laws requiring or permitting segregation according to race. This segregation was alleged to deprive the plaintiffs of the equal protection of the laws under the Fourteenth Amendment. In each of the cases other than the Delaware case, a three-judge federal district court denied relief to the plaintiffs on the so-called "separate but equal" doctrine announced by this Court in *Plessy v. Ferguson*. Under that doctrine, equality of treatment is accorded when the races are provided substantially equal facilities, even though these facilities be separate. In the Delaware case, the Supreme Court of Delaware adhered to that doctrine, but ordered that the plaintiffs be admitted to the white schools because of their superiority to the Negro schools.

The plaintiffs contend that segregated public schools are not "equal" and cannot be made "equal," and that hence they are deprived of the equal protection of the laws. Because of the obvious importance of the question presented, the Court took jurisdiction. Argument was heard in the 1952 Term, and reargument was heard this Term on certain questions propounded by the Court.

Reargument was largely devoted to the circumstances surrounding the adoption of the Fourteenth Amendment in 1868. It covered exhaustively consideration of the Amendment in Congress, ratification by the states, then-existing practices in racial segregation, and the views of proponents and opponents of the Amendment. This discussion and our own investigation convince us that, although these sources cast some light, it is not enough to resolve the problem with which we are faced. At best, they are inconclusive. The most avid proponents of the post-War Amendments undoubtedly intended them to remove all legal distinctions among "all persons born or naturalized in the United States." Their opponents, just as certainly, were antagonistic to both the letter and the spirit of the Amendments and wished them to have the most limited effect. What others in Congress and the state legislatures had in mind cannot be determined with any degree of certainty.

An additional reason for the inconclusive nature of the Amendment's history with respect to segregated schools is the status of public education at that time. In the South, the movement toward free common schools, supported by general taxation, had not yet taken hold. Education of white children was largely in the hands of private groups. Education of Negroes was almost nonexistent, and practically all of the race were illiterate. In fact, any education of Negroes was forbidden by law in some states. Today, in contrast, many Negroes have achieved outstanding success in the arts and sciences, as well as in the business and professional world. It is true that public school education at the time of the Amendment had advanced further in the North, but the effect of the Amendment on Northern States was generally ignored in the congressional debates. Even in the North, the conditions of public education did not approximate those existing today. The curriculum was usually rudimentary; ungraded schools were common in rural areas; the school term was but three months a year in many states, and compulsory school attendance was virtually unknown. As a consequence, it is not surprising that there should be so little in the history of the Fourteenth Amendment relating to its intended effect on public education.

In the first cases in this Court construing the Fourteenth Amendment, decided shortly after its adoption, the Court interpreted it as proscribing all state-imposed discriminations against the Negro race.[1] The doctrine of "separate but equal" did not make its appearance in this Court until 1896 in the case of *Plessy v. Ferguson*, involving not education but transportation.[2] American courts have since labored with the doctrine for over half a century. In this Court, there have been six cases involving the "separate but equal" doctrine in the field of public education. In *Cumming v. County Board of Education*, and *Gong Lum v. Rice*, the validity of the doctrine itself was not challenged. In more recent cases, all on the graduate school level, inequality was found in that specific benefits enjoyed by white students were denied to Negro students of the same educational qualifications. *Missouri ex rel. Gaines v. Canada, Sipuel v. Oklahoma, Sweatt v. Painter, McLaurin v. Oklahoma State Regents*. In none of these cases was it necessary to reexamine the doctrine to grant relief to the

Negro plaintiff. And in *Sweatt v. Painter, supra,* the Court expressly reserved decision on the question whether *Plessy v. Ferguson* should be held inapplicable to public education.

In the instant cases, that question is directly presented. Here, unlike *Sweatt v. Painter,* there are findings below that the Negro and white schools involved have been equalized, or are being equalized, with respect to buildings, curricula, qualifications and salaries of teachers, and other "tangible" factors. Our decision, therefore, cannot turn on merely a comparison of these tangible factors in the Negro and white schools involved in each of the cases. We must look instead to the effect of segregation itself on public education.

In approaching this problem, we cannot turn the clock back to 1868, when the Amendment was adopted, or even to 1896, when *Plessy v. Ferguson* was written. We must consider public education in the light of its full development and its present place in American life throughout the Nation. Only in this way can it be determined if segregation in public schools deprives these plaintiffs of the equal protection of the laws.

Today, education is perhaps the most important function of state and local governments. Compulsory school attendance laws and the great expenditures for education both demonstrate our recognition of the importance of education to our democratic society. It is required in the performance of our most basic public responsibilities, even service in the armed forces. It is the very foundation of good citizenship. Today it is a principal instrument in awakening the child to cultural values, in preparing him for later professional training, and in helping him to adjust normally to his environment. In these days, it is doubtful that any child may reasonably be expected to succeed in life if he is denied the opportunity of an education. Such an opportunity, where the state has undertaken to provide it, is a right which must be made available to all on equal terms.

We come then to the question presented: Does segregation of children in public schools solely on the basis of race, even though the physical facilities and other "tangible" factors may be equal, deprive the children of the minority group of equal educational opportunities? We believe that it does.

In *Sweatt v. Painter,* in finding that a segregated law school for Negroes could not provide them equal educational opportunities, this Court relied in large part on "those qualities which are incapable of objective measurement but which make for greatness in a law school." In *McLaurin v. Oklahoma State Regents,* the Court, in requiring that a Negro admitted to a white graduate school be treated like all other students, again resorted to intangible considerations: ". . . his ability to study, to engage in discussions and exchange views with other students, and, in general, to learn his profession." Such considerations apply with added force to children in grade and high schools. To separate them from others of similar age and qualifications solely because of their race generates a feeling of inferiority as to their status in the community that may affect their hearts and minds in a way unlikely ever to be undone. The effect of this separation on their educational opportunities was well stated by a finding in the Kansas case by a court which nevertheless felt compelled to rule against the Negro plaintiffs: Segregation of white and colored children in public schools has a detrimental effect upon the colored children. The impact is greater when it has the sanction of the law, for the policy of separating the races is usually interpreted as denoting the inferiority of the negro group. A sense of inferiority affects the motivation of a child to learn. Segregation with the sanction of law, therefore, has a tendency to [retard] the educational and mental development of negro children and to deprive them of some of the benefits they would receive in a racial[ly] integrated school system.[3] Whatever may have been the extent of psychological knowledge at the time of *Plessy v. Ferguson*, this finding is amply supported by modern authority. Any language in *Plessy v. Ferguson* contrary to this finding is rejected.

We conclude that, in the field of public education, the doctrine of "separate but equal" has no place. Separate educational facilities are inherently unequal. Therefore, we hold that the plaintiffs and others similarly situated for whom the actions have been brought are, by reason of the segregation complained of, deprived of the equal protection of the laws guaranteed by the Fourteenth Amendment. This disposition makes unnecessary any discussion whether such segregation also violates the Due Process Clause of the Fourteenth Amendment.[4]

Because these are class actions, because of the wide applicability of this decision, and because of the great variety of local conditions, the formulation of decrees in these cases presents problems of considerable complexity. On reargument, the consideration of appropriate relief was necessarily subordinated to the primary question—the constitutionality of segregation in public education. We have now announced that such segregation is a denial of the equal protection of the laws. In order that we may have the full assistance of the parties in formulating decrees, the cases will be restored to the docket, and the parties are requested to present further argument on Questions 4 and 5 previously propounded by the Court for the reargument this Term.[5] The Attorney General of the United States is again invited to participate. The Attorneys General of the states requiring or permitting segregation in public education will also be permitted to appear as *amici curiae* upon request to do so by September 15, 1954, and submission of briefs by October 1, 1954.

It is so ordered.

NOTES

1. *Slaughter-House Cases*, 16 Wall. 36, 67–72 (1873); *Strauder v. West Virginia*, 100 U.S. 303, 307–308 (1880): It ordains that no State shall deprive any person of life, liberty, or property, without due process of law, or deny to any person within its jurisdiction the equal protection of the laws. What is this but declaring that the law in the States shall be the same for the black as for the white; that all persons, whether colored or white,

shall stand equal before the laws of the States, and, in regard to the colored race, for whose protection the amendment was primarily designed, that no discrimination shall be made against them by law because of their color? The words of the amendment, it is true, are prohibitory, but they contain a necessary implication of a positive immunity, or right, most valuable to the colored race—the right to exemption from unfriendly legislation against them distinctively as colored—exemption from legal discriminations, implying inferiority in civil society, lessening the security of their enjoyment of the rights which others enjoy, and discriminations which are steps towards reducing them to the condition of a subject race.

2. The doctrine apparently originated in *Roberts v. City of Boston*, 59 Mass.198, 206 (1850), upholding school segregation against attack as being violative of a state constitutional guarantee of equality. Segregation in Boston public schools was eliminated in 1855. Mass.Acts 1855, c. 256. But elsewhere in the North, segregation in public education has persisted in some communities until recent years. It is apparent that such segregation has long been a nationwide problem, not merely one of sectional concern.

3. A similar finding was made in the Delaware case: I conclude from the testimony that, in our Delaware society, State-imposed segregation in education itself results in the Negro children, as a class, receiving educational opportunities which are substantially inferior to those available to white children otherwise similarly situated.87 A.2d 862, 865.

4. See *Bolling v. Sharpe*, post, p. 497, concerning the Due Process Clause of the Fifth Amendment.

5. Assuming it is decided that segregation in public schools violates the Fourteenth Amendment(a) would a decree necessarily follow providing that, within the limits set by normal geographic school districting, Negro children should forthwith be admitted to schools of their choice, or(b) may this Court, in the exercise of its equity powers, permit an effective gradual adjustment to be brought about from existing segregated systems to a system not based on color distinctions?

4.3

Roe v. Wade (1973)

Still a controversial decision, this 1973 Supreme Court ruling established that the constitutional right to privacy implied that a woman has the right to have an abortion in the first trimester of her pregnancy. In a set of previous rulings, the Court had defined a right to privacy as emanating from several of the rights granted in the Bill of Rights.

Justice Blackmun delivered the opinion of the Court.

This Texas federal appeal and its Georgia companion, *Doe v. Bolton, post*, p. 179, present constitutional challenges to state criminal abortion legislation. The Texas statutes under attack here are typical of those that have been in effect in many States for approximately a century. The Georgia statutes, in contrast, have a modern cast, and are a legislative product that, to an extent at least, obviously reflects the influences of recent attitudinal change, of advancing medical knowledge and techniques, and of new thinking about an old issue.

We forthwith acknowledge our awareness of the sensitive and emotional nature of the abortion controversy, of the vigorous opposing views, even among physicians, and of the deep and seemingly absolute convictions that the subject inspires. One's philosophy, one's experiences, one's exposure to the raw edges of human existence, one's religious training, one's attitudes toward life and family and their values, and the moral standards one establishes and seeks to observe, are all likely to influence and to color one's thinking and conclusions about abortion.

In addition, population growth, pollution, poverty, and racial overtones tend to complicate and not to simplify the problem.

Our task, of course, is to resolve the issue by constitutional measurement, free of emotion and of predilection. We seek earnestly to do this, and, because we do, we have inquired into, and in this opinion place some emphasis upon, medical and medical-legal history and what that history reveals about man's attitudes toward the abortion procedure over the centuries. We bear in mind, too, Mr. Justice Holmes' admonition in his now-vindicated dissent in *Lochner v. New York*, (1905):

[The Constitution] is made for people of fundamentally differing views, and the accident of our finding certain opinions natural and familiar or novel and even shocking ought not to conclude our judgment upon the question whether statutes embodying them conflict with the Constitution of the United States.

I

The Texas statutes that concern us here are Arts. 1191–1194 and 1196 of the State's Penal Code.[1] These make it a crime to "procure an abortion," as therein defined, or to attempt one, except with respect to "an abortion procured or attempted by medical advice for the purpose of saving the life of the mother." Similar statutes are in existence in a majority of the States.

Texas first enacted a criminal abortion statute in 1854. . . . This was soon modified into language that has remained substantially unchanged to the present time. . . .

II

Jane Roe, a single woman who was residing in Dallas County, Texas, instituted this federal action in March 1970 against the District Attorney of the county. She sought a declaratory judgment that the Texas criminal abortion statutes were unconstitutional on their face, and an injunction restraining the defendant from enforcing the statutes.

Roe alleged that she was unmarried and pregnant; that she wished to terminate her pregnancy by an abortion "performed by a competent, licensed physician, under safe, clinical conditions"; that she was unable to get a "legal" abortion in Texas because her life did not appear to be threatened by the continuation of her pregnancy; and that she could not afford to travel to another jurisdiction in order to secure a legal abortion under safe conditions. She claimed that the Texas statutes were unconstitutionally vague and that they abridged her right of personal privacy, protected by the First, Fourth, Fifth, Ninth, and Fourteenth Amendments. By an amendment to her complaint, Roe purported to sue "on behalf of herself and all other women" similarly situated.

James Hubert Hallford, a licensed physician, sought and was granted leave to intervene in Roe's action. In his complaint, he alleged that he had been arrested previously for violations of the Texas abortion statutes, and that two such prosecutions were pending against him. He described conditions of patients who came to him seeking abortions, and he claimed that for many cases he, as a physician, was unable to determine whether they fell within or outside the exception recognized by Article 1196. He alleged that, as a consequence, the statutes were vague and uncertain, in violation of the Fourteenth Amendment, and that they violated his own and his patients' rights to privacy in the doctor-patient relationship and his own right to practice medicine, rights he claimed were guaranteed by the First, Fourth, Fifth, Ninth, and Fourteenth Amendments.

John and Mary Doe, a married couple, filed a companion complaint to that of Roe. They also named the District Attorney as defendant, claimed like constitutional deprivations, and sought declaratory and injunctive relief. The Does alleged that they were a childless couple; that Mrs. Doe was suffering from a "neural-chemical" disorder; that her physician had "advised her to avoid pregnancy until such time as her condition has materially improved" (although a pregnancy at the present time would not present "a serious risk" to her life); that, pursuant to medical advice, she had discontinued use of birth control pills; and that, if she should become pregnant, she would want to terminate the pregnancy by an abortion performed by a competent, licensed physician under safe, clinical conditions. By an amendment to their complaint, the Does purported to sue "on behalf of themselves and all couples similarly situated."

The two actions were consolidated and heard together by a duly convened three-judge district court. The suits thus presented the situations of the pregnant single woman, the childless couple, with the wife not pregnant, and the licensed practicing physician, all joining in the attack on the Texas criminal abortion statutes. Upon the filing of affidavits, motions were made for dismissal and for summary judgment. The court held that Roe and members of her class, and Dr. Hallford, had standing to sue and presented justiciable controversies, but that the Does had failed to allege facts sufficient to state a present controversy, and did not have standing. It concluded that, with respect to the requests for a declaratory judgment, abstention was not warranted. On the merits, the District Court held that the "fundamental right of single women and married persons to choose whether to have children is protected by the Ninth Amendment, through the Fourteenth Amendment," and that the Texas criminal abortion statutes were void on their face because they were both unconstitutionally vague and constituted an overbroad infringement of the plaintiffs' Ninth Amendment rights. The court then held that abstention was warranted with respect to the requests for an injunction. It therefore dismissed the Does' complaint, declared the abortion statutes void, and dismissed the application for injunctive relief. . . .

The plaintiffs Roe and Doe and the intervenor Hallford, pursuant to 28 U.S.C. § 1253 have appealed to this Court from that part of the District Court's judgment denying the injunction. The defendant District Attorney has purported to cross-appeal, pursuant to the same statute, from the court's grant of declaratory relief to Roe and Hallford. Both sides also have taken protective appeals to the United States Court of Appeals for the Fifth Circuit. That court ordered the appeals held in abeyance pending decision here. We postponed decision on jurisdiction to the hearing on the merits.

▪ ▪ ▪

VII

Three reasons have been advanced to explain historically the enactment of criminal abortion laws in the 19th century and to justify their continued existence.

It has been argued occasionally that these laws were the product of a Victorian social concern to discourage illicit sexual conduct. Texas, however, does not advance this justification in the present case, and it appears that no court or commentator has taken the argument seriously. The appellants and *amici* contend, moreover, that this is not a proper state purpose, at all and suggest that, if it were, the Texas statutes are overbroad in protecting it, since the law fails to distinguish between married and unwed mothers.

A second reason is concerned with abortion as a medical procedure. When most criminal abortion laws were first enacted, the procedure was a hazardous one for the woman. This was particularly true prior to the development of antisepsis. Antiseptic techniques, of course, were based on discoveries by Lister, Pasteur, and others first announced in 1867, but were not generally accepted and employed until about the turn of the century. Abortion mortality was high. Even after 1900, and perhaps until as late as the development of antibiotics in the 1940's, standard modern techniques such as dilation and curettage were not nearly so safe as they are today. Thus, it has been argued that a State's real concern in enacting a criminal abortion law was to protect the pregnant woman, that is, to restrain her from submitting to a procedure that placed her life in serious jeopardy.

Modern medical techniques have altered this situation. Appellants and various *amici* refer to medical data indicating that abortion in early pregnancy, that is, prior to the end of the first trimester, although not without its risk, is now relatively safe. Mortality rates for women undergoing early abortions, where the procedure is legal, appear to be as low as or lower than the rates for normal childbirth. Consequently, any interest of the State in protecting the woman from an inherently hazardous procedure, except when it would be equally dangerous for her to forgo it, has largely disappeared. Of course, important state interests in the areas of health and medical standards do remain. The State has a legitimate interest in seeing to it that abortion, like any other medical procedure, is performed under circumstances that insure maximum safety for the patient. This interest obviously extends at least to the performing physician and his staff, to the facilities involved, to the availability of after-care, and to adequate provision for any complication or emergency that might arise. The prevalence of high mortality rates at illegal "abortion mills" strengthens, rather than weakens, the State's interest in regulating the conditions under which abortions are performed. Moreover, the risk to the woman increases as her pregnancy continues. Thus, the State retains a definite interest in protecting the woman's own health and safety when an abortion is proposed at a late stage of pregnancy.

The third reason is the State's interest—some phrase it in terms of duty—in protecting prenatal life. Some of the argument for this justification rests on the theory that a new human life is present from the moment of conception. The State's interest and general obligation to protect life then extends, it is argued, to prenatal life. Only when the life of the pregnant mother herself is at stake, balanced against the life she carries within her, should the interest of the embryo or fetus not prevail. Logically, of course, a legitimate state interest in this area need not stand or fall on acceptance of the belief that life begins at conception or at some other point prior to live birth. In assessing the State's interest, recognition may be given to the less rigid claim that as long as at least potential life is involved, the State may assert interests beyond the protection of the pregnant woman alone.

Parties challenging state abortion laws have sharply disputed in some courts the contention that a purpose of these laws, when enacted, was to protect prenatal life. Pointing to the absence of legislative history to support the contention, they claim that most state laws were designed solely to protect the woman. Because medical advances have lessened this concern, at least with respect to abortion in early pregnancy, they argue that with respect to such abortions the laws can no longer be justified by any state interest. There is some scholarly support for this view of original purpose. The few state courts called upon to interpret their laws in the late 19th and early 20th centuries did focus on the State's interest in protecting the woman's health, rather than in preserving the embryo and fetus. Proponents of this view point out that in many States, including Texas, by statute or judicial interpretation, the pregnant woman herself could not be prosecuted for self-abortion or for cooperating in an abortion performed upon her by another. They claim that adoption of the "quickening" distinction through received common law and state statutes tacitly recognizes the greater health hazards inherent in late abortion and impliedly repudiates the theory that life begins at conception.

It is with these interests, and the eight to be attached to them, that this case is concerned.

VIII

The Constitution does not explicitly mention any right of privacy. In a line of decisions, however, going back perhaps as far as *Union Pacific R. Co. v. Botsford,* (1891), the Court has recognized that a right of personal privacy, or a guarantee of certain areas or zones of privacy, does exist under the Constitution. In varying contexts, the Court or individual Justices have, indeed, found at least the roots of that right in the First Amendment, *Stanley v. Georgia,* (1969); in the Fourth and Fifth Amendments, *Terry v. Ohio,* (1968), *Katz v. United States,* (1967), *Boyd v. United States,* (1886), in the penumbras of the Bill of Rights, *Griswold v. Connecticut,* in the Ninth Amendment, (Goldberg, J., concurring); or in the concept of liberty guaranteed by the first section of the Fourteenth Amendment, (1923). These decisions make it clear that only personal rights that can be deemed "fundamental" or "implicit in the concept of ordered liberty," *Palko v. Connecticut*, (1937), are included in this guarantee of personal privacy. They also make it clear that the right has some extension to activities relating to marriage, *Loving v. Virginia*, (1967); procreation, *Skinner v. Oklahoma*, (1942); contraception, *Eisenstadt v. Baird*, (White, J., concurring in result); family relationships, *Prince v. Massachusetts*, (1944); and childrearing and education, *Pierce v. Society of Sisters*, (1925), *Meyer v. Nebraska*.

This right of privacy, whether it be founded in the Fourteenth Amendment's concept of personal liberty and restrictions upon state action, as we feel it is, or, as the District Court determined, in the Ninth Amendment's reservation of rights to the people, is broad enough to encompass a woman's decision whether or not to terminate her pregnancy. The detriment that the State would impose upon the pregnant woman by denying this choice altogether is apparent. Specific and direct harm medically diagnosable even in early pregnancy may be involved. Maternity, or additional offspring, may force upon the woman a distressful life and future. Psychological harm may be imminent. Mental and physical health may be taxed by child care. There is also the distress, for all concerned, associated with the unwanted child, and there is the problem of bringing a child into a family already unable, psychologically and otherwise, to care for it. In other cases, as in this one, the additional difficulties and continuing stigma of unwed motherhood may be involved. All these are factors the woman and her responsible physician necessarily will consider in consultation.

On the basis of elements such as these, appellant and some *amici* argue that the woman's right is absolute and that she is entitled to terminate her pregnancy at whatever time, in whatever way, and for whatever reason she alone chooses. With this we do not agree. Appellant's arguments that Texas either has no valid interest at all in regulating the abortion decision, or no interest strong enough to support any limitation upon the woman's sole determination, are unpersuasive. The Court's decisions recognizing a right of privacy also acknowledge that some state regulation in areas protected by that right is appropriate. As noted above, a State may properly assert important interests in safeguarding health, in maintaining medical standards, and in protecting potential life. At some point in pregnancy, these respective interests become sufficiently compelling to sustain regulation of the factors that govern the abortion decision. The privacy right involved, therefore, cannot be said to be absolute. In fact, it is not clear to us that the claim asserted by some *amici* that one has an unlimited right to do with one's body as one pleases bears a close relationship to the right of privacy previously articulated in the Court's decisions. The Court has refused to recognize an unlimited right of this kind in the past. *Jacobson v. Massachusetts*, (1905) (vaccination); *Buck v. Bell*, (1927) (sterilization).

We, therefore, conclude that the right of personal privacy includes the abortion decision, but that this right is not unqualified, and must be considered against important state interests in regulation.

We note that those federal and state courts that have recently considered abortion law challenges have reached the same conclusion. A majority, in addition to the District Court in the present case, have held state laws unconstitutional, at least in part, because of vagueness or because of overbreadth and abridgment of rights. . . .

Others have sustained state statutes. . . .

Although the results are divided, most of these courts have agreed that the right of privacy, however based, is broad enough to cover the abortion decision; that the right, nonetheless, is not absolute, and is subject to some limitations; and that, at some point, the state interests as to protection of health, medical standards, and prenatal life, become dominant. We agree with this approach.

Where certain "fundamental rights" are involved, the Court has held that regulation limiting these rights may be justified only by a "compelling state interest," . . . and that legislative enactments must be narrowly drawn to express only the legitimate state interests at stake. . . .

In the recent abortion cases . . . courts have recognized these principles. Those striking down state laws have generally scrutinized the State's interests in protecting health and potential life, and have concluded that neither interest justified broad limitations on the reasons for which a physician and his pregnant patient might decide that she should have an abortion in the early stages of pregnancy. Courts sustaining state laws have held that the State's determinations to protect health or prenatal life are dominant and constitutionally justifiable.

I X

The District Court held that the appellee failed to meet his burden of demonstrating that the Texas statute's infringement upon Roe's rights was necessary to support a compelling state interest, and that, although the appellee presented "several compelling justifications for state presence in the area of abortions," the statutes outstripped these justifications and swept "far beyond any areas of compelling state interest." Appellant and appellee both contest that holding. Appellant, as has been indicated, claims an absolute right that bars any state imposition of criminal penalties in the area. Appellee argues that the State's determination to recognize and protect prenatal life from and after conception constitutes a compelling state interest. As noted above, we do not agree fully with either formulation.

A. The appellee and certain *amici* argue that the fetus is a "person" within the language and meaning of the Fourteenth Amendment. In support of this, they outline at length and in detail the well known facts of fetal development.

If this suggestion of personhood is established, the appellant's case, of course, collapses, for the fetus' right to life would then be guaranteed specifically by the Amendment. The appellant conceded as much on reargument. On the other hand, the appellee conceded on reargument that no case could be cited that holds that a fetus is a person within the meaning of the Fourteenth Amendment.

The Constitution does not define "person" in so many words. Section 1 of the Fourteenth Amendment contains three references to "person." The first, in defining "citizens," speaks of "persons born or naturalized in the United States." The word also appears both in the Due Process Clause and in the Equal Protection Clause. "Person" is used in other places in the Constitution: in the listing of qualifications for Representatives and Senators, Art. I, § 2, cl. 2, and § 3, cl. 3; in the Apportionment Clause, Art. I, § 2, cl. 3; in the Migration and Importation provision, Art. I, § 9, cl. 1; in the Emolument Clause, Art. I, § 9, cl. 8; in the Electors provisions, Art. II, § 1, cl. 2, and the superseded cl. 3; in the provision outlining qualifications for the office of President, Art. II, § 1, cl. 5; in the Extradition provisions, Art. IV, § 2, cl. 2, and the superseded Fugitive Slave Clause 3; and in the Fifth, Twelfth, and Twenty-second Amendments, as well as in §§ 2 and 3 of the Fourteenth Amendment. But in nearly all these instances, the use of the word is such that it has application only post-natally. None indicates, with any assurance, that it has any possible pre-natal application.[2]

All this, together with our observation, that, throughout the major portion of the 19th century, prevailing legal abortion practices were far freer than they are today, persuades us that the word "person," as used in the Fourteenth Amendment, does not include the unborn. This is in accord with the results reached in those few cases where the issue has been squarely presented. . . . Indeed, our decision in *United States v. Vuitch* (1971), inferentially is to the same effect, for we there would not have indulged in statutory interpretation favorable to abortion in specified circumstances if the necessary consequence was the termination of life entitled to Fourteenth Amendment protection.

This conclusion, however, does not of itself fully answer the contentions raised by Texas, and we pass on to other considerations.

B. The pregnant woman cannot be isolated in her privacy. She carries an embryo and, later, a fetus, if one accepts the medical definitions of the developing young in the human uterus. The situation therefore is inherently different from marital intimacy, or bedroom possession of obscene material, or marriage, or procreation, or education, with which *Eisenstadt* and *Griswold*, *Stanley*, *Loving*, *Skinner*, and *Pierce* and *Meyer* were respectively concerned. As we have intimated above, it is reasonable and appropriate for a State to decide that, at some point in time another interest, that of health of the mother or that of potential human life, becomes significantly involved. The woman's privacy is no longer sole and any right of privacy she possesses must be measured accordingly.

Texas urges that, apart from the Fourteenth Amendment, life begins at conception and is present throughout pregnancy, and that, therefore, the State has a compelling interest in protecting that life from and after conception. We need not resolve the difficult question of when life begins. When those trained in the respective disciplines of medicine, philosophy, and theology are unable to arrive at any consensus, the judiciary, at this point in the development of man's knowledge, is not in a position to speculate as to the answer.

It should be sufficient to note briefly the wide divergence of thinking on this most sensitive and difficult question. There has always been strong support for the view that life does not begin until live birth. This was the belief of the Stoics. It appears to be the predominant, though not the unanimous, attitude of the Jewish faith. It may be taken to represent also the position of a large segment of the Protestant community, insofar as that can be ascertained; organized groups that have taken a formal position on the abortion issue have generally regarded abortion as a matter for the conscience of the individual and her family. As we have noted, the common law found greater significance in quickening. Physician and their scientific colleagues have regarded that event with less interest and have tended to focus either upon conception, upon live birth, or upon the interim point at which the fetus becomes "viable," that is, potentially able to live outside the mother's womb, albeit with artificial aid. Viability is usually placed at about seven months (28 weeks) but may occur earlier, even at 24 weeks. The Aristotelian theory of "mediate animation," that held sway throughout the Middle Ages and the Renaissance in Europe, continued to be official Roman Catholic dogma until the 19th century, despite opposition to this "ensoulment" theory from those in the Church who would recognize the existence of life from the moment of conception. The latter is now, of course, the official belief of the Catholic Church. As one brief *amicus* discloses, this is a view strongly held by many non-Catholics as well, and by many physicians. Substantial problems for precise definition of this view are posed, however, by new embryological data that purport to indicate that conception is a "process" over time, rather than an event, and by new medical techniques such as menstrual extraction, the "morning-after" pill, implantation of embryos, artificial insemination, and even artificial wombs.

In areas other than criminal abortion, the law has been reluctant to endorse any theory that life, as we recognize it, begins before live birth, or to accord legal rights to the unborn except in narrowly defined situations and except when the rights are contingent upon live birth. For example, the traditional rule of tort law denied recovery for prenatal injuries even though the child was born alive. That rule has been changed in almost every jurisdiction. In most States, recovery is said to be permitted only if the fetus was viable, or at least quick, when the injuries were sustained, though few courts have squarely so held. In a recent development, generally opposed by the commentators, some States permit the parents of a stillborn child to maintain an action for wrongful death because of prenatal injuries. Such an action, however, would appear to be one to vindicate the parents' interest and is thus consistent with the view that the fetus, at most, represents only the potentiality of life. Similarly, unborn children have been recognized as acquiring rights or interests by way of inheritance or other devolution of property, and have been represented by guardians *ad litem*. Perfection of the interests involved, again, has generally been contingent upon live birth. In short, the unborn have never been recognized in the law as persons in the whole sense.

X

In view of all this, we do not agree that, by adopting one theory of life, Texas may override the rights of the pregnant woman that are at stake. We repeat, however, that the State does have an important and legitimate interest in preserving and protecting the health of the pregnant woman, whether she be a resident of the State or a nonresident who seeks medical consultation and treatment there, and that it has still *another* important and legitimate interest in protecting the potentiality of human life. These interests are separate and distinct. Each grows in substantiality as the woman approaches term and, at a point during pregnancy, each becomes "compelling."

With respect to the State's important and legitimate interest in the health of the mother, the "compelling" point, in the light of present medical knowledge, is at approximately the end of the first trimester. This is so because of the now-established medical fact that, until the end of the first trimester mortality in abortion may be less than mortality in normal childbirth. It follows that, from and after this point, a State may regulate the abortion procedure to the extent that the regulation reasonably relates to the preservation and protection of maternal health. Examples of permissible state regulation in this area are requirements as to the qualifications of the person who is to perform the abortion; as to the licensure of that person; as to the facility in which the procedure is to be performed, that is, whether it must be a hospital or may be a clinic or some other place of less-than-hospital status; as to the licensing of the facility; and the like.

This means, on the other hand, that, for the period of pregnancy prior to this "compelling" point, the attending physician, in consultation with his patient, is free to determine, without regulation by the State, that, in his medical judgment, the patient's pregnancy should be terminated. If that decision is reached, the judgment may be effectuated by an abortion free of interference by the State.

With respect to the State's important and legitimate interest in potential life, the "compelling" point is at viability. This is so because the fetus then presumably has the capability of meaningful life outside the mother's womb. State regulation protective of fetal life after viability thus has both logical and biological justifications. If the State is interested in protecting fetal life after viability, it may go so far as to proscribe abortion during that period, except when it is necessary to preserve the life or health of the mother.

Measured against these standards, Art. 1196 of the Texas Penal Code, in restricting legal abortions to those "procured or attempted by medical advice for the purpose of saving the life of the mother," sweeps too broadly. The statute makes no distinction between abortions performed early in pregnancy and those performed later, and it limits to a single reason, "saving" the mother's life, the legal justification for the procedure. The statute, therefore, cannot survive the constitutional attack made upon it here.

This conclusion makes it unnecessary for us to consider the additional challenge to the Texas statute asserted on grounds of vagueness.

XI

To summarize and to repeat:

1. A state criminal abortion statute of the current Texas type, that excepts from criminality only a lifesaving procedure on behalf of the mother, without regard to pregnancy stage and without recognition of the other interests involved, is violative of the Due Process Clause of the Fourteenth Amendment.

    (a) For the stage prior to approximately the end of the first trimester, the abortion decision and its effectuation must be left to the medical judgment of the pregnant woman's attending physician.

    (b) For the stage subsequent to approximately the end of the first trimester, the State, in promoting its interest in the health of the mother, may, if it chooses, regulate the abortion procedure in ways that are reasonably related to maternal health.

    (c) For the stage subsequent to viability, the State in promoting its interest in the potentiality of human life may, if it chooses, regulate, and even proscribe, abortion except where it is necessary, in appropriate medical judgment, for the preservation of the life or health of the mother.

2. The State may define the term "physician," as it has been employed in the preceding paragraphs of this Part XI of this opinion, to mean only a physician currently licensed by the State, and may proscribe any abortion by a person who is not a physician as so defined.

In *Doe v. Bolton*, procedural requirements contained in one of the modern abortion statutes are considered. That opinion and this one, of course, are to be read together.[3]

This holding, we feel, is consistent with the relative weights of the respective interests involved, with the lessons and examples of medical and legal history, with the lenity of the common law, and with the demands of the profound problems of the present day. The decision leaves the State free to place increasing restrictions on abortion as the period of pregnancy lengthens, so long as those restrictions are tailored to the recognized state interests. The decision vindicates the right of the physician to administer medical treatment according to his professional judgment up to the points where important state interests provide compelling justifications for intervention. Up to those points, the abortion decision in all its aspects is inherently, and primarily, a medical decision, and basic responsibility for it must rest with the physician. If an individual practitioner abuses the privilege of exercising proper medical judgment, the usual remedies, judicial and intra-professional, are available.

XII

Our conclusion that Art. 1196 is unconstitutional means, of course, that the Texas abortion statutes, as a unit, must fall. The exception of Art. 1196 cannot be struck down separately, for then the State would be left with a statute proscribing all abortion procedures no matter how medically urgent the case.

Although the District Court granted appellant Roe declaratory relief, it stopped short of issuing an injunction against enforcement of the Texas statutes. . . .

We find it unnecessary to decide whether the District Court erred in withholding injunctive relief, for we assume the Texas prosecutorial authorities will give full credence to this decision that the present criminal abortion statutes of that State are unconstitutional.

The judgment of the District Court as to intervenor Hallford is reversed, and Dr. Hallford's complaint in intervention is dismissed. In all other respects, the judgment of the District Court is affirmed. . . .

It is so ordered.

NOTES

1. Article 1191. Abortion

If any person shall designedly administer to a pregnant woman or knowingly procure to be administered with her consent any drug or medicine, or shall use towards her any violence or means whatever externally or internally applied, and thereby procure an abortion, he shall be confined in the penitentiary not less than two nor more than five years; if it be done without her consent, the punishment shall be doubled. By "abortion" is meant that the life of the fetus or embryo shall be destroyed in the woman's womb or that a premature birth thereof be caused.

Art. 1192. Furnishing the means

Whoever furnishes the means for procuring an abortion knowing the purpose intended is guilty as an accomplice.

Art. 1193. Attempt at abortion

If the means used shall fail to produce an abortion, the offender is nevertheless guilty of an attempt to produce abortion, provided it be shown that such means were calculated to produce that result, and shall be fined not less than one hundred nor more than one thousand dollars.

Art. 1194. Murder in producing abortion

If the death of the mother is occasioned by an abortion so produced or by an attempt to effect the same it is murder.

Art. 1196. By medical advice

Nothing in this chapter applies to an abortion procured or attempted by medical advice for the purpose of saving the life of the mother.

The foregoing Articles, together with Art. 1195, compose Chapter 9 of Title 15 of the Penal Code. Article 1195, not attacked here, reads:

Art. 1195. Destroying unborn child

Whoever shall during parturition of the mother destroy the vitality or life in a child in a state of being born and before actual birth, which child would otherwise have been born alive, shall be confined in the penitentiary for life or for not less than five years.

2. When Texas urges that a fetus is entitled to Fourteenth Amendment protection as a person, it faces a dilemma. Neither in Texas nor in any other State are all abortions prohibited. Despite broad proscription, an exception always exists. The exception contained in Art. 1196, for an abortion procured or attempted by medical advice for the purpose of saving the life of the mother, is typical. But if the fetus is a person who is not to be deprived of life without due process of law, and if the mother's condition is the sole determinant, does not the Texas exception appear to be out of line with the Amendment's command?

There are other inconsistencies between Fourteenth Amendment status and the typical abortion statute. It has already been pointed out, that, in Texas, the woman is not a principal or an accomplice with respect to an abortion upon her. If the fetus is a person, why is the woman not a principal or an accomplice? Further, the penalty for criminal abortion specified by Art. 1195 is significantly less than the maximum penalty for murder prescribed by Art. 1257 of the Texas Penal Code. If the fetus is a person, may the penalties be different?

3. Neither in this opinion nor in *Doe v. Bolton*, post, p. 179, do we discuss the father's rights, if any exist in the constitutional context, in the abortion decision. No paternal right has been asserted in either of the cases, and the Texas and the Georgia statutes on their face take no cognizance of the father. We are aware that some statutes recognize the father under certain circumstances. North Carolina, for example, N.C.Gen. Stat. § 14–45.1 (Supp. 1971), requires written permission for the abortion from the husband when the woman is a married minor, that is, when she is less than 18 years of age, 41 N.C.A.G. 489 (1971); if the woman is an unmarried minor, written permission from the parents is required. We need not now decide whether provisions of this kind are constitutional.

4.4

Grutter v. Bollinger (2003)

The Supreme Court in this case let stand a University of Michigan Law School practice of using race as one factor to consider in admitting students. In a 5–4 ruling in 2003, the majority decided that a narrowly tailored affirmative action program like the one at the law school was permissible under constitutional law.

Justice O'Connor delivered the opinion of the Court.

This case requires us to decide whether the use of race as a factor in student admissions by the University of Michigan Law School (Law School) is unlawful.

I

A

The Law School ranks among the Nation's top law schools. It receives more than 3,500 applications each year for a class of around 350 students. Seeking to "admit a group of students who individually and collectively are among the most capable," the Law School looks for individuals with "substantial promise for success in law school" and "a strong likelihood of succeeding in the practice of law and contributing in diverse ways to the well-being of others." More broadly, the Law School seeks "a mix of students with varying backgrounds and experiences who will respect and learn from each other." In 1992, the dean of the Law School charged a faculty committee with crafting a written admissions policy to implement these goals. In particular, the Law School sought to ensure that its efforts to achieve student body diversity complied with this Court's most recent ruling on the use of race in university admissions. (1978). Upon the unanimous adoption of the committee's report by the Law School faculty, it became the Law School's official admissions policy.

The hallmark of that policy is its focus on academic ability coupled with a flexible assessment of applicants' talents, experiences, and potential "to contribute to the learning of those around them." The policy requires admissions officials to evaluate each applicant based on all the information available in the file, including a personal statement, letters of recommendation, and an essay describing the ways in which the applicant will contribute to the life and diversity of the Law School. In reviewing an applicant's file, admissions officials must consider the applicant's undergraduate grade point average (GPA) and Law School Admissions Test (LSAT) score because they are important (if imperfect) predictors of academic success in law school. The policy stresses that "no applicant should be admitted unless we expect that applicant to do well enough to graduate with no serious academic problems."

The policy makes clear, however, that even the highest possible score does not guarantee admission to the Law School. Nor does a low score automatically disqualify an applicant. Rather, the policy requires admissions officials to look beyond grades and test scores to other criteria that are important to the Law School's educational objectives. So-called "'soft' variables" such as "the enthusiasm of recommenders, the quality of the undergraduate institution, the quality of the applicant's essay, and the areas and difficulty of undergraduate course selection" are all brought to bear in assessing an "applicant's likely contributions to the intellectual and social life of the institution."

The policy aspires to "achieve that diversity which has the potential to enrich everyone's education and thus make a law school class stronger than the sum of its parts." The policy does not restrict the types of diversity contributions eligible for "substantial weight" in the admissions process, but instead recognizes "many possible bases for diversity admissions." The policy does, however, reaffirm the Law School's longstanding commitment to "one particular type of diversity," that is, "racial and ethnic diversity with special reference to the inclusion of students from groups which have been historically discriminated against, like African-Americans, Hispanics and Native Americans, who without this commitment might not be represented in our student body in meaningful numbers." By enrolling a "'critical mass' of [underrepresented] minority students," the Law School seeks to "ensur[e] their ability to make unique contributions to the character of the Law School."

The policy does not define diversity "solely in terms of racial and ethnic status." Nor is the policy "insensitive to the competition among all students for admission to the [L]aw [S]chool." Rather, the policy seeks to guide admissions officers in "producing classes both diverse and academically outstanding, classes made up of students who promise to continue the tradition of outstanding contribution by Michigan Graduates to the legal profession."

B

Petitioner Barbara Grutter is a white Michigan resident who applied to the Law School in 1996 with a 3.8 grade point average and 161 LSAT score. The Law School initially placed petitioner on a waiting list, but subsequently rejected her application. In December 1997, petitioner filed suit in the United States District Court for the Eastern District of Michigan against the Law

School, the Regents of the University of Michigan, Lee Bollinger (Dean of the Law School from 1987 to 1994, and President of the University of Michigan from 1996 to 2002), Jeffrey Lehman (Dean of the Law School), and Dennis Shields (Director of Admissions at the Law School from 1991 until 1998). Petitioner alleged that respondents discriminated against her on the basis of race in violation of the Fourteenth Amendment; Title VI of the Civil Rights Act of 1964, and Rev. Stat. §1977, as amended, 42 U.S.C. § 1981.

Petitioner further alleged that her application was rejected because the Law School uses race as a "predominant" factor, giving applicants who belong to certain minority groups "a significantly greater chance of admission than students with similar credentials from disfavored racial groups." Petitioner also alleged that respondents "had no compelling interest to justify their use of race in the admissions process." Petitioner requested compensatory and punitive damages, an order requiring the Law School to offer her admission, and an injunction prohibiting the Law School from continuing to discriminate on the basis of race. Petitioner clearly has standing to bring this lawsuit.

The District Court granted petitioner's motion for class certification and for bifurcation of the trial into liability and damages phases. The class was defined as "'all persons who (A) applied for and were not granted admission to the University of Michigan Law School for the academic years since (and including) 1995 until the time that judgment is entered herein; and (B) were members of those racial or ethnic groups, including Caucasian, that Defendants treated less favorably in considering their applications for admission to the Law School.'"

The District Court heard oral argument on the parties' cross-motions for summary judgment on December 22, 2000. Taking the motions under advisement, the District Court indicated that it would decide as a matter of law whether the Law School's asserted interest in obtaining the educational benefits that flow from a diverse student body was compelling. The District Court also indicated that it would conduct a bench trial on the extent to which race was a factor in the Law School's admissions decisions, and whether the Law School's consideration of race in admissions decisions constituted a race-based double standard.

During the 15-day bench trial, the parties introduced extensive evidence concerning the Law School's use of race in the admissions process. Dennis Shields, Director of Admissions when petitioner applied to the Law School, testified that he did not direct his staff to admit a particular percentage or number of minority students, but rather to consider an applicant's race along with all other factors. Shields testified that at the height of the admissions season, he would frequently consult the so-called "daily reports" that kept track of the racial and ethnic composition of the class (along with other information such as residency status and gender). This was done, Shields testified, to ensure that a critical mass of underrepresented minority students would be reached so as to realize the educational benefits of a diverse student body. Shields stressed, however, that he did not seek to admit any particular number or percentage of underrepresented minority students.

▪   ▪   ▪

We granted certiorari, to resolve the disagreement among the Courts of Appeals on a question of national importance: Whether diversity is a compelling interest that can justify the narrowly tailored use of race in selecting applicants for admission to public universities.

II

A

We last addressed the use of race in public higher education over 25 years ago. In the landmark *Bakke* case, we reviewed a racial set-aside program that reserved 16 out of 100 seats in a medical school class for members of certain minority groups. (1978). The decision produced six separate opinions, none of which commanded a majority of the Court. Four Justices would have upheld the program against all attack on the ground that the government can use race to "remedy disadvantages cast on minorities by past racial prejudice." Four other Justices avoided the constitutional question altogether and struck down the program on statutory grounds. Justice Powell provided a fifth vote not only for invalidating the set-aside program, but also for reversing the state court's injunction against any use of race whatsoever. The only holding for the Court in *Bakke* was that a "State has a substantial interest that legitimately may be served by a properly devised admissions program involving the competitive consideration of race and ethnic origin." Thus, we reversed that part of the lower court's judgment that enjoined the university "from any consideration of the race of any applicant."

Since this Court's splintered decision in *Bakke*, Justice Powell's opinion announcing the judgment of the Court has served as the touchstone for constitutional analysis of race-conscious admissions policies. Public and private universities across the Nation have modeled their own admissions programs on Justice Powell's views on permissible race-conscious policies. We therefore discuss Justice Powell's opinion in some detail.

Justice Powell began by stating that "[t]he guarantee of equal protection cannot mean one thing when applied to one individual and something else when applied to a person of another color. If both are not accorded the same protection, then it is not equal." In Justice Powell's view, when governmental decisions "touch upon an individual's race or ethnic background, he is entitled to a judicial determination that the burden he is asked to bear on that basis is precisely tailored to serve a compelling governmental interest." Under this exacting standard, only one of the interests asserted by the university survived Justice Powell's scrutiny.

First, Justice Powell rejected an interest in "'reducing the historic deficit of traditionally disfavored minorities in medical schools and in the medical profession'" as an unlawful interest in racial balancing. Second, Justice Powell rejected an interest in remedying societal discrimination because such measures would risk placing unnecessary burdens on innocent third parties "who bear no responsibility for whatever harm the beneficiaries of the special admissions program are thought to have suffered." Third, Justice Powell rejected an interest in "increasing the number of physicians who will practice in communities currently underserved," concluding that even if such an interest could be compelling in some circumstances the program under review was not "geared to promote that goal."

Justice Powell approved the university's use of race to further only one interest: "the attainment of a diverse student body." With the important proviso that "constitutional limitations protecting individual rights may not be disregarded," Justice Powell grounded his analysis in the academic freedom that "long has been viewed as a special concern of the First Amendment." Justice Powell emphasized that nothing less than the "'nation's future depends upon leaders trained through wide exposure' to the ideas and mores of students as diverse as this Nation of many peoples." In seeking the "right to select those students who will contribute the most to the 'robust exchange of ideas,'" a university seeks "to achieve a goal that is of paramount importance in the fulfillment of its mission." Both "tradition and experience lend support to the view that the contribution of diversity is substantial."

Justice Powell was, however, careful to emphasize that in his view race "is only one element in a range of factors a university properly may consider in attaining the goal of a heterogeneous student body." For Justice Powell, "[i]t is not an interest in simple ethnic diversity, in which a specified percentage of the student body is in effect guaranteed to be members of selected ethnic groups," that can justify the use of race. Rather, "[t]he diversity that furthers a compelling state interest encompasses a far broader array of qualifications and characteristics of which racial or ethnic origin is but a single though important element."

In the wake of our fractured decision in *Bakke*, courts have struggled to discern whether Justice Powell's diversity rationale, set forth in part of the opinion joined by no other Justice, is nonetheless binding precedent under *Marks*. In that case, we explained that "[w]hen a fragmented Court decides a case and no single rationale explaining the result enjoys the assent of five Justices, the holding of the Court may be viewed as that position taken by those Members who concurred in the judgments on the narrowest grounds." As the divergent opinions of the lower courts demonstrate, however, "[t]his test is more easily stated than applied to the various opinions supporting the result in [*Bakke*]."

We do not find it necessary to decide whether Justice Powell's opinion is binding under *Marks*. It does not seem "useful to pursue the *Marks* inquiry to the utmost logical possibility when it has so obviously baffled and divided the lower courts that have considered it." *Nichols v. United States*. More important, for the reasons set out below, today we endorse Justice Powell's view that student body diversity is a compelling state interest that can justify the use of race in university admissions.

B

The Equal Protection Clause provides that no State shall "deny to any person within its jurisdiction the equal protection of the laws." U.S. Const., Amdt. 14, §2. Because the Fourteenth Amendment "protect[s] *persons*, not *groups*," all "governmental action based on race—a *group* classification long recognized as in most circumstances irrelevant and therefore prohibited—should be subjected to detailed judicial inquiry to ensure that the *personal* right to equal protection of the laws has not been infringed." *Adarand Constructors, Inc. v. Peña,* (1995). We are a "free people whose institutions are founded upon the doctrine of equality." *Loving v. Virginia,* (1967). It follows from that principle that "government may treat people differently because of their race only for the most compelling reasons." *Adarand Constructors, Inc. v. Peña.*

We have held that all racial classifications imposed by government "must be analyzed by a reviewing court under strict scrutiny." This means that such classifications are constitutional only if they are narrowly tailored to further compelling governmental interests. "Absent searching judicial inquiry into the justification for such race-based measures," we have no way to determine what "classifications are 'benign' or 'remedial' and what classifications are in fact motivated by illegitimate notions of racial inferiority or simple racial politics." *Richmond v. J. A. Croson Co.,* (1989) (plurality opinion). We apply strict scrutiny to all racial classifications to "'smoke out' illegitimate uses of race by assuring that [government] is pursuing a goal important enough to warrant use of a highly suspect tool."

Strict scrutiny is not "strict in theory, but fatal in fact." *Adarand Constructors, Inc. v. Peña.* Although all governmental uses of race are subject to strict scrutiny, not all are invalidated by it. As we have explained, "whenever the government treats any person unequally because of his or her race, that person has suffered an injury that falls squarely within the language and spirit of the Constitution's guarantee of equal protection." But that observation "says nothing about the ultimate validity of any particular law; that determination is the job of the court applying strict scrutiny." When race-based action is necessary to further a compelling governmental interest, such action does not violate the constitutional guarantee of equal protection so long as the narrow-tailoring requirement is also satisfied.

Context matters when reviewing race-based governmental action under the Equal Protection Clause. In *Adarand Constructors, Inc. v. Peña*, we made clear that strict scrutiny must take "'relevant differences' into account." Indeed, as we explained, that is its "fundamental purpose." Not every decision influenced by race is equally objectionable and strict scrutiny is designed to provide a framework for carefully examining the importance and the sincerity of the reasons advanced by the governmental decisionmaker for the use of race in that particular context.

III

A

With these principles in mind, we turn to the question whether the Law School's use of race is justified by a compelling state interest. Before this Court, as they have throughout this litigation, respondents assert only one justification for their use of race in the admissions process: obtaining "the educational benefits that flow from a diverse student body." Brief for Respondents Bollinger et al. i. In other words, the Law School asks us to recognize, in the context of higher education, a compelling state interest in student body diversity.

We first wish to dispel the notion that the Law School's argument has been foreclosed, either expressly or implicitly, by our affirmative-action cases decided since *Bakke*. It is true that some language in those opinions might be read to suggest that remedying past discrimination is the only permissible justification for race-based governmental action. But we have never held that the only governmental use of race that can survive strict scrutiny is remedying past discrimination. Nor, since *Bakke*, have we directly addressed the use of race in the context of public higher education. Today, we hold that the Law School has a compelling interest in attaining a diverse student body.

The Law School's educational judgment that such diversity is essential to its educational mission is one to which we defer. The Law School's assessment that diversity will, in fact, yield educational benefits is substantiated by respondents and their *amici*. Our scrutiny of the interest asserted by the Law School is no less strict for taking into account complex educational judgments in an area that lies primarily within the expertise of the university. Our holding today is in keeping with our tradition of giving a degree of deference to a university's academic decisions, within constitutionally prescribed limits.

We have long recognized that, given the important purpose of public education and the expansive freedoms of speech and thought associated with the university environment, universities occupy a special niche in our constitutional tradition. In announcing the principle of student body diversity as a compelling state interest, Justice Powell invoked our cases recognizing a constitutional dimension, grounded in the First Amendment, of educational autonomy: "The freedom of a university to make its own judgments as to education includes the selection of its student body." *Bakke*. From this premise, Justice Powell reasoned that by claiming "the right to select those students who will contribute the most to the 'robust exchange of ideas,'" a university "seek[s] to achieve a goal that is of paramount importance in the fulfillment of its mission." Our conclusion that the Law School has a compelling interest in a diverse student body is informed by our view that attaining a diverse student body is at the heart of the Law School's proper institutional mission, and that "good faith" on the part of a university is "presumed" absent "a showing to the contrary."

As part of its goal of "assembling a class that is both exceptionally academically qualified and broadly diverse," the Law School seeks to "enroll a 'critical mass' of minority students." Brief for Respondents Bollinger et al. 13. The Law School's interest is not simply "to assure within its student body some specified percentage of a particular group merely because of its race or ethnic origin." *Bakke*, (opinion of Powell, J.). That would amount to outright racial balancing, which is patently unconstitutional. Rather, the Law School's concept of critical mass is defined by reference to the educational benefits that diversity is designed to produce.

These benefits are substantial. As the District Court emphasized, the Law School's admissions policy promotes "cross-racial understanding," helps to break down racial stereotypes, and "enables [students] to better understand persons of different races." These benefits are "important and laudable," because "classroom discussion is livelier, more spirited, and simply more enlightening and interesting" when the students have "the greatest possible variety of backgrounds."

■   ■   ■

We have repeatedly acknowledged the overriding importance of preparing students for work and citizenship, describing education as pivotal to "sustaining our political and cultural heritage" with a fundamental role in maintaining the fabric of society. *Plyler v. Doe*, (1982). This Court has long recognized that "education . . . is the very foundation of good citizenship." *Brown v. Board of Education*, (1954). For this reason, the diffusion of knowledge and opportunity through public institutions of higher education must be accessible to all individuals regardless of race or ethnicity. The United States, as *amicus curiae*, affirms that "[e]nsuring that public institutions are open and available to all segments of American society, including people of all races and ethnicities, represents a paramount government objective." And, "[n]owhere is the importance of such openness more acute than in the context of higher education." Effective participation by members of all racial and ethnic groups in the civic life of our Nation is essential if the dream of one Nation, indivisible, is to be realized.

Moreover, universities, and in particular, law schools, represent the training ground for a large number of our Nation's leaders. *Sweatt v. Painter*, (1950) (describing law school as a "proving ground for legal learning and practice"). Individuals with law degrees occupy roughly half the state governorships, more than half the seats in the United States Senate, and more than a third of the seats in the United States House of Representatives. The pattern is even more striking when it comes to highly selective law schools. A handful of these schools accounts for 25 of the 100 United States Senators, 74 United States Courts of Appeals judges, and nearly 200 of the more than 600 United States District Court judges.

In order to cultivate a set of leaders with legitimacy in the eyes of the citizenry, it is necessary that the path to leadership be visibly open to talented and qualified individuals of every race and ethnicity. All members of our heterogeneous society must have confidence in the openness and integrity of the educational institutions that provide this training. As we have recognized, law schools "cannot be effective in isolation from the individuals and institutions with which the law interacts." Access to legal education (and thus the legal profession) must be inclusive of talented and qualified individuals of every race and ethnicity, so that all members of our heterogeneous society may participate in the educational institutions that provide the training and education necessary to succeed in America.

The Law School does not premise its need for critical mass on "any belief that minority students always (or even consistently) express some characteristic minority viewpoint on any issue." To the contrary, diminishing the force of such stereotypes is both a crucial part of the Law School's mission, and one that it cannot accomplish with only token numbers of minority students. Just as growing up in a particular region or having particular professional experiences is likely to affect an individual's views, so too is one's own, unique experience of being a racial minority in a society, like our own, in which race unfortunately still matters. The Law School has determined, based on its experience and expertise, that a "critical mass" of underrepresented minorities is necessary to further its compelling interest in securing the educational benefits of a diverse student body.

B

Even in the limited circumstance when drawing racial distinctions is permissible to further a compelling state interest, government is still "constrained in how it may pursue that end: [T]he means chosen to accomplish the [government's] asserted purpose must be specifically and narrowly framed to accomplish that purpose." *Shaw v. Hunt*, (1996). The purpose of the narrow tailoring requirement is to ensure that "the means chosen 'fit' . . . th[e] compelling goal so closely that there is little or no possibility that the motive for the classification was illegitimate racial prejudice or stereotype." *Richmond v. J. A. Croson Co.*

Since *Bakke*, we have had no occasion to define the contours of the narrow-tailoring inquiry with respect to race-conscious university admissions programs. That inquiry must be calibrated to fit the distinct issues raised by the use of race to achieve student body diversity in public higher education. Contrary to Justice Kennedy's assertions, we do not "abandon[ ] strict scrutiny," (dissenting opinion). Rather, as we have already explained, we adhere to *Adarand*'s teaching that the very purpose of strict scrutiny is to take such "relevant differences into account."

To be narrowly tailored, a race-conscious admissions program cannot use a quota system—it cannot "insulat[e] each category of applicants with certain desired qualifications from competition with all other applicants." *Bakke* (opinion of Powell, J.). Instead, a university may consider race or ethnicity only as a "'plus' in a particular applicant's file," without "insulat[ing] the individual from comparison with all other candidates for the available seats." In other words, an admissions program must be "flexible enough to consider all pertinent elements of diversity in light of the particular qualifications of each applicant, and to place them on the same footing for consideration, although not necessarily according them the same weight."

We find that the Law School's admissions program bears the hallmarks of a narrowly tailored plan. As Justice Powell made clear in *Bakke*, truly individualized consideration demands that race be used in a flexible, non-mechanical way. It follows from this mandate that universities cannot establish quotas for members of certain racial groups or put members of those groups on separate admissions tracks. Nor can universities insulate applicants who belong to certain racial or ethnic groups from the competition for admission. Universities can, however, consider race or ethnicity more flexibly as a "plus" factor in the context of individualized consideration of each and every applicant.

We are satisfied that the Law School's admissions program, like the Harvard plan described by Justice Powell, does not operate as a quota. Properly understood, a "quota" is a program in which a certain fixed number or proportion of opportunities are "reserved exclusively for certain minority groups." *Richmond v. J. A. Croson Co.* (plurality opinion). Quotas "'impose a fixed number or percentage which must be attained, or which cannot be exceeded,'" *Sheet Metal Workers v. EEOC,* (1986) (O'Connor, J., concurring in part and dissenting in part), and "insulate the individual from comparison with all other candidates for the available seats." *Bakke* (opinion of Powell, J.). In contrast, "a permissible goal . . . require[s] only a good-faith effort . . . to come within a range demarcated by the goal itself," *Sheet Metal Workers v. EEOC,* and permits consideration of race as a "plus" factor in any given case while still ensuring that each candidate "compete[s] with all other qualified applicants," *Johnson v. Transportation Agency, Santa Clara Cty.,* (1987).

Justice Powell's distinction between the medical school's rigid 16-seat quota and Harvard's flexible use of race as a "plus" factor is instructive. Harvard certainly had minimum *goals* for minority enrollment, even if it had no specific number firmly in mind. ("10 or 20 black students could not begin to bring to their classmates and to each other the variety of points of view, backgrounds and experiences of blacks in the United States"). What is more, Justice Powell flatly rejected the argument that Harvard's program was "the functional equivalent of a quota" merely because it had some "'plus'" for race, or gave greater "weight" to race than to some other factors, in order to achieve student body diversity.

The Law School's goal of attaining a critical mass of underrepresented minority students does not transform its program into a quota. As the Harvard plan described by Justice Powell recognized, there is of course "some relationship between numbers and achieving the benefits to be derived from a diverse student body, and between numbers and providing a reasonable environment for those students admitted." "[S]ome attention to numbers," without more, does not transform a flexible admissions system into a rigid quota. Nor, as Justice Kennedy posits, does the Law School's consultation of the "daily reports," which keep track of the racial and ethnic composition of the class (as well as of residency and gender), "suggest[ ] there was no further attempt at individual review save for race itself" during the final stages of the admissions process. To the contrary, the Law School's admissions officers testified without contradiction that they never gave race any more or less weight based on the information contained in these reports. Moreover, as Justice Kennedy concedes, between 1993 and 2000, the number of African-American, Latino, and Native-American students in each class at the Law School varied from 13.5 to 20.1 percent, a range inconsistent with a quota.

■ ■ ■

Here, the Law School engages in a highly individualized, holistic review of each applicant's file, giving serious consideration to all the ways an applicant might contribute to a diverse educational environment. The Law School affords this individualized consideration to applicants of all races. There is no policy, either *de jure* or *de facto*, of automatic acceptance or rejection based on any single "soft" variable. Unlike the program at issue in *Gratz v. Bollinger, ante*, the Law School awards no mechanical, predetermined diversity "bonuses" based on race or ethnicity. Like the Harvard plan, the Law School's admissions policy "is flexible enough to consider all pertinent elements of diversity in light of the particular qualifications of each applicant, and to place them on the same footing for consideration, although not necessarily according them the same weight." *Bakke* (opinion of Powell, J.).

We also find that, like the Harvard plan Justice Powell referenced in *Bakke*, the Law School's race-conscious admissions program adequately ensures that all factors that may contribute to student body diversity are meaningfully considered alongside race in admissions decisions. With respect to the use of race itself, all underrepresented minority students admitted by the Law School have been deemed qualified. By virtue of our Nation's struggle with racial inequality, such students are both likely to have experiences of particular importance to the Law School's mission, and less likely to be admitted in meaningful numbers on criteria that ignore those experiences.

The Law School does not, however, limit in any way the broad range of qualities and experiences that may be considered valuable contributions to student body diversity. To the contrary, the 1992 policy makes clear "[t]here are many possible bases for diversity admissions," and provides examples of admittees who have lived or traveled widely abroad, are fluent in several languages, have overcome personal adversity and family hardship, have exceptional records of extensive community service, and have had successful careers in other fields. The Law School seriously considers each "applicant's promise of making a notable contribution to the class by way of a particular strength, attainment, or characteristic *e.g.*, an unusual intellectual achievement, employment experience, nonacademic performance, or personal background." All applicants have the opportunity to highlight their own potential diversity contributions through the submission of a personal statement, letters of recommendation, and an essay describing the ways in which the applicant will contribute to the life and diversity of the Law School.

What is more, the Law School actually gives substantial weight to diversity factors besides race. The Law School frequently accepts nonminority applicants with grades and test scores lower than underrepresented minority applicants (and other nonminority applicants) who are rejected. This shows that the Law School seriously weighs many other diversity factors besides race that can make a real and dispositive difference for nonminority applicants as well. By this flexible approach, the Law School sufficiently takes into account, in practice as well as in theory, a wide variety of characteristics besides race and ethnicity that contribute to a diverse student body. Justice Kennedy speculates that "race is likely outcome determinative for many members of minority groups" who do not fall within the upper range of LSAT scores and grades. But the same could be said of the Harvard plan discussed approvingly by Justice Powell in *Bakke*, and indeed of any plan that uses race as one of many factors.

Petitioner and the United States argue that the Law School's plan is not narrowly tailored because race-neutral means exist to obtain the educational benefits of student body diversity that the Law School seeks. We disagree. Narrow tailoring does not require exhaustion of every conceivable race-neutral alternative. Nor does it require a university to choose between maintaining a reputation for excellence or fulfilling a commitment to provide educational opportunities to members of all racial groups. Narrow tailoring does, however, require serious, good faith consideration of workable race-neutral alternatives that will achieve the diversity the university seeks.

We agree with the Court of Appeals that the Law School sufficiently considered workable race-neutral alternatives. The District Court took the Law School to task for failing to consider race-neutral alternatives such as "using a lottery system" or "decreasing the emphasis for all applicants on undergraduate GPA and LSAT scores." But these alternatives would require a dramatic sacrifice of diversity, the academic quality of all admitted students, or both.

The Law School's current admissions program considers race as one factor among many, in an effort to assemble a student body that is diverse in ways broader than race. Because a lottery would make that kind of nuanced judgment impossible, it would effectively sacrifice all other educational values, not to mention every other kind of diversity. So too with the suggestion that the Law School simply lower admissions standards for all students, a drastic remedy that would require the Law School to become a much different institution and sacrifice a vital component of its educational mission. The United States advocates "percentage plans," recently adopted by public undergraduate institutions in Texas, Florida, and California to guarantee admission to all students above a certain class-rank threshold in every high school in the State. The United States does not, however, explain how such plans could work for graduate and professional schools. More-over, even assuming such plans are race-neutral, they may preclude the university from conducting the individualized assessments necessary to assemble a student body that is not just racially diverse, but diverse along all the qualities valued by the university. We are satisfied that the Law School adequately considered race-neutral alternatives currently capable of producing a critical mass without forcing the Law School to abandon the academic selectivity that is the cornerstone of its educational mission.

▪ ▪ ▪

We agree that, in the context of its individualized inquiry into the possible diversity contributions of all applicants, the Law School's race-conscious admissions program does not unduly harm nonminority applicants.

▪ ▪ ▪

We take the Law School at its word that it would "like nothing better than to find a race-neutral admissions formula" and will terminate its race-conscious admissions program as soon as practicable. It has been 25 years since Justice Powell first approved the use of race to further an interest in student body diversity in the context of public higher education. Since that time, the number of minority applicants with high grades and test scores has indeed increased. We expect that 25 years from now, the use of racial preferences will no longer be necessary to further the interest approved today.

IV

In summary, the Equal Protection Clause does not prohibit the Law School's narrowly tailored use of race in admissions decisions to further a compelling interest in obtaining the educational benefits that flow from a diverse student body. Consequently, petitioner's statutory claims based on Title VI and 42 U.S.C. § 1981 also fail. The judgment of the Court of Appeals for the Sixth Circuit, accordingly, is affirmed.

It is so ordered.

5

CONGRESS

5.1

DAVID MAYHEW

From *Congress: The Electoral Connection*

In this classic work on Congress, Mayhew asks, what would Congress look like, and how would members of Congress behave, if members were solely interested in one thing: getting reelected? Mayhew says they would posture and preen, but also occasionally produce valuable legislation. In other words, it would look like the Congress we actually observe in the United States.

. . . Mostly through personal experience on Capitol Hill, I have become convinced that scrutiny of purposive behavior offers the best route to an understanding of legislatures—or at least of the United States Congress. In the fashion of economics, I shall make a simple abstract assumption about human motivation and then speculate about the consequences of behavior based on that motivation. Specifically, I shall conjure up a vision of United States congressmen as single-minded seekers of reelection, see what kinds of activity that goal implies, and then speculate about how congressmen so motivated are likely to go about building and sustaining legislative institutions and making policy. At all points I shall try to match the abstract with the factual.

I find an emphasis on the reelection goal attractive for a number of reasons. First, I think it fits political reality rather well. Second, it puts the spotlight directly on men rather than on parties and pressure groups, which in the past have often entered discussions of American politics as analytic phantoms. Third, I think politics is best studied as a struggle among men to gain and maintain power and the consequences of that struggle. Fourth—and perhaps most important—the reelection quest establishes an accountability relationship with an electorate, and any serious thinking about democratic theory has to give a central place to the question of accountability. The abstract assumption notwithstanding, I regard this venture as an exercise in political science rather than economics. Leaving aside the fact that I have no economics expertise to display, I find that economists who study legislatures bring to bear interests different from those of political scientists. Not surprisingly the public finance scholars tend to look upon government as a device for spending money. I shall give some attention to spending, but also to other governmental activities such as the production of binding rules. And I shall touch upon such traditional subjects of political science as elections, parties, governmental structure, and regime stability. Another distinction here is that economics research tends to be infused with the normative assumption that policy decisions should be judged by how well they meet the standard of Pareto optimality. This is an assumption that I do not share and that I do not think most political scientists share. There will be no need here to set forth any alternative assumption. . . .

My subject of concern here is a single legislative institution, the United States Congress. In many ways, of course, the Congress is a unique or unusual body. It is probably the most highly "professionalized" of legislatures, in the sense that it promotes careerism among its members and gives them the salaries, staff, and other resources to sustain careers. Its parties are exceptionally diffuse. It is widely thought to be especially "strong" among legislatures as a checker of executive power. Like most Latin American legislatures but unlike most European ones, it labors in the shadow of a separately elected executive. My decision to focus on the Congress flows from a belief that there is something to be gained in an intensive analysis of a particular and important institution. But there is something general to be gained as well, for the exceptionalist argument should not be carried too far. In a good many ways the Congress is just one in a large family of legislative bodies. I shall find it useful at various points in the analysis to invoke comparisons with European parliaments and with American state legislatures and city councils. I shall ponder the question of what "functions" the Congress performs or is capable of performing—a question that can be answered only with the records of other legislatures in mind. Functions to be given special attention are those of legislating, overseeing the executive, expressing public opinion, and servicing constituents. No functional capabilities can be automatically assumed.[1] Indeed the very term *legislature* is an unfortunate one because it confuses structure and function. Accordingly I shall here on use the more awkward but more neutral term *representative assembly* to refer to members of the class of entities inhabited by the United States House and Senate. Whatever the noun, the identifying characteristics of institutions in the class have been well stated by Loewenberg: it is true of all such entities that (1) "their members are formally equal to each other in status, distinguishing parliaments from hierarchically ordered organizations," and (2) "the authority of their members depends on their claim to representing the rest of the community, in some sense of that protean concept, representation."[2]

The following discussion will take the form of an extended theoretical essay. Perforce it will raise more questions than it answers. As is the custom in mono-causal ventures, it will no doubt carry arguments to the point of exaggeration; finally, of course, I shall be satisfied to explain a significant part of the variance rather than all of it. What the discussion will yield, I hope, is a picture of what the United States Congress looks like if the reelection quest is examined seriously.

■　■　■

The ultimate concern here is not how probable it is that legislators will lose their seats but whether there is a connection between what they do in office and their need to be reelected. It is possible to conceive of an assembly in which no member ever comes close to losing a seat but in which the need to be reelected is what inspires members' behavior. It would be an assembly with no saints or fools in it, an assembly packed with skilled politicians going about their business. When we say "Congressman Smith is unbeatable," we do not mean that there is nothing he could do that would lose him his seat. Rather we mean, "Congressman Smith is unbeatable as long as he continues to do the things he is doing." If he stopped answering his mail, or stopped visiting his district, or began voting randomly on roll calls, or shifted his vote record eighty points on the ADA scale, he would bring on primary or November election troubles in a hurry. It is difficult to offer conclusive proof that this last statement is true, for there is no congressman willing to make the experiment. But normal political activity among politicians with healthy electoral margins should not be confused with inactivity. What characterizes "safe" congressmen is not that they are beyond electoral reach, but that their efforts are very likely to bring them uninterrupted electoral success.

Whether congressmen think their activities have electoral impact, and whether in fact they have impact, are of course two separate questions. Of the former there can be little doubt that the answer is yes. In fact in their own minds successful politicians probably overestimate the impact they are having. Kingdon found in his Wisconsin candidates a "congratulation-rationalization effect," a tendency for winners to take personal credit for their victories and for losers to assign their losses to forces beyond their control. The actual impact of politicians' activities is more difficult to assess. The evidence on the point is soft and scattered. It is hard to find variance in activities undertaken, for there are no politicians who consciously try to lose. There is no doubt that the electorate's general awareness of what is going on in Congress is something less than robust. Yet the argument here will be that congressmen's activities in fact do have electoral impact. Pieces of evidence will be brought in as the discussion proceeds.

The next step here is to offer a brief conceptual treatment of the relation between congressmen and their electorates. In the Downsian analysis what national party leaders must worry about is voters' "expected party differential." But to congressmen this is in practice irrelevant, for reasons specified earlier. A congressman's attention must rather be devoted to what can be called an "expected incumbent differential." Let us define this "expected incumbent differential" as any difference perceived by a relevant political actor between what an incumbent congressman is likely to do if returned to office and what any possible challenger (in primary or general election) would be likely to do. And let us define "relevant political actor" here as anyone who has a resource that might be used in the election in question. At the ballot box the only usable resources are votes, but there are resources that can be translated into votes: money, the ability to make persuasive endorsements, organizational skills, and so on. By this definition a "relevant political actor" need not be a constituent; one of the most important resources, money, flows all over the country in congressional campaign years.

It must be emphasized that the average voter has only the haziest awareness of what an incumbent congressman is actually doing in office. But an incumbent has to be concerned about actors who do form impressions about him, and especially about actors who can marshal resources other than their own votes. Senator Robert C. Byrd (D., W.Va.) has a "little list" of 2,545 West Virginians he regularly keeps in touch with. A congressman's assistant interviewed for a Nader profile in 1972 refers to the "thought leadership" back in the district. Of campaign resources one of the most vital is money. An incumbent not only has to assure that his own election funds are adequate, he has to try to minimize the probability that actors will bankroll an expensive campaign against him. There is the story that during the first Nixon term Senator James B. Pearson (R., Kans.) was told he would face a well-financed opponent in his 1972 primary if he did not display more party regularity in his voting. Availability of money can affect strength of opposition candidacy in both primary and general elections.

Another resource of significance is organizational expertise, probably more important than money among labor union offerings. Simple ability to do electioneering footwork is a resource the invoking of which may give campaigns an interesting twist. Leut-hold found in studying ten 1962 House elections in the San Francisco area that 50 percent of campaign workers held college degrees (as against 12 percent of the Bay area population), and that the workers were more issue oriented than the general population. The need to attract workers may induce candidates to traffic in issues more than they otherwise would. Former Congressman Allard K. Lowenstein (D., N.Y.) has as his key invokable resource a corps of student volunteers who will follow him from district to district, making him an unusually mobile candidate.

Still another highly important resource is the ability to make persuasive endorsements. Manhattan candidates angle for the imprimatur of the

New York Times. New Hampshire politics rotates around endorsements of the *Manchester Union Leader.* Labor union committees circulate their approved lists. Chicago Democratic politicians seek the endorsement of the mayor. In the San Francisco area and elsewhere House candidates try to score points by winning endorsements from officials of the opposite party. As Neustadt argues, the influence of the president over congressmen (of both parties) varies with his public prestige and with his perceived ability to punish and reward. One presidential tool is the endorsement, which can be carefully calibrated according to level of fervor, and which can be given to congressmen or to challengers running against congressmen. In the 1970 election Senator Charles Goodell (R., N.Y.), who had achieved public salience by attacking the Nixon administration, was apparently done in by the resources called forth by that attack; the vice president implicitly endorsed his Conservative opponent, and the administration acted to channel normally Republican money away from Goodell.

What a congressman has to try to do is to insure that in primary and general elections the resource balance (with all other deployed resources finally translated into votes) favors himself rather than somebody else. To maneuver successfully he must remain constantly aware of what political actors' incumbent differential readings are, and he must act in a fashion to inspire readings that favor himself. Complicating his task is the problem of slack resources. That is, only a very small proportion of the resources (other than votes) that are conceivably deployable in congressional campaigns are ever in fact deployed. But there is no sure way of telling who will suddenly become aroused and with what consequence. For example, just after the 1948 election the American Medical Association, unnerved by the medical program of the Attlee Government in Britain and by Democratic campaign promises here to institute national health insurance, decided to venture into politics. By 1950 congressmen on record as supporters of health insurance found themselves confronted by a million-dollar AMA advertising drive, local "healing arts committees" making candidate endorsements, and even doctors sending out campaign literature with their monthly bills. By 1952 it was widely believed that the AMA had decided some elections, and few congressmen were still mentioning health insurance.

In all his calculations the congressman must keep in mind that he is serving two electorates rather than one—a November electorate and a primary electorate nested inside it but not a representative sample of it. From the standpoint of the politician a primary is just another election to be survived. A typical scientific poll of a constituency yields a congressman information on the public standing of possible challengers in the other party but also in his own party. A threat is a threat. For an incumbent with a firm "supporting coalition" of elite groups in his party the primary electorate is normally quiescent. But there can be sudden turbulence. And it sometimes happens that the median views of primary and November electorates are so divergent on salient issues that a congressman finds it difficult to hold both electorates at once. This has been a recurrent problem among California Republicans.

A final conceptual point has to do with whether congressmen's behavior should be characterized as "maximizing" behavior. Does it make sense to visualize the congressman as a maximizer of vote percentage in elections— November or primary or, with some complex trade-off, both? For two reasons the answer is probably no. The first has to do with his goal itself, which is to stay in office rather than to win all the popular vote. More precisely his goal is to stay in office over a number of future elections, which does mean that "winning comfortably" in any one of them (except the last) is more desirable than winning by a narrow plurality. The logic here is that a narrow victory (in primary or general election) is a sign of weakness that can inspire hostile political actors to deploy resources intensively the next time around. By this reasoning the higher the election percentages the better. No doubt any congressman would engage in an act to raise his November figure from 80 percent to 90 percent if he could be absolutely sure that the act would accomplish the end (without affecting his primary percentage) and if it could be undertaken at low personal cost. But still, trying to "win comfortably" is not the same as trying to win all the popular vote. As the personal cost (e.g. expenditure of personal energy) of a hypothetical "sure gain" rises, the congressman at the 55 percent November level is more likely to be willing to pay it than his colleague at the 80 percent level.

■ ■ ■

Whether they are safe or marginal, cautious or audacious, congressmen must constantly engage in activities related to reelection. There will be differences in emphasis, but all members share the root need to do things—indeed, to do things day in and day out during their terms. The next step here is to present a typology, a short list of the *kinds* of activities congressmen find it electorally useful to engage in. The case will be that there are three basic kinds of activities. . . .

One activity is *advertising*, defined here as any effort to disseminate one's name among constituents in such a fashion as to create a favorable image but in messages having little or no issue content. A successful congressman builds what amounts to a brand name, which may have a generalized electoral value for other politicians in the same family. The personal qualities to emphasize are experience, knowledge, responsiveness, concern, sincerity, independence, and the like. Just getting one's name across is difficult enough; only about half the electorate, if asked, can supply their House members' names. It helps a congressman to be known. "In the main, recognition carries a positive valence; to be perceived at all is to be perceived favorably." A vital advantage enjoyed by House incumbents is that they are much better known among voters than their November challengers. They are better known because they spend a great deal of time, energy, and money trying to make themselves better known. There are standard routines—frequent visits to the constituency, nonpolitical speeches to home audiences, the sending out of infant care booklets and letters of condolence and congratulation. Of 158 House members questioned in the mid-1960s, 121 said that they regularly sent newsletters to their constituents; 48 wrote separate news or opinion columns for newspapers; 82 regularly reported to their constituencies by radio or television; 89 regularly sent out mail questionnaires. Some routines are less standard. Congressman George E. Shipley (D., Ill.) claims to have met personally about half his constituents (i.e. some 200,000 people). For over twenty years Congressman Charles C. Diggs, Jr. (D., Mich.) has run a radio program featuring himself as a "combination disc jockey-commentator and minister." Congressman Daniel J. Flood (D., Pa.) is "famous for appearing unannounced and often uninvited at wedding anniversaries and other events." Anniversaries and other events aside, congressional advertising is done largely at public expense. Use of the franking privilege has mushroomed in recent years; in early 1973 one estimate predicted that House and Senate members would send out about 476 million pieces of mail in the year 1974, at a public cost of $38.1 million—or about 900,000 pieces per member with a subsidy of $70,000 per member. By far the heaviest mailroom traffic comes in Octobers of even-numbered years. There are some differences between House and Senate members in the ways they go about getting their names across. House members are free to blanket their constituencies with mailings for all boxholders; senators are not. But senators find it easier to appear on national television—for example, in short reaction statements on the nightly news shows. Advertising is a staple congressional activity, and there is no end to it. For each member there are always new voters to be apprised of his worthiness and old voters to be reminded of it.

A second activity may be called *credit claiming*, defined here as acting so as to generate a belief in a relevant political actor (or actors) that one is personally responsible for causing the government, or some unit thereof, to do something that the actor (or actors) considers desirable. The political logic of this, from the congressman's point of view, is that an actor who believes that a member can make pleasing things happen will no doubt wish to keep him in office so that he can make pleasing things happen in the future. The emphasis here is on individual accomplishment (rather than, say, party or governmental accomplishment) and on the congressman as doer (rather than as, say, expounder of constituency views). Credit claiming is highly important to congressmen, with the consequence that much of congressional life is a relentless search for opportunities to engage in it.

Where can credit be found? If there were only one congressman rather than 535, the answer would in principle be simple enough. Credit (or blame) would attach in Downsian fashion to the doings of the government as a whole. But there are 535. Hence it becomes necessary for each congressman to try to peel off pieces of governmental accomplishment for which he can believably generate a sense of responsibility. For the average congressman the staple way of doing this is to traffic in what may be called "particularized benefits." Particularized governmental benefits, as the term will be used here, have two properties: (1) Each benefit is given out to a specific individual, group, or geographical constituency, the recipient unit being of a scale that allows a single congressman to be recognized (by relevant political actors and other congressmen) as the claimant for the benefit (other congressmen being perceived as indifferent or hostile). (2) Each benefit is given out in apparently ad hoc fashion (unlike, say, social security checks) with a congressman apparently having a hand in the allocation. A particularized benefit can normally be regarded as a member of a class. That is, a benefit given out to an individual, group, or constituency can normally be looked upon by congressmen as one of a class of similar benefits given out to sizable numbers of individuals, groups, or constituencies. Hence the impression can arise that a congressman is getting "his share" of whatever it is the government is offering. (The classes may be vaguely defined. Some state legislatures deal in what their members call "local legislation.")

In sheer volume the bulk of particularized benefits come under the heading of "casework"—the thousands of favors congressional offices perform for supplicants in ways that normally do not require legislative action. High school students ask for essay materials, soldiers for emergency leaves, pensioners for location of missing checks, local governments for grant information, and on and on. Each office has skilled professionals who can play the bureaucracy like an organ—pushing the right pedals to produce the desired effects. But many benefits require new legislation, or at least they require important allocative decisions on matters covered by existent legislation. Here the congressman fills the traditional role of supplier of goods to the home district. It is a believable role; when a member claims credit for a benefit on the order of a dam, he may well receive it. Shiny construction projects seem especially useful. In the decades before 1934, tariff duties for local industries were a major commodity. In recent years awards given under grant-in-aid programs have become more useful as they have become more numerous. Some quests for credit are ingenious; in 1971 the story broke that congressmen had been earmarking foreign aid money for specific projects in Israel in order to win favor with home constituents. It should be said of constituency benefits that congressmen are quite capable of taking the initiative in drumming them up; that is, there can be no automatic assumption that a congressman's activity is the result of pressures brought to bear by organized interests. Fenno shows the importance of member initiative in his discussion of the House Interior Committee.

A final point here has to do with geography. The examples given so far are all of benefits conferred upon home constituencies or recipients therein (the latter including the home residents who applauded the Israeli projects). But the properties of particularized benefits were carefully specified so as not

to exclude the possibility that some benefits may be given to recipients outside the home constituencies. Some probably are. Narrowly drawn tax loopholes qualify as particularized benefits, and some of them are probably
conferred upon recipients outside the home districts. (It is difficult to find
solid evidence on the point.) Campaign contributions flow into districts
from the outside, so it would not be surprising to find that benefits go where
the resources are.

How much particularized benefits count for at the polls is extraordinarily
difficult to say. But it would be hard to find a congressman who thinks he can
afford to wait around until precise information is available. The lore is that
they count—furthermore, given home expectations, that they must be supplied in regular quantities for a member to stay electorally even with the
board. Awareness of favors may spread beyond their recipients, building for a
member a general reputation as a good provider. "Rivers Delivers." "He Can
Do More For Massachusetts." A good example of Capitol Hill lore on electoral
impact is given in this account of the activities of Congressman Frank Thomp-
son, Jr. (D., N.J., 4th district):

> In 1966, the 4th was altered drastically by redistricting; it lost Burl-
> ington County and gained Hunterdon, Warren, and Sussex. Thomp-
> son's performance at the polls since 1966 is a case study of how an
> incumbent congressman, out of line with his district's ideological per-
> suasions, can become unbeatable. In 1966, Thompson carried Mercer
> by 23,000 votes and lost the three new counties by 4,600, winning
> reelection with 56% of the votes. He then survived a district-wide drop
> in his vote two years later. In 1970, the Congressman carried Mercer
> County by 20,000 votes and the rest of the district by 6,000, finishing
> with 58%. The drop in Mercer resulted from the attempt of his hard-
> line conservative opponent to exploit the racial unrest which had
> developed in Trenton. But for four years Thompson had been making
> friends in Hunterdon, Warren, and Sussex, busy doing the kind of
> chores that congressmen do. In this case, Thompson concerned himself
> with the interests of dairy farmers at the Department of Agriculture.
> The results of his efforts were clear when the results came in from the
> 4th's northern counties.

So much for particularized benefits. But is credit available elsewhere? For
governmental accomplishments beyond the scale of those already discussed?
The general answer is that the prime mover role is a hard one to play on
larger matters—at least before broad electorates. A claim, after all, has to be
credible. If a congressman goes before an audience and says, "I am responsible for passing a bill to curb inflation," or "I am responsible for the highway
program," hardly anyone will believe him. There are two reasons why people
may be skeptical of such claims. First, there is a numbers problem. On an

accomplishment of a sort that probably engaged the supportive interest of more than one member it is reasonable to suppose that credit should be apportioned among them. But second, there is an overwhelming problem of information costs. For typical voters Capitol Hill is a distant and mysterious place; few have anything like a working knowledge of its maneuverings. Hence there is no easy way of knowing whether a congressman is staking a valid claim or not. The odds are that the information problem cuts in different ways on different kinds of issues. On particularized benefits it may work in a congressman's favor; he may get credit for the dam he had nothing to do with building. Sprinkling a district with dams, after all, is something a congressman is supposed to be able to do. But on larger matters it may work against him. For a voter lacking an easy way to sort out valid from invalid claims the sensible recourse is skepticism. Hence it is unlikely that congressmen get much mileage out of credit claiming on larger matters before broad electorates.

Yet there is an obvious and important qualification here. For many congressmen credit claiming on non-particularized matters is possible in specialized subject areas because of the congressional division of labor. The term "governmental unit" in the original definition of credit claiming is broad enough to include committees, subcommittees, and the two houses of Congress itself. Thus many congressmen can believably claim credit for blocking bills in subcommittee, adding on amendments in committee, and so on. The audience for transactions of this sort is usually small. But it may include important political actors (e.g. an interest group, the president, the *New York Times*, Ralph Nader) who are capable of both paying Capitol Hill information costs and deploying electoral resources. There is a well-documented example of this in Fenno's treatment of post office politics in the 1960s. The postal employee unions used to watch very closely the activities of the House and Senate Post Office Committees and supply valuable electoral resources (money, volunteer work) to members who did their bidding on salary bills. Of course there are many examples of this kind of undertaking, and there is more to be said about it.

The third activity congressmen engage in may be called *position taking*, defined here as the public enunciation of a judgmental statement on anything likely to be of interest to political actors. The statement may take the form of a roll call vote. The most important classes of judgmental statements are those prescribing American governmental ends (a vote cast against the war; a statement that "the war should be ended immediately") or governmental means (a statement that "the way to end the war is to take it to the United Nations"). The judgments may be implicit rather than explicit, as in: "I will support the president on this matter." But judgments may range far beyond these classes to take in implicit or explicit statements on what almost anybody should do or how he should do it: "The great Polish scientist Copernicus has been unjustly neglected"; "The way for Israel to achieve peace is to give up the Sinai." The congressman as position taker is a speaker rather than a doer. The electoral requirement is not that he make pleasing things happen but that he make pleasing judgmental statements. The position itself is the political commodity. Especially on matters where governmental responsibility is widely diffused it is not surprising that political actors should fall back on positions as tests of incumbent virtue. For voters ignorant of congressional processes the recourse is an easy one. The following comment by one of Clapp's House interviewees is highly revealing: "Recently, I went home and began to talk about the ——— act. I was pleased to have sponsored that bill, but it soon dawned on me that the point wasn't getting through at all. What was getting through was that the act might be a help to people. I changed the emphasis: I didn't mention my role particularly, but stressed my support of the legislation."

The ways in which positions can be registered are numerous and often imaginative. There are floor addresses ranging from weighty orations to mass-produced "nationality day statements." There are speeches before home groups, television appearances, letters, newsletters, press releases, ghostwritten books, *Playboy* articles, even interviews with political scientists. On occasion congressmen generate what amount to petitions; whether or not to sign the 1956 Southern Manifesto defying school desegregation rulings was an important decision for southern members. Outside the roll call process the congressman is usually able to tailor his positions to suit his audiences. A solid consensus in the constituency calls for ringing declarations; for years the late Senator James K. Vardaman (D., Miss.) campaigned on a proposal to repeal the Fifteenth Amendment. Division or uncertainty in the constituency calls for waffling; in the late 1960s a congressman had to be a poor politician indeed not to be able to come up with an inoffensive statement on Vietnam ("We must have peace with honor at the earliest possible moment consistent with the national interest"). On a controversial issue a Capitol Hill office normally prepares two form letters to send out to constituent letter writers—one for the pros and one (not directly contradictory) for the antis. Handling discrete audiences in person requires simple agility, a talent well demonstrated in this selection from a Nader profile:

> "You may find this difficult to understand," said Democrat Edward R. Roybal, the Mexican-American representative from California's thirtieth district, "but sometimes I wind up making a patriotic speech one afternoon and later on that same day an anti-war speech. In the patriotic speech I speak of past wars but I also speak of the need to prevent more wars. My positions are not inconsistent; I just approach different people differently." Roybal went on to depict the diversity of crowds he speaks to: one afternoon he is surrounded by balding men wearing Veterans' caps and holding American flags; a few hours later he speaks to a crowd of Chicano youths, angry over American involvement in Vietnam.

Such a diverse constituency, Roybal believes, calls for different methods of expressing one's convictions.

Indeed it does. Versatility of this sort is occasionally possible in roll call voting. For example a congressman may vote one way on recommittal and the other on final passage, leaving it unclear just how he stands on a bill. Members who cast identical votes on a measure may give different reasons for having done so. Yet it is on roll calls that the crunch comes; there is no way for a member to avoid making a record on hundreds of issues, some of which are controversial in the home constituencies. Of course, most roll call positions considered in isolation are not likely to cause much of a ripple at home. But broad voting patterns can and do; member "ratings" calculated by the Americans for Democratic Action, Americans for Constitutional Action, and other outfits are used as guidelines in the deploying of electoral resources. And particular issues often have their alert publics. Some national interest groups watch the votes of all congressmen on single issues and ostentatiously try to reward or punish members for their positions; over the years some notable examples of such interest groups have been the Anti-Saloon League, the early Farm Bureau, the American Legion, the American Medical Association, and the National Rifle Association. On rare occasions single roll calls achieve a rather high salience among the public generally. This seems especially true of the Senate, which every now and then winds up for what might be called a "showdown vote," with pressures on all sides, presidential involvement, media attention given to individual senators' positions, and suspense about the outcome. Examples are the votes on the nuclear test-ban treaty in 1963, civil rights cloture in 1964, civil rights cloture again in 1965, the Haynsworth appointment in 1969, the Carswell appointment in 1970, and the ABM in 1970. Controversies on roll calls like these are often relived in subsequent campaigns, the southern Senate elections of 1970 with their Haynsworth and Carswell issues being cases in point.

Probably the best position-taking strategy for most congressmen at most times is to be conservative—to cling to their own positions of the past where possible and to reach for new ones with great caution where necessary. Yet in an earlier discussion of strategy the suggestion was made that it might be rational for members in electoral danger to resort to innovation. The form of innovation available is entrepreneurial position taking, its logic being that for a member facing defeat with his old array of positions it makes good sense to gamble on some new ones. It may be that congressional marginals fulfill an important function here as issue pioneers—experimenters who test out new issues and thereby show other politicians which ones are usable. An example of such a pioneer is Senator Warren Magnuson (D., Wash.), who responded to a surprisingly narrow victory in 1962 by reaching for a reputation in the area of consumer affairs. Another example is Senator Ernest Hollings (D., S.C.), a servant of a shaky and racially heterogeneous southern constituency who launched "hunger" as an issue in 1969—at once pointing to a problem and giving it a useful nonracial definition. One of the most successful issue entrepreneurs of recent decades was the late Senator Joseph McCarthy (R., Wis.); it was all there—the close primary in 1946, the fear of defeat in 1952, the desperate casting about for an issue, the famous 1950 dinner at the Colony Restaurant where suggestions were tendered, the decision that "Communism" might just do the trick.

NOTES

1. "But it is equally true, though only of late and slowly beginning to be acknowledged, that a numerous assembly is as little fitted for the direct business of legislation as for that of administration." John Stuart Mill, *Considerations on Representative Government* (Chicago: Regency, 1962), p. 104.

2. Gerhard Loewenberg, "The Role of Parliaments in Modern Political Systems," in Loewenberg (ed.), *Modern Parliaments: Change or Decline?* (Chicago: Aldine-Atherton, 1971), p. 3.

5.2

R. DOUGLAS ARNOLD

From *The Logic of Congressional Action*

How do ordinary citizens hold members of Congress accountable? Arnold argues that the American political parties are too undisciplined and weak to enable citizens to reward or punish the parties at election time. Instead, members of Congress tend to be held accountable by small numbers of citizens who pay close attention to what individual legislators, not necessarily parties, are doing in Congress.

CITIZENS' CONTROL OF GOVERNMENT

To what extent are citizens able to control their government in a representative system? This is—or should be—one of the central questions in political science, one that should occupy the combined talents of democratic theorists and institutional specialists. All too often scholars avoid addressing the issue directly, hoping that their results speak for themselves (they rarely do). The question is especially difficult to answer for the American system. In the United States, the sharing of power among legislators and an elected executive, coupled with the lack of strong parties to unite the two branches, makes the links among citizens, elected officials, and policy outcomes more complicated than in, say, a parliamentary system.

The Role of Parties

It is easy to see how citizens could achieve control in a representative system where most citizens choose among legislative candidates according to the party performance rule. This rule posits that a citizen first evaluates current conditions in society, decides how well he or she likes those conditions, and then either rewards or punishes the governing party by supporting or opposing its legislative candidates. If all voters employed the party performance rule, legislators from the governing party would have a powerful incentive to anticipate citizens' needs, to devise and enact effective programs for fulfilling those needs, and to produce pleasing outcomes by election day. [T]he party performance rule requires the least information and analysis on the part of citizens and demands the most in performance on the part of legislators.

Even though the evidence is strong that at least some citizens use some-thing like the party performance rule in congressional elections, this rule does not provide a firm basis for citizens' control unless it is the predominant decision rule in congressional elections. Legislators work together to produce pleasing effects only if they believe citizens will reward them for their team successes and punish them for their team failings. If citizens use the party performance rule in conjunction with the various candidate-centered rules, or if many citizens reject the rule completely, then legislators have every incentive to emphasize their personal attributes and positions and no incen-tive to behave as loyal team members. Whenever legislators see a conflict between making themselves look good and making their party look good they naturally choose the former, for as individuals calculating at the margin, they can always do more to affect their own images than they can to affect their party's performance in office.

For similar reasons the party position rule offers an inadequate founda-tion for citizens' control of government. Although it appears that some citi-zens choose their legislators according to where the parties stand on the issues, this method of choosing provides only a weak link between citizens' preferences and legislators' actions. If many citizens shift their allegiance from one party to the other, whether in response to the issues of the day or as part of a longer-term realignment, then the new cohort of legislators may have different policy preferences from those of the legislators they replace. The defect in the party position rule as a mechanism for citizens' control is that nothing impels new legislators to enact their parties' promises. Citizens' evaluations are prospective judgments about what the parties promise rather than retrospective appraisals of their performance. Once in office, legislators can distance themselves from their parties' positions and concentrate on their own individual positions and accomplishments.

Under current conditions in American politics, then, it is difficult to see how either the party performance rule or the party position rule provides an adequate mechanism for citizens' control of government. In order to work properly, these mechanisms require the subordination of candidates to par-ties; yet citizens have proven themselves increasingly independent of party. Meanwhile legislators do everything in their power to insure that citizens focus on the legislators rather than on their party teams.

Individual Legislators

If party no longer provides a mechanism for citizens' control of American government (and perhaps it never did), does this leave citizens powerless to affect governmental decisions? It does not. Both the incumbent performance rule and the candidate position rule permit a certain degree of control. In a system with weak parties, however, citizens' control is necessarily a multistep process in which influence may be exerted over legislators' individual decisions, over the setting of the agenda, and over policy outcomes. These three matters of individual responsiveness, agenda control, and policy responsiveness require separate investigation.

Individual responsiveness refers to the degree to which legislators' individual actions reflect their constituents' policy preferences. Here the incentives are strong for individual legislators to keep their public positions and actions within the bounds of what their constituents find acceptable. There need not be a one-to-one correspondence between a legislator's positions and those of his or her constituents on every issue that comes before Congress, or even a strong correlation between constituency opinion and roll-call voting. What *is* required is that legislators work hard to identify issues that could be used against them and to discover the safest position on each issue. At times these calculations impel legislators to follow the intense preferences of a small minority, at times they encourage legislators to anticipate the potential preferences of a larger group, at times they make legislators attentive to the special needs of their core supporters, and at times they encourage legislators to reach out to their regular opponents.

The central question is not really whether legislators are responsive to citizens, but rather *which* citizens legislators respond to and under what conditions responsiveness varies. [L]egislators are responsive to narrow and organized interests when they are asked to decide about issues for which the group costs and benefits are both visible and directly traceable to their actions while the general costs and benefits are less visible. The power of the National Rifle Association, the dairy lobby, and the banking industry over legislation affecting gun control, dairy price supports, and financial regulation illustrates the point. Yet legislators can also feel bound by the potential preferences of broader and inattentive publics. They are especially responsive to inattentive publics when they are asked to decide about an issue for which the group costs could become visible and traceable if Congress enacted the wrong policy. The degree to which legislators followed the potential preferences of sugar consumers in 1974 or natural gas consumers throughout the 1970s supports this point.

Although it is easy to demonstrate that under the proper conditions legislators respond to citizens' preferences and potential preferences, responsiveness by itself does not guarantee citizens' control over policy outcomes. If the agenda is controlled by other forces, then citizens' influence over the final stage in decision making may offer them little real influence over the important decisions in society. This was the essential insight of Peter Bachrach and Morton Baratz, who argued that the power to keep something off the governmental agenda is at least as important as the power to choose among the few policy options that do make the agenda.[1] Their insight is usually used to support the assertion that corporations or other powerful elites control governmental decision making by keeping all the interesting and important issues off the agenda. In this view, elites are powerful not because they affect the final choices in government but because they guarantee that these choices are between Tweedledum and Tweedledee.

Even if one accepts the basic argument that the ability to keep items off the governmental agenda is an important source of power, it should be noted that the argument also applies to ordinary citizens. Congress frequently avoids acting on problems or considering specific policy options because legislators fear retribution by ordinary citizens. A few examples make the point. Throughout the 1970s Congress refused to consider imposing a massive gasoline tax, despite the evidence that, if coupled with an income tax rebate to avoid either redistribution among income groups or growth in tax revenues, it would be the least intrusive method for curbing demand for imported oil. Throughout the 1980s Congress refused to consider any reductions in Social Security payments for current beneficiaries, despite the massive budget deficit and despite the fact that Social Security expenditures accounted for nearly a quarter of federal expenditures. When Congress considered tax reform in 1986, no one proposed eliminating the deduction for mortgage interest, despite the fact that eliminating this very expensive tax preference would have allowed Congress to reduce tax rates by a few extra points. None of these proposals made it on the congressional agenda because legislators believed that ordinary citizens would not tolerate the imposition of such large, visible, and traceable costs.

The power of the electoral connection may actually be greater at earlier stages of decision making, when legislators are deciding which problems to pursue or which alternatives to consider, rather than at the final stages, when legislators are voting on particular amendments or on a bill's final passage. After sifting through all the roll-call votes taken in Congress over several years, I am struck by how inconsequential many of these decisions really are. Legislators often vote on the trivia in political life—whether to increase or decrease slightly the funding for some program or whether to move the cost of the savings and loan bailout "off budget" rather than counting it as part of the federal deficit. Yet scores of political scientists occupy themselves analyzing these roll-call votes and attempting to determine (among other things) how much constituency opinion affects legislators' decisions. Not surprisingly, they often find that the correlations are weak or nonexistent. Their findings do not, however, prove that legislators are unresponsive to constituency opinion.

Consider the case of the nuclear freeze resolution, which the House debated in 1982 and 1983. Marvin Overby demonstrates that constituency opinion, as measured by the results of ten statewide referenda, had only a modest impact on the first roll-call vote in 1982 and no impact at all on two votes taken in 1983.[2] Initially this seems very puzzling, because the nuclear freeze movement was one of the great grass-roots movements of recent decades. How is it possible that a movement that forced ten states to hold referenda, and achieved strong majorities in nine of them, could not then influence legislators' decisions? The answer is that the movement won most of its points at earlier stages in the legislative process. Its first victory was in forcing the nuclear freeze on the agenda over the determined opposition of the Reagan administration. Its second victory was in forcing opponents of the measure to thwart the proponents by drafting a substitute resolution that was actually a variant of the original freeze proposal. By the time House members were asked to vote on the nuclear freeze, they were essentially choosing between the very strong original proposal and a somewhat weaker proposal backed by the Reagan administration.[3] Legislators could vote as they pleased because most citizens could not tell the difference between the two resolutions. Moreover, the movement actually won the major battle, even though in the end it failed to enact its most-preferred version.

The story of tax reform also supports the argument that constituency opinion can have powerful effects on congressional policy making without ever revealing itself in voting decisions. Those who search for constituency influence by studying roll-call votes would be hard pressed to find it by analyzing all the recorded votes on tax reform. In the House there were only two votes on procedural matters, no recorded votes on amendments, no recorded votes on final passage, and only a single roll call on the conference report. Although the Senate conducted roll-call votes on twenty-four amendments, most of these amendments were on relatively minor matters. Despite the lack of significant divisions that might be related to constituency pressures, and despite the overwhelming majorities that eventually approved the bill, the complete story of tax reform demonstrates that legislators were constantly calculating electoral effects and that most of their initial calculations suggested that the whole enterprise was politically dangerous. One cannot begin to understand how coalition leaders managed to produce a winning coalition in this environment, nor why they incorporated into the bill the specific provisions that they did, without first understanding how legislators balanced various constituency pressures. Unfortunately for those who assess constituency influence by analyzing roll-call votes, virtually all of the relevant decisions were made early in the legislative process, behind closed doors, and without recorded votes.

Although both attentive and inattentive publics can affect the governmental agenda, attentive publics have the clear advantage. Inattentive publics manage to keep some items off the agenda because legislators believe that adopting particular proposals would impose costs on these groups and thereby rouse them to political action. These inattentive publics are unable to force legislators to place items on the governmental agenda, however, because legislators know that inactivity leaves no evidence that can be used to rouse inattentive publics against them. Attentive publics have advantages on both fronts because they do not have to rely on the rule of anticipated reactions. They can monitor exactly who is doing what on Capitol Hill and attempt to nudge policy makers toward including (or excluding) specific items on the agenda.

They can also monitor inactivity on Capitol Hill and pressure the appropriate legislators to initiate action. The constant surveillance by attentive publics is a more precise form of control than the possibility of detection by inattentive publics, and it is symmetric with respect to promoting or preventing action.

Does influence over the agenda and influence over legislators' individual decisions translate into influence over policy outcomes? Are these mechanisms sufficient for citizens to obtain the policy outcomes they really want? Under the proper conditions these mechanisms do help to provide such control, but their success depends in part on the length and complexity of the causal chain connecting a policy instrument with its policy effects. When a causal chain is short and simple, citizens are more likely to know which policy instrument will produce the appropriate effects and are better able to monitor the performance of their representatives. When a causal chain is long and complex, or when a problem in society stems from multiple causes, citizens may be incapable of doing the appropriate policy analysis and political analysis.

Consider the ease with which citizens can hold their representatives accountable on an issue like flag burning. Once the Supreme Court ruled that flag burning was constitutionally protected, it became only a matter of time before Congress would pass a bill attempting to prohibit flag desecration, for both the bill and the procedures required to enact it were simple and easy for citizens to understand. With public opinion strongly in favor, with veterans' groups and the president pushing for action, and with the news media covering the story closely, legislators had little choice but to grant citizens' demands.[4]

Contrast this with the difficulty of holding representatives accountable on complex issues, such as energy or the economy. Most problems in these areas stem from multiple causes, and most of the standard solutions involve long and complicated causal chains. It is difficult for citizens to know what the best solution would be to a problem like inflation, and it is equally difficult for them to monitor legislators' actions on these matters. To the extent that citizens are poor policy analysts, they may obtain the policy instruments they favor but fail to get the policy outcomes they really want because their chosen instruments are incapable of producing the desired effect. Some would argue that this was the case for natural gas in the 1970s. Consumers obtained the regulations they seemed to prefer, but these regulations inhibited rather than promoted the supply of affordable natural gas.

The degree of citizens' control also depends on what procedures Congress employs. As previous chapters have shown repeatedly, legislators' responsiveness to both attentive and inattentive publics varies depending on the procedures that govern how legislators record their positions. When legislators are asked to vote on narrow matters for which the group effects are large and the general effects negligible, they quite naturally pay greater attention to the group effects. When many narrow issues are combined into an omnibus bill that helps to camouflage the group effects and accentuate the general effects, legislators pay greater attention to the general effects. Despite the importance of procedures, citizens seldom have much influence over procedural strategies. Coalition leaders usually select the terms for debate and action. Even when legislators must ratify the chosen procedures with a recorded vote, legislators are generally free of scrutiny. Few citizens have acquired a proper appreciation for the importance of closed or restrictive rules.[5]

The model of citizens' control that I have been discussing is essentially an auditing model. Citizens do not instruct legislators on how to vote, nor do they necessarily have well-defined policy preferences in advance of congressional action. Legislators nevertheless have strong incentives to consider citizens' potential preferences when they are deciding how to vote for fear that making the wrong choice might trigger an unfavorable audit. The fear is not simply that citizens will notice on their own when a legislator errs, but that challengers will investigate fully a legislator's voting record and then share with citizens their interpretations of how he or she has gone wrong.[6]

Those who doubt the power of infrequent audits to affect politicians' behavior should first consider their own behavior when filling out their federal tax returns. Most taxpayers know that the probability of being audited is quite small; yet they nevertheless report most of their income and keep their deductions within the bounds of what they believe future IRS auditors will allow. The probability of audit may be small, but the potential sanctions for failing to anticipate what auditors will allow is very large—ranging from penalties and interest to fines and imprisonment. Although legislators do not face fines and imprisonment (at least for their roll-call decisions), they do face the severe sanction of electoral defeat if they repeatedly fail to anticipate what actions their constituents will allow. Moreover, citizens, like IRS agents, have help in monitoring compliance. Tax auditors receive reports from employers, banks, and brokers about taxpayers' financial transactions, from which they can make inferences about how faithful taxpayers are in reporting their income and deductions. Citizens receive reports from challengers, interest groups, and the media about legislators' positions and actions, and they too can make inferences about how faithful legislators are in representing their policy preferences.

The incumbent performance rule clearly requires more information and analysis than the party performance rule in order for citizens to control their government. Under the party performance rule, citizens can achieve control simply by knowing which party is in power and deciding whether or not they like current conditions in society. In contrast, the incumbent performance rule requires that citizens be both policy analysts and political analysts. They need to know something about the causes of society's problems and something about how various proposals would affect their interests. They also need to know something about what their legislators are doing to advance or retard those interests.

Reforms

The complexity of the incumbent performance rule and the inequitable distribution of information required for its proper use make this a far less effective mechanism for controlling government than the party performance rule. This fact usually impels political scientists to close with a call for strengthening the parties. If only we had strong parties (they argue), then government would be more responsive, responsible, and accountable. Unfortunately, the tide has been moving in the opposite direction for several decades. Political parties today are weak, and no one has set forth a politically feasible plan for reversing the tide.

If parties are weak and the prospects for strengthening them are slim, then the alternative route for those who seek to increase citizens' control of government is to reform congressional procedures so that the incumbent performance rule functions more effectively and so that legislators are responsive to general interests as well as group interests. Although this was the intent of those who reformed procedures in the 1970s, many of the reforms have had the opposite effect. Reformers demanded that all committee meetings must be open, but all this openness has actually allowed narrowly based interest groups to monitor legislators more closely and has thereby made legislators more responsive to group interests. Reformers demanded an end to the closed rule because it was antidemocratic, but most of the amendments proposed without benefit of the rule have been particularistic proposals that serve group interests. Reformers demanded an end to secret, unrecorded votes, but the increased reliance on recorded votes has actually made it easier for narrow groups to hold legislators accountable because most of these votes are on particularistic amendments.

Several reforms have been more effective in promoting citizens' control and reducing the dominance of particularistic interests. The creation of budget committees and a congressional budget process has forced legislators to consider and act on the larger questions of economic policy rather than just on the narrower questions of how much to spend on specific programs. Changes in the selection process for the House Rules Committee have made this committee an ally of the party leadership and have thereby forced it to write rules that accommodate more general interests. Ad hoc committees have allowed Congress to handle questions that span many committees (such as energy), and special governmental commissions have helped legislators to act on issues that are too hot for existing committees to handle (such as Social Security). All of these changes and innovations allow both legislators and citizens to focus on the larger policy issues.

Most important, perhaps, is that legislators have been willing to ignore some of the reforms that have not worked. Committees now regularly close their doors when they are writing difficult bills, such as tax increases, that impose substantial costs on citizens. Even when they do meet in public, they sometimes work out the difficult issues in a huddle at the front of the room and then announce their decisions to the assembled reporters and lobbyists at the rear. The House Rules Committee has also refined the art of writing restrictive rules so that complicated bills do not unravel in a flurry of particularistic amendments, while still preserving both legislators' ability to make choices about the larger issues and citizens' ability to monitor legislators' choices.

Legislators have discovered the strengths and weaknesses of specific procedures by trial and error. Open meetings, open rules, and unlimited recorded votes seemed like good ideas when they were proposed, and they were backed by Common Cause and others who sought to reduce the power of special interests. Unfortunately, these reforms were based on a faulty understanding of the mechanisms that allow for citizens' control. We now know that open meetings filled with lobbyists, and recorded votes on scores of particularistic amendments, serve to increase the powers of special interests, not to diminish them.

A proper understanding of the incumbent performance rule suggests how procedures can be designed to reduce the power of special interests. The key is to ask legislators to stand up and be counted on the broader policy issues, issues for which the general effects overshadow the group and geographic effects, and to curtail the ability of legislators to propose endless particularistic amendments. Restrictive procedures of this kind need not be antidemocratic. Senator Packwood's proposal that all amendments to the tax reform bill must be revenue neutral had to be approved by his colleagues before it became effective. Once approved, it prevented senators from proposing a series of attractive amendments that would have gradually undermined the entire bill. Similarly, legislators must approve closed and restrictive rules before they are bound by their provisions. Presumably they approve such restrictions on their own autonomy only if they believe that the resulting bills are politically acceptable.

I am convinced that it is possible to increase the potential for citizens' control of government without first transforming weak parties into strong parties. In order to do so, however, one needs to understand the links among citizens, legislators, and policy outcomes. The more one understands how those links operate, the more likely it is that reform efforts will actually contribute to democratic control of government.

NOTES

1. See Peter Bachrach and Morton S. Baratz, "Two Faces of Power," *American Political Science Review* 56 (1962): 947–952; and Bachrach and Baratz, "Decisions and Nondecisions: An Analytical Framework," *American Political Science Review* 57 (1963): 641–651.

2. L. Marvin Overby, "Assessing Constituency Influence: A Loglinear Model of Congressional Voting on the Nuclear Freeze, 1982–1983" (paper presented at the annual meeting of the Southwestern Political Science Association, March, 1989).

3. Ibid.

4. The House approved the bill on flag desecration 380 to 38, and the Senate followed, 91 to 9. Once Congress passed this bill, it became much easier to block a constitutional amendment on the same subject—especially in the Senate, where the electoral clock ticks more slowly—because most senators had used the previous vote to establish their position against flag burning. The Senate rejected the proposed constitutional amendment 51 to 48 (15 votes short of the two-thirds required). For the complete story, see Martha Angle, "Flag-Desecration Legislation Passed by House," *Congressional Quarterly Weekly Report* 47 (September 16, 1989): 2400; Joan Biskupic, "Senate Amends, Then Passes Bill on Flag Desecration," *Congressional Quarterly Weekly Report* 47 (October 7, 1989): 2646; and Joan Biskupic, "Anti–Flag Burning Amendment Falls Far Short in Senate," *Congressional Quarterly Weekly Report* 47 (October 21, 1989): 2803–2804.

5. Presidents and journalists could easily raise citizens' consciousness on the importance of some procedural votes. President Reagan did so in 1981 and thereby pressured House members to support the closed rule on his budget proposal. The *Wall Street Journal* did so in 1989 by including in an editorial the names of more than a hundred Democrats in the House who claimed to support the repeal of a tax provision that was particularly burdensome for small businesses but who had actually opposed the procedural device that was required to include the repeal amendment in the pending bill. Several weeks after the editorial appeared, House members passed the repeal amendment, 390 to 36. See Paul Starobin, "Section 89 Repeal Drive: Taking No Prisoners," *Congressional Quarterly Weekly Report* 47 (September 30, 1989): 2543–2547.

6. For a contrary view of citizens' control of government—one that asserts that it is practically nonexistent—see Robert A. Bernstein, *Elections, Representation, and Congressional Voting Behavior: The Myth of Constituency Control* (Englewood Cliffs, N.J.: Prentice Hall, 1989). My own views diverge from Bernstein's in several important respects. First, I do not require that citizens have policy preferences in advance of congressional action but rather argue that legislators anticipate how citizens might react if legislators failed to anticipate citizens' potential preferences. Second, I do not accept as evidence that legislators have failed to heed constituents' preferences on an issue the fact that there is no relationship between constituency opinion and reelection results, for such findings are equally consistent with the notion that legislators anticipate the likelihood of electoral retribution and adjust their decisions accordingly.

5.3

GERALD STROM

From *The Logic of Lawmaking*

Strom offers a set of concepts to help us understand legislative politics. Adopting a "rational actor" approach to legislative behavior, he describes theories from political science that indicate how the median voter is a key actor in collective decision making. Often, legislation is determined by how the most moderate legislator (the median) votes.

1. DEFINITIONS AND ASSUMPTIONS

The Nature of Legislative Preferences

Once it is taken as given that legislative actors have preferences for legislative outcomes (regardless of the source of these preferences) and can adopt maximizing strategies to attain them, the next step is to examine the relationships among these given preferences. A core element of the rational actor theory is a set of assumptions about people's preferences. If you prefer both to read this essay and not to read it, you have a problem because your preferences are contradictory. In such circumstances, it is impossible to act rationally to pursue your preferences because you cannot develop a strategy that simultaneously allows you to read and not read this essay. Presumably, the fact that you got this far indicates that your preference for reading this essay outweighs your preference for not reading it (of course, this might change as you proceed). Moreover, in continuing to read, you are giving up opportunities to do other things you might also prefer, like reading a different book, watching television, or going to a movie. What this example illustrates is that, at any given time, people have many different preferences, and these preferences are related to each other. It is these relationships among preferences which the assumptions discussed below concern.

If you were a member of the U.S. House of Representatives in 1986 and could choose between voting for or against the higher education bill as it emerged from committee, only one of three possible conditions logically must characterize your preferences for these two options. (1) You can prefer the bill to the status quo of no bill; (2) you can prefer the status quo to the bill; or (3) you can prefer them equally (in which case, you are said to be indifferent between the bill and the status quo.)[1] The fact that only one of these relations must hold between the two preferences is referred to as the *connectedness* axiom. In requiring connectedness, rational actor theories are requiring that an actor's preferences concerning a given set of outcomes are connected or related to each other so they can be compared. More technically, if we let $u(B)$ represent the amount of utility or satisfaction a person would receive if the bill passes and $u(Q)$ the amount of utility if no bill passes, then we can express the connectedness axiom as implying that only one of the following relations holds:

$$u(B) > u(Q)$$
$$u(B) < u(Q)$$
$$u(B) = u(Q)$$

Also, by letting P stand for *is preferred to*, the first of these relations could have been written BPQ; and by letting I represent *is indifferent to*, the last one could have been expressed as BIQ. Finally, the relation R is defined as *is preferred to or is indifferent to* and can be defined formally as either P or I. Using this new symbol, the connectedness axiom can be written as either BRQ or QRB. Expressions like $u(B)$ occur frequently in the literature of rational actor theory, and it is important to be clear about what such terms mean. Above, $u(B)$ was defined as *the utility that an actor associates with outcome B*. What does this mean? As used in rational actor theory, utility is an abstract concept. Utility itself is never observed, and there is no need to measure it precisely because there is no need to know just what value $u(B)$ has.[2] Rather, all one needs to know is whether $u(B)$ is greater than, less than, or equal to the utility associated with some other outcome. That is, it is the *relationships* among the utilities associated with various outcomes which are important. One wants to know whether $u(B) > u(Q)$, or $u(B) < u(Q)$, or $u(B) = u(Q)$, not the precise values of $u(B)$ or $u(Q)$. All one needs to know, in other words, are ordinal relationships, not interval values.

Also note that as a consequence of the precise value of $u(B)$ being unobserved and unmeasured, there is no way one can compare the utility of two different actors. It can be said that two actors both prefer $u(B)$ to $u(Q)$, but one cannot say that one of them prefers B to Q more than the other one does.[3] Because such interpersonal comparisons of utility are not possible, the only utility comparisons made are for a single actor; and if many actors are involved in a decision, a separate set of comparisons is made for each person.

Now, consider a choice among three alternatives: a bill reported from a committee (B), an amended version of this bill (A), and no bill (or the status quo, Q). If a legislator prefers the bill over the amended version of the bill and prefers the amended version over no bill, should the legislator also prefer the bill over no bill? If so, this legislator would be said to have *transitive* preferences. Rational action presumes transitive preferences so that BPA and APQ

implies *BPQ*.[4] Without it, a legislator cannot develop a strategy to pursue his or her preferences effectively. If the legislator prefers the bill to the amended version, the amended version to no bill, and no bill to the bill, his or her preferences are *intransitive*. Therefore, this legislator, with *BPA*, *APQ*, and *QPB*, cannot make a rational choice because regardless of what alternative he or she chooses, there will always be a better alternative available. Thus, if the legislator thought about voting for the bill, he or she would not because no bill is preferred; but the legislator would not vote against the bill either because the amended version is preferable to no bill; and finally, the legislator would not vote for the amended version because the bill is preferable to the amended version. Theories of rational action, through the transitivity assumption, assume that such vicious circles do not exist.[5]

These two assumptions or axioms, connectedness and transitivity, are the core of all theories of rational action. They imply that a rational actor has a consistent and noncontradictory set of preferences over any set of alternatives. It is thus assumed that the choices a rational actor makes as a consequence of these preferences will also be consistent. This consistency, in turn, implies that the behavior of a rational actor is predictable from a knowledge of his or her preferences.

Note, finally, that rational actor theory as described here assumes a relatively short time perspective within which actors do not change their preferences. Thus, the consistency referred to above is a short-term consistency resulting from a fixed set of preferences over a set of alternatives. This is consistent with the fact that rational actor theories take preferences as given and do not try to explain why people hold the preferences they do. Nothing in the assumptions, however, precludes rational actors from changing their preferences over time. All that is required here is that actors do not change their preferences while in the process of deciding among a particular set of alternatives. In other words, preferences are assumed to be fixed during the duration of a given decision-making process.

Representing Preferences

A useful way to examine and analyze preferences (and the behaviors they cause) is to represent them pictorially or spatially. One very useful way this can be done was suggested by Black (1958). On a two-dimensional graph, let the *horizontal axis* (the *abscissa*) represent outcomes on which actors have preferences, and let the *vertical axis* (the *ordinate*) represent their preference rankings. With the higher education bill, for example, the three options of no bill, reported bill, and amended bill can be represented along the horizontal axis, and the preference ranking of legislators for these alternatives can be represented on the vertical axis as in Figure 1. It does not matter (at this stage) in what order the alternatives are placed on the horizontal axis, nor is it presumed here that distance has any significance on either axis. The prefer-

FIGURE 1 Individual Preference Curve over Three Alternatives

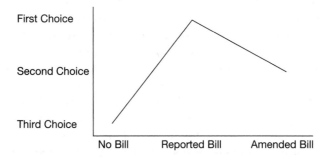

FIGURE 2 Individual Preference Curve with Indifference between Two Alternatives

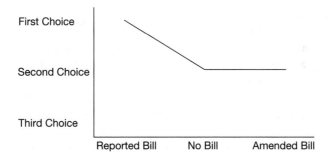

ences of a legislator who most preferred the reported bill can be represented by placing a dot at the point at which lines drawn from *reported bill* and *first choice* meet and similarly for the legislator's other preferences. If these points are now connected by a line, always moving from left to right (and knowing that the spaces between the alternatives are meaningless), a preference curve for this individual is created (as in Figure 1).

Note that the ability to represent preferences in this way requires that these preferences be both connected and transitive. Connectedness implies that preferences over outcomes are related to each other and hence can be represented together on the same graph. Transitivity, in turn, actually allows one to place the points in the figure. To see this, consider what would happen if a legislator did not have transitive preferences. In the case illustrated in Figure 1, for example, if a legislator held the preference order no bill > amended bill > reported bill > no bill, which outcome is his or her first choice? It cannot be no bill because both the amended bill and the reported bill are preferred to no bill. Likewise, it cannot be either of these others because no bill is preferred to them. Thus, in representing preferences as in Figure 1, the set of preferences needs to be both connected and transitive.

Also note in Figure 2 how indifference between two alternatives can be represented as a horizontal line. Thus, given the ordering of the alternatives in this figure, a legislator who preferred the reported bill to both an amended bill and no bill and was indifferent between the latter two would have a preference curve that fell from the first choice of the reported bill to the no bill position and then was horizontal to the amended bill position. Alternatively, given the order of alternatives in Figure 2, if a legislator were indifferent between the bill and an amended bill and preferred both to no bill, the curve would be horizontal between the location of the reported bill and amended bill alternatives and would then fall to the no bill alternative.

In both Figures 1 and 2, it can be seen that the preference curves have a single peak (in both cases, it is over the reported bill alternative). Note that the preference curve would also have one peak if the alternatives were rearranged with the reported bill alternative on the left, the amended bill alternative in the middle, and no bill on the right. More generally, a curve will have only one peak if, in moving from left to right, one never draws the line up after drawing it down. Although the number of peaks in a preference curve may seem like a strange thing with which to be concerned, Black (1958) recognized that the single peakedness of a set of preference curves is very significant; and because of this, one always tries, if possible, to draw curves that are single peaked (rearranging the alternatives on the horizontal axis if necessary to produce a single-peaked curve).

For one individual, it is always possible to find a way to arrange the alternatives, regardless of how many there are, so that the preference curve is single peaked. One way this can be done is to put the most preferred alternative on the left, the second most preferred outcome next to it, and so forth so that the least preferred alternative is on the right. It is also possible with some orderings of preferences to do this simultaneously for multiple individuals. For example, consider a hypothetical case in which the 435-member House is divided into three equal groups on a bill like the higher education bill. The 145 members of each of these groups might have the following preference orders:

> Group 1: reported bill > amended bill > no bill
> Group 2: amended bill > reported bill > no bill
> Group 3:   no bill   > amended bill > reported bill

Given these preference orders, if the alternatives are arrayed on the abscissa so that *reported bill* is on the left, *amended bill* is in the middle, and *no bill* is on the right, it can be seen in Figure 3 that the preference curves for all three groups are simultaneously single peaked.[6]

Sometimes, however, for a given set of preference orders, it is not possible to represent all the orders simultaneously with single-peaked preference curves. Consider, for example, that if instead of the preference orders seen in Figure 3, the preference orders for the three groups are as follows:

FIGURE 3   Preference Curves for Three Groups over Three Alternatives

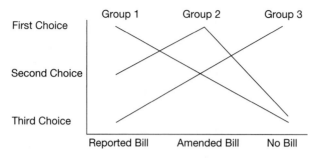

FIGURE 4   Preference Curves for Three Groups over Three Alternatives

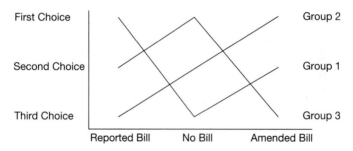

Group 1:   reported bill > amended bill > no bill
Group 2:   amended bill > no bill   > reported bill
Group 3:   no bill   > reported bill > amended bill

In this case, it is impossible to find an ordering of the alternatives which makes all curves simultaneously single peaked. Thus, in Figure 4, the preference curve for group 1 is not single peaked. With a different ordering of the alternatives on the abscissa, the preferences curve for group 1 can be made to have a single peak; but in the process of doing this, one of the other curves becomes non-single peaked. For example, in Figure 5, the order of alternatives is changed from that in Figure 4, and now group 2 has a non-single-peaked preference curve.

Single-Peaked Preference Curves and Equilibrium Outcomes

The basic reason for the concern in the spatial models of legislatures with single-peaked preference curves is that Black (1958) was able to show that if an ordering of the alternatives can be found so that all the preference curves are single peaked, the outcome under the median (or middle) peak will receive a majority against any other outcome.[7] Thus, in Figure 3, the amended bill outcome would receive the votes of groups 2 and 3 in a vote between this

FIGURE 5 Preference Curves for Three Groups over Three Alternatives

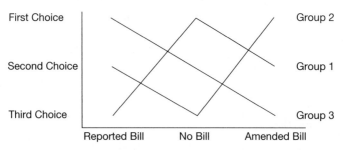

alternative and the reported bill alternative because the preference curves for these two groups rise in moving from the reported bill position to the amended bill position, which implies that both prefer the amended bill to the reported bill. Similarly, the curves for groups 1 and 2 rise in going from the no bill position to the amended bill position, and so the members of these two groups prefer the amended bill to no bill and would vote for the amended bill alternative. Thus, of these three alternatives, the amended bill, because it is under the middle preference curve, cannot be defeated by either of the other two alternatives.

The importance of this conclusion can be seen by contrasting the case of the preferences in Figure 3 with those illustrated in Figure 4. In the former case, all the preference curves are simultaneously single peaked, and a single outcome was shown to defeat each of the other alternatives. However, for the preferences illustrated in Figure 4, the curves are not all simultaneously single peaked. From these curves it can be seen that the reported bill alternative defeats the amended bill alternative; the no bill alternative defeats the reported bill; and the amended bill alternative defeats no bill (which, in turn, is defeated by the reported bill alternative). Thus, in this case, there is no alternative that defeats all of the other alternatives. Rather, there is a circular pattern among the three alternatives such that any given alternative is defeated by one of the others. In this case, it is impossible to know which alternative the legislature would select.

In Figure 3, in which all the preference curves are single peaked and the amended bill alternative is the one located under the median preference peak, this alternative can be referred to as an *equilibrium outcome*. Just as in economics wherein the intersection of supply and demand curves defines a market equilibrium, a voting equilibrium is one toward which the voting system will generally move if it is not there already; and once there, it will not depart.[8] Viewed in this way, the notion of an equilibrium is important for predicting what is likely to happen in a decision-making process such as voting. When an equilibrium exists, it is generally predicted that the process will move to the equilibrium position and then remain there. The equilibrium, in other words, represents the predicted outcome. It is for this reason that legislative decision models (like other models of dynamic processes) generally try to identify the conditions under which an equilibrium will exist and then to identify what the specific equilibrium will be.

In trying to determine the conditions under which legislative policy processes will or will not have an equilibrium, one must be careful to specify the kind of decision rule (e.g., majority rule) under which voting will be conducted. In the above example, it was assumed that all voting takes place as a choice between two alternatives. A variant of what is often called Condorcet voting, this is the typical type of voting specified in parliamentary procedure, and it will be referred to here as the *legislative voting process*.[9] With such a voting procedure, votes can be taken on whether or not to amend a bill, whether or not to pass a bill, whether or not to adopt a particular motion, and whether or not to end consideration of an issue. All these are dichotomous choices between only two options. This does not imply, however, that a legislature cannot consider more than two alternatives. Legislators can consider as many different alternatives (or motions) as they want; but with the legislative voting process, they must consider them two at a time.[10]

Thus, what Black (1958) proved is that if a committee or legislature is making a unidimensional decision under the legislative voting process, and if an ordering of the alternatives on the abscissa can be found so that the preference curves of all voters are single peaked, the outcome under the median (or middle) peak is a voting equilibrium that can defeat all other alternatives.[11] This equilibrium outcome is also the Condorcet winner or the Condorcet winning alternative. In Figure 3, the amended bill alternative is the alternative under the median peak; and hence by Black's theorem, it must be the voting equilibrium. It would be possible to rearrange the alternatives in Figure 3 so that the amended bill alternative is no longer under the median peak; but in this case, the result would be that the preference curves are no longer all single peaked.

Note, too, that the examples in this chapter have used a discrete, and usually small, number of alternatives on the horizontal axis. The application of Black's theorem, however, is not restricted only to discrete cases because restriction on the number of alternatives considered is not a part of the assumptions behind the theorem. Because of this, the theorem is applicable to any number of alternatives, even an infinite number, as long as the preference curves over these alternatives are single peaked.

2. THE UNIDIMENSIONAL MODEL OF LEGISLATIVE DECISION MAKING

. . . How can a Black-type unidimensional model be used to analyze actual legislative decision making? As will be shown here, such a model is useful for examining both the outcomes of legislative decision making and the impact of various rules and structures on such outcomes.

FIGURE 6 Preference Curves of a Seven-Person School Board with Respect to the Salary Increase of the Superintendent

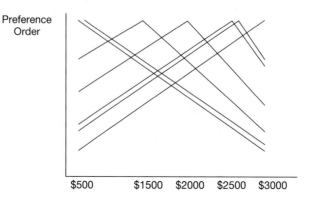

Consider first how the model can be used to analyze legislative outcomes. Several years ago, the seven-members school board on which I serve was trying to determine the amount of a salary increase for superintendent of schools. Two of the members favored a $500 increase, one favored $1500, one favored $2000, two favored $2500, and one favored $3000. As there was no other issue involved, this was a unidimensional decision, and it seems appropriate to assume that all the board members had transitive and single-peaked preferences (e.g., the members who favored a $500 increase preferred it to an increase of $1500, $2000, or larger). Thus, it is possible to use the model of the previous chapter and represent the preferences of the seven members as in Figure 6.[12] By examining the preference curves, it can be seen that the median peak is the one over *$2000*, making that the predicted outcomes of Black's median outcome model. In the actual case at hand, this turned out to be a very good prediction, because after much discussion and several votes, the board decided to give the superintendent a $2000 increase.

It might be thought that in a case like this, the members would simply split the difference between the high and low values; but the midpoint of the $500–$3000 range is $1750, and that was not the correct outcome. Alternatively, the members could have added all their preferred positions together and divided by 7 to give the mean, or average outcome; but in this case, the yield would have been $1789, which again is not a correct prediction. Thus, in this case, there is fairly strong evidence that a Black-type median outcome model is the most appropriate and accurate way to characterize the outcome.

Note also that, in this case, it makes no difference in which order the alternatives are considered. Because all the preference curves are single peaked and the $2000 outcome is under the median peak, it can defeat any of the other outcomes in a majority vote. Thus, the $2000 outcome will win regard-

FIGURE 7 Preference Curves of Five Groups of Legislators Concerning Five Weapons Systems

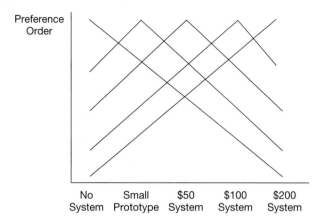

less of the order of voting, and this is generally true when all the preference curves are simultaneously single peaked.

As a second example of using the unidimensional model to predict legislative policy outcome, consider a hypothetical case of decision making in the U.S. House of Representatives. Assume that the president has proposed a new weapons system for the Army which will cost between $50 and $200 million dollars over three years (and assume that the actual costs are not currently known). It is known, however, that 178 members of the House are opposed to building the system whatever its cost, that 40 members favor only building a small prototype so that better cost and effectiveness estimates can be made, that 190 members favor the system if it can be built for $50 million or less, that only 17 members favor building it if it costs $100 million or less, and that 10 members favor it even if it costs $200 million. Note that these preferences are arranged in Figure 7 from *no system* through various partial systems to a full $200 million system. The question then is which position the House is likely to adopt if all the preference curves are single peaked. With 435 members, a House majority consists of 218 members. With a Black-type model, then, one needs to find the position of the 218th preference curves (counting from either side). Here, 178 plus 40 is exactly 218, so the median peak is over the *small prototype* position, and that would be the expected outcome.

Of course, it could be argued here that anyone can add 178 and 40 and get 218 and does not need a spatial model or Black's theorem to do so. However, it is the logic of Black's theorem which allows this addition to make sense. The assumptions from which the theorem is derived allow one to predict that the 178 members who wanted no system would vote in favor of the prototype alternative against all other proposals except the one to build no system. Similarly, the assumptions are that all those who wanted to build more than a prototype would vote against the prototype in a vote against a more than prototype system but would favor the prototype over no system. Thus, the single-peak assumption provides a reason for adding 178 to 40 which otherwise would not exist. Note also that if all the curves were not single peaked, the adding of 40 and 178 would likely produce the wrong answer, as subsequent results will show.

Consider now a second use of a Black-type model which can be found in the literature on legislative decision making. This concerns attempts to determine what effects various institutional arrangements have on legislative outcomes. Both Denzau and Mackay (1983) and Krehbiel (1987), for example, used such a model to examine the powers of committees to affect legislation. By assuming that bills can be treated as unidimensional phenomena and that legislators have single-peaked preferences, they can employ Black's theorem about the outcome under the median peak to determine whether committees will be influential in Congress. Consider, for example, Figure 8, in which the *horizontal line* represents positions on a single-issue dimension. Let Q represent the current law on the dimension (the status quo position) that remains in effect if no new law is passed. Similarly, let *CM* represent the outcome under the median peak for the committee on this dimension, and let *FM* represent the median for a full legislative chamber.[13] This means that in the committee, a majority prefer position *CM* to all other positions, and the committee would be expected to report a bill corresponding to position *CM*.[14] If there are no rules limiting full chamber amendments, the position *CM* reported by the committee will then be amended in the full chamber to position *FM*. Note, too, that in this case, the status quo position Q has no impact on the outcome, and this would be true regardless of the location of Q in the issue space. In this case, it is clear that neither the committee nor the status quo has any independent influence on the legislative outcome. The full chamber median *FM* would win whether or not a committee existed which reported *CM* to the full chamber, and *FM* would also win regardless of the location of the status quo position. Thus, this straightforward application of the median voter theorem shows that if committees are indeed powerful in Congress, it must be because of other characteristics of committees or the chambers themselves.

One set of such characteristics includes various sophisticated strategies employed by committees to win in the full chamber, and we will consider these in the next chapter. Another set includes the various rules and procedures governing the legislative process in the Congress. One of these, which is considered here, is a closed rule, which bars the full chamber from amending bills reported from committee.

In Figure 8, it was seen that with an open rule, the committee bill was amended in the full chamber to the position *FM* and that the status quo position Q had no impact on the result. However, if a closed rule were in effect for this case, both these conclusions would become invalid. With a closed rule, the full chamber cannot amend position *CM*, and so full chamber actors

FIGURE 8 Location of the Floor Median (*FM*), the Status Quo (Q), and the Committee Median (*CM*) in a One-Dimensional Issue Space

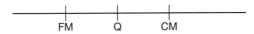

FIGURE 9 Location of the Floor Median (*FM*), the Status Quo (Q), and the Committee Median (*CM*) in a One-Dimensional Issue Space

are faced with a choice between accepting or rejecting *CM*. Moreover, if *CM* is rejected, the status quo position Q wins by default. In Figure 8, it can be seen that the status quo Q is between *FM* and *CM*, which means that a full chamber majority prefer Q to *CM*; so in this case, they could be expected to reject the committee bill.

Consider now the case illustrated in Figure 9, in which Q is not between *CM* and *FM*. As in the previous case, Black's theorem predicts that the committee would report *CM* to the full chamber. In this case, however, it can be seen that *CM* is closer to *FM* than is Q, so a full chamber majority would prefer *CM* to Q and would vote to adopt *CM*. Thus, in this case, the committee wins, and this result was made possible by the closed rule barring the full chamber from amending *CM* to position *FM*. The presence or absence of such a rule, in other words, can determine outcomes as much as the preferences of the actors themselves. Moreover, note that the closed rule and others like it also make the position of the status quo an important factor in determining outcomes. With no restrictive rules, the position of the status quo was irrelevant; but with a restrictive rule, this position can be important. In particular, for the examples here, a status quo between *CM* and *FM* will always be adopted under a closed rule because a full chamber majority prefers such a Q to *CM*. Similarly, when *CM* is between *FM* and Q, as in Figure 9, Q will never be adopted because *CM* is closer to *FM* than is Q. Finally, when *FM* is between *CM* and Q, the outcome will be Q if the preference curves of full chamber actors fall more rapidly in the *FM–CM* interval than they do in the *FM–Q* interval, and it will be *CM* if they fall faster in *FM–Q* than in *FM–CM*.

The Problem of Non-Single-Peaked Preference Curves

In the preceding section, it was shown how a simple, unidimensional spatial model can be used to represent legislative decision making. In doing this, it was assumed that the alternatives could be arranged on the single dimension so that the preference curves of all the legislators were single peaked. In turn, this allowed the use of Black's theorem to predict which alternative would be chosen. What happens when the single-peaked assumption does not hold, and it is not possible to find an arrangement of alternatives which produces single-peaked preference curves for all actors? In the higher education bill, for example, such would be the case if many but not all of the members who wanted to provide more money for student loans ranked positions lower, the less money they provided, but some also preferred a "do it right or don't do it at all" philosophy and ranked spending no money second to spending a great deal of money. There is no way the alternatives on this dimension can be arranged so that the preference curves of both sets of legislators are simultaneously single peaked.

Note first that single peakedness is a sufficient, but not a necessary, condition for a stable equilibrium outcome in unidimensional decision making. This means that if all the curves are single peaked, a stable outcome is predicted to exist, but such an outcome *might* also occur when all the curves are not single peaked. Because of this, nothing very drastic may happen if all the preference curves are not single peaked. However, since the additional conditions needed to guarantee an equilibrium (see Sen and Pattanaik 1969) are fairly stringent and are seldom likely to occur, it appears that majority voting schemes are likely to produce unpredictable results when preference curves are not single peaked.[15]

As a simple illustration of the problems that can result from majority voting processes when all the curves are not single peaked, consider again a simple three-person legislature weighing three different alternatives. Assume that the preferences of the three legislators for the three alternatives are as follows:

$$
\begin{array}{ll}
\text{Legislator 1:} & X > Y > Z \\
\text{Legislator 2:} & Y > Z > X \\
\text{Legislator 3:} & Z > X > Y
\end{array}
$$

There is no arrangement of these three alternatives on the horizontal axis which will produce single-peaked preferences for all three legislators. As in Figure 4, of Chapter 1, one of the curves will always have more than one peak. Here, let alternative Z be the status quo position, and assume that this three-person legislature uses the legislative voting process whereby all votes are between only two alternatives. What outcome will be adopted?

In a legislature like Congress, the status quo motion is voted on last—that is, the final vote is on whether or not to pass the bill, which is equivalent to a decision between adopting the bill or the status quo of no bill. Thus, here, if legislator 1 first proposes that X be adopted, and legislator 2 then proposes Y (e.g., as an amendment to X), the first vote will be between X and Y. Legislators 1 and 3 prefer X to Y, so the outcome of this first vote will be X (i.e., the amendment is defeated). Now, X is put against the status quo Z, and because legislators 2 and 3 prefer Z to X, they will vote against X, and the status quo Z will be implicitly adopted. This all looks fine, but consider now what happens if the order in which the outcomes are voted on is altered. Assume that instead of the status quo entering last, the legislative rules specify that after a motion is made, it is immediately put against the status quo. The winner of this vote then defines the new (or same) status quo, and a new motion can be made to change this outcome. In the example, this rule implies that if legislator 1 first proposes X, the initial vote will be between X and Z. As legislators 2 and 3 prefer Z to X, Z will win; and then, after legislator 2 proposes Y, a second vote will be held between Y and Z. In this case, legislators 1 and 2 both prefer Y to Z, so the final outcome will be Y.

Working with the non-single-peaked preferences given above, majority voting produced two different outcomes. In one case, alternative Z won; and in another, alternative Y won. The preferences were the same, and the same majority voting system was used both times, but two different outcomes resulted when all that changed were the rules specifying the order in which votes would occur. Thus, in this case, it is impossible to predict which outcome will be adopted from the preferences of the three legislators; one also needs to know the order in which the alternatives will be considered. The basic reason for this outcome can be seen by examining closely the preference orders of the three legislators. A majority prefers X to Y, another majority prefers Y to Z, and still a third majority prefers Z to X. Here, the group level preference ordering is intransitive. Thus, an intransitive social ordering results from the voting system even though all the individuals held transitive individual preference orderings. As a whole, the legislature in this case cannot decide what outcome to enact. Whichever alternative is chosen, one majority will prefer something else: if X is chosen, a majority prefers Z; if Z is chosen, a majority prefers Y; and if Y is chosen, a majority prefers X.

Kenneth Arrow (1951) showed that in general, there is no way to guarantee a transitive social preference ordering for outcomes. A transitive order may exist with a Condorcet alternative that defeats all others, but one cannot be sure of this without violating some rules usually considered fundamental to democratic voting systems.[16] If the social preference orderings are intransitive, no equilibrium may exist, so that the outcome chosen is likely to be both unstable and unpredictable, depending upon such things as the order in which the alternatives are considered.[17] Because of the importance of this problem, almost all the subsequent work on legislative and other forms of collective decision making has in one way or another sought to deal with this *paradox of voting* or the *Arrow paradox*.

Another even more devastating demonstration of the paradox has been described by Plott (1976). He considers the case of three legislators and four alternatives. Let the preference orders for the three legislators be as follows for the four alternatives W, X, Y, and Z:

Legislator 1: $Y > X > W > Z$
Legislator 2: $X > W > Z > Y$
Legislator 3: $W > Z > Y > X$

If the other of voting is such that W is first put against X, with the winner against Y, and then the winner of this second round against Z, the outcome can be seen to be Z (X defeats W, Y defeats X, and Z defeats Y). Notice, however, that all three legislators prefer W to Z. In other words, the outcome W that was unanimously preferred to Z lost to Z in the voting. Clearly, there is a major problem here. How, for example, would we explain why Z won when every legislator preferred W to Z? The answer is that Z won because it was one of the last two alternatives on which a vote was taken. Had Z entered first against either X or W, it would have been eliminated in the first round. Thus, given a set of preference orders, the order of voting on alternatives turns out to be the major factor in determining which alternative is chosen.

Note also that these problems are not just artificial, resulting from the preferences specifically used in the example above. These are real problems that can arise in real decision-making situations. Riker (1958), for example, discovered a case in which just such a problem arose. In 1953, the House of Representatives was considering the Agriculture Appropriations Act of 1953 where "the most significant and controversial subject was the amount of money for the Soil Conservation Service" (p. 357). As reported by the committee on appropriations, $250 million was allocated for the service. During full House consideration, Representative Javits (Republican, New York) offered an amendment to change this $250 million to $142.41 million. Representative O'Toole (Democrat, New York) then moved to amend the Javits amendment by setting the figure at $100 million. House rules prohibited further amendments to the O'Toole amendment, but did permit a substitute to the first (Javits) amendment and then an amendment to this substitute amendment. Thus, under the rules, Representative Anderson (Republican, Minnesota) was able to offer a substitute amendment setting the figure at $200 million. Finally, Representative Whitten (Democrat, Mississippi), the subcommittee chairman, offered an amendment to the Anderson substitute setting the figure at $225 million.

As is shown in Table 1, at this stage, there were five separate proposals before the House. By House rules, the first vote was held on whether or not the Javits amendment should be amended with the one offered by O'Toole. On this vote, the O'Toole amendment failed, so the Javits amendment was not amended. The second vote was then held on whether or not the Anderson substitute should be amended by the Whitten amendment. On this vote, the Whitten amendment failed. The third vote was thus between the unamended Javits amendment and the unamended Anderson substitute. On this vote, the Anderson substitute lost, and a final vote (before passage of the whole bill) was held between the Javits amendment and the original committee proposal. On this vote, the Javits amendment lost, so the original committee proposal was not changed.

By themselves, these various votes do not demonstrate the existence of an intransitive social preference ordering. However, as Riker (1958) noted (p. 358):

TABLE 1 Proposals before the House Concerning the Soil
Conservation Service Appropriations in 1953

Proposal	Amount
Committee recommendation	$250 million
Javits amendment	$142 million
O'Toole amendment to Javits	$100 million
Anderson substitute to Javits	$200 million
Whitten amendment to Anderson	$225 million

From the fact that all amendments failed one might infer that a majority favored the original proposal. Nevertheless, one awkward fact casts
doubt on this inference: although the largest amount stayed in the bill,
the third largest amount (Anderson) beat the second largest amount
(Whitten). From this fact one may reasonably suspect an intransitivity
here, for if the largest amount were really favored over all others, and
the amount was the dominant criterion, then logically the second largest sum should have defeated the third largest.

Further, from a more detailed analysis of voting patterns, Riker showed that
none of the alternatives in this case could get a majority against each of the
others. The committee proposal that eventually won, for example, would have
been defeated by the Whitten amendment, but such a vote was never held
because the Anderson substitute defeated the Whitten proposal, and it was
not considered again. Similarly, each of the other alternatives could have
been defeated by some other alternative, as Table 2 shows.

Thus, in this complex but realistic case, a paradox of voting existed in the
House. Nevertheless, the House, by not putting each of the alternatives against
each of the others could not discover the existence of the paradox, and the consequence was that no matter which proposal was adopted, a majority would
have preferred another.

As a second example, consider the case examined by Blydenburgh (1971) in
which a sequence of votes allowed him to reconstruct the preferences of the
members of the House of Representatives. In trying to balance the 1932 budget, the House was considering raising revenue by imposing a sales tax (*ST*),
an excise tax (*ET*), or an income tax increase (*IT*). Ignoring those who were
indifferent in preference to all three alternatives, Blydenburgh concluded
that the following groups of representatives existed:

> Group 1 (162 members): *IT* > *ET* > *ST*
> Group 2 (38 members):   *ET* > *ST* > *IT*
> Group 3 (16 members):   *ST* > *IT* > *ET*
> Group 4 (69 members):   *ST* > *ET* > *IT*
> Group 5 (71 members):   *ST* > (*ET IT*)

TABLE 2 Winning Proposals before the House Concerning the Soil Conservation Service Appropriations in 1953

	Original	Javits	Anderson	Whitten	O'Toole
Original	X	R	R	C	R
Javits	C	X	C	C	R
Anderson	C	R	X	R	R
Whitten	R	R	C	X	R
O'Toole	C	C	C	C	X

Here, the parentheses for group 5 indicated an inability to determine from their votes their preferences between the excise tax and income tax alternatives. A plausible interpretation is that all the members of this group were indifferent to the two alternatives; but if only four of these members were actually indifferent, a cyclical social preference order existed in this case whereby $ST > IT > ET > ST$.[18] In this case, the House adopted the excise tax alternative, the last alternative proposed, even though a majority preferred an income tax increase. Moreover, had the excise tax proposal been voted on first against the income tax alternative, it would not have been adopted.

Blydenburgh identified the existence of a cyclical social preference order in this case because there was a sequence of votes on the three tax alternatives. However, such a sequence of votes does not often exist, and therefore the cyclical majority problem will not likely be recognized by either participants or observers. In the hypothetical example above, the three legislators would probably not have recognized the paradox because they would not have voted first on X against W, then the winner against Y, the winner of this second round against Z, and Z against either X or W. Real-world legislative decision making would have stopped after selecting Z, just as the House stopped after adopting the excise tax.

The cyclical majority problem is usually illustrated by using relatively simple examples; but this does not mean that it is a problem only in these cases. In fact, it is known that the *à priori* probability of the paradox increases rather dramatically with increases in both the number of alternatives considered and the number of voters (Niemi and Weisberg 1968; DeMayer and Plott 1970; Gehrlein and Fishburn 1976). Niemi and Weisberg, for example, showed that for three alternatives, the *à priori* probability of a paradox with three actors is .056. This rises to .082 for fifteen actors and rises again to .088 for an infinite number of actors. In this case, it can be seen that the probabilities of a paradox rise but not very rapidly with increases in the number of actors. Now consider what happens if the number of actors is held constant at three, and the number of alternatives is increased. For three actors and three alternatives, the *à priori* probability is again. .056. This rises to .111 for four alternatives, .16

for five alternatives, and .20 for six alternatives. For more alternatives, the probability continues to increase so that for many actors and many alternatives, the *à priori* probability of a paradox can be as high as .84. This means that for a realistic number of actors and alternatives in decision-making settings such as in Congress, the *à priori* probability of a paradox is well in excess of .50 so that it is much more likely that a paradox will exist than that it will not. Thus, the cyclical majorities problem is more likely to occur in complex real-world decision making than in the simple examples constructed to illustrate the problem.

Also note that if James Madison was correct in his analysis in *Federalist 10*, the probability of a paradox should be larger at the national level than at the state or local levels of government. Madison's basic argument was, "Extend the sphere and you take in a greater variety of parties and interests; you make it less probable that a majority of the whole will have a common motive to invade the rights of other citizens; or if such a common motive exists, it will be more difficult for all who feel it to discover their own strength and to act in union with each other." In more modern language, this means that the larger the geographic area represented in a legislature, the more likely it is that the preference orderings of legislators will differ from each other. In turn, this implies that it is more likely that not all of these differences can be represented simultaneously by single-peaked preference curves. On the other hand, the more homogeneous the are represented in a legislature (and to Madison, homogeneous was associated with a smaller geographic area), the more similarity is likely to exist, and hence the more likely the preferences can be simultaneously represented with single-peaked curves. It is thus more likely that a paradox of voting will occur in Congress than in a local municipal legislature (e.g., a city council or school board).

Finally, note that in these examples of intransitive social preferences, it has been shown implicitly that parliamentary rules can have an important impact on outcome. Thus, rules that specify the order in which the alternatives are voted upon or rules that limit the kind or number of amendments that can be offered seem to be as important as the preferences of the legislators in determining outcome. This is indeed the case; and as will be shown in subsequent chapters, a major part of the spatial theory of legislative decision making concerns the interaction of preferences and rules in determining legislative outcomes.

Conclusions

The unidimensional spatial model considered in this chapter is relatively simple, but it is sufficient to illustrate the general approach of spatial theory to legislative decision making. With the aid of a few simplifying assumptions, spatial theorists have sought to isolate the essential elements of the legislative decision-making process so they become susceptible to intensive logical and mathematical analysis. These efforts have been repaid by a deeper understanding of how legislative processes work and by an identification of a series of fundamental problems at the heart of any form of democratic collective decision making. In particular, there is a possibility that there may be no alternative that is majority preferred to all others. In such circumstances, legislatures may still make a decision, which implies that at times an outcome may be selected even though there are others that would defeat it in a majority vote.

In many ways, however, the unidimensional spatial model discussed in this chapter is not realistic in terms of real-world legislative decision making. For example, the model assumes that legislators always vote their true preferences. It also assumes that the issues involved in legislative decision making can be reduced to a single dimension. Although these are both serious problems, they are not fatal for the theory, for both can be adequately managed within its confines.

NOTES

1. It might be thought that an additional relationship of "I don't know which I prefer" could exist among these alternatives. However, this relationship is equivalent to preferring them equally because if one does not know which alternative he or she prefers, it is impossible for one alternative to be ranked before another, and hence they must be ranked equally.

2. von Neumann and Morgenstern (1944) have shown how, through the use of a lottery over the alternatives, cardinal (or interval level) utility can be measured (see also Riker and Ordeshook 1973). However, their proposal is theoretically controversial; practically, for the case of real-world legislatures, implementing such a procedure would be impossible. Therefore, here, as in the spatial theory generally, only ordinal utility will be assumed.

3. An additional consequence is that one cannot add the utilities of different actors to get an aggregate level of satisfaction from a given outcome.

4. More generally, where R represents "preferred to or indifferent to," transitive preferences imply that BRA and ARQ implies BRQ.

5. In making this assumption, it is not denied that people may at times hold intransitive preferences. However, because people cannot act rationally on the basis of such preferences, they cannot logically be a part of a theory of rational action.

6. Note in the figure that there are just three preference curves, one for each of the groups. This is permissible here as the groups are of equal size. Normally, however, one would draw a separate indifference curve for each legislator. Thus, in Figure 1.3, one would draw 435 separate indifference curves.

7. Technically, the single-peak condition is sufficient for the existence of a majority preferred outcome. It is not, however, a necessary condition. The (technical) necessary conditions are given in Sen and Pattanaik (1969).

8. Technically, the equilibrium noted in the text is attractive and stable. It is attractive in the sense that it is the alternative toward which the outcome will move, and it is stable in the sense that once this alternative is reached, it will not be departed from. As shown later, however, not all voting equilibria need be attractive. For a detailed analysis of the meaning of a spatial equilibrium, see Krehbiel (1988).

9. Condorcet voting is named after the Marquis de Condorcet (1743–94), a French mathematician, philosopher, and social scientist who was the first to examine such a

voting scheme systematically. For an analysis of Condorcet's work, see Black (1958). The specific method described here differs from pure Condorcet voting in that all logical combinations are not paired against each other. Here, only winners make it to the next round.

10. Alternative voting schemes are discussed in Riker and Ordeshook (1973), Riker (1982), and Ordeshook (1986).

11. One other condition is needed here, and that is that all the voters vote their true preferences. As will be seen subsequently, there are reasons that actors might not do this in a legislature.

12. What is not known are the second most preferred positions for members in the middle, so it is unclear, for example, whether the preference curve for the member who most prefers the $2000 increase should decline faster on the left or right of the $2000 point. However, in this case (and in many similar cases), this issue is not a problem and does not affect the conclusions reached.

13. *CM*, in other words, is the outcome corresponding to the median preference curve peak when only the preferences of committee members are considered. Similarly, *FM* is the median peak at which the preferences of all the members of a chamber are considered.

14. Under congressional rules in which the full chamber does not consider bills until they have been reported by a committee, it might seem here that the optimal strategy for the committee might be to report no bill, ensuring themselves the status quo outcome. However, such a strategy presumes that a committee majority will adopt a sophisticated strategy, and such strategies will not be considered until the next chapter. Thus, here, it is assumed that the committee majority is myopic and reports the *CM* bill.

15. See also Niemi (1983) for the effects of partially relaxing the single peakedness requirement.

16. Arrow's conditions are somewhat technical and will not be discussed here. For a discussion and analysis of them, see Plott (1976).

17. Note that the existence of a social preference cycle does not always imply that an equilibrium does not exist. There may exist, for example, an alternative that defeats all others even when there are cycles among these latter alternatives.

18. *ST* is preferred to *IT* by groups 2, 3, 4, and 5, which have a total of 194 members. *IT* is preferred to *ST* only by group 1, with 162 members. Thus, *ST* > *IT*. Similarly, *IT* is preferred to *ET* by groups 1 and 3, with a total of 178 members; *ET* is preferred by groups 2 and 4, with 107 members; and it is unclear which order is preferred by group 5. However, if only one member of group 5 prefers *IT* to *ET*, there would be 179 members preferring *IT* to *ET* and only 177 members preferring *ET* to *IT*. Thus, it is reasonable to presume that *IT* > *ET*. Finally, groups 1 and 2, with 200 members, prefer *ET* to *ST*, whereas groups 3, 4, and 5, with 156 members, prefer *ST* to *ET*. Thus, *ET* > *ST*, and the whole social preference order is intransitive.

REFERENCES

Arrow, Kenneth J. 1951. *Social choice and individual value.* New Haven: Yale University Press.

Black, Duncan. 1958. *The theory of committees and elections.* Cambridge: Cambridge University Press.

Blydenburgh, John. 1971. The closed rule and the paradox of voting. *Journal of Politics* 33:57–71.

DeMayer, Frank, and Charles Plott. 1970. The probability of a cyclical majority. *Econometrica* 38:345–54.

Denzau, Arthur T., and Robert J. Mackay. 1983. Gatekeeping and monopoly power of committees: An analysis of sincere and sophisticated behavior. *American Journal of Political Science* 27:740–61.

Gehrlein, William V., and Peter C. Fishburn. 1976. The probability of the paradox of voting. *Journal of Economic Theory* 13:14–25.

Krehbiel, Keith. 1987. Sophisticated committees and structure-induced equilibria in Congress. In *Congress: Structure and policy*, ed. Mathew McCubbins and Terry Sullivan. Cambridge: Cambridge University Press.

———. 1988. Spatial models of legislative choice. *Legislative Studies Quarterly* 13: 259–319.

Niemi, Richard G. 1983. Why so much stability: Another opinion. *Public Choice* 41: 261–70.

Niemi, Richard G., and Herbert Weisberg. 1968. A mathematical solution for the probability of the paradox of voting. *Behavioral Science* 13:317–23.

Ordeshook, Peter C. 1986. *Game theory and political theory.* Cambridge: Cambridge University Press.

Plott, Charles R. 1976. Axiomatic social choice theory: An interpretation and overview. *American Journal of Political Science* 20:511–56.

Riker, William H. 1958. The paradox of voting and congressional rules for voting amendments. *American Political Science Review* 52:349–66.

———. 1982. *Liberalism against populism.* San Francisco: W. H. Freeman.

Riker, William H., and Peter C. Ordeshook. 1973. *An introduction to positive political theory.* Englewood Cliffs: Prentice-Hall.

Sen, A. K., and P. K. Pattanaik. 1969. Necessary and sufficient conditions for rational choice under majority decision. *Journal of Economic Theory* 1:178–202.

von Neumann, John, and Oskar Morgenstern. 1944. *The theory of games and economic behavior.* New York: John Wiley.

5.4

GARY W. COX AND MATHEW D. McCUBBINS

From *Setting the Agenda: Responsible Party Government in the U.S. House of Representatives*

The majority party in the House of Representatives closely controls legislative business, but to do so the party needs the cooperation of its members. How do majority political parties in Congress keep their coalitions together to pass legislation? Cox and McCubbins argue that party leaders, first, offer plum committee assignments and pork barrel benefits to rank-and-file members, and second, keep tight control over the agenda to ensure that no bills are voted upon that would potentially divide the party.

2. PROCEDURAL CARTEL THEORY

> The job of speaker is not to expedite legislation that runs counter to the wishes of the majority of his majority.
>
> —Speaker Dennis Hastert (R-IL)[1]

In this chapter, we present and discuss the assumptions that undergird procedural cartel theory. To provide a context for comparison, however, we first briefly survey the literature on partisan legislative organization.

Theories of Partisan Legislative Organization

Much of the literature on legislative organization focuses on why political parties are created within legislatures in the first place. We divide extant explanations into those that hinge primarily on the internal legislative payoffs to forming parties and those that hinge primarily on the external electoral payoffs. We then turn to survey the literature on how parties are organized and what parties do.

Why are there parties in legislatures?

PARTIES ARE CREATED TO SOLVE INTERNAL COLLECTIVE ACTION PROBLEMS. One line of theorizing about why parties exist is similar to the distributive line of argument regarding committees. Absent any organization (other than a voting rule for floor decisions), legislators face a chaotic and unpredictable agenda. They cannot be sure that the legislature will not vote tomorrow to strip them of benefits conferred today. Nor is it clear how to ensure that the benefits are conferred to begin with, given a world where any legislator can move any amendment at any time.

In order to deal with the unpredictability—and unprofitability—of the unorganized legislature, legislators form political parties to bind themselves together in durable coalitions. Gains from legislative trade that could not be accrued without parties are thus accrued.

PARTIES ARE CREATED TO SOLVE EXTERNAL COLLECTIVE ACTION PROBLEMS. An alternative theory views legislative parties as being formed primarily to accrue electoral gains. Modern political parties facing mass electorates, similar to modern corporations facing mass markets, have a strong incentive to fashion and maintain a brand name. Such brand names are, however, public goods to all politicians running under the party's label. Thus, parties arise in order to ensure that the usual problems of providing and maintaining public goods are overcome—and in particular to internalize electoral externalities that would otherwise arise.

How are parties organized?

If parties exist to solve collective action problems, as seems the main tenet in the literature, then how do they organize to solve these problems? The literature has several suggestions, which we now survey.

PARTIES AS FIRMS. Many scholars envision parties as being similar to the firms depicted in the literature on industrial organization (cf. Alchian and Demsetz 1972; Tirole 1988), in that they involve delegation to central agents (party leaders) in order to reduce transaction costs and ameliorate collective action problems. Scholars in this tradition implicitly accept the industrial organization literature's focus on hierarchical firms with single chief executive officers.

PARTIES AS PARTNERSHIPS. In the case of the political party, we believe a more fruitful analogy is to partnerships, such as law or accountancy firms, in which various gradations of senior partners provide overall strategic and tactical direction to the firm. The "senior partners" in our story—at least as regards the majority party—will be committee and subcommittee chairs, majority party floor leaders, campaign finance committee chairs, and the like. Agenda-setting and other powers are distributed across the offices held by these senior partners rather than fully concentrated in the hands of the speaker, just as the right to recruit new clients and take on new jobs is distributed among the senior partners in a law or accountancy firm, rather than fully concentrated in the hands of the firm's president. Similarly, just as the job of ensuring that no senior partner's actions impinge too unfavorably on a law firm's overall reputation falls not just on the firm's president but also on the other senior partners collectively, so too the job of policing committee chairs falls partly to the speaker and partly to informal politics centered on the party caucus.

What do parties do?

Once organized, what do parties do to mitigate the collective action problems that are assumed to be the reason for their existence?

PARTIES AS FLOOR VOTING COALITIONS. Some partisan theories view parties primarily as floor voting coalitions. In such theories, the central issue is the degree to which parties can discipline their members, ensuring a cohesive voting bloc on the floor, even when there are internal disagreements over policy.

The best-known model that seeks to explain variations in American parties' ability to discipline their members, and hence enact programs, is the conditional party government model of Aldrich (1995), Rohde (1991), and Aldrich and Rohde (2001). In this model, majority party backbenchers delegate more power to their party leaders, when preferences vary less within each party and more between the parties. Party government is thus conditional on a sufficient disagreement in preferences between the parties (relative to their internal disagreements) arising. When this condition is met, American parties act more in accord with the traditional model of responsible party government.

PARTIES AS PROCEDURAL COALITIONS. Other partisan theories, including our own, view parties primarily as procedural coalitions. For such theories, the central issue is the majority party's ability to control the legislative agenda, defined as the set of bills considered and voted on the floor.

How do majority parties control the agenda?

Strict party discipline, at least on important votes, is one method for the majority party or coalition to control legislative outcomes. When party leaders have the means to impose discipline on their backbenchers, agenda control is attained by the extension of the will of the party leadership. But, where discipline is costly, other methods may be substituted. In considering these other methods, there is an important distinction to be made between positive and negative agenda power. Positive agenda power is the ability to push bills through the legislative process to a final-passage vote on the floor. Negative agenda power is the ability to block bills from reaching a final passage vote on the floor. Formal and informal models of legislative parties differ in whether they depict parties as controlling the agenda via the allocation of proposal rights (positive agenda power) or veto rights (negative agenda power).

PARTIES AS ALLOCATING PROPOSAL RIGHTS. Two examples of theories in which proposal rights are the key resource allocated by parties to their members are Laver and Shepsle's (1996) model of ministerial government and Diermeier and Feddersen's (1998) model of the vote of confidence. In a common interpretation of Laver and Shepsle's model, multiparty coalition governments allocate ministerial portfolios to their various member parties, with each minister then possessing both positive and negative agenda power in his respective jurisdiction. Thus, each minister can make proposals directly to the assembly, without needing cabinet clearance. In Diermeier and Feddersen's model, coalitions of legislators allocate increased "recognition probabilities" to their members, thereby increasing their ability to make proposals. Once recognized, a given member of a coalition again needs no preclearance by other members of the coalition for his proposals: They go straight to a final-passage vote in the plenary.

PARTIES AS ALLOCATING VETO RIGHTS. An alternative view of parties is that they allocate negative agenda power, or veto rights, among their members. Tsebelis (2002) takes this view of parliamentary coalitions. Rather than view individual parties as possessing both negative and positive agenda power across a range of issues (those under the jurisdiction of the party's ministers), Tsebelis views parties as possessing a general veto over the entire range of issues the coalition must face—therefore no coalition partner possesses unilateral proposal power. Similarly, Cox and McCubbins (2002) view majority parties primarily as allocating veto (or delaying) power to various offices held by their senior partners, such as committee chairs and speakers, thus necessarily lessening the proposal power of any given party member or subset of members.

Procedural Cartel Theory

In this section, we list the assumptions and motivating principles of procedural cartel theory. Assumptions 1–5 are from our previous book, *Legislative Leviathan*, and are defended at length in the second edition of that volume. Assumption 6 is new to this reading, and, accordingly, we expand on it here. . . . After elaborating the assumptions of our theory, we sketch some of the intuitions that have steered our research (. . .) and conclude. . . . In subsequent chapters, we will present and test simplified and formalized models consistent with the broader theory presented here.

> **Assumption 1:** Members of Congress seek reelection to the House, internal advancement within the House, good public policy, and majority status.

In our previous work (Cox and McCubbins 1993), our formal statement of members' goals included three of the motivations just discussed: reelection, internal advancement, and majority status.[2] Key to our approach was the assumption that majority status confers substantial benefits. In particular, advancement to committee chairs and other key posts in the House is possible only if one's party gains a majority, and advancement of one's legislative projects is greatly facilitated by majority status.[3] Thus, majority status is arguably an essential gateway to internal advancement and policy goals. The more substantial the benefits of majority status are, the more incentive they provide to the senior partners in a given party to pursue majority status—hence to undertake the sorts of agenda-setting actions that we describe in the remainder of the reading.

> **Assumption 2:** The reputation (or brand name) of a member's party affects both the member's personal probability of reelection and, more substantially, the party's probability of securing a majority.

We have discussed this premise at length in our previous work (see Cox and McCubbins 1993, Chapter 5). To the extent that this assumption holds, a political party's reputation is a *public good* to all candidates sharing the party's label. More specifically, if a party's reputation improves or worsens, all members benefit or suffer together, regardless of whether they contributed to the improvement or worsening.

> **Assumption 3:** A party's reputation depends significantly on its record of legislative accomplishment.

The policies with which a particular party and its leaders are associated—both those it promotes and those it opposes—can significantly affect the party's reputation. A recent example of this is the budget battle waged between Speaker of the House Newt Gingrich and President Bill Clinton in 1995. This battle led to the opening of the new fiscal year without a federal budget, causing the closure of nonessential government services. For present purposes, the important point about this budgetary stand-off is simply that it led to a sharp reduction in the popularity of congressional Republicans and their leaders, as measured by thermometer ratings in mass surveys (Jacobson 1996). In other words, in this instance a leader's legislative policy—that of refusing to compromise on the budget—led directly to a decline in the party's overall popularity.

We assume that this anecdote points to a more general phenomenon, in which legislative actions taken by various members of the party can affect the overall party's reputation on the margin. There is some disagreement about how much and how quickly party identification incorporates new events and evaluations. For our purposes, we need simply to assert a position similar to that adopted by V. O. Key (1966), in which parties' legislative actions *do* consequentially affect voters' behavior. Whether the path by which legislative actions influence votes is through party reputations (party identification) or through some shorter-term partisan pathways is less important.

Assumption 4: Legislating—hence compiling favorable records of legislative accomplishment—is akin to team production and entails overcoming an array of cooperation and coordination problems.

Achieving their goals—reelection, internal advancement, and majority status—requires passage of legislation, yet legislators' ability to accomplish things on their own is quite limited. Legislation must be accepted by majorities in both houses of Congress and be signed by the president to become law.[4] To get through even one house, moreover, a bill needs to get scarce floor time and the support of a majority coalition, both of which are costly and difficult to achieve. Legislating thus requires that members somehow join forces, cooperate, and engage in "team production" (Alchian and Demsetz 1972).

Team production, however, means confronting and overcoming a variety of collective action and coordination problems. For example, all members would like to spend more money on their own districts than might be optimal from their party's perspective (Cox and McCubbins 1993); all members would like to have free access to floor time, but the result could be that nothing can get done reliably; divergent national, regional, and partisan interests might lead members to pursue different policies in the absence of some coordinating mechanism. Most important for our theory, as noted above, the party label itself is a public good (for party members) that is subject to free-rider problems. Managing the party label is the primary collective action problem that members of a party must solve, and their collective goal of solving this and other collective action problems is the sense in which they are members of a partnership.

Assumption 5: The primary means by which a (majority) party regulates its members' actions, in order to overcome problems of team production in the legislative process, is by delegating to a central authority.

Though other solutions for collective action problems exist, the most common solution seems to be delegation to a central authority—an idea that appears in a wide variety of literatures.[5] Three common elements in all these works are that the central authority to whom power is delegated monitors individual behavior, controls carrots and sticks with which to reward and punish individuals, and is motivated to solve the collective action problem(s) faced by the group. Along these lines, the core point of our previous book (Cox and McCubbins 1993) is that majority party members delegate to party leaders the authority to manage legislative resources and the legislative process in order to solve the cooperation and coordination problems they face, including maintaining the value of the party label.[6]

How are party leaders motivated to use their delegated powers for collective, rather than purely personal, gain? We argue that members wishing to hold important offices in the House (such as the speakership and committee chairs) know that the only realistic route to getting these offices is for their party to attain a majority of seats and for them to be in sufficiently good standing with their caucus to be (re)nominated for such offices.[7] Thus, the more valuable are the top posts going to the majority party's senior members, the more motivated are those members to ensure the party's continued majority status (and their own good standing).

As noted in the previous chapter, we believe that political parties are more fruitfully analogized to legal or accountancy partnerships than to strictly hierarchical single-leader firms (or armies). Thus, when we speak of delegation to a central authority, we do not mean literally to a single person but instead to a group of "senior partners."

> **Assumption 6:** The key resource that majority parties delegate to their senior partners is the power to set the legislative agenda; the majority party forms a procedural cartel that collectively monopolizes agenda-setting power.

This is our key assumption, and our point of departure from most of the previous literature. A *procedural cartel* is a coalition of legislators who constitute a majority in the assembly, share a common label (at least in the United States), and cartelize the agenda via the following basic strategy. First, the cartel creates (or, more typically, inherits) a set of offices endowed with special agenda-setting powers. In the case of the U.S. House, the main agenda-setting offices are the committee chairs, slots on the Rules Committee, and the speakership.[8] Second, the cartel ensures that its members get all, or nearly all, of the agenda-setting offices.[9] Third, cartel members expect those appointed to agenda-setting offices to *always* obey "the first commandment of party leadership"—*Thou shalt not aid bills that will split thy party*—and to sometimes obey the second commandment—*Thou shalt aid bills that most in thy party like*. Fourth, cartel members expect rank-and-file members to support the agenda-setting decisions rendered by officeholders when those decisions are made in conformity to the expectations just noted. Fifth, the cartel's leadership takes action to maintain cooperation and coordination within the cartel.

We use the term "cartel" because procedural cartels, like economic cartels, seek to establish a collective monopoly on a particular resource (in this case, agenda-setting power), seek to restrict supply of products made with this resource (in this case, bills that are placed on the floor agenda), and face problems of free-riding (in this case, members reluctant to vote for a party measure when such a vote will not sell well back home, or members eager to use their delegated agenda powers for personal gain). We have also used the term "legislative leviathan" to describe party organizations within legislatures, in order to emphasize their sometimes considerable degree of centralized authority.[10] Indeed, even during their relatively decentralized periods, parties in the U.S. House have been more hierarchical and stable than the typical economic cartel. Even though neither term's connotations are fully satisfactory, in this reading we will refer to party organizations as forming procedural cartels (and we will stress the analogy of a group of senior partners directing a law or accountancy firm rather than of a CEO running a corporation or a general commanding an army).

How Does the Majority Cartelize the Agenda?

In this section, we reconsider the defining features of "procedural cartels," as mentioned in Assumption 6. At this point, we wish only to argue that these features *plausibly* characterize the modern (i.e., post-Reed) House of Representatives; we will return to them in greater detail later in the reading.

The structure of agenda-setting offices

An initial question is whether there exist offices endowed with special agenda-setting powers in the House and whether these offices' powers were in some sense chosen by the majority party. By "special agenda-setting powers," or agenda power for short, we refer to any *special* ability to determine which bills are considered on the floor and under what procedures. Because any member can participate in an attempt to discharge a bill, we would not count "the ability to participate in a discharge attempt" as an "agenda power" in our sense. Such an ability is not special; it is general. In contrast, only members of the Rules Committee can participate in fashioning special rules,[11] and only chairs can delay bills merely by not scheduling them—to mention two examples of agenda power as we define it.

Given this definition, there obviously do exist offices in the House endowed with agenda power. As noted previously, the most important of these include the committee and subcommittee chairs, the seats on the Rules Committee, and the speakership.

Did the majority party in some sense choose the level of agenda power delegated to the various agenda-setting offices? Yes, in two senses.

First, the House adopts rules anew in each Congress. These rules are proposed by the majority party and are usually adopted on a straight party-line vote. Thus, among other things, the majority chooses (or reaffirms) the delegation of agenda power in those rules.

Second, the modern structure of agenda power in the House was erected in the period 1880–94 to enable the majority party to legislate, even against the wishes of the minority. . . . We will show that the House's rules have not, since 1894, changed so as to erase the majority party advantages accrued in this period. In particular, the minority party's ability to delay has not been restored, nor has the central position of the Rules Committee been significantly altered.[12] The powers of the speaker have waxed and waned, but when they have changed, they have simply been redistributed within the majority party, not allocated to any minority party members. In this sense, the majority party chose the structure of agenda power and the majority's overall advantage has remained largely constant since the 1890s (a claim we defend at length. . . .

Who gets the agenda-setting offices?

A second question is whether the majority party sets up a procedure for selecting the occupants of the agenda-setting offices that is likely to lead in principle, and does lead in practice, to its members winning most of the agenda-setting offices. The answer in practice is clear: the majority party secures all chairs, the speakership, and a super-proportional share of seats on the Rules Committee. It also secures super-proportional shares on the major committees that enjoy privileged access to the floor and on conference committees (which also exercise special agenda-setting powers) (Cox and McCubbins 1993).

As for the procedures regulating access to the House's agenda-setting posts, they all include an initial stage in which each party decides on nominees for the various posts, followed by a choice between, or ratification of, the parties' nominees in the House. The choice of a speaker is largely unregulated, as this is the first vote in each Congress and occurs before the adoption of rules. The choice of all other agenda-setting posts—committee positions of various sorts—is regulated. In particular, since 1917 the procedure has been as follows. First, the majority party informs the minority of how many seats each party will receive on each committee. Second, each party submits a slate specifying its nominees for its designated committee positions. Third, the two party slates are combined into a single resolution that is then voted up or down (since 1917 it has not been permissible to amend the slates on the floor). Given these procedures, it is not surprising that the majority party has never failed to secure a monopoly on chairs, the speakership, and a disproportionally large share of seats on the control and conference committees.[13]

Fiduciary behavior of officeholders

A third question is whether party members expect that party officeholders will exercise their official powers partly for the benefit of the party, rather than purely to pursue personal goals, and whether officeholders who do not act as expected are sanctioned in some way. Since agenda cartelization entails delegation of authority from party backbenchers to party leaders, cartelization creates the possibility of mischief by party leaders (i.e., not serving the collective interests of the party). Much of the literature implicitly adopts a strict standard by which to judge when officeholders act in the interest of their party, according to which they must aid legislation favored by significant majorities of their party. For example, the well-known accounts of Judge Smith's tenure on the Rules Committee point out—quite accurately—that he frequently obstructed legislation desired by large portions of his own party, and they conclude from this that Smith was acting in pursuit of his own or his faction's interests, not his party's.

Delay or outright obstruction of bills that significant portions of one's party want to turn into "party issues" represents an agency loss, but it does not mean that the persons in question have utterly abandoned representing or serving their party. After all, the wets in Thatcher's government delayed and obstructed when they could, and many other examples of hard bargaining over tough issues in coalition governments involve such tactics. Are we to conclude from every instance of persistent obstruction by elements of the governing coalition that the coalition is entirely toothless?

We think that would be premature. There are less stringent standards that might serve as "lines in the sand" demarcating behavior that is minimally fiduciary from behavior that is treasonous. Here, we wish to characterize such a standard, one that we believe has been expected of officeholders in the House at least since the late nineteenth century. This standard focuses on crimes of commission—pushing legislation one's party mostly dislikes—not on crimes of omission—failing to aid (or actively blocking) legislation one's party mostly likes. Crimes of commission increase in seriousness (1) with the proportion of the party that dislikes it and (2) if the bill actually passes. As a specific benchmark, *we claim that officeholders are expected never to push bills that would pass despite the opposition of a majority of their party.* We call such an event—passage of a bill against the votes of a majority of a given party—a *roll* of that party. If the majority's officeholders are not held to even the minimal standard of not using their powers to roll their own party, then they do indeed look like nonpartisan figures willing (and able with impunity) to build shifting coalitions in support of their projects.

An example of a violator of our proposed standard is Representative Phil Gramm (D-TX) who, during the negotiations leading to the first Reagan budget, clearly used his position in a way intended to roll his own party. In this specific instance, Democratic party leaders branded Gramm's behavior as unconscionable after they discovered it and took quick actions to sanction him, including stripping him of the posts he had abused (Roberts 1983a).[14]

Other similar examples can be cited. In 1924, eight Republicans on the Rules Committee cooperated on the passage of a strengthened discharge procedure, which most majority party members opposed; six of them were removed from the committee in the next Congress (in which the offending rule was also eviscerated cf. Hasbrouck 1927: 163–4). In 1975, Chairman Richard Ichord of the Internal Security Committee, a longtime thorn in the side of liberal Democrats, found that the committee had essentially been disestablished, due largely to actions taken in the Democratic Caucus (Jacobs 1995). In all these cases, the majority party caucus essentially *denied renomination* to wayward officeholders. There was no House vote needed to ratify the majority's decision; moreover, it would have been difficult to reject those decisions in the House, given that each party's slate of committee nominations is unamendable under House rules. To the extent that threats to deny renomination are credible, they induce officeholders to abandon, or at least sweeten, bills that substantial portions of their party dislike.

Our position is that these anecdotes generalize. In any period of congressional history, an officeholder behaving as Gramm did would have met with comparable reactions. In any period, it would be common knowledge that the standard of "not conspiring, explicitly or implicitly, with the enemy to roll one's own party" would apply to officeholders and that violators of this standard could expect to lose their offices and/or face other sanctions.

Many in the congressional literature seem to believe that sanctions against officeholders, especially against committee chairs, were simply not feasible in the period from 1937 to 1960. If this were so, then one should expect that Southern Democrats in this period used their agenda powers with impunity to push bills that they and the Republicans agreed on. Such "conservative coalition" bills, moving policy rightward, would have provoked splits in committees chaired by Southerners—with Northern Democrats outvoted by a combination of Southern Democrats and Republicans. Moreover, such bills would easily have made it to the floor, with the help of a Rules Committee often seen as controlled by the conservative coalition in this period. Once on the floor, conservative coalition bills would have *both* split the majority party *and* passed. Passage would follow as long as the number of conservative Southern Democrats plus regular Republicans exceeded the number of Northern Democrats plus liberal Republicans. Put another way, as long as the policy being changed lay to the left of the House median, the conservative coalition would have outvoted a majority of the Democratic Party. We assess the impact of the conservative coalition in detail, and evaluate these predictions, ... For now, suffice it to say that we do not find significant evidence of Southern Democrats defecting from their party and joining with Republicans to successfully push an agenda unpalatable to Northern Democrats.

Loyalty from the rank and file

A final question is: how does a procedural cartel ensure that its rank-and-file members support the agenda-setting decisions of its officeholders, even though at least some members' short-term interests would be better served by voting against those decisions? A key to the answer is that votes taken on procedural decisions (e.g., a vote to ratify a special rule proposed by the Rules Committee or to sustain a decision rendered by the speaker) are more obscure to constituents than are ordinary substantive votes (cf. Froman and Ripley 1965). If a member votes for a bill her constituents oppose on final passage, she runs a clear risk. If she supports a special rule filled with arcane boilerplate that helps ensure the bill's success, she runs a smaller risk.[15] Thus, party pressures can affect members' decisions on procedure more than their decisions on substance, even though all legislators know that procedural motions directly affect substantive outcomes.[16]

Another key point is that the cartel does not need the loyalty of every member on every vote. Often, it needs only enough votes to snatch victory from the jaws of defeat on close and important votes (cf. King and Zeckhauser 2003). This is a much more limited and manageable task than enforcing some minimum standard of cohesion across the board, which some mistakenly take to be what any "partisan" model must predict.

Is there evidence that cartels in the U.S. House do demand loyalty? Alexander (1970 [1916]: 210) notes that, soon after Reed's elevation of the Rules Committee to its modern status, members chafed under the expectation that "one must support whatever the Rules Committee brought forward or become irregular." More recently, Republican Whip Tom DeLay (R-TX) has made the party's expectations regarding behavior on procedural motions clear to his freshmen (Burger 1995).

To buttress such anecdotal evidence that majority parties do expect loyalty on key procedural votes, one can also point to more systematic evidence that the majority party's rank and file support their officeholders' agenda-setting decisions, while minority party members oppose them. First, after the packing of the Rules Committee in 1961 (and especially after the procedural reforms of 1973), members have voted with their parties significantly more than would be expected on the basis of their left–right position on a wide range of procedural and organizational votes (Cox and Poole 2002).[17] Second, in the postreform Congress, majority party members have been prone to support special rules, even when they then vote against the bill in question, while minority party members have exhibited the opposite tendency (Sinclair 2002). Sinclair's interpretation of this evidence is that majority party members are supporting their leaders' agenda-setting decisions, even when they oppose the substance of the proposals aided by the special rule in question, while minority party members oppose the Rules Committee's resolutions, even when they support the measure being aided. Third, more evidence of parties' influence over their members' voting behavior is reviewed. . . .

In addition, party leaders reward party members' loyalty on key votes, and especially on "agenda votes" in which the leaders of the two parties take opposing positions.[18] More loyal members are more likely to be appointed to the most desirable committees and to have committee transfers granted than are less loyal party members (Cox and McCubbins 1993, Chapter 7).

In summary, majority party leaders make clear their expectations of loyalty on certain key procedural votes; there is evidence that party pressures are greater on such votes; and there is evidence that more loyal members get better committee assignments. These findings are all consistent with a picture in which majority party leaders both *expect* and *get* "loyalty on the margin," enough to make the difference between winning and losing on close votes (King and Zeckhauser 2003).

Nevertheless, it is the very costliness of enforcing discipline in the U.S. House that helps to explain why U.S. parties principally rely on controlling the legislative agenda to achieve their legislative goals. In the model of responsible party government (American Political Science Association 1950), parties ensure cohesive voting blocs through a combination of control over nominations and disciplining their members. U.S. parties, however, have relatively weak nominating powers. Similarly, discipline is weaker in the United States than in some other countries. This puts more emphasis on agenda control, or influencing the bills and motions on which members must vote, as the single most powerful mechanism by which legislative outcomes can be affected in the U.S. House. By using agenda control, the party can prevent votes on which its disciplinary abilities would be strained or broken.

What about quitting the party?

In the discussion of fiduciary behavior and loyalty . . . , we did not address the issue of why members of a cartel do not quit their party, join the other side, and form a new cartel (with a better share of the spoils for themselves). In particular, one might wonder why centrist members cannot extract a better deal. Why are not all the committee chairs centrists, for example? Alternatively, why are not centrist chairs free to exercise agenda power in any way they see fit, subject only to majoritarian and not specifically partisan constraints?

There are three points we would urge in answer to this line of inquiry. First, it is rare for a single member to be pivotal (Senator James Jeffords in May 2001 being the most notable exception). Typically several members must simultaneously switch parties in order to bring down the current cartel. Potential defectors must thus *coordinate*, not just in the sense of jumping at the same time but also in the sense of negotiating, *before* actually defecting, with their prospective new partners over the division of the spoils.[19]

Second, and more important, it is ex ante costly to switch parties. The Grenvillite faction in late eighteenth-century English politics could pivot freely, little constrained by electoral considerations, because they literally owned their seats. In the modern U.S. House, however, elections are partisan, and party labels count for a lot. When a member switches party labels, can he communicate that fact—and at what cost—to his constituents? How many voters in his former party will continue out of habit or loyalty to support that party? How many voters in the new party will remember that he used to be in the other party and refuse to support him on that ground? Among those voters who do learn of the member's switch, how many will view it as purely opportunistic, making the representative seem unreliable? Can he combat such ideas at low cost? How many names on the member's donor list will stop contributing? Who has been planning to run for the other party and how will they react to the incumbent's switch? All these questions about electoral ramifications—and more besides—would have to be considered by prospective defectors, at least if they are prudent.

Third, it is ex post costly to switch parties. Grose and Yoshinaka (2003) report "that incumbent legislators who switch parties have poorer showings after their switch in both general and primary election contests." Moreover, if one regresses the number of terms remaining in a legislator's career in Congress t on her seniority (i.e., the number of terms already served through Congress t) and a dummy variable equal to 1 if the member switched parties in Congress t, one finds the switched party dummy variable to have a statistically significant coefficient of roughly—3. In other words, by one crude estimate, the cost of switching parties is three fewer terms in the House than would otherwise be expected, given a member's current seniority.[20]

These various costs help explain why actual party switching has been rare in the House and Senate. To the extent that the exogenous electoral costs of switching are large, moreover, it would follow that the threat of switching parties would not be as effective as it would be in a pure spatial representation of politics.

2.4. Conclusion

In this chapter, we have laid out the main assumptions underpinning our theory of legislative parties. In our view, U.S. legislators seek not just reelection but also advancement in the internal hierarchy of posts within the House, good public policy, and majority status for their parties. Their parties compete in mass elections, as business firms compete in mass markets, by developing brand names. The value of a party's brand name depends on its legislative record of accomplishment. Thus, a key problem for majority parties is to manage the legislative process, in order to secure the best possible record, hence contributing to the best possible reputation.

This much was already evident in our original exploration of congressional organization, *Legislative Leviathan*. In this reading, we develop several additional themes.

First, we portray agenda control as the key to the majority party's influence over the legislative process. In the responsible party government model, the primary mechanisms by which a party overcomes collective action problems, so that it can enact a program, are screening candidates and disciplining legislators. In the U.S. context, however, both screening and discipline are—although utilized to some extent-relatively costly. This raises the importance of a third technique to manage conflicts between collective and individual goals; controlling the agenda so that the sharpest conflicts are never even considered on the floor.

How does a legislative majority party work to control the agenda? The mechanism is similar to that portrayed in *Legislative Leviathan*. Certain members of the party—whom we have here dubbed the "senior partners"—are given valuable offices wielding substantial agenda-setting powers. In order to secure their party's (re)nomination for these offices, senior partners are expected to obey a minimal commandment of party loyalty—namely, not using their official powers in order to promote bills that will, if considered on the floor, lead to serious splits in the party (operationalized as *rolls* in the coming chapters). The rank and file, meanwhile, are also expected to obey a minimal commandment of party loyalty—namely, supporting their office-holders' agenda-setting decisions, especially on the more procedurally arcane (yet substantively critical) votes. Their incentive to support such procedural maneuvers is the prospect of better internal advancement and a greater chance of majority status for the party as a whole.

Analogizing parties to partnerships is our second main point of departure from *Legislative Leviathan,* where we more often focused on the speaker and the top few leaders rather than the entire set of party members holding agenda-setting offices. Law and accountancy partnerships are designed to allow their senior partners considerable autonomy. By stressing the analogy to a partnership and the importance of agenda power, our approach naturally raises the question of how specific agenda powers are distributed among senior partners.

There are many theoretical possibilities, such as allocating *all* agenda power to the top party leader, allocating proposal power(s) to various senior partners, or allocating veto power(s) to various senior partners. We have argued that, whatever the details of agenda-power allocation, all majority parties in the U.S. House since adoption of Reed's Rules have structured agenda power in such a way that it is very difficult to roll them.

Closely related to the issue of what powers are distributed to which senior partners is the question of what standards of behavior those partners are expected to uphold. At one theoretical extreme, senior partners may have no fiduciary responsibilities to their parties. Agenda power is clearly allocated in these models but officeholders are then free to act in pursuit of their own interests, with neither formal checks (e.g., the necessity of securing their party's renomination) nor informal norms to constrain them. At the other theoretical extreme, senior partners may be expected completely to subordinate their personal goals to the party's. This is implicitly the case, for example, in Ranney's (1951) or the American Political Science Association's (1950) portrayal of responsible party government. Agenda power is not mentioned in such models, but officeholders are clearly enjoined to marshal their parties behind a coherent party platform.

We have opted for a theoretical middle ground of sorts, in which the norm to which senior partners are held depends on the internal homogeneity of the party. If the party is extremely heterogeneous (perhaps similar to a multi-party coalition government in other countries), then only a minimal standard can be realistically enforced: that of not using one's official powers to push legislation that will roll the party. As the party becomes more homogeneous, its senior partners are held to a higher standard, in which they must also use their official posts to help push legislation that most in the party support. Thus, for example, Jamie Whitten (D-MI) continued as chair of the powerful Appropriations Committee in the 1970s because he considerably increased his willingness to cooperate with the party leadership in pushing through

Democratic priorities, even those he personally found distasteful (Crook and Hibbing 1985).

Why does the fiduciary standard become higher for more homogeneous parties? This prediction is entailed by our theory because procedural cartels, as we describe them, primarily distribute veto power among the senior partners of the party. Distributing veto power necessarily interferes with pushing through an ambitious program of legislation, as each senior partner with a veto in a particular policy area has to be brought on board. Thus, the ability of a procedural cartel to legislate necessarily depends on how similar their senior partners' preferences are.

Even when a majority's senior partners disagree on a wide range of issues, however, it becomes no easier to roll the majority party (i.e., pass bills that most majority party members dislike) because some senior partner or partners with relevant veto power will derail the bill. Thus, even internally divided majority parties do not surrender their *negative* agenda-setting power. They simply avoid bills that cannot be passed and move on to bills that can be passed, which tend to be less ideological and more porcine. The minority benefits from the internal divisions of the majority, in the sense that the bills the senior partners can agree on are less likely to have a clear ideological bite to them, hence less likely to roll the minority. But the minority is no more successful in dismantling the majority's previous accomplishments than before. Nor does it benefit by receiving a larger share of chairs, of staff, or of pork.

Because negative agenda power is the bedrock and "first story" of party government, in our view, most of this reading considers the consequences of such power. We return to the "second story" of party government, and discuss when a majority party might wish to build up such a story by readjusting the mix of positive and negative agenda power. . . .

NOTES

1. Quoted in Babington (2004).

2. We did not there formally incorporate the third of Fenno's (1973) famous trio of goals: the pursuit of good public policy. . . . [H]owever, we adapt the standard spatial model of policy making for much of our argument, and this model is sufficiently abstract so that one can easily read personal policy goals into it. Thus, one can add the pursuit of policy as one of the goals that is consistent with the model we present here—although we do not insist on that interpretation.

3. As an example of the importance of majority status for members' legislative projects, consider the statements that Representative Ralph Hall made as he switched from being a member of the Democratic minority to being a member of the Republican majority: "This is the first time, I've just been zeroed out [by the Appropriations Committee]. . . . I've always said that if being a Democrat hurt my district, I'd either resign, retire or switch parties. . . . And it hurt my district this time [because I was denied funds]" (Wolf 2004).

4. Alternatively, of course, a bill can be vetoed, and the veto can be overridden by two thirds of both houses.

5. Among the other solutions suggested in the literature are preplay communication, repeated play, and property rights (Tirole 1988; Friedman 1971).

6. Describing the authority associated with party leadership, Dennis Hastert stated, "So I have two functions. One is governmental, the other political. The governmental function is to run the House, move legislation through, make sure the chairmen and the committees are all operating smoothly. . . . The other function is political. I have to recruit the best possible candidates for Congress and make sure they have the financial and other resources they need to run or, if they're already in Congress, to make sure they have enough to stave off potential challengers" (Hastert 2004: 181–2).

7. Speaker Dennis Hastert clearly recognized the importance of majority status and being in good standing with his party. He emphasized, "Stripped to its essentials, my job is to run the House and make sure we [Republicans] hold the House" (Hastert 2004: 181).

8. Although the speakership is a constitutional office, its agenda-setting powers, as well as those of the other offices mentioned, are stipulated in House rules and precedents. The cartel controls the allocation of agenda power to the various offices to the extent that it can control votes on the adoption of rules.

9. In the United States, the cartel ensures a near-monopoly on agenda-setting offices to the extent that it can control the relevant votes on the floor (on election of the speaker and appointment of committees). To aid in controlling these floor votes, the cartel establishes an intracartel procedure to decide on the nominee for speaker and on a slate of committee appointments.

10. The role of the majority party has also been analogized to former Soviet Congresses. Indeed, as Hastert (2004: 250) notes, "Representative David Obey . . . compares the way the House is run today to 'the old Soviet Congresses—stamp of approval and ratify' rather than using your own judgment. Well, Obey was here when Democrats ran the place. . . . Talk about rubber stamps and domination by a party that had lots of votes and squish room. They were ruthless. They did things like the old Soviet Congresses, such as removing offenders from their hideaway offices, grabbing their office furniture, and taking their parking spots away."

11. A "special rule" is a resolution reported by the Rules Committee that regulates the consideration of a bill or resolution.

12. We are talking here about the powers of the Rules Committee, not its membership.

13. Decrying this monopoly power of the majority party, Dennis Hastert stated, "The truth is that since the last time we had a majority in 1954 only one Republican, Missouri's Bill Emerson, had ever stood on the House Floor—and he stood there as a page. We [the Republicans] had been in the wilderness so long that nobody remembered anything about being in the leadership. We didn't even know where the special back rooms were; we didn't even know where the *keys* to those rooms were" (Hastert 2004: 118).

14. A number of his coconspirators, the so-called Boll Weevils, were also punished by then-Speaker Tip O'Neill. For example, John Breaux of Louisiana and Roy Dyson of Maryland failed to win spots on the Budget and Appropriations committees, respectively (Roberts 1983a). In Breaux's place, the Democratic Party awarded the Budget Committee position to Martin Frost, a Texas Democrat who had "proven himself to be a national Democrat" (Roberts 1983b). Although G. V. Montgomery of Mississippi was reelected chairman of Veterans' Affairs, he lost 53 votes in the party caucus and remarked that conservatives would henceforth likely be more cooperative with their party leaders in Congress (Roberts 1983a).

15. In Arnold's (1990) terms, procedural votes are less "traceable."

16. Nokken's (2004) analysis demonstrates that departing members of Congress in lame duck sessions increasingly vote with their party (as opposed to their constituency). The explanation for this phenomenon is that when constituency constraints are severed (as they are in this situation), members vote with their party in hopes that the party will reward them for their loyalty by aiding them in their future career moves.

17. Quantitatively, Cox and Poole estimate about five to 10 votes switching on key procedural votes, which is consistent with qualitative evidence regarding vest pocket votes.

18. Loyalty is always important in committee assignments, but during times of high homogeneity within the majority party, there may be an increased premium placed on legislative competence. High levels of intraparty homogeneity decrease the relative importance of high loyalty and increase the importance of competence (Wawro 2000, Crook and Hibbing 1985).

19. The Jeffords case is informative here, as it demonstrates the costs of negotiating a defection. The Democrats gave Senator Jeffords the chairmanship of the Environment and Public Works Committee as an inducement to switch parties, which required Harry Reid to give up his status as the ranking Democrat on the committee (Lancaster 2001).

20. The analysis covers only the 80th through 100th Congresses. It is a crude estimate for two main reasons. First, the (negative) correlation between whether a member switches parties and how long that member continues in the House may be only partly due to switching being bad pre se. Perhaps members who switched had very poor electoral prospects, had they remained in their parties, and switched for this reason. So far as we know, however, there is no systematic evidence that party switchers did face greater electoral risks than the typical nonswitching member. Indeed, Ansolabehere, Snyder, and Stewart (2001) find qualitative evidence that discomfort with being ideological misfits accounts for legislators' switching; however, Castle and Fett (2000: 236–7) find that switching is more likely the more ideologically out of step a member is with his copartisans, controlling for a measure of primary electoral risk. Second, our data do not include the full number of terms served by members whose careers continue past the 100th Congress. For these members, the number of terms remaining is coded as zero. As there were no members who switched parties in the 100th Congress, this defect of the data biases our estimate of the cost of switching downward. In other words, if we knew the correct total terms remaining for all members whose careers reached the 100th Congress, the difference between switchers and nonswitchers would be even larger than we report here.

BIBLIOGRAPHY

Alchian, Armen, and Harold Demsetz. 1972. "Production, Information Costs, and Economic Organization." *The American Economic Review* 62: 777–95.

Aldrich, John H. 1995. *Why Parties? The Origin and Transformation of Party Politics in America.* Chicago: University of Chicago Press.

Aldrich, John H., and David W. Rohde. 2001. "The Logic of Conditional Party Government." In *Congress Reconsidered*, 7th ed., eds. Lawrence C. Dodd and Bruce I. Oppenheimer. Washington, DC: Congressional Quarterly, pp. 269–92.

Alexander, DeAlva Stanwood. 1970 [1916]. *History and Procedure of the House of Representatives.* New York: Houghton Mifflin Company.

American Political Science Association. 1950. *Toward a More Responsible Party System, A Report.* New York: Rinehart.

Ansolabehere, Stephen, James Snyder, and Charles Stewart. 2001. "The Effects of Party and Preferences on Congressional Roll-Call Voting." *Legislative Studies Quarterly* 26: 533–72.

Arnold, R. Douglas. 1990. *The Logic of Congressional Action.* New Haven, CT: Yale University Press.

Babington, Charles. 2004. "Hastert Launches a Partisan Policy." Downloaded 11/27/04 from: www.washingtonpost.com.

Burger, Timothy. 1995. "After a Defeat, House Leaders Must Regroup." *Roll Call,* July 17.

Castle, David, and Patrick Fett. 2000. "Member Goals and Party Switching in the U.S. Congress." In *Congress on Display, Congress at Work,* ed. William T. Bianco. Ann Arbor: University of Michigan Press, pp. 231–42.

Cox, Gary W., and Mathew D. McCubbins. 1993. *Legislative Leviathan: Party Government in the House.* Berkeley: University of California Press.

2002. "Agenda Power in the U.S. House of Representatives, 1877 to 1986." In *Party, Process, and Political Change in Congress: New Perspectives on the History of Congress,* eds. David Brady and Mathew D. McCubbins. Stanford, CA: Stanford University Press.

Cox, Gary W., and Keith T. Poole. 2002. "On Measuring Partisanship in Roll-Call Voting: The U.S. House of Representatives, 1877–1999." *American Journal of Political Science* 46: 477–89.

Crook, Sara Brandes, and John R. Hibbing. 1985. "Congressional Reform and Party Discipline: The Effects of Changes in the Seniority System on Party Loyalty in the U.S. House of Representatives." *British Journal of Political Science* 15: 207–26.

Diermeier, Daniel, and Timothy J. Feddersen. 1998. "Cohesion in Legislatures and the Vote of Confidence Procedure." *American Political Science Review* 92: 611–21.

Fenno, Richard F. 1973. *Congressmen in Committees.* Boston: Little, Brown.

Friedman, James. 1971. "A Non-cooperative Equilibrium for Supergames." *Review of Economic Studies* 38: 1–12.

Froman, Lewis A., Jr., and Randall B. Ripley. 1965. "Conditions for Party Leadership: The Case of the House Democrats." *American Political Science Review* 59: 52–63.

Grose, Christian, and Antoine Yoshinaka. 2003. "The Electoral Consequences of Party Switching by Incumbent Members of Congress, Incumbent Legislators Who Switched Parties, 1947–2000." *Legislative Studies Quarterly* 27(1): 55–75.

Hasbrouck, Paul DeWitt. 1927. *Party Government in the House of Representatives.* New York: Macmillan.

Hastert, Dennis. 2004. *Speaker: Lessons from Forty Years in Coaching and Politics.* Washington, DC: Regnery.

Jacobs, John. 1995. *A Rage for Justice.* Berkeley: University of California Press.

Jacobson, Gary C. 1996. "The 1994 House Elections in Perspective." *Political Scien Quarterly* 111: 203–23.

Key, V. O. 1966. *The Responsible Electorate.* Cambridge, MA: Harvard University Press.

King, David C., and Richard Zeckhauser. 2003. "Congressional Vote Options." *Legislative Studies Quarterly* 28: 387–411.

Lancaster, John. 2001. "Senate Republicans Try to Regroup: GOP Caucus Unites Behind Lott as Leader in the Wake of Jeffords's Defection," *The Washington Post,* May 26, p. A.18

Laver, Michael, and Kenneth A. Shepsle. 1996. *Making and Breaking Governments: Cabinets and Legislatures in Parliamentary Democracies*. Cambridge and New York: Cambridge University Press.

Nokken, Timothy P. 2004. "Roll Call Behavior in the Absence of Electoral Constraints: Shirking in Lan??? Duck Sessions of the House of Representatives, 1879–1933." Unpublished paper.

Ranney, Austin. 1951. "Toward A More Responsible Two-Party System: A Commentary." *American Political Science Review* 45: 488–99.

Roberts, Steven V. 1983a. "The Democrats Get Even." *New York Times*, January 9, p. E1.

1983b. "Democrats Reward Loyalty in Giving Assignments," *New York Times*, January 6, p. A25.

Rohde, David W. 1991. *Parties and Leaders in the Postreform House*. Chicago: University of Chicago Press.

Sinclair, Barbara. 2002. "Do Parties Matter?" In *Party, Process, and Political Change: New Perspectives on the History of Congress*, eds. David Brady and Mathew D. McCubbins. Stanford, CA: Stanford University Press, pp. 36–63.

Tirole, Jean. 1988. *The Theory of Industrial Organization*. MIT, Press: Cambridge, MA.

Tsebelis, George. 2002. *Veto Players: How Political Institutions Work*. Princeton, NJ: Princeton University Press.

Wawro, Gregory. 2000. *Legislative Entrepreneurship in the U.S. House of Representatives*. Ann Arbor: University of Michigan Press.

Wolf, Jim. 2004. "Veteran Texas Democrat Switches to Republicans." Washington, DC Reuters.

6

THE PRESIDENCY

6.1

RICHARD E. NEUSTADT

From *Presidential Power and the Modern Presidents: The Politics of Leadership from Roosevelt to Reagan*

In leading a vast executive branch with millions of employees, the president cannot monitor all those who work for him, nor can he or she compel many people to act. This excerpt from the famous book by Neustadt makes the simple point that presidents lead by persuading others that their interests coincide with the president's interests. According to Neustadt, presidential power ebbs and flows with each president's credibility as a persuader.

3. THE POWER TO PERSUADE

. . . The Constitutional Convention of 1787 is supposed to have created a government of "separated powers." It did nothing of the sort. Rather, it created a government of separated institutions *sharing* powers. "I am part of the legislative process," Eisenhower often said in 1959 as a reminder of his veto. Congress, the dispenser of authority and funds, is no less part of the administrative process. Federalism adds another set of separated institutions. The Bill of Rights adds others. Many public purposes can only be achieved by voluntary acts of private institutions; the press, for one, in Douglass Cater's phrase, is a "fourth branch of government." And with the coming of alliances abroad, the separate institutions of a London, or a Bonn, share in the making of American public policy.

What the Constitution separates our political parties do not combine. The parties are themselves composed of separated organizations sharing public authority. The authority consists of nominating powers. Our national parties are confederations of state and local party institutions, with a headquarters that represents the White House, more or less, if the party has a President in office. These confederacies manage presidential nominations. All other public offices depend upon electorates confined within the states. All other nominations are controlled within the states. The President and congressmen who bear one party's label are divided by dependence upon different sets of voters. The differences are sharpest at the stage of nomination. The White House has too small a share in nominating congressmen, and Congress has too little weight in nominating presidents for party to erase their constitutional separation. Party links are stronger than is frequently supposed, but nominating processes assure the separation.

The separateness of institutions and the sharing of authority prescribe the terms on which a President persuades. When one man shares authority with another, but does not gain or lose his job upon the other's whim, his willingness to act upon the urging of the other turns on whether he conceives the action right for him. The essence of a President's persuasive task is to convince such men that what the White House wants of them is what they ought to do for their sake and on their authority. (Sex matters not at all; for *man* read *woman*.)

Persuasive power, thus defined, amounts to more than charm or reasoned argument. These have their uses for a President, but these are not the whole of his resources. For the individuals he would induce to do what he wants done on their own responsibility will need or fear some acts by him on his responsibility. If they share his authority, he has some share in theirs. Presidential "powers" may be inconclusive when a President commands, but always remain relevant as he persuades. The status and authority inherent in his office reinforce his logic and his charm.

Status adds something to persuasiveness; authority adds still more. . . . In Walter Bagehot's charming phrase "no man can *argue* on his knees." Although there is no kneeling in this country, few men—and exceedingly few cabinet officers—are immune to the impulse to say "yes" to the President of the United States. It grows harder to say "no" when they are seated in his Oval Office at the White House, or in his study on the second floor, where almost tangibly he partakes of the aura of his physical surroundings. In Sawyer's case, moreover, the President possessed formal authority to intervene in many matters of concern to the secretary of commerce. These matters ranged from jurisdictional disputes among the defense agencies to legislation pending before Congress and, ultimately, to the tenure of the secretary, himself. . . .

A President's authority and status give him great advantages in dealing with the men he would persuade. Each "power" is a vantage point for him in the degree that other men have use for his authority. From the veto to appointments, from publicity to budgeting, and so down a long list, the White House now controls the most encompassing array of vantage points in the American political system. With hardly an exception, those who share in governing this country are aware that at some time, in some degree, the doing of *their* jobs, the furthering of *their* ambitions, may depend upon the President of the United States. Their need for presidential action, or their fear of it, is bound to be recurrent if not actually continuous. Their need or fear is his advantage.

A President's advantages are greater than mere listing of his "powers" might suggest. Those with whom he deals must deal with him until the last day of his term. Because they have continuing relationships with him, his future, while it lasts, supports his present influence. Even though there is no need or fear of him today, what he could do tomorrow may supply today's advantage. Continuing relationships may convert any "power," any aspect of his status, into vantage points in almost any case. When he induces other people to do what he wants done, a President can trade on their dependence now and later.

The President's advantages are checked by the advantages of others. Continuing relationships will pull in both directions. These are relationships of mutual dependence. A President depends upon the persons whom he would persuade; he has to reckon with his need or fear of them. They too will possess status, or authority, or both, else they would be of little use to him. Their vantage points confront his own; their power tempers his.

■　　■　　■

The power to persuade is the power to bargain. Status and authority yield bargaining advantages. But in a government of "separated institutions sharing powers," they yield them to all sides. With the array of vantage points at his disposal, a President may be far more persuasive than his logic or his charm could make him. But outcomes are not guaranteed by his advantages. There remain the counter pressures those whom he would influence can bring to bear on him from vantage points at their disposal. Command has limited utility; persuasion becomes give-and-take. It is well that the White House holds the vantage points it does. In such a business any President may need them all—and more.

II

This view of power as akin to bargaining is one we commonly accept in the sphere of congressional relations. Every textbook states and every legislative session demonstrates that save in times like the extraordinary Hundred Days of 1933—times virtually ruled out by definition at midcentury—a President will often be unable to obtain congressional action on his terms or even to halt action he opposes. The reverse is equally accepted: Congress often is frustrated by the President. Their formal powers are so intertwined that neither will accomplish very much, for very long, without the acquiescence of the other. By the same token, though, what one demands the other can resist. The stage is set for that great game, much like collective bargaining, in which each seeks to profit from the other's needs and fears. It is a game played catch-as-catch-can, case by case. And everybody knows the game, observers and participants alike.

■ ■ ■

In spheres of party politics the same thing follows, necessarily, from the confederal nature of our party organizations. Even in the case of national nominations a President's advantages are checked by those of others. In 1944 it is by no means clear that Roosevelt got his first choice as his running mate. In 1948 Truman, then the President, faced serious revolts against his nomination. In 1952 his intervention from the White House helped assure the choice of Adlai Stevenson, but it is far from clear that Truman could have done as much for any other candidate acceptable to him. In 1956 when Eisenhower was President, the record leaves obscure just who backed Harold Stassen's efforts to block Richard Nixon from renomination as vice president. But evidently everything did not go quite as Eisenhower wanted, whatever his intentions may have been. The outcomes in these instances bear all the marks of limits on command and of power checked by power that characterize congressional relations. Both in and out of politics these checks and limits seem to be quite widely understood.

Influence becomes still more a matter of give-and-take when Presidents attempt to deal with allied governments. A classic illustration is the long unhappy wrangle over Suez policy in 1956. In dealing with the British and the French before their military intervention, Eisenhower had his share of bargaining advantages but no effective power of command. His allies had their share of counterpressures, and they finally tried the most extreme of all: action despite him. His pressure then was instrumental in reversing them. But had the British government been on safe ground at home, Eisenhower's wishes might have made as little difference after intervention as before. Behind the decorum of diplomacy—which was not very decorous in the Suez affair—relationships among allies are not unlike relationships among state delegations at a national convention. Power is persuasion, and persuasion becomes bargaining. The concept is familiar to everyone who watches foreign policy.

In only one sphere is the concept unfamiliar: the sphere of executive relations. Perhaps because of civics textbooks and teaching in our schools, Americans instinctively resist the view that power in this sphere resembles power in all others. Even Washington reporters, White House aides, and congressmen are not immune to the illusion that administrative agencies comprise a single structure, "the" executive branch, where presidential word is law, or ought to be. . . . When a President seeks something from executive officials his persuasiveness is subject to the same sorts of limitations as in the case of congressmen, or governors, or national committeemen, or private citizens, or foreign governments. There are no generic differences, no differences in kind and only sometimes in degree. The incidents preceding the dismissal of MacArthur and the incidents surrounding seizure of the steel mills make it plain that here as elsewhere influence derives from bargaining advantages; power is a give-and-take.

Like our governmental structure as a whole, the executive establishment consists of separated institutions sharing powers. The President heads one of these; cabinet officers, agency administrators, and military commanders head others. Below the departmental level, virtually independent bureau chiefs head many more. Under midcentury conditions, federal operations spill across dividing lines on organization charts; almost every policy entangles many agencies; almost every program calls for interagency collaboration. Everything somehow involves the President. But operating agencies owe their existence least of all to one another—and only in some part to him. Each has a separate statutory base; each has its statutes to administer; each deals with a different set of subcommittees at the Capitol. Each has its own peculiar set of clients, friends, and enemies outside the formal government. Each has a different set of specialized careerists inside its own bailiwick. Our Constitution gives the President the "take-care" clause and the appointive power. Our statutes give him central budgeting and a degree of personnel control. All agency administrators are responsible to him. But they also are responsible to Congress, to their clients, to their staffs, and to themselves. In short, they have five masters. Only after all of those do they owe any loyalty to each other.

"The members of the cabinet," Charles G. Dawes used to remark, "are a president's natural enemies." Dawes had been Harding's budget director, Coolidge's vice president, and Hoover's ambassador to London; he also had been General Pershing's chief assistant for supply in World War I. The words are highly colored, but Dawes knew whereof he spoke. The men who have to serve so many masters cannot help but be somewhat the "enemy" of any one of them. By the same token, any master wanting service is in some degree the "enemy" of such a servant. A President is likely to want loyal support but not to relish trouble on his doorstep. Yet the more his cabinet members cleave to him, the more they may need help from him in fending off the wrath of rival masters. Help, though, is synonymous with trouble. Many a cabinet officer, with loyalty ill rewarded by his lights and help withheld, has come to view the White House as innately hostile to department heads. Dawes's dictum can be turned around.

A senior presidential aide remarked to me in Eisenhower's time: "If some of these cabinet members would just take time out to stop and ask themselves, 'What would I want if I were President?' they wouldn't give him all the trouble he's been having." But even if they asked themselves the question, such officials often could not act upon the answer. Their personal attachment to the President is all too often overwhelmed by duty to their other masters.

Executive officials are not equally advantaged in their dealings with a President. Nor are the same officials equally advantaged all the time. . . . The vantage points conferred upon officials by their own authority and status vary enormously. The variance is heightened by particulars of time and circumstance. In mid-October 1950, Truman, at a press conference, remarked of the man he had considered firing in August and would fire the next April for intolerable insubordination:

> Let me tell you something that will be good for your souls. It's a pity that you . . . can't understand the ideas of two intellectually honest men when they meet. General MacArthur . . . is a member of the Government of the United States. He is loyal to that Government. He is loyal to the President. He is loyal to the President in his foreign policy. . . . There is no disagreement between General MacArthur and myself.

MacArthur's status in and out of government was never higher than when Truman spoke those words. The words, once spoken, added to the general's credibility thereafter when he sought to use the press in his campaign against the President. And what had happened between August and October? Near victory had happened, together with that premature conference on postwar plans, the meeting at Wake Island.

If the bargaining advantages of a MacArthur fluctuate with changing circumstances, this is bound to be so with subordinates who have at their disposal fewer powers, lesser status, to fall back on. And when officials have no powers in their own right, or depend upon the President for status, their counterpressure may be limited indeed. White House aides, who fit both categories, are among the most responsive men of all, and for good reason. As a director of the budget once remarked to me, "Thank God I'm here and not across the street. If the President doesn't call me, I've got plenty I can do right here and plenty coming up to me, by rights, to justify my calling him. But those poor fellows over there, if the boss doesn't call them, doesn't ask them to do something, what *can* they do but sit?" Authority and status so conditional are frail reliances in resisting a President's own wants. Within the White House precincts, lifted eyebrows may suffice to set an aide in motion; command, coercion, even charm aside. But even in the White House a President does not monopolize effective power. Even there persuasion is akin to bargaining. A former Roosevelt aide once wrote of cabinet officers:

> Half of a President's suggestions, which theoretically carry the weight of orders, can be safely forgotten by a Cabinet member. And if the President asks about a suggestion a second time, he can be told that it is being investigated. If he asks a third time, a wise Cabinet officer will give him at least part of what he suggests. But only occasionally, except about the most important matters, do Presidents ever get around to asking three times.

The rule applies to staff as well as to the cabinet, and certainly has been applied *by* staff in Truman's time and Eisenhower's.

Some aides will have more vantage points than a selective memory. Sherman Adams, for example, as the assistant to the President under Eisenhower, scarcely deserved the appelation "White House aide" in the meaning of the term before his time or as applied to other members of the Eisenhower entourage. Although Adams was by no means "chief of staff" in any sense so sweeping—or so simple—as press commentaries often took for granted, he apparently became no more dependent on the President than Eisenhower on him. "I need him," said the President when Adams turned out to have been remarkably imprudent in the Goldfine case, and delegated to him, at least nominally, the decision on his own departure. This instance is extreme, but the tendency it illustrates is common enough. Any aide who demonstrates to others that he has the President's consistent confidence and a consistent part in presidential business will acquire so much business on his own account that he becomes in some sense independent of his chief. Nothing in the Constitution keeps a well-placed aide from converting status into power of his own, usable in some degree even against the President—an outcome not unknown in Truman's regime or, by all accounts, in Eisenhower's.

The more an officeholder's status and his powers stem from sources independent of the President, the stronger will be his potential pressure on the President. Department heads in general have more bargaining power than do most members of the White House staff; but bureau chiefs may have still more, and specialists at upper levels of established career services may have almost unlimited reserves of the enormous power which consists of sitting still.

▪   ▪   ▪

In the right circumstances, of course, a President can have his way with any of these people. Chapter 2 includes three instances where circumstances were "right" and a presidential order was promptly carried out. But one need only note the favorable factors giving those three orders their self-executing quality to recognize that as between a President and his "subordinates," no less than others on whom he depends, real power is reciprocal and varies markedly with organization, subject matter, personality, and situation. The mere fact that persuasion is directed at executive officials signifies no necessary easing of his way. Any new congressman of the Administration's party, especially if narrowly elected, may turn out more amenable (though less useful) to the President than any seasoned bureau chief "downtown." *The probabilities of power do not derive from the literary theory of the Constitution.*

III

There is a widely held belief in the United States that were it not for folly or for knavery, a reasonable President would need no power other than the logic of his argument. No less a personage than Eisenhower has subscribed to that belief in many a campaign speech and press-conference remark. But faulty reasoning and bad intentions do not cause all quarrels with Presidents. The best of reasoning and of intent cannot compose them all. For in the first place, what the President wants will rarely seem a trifle to the people he wants it from. And in the second place, they will be bound to judge it by the standard of their own responsibilities, not his. However logical his argument according to his lights, their judgment may not bring them to his view.

Those who share in governing this country frequently appear to act as though they were in business for themselves. So, in a real though not entire sense, they are and have to be. When Truman and MacArthur fell to quarreling, for example, the stakes were no less than the substance of American foreign policy, the risks of greater war or military stalemate, the prerogatives of Presidents and field commanders, the pride of a proconsul and his place in history. Intertwined, inevitably, were other stakes as well: political stakes for men and factions of both parties; power stakes for interest groups with which they were or wished to be affiliated. And every stake was raised by the apparent discontent in the American public mood. There is no reason to suppose that in such circumstances men of large but differing responsibilities will see all things through the same glasses. On the contrary, it is to be expected that their views of what ought to be done and what they then should do will vary with the differing perspectives their particular responsibilities evoke. Since their duties are not vested in a "team" or a "collegium" but in themselves, as individuals, one must expect that they will see things for themselves. Moreover, when they are responsible to many masters and when an event or policy turns loyalty against loyalty—a day-by-day occurrence in the nature of the case—one must assume that those who have the duties to perform will choose the terms of reconciliation. This is the essence of their personal responsibility. When their own duties pull in opposite directions, who else but they can choose what they will do?

When Truman dismissed MacArthur, the latter lost three posts: the American command in the Far East, the Allied command for the occupation of Japan, and the United Nations command in Korea. He also lost his status as the senior officer on active duty in the United States armed forces. So long as he held those positions and that status, though, he had a duty to his troops, to his profession, to himself (the last is hard for any man to disentangle from the rest). As a public figure and a focus for men's hopes he had a duty to constituents at home, and in Korea and Japan. He owed a duty also to those other constituents, the UN governments contributing to his field forces. As a patriot he had a duty to his country. As an accountable official and an expert guide he stood at the call of Congress. As a military officer he had, besides, a duty to the President, his constitutional commander. Some of these duties may have manifested themselves in terms more tangible or more direct than others. But it would be nonsense to argue that the last negated all the rest, however much it might be claimed to override them. And it makes no more sense to think that anybody but MacArthur was effectively empowered to decide how he himself would reconcile the competing demands his duties made upon him.

■   ■   ■

The essence of a President's persuasive task, with congressmen and everybody else, is to induce them to believe that what he wants of them is what their own appraisal of their own responsibilities requires them to do in their interest, not his. Because men may differ in their views on public policy, because differences in outlook stem from differences in duty—duty to one's office, one's constituents, oneself—that task is bound to be more like collective bargaining than like a reasoned argument among philosopher kings. Overtly or implicitly, hard bargaining has characterized all illustrations offered up to now. This is the reason why: Persuasion deals in the coin of self-interest with men who have some freedom to reject what they find counterfeit.

6.2

CHARLES M. CAMERON

"Bargaining and Presidential Power"

The president is the executive of the national government, but he has a key leg-islative power that allows him to influence Congress: the veto. Cameron shows how presidents can use the veto effectively to shape legislation. The threat of a presidential veto can be enough; Congress will often write legislation specifically to avoid a veto.

"Presidential power" is a deceptive phrase. It suggests that the capacity to shape policy is an attribute of the *president*, and a single attribute at that. But power is not an attribute of an individual, like her height or weight. Instead, "power" describes something about the outcome of a strategic interaction (a "game"). In particular, a president has power in a game when its outcome resembles what the president wants and he causes the outcome to be that way.[1]

This way of thinking about power shifts attention from the attributes of presidents to the characteristics of the games they play. Among these many games are the Supreme Court nominations game, the veto game, the executive order game, the treaty ratification game, the legislative leadership game, the agency supervision and management game, the commander-in-chief game, the staffing game, the executive reorganization game, the opinion leadership game, and the impeachment game. *Understanding the presidency means under-standing these games.* I am tempted to add, "and that is all it means," but that would be too strong. Skill, personality, and charisma seem to matter, or so many people believe. But they always operate within the confines of specific games and strategic circumstances. Understanding the games presidents play is fundamental for understanding presidential power.

Presidents participate in so many games that it is hard to characterize them in a simple way. Broadly speaking, though, when presidents interact with Con-gress, they often play *coordination games* or *bargaining games*. Loosely speak-ing, coordination games require many players to act in one of several possible ways if they are to benefit themselves. If they do not all act in the same way, they work at cross-purposes. The politics of such games involve selecting the "focal points" coordinating the players' actions. A majority party setting its legislative agenda in Congress is a prime example of this situation, because many players—across committees in both houses and in the leadership—must focus on a few priorities if they are to accomplish much. Oft times, the selection of focal points involves loose norms and improvisation rather than formal procedures specified in law or the Constitution; this lies outside what Neustadt called the "literary theory of the Constitution," though hardly outside the reach of social science.

In contrast, bargaining games require players to divide among themselves a "pie," or set of benefits. The politics of bargaining involves gambits increasing one's share of the pie. Examples include haggling over the content of laws, pulling and hauling to determine the direction and vigor of agency decisions, and bickering over the appointment of executive officials and judges. These activities all involve give-and-take across the branches of government. Many bargaining games in which the president participates are quite formal, with a structure specified by the Constitution, by law, or by norms of long-standing precedent.[2]

▪ ▪ ▪

PRESIDENTIAL BARGAINING GAMES: WHAT DO WE KNOW?

Given the importance of bargaining games for the contemporary presidency, an obvious question is: What does the empirical record tell us about presidential bargaining games? This seems like it should be an easy question to answer, but unfortunately it is not. The problem is that data on the *process* of bargaining—the number of vetoes, of nominees rejected by Congress, the number of oversight hearings, the number of policy proposals in State of the Union messages, the number of bills introduced in Congress, the number of executive orders reversed by Congress, and so on—are relatively easy to collect but hard to interpret (I'll explain why shortly). Conversely, data on the *outputs* from bargaining games—for example, the number and content of important laws, executive orders, and treaties, the intensity and import of bureaucratic action, the ideological tenor and meaning of court decisions—are very hard to collect but much easier to interpret.

Why are process measures so much harder to interpret compared to output measures? The problem is that power in bargaining games often operates through *anticipation*. Congress anticipates a veto if it goes too far: in order to avoid the veto, it trims back a policy initiative. No veto occurs, but the president's preferences have altered what Congress would have done if could have operated without constraint. In other words, the game's structure allows the president to exercise power over the outcome, even absent a veto. As a second example, suppose the president anticipates a torrent of opposition if he nominates a controversial activist to head a regulatory agency. Accordingly, he eschews the controversial nominee in favor of a more moderate one, though he would prefer to put the activist in charge if he could do so without cost. The nomination then flies through Congress. In this case, the structure of the game allows Congress to exercise some power over the nominee's ideology even with no direct evidence of this in the public record.

Situations like this involve the "second face of power," power operating through anticipated response.[3] These situations are notoriously difficult to study using process measures since participants maneuver to avoid the most easily measured consequences of disagreement.

How can one find the traces of power when the second face of power is at work? There are two methods: the first direct, the second indirect. The direct method involves measuring policy outputs and relating them to the actors' preferences. If the president actually exercises power over the output, even without taking visible action, then a switch from a liberal president to a conservative one should result in a change in policy, *ceteris paribus*. If one collects data on policy outputs and proxies for preference changes (e.g., partisan affiliation of the president and key congressional actors), and the policy outputs change in a clear and simple way in response to changes in the preference proxies, then one has strong circumstantial evidence of power being exercised. Obviously, one needs to control for confounding influences, but the principle is clear enough.[4]

The indirect approach is more convoluted. It begins with process data, such as vetoes, rejected nominees, reversed executive orders, and blocked agency initiatives. The problem is interpreting such data. In order for events like vetoes to occur, there must be policy disagreement between the actors. But this is only a *necessary* condition. It is certainly not a *sufficient* condition, as arguments about the second face of power indicate. Instead, a process marker like a veto, a rejected nominee or treaty, or a reversed executive order, represents the impact of policy disagreement, *plus something else beyond mere disagreement*. Let us call this additional element "Factor X."[5] The essence of the indirect approach is to build an explicit model of bargaining *incorporating Factor X*. Using this model, one can interpret the process measures and even draw conclusions about presidential power. Absent such a model, all that can be concluded from process measures like counts of vetoes is that policy disagreement occurred—a very weak conclusion since policy disagreement may not trigger a veto without Factor X.[6]

■　　■　　■

The Indirect Approach: Studying Veto Bargaining

Absent a model of vetoes (actual vetoes, not just veto power), any number of vetoes is equally compatible with little, some, or a great deal of presidential power over legislative outputs. No vetoes may mean that Congress has capitulated to the president, or the president has capitulated to Congress; or that Congress has made some compromises before submitting the bill to the president, who compromises somewhat by accepting it. Many vetoes are equally ambiguous. The lesson is a general one—data on process measures simply do not speak for themselves. The idea of the indirect approach is to combine process measures with explicit models of bargaining, in the hope the data will speak more distinctly.

Veto threats

Matthews provides an elegant model of veto threats, beginning with a standard model of one-shot, take-it-or-leave-it bargaining over political issues.[7] Then he adds an explicit "Factor X"—congressional uncertainty about the president's policy preferences. In other words, Matthews assumes the president has a policy reputation, but the reputation is not so precise that Congress can predict with pinpoint accuracy the response of the president to every conceivable bill. Disagreement between the president and Congress, *plus* congressional uncertainty about how far it can push the president before triggering a veto, allows vetoes to occur within the model—they occur when the president turns out to be somewhat tougher (that is, more extreme) than Congress anticipated. Finally, Matthews allows the president to issue a veto threat before Congress writes a bill. Using quite sophisticated game theory, Matthews works out predictions about the behavior of Congress and president.

Within the confines of the model, one can evaluate the impact of the "institution" of the veto threat on presidential power. Broadly speaking, veto threats often enhance presidential power (relative to a world without veto threats), because they help the president and Congress strike bargains that they might not otherwise forge, for want of congressional concessions. Moreover, the concessions induced by threats often work to the advantage of the president.[8]

In our own research, my collaborators and I present systematic data on veto threats, congressional concessions after threats, and vetoes after threats, and use Matthews's model to interpret the data (and, to some extent, use the data to test the model).[9] The universe for the study consists of the 2,284 "nonminor" bills presented to the president between 1945 and 1992. We collected data on a random sample of 281 nonvetoed bills from the universe, stratified across three levels of "legislative significance" derived from an approach similar to Mayhew's. We also collected data on all vetoed bills in the universe, some 162 bills, for a total of 443 bills in all. We compiled data on threats and concessions from legislative histories of the bills, the public papers of the presidents, and newspaper accounts.

Statistical analysis of the data revealed the following patterns:

1. During unified government, veto threats rarely occur regardless of the significance of the legislation.
2. During divided government, veto threats occur frequently and increase in frequency with legislative significance. The frequency of veto threats for important legislation during divided government is surprisingly high: 34 percent of such bills received veto threats.
3. If a bill is not threatened, a veto is unlikely though not impossible.

4. If a bill is threatened, the probability of a veto increases dramatically, especially during divided government and at higher levels of legislative significance. But vetoes are not certain even after a threat.
5. Veto threats usually bring concessions.
6. Concessions deter vetoes. The bigger the concession the less likely a threatened bill is to be vetoed.

Although some of these findings lie outside the scope of Matthews's model (for example, the importance of legislative significance), for the most part these findings strongly resemble what the model predicts. Thus, the model "explains" the data, in the sense that it provides a detailed causal mechanism for the process. If one combines the import of the model—veto threats often enhance presidential power—with the data on the actual frequency of threats, one obtains a picture in which veto threats assume considerable importance in the armamentarium of presidents serving in periods of divided party government.

NOTES

1. This conclusion follows from the canonical definition of power: "power is a causal relationship between preferences and outcomes." For a thorough discussion, see Jack Nagal, *The Descriptive Analysis of Power* (New Haven, Conn.: Yale University Press, 1975).

2. The distinction I am drawing between coordination and bargaining is rooted more in presidential politics than abstract game theory. For example, there are bargaining games in which coordination is critical (e.g., Nash bargaining games, with a multitude of equilibria). So I am not drawing a logical or mathematical distinction but instead pointing to the character of different activities.

3. Peter Bachrach and Morton Baratz, "The Two Faces of Power," *American Political Science Review* (1962) 56: 947–952.

4. This method of studying power is laid out in the classics of the power literature, see Robert A. Dahl, *Modern Political Analysis*, 2nd ed. (Englewood Cliffs, N.J.: Prentice-Hall, 1970), and Jack Nagal, *The Descriptive Analysis of Power* (New Haven, Conn.: Yale University Press, 1975). It was first applied to studying presidential power in Terry Moe, "An Assessment of the Positive Theory of 'Congressional Dominance' of Bureaucracy," *Legislative Studies Quarterly* (1987) 12: 475, and Barry R. Weingast, and Mark J. Moran, "Bureaucracy Discretion or Congressional Control? Regulatory Policymaking by the Federal Trade Commission," *Journal of Political Economy* (1983) 91: 765–800.

5. For those who don't like suspense: "Factor X" often turns out to be some type of uncertainty, including uncertainty about what others will do (e.g., in the form of mixed strategies) or what they want (e.g., incomplete information about actors' preferences) and thus what they will do.

6. One cannot even conclude that vetoes are evidence of the most important or most intense disagreements. Drawing that conclusion requires a model of vetoes in which the statement is true; absent the model, it is not a valid inference.

7. Steven Matthews, "Veto Threats: Rhetoric in a Bargaining Game," *Quarterly Journal of Economics* (1989) 103: 347–369.

8. They don't always do so, for sometimes the concessions are inadequate to head off a veto. In this case, concessions don't actually advantage the president (neglecting veto overrides).

9. Charles M. Cameron, *Veto Bargaining: Presidents and the Politics of Negative Power* (New York: Cambridge University Press, 2000), and Charles Cameron, John S. Lapinski, and Charles Riemann, "Testing Formal Theories of Political Rhetoric," *Journal of Politics* (Forthcoming Winter 2000).

6.3

BRANDICE CANES-WRONE

From *Who Leads Whom? Presidents, Policy, and the Public*

Do presidents follow public opinion even when they believe it is wrong? Or do presidents do what they think is right even when doing so is unpopular? Canes-Wrone describes three important cases when presidents pandered; that is, they followed public opinion rather than do what they thought was the right thing to do. She argues that this happens often.

6. EXAMPLES OF POLICY PANDERING AND LEADERSHIP

Why did Jimmy Carter, a long-time proponent of expanding humanitarian assistance, suddenly propose to scale back the program? Why did Ronald Reagan, who was philosophically opposed to tax increases, recommend an unpopular one? And why did George H. W. Bush veto a bill extending unemployment benefits only to sign similar bills over the course of the following eight months?

. . . [T]he cases illustrate the behaviors of *policy pandering* and *policy leadership*. Pandering reflects circumstances in which a president supports a popular policy option despite the fact that he expects it to harm citizens' interests. Policy leadership, in comparison, occurs when a president endorses an unpopular option that he believes will advance societal welfare.

■   ■   ■

Case Selection

The primary motivation for developing the Conditional Pandering Theory was to assess the incentives of the president to pander to public opinion when forced to choose between endorsing a popular course of action or one he believes will produce a good outcome for society. Given this substantive aim, I focus the narrative analysis on executive decisions for which the president's beliefs regarding the optimal policy choice differed from those of the mass public. As previously discussed, the concept of policy pandering does not require that a president's beliefs regarding the optimal course of action are necessarily correct. Accordingly, in the cases, the fact that a president deemed the mass citizenry to be misguided does not mean that the reader will necessarily agree with the president's assessment.

The need to ascertain the president's beliefs in relation to public opinion made the selection of cases contingent on the availability of historical evidence on these factors. Even so, I imposed a number of additional restrictions regarding the selection. First, to illustrate how the theoretical predictions vary according to the president's popularity relative to that of his likely competition, I ensured that one case concerned a president far ahead of his likely competition, one a president far behind, and one a president who could expect a tight race. Using the language of chapter 5, at least one case involved a highly popular president, one an unpopular chief executive, and one a marginally popular president. Thus, in the narratives, presidential approval ratings are often employed as a proxy for a chief executive's popularity relative to that of his potential competition. Prior research establishes that this factor is correlated with a president's likelihood of retaining office (e.g., Brody and Sigelman 1983; Sigelman 1979). By comparison, trial heats are not particularly accurate assessments of a president's electoral prospects until the final months of a race; indeed, trial heats are not even routinely available throughout a president's term.

The second restriction is that the universe of potential cases was limited to the decisions of presidents since Nixon. The literature suggests that these presidents have been more likely than their predecessors to involve the mass public in policymaking (e.g., Kernell 1997; Skowronek 1993); the restriction enables showing that the Conditional Pandering Theory is germane to these presidencies. Third, to demonstrate that the theory is not limited in applicability to a given administration or personality, I selected a different chief executive for each case. Fourth, I chose only policy decisions that were significant enough to receive coverage in the *Congressional Quarterly Almanac*. This restriction was inspired by a desire to establish that the theory is relevant to relatively important policy decisions. Finally, the selection was influenced by the fact that presidents can more easily change public opinion in foreign as compared with domestic affairs. Because of this asymmetry, one might suppose that presidential pandering would be uncommon in foreign affairs and common in domestic matters. To demonstrate the relevance of the Conditional Pandering Theory across both domains, I illustrate the behavior of policy pandering with decisions involving foreign affairs and the behavior of policy leadership with decisions on domestic matters.

A substantial portion of each narrative is devoted to describing why seemingly plausible alternative explanations do not explain the sequence of events. This attention to alternative explanations is partially a function of the fact that one would not necessarily anticipate truth revelation by presidents and their advisors. Chief executives are not likely to admit, even in retrospect, that they followed public opinion despite having evidence suggesting the action would produce harmful effects. (Nor are presidents particularly likely to state that electoral motivations were what lead them to take an unpopular position, as occurs in the Conditional Pandering Theory when first-term presidents exercise policy leadership.) The narratives accordingly do not revolve around "smoking guns" of admissions by presidents but, instead, careful attention to their long-standing beliefs, public opinion, and possible alternative accounts.

President Carter and Foreign Aid: The Trustee Panders

Carter is reputed to have placed the public interest above other political objectives. For example, Erwin Hargrove (1988, 11) assesses in his biography of Carter: "The key of Carter's understanding of himself as a political leader was his belief that the essential responsibility of leadership was to articulate the good of the entire community rather than any part of it . . . Rather than being antipolitical or nonpolitical leadership, this was, for him, a different kind of leadership that eschewed the normal politician's preoccupation with representing private interests, bargaining, and short-term electoral goals." Similarly, Charles Jones (1988) characterizes Carter's regime as the "trustee-ship presidency," in which the chief executive viewed himself as a trustee of the people and sought to enact policies he believed were in the public interest even when they were not politically expedient. Precisely because of this reputation, I illustrate the behavior of pandering with a case study that concerns President Carter. By establishing that the Conditional Pandering Theory has relevance for his policy decisions, I show it is applicable even to presidents who are not thought to cater to public opinion.

The case study focuses on Carter's budgetary proposal for the policy issue of humanitarian assistance in 1980, the year he ran for reelection. Upon taking office, Carter had pledged to switch U.S. policy toward communist containment in the Third World. Instead of responding militarily whenever conflicts over communism arose, Carter espoused a "preventive" approach. He sought to lessen the appeal of communism to the citizens of Third World nations by solving their underlying problems (e.g., Deibel 1987; Skidmore 1996). Development assistance comprised a key component of this preventive approach.

For the first three years of Carter's term, his proposals for humanitarian assistance, or economic aid, were consistent with this philosophy. In each year, Carter requested an increase and he invariably achieved one, even if not for the full amount he had requested. He pursued this expansion despite a lack of public support for the program; according to responses to the General Social Survey, throughout his administration over 65 percent of the populace believed the United States spent too much on foreign aid.[1]

Carter knew that his policy position was unpopular. He acknowledged as much during a call-in radio show he hosted during the first few months in office. Stating his policy stance to a caller, Carter began, "Well, John [the caller], I'm going to take a position that's not very popular, politically speaking."[2] Likewise, in a session with media representatives during the second year of the administration, Carter remarked, "I don't know of any issue that has less political support than that program itself, foreign aid in all its forms."[3]

Carter's lack of pandering over foreign aid during his first three years in office is consistent with his reputation for placing the public interest above other, more political objectives. His behavior also, however, comports with the Conditional Pandering Theory. The theory suggests that a president will not pander to public opinion if he does not soon face a contest for reelection or if he is highly popular or unpopular. In the early months of 1977 and 1978, when Carter submitted his foreign aid proposals as a part of his annual budgetary requests, the presidential election was relatively distant. By the outset of 1979, when Carter offered his humanitarian aid proposal for the following fiscal year, the electoral race was approaching but Carter's popularity was weak. His public approval ratings for the past year had averaged 43 percent, a very low level by historical standards. His decision to exercise policy leadership is thus consistent with the Conditional Pandering Theory.

Of course, that Carter's policymaking on foreign aid between 1977 and 1979 comports with the Conditional Pandering Theory does not eliminate the possibility that his actions were entirely the consequence of his character. For this reason, we focus on the humanitarian aid proposal Carter offered in 1980, when he reversed his previous position and recommended that the United States cut economic assistance. Specifically, in his budget of January 1980 (which was for fiscal year 1981), Carter proposed cutting economic assistance by 2 percent in nominal terms. The cut constituted a nominal decline of 26 percent relative to his recommendation in the previous budget. Moreover, given the inflation rate predicted by the administration, his request signified a real reduction of 11 percent from the appropriations of last year and 39 percent from his earlier proposal.

The descriptive summaries accompanying the numbers in Carter's budgets reflect the change in his policy position. The budget submitted in 1979 stated that it contained "increases in foreign aid with emphasis on long-term development of poor countries, and reducing widespread poverty." In contrast, the budget submitted in 1980 characterized the proposals for foreign affairs as "designed to help meet the near-term challenges to stability." This budget was also printed in the colors of Carter's reelection campaign, emphasizing the linkage between the document and election year politics (Hargrove 1988).

When Carter submitted his election-year budget, he had reason to believe the impending presidential race would be competitive. His approval ratings were respectable at 58 percent but not remarkably high by historical standards. Moreover, economists were forecasting an imminent recession that would cause double-digit inflation and an increase in unemployment. Carter knew that the recession, assuming it materialized, could cause him serious problems in his campaign for reelection. As a result, he very much wanted his budget to appeal to voters (Kaufman 1993, 168–69).

Carter's policy reversal on foreign aid helped to achieve this goal. By proposing a reduction in economic assistance, he ensured that his position on this program would be consonant with public opinion. According to a Roper survey taken the month before he submitted his budget, 72 percent of the population thought foreign assistance should be decreased.[4] Had Carter continued trying to expand economic aid, he would have handed challengers an easy issue on which to criticize him.

Thus consistent with the Conditional Pandering Theory, Carter switched his position in the direction of public opinion once he was marginally popular and soon faced a contest for reelection. He could reasonably expect that the effects of cutting economic assistance would not be known by voters before the election, particularly since appropriations bills are not typically enacted until summer at the earliest. Moreover, the anticipated competitiveness of the race meant that his policy choice might affect his likelihood of winning. As a result, Carter had an electoral incentive to take the popular position of cutting humanitarian assistance, even if he believed that increasing it was in America's long-term interest.

Among seemingly plausible alternative explanations, none receives support on careful examination. Perhaps the most natural justification, and one that would comport with Carter's reputation for pursuing the public interest, is that his beliefs about the value of humanitarian assistance had changed. In fact, as Michael Genovese (1994) observes, there is a good deal of evidence that Carter shifted from a "Wilsonian idealist" to a "Cold War confrontationist" as his term progressed. David Skidmore (1996) also describes this transformation in an analysis that is fittingly entitled *Reversing Course*. However, as these scholars acknowledge, the transformation began as early as 1978. Thus if the change in philosophy were the primary cause of Carter's policy reversal on foreign aid, the policy reversal should have occurred earlier.

Moreover, the budget that Carter proposed in his final month in office, after his electoral defeat, reiterated his commitment to a substantial growth in humanitarian assistance. He recommended increasing it by 26 percent in nominal terms, which, given the projected inflation rate, comprised a real increase of 12 percent. The justification Carter gave for this request in his Budget Message highlighted his continued belief in the importance of humanitarian assistance. He stated, "I believe in the need for higher levels of aid to achieve foreign policy objectives, promote economic growth, and help needy people abroad. Foreign aid is not politically popular and represents an easy target for budget reduction. But it is not a wise one." Carter's election-year proposal to decrease development assistance therefore cannot be attributed to a fundamental change in his convictions regarding the benefits of foreign aid.

Given that the policy shift cannot be ascribed to a change in Carter's convictions, I consider whether it can be attributed to factors specific to the time period in which it occurred. These alternative explanations include the macroeconomy, anticipated congressional behavior, and international events. I consider each in turn.

In January 1980, inflation was a major concern for President Carter and the public. During the past year, the consumer price index had increased by 12.4

percent and according to Gallup's Most Important Problem survey, 36 percent of citizens (a plurality of respondents) considered inflation to be the most important problem in the nation.[5] Carter accordingly designed his election-year budget with the goal of curbing inflation (Hargrove 1988, 102–3; Kaufman 1993, 168–69). One could therefore argue that he proposed to cut humanitarian aid in order to help reduce inflation.

The key problem with this argument is that Carter's overall budget was not all that fiscally conservative. As Hargrove (1988, 103) assesses, the budget reflected that Carter was "not, in the final analysis, a conservative prepared to launch a period of austerity." In fact, Carter's budget entailed real increases in other, more popular programs. For example, Carter proposed conspicuous growth in funding for federal health programs and ground transportation, issues on which a majority of the public supported higher spending.[6] It is therefore difficult to conclude that Carter's desire to curb inflation was the primary determinant of his decision to recommend reducing humanitarian assistance.

A separate potential explanation for the policy shift involves Carter's congressional relations. In 1979, Congress failed to enact a Foreign Aid Appropriations Bill. The funding for international assistance programs came from continuing resolutions, which appropriated almost 20 percent less than the president had requested for the programs. Given these events, one might conjecture that Carter's policy reversal resulted from a change in his bargaining strategy.

The evidence suggests, however, that Carter's proposal to reduce international assistance did not reflect a general adjustment in his approach to budgetary negotiations. In fact, in the same budget he proposed expanding programs for which Congress had in the previous year appropriated far less than he had requested. For example, in 1979 Carter obtained 23 percent less funding than he had proposed for the District of Columbia, but in 1980 he still requested 9 percent more than he had in the previous budgetary cycle. Likewise, Congress appropriated 9 percent less than Carter recommended for agricultural spending in 1979, yet in 1980 the president recommended an increase of 20 percent relative to his proposal of the previous year. Carter thus did not systematically lower his budgetary requests in response to previous failures to expand the programs.

In keeping with this evidence that Carter's legislative negotiations differed by policy area, I consider as a final rationale for his policy shift an explanation particular to foreign aid. Specifically, I examine the possibility that an international event induced the president to desire a lower level of humanitarian assistance. In 1979 there were two major international incidents that affected U.S. interests: the abduction of American hostages in Iran in November 1979 and the Soviet invasion of Afghanistan in the following month. Ostensibly, these incidents could have affected Carter's beliefs concerning the value of bilateral assistance to the Soviet Union and Iran.

Regardless of the president's beliefs about such bilateral assistance, however, his proposal to reduce humanitarian aid could not be the consequence of them.

As documented in the 1981 *Country Report on Human Rights Practices* prepared by the State Department, the United States offered no bilateral assistance to the Soviet Union or Iran in 1979.[7] Thus, Carter could not recommend cutting assistance to these countries.[8] A related possibility is that the Soviet invasion of Afghanistan and the Iranian hostage crisis induced the president to disfavor the use of humanitarian aid as a means of solving the problems of the Third World. Yet, as previously discussed, soon after the 1980 elections, Carter proposed a massive increase in humanitarian assistance. Thus the international events seem to have, if anything, strengthened the president's belief that humanitarian assistance would promote U.S. interests.[9]

In sum, Carter's policy reversal on foreign aid in 1980 cannot be attributed to a change in his belief system, the state of the economy, congressional relations, or to the major foreign events of the day. Nor is the shift consistent with his subsequent policy proposals on foreign aid. The decision does, however, comport with the Conditional Pandering Theory. When the election was distant or Carter's approval ratings were low, he pursued the course of action he believed to be in the public interest. Yet when the election was near and his public standing was such that he seemed likely to face a tight race, the president pandered to public opinion.

President Bush and Unemployment Benefits: Policy Leadership from Ahead and Pandering

Throughout the summer of 1991, President Bush looked likely to sail to reelection. His approval ratings had hit historically high levels in the wake of the Gulf War victory earlier that year and still hovered in the high 60s and low 70s.[10] Front-runners for the Democratic nomination decided one after another not to challenge the president. By September, Al Gore, Richard Gephardt, and Jay Rockefeller IV had all dropped out of the race. As Robert E. Denton and Mary E. Stuckey (1994, 19) surmise, "Bush simply seemed unbeatable."

This popularity was noteworthy given the lackluster economy over which the president was presiding. The gross national product (GNP) had increased only 0.4 percent during the second quarter of 1991, and this relatively meager growth followed nine months of GNP retraction.[11] As of June, the unemployment rate was approaching 7 percent.[12] Much of the unemployment involved middle-management workers who had been downsized by corporations. These managers were having a particularly difficult time finding alternative employment; many remained jobless at the time their unemployment benefits expired. The unemployment rate thus reflected a substantial number of workers who were not only out of work but also not receiving government assistance. For instance, in July 1991 unemployment compensation expired for 350,000 jobless Americans (Cohen 1997, 218).

It was in this environment that Congress enacted a series of bills extending unemployment benefits. The first of these bills to reach Bush's desk was HR 3201, which arrived August 17. The legislation provided up to 20 weeks of extra benefits through July 1992 at an estimated cost of $5.3 billion. The legislation specified that for the compensation to be distributed, the president had to declare a state of emergency. Bush signed the bill but did not declare an emergency, thereby preventing the expenditure of the benefits.

The second unemployment bill to reach Bush's desk was S 1722, entitled the Emergency Unemployment Compensation Act of 1991. The bill, which was passed by Congress on October 1, again offered up to 20 weeks of extended benefits and had an estimated cost of $6.4 billion. Unlike the earlier legislation, S 1722 did not allow the president the option of signing the legislation without obligating the additional benefits. Bush could thus either veto the bill or enact the temporary extension.[13]

Surveys conducted around the time that Congress passed S 1722 suggest the bill was quite popular. A *Los Angeles Times* poll taken September 21 through 25 found that 63 percent of respondents favored the legislation strongly or at least somewhat, and only 33 percent opposed it.[14] Likewise, a Harris poll conducted September 27 through October 2 found that only 37 percent of respondents would rate the president's opposition to the bill as "excellent" or "pretty good."[15] These survey data suggest that to the extent Bush wished to placate the mass public, he had an incentive to endorse the legislation.

Bush's incentives were not straightforward, however, because he did not believe that the extension of unemployment benefits would promote a strong economy. As David Mervin (1996, 87) describes, the president was "particularly averse to government interference in the economy." This belief repeatedly put him in conflict with the Democratic-controlled Congress. Nicholas Calio, who was in charge of Bush's legislative relations, describes how the White House perceived congressional efforts to control the economy: "There were many things that, in our view, Congress got involved in [which] it really shouldn't—in micro managing markets . . . There were a lot of things we felt needed to be stopped."[16]

The legislation S 1722, the Emergency Unemployment Compensation Act, was apparently one of those things. While the legislation was being considered, Bush openly referred to it as part of "a bunch of garbage" that the Democrats were sending his way.[17] In a news conference, he argued that the measure would ultimately harm taxpayers. Furthermore, he exhorted citizens to implore their representatives to "do something that the President can sign that will help us with unemployment benefits but will also protect the other taxpayer."[18] On October 11, Bush vetoed S 1722, declaring in an accompanying memorandum that it would "threaten economic recovery and its associated job creation." He continued, "the Congress has . . . ignored my call for passage of measures that will increase the nation's competitiveness, productivity and growth.[19]

For all of this strong language, Bush agreed to a measure quite similar to S 1722, HR 3575, less than two months later. HR 3575 extended unemployment benefits for up to 20 weeks through mid-June at an estimated cost of $5.3

billion. When the president signed the bill on November 15, his electoral vulnerability was much greater than it had been when he had vetoed S 1722. Headlines from the preceding weeks had declared "Democrats Find Bush Is Vulnerable" and "Democrat Hopefuls See Bush Weakness."[20] Correspondingly, his popularity ratings had dropped to 56 percent.[21]

The possibility that Bush switched his policy position for electoral reasons did not go unnoticed at the time. For example, Senator George Mitchell of Maine, referring to Bush's apparent reversal, asserted the president was in "panic city."[22] The administration rebuked such criticism and claimed the legislative negotiations had in fact culminated in a victory for the president over the details of how the unemployment benefits would be funded. According to the administration, the bill that Bush had originally vetoed would have increased the deficit and thus violated the 1990 Budget Act, which required that any new program not add to the deficit. The bill he signed, in comparison, supposedly paid for itself through tax increases on the wealthy, the renewal of an employer tax, and a new policy of income confiscation from individuals who defaulted on school loans.[23]

Such a justification for Bush's action would have been more credible had the president not soon thereafter approved another temporary extension of unemployment benefits, HR 4095, which many believed would increase the deficit. Bush signed this subsequent legislation on February 7, 1992, after his popularity ratings had been hovering in the mid-40s for the past month.[24] HR 4095 provided an additional thirteen weeks of benefits, paying for them primarily through a "surplus" that the Office of Management and Budget (OMB) predicted would arise from 1991 tax bills.[25] The Congressional Budget Office (CBO) disputed the prediction of a surplus, and critics ridiculed the forecast.[26] For example, Representative Thomas J. Downey, a Democrat from Long Island, chided that "Only in the land of Oz could you take a $350 billion deficit and find $2 billion in savings."[27]

The claim that Bush did not switch his position seemed even more disingenuous in July 1992. On July 3, when the president was running neck-and-neck with Bill Clinton and Ross Perot in the pre-election polls, the president signed HR 5260, which permanently changed the unemployment system by allowing nonemergency benefits to take effect more easily during times of high unemployment. As recently as April, Bush had opposed making such permanent changes to the system.[28] Even the day before signing HR 5260, the president had threatened to veto the permanent expansion.[29] The champion of the bill in Congress, Representative Thomas J. Downey, offered an explanation for Bush's actions during the brief House debate over the legislation. He predicted, "The President is going to sign this bill for two reasons. Unemployment is up, and his popularity is down."[30]

Does the variation in Bush's policy decisions over unemployment benefits correspond to the predictions of the Conditional Pandering Theory? The theory suggests that a president will endorse policies that he believes are in the public interest when he is quite popular relative to his likely electoral competition, when he is relatively unpopular, or when he does not soon face a contest for reelection. In this case, Bush supported an unpopular policy that he believed would advance a strong economy so long as his electoral prospects were strong. Once he seemed vulnerable, however, he changed course and issued popular decisions that did not reflect his belief that preventing government interference in the economy would harm it and, by consequence, societal welfare. This variation in executive behavior is exactly what the Conditional Pandering Theory would predict.

Some readers may take issue with the notion that Bush was trying to advance societal welfare by vetoing unemployment benefits. It is accordingly worth reemphasizing that the Conditional Pandering Theory does not require that a president is actually advancing citizens' interests, only that he believes he is doing so; the president can be wrong in this assessment. The preceding description of events documented that Bush believed economic recovery, as well as long-term growth, would be best advanced by limiting government interference in the macroeconomy. The question of whether these beliefs were accurate, or whether they are in part a function of ideological biases, is not paramount to analyzing the predicative power of the theory. In the concluding section of this reading, I return to the issue of whether presidents are likely to have better information than citizens do about the expected consequences of policies. For now, I have a more precise goal, which is to show that the Conditional Pandering does a better job at predicting the variation in Bush's policy decisions than seemingly likely alternative explanations.

To realize this goal, four alternative rationales are evaluated, the last two of which are evaluated jointly. First, I examine whether Bush altered his policy beliefs in response to economic events. Second, the possibility that his claims of policy consistency were correct is considered. Third, I analyze executive-legislative negotiations that occurred after Clinton had taken a clear lead in order to assess whether Bush's likelihood of pandering was simply greater the sooner the election; and fourth, whether this likelihood was greater the lower his chances of retaining office.

During the course of the executive-legislative negotiations over the extension of unemployment benefits, the unemployment rate itself varied noticeably. When the president vetoed an extension of benefits in October 1991, the Labor Department had just announced that the rate had dropped a tenth of a percentage point to 6.7 percent. A month later, when Bush approved a temporary extension, the rate had risen back up to 6.8 percent. Furthermore, at the subsequent bill signings in February and July, the rate was estimated to be 7.1 percent and 7.8 percent respectively. It therefore seems plausible that changes in the economic situation caused Bush to believe greater government intervention in the economy was warranted.

Yet the evidence suggests otherwise. In June 1991 the unemployment rate was 6.9 percent and legislation temporarily extending compensation to the jobless was already making its way through Congress. Bush, who was enjoying approval ratings in the mid-70s, did not lend support to the bill. Then in July 1992, Bush threatened to veto a permanent expansion of unemployment benefits even after the Labor Department had announced that the unemployment rate was 7.8 percent, the highest level in eight years.[31]

Finally, Bush never intimated that he reversed course because of changes in the economy. Instead, he consistently stated that his willingness to approve extensions of compensation depended on whether they would increase the deficit. For example, during a news conference in August 1991, he promoted Senator Dole's proposed extension of unemployment benefits, which was less expensive than the Democratic proposals, claiming that the Dole plan had "fiscal integrity."[32] At a fundraising luncheon in November, the president expounded his position further, declaring that:

> The Democratic leaders know that I've been ready since August to sign an extension, but to sign one as proposed by most of the Republicans in the Senate and House that lives within the budget agreement. We don't have to add to the ever-increasing deficit and still do what is compassionate and correct. They passed a bill. They wanted to embarrass me politically. I vetoed that bill . . . Unemployed workers deserve this kind of support, but we need a change in the Congress if we're going to do it in a way that lives within the budget agreement.[33]

These assertions comport with the ones Bush gave eight months later with regards to permanently extending unemployment compensation. When the president was asked by Congressman Robert H. Michel, the Minority Leader of the House, whether he might veto such legislation, Bush responded that he had a "certain custodianship for trying to support reasonable expenditures." He continued, "If [Democratic congressional members] send me something that we view and the leadership here views as too expensive, we'll have to send it back and urge them to get one down there that we can support."[34]

In sum, Bush's actions as well as rhetoric indicate that changes in the unemployment rate did not alter his fundamental beliefs about the appropriateness of extending benefits to the jobless. The president's rhetoric highlights a separate alternative explanation, however, which is that substantive differences among the assorted bills explain the variation in his willingness to sign them. The president's decisions could accordingly be construed as an example of what Cameron (2000) terms "veto bargaining." This rationale for the seemingly disparate decisions has some merit. In fact, had the legislative matter ended after Bush's approval of the extension of benefits in November 1991, it would be relatively straightforward to argue that his policy actions reflected an aversion to increasing the deficit.

The president's behavior in February 1992 suggests that this alternative explanation cannot completely account for his behavior, however. As discussed previously, the extension Bush approved in February paid for itself only under highly disputed assumptions about unexpected revenues. In fact, during a congressional hearing on the legislation, Republican House members recommended that the unemployment trust fund be taken off-budget so that it could not affect the official deficit.[35] Bush's ostensible fiscal restraint thus not only entailed questionable assumptions about unexpected surpluses but also coincided with Republicans recommending score-keeping changes in the accounting of unemployment benefits. Given these circumstances, Bush's supposed fiscal responsibility appears more superficial than substantial. His desire for restraint may well have been sincere, but this desire appears to have been superseded by an impetus to enact a popular policy once he was facing a competitive electoral contest.

The final alternative hypotheses I consider are that Bush was simply more likely to pander to public opinion as the election neared, independent of his popularity; and that he was simply more likely to pander as his popularity declined, and thus would have pandered even if the preelection polls had indicated he was quite likely to lose reelection. The events described thus far do not allow one to distinguish between these explanations and the Conditional Pandering Theory. However, subsequent events shed light on the matter.

Clinton took a substantial lead in the polls following the Democratic Party Convention in mid-July. Throughout the remainder of the race, Bush was consistently the underdog, trailing the competition by as much as twenty-five points and sustaining approval ratings no higher than 40 percent.[36] While Congress did not enact other unemployment legislation during this period, the chambers did pass several bills that involved substantial government regulation of the private sector.

That legislation included the Family and Medical Leave Act of 1992 (S 5), which Congress enacted on September 10, and the Cable Television Consumer Protection and Competition Act of 1992 (S 12), which was sent to the president on September 22. The first bill granted workers up to twelve weeks of unpaid leave in order to care for a new baby or sick relative.[37] The second aided competitors to the cable industry, as well as bestowed the federal government with the power to set rates for the lowest-priced cable package.[38] Each of these bills appealed to popular sentiment. For instance, in a survey of registered voters, 63 percent of respondents stated that they would support a law requiring businesses to grant up to three months of unpaid leave for a new child or medical emergency, while only 31 percent opposed such a law.[39] Likewise, a Harris survey found that 87 percent of the national adult population believed most cable companies could overcharge customers owing to a lack of competition, and 70 percent favored allowing local telephone companies to provide cable services so that the cable industry would be more competitive.[40]

Despite the popularity of the policy issues, Bush vetoed the bills. In each case, his expressed rationale for doing so was consistent with his belief that government interference in the economy would harm it. The president professed that the Family and Medical Leave Act, if enacted, would become a "government-dictated mandate that increases costs and loses jobs."[41] He predicted the cable bill would "cost the economy jobs, reduce consumer programming choices, and retard the deployment of growth-oriented investment critical to the future of our Nation's communications infrastructure."[42]

Bush issued each veto within seven weeks of the election, by which time Clinton held a convincing lead in the preelection polls. When Bush delivered the Family Leave veto on September 22, Clinton maintained a ten percentage point advantage according to the Gallup trial heat.[43] At the time of the Cable Bill veto, on October 3, Bush trailed by eleven to twelve percentage points.[44] That the president vetoed the bills under these conditions suggests that he did not continually pander to public opinion as the election approached or as his popularity declined relative to his electoral competition.

Instead, as predicted by the Conditional Pandering Theory, Bush endorsed the policies he believed to be the right ones when he was unpopular compared with his electoral opposition. In combination with his decisions on unemployment legislation, Bush's behavior illustrates the theoretically predicted relationship between the likelihood of pandering and presidential popularity. When he was highly popular or unpopular relative to his competition, he supported the policies he believed would produce the best outcomes for the nation, despite the proximity of the presidential election. Only when he was in the midst of a seemingly tight race did he enact popular laws that he did not believe would ultimately advance citizens' interests.

Reagan and the Contingency Tax Proposal: Policy Leadership from Behind

In the beginning of 1983, Reagan's personal popularity was quite low. Throughout the month of January, his approval ratings hovered in the mid-30s.[45] This lack of popularity reflected the economic situation. In the previous year, the GNP had fallen 1.8 percent, the largest annual reduction since 1946.[46] Unemployment stood at 10.8 percent, the highest level since 1950.[47]

Many economists, including ones working in the executive branch, believed the projection of large deficits for years to come was holding back an economic recovery. As of January 1983, the projected deficits for the next five years were in the range of $185 to $300 billion, approximately 7 percent of GNP. In comparison, the deficit of the last full year before Reagan entered office was $60 billion, around 2 percent of GNP.[48] Paul Volcker, the Chairman of the Federal Reserve, publicly expressed his concerns about the projected deficits in January. He observed, "We are exposed to fears of 'out-of-control' structural deficits, and the result is upward pressure on interest rates."[49] Martin Feldstein, chairman of the Council of Economic Advisors, agreed with Volcker that the projection of large deficits was boosting interest rates and therefore impeding an economic recovery, particularly in sectors dependent on borrowing, such as housing and automobiles.[50] Indeed, interest rates were quite high; the prime rate was 11 percent and the rate for a conventional home loan was 13.25 percent.[51]

Reagan was deeply concerned about the economy and, moreover, realized that he would not win reelection in 1984 unless conditions improved. He acknowledged that if his administration could not move the country into a recovery it "obviously . . . would be a sign" that he should retire after one term.[52] Reagan also recognized the projected deficits as a problem. For example, in an administration briefing in May 1982, he claimed that "the only thing that's keeping the interest rates up and preventing a speedier recovery is the lack of confidence on the part of the private sector that government will stay the course" by progressing toward a balanced budget.[53]

Curbing the deficit was not a simple matter for the president, however. He desired significant increases in defense spending and the preservation of his recently enacted income tax cuts (e.g., Dallek 1984, 105; Feldstein 1994, 26 and 36–37). Furthermore, Reagan did not want to obtain the needed reductions through changes to Medicare, Social Security, or federal employee retirement programs, which together constituted a majority of the budget (Dallek 1984, 72–73). The president was willing, indeed wanted, to decrease spending on social welfare programs (e.g., Hogan 1990, 225), but congressional leaders had indicated that they would be unwilling to curtail these programs substantially.[54]

It was in this setting that Reagan proposed standby taxes that would be triggered in a couple of years if the deficit did not decline by then; specifically, the taxes were scheduled to take effect on October 1, 1985, if the estimated deficit for fiscal year 1986 turned out to be greater than $2\frac{1}{2}$ percent of the gross national product and Congress had approved the president's spending cuts. The taxes included an excise fee on oil of approximately five dollars a barrel as well as an increase in corporate and personal income tax payments of approximately 1 percent of taxable income.[55] Reagan promoted this proposal in his State of the Union address, a radio address, and several targeted addresses during the first two months of 1983.[56]

The evidence suggests that Reagan believed the policy was in citizens' interests because it would help to control the deficit and thereby improve the economy by reducing interest rates. Martin Feldstein, who helped to design the plan along with Reagan's domestic policy adviser Ed Harper, describes how the president came to espouse the idea. Feldstein recounts that the president supported the policy over the objections of others within the White House because, ultimately, he "recognized the need to project declining deficits and an eventual budget balance" (Feldstein 1994, 28). The president's statements support this assertion. For example, in remarks to the St. Louis Regional Commerce and Growth Association on February 1, the president promoted the standby tax proposal by claiming that "it will reassure many of those out in the money markets today that we do mean to control inflation and interest rates."[57]

Despite Reagan's public espousal of the policy, it was quite unpopular. In fact, survey data suggest it was even less popular than the option of eliminating Reagan's income tax reductions. When citizens were asked whether they would support "a standby program of increased personal and business taxes—as well as a special tax on oil" for the years 1986–88 in order to reduce the budget deficit, 60 percent opposed the proposal.[58] In comparison, only 39 percent of the population believed that "July's tax cut should be put into effect despite the size of the government deficit."[59]

Reagan's promotion of the contingency tax proposal is thus not a case of a president following public opinion. Instead, consistent with the Conditional Pandering Theory, Reagan advocated a policy he believed would serve the public interest even though it was unpopular. As documented earlier, the president knew that without an economic recovery, he would be unlikely to win reelection. He believed that the standby taxes, if enacted, would help the economy and thereby increase his likelihood of winning the upcoming race. His electoral incentive was therefore to promote the proposal despite its lack of popular support.

Of course, it remains plausible that Reagan's behavior was consistent with the Conditional Pandering Theory but that he promoted the proposal for other reasons. I discuss three plausible alternative explanations: that Reagan had a propensity to follow his policy beliefs regardless of the political circumstances; that the president was somehow catering to his conservative base; and that he was playing blame-game politics with the Democrats over who was responsible for the budget deficit. None of these explanations is corroborated under scrutiny.

A seemingly credible rationale for Reagan's behavior is that he generally advocated policies he thought were in the public interest, regardless of their popularity. Indeed, this claim receives some support from officials who worked for him. For example, Edwin Meese III, Reagan's attorney general from February 1985 through August 1988, observes that "Reagan was remarkably steadfast when pursuing his key objectives" (Meese 1992, 330). Martin Anderson, the chief domestic and policy adviser to the president in 1981 and 1982, similarly assesses that Reagan would "never alter his course" when he felt strongly about a decision (Pemberton 1997, 110).

Notwithstanding Reagan's dedication to his beliefs, there is evidence that he was not above catering to public opinion. For example, he was more than willing to fire agency heads who became unpopular while following his agenda. William Pemberton (1997, 121) notes that after the White House pressured Ann Gorsuch Burford to resign her post as head of the Environmental Protection Agency, she "felt betrayed" by the president because he had "abandoned her when she came under fire for carrying out his policy." Likewise, when James Watt, Reagan's first Secretary of Interior, told the president that he probably have to fire Watt at some point because of the unpopular agenda

Watt would be implementing, "Reagan, eyes sparkling with laughter, replied, 'I will'" (Pemberton 1997, 119).

Robert Dallek (1984, 33) reconciles the apparent tension between Reagan's faithfulness to his beliefs and capacity to make tactical modifications. "If Goldwater was ready to stand or fall on principle," Dallek observes, "Reagan, in his determination to be liked and to gain his personal goals, will compromise." As this assessment and Reagan's dealings with his officials imply, the president's support for the contingency taxes cannot be attributed to a universal unwillingness to take positions for purely political reasons.

Conclusion

The narratives on Carter's humanitarian assistance proposals, Bush's policy decisions on unemployment compensation, and Reagan's proposal for standby taxes establish that the Conditional Pandering Theory has explanatory power. In all of these analyses, the predictions of the theory were consistent with the president's policy decisions. Furthermore, the theory made sense of seemingly puzzling events; in each case a president switched positions and/or supported policies counter to his ideological leanings. In contrast, conventional explanations of presidential decision making—character, inside the beltway bargaining, and the appeasement of core constituencies, for example—did not account for the executive behavior.

NOTES

1. The survey asked, "We are faced with many problems in this country, none of which can be solved easily or inexpensively. I'm going to name some of these problems, and for each one I'd like you to tell me whether you think we're spending too much money on it, too little money, or about the right amount. Are we spending too much money, too little money, or about the right amount on foreign aid?"

2. Jimmy Carter, "'Ask President Carter' Remarks During a Telephone Call-in Program on the CBS Radio Network," March 5, 1977, *Public Papers of the Presidents of the United States, 1977 Book 1* (Washington, DC: Government Printing Office, 1977).

3. Jimmy Carter, "Remarks and a Question-and-Answer Session with a Group of Editors and News Directors," May 19, 1978, *Public Papers of the Presidents of the United States, 1978 Book 1* (Washington, DC: Government Printing Office, 1978).

4. Survey conducted December 1–8, 1979. The question wording is identical to that in footnote 1 of this chapter.

5. Survey conducted by the Gallup organization January 25–28, 1980. The survey asked the standard most important problem question, "What do you think is the most important problem in the nation today?" Responses were open-ended.

6. Carter proposed real increases of 9 percent in health programs and 4 percent in ground transportation. The public opinion data are from a Roper survey conducted December 1–8, 1979. Respondents were asked the (by-now familiar) question, "We are faced with many problems in this country, none of which can be solved easily or inexpensively. I'm going to name some of these problems, and for each one I'd like you to

tell me whether you think we're spending too much money on it, too little money or about the right amount." For health, the question ended with "improving and protecting the nation's health" and for ground transportation, it ended with "improving the public transportation." The responses suggest that 59 percent of adults believed the government was spending too little on health and that 50 percent believed too little was being spent on public transportation.

7. *Country Reports on Human Rights Practices,* report submitted to the Committee on Foreign Relations, U.S. Senate, and Committee on Foreign Affairs, U.S. House of Representatives, by the Department of State, February 2, 1981.

8. Carter did impose an embargo on the sale of grain to the Soviet Union, but this embargo did not affect appropriations for foreign assistance.

9. Nor did Carter shift his requests for humanitarian aid into security assistance; in nominal terms, Carter proposed a measly 0.002 percent increase in security aid.

10. Ragsdale (1998, 213).

11. Peter G. Gosselin, "Economy Rolling Again . . . But Slowly: Slight Gain in Gross National Product Worries Analysts," *Boston Globe,* July 27, 1991, 12.

12. U.S. Department of Labor, Bureau of Labor Statistics.

13. *Congressional Quarterly Almanac,* vol. 47 (1991), 304–8.

14. The question was: "Congress recently passed a bill to extend unemployment benefits beyond the regular 25-week period. To provide the 6.4 billion dollars needed to extend benefits, a budget emergency would have to be declared that President Bush says is not justified. Would you like to see Bush sign this bill into law, or do you think he should veto it?"

15. The question was: "Now let me ask you some specifics about President Bush. How would you rate him on . . . his opposition to a bill that would extend for 20 weeks unemployment insurance to unemployed workers whose benefits have run out . . . —excellent, pretty good, only fair or poor?" The responses of "only fair" and "poor" are reported jointly by Harris, with 59 percent of the population assigning Bush one of these ratings.

16. Quoted in Mervin (1996, 114).

17. George Bush, "Remarks at a Republican Party Fundraising Dinner in East Brunswick, New Jersey," September 24, 1991, *Public Papers of the Presidents, 1991 Book 2* (Washington, DC: Government Printing Office, 1992).

18. George Bush, "The President's News Conference," October 4, 1991, *Public Papers of the Presidents, 1991 Book 2.*

19. George Bush, "Memorandum of Disapproval for the Emergency Unemployment Compensation Act of 1991," October 11, 1991, *Public Papers of the Presidents, 1991 Book 2.*

20. Andrew J. Glass, "Democrats Find Bush is Vulnerable," *Atlanta Journal and Constitution,* November 3, 1991, O5; Adam Pertman, "Democrat Hopefuls See Bush Weakness," *Boston Globe,* November 3, 1991, 213.

21. Ragsdale (1998, 213).

22. Michael Kranish, "Bush Bristles at Claims He Has Shifted," *Boston Globe,* November 17, 1991, 1.

23. *Congressional Quarterly Almanac,* vol. 48 (1992), 347–48.

24. Ragsdale (1998, 213).

25. *Congressional Quarterly Almanac,* vol. 48 (1992), 347.

26. Ibid.

27. To deal with the possibility that the additional unemployment compensation would add to the deficit, Congress voted to waive the 1990 Budget Act, which required that every new program pay for itself (*Congressional Quarterly Almanac,* vol. 48 [1992], 352).

28. Adam Clymer, "Bush Fights Long-Term Change in Jobless Benefits," *New York Times,* April 9, 1992, D20.

29. Adam Clymer, "Congress Passes Jobless Aid and Bush Says He Will Sign," *New York Times,* July 3, 1992, A13.

30. Ibid.

31. Jill Zuckman, "Bush Relents, Agrees to Sign Jobless Benefits Extension," *Congressional Quarterly Weekly,* July 4, 1992, 1961–62.

32. George Bush, "The President's News Conference," August 2, 1991, *Public Papers of the Presidents, 1991 Book 2.*

33. George Bush, "Remarks at a Bush-Quayle Fundraising Luncheon in New York City," November 12, 1991, *Public Papers of the Presidents, 1991 Book 2.*

34. George Bush, "Remarks and an Exchange with Reporters in a Meeting with the House Republican Conference on Health Care," July 2, 1992, *Public Papers of the Presidents, 1992–93 Book 1* (Washington, DC: Government Printing Office, 1993).

35. Ways and Means Committee Subcommittee on Human Resources Hearing. "Extending Unemployment Benefits." Panel of Congressional Witnesses, B-318 Rayburn House Office Building, January 23, 1992.

36. The 1992 Gallup Poll Presidential Candidate Trial Heats are available in the Roper Center for Public Opinion Research database on polls and surveys (commonly referred to as RPOLL). For Bush's approval ratings, see Ragsdale (1998, 213–14).

37. Jill Zuckman, "Family Leave Act Falls Again: Veto Override Fails in House," *Congressional Quarterly Weekly,* October 3, 1992, 3059.

38. Mike Mills, "Bush Asks for a Sign of Loyalty: Congress Changes the Channel," *Congressional Quarterly Weekly,* October 10, 1992, 3149–51.

39. NBC News and Wall Street Journal Poll conducted September 12–15, 1992. The survey asked: "Congress has passed a law that would require companies to give employees up to three months of unpaid leave for the birth or adoption of a child, or to care for a seriously ill family member, while protecting their job. Would you favor or oppose this law, even if it means additional costs for business?"

40. Harris survey conducted March 19–24, 1992. The first question was, "Here are some statements people have made about the cable television industry in American today. For each one, please tell me whether you agree or disagree . . . Because most cable T.V. companies have local monopolies, they can charge too much for the service they provide." The second question was, "Would you favor or oppose changing the regulations so that your telephone company could provide cable television service in competition with the company that provides now?"

41. George Bush, "Remarks and an Exchange with Reporters on Family Leave Legislation," September 16, 1992, *Public Papers of the Presidents, 1992–93 Book 2.*

42. George Bush, "Letter to Congressional Leaders on Cable Television Legislation," September 17, 1992, *Public Papers of the Presidents, 1992–93 Book 2.*

43. Each of the following trial heats, conducted September 17–20 of registered voters and those who could vote without having yet registered, gave Clinton a ten-point lead. The questions were "If the (1992) presidential election were being held today, would you vote for the Republican ticket of George Bush and Dan Quayle or for the Democratic ticket of Bill Clinton and Al Gore? (If Perot (vol.)/Other (vol.)/Don't know/ Refused, ask:) As of today, do you lean more to Bush and Quayle, the Republicans, or to Clinton and Gore, the Democrats?" and "If the (1992) presidential election were being held today, would you vote for the Republican ticket of George Bush and Dan Quayle or for the Democratic ticket of Bill Clinton and Al Gore?" In the first case,

Clinton received support from 50 percent of respondents, and in the second, he received support from 44 percent.

44. These trial heats were conducted by the Gallup Organization on October 1–3 using the questions in the format of footnote 55 of this chapter. The only difference in the questions is that Ross Perot was explicitly mentioned as a candidate, a result of the fact that he had reentered the race. In the survey that did not urge the leaners to make a choice, Clinton was favored by 47 percent of respondents and Bush by 35 percent. In the survey that pushed the leaners to choose a candidate, Clinton received support from 44 percent of the respondents and Bush from 33 percent.

45. Ragsdale (1998, 210).

46. Anantole Kaletsky, "GNP in U.S. Fell 1.8% Last Year," *Financial Times* (London ed.), January 20, 1983, I1.

47. "Unemployment Claims Rose at End of the Year," *New York Times*, January 14, 1983, D15.

48. Jonathan Fuerbringer, "Do Deficits Impede Recovery?" *New York Times*, January 20, 1983, D1.

49. Volcker's statement was made at a meeting of the American Council for Capital Formation. Kenneth B. Noble, "Deficits Criticized by Volcker," *New York Times*, January 21, 1983, D3.

50. Fuerbringer, "Do Deficits Impede Recovery?"

51. "Current Interest Rates," *New York Times*, January 10, 1983, D7; Kenneth R. Harney, "Interest Rates May Rise Along with Economy," *Washington Post*, January 15, 1983, F1.

52. Rich Jaroslovsky, "Economic Upturn Aids President's Popularity, but It Is Not Panacea," *Wall Street Journal*, April 28, 1983, 1. Cited in Kernell (1997, 224).

53. Ronald Reagan, "Meeting with Editors from the Midwestern Region," May 10, 1982, *Public Papers of the Presidents, 1982 Book 1* (Washington, DC: Government Printing Office, 1983).

54. Hedrick Smith, "Deficit in the $185 Billion Range Expected in 1984 Reagan Budget," *New York Times*, January 18, 1983, A1.

55. Robert D. Hershey Jr., "President to Seek Contingent Taxes," *New York Times*, January 26, 1983, A15.

56. These addresses include the State of the Union on January 25, a national radio address entitled "Fiscal Year 1984 Budget" on January 29, "Remarks and a Question-and-Answer Session at the St. Louis Regional Commerce and Growth Association" on February 1, "Remarks and a Question-and-Answer Session via Satellite to the Young Presidents Organization" on February 14. All of these addresses are in the *Public Papers of the Presidents, 1983 Book 1* (Washington, DC: Government Printing Office, 1984).

57. Ibid.

58. Cambridge Reports, Research International survey conducted in January of 1983. The full question was "Last month, in his State of the Union and Budget Messages to Congress, President (Ronald) Reagan proposed the following actions as ways of reducing these budget deficits for the next few years. Please tell me whether you would favor or oppose each of them. . . . Putting in effect a standby program of increased personal and business taxes—as well as a special tax on oil—for the years 1986–88."

59. Roper survey conducted January 8–22, 1983. The full question was, "A 5% cut in income taxes took effect in October 1981, and another 10% cut in income taxes took effect this past July. An additional 10% cut in income taxes is due to take effect this coming July. Do you think next July's tax cut should be put into effect despite the size of the government deficit, or do you think next July's tax cut should be cancelled to help reduce the deficit?"

REFERENCES

Brody, Richard A., and Lee Sigelman. 1983. "Presidential Popularity and Presidential Elections: An Update and Extension." *Public Opinion Quarterly* 47: 325–28.

Cameron, Charles M. 2000. *Veto Bargaining: President and the Politics of Negative Power.* Cambridge, UK: Cambridge University Press.

Cohen, Jeffrey E. 1997. *Presidential Responsiveness and Public Policy-Making: The Public and the Policies that Presidents Choose.* Ann Arbor: University of Michigan Press.

Dallek, Robert. 1984. *Ronald Reagan: The Politics of Symbolism.* Cambridge, MA: Harvard University Press.

Deibel, Terry L. 1987. *Presidents, Public Opinion, and Power: The Nixon, Carter and Reagan Years.* New York: Foreign Policy Association.

Denton, Robert E., Jr., and Mary E. Stuckey. 1994. "A Communication Model of Presidential Campaigns: A 1992 Overview." In *The 1992 Presidential Campaign: A Communication Perspective,* ed. Robert E. Denton, Jr., 1–42. Westport, CT: Praeger.

Feldstein, Martin. 1994. Introductory chapter of *American Economic Policy in the 1980s,* ed. Martin Feldstein, 1–79. Chicago: University of Chicago Press.

Genovese, Michael A. 1994. "Jimmy Carter and the Age of Limits: Presidential Power in a Time of Decline and Diffusion." In *The Presidency and Domestic Politics of Jimmy Carter,* ed. Herbert D. Rosenbaum and Alexej Ugrinsky, 187–221. Westport, CT: Greenwood Press.

Hargrove, Erwin C. 1988. *Jimmy Carter as President: Leadership and the Politics of the Public Good.* Baton Rouge: Louisiana State University Press.

Hogan, Joseph. 1990. *The Reagan Years: The Record in Presidential Leadership.* Ed. Joseph Hogan. Manchester, NY: Manchester University Press.

Jones, Charles O. 1988. *The Trusteeship Presidency: Jimmy Carter the United States Congress.* Baton Rouge: Louisiana State University Press.

Kaufman, Burton Ira. 1993. *The Presidency of James Earl Carter, Jr.* Lawrence: University Press of Kansas.

Kernell, Samuel. 1997. *Going Public: New Strategies of Presidential Leadership,* 3rd ed. Washington, DC: Congressional Quarterly Press.

Meese, Edwin III. 1992. *With Reagan: The Inside Story.* Washington, DC: Regnery Gateway.

Mervin, David. 1996. *George Bush and the Guardianship Presidency.* New York: St. Martin's Press.

Pemberton, William E. 1997. *Exit with Honor: The Life and Presidency of Ronald Reagan.* Armonk, NY: M. E. Sharpe.

Ragsdale, Lyn. 1998. *Vital Statistics on the Presidency: Washington to Clinton.* Washington, DC: Congressional Quarterly, Inc.

Sigelman, Lee. 1979. "Presidential Popularity and Presidential Elections." *Public Opinion Quarterly* 43: 532–34.

Skidmore, David. 1996. *Reversing Course: Carter's Foreign Policy, Domestic Politics, and the Failure of Reform.* Nashville, TN: Vanderbilt University Press.

Skowronek, Stephen. 1993. *The Politics Presidents Make: Leadership from John Adams to George Bush.* Cambridge, MA: Harvard University Press.

6.4

WILLIAM G. HOWELL

From *Power without Persuasion: The Politics of Direct Presidential Action*

Presidents have increasingly used unilateral actions, such as executive orders, to make policy independent of Congress. Howell describes the trends in these unilateral actions and offers a historical explanation. Over the course of the twentieth century, both Congress and the Supreme Court permitted presidents more latitude because the problems they faced became more complicated.

1. PRESIDENTIAL POWER IN THE MODERN ERA

... Throughout the twentieth century, presidents have used their powers of unilateral action to intervene into a whole host of policy arenas. Examples abound:

- During World War II, Roosevelt issued dozens of executive orders that nationalized aviation plants, shipbuilding companies, thousands of coal companies and a shell plant—all clear violations of the Fifth Amendment's "taking" clause. The courts overturned none of these actions.
- With executive order 9066, Roosevelt ordered the evacuation, relocation, and internment of over 110,000 Japanese Americans living on the West Coast.
- In 1948, Truman desegregated the military via executive order 9981.
- After congressional efforts to construct a program that would send American youth abroad to do charitable work faltered three years in a row, Kennedy unilaterally created the Peace Corps and then financed it using discretionary funds.
- Johnson instituted the first affirmative action policy with executive order 11246.
- Preempting Congress, Nixon used an executive order to design the Environmental Protection Agency not as an independent commission, as Congress would have liked, but as an agency beholden directly to the president.
- By subjecting government regulations to cost-benefit analyses with executive order 12291, Reagan centralized powers of regulatory review.
- In 1992, George Bush federalized the National Guard and used its members to quell the Los Angeles riots.

While the majority of unilateral directives may not resonate quite so loudly in the telling of American history, a growing proportion involve substantive policy matters. Rather than being simply "daily grist-of-the-mill diplomatic matter," presidential directives have become instruments by which presidents actually set all sorts of consequential domestic and foreign policy (Paige 1977). . . .

Between 1920 and 1998, presidents issued 10,203 executive orders, or roughly 130 annually. As might be expected, presidents issued more civil service orders than orders in any other policy arena. On average, presidents issued thirty-three such orders, most of which dealt with the management of government personnel. This proportion, however, declined precipitously after World War II, when executive orders were no longer used to perform such trivial administrative practices as exempting individuals from mandatory retirement requirements.

Outside of those orders relating directly to the civil service, each year presidents issued on average thirty-two orders in foreign affairs, another eight on social welfare policy, sixteen on regulations of the domestic economy, and fully thirty-three that concerned the management of public lands and energy policy, though the number in this last category has declined markedly over the past few decades. The majority of orders, it seems, have substantive policy content, both foreign and domestic.

These figures only concern executive orders, which represent but one tool among many that presidents have at their disposal. When negotiating with foreign countries, presidents can bypass the treaty ratification process by issuing executive agreements; not surprisingly, the ratio of executive agreements to treaties, which hovered between zero and one in the nineteenth century, now consistently exceeds thirty (King and Ragsdale 1988). If presidents choose to avoid the reporting requirements Congress has placed on executive orders, they can repackage their policies as executive memoranda, determinations, administrative directives, or proclamations. And if they prefer to keep their decisions entirely secret, they can issue national security directives, which neither Congress nor the public has an opportunity to review (Cooper 2002).

The U.S. Constitution does not explicitly recognize any of these policy vehicles. Over the years, presidents have invented them, citing national security or expediency as justification. Taken as a whole, though, they represent one of the most striking, and underappreciated, aspects of presidential power in the modern era. Born from a truly expansive reading of Article II powers, these policy mechanisms have radically impacted how public policy is made in America today. The president's powers of unilateral action exert just as much influence over public policy, and in some cases more, than the formal powers that presidency scholars have examined so carefully over the past several decades.

▪   ▪   ▪

If we want to account for the influence that presidents wield over the construction of public policy, we must begin to pay serious attention to the president's capacity to create law on his own.

"Presidential Power Is the Power to Persuade"

The image of presidents striking out on their own to conduct a war on terrorism or revamp civil rights policies or reconstruct the federal bureaucracy stands in stark relief to scholarly literatures that equate executive power with persuasion and, consequently, place presidents at the peripheries of the law-making process.

Richard Neustadt sets the terms by which every student of American politics has come to understand presidential power in the modern era. When thinking about presidents since FDR, Neustadt argues, "weak remains the word with which to start" (1991 [1960], xix). Presidents are much like Shakespearean kings, marked more by tragedy than grandeur. Each is held captive by world events, by competing domestic interests and foreign policy pressures, by his party, his cabinet, the media, a fickle public and partisan Congress. To make matters worse, the president exercises little control over any of these matters—current events and the political actors who inhabit them regularly disregard his expressed wishes. As a result, the pursuit of the president's policy agenda is marked more by compromise than conviction; and his eventual success or failure (as determined by either the public at the next election or historians over time) ultimately rests with others, and their willingness to extend a helping hand.

The public now expects presidents to accomplish far more than their formal powers alone permit. This has been especially true since the New Deal, when the federal government took charge of the nation's economy, commerce, and the social welfare of its citizens. Now presidents must address almost every conceivable social and economic problem, from the impact of summer droughts on midwestern farmers to the spread of nuclear weapons in the former Soviet Union. Armed with little more than the powers to propose and veto legislation and recommend the appointment of bureaucrats and judges, however, modern presidents appear doomed to failure from the very beginning. As one recent treatise on presidential. "greatness" puts it, "modern presidents bask in the honors of the more formidable office that emerged from the New Deal, but they find themselves navigating a treacherous and lonely path, subject to a volatile political process that makes popular and enduring achievement unlikely" (Landy and Milkis 2000, 197).

If a president is to enjoy any measure of success, Neustadt counsels, he must master the art of persuasion. Indeed, according to Neustadt, power and persuasion are synonymous. The ability to persuade, to convince other political actors that his interests are their own, defines political power and is the key to presidential achievement. Power is about bargaining and negotiating; about brokering deals and trading promises; and about cajoling legislators, bureaucrats, and justices to do things that the president cannot accomplish on his own. . . . The president wields influence when he manages to enhance his bargaining stature and build governing coalitions; and the principal way to accomplish as much, Neustadt claims, is to draw upon the bag of experiences, skills, and qualities that he brings to the office.

Intentionally or not, Neustadt set off a behavioral revolution. . . . Self-confidence, an instinct for power, an exalted reputation within the Washington community, and prestige among the general public were considered the foundations of presidential success. Without certain personal qualities, presidents could not hope to build the coalitions necessary for action. Power was contingent upon persuasion, and persuasion was a function of all the personal qualities individual presidents bore; and so, the argument ran, what the presidency was at any moment critically depended upon who filled the office.

By these scholars' accounts, a reliance on formal powers actually signals weakness. What distinguishes great presidents is not a willingness to act upon the formal powers of the presidency but an ability to rally support precisely when and where such formal powers are lacking. As Neustadt argues, formal powers constitute a "painful last resort, a forced response to the exhaustion of other remedies, suggestive less of mastery than of failure—the failure of attempts to gain an end by softer means" (1991 [1960], 24). Presidents who veto bill after bill (think Ford) do so because their powers to persuade have faltered. The presidents who effectively communicate (Reagan) or who garner strong professional reputations (Roosevelt) stand out in the eyes of history.

Although the notion of the personal presidency dominated the field for decades, its influence is on the decline. The principal reason is that it no longer matches up with the facts. The personal presidency became a popular theoretical notion just as the American presidency was experiencing tremendous growth and development as an institution: in its staffing, its budget, and the powers delegated to it by Congress. As time went on, it became increasingly clear that the field needed to take more seriously the formal structures and powers that define the modern presidency.

If the personal presidency literature is correct, executive power should rise and fall according to the personal qualities of each passing president. Presidential power should expand and contract according to the individual skills and reputations that each president brings to the office. The constituent elements of the personal presidency may be important. Prestige and reputation may matter. But if we are to build a theory of presidential power, it seems reasonable to start with its most striking developments during the modern era. And these developments have little to do with the personalities of the men who, since Roosevelt, have inhabited the White House.

By virtually any objective measure, the size and importance of the "presidential branch" has steadily increased over the past century (Hart 1995). According to Thomas Cronin, "for almost 150 years the executive power of the presidency has steadily expanded" (1989, 204). Edward Corwin echoes this sentiment, arguing that "taken by and large, the history of the Presidency is a history of aggrandizement" (1957, 238). How can such trends persist if presidential powers are fundamentally personal in nature? It cannot be that the caliber of presidents today is markedly higher than a century ago, and for that reason alone presidents have managed to exert more and more influence. Does it really make sense to say that successful twentieth-century presidents (e.g., the Roosevelts or Reagan) distinguish themselves from great nineteenth-century presidents (e.g., Jackson, Polk, or Lincoln) by exhibiting stronger personalities? And if not, how can we argue that the roots of modern presidential power are fundamentally personal in nature? While Neustadt may illuminate short-term fluctuations at the boundaries of presidential influence—skill in the art of persuasion surely plays some part in political power—he cannot possibly explain the general growth of presidential power.

During the past twenty years, scholars have revisited the more formal components of presidential power. Work on the institutional presidency has regained the stature it held in political science during the first half of the twentieth century. This work is far more rigorous than the personal presidency literature and, for that matter, the institutional literature's earlier incarnations. A science of politics is finally taking hold of presidential studies: empirical tests now are commonplace; theoretical assumptions are clearly specified; and hypotheses are subject to independent corroboration. Perhaps more important than its methodological contributions, though, the institutional literature has successfully refocused scholarly attention on the office of the presidency and the features that make it distinctly modern: its staff and budget, the powers and responsibilities delegated to it by Congress, and the growth of agencies and commissions that collect and process information within it.

Nothing in the institutional literature, however, fundamentally challenges Neustadt's original claim that "presidential power is the power to persuade" (1991 [1960], 11). Scholars continue to equate presidential power with an ability to bargain, negotiate, change minds, turn votes, and drive legislative agendas through Congress. Not surprisingly, the president remains secondary throughout this work. He continues to play second fiddle to the people who make real policy decisions: committee members writing bills, congressional representatives offering amendments, bureaucrats enforcing laws, judges deciding cases.

To legislate, to build a record of accomplishments about which to boast at the next election, and to find their place in history, presidents above all rely upon Congress—so the institutional literature argues. Without Congress's active support, and the endorsement of its members, presidents cannot hope to achieve much at all. . . . The struggle for votes is perennial; and success is always fleeting. Should Congress lock up, or turn away, the president has little or no recourse. Ultimately, presidents depend upon Congress to delegate authority, ratify executive decisions, and legislate when, and where, presidents cannot act at all.

■   ■   ■

Because of his unique position within a system of separated powers, the president has numerous opportunities to take independent action, with or without the expressed consent of either Congress or the courts. Sometimes he does so by issuing executive orders, proclamations, or executive agreements; other times by handing down general memoranda to agency heads; and still other times by dispensing national security directives. The number of these unilateral directives, and of opportunities to use them, has literally skyrocketed during the modern era (Moe and Howell 1999a, 1999b). While presidents freely exercise these powers during periods of national crises, as the events following September 11th have made clear, they also rely upon executive orders and executive agreements during periods of relative calm, effecting policy changes that never would survive the legislative process. And to the extent that presidents use these "power tools of the presidency" more now than they did a century ago, the ability to act unilaterally speaks to what is distinctively "modern" about the modern presidency (Cooper 1997, 2002).

Rather than hoping to influence at the margins what other political actors do, the president can make all kinds of public policies without the formal consent of Congress. While the growth of the presidency as an institution (its staffs, budgets, departments, and agencies) augments presidential power, it is the ability to set policy unilaterally that deserves our immediate and sustained attention.

■   ■   ■

Thinking about Unilateral Powers

From the beginning, it is worth highlighting what makes unilateral powers distinctive. For the ability to act unilaterally is unlike any other power formally granted the president. Two features stand out.

The most important is that the president moves policy first and thereby places upon Congress and the courts the burden of revising a new political landscape. Rather than waiting at the end of an extended legislative process to sign or veto a bill, the president simply sets new policy and leaves it up to Congress and the courts to respond. If they choose not to retaliate, either by passing a law or ruling against the president, then the president's order stands. Only by taking (or credibly threatening to take) positive action can either adjoining institution limit the president's unilateral powers.

. . . By moving first, and anticipating the moves of future actors, legislators of all stripes and in very different political systems influence the kinds of policies governments produce. . . . But gains to the president are twice over. While agenda setters in Congress only propose bills, the president moves first and creates legally binding public policies. And he does so without ever having to wait on coalitions subsequently forming, committee chairs cooperating, or party leaders endorsing.

The second important feature of unilateral powers is that the president acts alone. There is no need to rally majorities, compromise with adversaries, or wait for some interest group to bring a case to court. Rather than depending upon Congress to enact his legislative agendas, the president frequently can strike out on his own, occasionally catching even his closest advisors off guard (recall Clinton's unilateral decision to bomb Iraq in the fall of 1998, the day before his scheduled impeachment hearing in the House Judiciary Committee). As the chief of state, the modern president is in a unique position to lead, to define a national agenda, and to impose his will in more and more areas of governance.

■　　■　　■

The ability to move first and act alone, then, distinguishes unilateral powers from all other sources of influence. In this sense, Neustadt is turned upside-down, for unilateral action is the virtual antithesis of bargaining and persuading. Here, presidents just act; their power does not hinge upon their capacity to "convince [political actors] that what the White House wants of them is what they ought to do for their sake and for their authority" (Neustadt 1991 [1960], 30). To make policy, presidents need not secure the formal consent of Congress, the active support of bureaucrats, or the official approval of justices. Instead, presidents simply set public policy and dare others to counter. For as long as Congress lacks the votes (usually two-thirds of both chambers) to overturn him, the president can be confident that his policy will stand.

The presidency literature's traditional distinction between formal and informal powers does not contribute much insight here. Because the Constitution does not mandate them, powers of unilateral action cannot be considered formal. It is by reference to what presidents have done (or gotten away with) that these powers take form. But nor are these discretionary powers informal. They are not rooted in personal qualities that vary with each passing president. Rather, these powers emerge from specific institutional advantages within the office of the presidency itself: its structure, resources, and location in a system of separated powers. The promise of a sustained analysis of unilateral powers, then, is great. To the extent that presidents act unilaterally with increasing frequency and effect in the postwar era, an institutional theory of unilateral action enables scholars to see beyond Neustadt's original conception of presidential influence in the modern era.

The Tool Chest

. . . Presidents in . . . times have manufactured a number of policy instruments that give shape and meaning to . . . prerogative powers. The most common include executive orders, proclamations, national security directives, and executive agreements. There are few hard and fast rules about how policies are classified, affording presidents a fair measure of liberty to select the instrument that best serves their objectives. Still, some basic distinctions generally apply.

Among all unilateral directives, "executive orders combine the highest levels of substance, discretion, and direct presidential involvement" (Mayer 2001, 35). Executive orders, for the most part, instruct government officials and administrative agencies to take specific actions with regard to both domestic and foreign affairs. "Executive orders are directives issued by the president to officers of the executive branch, requiring them to take an action, stop a certain type of activity, alter policy, change management practices, or accept a delegation of authority under which they will henceforth be responsible for the implementation of law" (Cooper 2002, 16). But while presidents direct executive orders to subordinates within the executive branch, the impact of these orders is felt well beyond the boundaries of the federal government. . . . Through executive orders, presidents have dictated the terms by which government contractors hire and fire their employees, set restrictions on where American citizens can travel abroad, frozen the financial holdings of private parties, reset trade, tariffs, and determined the kinds of recreational activities that are allowed on public lands.

If executive orders are typically directed to officials within the federal government, presidential proclamations almost always target individuals and groups outside of the government. Because Article II of the Constitution does not endow the president with clear and immediate authority over private parties (as it does over the federal bureaucracy), it is not surprising that proclamations tend to be less consequential than executive orders, most involving ceremonial and commemorative affairs. There are, however, numerous exceptions, such as Nixon's 1971 proclamations and orders temporarily freezing all wages, rents, and prices as part of the national economic stabilization program; Ford's 1973 proclamation granting pardons to draft dodgers; and Carter's 1980 proclamations imposing new surcharges on imported oil.

▪ ▪ ▪

Even the advent of the Cold War can be traced back to a national security directive. Issued in April 1950, N.S.C. 68 emphasized the historical importance of the mounting conflict between the United States and Soviet Union. The document, drafted by the director of the State Department's policy-planning staff, Paul Nitze, was a call to arms and defined the nation's military and political objectives as it waged an ongoing struggle against the world's only other superpower. . . . While it met some initial resistance within the Truman and Eisenhower administrations, N.S.C. 68, more than any other document, established the guiding doctrine for successive presidents' Cold War foreign policy.

Executive agreements stand apart from these other directives. While executive orders, proclamations, and (to a lesser degree) national security directives all are unilateral counterparts to legislation, executive agreements provide presidents with an alternative to the treaty ratification process. Rather than having to secure the consent of two-thirds of the Senate before entering into a bi- or multilateral agreement with foreign nations, presidents can use executive agreements to unilaterally commit the United States to deals involving such issues as international trade, ocean fishing rights, open air space, environmental standards, and immigration patterns. While most of these agreements concern very specific (and often technical) matters, the sheer number issued during the modern era has increased at such an astronomical rate that collectively they now constitute a vital means by which presidents unilaterally affect public policy.

When setting public policy, presidents frequently issue combinations of these various policy directives. To force the integration of schools in Little Rock, Arkansas, Eisenhower simultaneously issued a proclamation and an executive order. Carter relied upon a series of executive orders and executive agreements to negotiate the Iran Hostage Crisis. Presiding over World War II, the Korean War, and the Vietnam War, Roosevelt, Truman, Johnson, and Nixon all issued a wide array of secretive orders, national security directives and otherwise. Presidents frequently use executive orders, secretarial orders, and reorganization plans to create administrative agencies and then turn to other kinds of unilateral directives—for example, administrative directives, findings and determinations, and regulations—to monitor their behavior. The ease with which presidents can mix and match these unilateral directives to advance their policy goals is considerable.

The Legality of Unilateral Powers

The first Court challenge to a presidential order, *Little v. Barreme* (1804) concerned the legality of a seizure of a Danish ship, the *Flying Fish*. George Little, the captain of the *U.S.S. Boston,* had intercepted the ship at sea. At the time, Captain Little was complying with a John Adams presidential order that the Navy seize any and all ships sailing to or from French ports. Previously, however, Congress had only authorized the seizure of frigates sailing to French ports. Because the Danish brig was sailing *from* a French port and not *to* one (it was headed from Jérémie to St. Thomas), the Court for the first time had to resolve a discrepancy between a presidential order and congressional statute.

In a unanimous ruling written by Chief Justice John Marshall, the Court declared that had Adams' order stood alone, the Navy's actions would be constitutional. Because Congress had enacted a more restrictive statute, however, the Court was forced to rule in favor of the Danish captain. "Congressional policy announced in a statute necessarily prevails over inconsistent presidential orders. . . . Presidential orders, even those issued as Commander in Chief, are subject to restrictions by Congress." Marshall subsequently ordered Captain Little to pay damages. More importantly, though, Marshall established the clear principle that when an executive order blatantly conflicts with a law, the law prevails.

During the rest of the nineteenth century, the federal courts considered a host of challenges to unilateral directives issued by presidents, most of which involved military orders. It was not until the 1930s that the Supreme Court formally recognized the president's power to act unilaterally. Three cases— *United States v. Curtiss-Wright* (1936); *United States v. Belmont* (1937); and *United States v. Pink* (1942)—made the difference (Schubert 1973, 107).

Curtiss-Wright centrally involved the constitutionality of an executive agreement that forbade the sale of arms to countries involved in armed conflict. When it sold fifteen machine guns to the government of Bolivia, Curtiss-Wright Export Corporation was charged with violating the agreement. As part of its defense, the company argued that Congress had "abdicated its essential functions and delegated them to the Executive," and for that reason, the Court should overturn the executive agreement. Instead, the Supreme Court, in an oft-cited phrase, deemed the president the "sole organ of the federal government in the field of international relations" and upheld the constitutionality of this particular delegation of authority. Doing so, it formally recognized his legal right to issue executive agreements.

In *United States v. Belmont*, the Supreme Court extended this right to executive orders. When Russia reneged on debts owed to the United States in the 1930s, President Roosevelt seized Russian financial assets held in American banks. Arguing that Roosevelt's actions violated New York State law, a Russian investor asked the Court to overturn the executive order and to award compensation for his losses. The Court, however, refused. Doing so, it equated an executive order with federal law and reaffirmed its preeminence over state law.

The Supreme Court extended this reasoning to executive agreements in *United States v. Pink*, which again involved the seizure of Russian assets in American banks. This time, however, the focus concerned an exchange between the president and the Russian government known as the Litvinov Assignment. In a letter to Roosevelt, People's Commissar for Foreign Affairs Maxim Litvinov relinquished certain Russian claims to assets of Russian companies in New York banks. Roosevelt subsequently acknowledged the reassignment of property claims. In *Pink*, the question before the Court centered on the legal authority of this exchange. Ultimately, the Court ruled that because executive agreements have the same status as treaties, and because both override state laws, the plaintiffs could not use New York State law to try to recover their lost assets.

Collectively, *Curtiss-Wright, Belmont,* and *Pink* firmly established the president's authority to issue directives involving "external affairs." Their distinction between foreign and domestic policy, however, subsequently blurred. And for good reason. The list of exceptions to any definition of "foreign" or "domestic" policy is sufficiently long as to make the definitions themselves unworkable as elements of jurisprudence. "The original constitutional understanding that in domestic affairs Congress would make the law and presidents would see to its enforcement had never worked in practice and by the early 1990s it had largely been abandoned" (McDonald 1994, 314). The courts now fully recognize the president's power to issue executive orders and agreements that concern both foreign and domestic policy. Indeed, powers of unilateral action have become a veritable fixture of the American presidency in the modern era.

Writing Public Policy

Much can happen between the issuance of a presidential order and its implementation. Opportunities for shirking abound. Administrative agencies may read their mandates selectively; they may ignore especially objectionable provisions; they may report false or misleading information about initiatives' successes and failures. As we have already noted, the executive branch assuredly does not reduce to the president himself. Bureaucrats enjoy a fair measure of autonomy to do as they please.

Demanding a policy change does not make it so. As Neustadt himself forcefully argued, orders handed down from on high are not always self-executing (1991 [1960], 10–28). In 1948, for instance, Truman issued an executive order demanding the desegregation of the military, but decades passed before the outcome was finally realized. Presidents are engaged in a constant struggle to ensure compliance among members of the executive branch, and to advance the realization of their policy interests. Presidents appoint high-ranking officials who share their worldview, and whenever possible, presidents try to rally the support of their subordinates. This has important consequences for our understanding of presidential power; for when it comes to the implementation of public policy (whether enacted as a federal statute or issued as a unilateral directive), the power modern presidents wield very much depends upon their ability to persuade.

■ ■ ■

[W]hile presidents must build and sustain coalitions to pass laws, they can unilaterally issue policy directives over the vocal objections of congressional majorities. As one political observer instructs, "Forget Capitol Hill deliberations and back-room negotiations with industry titans. No need for endless debate and deal-making. For a president, an executive order can be as powerful as a law—and considerably easier to achieve." In the political fight over the content of public policy, presidents regularly exert power without persuasion.

▪   ▪   ▪

7. CONCLUSION

▪   ▪   ▪

Macrotrends in unilateral policy making

Since George Washington issued the Neutrality Proclamation in 1793, presidents have relied upon their unilateral powers to effect important policy changes. In the nineteenth century, Jefferson followed up with the Louisiana Purchase and Lincoln with the Emancipation Proclamation. In the early twentieth century, Theodore Roosevelt established the national parks system and Wilson issued more than 1,700 executive orders to guide the nation through World War I.

For the past fifty years, however, the trajectory of unilateral policy making has noticeably increased. While it was relatively rare, and for the most part inconsequential, during the eighteenth and nineteenth centuries, unilateral policy making has become an integral feature of the modern presidency. Presidents issue more unilateral directives today than ever before, steadily expanding their influence over all kinds of public policies, foreign and domestic. While there remain important fluctuations from year to year, and from administration to administration, the time-series of significant executive orders and executive agreements unmistakably rises.

In part, this is due to the overwhelming demands placed upon modern presidents. The public holds presidents responsible for all kinds of activities that previously either did not concern the federal government or rested solely within the domain of Congress. Presidents now develop policies on medical practices, racial discrimination, social welfare, labor and management relations, international trade, and education—areas that few presidents, prior to FDR, ever addressed. Indeed, it is difficult to think of a single area of governance that modern presidents can safely ignore. Modern presidents, in this sense, do more simply because the public expects them to.

In addition, presidential powers have expanded over the past half-century because the checks placed on them by Congress have subsided. As political parties have weakened, subcommittees have proliferated, and ideological divisions within Congress have heightened, Congress's ability to legislate has waned. So much so, in fact, that gridlock, while not constant, has become "a basic fact of U.S. lawmaking" (Krehbiel 1998, 4). This development has important implications for presidential power. As Congress weakens, the check it places on presidential power relaxes, and new opportunities arise for the president to strike out on his own. An expansion of presidential power then signals a shift in the overall division of powers—tipping the balance in favor of the president, and against Congress.

Two additional factors probably contributed to the overall increase in unilateral policy making during the latter half of the twentieth century. First, the time-series takes off in the late 1930s, just after the Supreme Court issued a series of rulings—*United States v. Curtiss-Wright* (1936); *United States v. Belmont* (1937); and *United States v. Pink* (1942)—that collectively fortified the president's legal authority to issue executive orders and executive agreements. With the official sanctioning of the Court, modern presidents proceeded with a greater measure of confidence when issuing executive orders and other unilateral directives. Second, many of these orders either created new administrative agencies or directed existing agencies to perform new functions. In this sense, the general trajectory of the significant executive order time-series maps the steady growth of the administrative state. Modern presidents did more simply because more needed to be done. Compared to their predecessors, modern presidents oversee more agencies that employ more employees that perform more tasks. As a consequence, it is little wonder that modern presidents rely upon the unilateral powers with greater frequency.

These trends, however, need not continue forever. There is nothing in the logic of the unilateral politics model that requires presidential power to increase monotonically over time. Quite the contrary, should a new consensus about policy matters emerge in Congress and legislative productivity displace gridlock, opportunities for presidents to act unilaterally may decline. Similarly, should executive actions attract heightened public scrutiny, judges may feel emboldened to overturn presidents with greater frequency.

BIBLIOGRAPHY

Cooper, Phillip. 2002. *By Order of the President: The Use and Abuse of Executive Direct Action.* Lawrence: University Press of Kansas.

———. 1997. "Power Tools for an Effective and Responsible Presidency." *Administration and Society* 29(5): 529–56.

Corwin, Edward. 1957. *The President, Office and Powers, 1787–1948: History and Analysis of Practice and Opinion.* New York: New York University Press.

Cronin, Thomas. 1989. *Inventing the American Presidency.* Lawrence: University of Kansas Press.

Hart, John. 1995. *The Presidential Branch From Washington to Clinton.* Chatham NJ: Chatham House Publishers, Inc.

King, Gary, and Lyn Ragsdale. 1988. *The Elusive Executive: Discovering Statistical Patterns in the Presidency.* Washington, DC: Congressional Quarterly Press.

Krehbiel, Keith. 1998. *Pivotal Politics: A Theory of U.S. Lawmaking.* Chicago: University of Chicago Press.

Landy, Marc, and Sidney Milkis. 2000. *Presidential Greatness.* Lawrence: University of Kansas Press.

Mayer, Kenneth. 2001. *With the Stroke of a Pen: Executive Orders and Presidentia Power.* Princeton, NJ: Princeton University Press.

McDonald, Forrest. 1994. *The American Presidency: An Intellectual History.* Lawrence: University of Kansas Press.

Moe, Terry, and William Howell. 1999a. "The Presidential Power of Unilateral Action." *Journal of Law, Economics and Organization* 15(1): 132–79.

———. 1999b. "Unilateral Action and Presidential Power: A Theory." *Presidential Studies Quarterly* 29(4): 850–72.

Neustadt, Richard E. 1991 [1960]. *Presidential Power and the Modern Presidents.* New York: Free Press.

Paige, Joseph. 1977. *The Law Nobody Knows: Enlargement of the Constitution—Treaties and Executive Agreements.* New York: Vantage Press.

Schubert, Glendon. 1973. *The Presidency in the Courts.* New York: Da Capo Press.

6.5

GEORGE W. BUSH

Signing Statement of H.R. 2863

In one of the most controversial signing statements by any president, George W. Bush made it clear that he believed a 2005 law regarding treatment of enemy combatants in U.S. custody would lead to Congress overstepping its role in national security operations.

Today, I have signed into law H.R. 2863, the "Department of Defense, Emergency Supplemental Appropriations to Address Hurricanes in the Gulf of Mexico, and Pandemic Influenza Act, 2006." The Act provides resources needed to fight the war on terror, help citizens of the Gulf States recover from devastating hurricanes, and protect Americans from a potential influenza pandemic.

Sections 8007, 8011, and 8093 of the Act prohibit the use of funds to initiate a special access program, a new overseas installation, or a new start program, unless the congressional defense committees receive advance notice. The Supreme Court of the United States has stated that the President's authority to classify and control access to information bearing on the national security flows from the Constitution and does not depend upon a legislative grant of authority. Although the advance notice contemplated by sections 8007, 8011, and 8093 can be provided in most situations as a matter of comity, situations may arise, especially in wartime, in which the President must act promptly under his constitutional grants of executive power and authority as Commander in Chief of the Armed Forces while protecting certain extraordinarily sensitive national security information. The executive branch shall construe these sections in a manner consistent with the constitutional authority of the President.

Section 8059 of the Act provides that, notwithstanding any other provision of law, no funds available to the Department of Defense for fiscal year 2006 may be used to transfer defense articles or services, other than intelligence services, to another nation or an international organization for international peacekeeping, peace enforcement, or humanitarian assistance operations, until 15 days after the executive branch notifies six committees of the Congress of the planned transfer. To the extent that protection of the U.S. Armed Forces deployed for international peacekeeping, peace enforcement, or humanitarian assistance operations might require action of a kind covered by section 8059 sooner than 15 days after notification, the executive branch shall construe the section in a manner consistent with the President's constitutional authority as Commander in Chief.

A proviso in the Act's appropriation for "Operation and Maintenance, Defense-Wide" purports to prohibit planning for consolidation of certain offices within the Department of Defense. Also, sections 8010(b), 8032, 8037(b), and 8100 purport to specify the content of portions of future budget requests to the Congress. The executive branch shall construe these provisions relating to planning and making of budget recommendations in a manner consistent with the President's constitutional authority to require the opinions of the heads of departments, to supervise the unitary executive branch, and to recommend for congressional consideration such measures as the President shall judge necessary and expedient.

Section 8005 of the Act, relating to requests to congressional committees for reprogramming of funds, shall be construed as calling solely for notification, as any other construction would be inconsistent with the constitutional principles enunciated by the Supreme Court of the United States in INS v. Chadha.

The executive branch shall construe section 8104, relating to integration of foreign intelligence information, in a manner consistent with the President's constitutional authority as Commander in Chief, including for the conduct of intelligence operations, and to supervise the unitary executive branch. Also, the executive branch shall construe sections 8106 and 8119 of the Act, which purport to prohibit the President from altering command and control relationships within the Armed Forces, as advisory, as any other construction would be inconsistent with the constitutional grant to the President of the authority of Commander in Chief.

The executive branch shall construe provisions of the Act relating to race, ethnicity, gender, and State residency, such as sections 8014, 8020 and 8057, in a manner consistent with the requirement to afford equal protection of the laws under the Due Process Clause of the Constitution's Fifth Amendment.

The executive branch shall construe Title X in Division A of the Act, relating to detainees, in a manner consistent with the constitutional authority of the President to supervise the unitary executive branch and as Commander in Chief and consistent with the constitutional limitations on the judicial power, which will assist in achieving the shared objective of the Congress and the President, evidenced in Title X, of protecting the American people from further terrorist attacks. Further, in light of the principles enunciated by the Supreme Court of the United States in 2001 in Alexander v. Sandoval, and noting that the text and structure of Title X do not create a private right of action to enforce Title X, the executive branch shall construe Title X not to create a private right of action. Finally, given the decision of the Congress reflected in subsections 1005(e) and 1005(h) that the amendments made to section 2241 of title 28, United States Code, shall apply to past, present, and future actions, including applications for writs of habeas corpus, described in that section, and noting that section 1005 does not confer any constitutional right upon an alien detained abroad as an enemy combatant, the executive branch shall construe section 1005 to preclude the Federal courts from exercising subject matter jurisdiction over any existing or future action, including applications for writs of habeas corpus, described in section 1005.

Language in Division B of the Act, under the heading "Office of Justice Programs, State and Local Law Enforcement Assistance," purports to require the Attorney General to consult congressional committees prior to allocating appropriations for expenditure to execute the law. Because the President's constitutional authority to supervise the unitary executive branch and take care that the laws be faithfully executed cannot be made by law subject to a requirement to consult with congressional committees or to involve them in executive decision- making, the executive branch shall construe the provision to require only notification. At the same time, the Attorney General shall, as a matter of comity between the executive and legislative branches, seek and consider the views of appropriate committees in this matter as the Attorney General deems appropriate.

Certain provisions in the Act purport to allocate funds for specified purposes as set forth in the joint explanatory statement of managers that accompanied the Act or other Acts; to make changes in statements of managers that accompanied various appropriations bills reported from conferences in the past; or to direct compliance with a committee report. Such provisions include section 8044 in Division A, and sections 5022, 5023, and 5024 and language under the heading "Natural Resources Conservation Service, Conservation Operations" in Division B, of the Act. Other provisions of the Act, such as sections 8073 and 8082 in Division A, purport to give binding effect to legislative documents not presented to the President. The executive branch shall construe all these provisions in a manner consistent with the bicameral passage and presentment requirements of the Constitution for the making of a law.

GEORGE W. BUSH
THE WHITE HOUSE
DECEMBER 30, 2005

7

THE BUREAUCRACY

7.1

JAMES Q. WILSON

From *Bureaucracy: What Government Agencies
Do and Why They Do It*

Wilson writes convincingly that bureaucracies can vary greatly in their effectiveness. He pokes holes in standard complaints about bureaucracies by indicating how some of the inefficiencies that people complain about are either unavoidable or by design.

20. BUREAUCRACY AND THE PUBLIC INTEREST

The German army beat the French army in 1940; the Texas prisons for many years did a better job than did the Michigan prisons; Carver High School in Atlanta became a better school under Norris Hogans. These successes were the result of skilled executives who correctly identified the critical tasks of their organizations, distributed authority in a way appropriate to those tasks, infused their subordinates with a sense of mission, and acquired sufficient autonomy to permit them to get on with the job. The critical tasks were different in each case, and so the organizations differed in culture and patterns of authority, but all three were alike in one sense: incentives, culture, and authority were combined in a way that suited the task at hand.

By now, . . . the reader may find all this painfully obvious. If [these points] are obvious to the reader, then surely they are obvious to government officials. Intellectually perhaps they are. But whatever lip service may be given to the lessons . . . the daily incentives operating in the political world encourage a very different course of action.

Armies

Though the leadership and initiative of field officers and noncoms is of critical importance, the Pentagon is filled with generals who want to control combat from headquarters or from helicopters, using radios to gather information and computers to process it. Though the skill of the infantryman almost always has been a key to military success, the U.S. Army traditionally has put its best people in specialized units (intelligence, engineering, communications), leaving the leftovers for the infantry.[1] Though it has fought wars since 1945 everywhere except in Europe, the army continues to devote most of its planning to big-tank battles on the West German plains.

Prisons

The success of George Beto in the Texas DOC was there for everyone to see, but many observers gave the most favorable attention to prison executives who seemed to voice the best intentions (rehabilitation, prisoner self-governance) rather than the best accomplishments (safe, decent facilities).

Schools

Especially in big cities, many administrators keep principals weak and teachers busy filling out reports, all with an eye toward minimizing complaints from parents, auditors, interest groups, and the press. Teachers individually grumble that they are treated as robots instead of professionals, but collectively they usually oppose any steps—vouchers, merit pay, open enrollment, strengthened principals—that in fact have given teachers a larger role in designing curricula and managing their classrooms. Norris Hogans received little help from the Atlanta school system; politically, extra resources had to go to all schools "equally" rather than disproportionately to those schools that were improving the most.

These generals, wardens, administrators, and teachers have not been behaving irrationally; rather, they have been responding to the incentives and constraints that they encounter on a daily basis. Those incentives include the need to manage situations over which they have little control on the basis of a poorly defined or nonexistent sense of mission and in the face of a complex array of constraints that seems always to grow, never to shrink. Outside groups—elected officials, interest groups, professional associations, the media—demand a voice in the running of these agencies and make that demand effective by imposing rules on the agencies and demanding that all these rules be enforced all of the time. Moreover, habitual patterns of action—the lessons of the past, the memories of earlier struggles, the expectations of one's co-workers—narrow the area within which new courses of action are sought.

Bureaucrats often complain of "legislative micromanagement," and indeed it exists. . . . with respect to the armed forces. There has been a dramatic

increase in the number of hearings, reports, investigations, statutory amendments, and budgetary adjustments with which the Pentagon must deal.[2] But
there also has been a sharp increase in presidential micromanagement. Herbert Kaufman notes that for a half century or more the White House has
feared agency independence more than agency paralysis, and so it has multiplied the number of presidential staffers, central management offices, and
requirements for higher-level reviews. Once you start along the path of congressional or White House control, the process acquires a momentum of its
own. "As more constraints are imposed, rigidities fixing agencies in their
established ways intensify. As a result, complaints that they do not respond to
controls also intensify. Further controls, checkpoints, and clearances are
therefore introduced."[3] Much the same story can be told with respect to the
growing involvement of the courts in agency affairs.

With some conspicuous exceptions the result of this process has been to
deflect the attention of agency executives away from how the tasks of their
agencies get defined and toward the constraints that must be observed no matter what the tasks may be. Who then decides what tasks shall be performed? In
a production agency with observable outputs and routinized work processes,
the answer is relatively simple: The laws and regulations that created the agency
also define its job. But in procedural, coping, and craft agencies, the answer
seems to be nobody in particular and everybody in general. The operating-level
workers define the tasks, occasionally by design, as in those cases where operator ideology makes a difference, but more commonly by accident, as in those
instances where prior experiences, professional norms, situational and technological imperatives, and peer-group expectations shape the nature of the work.

From time to time a gifted executive appears at a politically propitious time
and makes things happen differently. He or she creates a new institution that
acquires a distinctive competence, a strong sense of mission, and an ability to
achieve socially valued goals. The Army Corps of Engineers, the Social Security Administration, the Marine Corps, the Forest Service, the FBI: For many
years after they were created, and in many instances still today, these agencies, along with a few others that could be mentioned, were a kind of elite service that stood as a living refutation of the proposition that "all bureaucrats
are dim-witted paper-shufflers." And these are only the federal examples; at
the local level one can find many school systems and police departments that
have acquired a praiseworthy organizational character.

But one must ask whether today one could create from scratch the Marine
Corps, or the FBI, or the Forest Service; possibly, but probably not. Who
would dare suggest that a new agency come into being with its own personnel
system (and thus with fewer opportunities for civil servants to get tenure),
with a single dominant mission (and thus with little organizational deference
to the myriad other goals outsiders would want it to serve), and with an ardu-
ous training regime designed to instill *esprit de corps* (and thus with less
regard for those niceties and conveniences that sedentary people believe to be

important)? Or how optimistic should we be that today we could organize a Social Security Administration in a way that would bring to Washington men and women of exceptional talent? Might not many of those people decide today that they do not want to risk running afoul of the conflict-of-interest laws, that they have no stomach for close media and congressional scrutiny, and that they would not accept the federal pay levels pegged to the salaries of members of Congress fearful of raising their own compensation?

It would be a folly of historical romanticism to imagine that great agencies were created in a golden age that is destined never to return, but it would be shortsighted to deny that we have paid a price for having emphasized rules and constraints to the neglect of tasks and mission. At the end of her careful review of the problems the SSA has had in managing disability insurance and supplemental security income, Martha Derthick makes the same point this way: "If the agencies repeatedly fall short, one ought at least to consider the possibility that there is a systematic mismatch between what they are instructed to do and their capacity to do it."[4] In recent years, when Congress has been creating new programs and modifying old ones at a dizzying rate, often on the basis of perfunctory hearings (or, as with the Senate's consideration of the 1988 drug bill, no hearings at all), a government agency capable of responding adequately to these endless changes would have to be versatile and adaptable, "capable of devising new routines or altering old ones very quickly." These qualities, she concludes, "are rarely found in large formal organizations."[5] I would only add that government agencies are far less flexible than formal organizations generally.

Things are not made much better by our national tendency to engage in bureaucrat-bashing. One has to have some perspective on this. It is true that bureaucracies prefer the present to the future, the known to the unknown, and the dominant mission to rival missions; many agencies in fact are skeptical of things that were "NIH"—Not Invented Here. Every social grouping, whether a neighborhood, a nation, or an organization, acquires a culture; changing that culture is like moving a cemetery: it is always difficult and some believe it is sacrilegious. It is also true, as many conservatives argue, that the government tries to do things that it is incapable of doing well, just as it is true, as many liberals allege, that the government in fact does many things well enough. As Charles Wolf has argued, both markets and governments have their imperfections; many things we might want to do collectively require us to choose between unsatisfactory alternatives.[6]

A Few Modest Suggestions That May Make a Small Difference

To do better we have to deregulate the government.[7] If deregulation of a market makes sense because it liberates the entrepreneurial energies of its members, then it is possible that deregulating the public sector also may help energize it. The difference, of course, is that both the price system and the profit motive provide a discipline in markets that is absent in non-markets.

Whether any useful substitutes for this discipline can be found for public-sector workers is not clear, though I will offer some suggestions. But even if we cannot expect the same results from deregulation in the two sectors we can agree at a minimum that detailed regulation, even of public employees, rarely is compatible with energy, pride in workmanship, and the exercise of initiative. The best evidence for this proposition, if any is needed, is that most people do not like working in an environment in which every action is second-guessed, every initiative viewed with suspicion, and every controversial decision denounced as malfeasance.

James Colvard, for many years a senior civilian manager in the navy, suggests that the government needs to emulate methods that work in the better parts of the private sector: "a bias toward action, small staffs, and a high level of delegation which is based on trust."[8] A panel of the National Academy of Public Administration (NAPA), consisting of sixteen senior government executives holding the rank of assistant secretary, issued a report making the same point:

> Over many years, government has become entwined in elaborate management control systems and the accretion of progressively more detailed administrative procedures. This development has not produced superior management. Instead, it has produced managerial overburden. . . . Procedures overwhelm substance. Organizations become discredited, along with their employees. . . . The critical elements of leadership in management appear to wither in the face of a preoccupation with process. The tools are endlessly "perfected"; the manager who is expected to use these tools believes himself to be ignored. . . . Management systems are not management. . . . The attitude of those who design and administer the rules . . . must be reoriented from a "control mentality" to one of "how can I help get the mission of this agency accomplished."[9]

But how can government "delegate" and "trust" and still maintain accountability? If it is a mistake to foster an ethos that encourages every bureaucrat to "go by the book," is it not an equally serious problem to allow zealots to engage in "mission madness," charging off to implement their private versions of some ambiguous public goal? (Steven Emerson has written a useful account of mission madness in some highly secret military intelligence and covert-action agencies.)[10] Given everything we know about the bureaucratic desire for autonomy and the political rewards of rule making, is there any reason to suppose that anybody will find it in his or her interest to abandon the "control mentality" and adopt the "mission accomplishment" mentality?

Possibly not. But it may be worth thinking about what a modestly deregulated government might look like. It might look as it once did, when some of the better federal agencies were created. At the time the Corps of Engineers, the Forest Service, and the FBI were founded much of the federal government was awash in political patronage, petty cabals, and episodic corruption.

Organizing an elite service in those days may have been easier than doing so today, when the problems are less patronage and corruption than they are officiousness and complexity. But the keys to organizational success have not changed. The agencies were started by strong leaders who were able to command personal loyalty, define and instill a clear and powerful sense of mission, attract talented workers who believed they were joining something special, and make exacting demands on subordinates.

Today there is not much chance to create a new agency; almost every agency one can imagine already has been created. Even so, the lessons one learns from changing agencies confirm what can be inferred from studying their founding.

First: Executives should understand the culture of their organizations—that is, what their subordinates believe constitute the core tasks of the agency—and the strengths and limitations of that culture. If members widely share and warmly endorse that culture the agency has a sense of mission. This permits the executive to economize on scarce incentives (people want to do certain tasks even when there are no special rewards for doing it); to state general objectives confident that subordinates will understand the appropriate ways of achieving them; and to delegate responsibility knowing that lower-level decisions probably will conform to higher-level expectations.

A good executive realizes that workers can make subtle, precise, and realistic judgments, but only if those judgments refer to a related, coherent set of behaviors. People cannot easily keep in mind many quite different things or strike reasonable balances among competing tasks. People want to know what is expected of them; they do not want to be told, in answer to this question, that "on the one hand this, but on the other hand that."

In defining a core mission and sorting out tasks that either fit or do not fit with this mission, executives must be aware of their many rivals for the right to define it. Operators with professional backgrounds will bring to the agency their skills but also their biases: Lawyers, economists, and engineers see the world in very different ways. You cannot hire them as if they were tools that in your skilled hands will perform exactly the task you set for them. Black and Decker may make tools like that, but Harvard and MIT do not. Worker peer groups also set expectations to which operators conform, especially when the operators work in a threatening, unpredictable, or confrontational environment. You may design the ideal patrol officer or schoolteacher, but unless you understand the demands made by the street and the classroom, your design will remain an artistic expression destined for the walls of some organizational museum.

These advantages of infusing an agency with a sense of mission are purchased at a price. An agency with a strong mission will give perfunctory attention, if any at all, to tasks that are not central to that mission. Diplomats in the State Department will have little interest in embassy security; intelligence officers in the CIA will not worry as much as they should about counter-intelligence; narcotics agents in the DEA will minimize the importance of improper prescriptions written by physicians; power engineers in the TVA will not think as hard about environmental protection or conservation as about maximizing the efficiency of generating units; fighter pilots in the USAF will look at air transport as a homely stepchild; and navy admirals who earned their flag serving on aircraft carriers will not press zealously to expand the role of minesweepers.

If the organization must perform a diverse set of tasks, those tasks that are not part of the core mission will need special protection. This requires giving autonomy to the subordinate tasks subunit (for example, by providing for them a special organizational niche) and creating a career track so that talented people performing non-mission tasks can rise to high rank in the agency. No single organization, however, can perform well a wide variety of tasks; inevitably some will be neglected. In this case, the wise executive will arrange to devolve the slighted tasks onto another agency, or to a wholly new organization created for the purpose. Running multitask conglomerates is as risky in the public as in the private sector. There are limits to the number of different jobs managers can manage. Moreover, conglomerate agencies rarely can develop a sense of mission; the cost of trying to do everything is that few things are done well. The turf-conscious executive who stoutly refuses to surrender any tasks, no matter how neglected, to another agency is courting disaster; in time the failure of his or her agency to perform some orphan task will lead to a political or organizational crisis. Long ago the State Department should have got out of the business of building embassies. Diplomats are good at many things, but supervising carpenters and plumbers is not one of them. Let agencies whose mission is construction—the Army Corps of Engineers or the navy's Seabees—build buildings.

Second: Negotiate with one's political superiors to get some agreement as to which are the *essential* constraints that must be observed by your agency and which the marginal constraints. This, frankly, may be impossible. The decentralization of authority in Congress (and in some state legislatures) and the unreliability of most expressions of presidential or gubernatorial backing are such that in most cases you will discover, by experience if not by precept, that all constraints are essential all of the time. But perhaps with effort some maneuvering room may be won. A few agencies obtained the right to use more flexible, less cumbersome personnel systems modeled on the China Lake experiment, and Congress has the power to broaden those opportunities. Perhaps some enlightened member of Congress will be able to get statutory authority for the equivalent of China Lake with respect to procurement regulations. An executive is well advised to spend time showing that member how to do it.

Third: Match the distribution of authority and the control over resources to the tasks your organization is performing. In general, authority should be placed at the lowest level at which all essential elements of information are available. Bureaucracies will differ greatly in what level that may be. At one extreme are agencies such as the Internal Revenue Service or maximum-security prisons, in which uniformity of treatment and precision of control are so important as to make it necessary for there to be exacting, centrally determined rules for most tasks. At the other extreme are public schools, police departments, and armies, organizations in which operational uncertainties are so great that discretion must be given to (or if not given will be taken by) lower-level workers.

A good place in which to think through these matters is the area of weapons procurement. The overcentralization of design control is one of the many criticisms of such procurement on which all commentators seem agreed. Buying a new aircraft may be likened to remodeling one's home: You never know how much it will cost until you are done; you quickly find out that changing your mind midway through the work costs a lot of money; and you soon realize that decisions have to be made by people on the spot who can look at the pipes, wires, and joists. The Pentagon procures aircraft as if none of its members had ever built or remodeled a house. It does so because both it and its legislative superiors refuse to allow authority to flow down to the point where decisions rationally can be made.

The same analysis can be applied to public schools. As John Chubb and Terry Moe have shown, public and private schools differ in the locus of effective control.[11] At least in big cities, decisions in private schools that are made by headmasters or in Catholic schools that are made by small archdiocesan staffs are made in public schools by massive, cumbersome headquarters bureaucracies. Of course, there are perfectly understandable political reasons for this difference, but not very many good reasons for it. Many sympathetic critics of the public schools believe that the single most useful organizational change that could be made would be to have educational management decisions—on personnel, scheduling, and instructional matters—made at the school level.[12]

Fourth: Judge organizations by results. This reading has made it clear that what constitutes a valued result in government usually is a matter of dispute. But even when fairly clear performance standards exist, legislatures and executives often ignore them with unhappy results. William E. Turcotte compared how two state governments oversaw their state liquor monopolies. The state that applied clear standards to its liquor bureaucrats produced significantly more profit and lower administrative costs than did the state with unclear or conflicting standards.[13]

Even when results are hard to assess more can be done than is often the case. If someone set out to evaluate the output of a private school, hospital, or security service, he or she would have at least as much trouble as would someone trying to measure the output of a public school, hospital, or police department. Governments are not the only institutions with ambiguous products.

There are two ways to cope with the problem in government One . . . is to supply the service or product in a marketlike environment. Shift the burden of evaluation off the shoulders of professional evaluators and onto the shoulders of clients and customers, and let the latter vote with their feet. The "client" in these cases can be individual citizens or government agencies; what is important is that the client be able to choose from among rival suppliers.

But some public services cannot be supplied, or are never going to be supplied, by a market. We can imagine allowing parents to choose among schools but we cannot imagine letting them choose (at least for most purposes) among police departments or armies. In that case one should adopt the second way of evaluating a public service: carry out a demonstration project or conduct a field experiment. (I will use the two ideas interchangeably, though some scholars distinguish between them.)[14] An experiment is a planned alteration in a state of affairs designed to measure the effect of the intervention. It involves asking the question, "if I change X, what will happen to Y, having first made certain that everything else stays the same?" It sounds easy, but it is not.

A good experiment (bad ones are worse than no experiment at all) requires that one do the following: First, identify a course of action to be tested; call it the treatment. A "treatment" can be a police tactic, a school curriculum, or a welfare program. Second, decide what impact the treatment is intended to have; call this the outcome. The outcome can be a crime rate, an achievement score, a work effort, a housing condition, or an income level. Third, give the treatment to one group (the experimental group) and withhold it from another (the control group). A group might be a police precinct, a class of students, the tenants in a housing project, or people who meet some eligibility requirement (say, having low incomes). It is quite important how the membership in these groups is determined. It should be done randomly; that is, all eligible precincts, schools, tenants, or people should be randomly sorted into experimental and control groups. Random assignment means that all the characteristics of the members of the experimental and control groups are likely to be identical. Fourth, assess the condition of each group before and after the treatment. The first assessment describes the baseline condition, the second the outcome condition. This outcome assessment should continue for some time after the end of the treatment, because experience has shown that many treatments seem to have a short-term effect that quickly disappears. Fifth, make certain that the evaluation is done by people other than those providing the treatment. People like to believe that their efforts are worthwhile, so much so that perhaps unwittingly they will gather data in ways that make it look like the treatment worked even when it did not.[15]

The object of all this is to find out what works. Using this method we have discovered that tripling the number of patrol cars on a beat does not lower the crime rate; that foot patrol reduces the fear of crime but not (ordinarily) its incidence; and that arresting spouse-beaters reduces (for a while) future assaults more than does counseling the assaulters.[16] We have learned that giving people an income supplement (akin to the negative income tax) reduces work effort and in some cases encourages families to break up.[17] We have learned that giving special job training and support to welfare mothers, ex-offenders, and school drop-outs produces sizable gains in the employment records of the welfare recipients but no gain for the ex-offenders and school drop-outs.[18] We have learned that a housing allowance program increases the welfare of poor families even though it does not improve the stock of housing. We have learned that more flexible pay and classification systems greatly benefit the managers of navy research centers and improve the work atmosphere at the centers.

There also have been many failed or flawed management experiments. In the 1930s, Herbert Simon carried out what may have been the first serious such experiment when he tried to find out how to improve the performance of welfare workers in the California State Relief Administration. Though elegantly designed, the experimental changes proved so controversial and the political environment of the agency so unstable that it is not clear that any useful inferences can be drawn from the project.[19] The attempt to evaluate educational vouchers at Alum Rock was undercut by the political need to restrict participation by private schools . . . . There are countless other "studies" that are evaluations in name only; in reality they are self-congratulatory conclusions written by program administrators. The administrative world is a political world, not a scientific laboratory, and evaluators of administration must come to terms with that fact. Often there are no mutually acceptable terms. But where reasonable terms can be struck it is possible to learn more than untutored experience can tell us about what works.

Such dry and dusty research projects probably seem thin fare to people who want Big Answers to Big Questions such as "How can we curb rampant bureaucracy?" or "How can we unleash the creative talents of our dedicated public servants?" But public management is not an arena in which to find Big Answers; it is a world of settled institutions designed to allow imperfect people to use flawed procedures to cope with insoluble problems.

The fifth and final bit of advice flows directly from the limits on judging agencies by their results. All organizations seek the stability and comfort that comes from relying on standard operating procedures—"SOPs." When results are unknown or equivocal, bureaus will have no incentive to alter those SOPs so as better to achieve their goals, only an incentive to modify them to conform to externally imposed constraints. The SOPs will represent an internally defined equilibrium that reconciles the situational imperatives, professional norms, bureaucratic ideologies, peer-group expectations, and (if present) leadership demands unique to that agency. The only way to minimize the adverse effect of allowing human affairs to be managed by organizations driven by their autonomous SOPs is to keep the number, size, and authority of such organizations as small as possible. If none of the four preceding bits of advice work, the reader must confront the realization that there are no solutions for the bureaucracy problem that are not also "solutions" to the government problem. More precisely: All complex organizations display bureaucratic problems of confusion, red tape, and the avoidance of responsibility. Those problems are much greater in government bureaucracies because government itself is the institutionalization of confusion (arising out of the need to moderate competing demands); of red tape (arising out of the need to satisfy demands that cannot be moderated); and of avoided responsibility (arising out of the desire to retain power by minimizing criticism).

In short, you can have less bureaucracy only if you have less government. Many, if not most, of the difficulties we experience in dealing with government agencies arise from the agencies being part of a fragmented and open political system. If an agency is to have a sense of mission, if constraints are to be minimized, if authority is to be decentralized, if officials are to be judged on the basis of the outputs they produce rather than the inputs they consume, then legislators, judges, and lobbyists will have to act against their own interests. They will have to say "no" to influential constituents, forgo the opportunity to expand their own influence, and take seriously the task of judging the organizational feasibility as well as the political popularity of a proposed new program. It is hard to imagine this happening, partly because politicians and judges have no incentive to make it happen and partly because there are certain tasks a democratic government must undertake even if they cannot be performed efficiently. The greatest mistake citizens can make when they complain of "the bureaucracy" is to suppose that their frustrations arise simply out of management problems; they do not—they arise out of governance problems.

Bureaucracy and the American Regime

The central feature of the American constitutional system—the separation of powers—exacerbates many of these problems. The governments of the United States were not designed to be efficient or powerful, but to be tolerable and malleable. Those who devised these arrangements always assumed that the federal government would exercise few and limited powers. As long as that assumption was correct (which it was for a century and a half) the quality of public administration was not a serious problem except in the minds of those reformers (Woodrow Wilson was probably the first) who desired to rationalize government in order to rationalize society. The founders knew that the separation of powers would make it so difficult to start a new program or to create a new agency that it was hardly necessary to think about how those agencies would be administered. As a result, the Constitution is virtually silent on what kind of administration we should have. At least until the Civil War thrust the problem on us, scarcely anyone in the country would have known what you were talking about if you spoke of the "problem of administration."

Matters were very different in much of Europe. Kings and princes long had ruled; when their authority was captured by parliaments, the tradition of ruling was already well established. From the first the ministers of the parliamentary regimes thought about the problems of administration because in those countries there was something to administer. The centralization of executive authority in the hands of a prime minister and the exclusion (by and large) of parliament from much say in executive affairs facilitated the process of controlling the administrative agencies and bending them to some central will. The constitutions of many European states easily could have been written by a school of management.

Today, the United States at every level has big and active governments. Some people worry that a constitutional system well-designed to preserve liberty when governments were small is poorly designed to implement policy now that governments are large. The contrast between how the United States and the nations of Western Europe manage environmental and industrial regulation . . . is illuminating: Here the separation of powers insures, if not causes, clumsy and adversarial regulation; there the unification of powers permits, if not causes, smooth and consensual regulation.

I am not convinced that the choice is that simple, however. It would take another book to judge the advantages and disadvantages of the separation of powers. The balance sheet on both sides of the ledger would contain many more entries than those that derive from a discussion of public administration. But even confining our attention to administration, there is more to be said for the American system than many of its critics admit.

America has a paradoxical bureaucracy unlike that found in almost any other advanced nation. The paradox is the existence in one set of institutions of two qualities ordinarily quite separate: the multiplication of rules and the opportunity for access. We have a system laden with rules; elsewhere that is a sure sign that the bureaucracy is aloof from the people, distant from their concerns, and preoccupied with the power and privileges of the bureaucrats—an elaborate, grinding machine that can crush the spirit of any who dare oppose it. We also have a system suffused with participation: advisory boards, citizen groups, neighborhood councils, congressional investigators, crusading journalists, and lawyers serving writs; elsewhere this popular involvement would be taken as evidence that the administrative system is no system at all, but a bungling, jerry-built contraption wallowing in inefficiency and shot through with corruption and favoritism.

That these two traits, rules and openness, could coexist would have astonished Max Weber and continues to astonish (or elude) many contemporary students of the subject. Public bureaucracy in this country is neither as rational and predictable as Weber hoped nor as crushing and mechanistic as he feared. It is rule-bound without being overpowering, participatory without being corrupt. This paradox exists partly because of the character and mores of the American people: They are too informal, spontaneous, and other-directed to be either neutral arbiters or passionless Gradgrinds. And partly it exists because of the nature of the regime: Our constitutional system, and above all the exceptional power enjoyed by the legislative branch, makes it impossible for us to have anything like a government by appointed experts but easy for individual citizens to obtain redress from the abuses of power.

Anyone who wishes it otherwise would have to produce a wholly different regime, and curing the mischiefs of bureaucracy seems an inadequate reason for that. Parliamentary regimes that supply more consistent direction to their bureaucracies also supply more bureaucracy to their citizens. The fragmented American regime may produce chaotic government, but the coherent European regimes produce bigger governments.

In the meantime we live in a country that despite its baffling array of rules and regulations and the insatiable desire of some people to use government to rationalize society still makes it possible to get drinkable water instantly, put through a telephone call in seconds, deliver a letter in a day, and obtain a passport in a week. Our Social Security checks arrive on time. Some state prisons, and most of the federal ones, are reasonably decent and humane institutions. The great majority of Americans, cursing all the while, pay their taxes. One can stand on the deck of an aircraft carrier during night flight operations and watch two thousand nineteen-year-old boys faultlessly operate one of the most complex organizational systems ever created. There are not many places where all this happens. It is astonishing it can be made to happen at all.

NOTES

1. Arthur T. Hadley, *The Straw Giant* (New York: Random House, 1986), 53–57, 249–52.

2. CSIS, *U.S. Defense Acquisition: A Process in Trouble* (Washington, D.C.: Center for Strategic and International Studies, March 1987), 13–16.

3. Herbert Kaufman, *The Administrative Behavior of Federal Bureau Chiefs* (Washington, D.C.: The Brookings Institution, 1981), 192.

4. Martha Derthick, *Agency Under Stress: The Social Security Administration and American Government* (Washington, D.C.: Brookings Institution, forthcoming).

5. Ibid., chap. 3.

6. Charles Wolf, Jr., *Markets or Governments: Choosing Between Imperfect Alternatives* (Cambridge, Mass.: MIT Press, 1988).

7. I first saw this phrase in an essay by Constance Horner, then director of the federal Office of Personnel Management: "Beyond Mr. Gradgrind: The Case for Deregulating the Public Sector," *Policy Review* 44 (Spring 1988): 34–38. It also appears in Gary C. Bryner, *Bureaucratic Discretion* (New York: Pergamon Press, 1987), 215.

8. James Colvard, "Procurement: What Price Mistrust?" *Government Executive* (March 1985): 21.

9. NAPA, *Revitalizing Federal Management: Managers and Their Overburdened Systems* (Washington, D.C.: National Academy of Public Administration, November 1983), vii, viii, 8.

10. Steven Emerson, *Secret Warriors* (New York: G. P. Putnam's Sons, 1988).

11. John E. Chubb and Terry M. Moe, "Politics, Markets, and the Organization of Schools," *American Political Science Review* 82 (1988): 1065–87.

12. Chester E. Finn, Jr., "Decentralize, Deregulate, Empower," *Policy Review* (Summer 1986): 60; Edward A. Wynne, *A Year in the Life of a School* (forthcoming).

13. William E. Turcotte, "Control Systems, Performance, and Satisfaction in Two State Agencies," *Administrative Science Quarterly* 19 (1974): 60–73.

14. Richard P. Nathan, *Social Science in Government: Uses and Misuses* (New York: Basic Books, 1988), chap. 3.

15. Matters are, of course, a bit more complicated than this summary might suggest. There is a small library of books on evaluative research that go into these matters in more detail; a good place to begin is Richard P. Nathan, *Social Science in Government* (New York: Basic Books, 1988). On the political aspects of evaluation, see Henry J. Aaron, *Politics and the Professors* (Washington, D.C.: The Brookings Institution, 1978). On the technical side see Thomas D. Cook and Donald T. Campbell, *Quasi-Experimentation* (Chicago: Rand McNally, 1979). There is even a journal, *Evaluation Review*, specializing in these issues.

16. These projects were all done by the Police Foundation and are described in James Q. Wilson, *Thinking About Crime*, rev. ed. (New York: Basic Books, 1983).

17. See Joseph A. Pechman and P. Michael Timpane, eds., *Work Incentives and Income Guarantees* (Washington, D.C.: Brookings Institution, 1975); and R. Thayne Robson, ed., *Employment and Training R&D* (Kalamazoo, Mich.: Upjohn Institute for Employment Research, 1984).

18. Nathan, *Social Science,* chap. 5; and Manpower Demonstration Research Corporation, *Summary and Findings of the National Supported Work Demonstration* (Cambridge, Mass.: Ballinger, 1980).

19. Clarence E. Ridley and Herbert A. Simon, *Measuring Municipal Activities* (Chicago: International City Managers' Association, 1938).

7.2

MATHEW D. McCUBBINS AND THOMAS SCHWARTZ

"Congressional Oversight Overlooked: Police Patrols versus Fire Alarms"

In this classic article, McCubbins and Schwartz compare two kinds of oversight of executive agencies by Congress. Under the police patrol model, Congress provides resources for constant monitoring of bureaucratic behavior. Under the fire alarm model, Congress waits for complaints from constituents and groups in society about the bureaucracies and then holds them accountable. The fire alarm model is often the more efficient method of oversight.

Scholars often complain that Congress has neglected its oversight responsibility: despite a large and growing executive branch, Congress has done little or nothing to oversee administrative compliance with legislative goals. As a consequence, we are told, Congress has largely lost control of the executive branch: it has allowed the executive branch not only to grow but to grow irresponsible. In popular debate as well as congressional scholarship, this neglect of oversight has become a stylized fact: widely and dutifully reported, it is often bemoaned, sometimes explained, but almost never seriously questioned.[1]

We question it. What has appeared to scholars to be a neglect of oversight, we argue, really is a preference for one form of oversight over another, less-effective form. In so arguing, we develop a simple model of congressional choice of oversight policy, offer evidence to support the model, and draw from it further implications regarding bureaucratic discretion and regulatory legislation. More generally, we model the choice by policy makers of an optimal enforcement strategy, given opportunity costs, available technology, and human cognitive limits.

THE MODEL

Congressional oversight policy concerns whether, to what extent, and in what way Congress attempts to detect and remedy executive-branch violations of legislative goals. Our model of congressional choice of oversight policy rests on a distinction between two forms or techniques of oversight:

Police-Patrol Oversight

Analogous to the use of real police patrols, police-patrol oversight is comparatively centralized, active, and direct: at its own initiative, Congress examines a sample of executive-agency activities, with the aim of detecting and remedying any violations of legislative goals and, by its surveillance, discouraging such violations. An agency's activities might be surveyed by any of a number of means, such as reading documents, commissioning scientific studies, conducting field observations, and holding hearings to question officials and affected citizens.

Fire-Alarm Oversight

Analogous to the use of real fire alarms, fire-alarm oversight is less centralized and involves less active and direct intervention than police-patrol oversight: instead of examining a sample of administrative decisions, looking for violations of legislative goals, Congress establishes a system of rules, procedures, and informal practices that enable individual citizens and organized interest groups to examine administrative decisions (sometimes in prospect), to charge executive agencies with violating congressional goals, and to seek remedies from agencies, courts, and Congress itself. Some of these rules, procedures, and practices afford citizens and interest groups access to information and to administrative decision-making processes. Others give them standing to challenge administrative decisions before agencies and courts, or help them bring alleged violations to congressmen's attention. Still others facilitate collective action by comparatively disorganized interest groups. Congress's role consists in creating and perfecting this decentralized system and, occasionally, intervening in response to complaints. Instead of sniffing for fires, Congress places fire-alarm boxes on street corners, builds neighborhood fire houses, and sometimes dispatches its own hook-and-ladder in response to an alarm.

The distinction between police-patrol and fire-alarm oversight should not be confused with the distinction that sometimes is drawn between *formal* and *informal* oversight, which differ in that formal oversight activities have oversight as their principal and official purpose, whereas informal oversight activities are incidental to other official functions, such as appropriations hearings. Both can involve direct and active surveillance rather than responses to alarms. (See Dodd and Schott, 1977; Ogul, 1977.)

Our model consists of three assumptions:

Technological Assumption

Two forms of oversight are available to Congress: police-patrol oversight and fire-alarm oversight. Congress can choose either form or a combination of the two, making tradeoffs between them in two circumstances: (1) When writing legislation, Congress can include police-patrol features, such as sunset review, or fire-alarm features, such as requirements for public hearings. (2) When it evaluates an agency's performance, Congress can either call oversight hearings to patrol for violations of legislative goals or else wait for alarms to signal potential violations.

Motivational Assumption

A congressman seeks to take as much credit as possible for the net benefits enjoyed by his potential supporters—by citizens and interest groups, within his constituency and elsewhere, whose support can help him win reelection. This means, in part, that a congressman seeks to avoid as much blame as possible for the net costs borne by his potential supporters.

Institutional Assumption

Executive agencies act as agents of Congress and especially of those subcommittees on which they depend for authorizations and appropriations.

The Motivational Assumption is closely tied to Mayhew's celebrated reelection model (1974) and to the blame-shirking model of Fiorina (1982a). The Institutional Assumption is found in Baldwin (1975), Ferejohn (1981), Joskow (1974), McCubbins (1982a,b), and Mitnick (1980). Although not previously stated, the Technological Assumption seems to us to be uncontroversial.

That cannot be said of the Motivational Assumption, which depicts congressmen as pure politicians, single-mindedly pursuing reelection. To this picture one might object that real congressmen are not just politicians but statesmen, pursuing justice and the public interest, acting according to various moral and ideological principles, even at some cost to their reelection prospects.

We will argue, however, that if the Motivational Assumption were replaced by the assumption that congressmen act strictly as statesmen, our conclusions regarding oversight would still be derivable, although in a somewhat different way. Our analysis has less to do with specific legislative goals than with optimal strategies for enforcing compliance with legislative goals of any sort.

CONSEQUENCES

Three important consequences follow from our model:

Consequence 1

To the extent that they favor oversight activity of any sort, congressmen tend to prefer fire-alarm oversight to police-patrol oversight.

Our argument for Consequence 1 is that a congressman's objective, according to the Motivational Assumption, is to take as much credit as possible for net benefits enjoyed by his potential supporters and that he can do so more efficiently under a policy of fire-alarm oversight than under a police-patrol policy, for three reasons:

First, congressmen engaged in police-patrol oversight inevitably spend time examining a great many executive-branch actions that do not violate legislative goals or harm any potential supporters, at least not enough to occasion complaints. They might also spend time detecting and remedying arguable violations that nonetheless harm no potential supporters. For this they receive scant credit from their potential supporters. According to the Motivational Assumption, then, their time is largely wasted, so they incur opportunity costs. But under a fire-alarm policy, a congressman does not address concrete violations unless potential supporters have complained about them, in which case he can receive credit for intervening. So a unit of time spent on oversight is likely to yield more benefit for a congressman under a fire-alarm policy than under a policy-patrol policy. As a result, a fire-alarm policy enables congressmen to spend less time on oversight, leaving more time for other profitable activities, or to spend the same time on more personally profitable oversight activities—on addressing complaints by potential supporters. Justly or unjustly, time spent putting out visible fires gains one more credit than the same time spent sniffing for smoke.

Second, under a realistic police-patrol policy, congressmen examine only a small sample of executive-branch actions. As a result, they are likely to miss violations that harm their potential supporters, and so miss opportunities to take credit for redressing grievances, however fair the sample. Under a fire-alarm policy, by contrast, potential supporters can in most cases bring to congressmen's attention any violations that harm them and for which they have received no adequate remedy through the executive or judicial branch.

Third, although fire-alarm oversight can be as costly as police-patrol oversight, much of the cost is borne by the citizens and interest groups who sound alarms and by administrative agencies and courts rather than by congressmen themselves. A congressman's responsibility for such costs is sufficiently remote that he is not likely to be blamed for them by his potential supporters.

Consequence 2

Congress will not neglect its oversight responsibility. It will adopt an extensive and somewhat effective (even if imperfect) oversight policy.

This is because one of the two forms of oversight—the fire-alarm variety—serves congressmen's interests at little cost. When his potential supporters complain of a violation of legislative goals, a congressman gains credit if he eliminates the cause of the complaint. By virtue of the Institutional Assumption, he often can be reasonably effective in eliminating such causes. Beyond establishing and perfecting the system and addressing some complaints, fire-alarm oversight is almost costless to congressmen: others bear most of the cost.

Consequence 3

Congress will adopt an extensive and somewhat effective policy of fire-alarm oversight while largely neglecting police-patrol oversight.

This just summarizes Consequences 1 and 2.

MISPERCEPTION

Faced with an apparent fact he finds puzzling, unfortunate, or otherwise worthy of attention, a scientist has two alternatives: (a) to accept the fact and try to explain it, or (b) to question the *apparent* fact and try to explain its appearance. In the case at hand, students of Congress have, for the most part, chosen (a): they have uncritically agreed that Congress neglects its oversight responsibility and have tried to explain this neglect.

Here are the three main explanations found in the literature, along with a brief critical comment on each:

Complexity

Because public-policy issues are so complex, Congress has had to delegate authority over them to a large, complex, technically expert bureaucracy, whose actions it is unable effectively to oversee (Lowi, 1969; Ogul, 1977; Ripley, 1969; Seidman, 1975; Woll, 1977).

Comment

Given sufficient incentives, as Fiorina (1982a) observes, Congress has found the capacity to tackle a number of complex issues itself. A striking example is the tax code (Jaffe, 1973, pp. 1189–90). What is more, there is no evident reason why Congress should respond to the complexity of issues by creating a large, expert bureaucracy without also creating a large, expert congressional staff—one sufficiently large and expert, not only to help decide complex issues, but to help oversee a large, expert bureaucracy.

Good Government

To serve the public interest, Congress has established regulatory and other executive-branch agencies based on expertise and divorced from politics. Because these agencies are designed to serve the public interest, whereas Congress is influenced by special-interest lobbies, oversight not only is unnecessary but might be regarded as political meddling in processes that ought to remain nonpolitical (Lowi, 1969).

Comment

Whatever the original intent, it is no longer plausible in most cases to suppose that the public interest is best served by a bureaucracy unaccountable to Congress and, therefore, unaccountable to the electorate.

Decentralization

Because congressional decisions are made, for the most part, by a large number of small, relatively autonomous subcommittees with narrow jurisdictions, general oversight committees tend to be weak (Dodd and Schott, 1979).

Comment

At most this explains why congressional oversight responsibilities are not centralized. It does not explain why they are neglected. If anything, subcommittee specialization should enhance congressional oversight over individual agencies. Subcommittees controlling authorizations and appropriations might be in a better position to do oversight than so-called oversight committees.

Regarding the apparent fact that Congress neglects oversight, we choose alternative (b) over (a): what appears to be a neglect of oversight can be explained as a preference by congressmen for fire-alarm over police-patrol oversight. We have already argued that congressmen have this preference. Scholars who decry the neglect of oversight have, we suggest, focused on an single form of oversight: they have looked only for police-patrol oversight, ignoring the fire-alarm alternative—and therewith the major part of actual oversight activity. Observing a neglect of *police-patrol* oversight, they have mistakenly concluded that *oversight* is neglected.

It has been suggested to us that scholars who have remarked congressional neglect of oversight were using the word more narrowly than we are—that they were *defining* "oversight" to mean police-patrol oversight, contrary to our Technological Assumption.

To this we have three replies: First, established usage equates oversight with the task of detecting and remedying violations of legislative goals by the executive branch.[2] No technique for accomplishing this task can be ruled out by definition. Second, the definitional equation of oversight with police-patrol oversight reflects the odd view that it is less important for Congress to make a serious attempt to detect and remedy violations of legislative goals than to employ a specific technique for doing so. Third, it would be odd to have a name for one way of detecting and remedying executive-branch violations of legislative goals but none for the general task of detecting and remedying such violations.

It has also been suggested to us that fire-alarm activities were never conceived or intended to be a form of oversight, whatever their effects.

We agree that congressmen rarely if ever refer to fire-alarm activities as "oversight," a term officially applied to subcommittees engaged in direct surveillance—in police-patrol oversight. Still, there is no evident reason for congressmen to engage in most fire-alarm activities unless they aim thereby to detect and remedy certain administrative violations of legislative goals.

Those who equate oversight with police-patrol oversight might argue that redressing grievances against the executive branch is not the same as enforcing compliance with congressional goals: the goals congressmen pursue in answering alarms related to particular laws need not be the goals they had in mind when they enacted those laws.

We see no reason to believe, however, that acts of legislation reflect well-defined or unalterable legislative goals—especially in view of the classical voting paradox and similar anomalies (Arrow, 1963; Plott, 1967; Schwartz, 1970,

1981, 1982a). Rather, legislative goals are refined, elaborated, and even changed over time in response to new problems—including complaints against executive agencies—and to changes in preferences and political alignments. In answering fire alarms, congressmen not only enforce compliance with legislative goals; they help decide what those goals are.

Possibly those who bemoan congressional neglect of oversight would agree that fire-alarm oversight is extensively practiced but argue that it is not *effective*.

We have argued already that fire-alarm oversight is likely to be somewhat effective. The evidence presented two sections hence supports this conclusion.

Even granting that fire-alarm oversight is extensively practiced and *somewhat* effective, hence that Congress does not *neglect* its oversight responsibility, one might still wonder which form of oversight is the *more* effective. To this question we now turn.

THE GREATER EFFECTIVENESS OF FIRE-ALARM OVERSIGHT

We will argue that fire-alarm oversight is likely to be more effective, on balance, than police-patrol oversight. But this requires two qualifications: First, we do not contend that the most effective oversight policy is likely to contain no police-patrol features, only that fire-alarm techniques are likely to predominate. Second, we do not contend that a predominantly fire-alarm policy is more likely than a predominantly police-patrol policy to serve the public interest, only that it is likely to secure greater compliance with legislative goals; whether such compliance serves the public interest depends on what those goals are.

A predominantly fire-alarm oversight policy is likely to be more effective— to secure greater compliance with legislative goals—than a predominantly police-patrol policy for two main reasons:

First, legislative goals often are stated in such a vague way that it is hard to decide whether any violation has occurred unless some citizen or group registers a complaint. Such a complaint gives Congress the opportunity to spell out its goals more clearly—just as concrete cases and controversies give courts the opportunity to elucidate legal principles that would be hard to make precise in the abstract.

Second, whereas a fire-alarm policy would almost certainly pick up any violation of legislative goals that seriously harmed an organized group, a police-patrol policy would doubtless miss many such violations, since only a sample of executive-branch actions would be examined.

One who agrees with this point might still argue, on behalf of the greater efficacy of police-patrol oversight, that the citizens harmed by violations of legislative goals are not always represented by organized groups and, hence, cannot always sound a loud enough alarm to secure a redress of grievances.

Our reply is fourfold: First, nowadays even "disadvantaged" groups often have public spokesmen. Second, as we show in the following section, sometimes

Congress passes legislation, as part of its fire-alarm policy, that helps comparatively disorganized groups to act collectively. Third, congressmen's extensive constituent-service activities provide even individual citizens with an effective voice against administrative agencies: case work is part (but only part) of the fire-alarm system. Finally, if the point is merely that fire-alarm oversight can be biased in various ways, then the same is true of police-patrol oversight; and although a good enough police-patrol policy would avoid bias, so would a good enough fire-alarm policy.

To be sure, fire-alarm oversight tends to be *particularistic* in the sense of Mayhew (1974): it arguably emphasizes the interests of individuals and interest groups more than those of the public at large. This is an important difference—the essential difference, we think, between the respective products of police-patrol and fire-alarm oversight. But whether it is a shortcoming of fire-alarm oversight depends on one's ideological point of view: even if fire-alarm oversight deemphasizes some public-interest concerns, it gives special emphasis to a concern for the interests and rights of individual citizens and small groups—a concern well founded in American political values.

Although our model refers only to Congress, we hazard to hypothesize that as most organizations grow and mature, their top policy makers adopt methods of control that are comparatively decentralized and incentive based. Such methods, we believe, will work more efficiently (relative to accepted policy goals) than direct, centralized surveillance. This is sufficiently plausible that we wonder why students of Congress have generally assumed that congressional oversight must be of the direct, centralized police-patrol variety. Part of the reason, perhaps, is that Congress itself applies the label "oversight" to subcommittees charged with police-patrol responsibilities.

As we stated earlier, Consequences 1–3 do not depend on our Motivational Assumption, which depicts congressmen as pure politicians rather than statesmen. This is because statesmen, wishing to secure compliance with their legislative goals, would presumably adopt the most effective oversight policy, and that is likely to be one in which fire-alarm techniques predominate.

EVIDENCE

Evidence for Consequence 3—and therewith our model—is plentiful and well known. Scholars who bemoan congressional neglect of oversight have not ignored this evidence. Rather, they have missed its significance: lacking the concept of fire-alarm oversight, they have failed to see the details of our fire-alarm system as instances of oversight activity. Here is a brief summary of the available evidence:

1. Under a fire-alarm system, complaints against administrative agencies are often brought to the attention of congressional subcommittees by lobbyists for organized groups, and to the attention of

administrative agencies by congressional subcommittees. The functioning of this "subgovernmental triangle" has been well documented (Dodd and Oppenheimer, 1977; Fenno, 1966, 1973a,b; Goodwin, 1970; Ornstein, 1975; Ripley, 1969; Huitt, 1973; Matthews, 1960; Ripley and Franklin, 1976).

2. Congress has passed legislation to help comparatively disorganized groups to press their grievances against the federal government. McConnell (1966) shows how the Agriculture, Labor, and Commerce Departments act as lobbyists for farm, labor, and small-business interests. Congress has also created new programs, such as the Legal-Services Corporation, to organize and press the claims of comparatively voiceless citizens.

3. Constituent-service activities are not limited to unsnarling procedural knots. As part of the fire-alarm system, district staff and casework help individuals and groups—some of them otherwise powerless—to raise and redress grievances against decisions by administrative agencies. This casework component of legislative policy making has been examined only recently, with a primary focus on the electoral connection (Cain, Ferejohn, and Fiorina, 1979a,b; Fenno, 1978; Fiorina, 1977a; Mayhew, 1974; Parker and Davidson, 1979) and with a secondary focus on policy consequences (Fiorina, 1977a, 1982b; Fiorina and Noll, 1978, 1979a,b).

4. Often the fire-alarm system allows for the redress of grievances by administrative agencies and courts; Congress itself need not always get involved. To facilitate such redress, Congress has passed several laws, notably the Administrative Procedures Act of 1946 and the Environmental Procedures Act of 1969, that have substantially increased the number of groups with legal standing before administrative agencies and district courts regarding bureaucratic controversies (Lowi, 1969).[3] Congress has also, as in sections 4–7 of the Toxic Substances Control Act of 1976, increased the courts' powers to issue injunctions in response to alarms and has required administrative agencies to hold hearings, publish information, and invite public comment on agency decision making (McCubbins, 1982a).

5. There are numerous cases in which violations of legislative goals were brought to the attention of Congress, which responded with vigorous remedial measures. For example, Congress dismantled the Area Redevelopment Administration (ARA) in 1963, even though it had just been authorized in 1961. The ARA was encouraging industries to relocate in redevelopment areas despite clear provisions in the law to the contrary. Congress also can redefine or reaffirm its goals by redefining or explicating the jurisdictional authority of an administrative agency. This happened with the Federal Trade Commission when it first sought to regulate cigarette advertising, children's

television, and funeral homes. Sometimes such congressional intervention is legislatively mandated. Before taking action on a pending
case, for example, the National Labor Relations Board must consult
with the appropriate congressional committees.

6. The general impression that Congress neglects oversight, we have
argued, really is a perception that Congress neglects police-patrol
over-sight. That impression and the evidence adduced to support it
constitute further evidence for Consequences 1 and 3: they show that
congressmen tend to prefer an oversight policy in which fire-alarm
techniques predominate.

FURTHER IMPLICATIONS: HAS BUREAUCRATIC DISCRETION INCREASED?

Hand in glove with our stylized fact (neglect of oversight) goes another: Congress has increasingly relinquished its legislative authority to the executive
branch, allowing the bureaucracy to make law (Dodd and Schott, 1979; Hess,
1976; Lowi, 1969; Woll, 1977).[4]

Although Congress may, to some extent, have allowed the bureaucracy to
make law, it may also have devised a reasonably effective and noncostly way to
articulate and promulgate its own legislative goals—a way that depends on the
fire-alarm oversight system. It is convenient for Congress to adopt broad legislative mandates and give substantial rule-making authority to the bureaucracy. The problem with doing so, of course, is that the bureacracy might not
pursue Congress's goals. But citizens and interest groups can be counted on to
sound an alarm in most cases in which the bureaucracy has arguably violated
Congress's goals. Then Congress can intervene to rectify the violation. Congress has not necessarily relinquished legislative responsibility to anyone else.
It has just found a more efficient way to legislate.

When legislators try to write laws with sufficient detail and precision to
preclude administrative discretion, they quickly run up against their own
cognitive limits: beyond a certain point, human beings just cannot anticipate
all the contingencies that might arise. The attempt to legislate for all contingencies can entail unintended (and undesired) consequences. In his classic
study of Anglo-American judicial reasoning, Levi (1948) makes this point
about judges (lawmakers of a sort), who lay down imprecise rules, which they
subsequently and gradually elaborate in response to concrete legal disputes.
Oakeshott (1973) makes a similar point about political activity of all sorts: it
cannot be based on precise, detailed blueprints, and so policy formulations
can at best be rough summaries of experience, requiring elaboration and judicious application case by case.

The ostensible shifting of legislative responsibility to the executive branch
may simply be the responsible adoption of efficient legislative techniques and

the responsible acceptance of human cognitive limits—both facilitated by the fire-alarm system.

FURTHER IMPLICATIONS: THE CHOICE OF REGULATORY POLICY

When it decides regulatory issues, Congress tends to choose one of two types of regulatory instrument: command-and-control instruments and incentive-based instruments. Congress faces a similar choice when it decides, not how to regulate society, but how to regulate the regulators—when it decides, in other words, on oversight policy. For police-patrol oversight is similar to command-and-control regulatory instruments, while fire-alarm oversight is similar to incentive-based instruments.

Offhand one might suppose that just as congressmen tend to prefer fire-alarm to police-patrol oversight policies, so they would tend to prefer incentive-based to command-and-control regulatory policies. Our observations, of course, do not support this supposition (Breyer, 1982; Fiorina, 1982a; Joskow and Noll, 1978; McCubbins, 1982a; McCubbins and Page, 1982; Schultze, 1977).

Paradoxically, Congress's very preference for fire-alarm oversight entails a preference for command-and-control regulatory policy. For command-and-control agencies are more susceptible of case-by-case congressional intervention in response to complaints, hence more susceptible of fire-alarm control, than are courts, taxing authorities, and private individuals and firms—the principal participants in incentive-based regulatory policy.

CONCLUSION

The widespread perception that Congress has neglected its oversight responsibility is a widespread mistake. Congressional scholars have focused their attention on police-patrol oversight. What has appeared to many of them to be a neglect of oversight is really a preference—an eminently rational one—for fire-alarm oversight. That a decentralized, incentive-based control mechanism has been found more effective, from its users' point view, than direct, centralized surveillance should come as no surprise.

Besides criticizing the received wisdom regarding congressional oversight, we hope to have highlighted a neglected way of looking at congressional behavior. Sometimes Congress appears to do little, leaving important policy decisions to the executive or judicial branch. But appearances can deceive. A perfectly reasonable way for Congress to pursue its objectives is by ensuring that fire alarms will be sounded, enabling courts, administrative agencies, and ultimately Congress itself to step in, whenever executive compliance with congressional objectives is called in question. In examining congressional policies and their impact, do not just ask how clear, detailed, or far-sighted congressional legislation is. Ask how likely it is that fire alarms will signal putative violations of legislative goals and how Congress is likely to respond to such alarms.

NOTES

1. See Bibby, 1966, 1968; Dodd and Schott, 1979; Fiorina, 1977a,b, 1982b; Hess, 1976; Huntington, 1973; Lowi, 1969; Mitnick, 1980; Ogul, 1976, 1977; Ripley, 1978; Scher, 1963; Seidman, 1975; Woll, 1977. The following remarks by Pearson (1975) succinctly exemplify this view: "Paradoxically, despite its importance, congressional oversight remains basically weak and ineffective" (p. 281). "Oversight is a vital yet neglected congressional function" (p. 288).

2. A 1977 report by the U.S. Senate Committee on Government Operations stated that "Oversight involves a wide range of congressional efforts to review and control policy implementation . . ." (pp. 4–5). According to Dodd and Schott (1979), "Oversight . . . involves attempts by Congress to review and control policy implementation" (p. 156). Ogul (1976) defines oversight as the process by which Congress determines, among other things, whether agencies are complying with congressional intent. See also Bibby, 1966; Harris, 1964; Lees, 1977; Lowi, 1969; Ripley, 1978; Woll, 1977.

3. Ferejohn (1974) provides a good example of how the decision-making procedures of the Army Corps of Engineers were expanded to include wilderness, wildlife, and environmental group interests by the passage of the 1969 Environmental Procedures Act.

4. On related points see Fiorina (1977b), Weingast and Moran (1981), McCubbins (1982a,b), and McCubbins and Page (1982). Weingast has argued that Congress employs a number of its constitutionally defined powers in a decentralized and often unobserved way in order to exercise control over the actions of administrative agencies (Calvert, Moran, and Weingast, 1982; Weingast and Moran, 1981).

REFERENCES

Arrow, Kenneth. 1963. *Social choice and individual values.* 2nd ed. New York: Wiley.

Baldwin, John. 1975. *The regulatory agency and the public corporation: The Canadian air transport industry.* Cambridge, Mass.: Ballinger.

Bibby, John. 1966. Committee characteristics and legislative oversight of administration. *Midwest Journal of Political Science,* 10 (February 1966): 78–98.

———. 1968. Congress' neglected function. In *Republican papers,* edited by Melvin Laird. New York: Praeger.

Breyer, Stephen. 1982. *Regulation and its reform.* Cambridge, Mass.: Harvard University Press.

Cain, Bruce, John Ferejohn, and Morris Fiorina. 1979a. The roots of legislator popularity in Great Britain and the United States. Social Science Working Paper No. 288, California Institute of Technology, Pasadena, Calif.

———. 1979b. Casework service in Great Britain and the United States. California Institute of Technology, Pasadena, Calif. Mimeo.

Calvert, Randall, Mark Moran, and Barry Weingast. 1982. Congressional influence over policymaking: The case of the FTC. Paper presented at the annual meeting of the American Political Science Association, Chicago, September 1982.

Dodd, Lawrence, and Bruce Oppenheimer, eds. 1977. *Congress reconsidered.* New York: Praeger.

Dodd, Lawrence, and Richard Schott. 1979. *Congress and the administrative state*. New York: Wiley.

Fenno, Richard, Jr. 1966. *The power of the purse*. Boston: Little, Brown.

———. 1973a. *Congressmen in committees*. Boston: Little, Brown.

———. 1973b. The internal distribution of influence: The house. In *The Congress and America's future*, 2nd ed, edited by David Truman, pp. 52–76. Englewood Cliffs, N.J.: Prentice-Hall.

———. 1978. *Home style*. Boston: Little, Brown.

Ferejohn, John. 1974. *Pork barrel politics*. Stanford, Calif.: Stanford University Press.

———. 1981. A note on the structure of administrative agencies. California Institute of Technology, Pasadena, Calif. Mimeo.

Fiorina, Morris, 1977a. *Congress: Keystone of the Washington establishment*. New Haven, Conn.: Yale University Press.

———. 1977b. Control of the bureaucracy: A mismatch of incentives and capabilities. Social Science Working Paper No. 182, California Institute of Technology, Pasadena, Calif.

———. 1982a. Legislative choice of regulatory forms: Legal process or administrative process? *Public Choice* 39 (September 1982): 33–66.

———. 1982b. Group concentration and the delegation of legislative authority. California Institute of Technology, Pasadena, Calif. Mimeo.

Fiorina, Morris, and Roger Noll. 1978. Voters, bureaucrats and legislators: A rational choice perspective on the growth of bureaucracy, *Journal of Public Economics* 9 (June 1978): 239–54.

———. 1979a. Voters, legislators and bureaucracy: Institutional design in the public sector. In *Problemi di administrazione publica, Centro di formazione e studi per il Messogiorno*, Naples, Italy, Formes 4 (2): 69–89.

———. 1979b. Majority rule models and legislative election. *Journal of Politics* 41: 1081–1104.

Goodwin, George, Jr. 1970. *The little legislatures*. Amherst: University of Massachusetts Press.

Harris, Joseph. 1964. *Congressional control of administration*. Washington, D.C.: Brookings.

Hess, Stephen. 1976. *Organizing the presidency*. Washington, D.C.: Brookings.

Huitt, Ralph. 1973. The internal distribution of influence: The Senate. In *The Congress in America's future*, 2nd ed., edited by David Truman, pp. 77–101. Englewood Cliffs, N.J.: Prentice-Hall.

Huntington, Samuel. 1973. Congressional responses to the twentieth century. In *The Congress in America's future*, 2nd ed., edited by David Truman, pp. 5–31. Englewood Cliffs, N.J.: Prentice-Hall.

Jaffe, Louis. 1973. The illusion of the ideal administration. *Harvard Law Review* 86: 1183–99.

Joskow, Paul. 1974. Inflation and environmental concern: Structural change is the process of public utility price regulation. *Journal of Law and Economics* 17 (October 1974): 291–327.

Joskow, Paul, and Roger Noll. 1978. Regulation in theory and practice: An overview. California Institute of Technology, Social Science Working Paper No. 213, Pasadena, Calif.

Lees, John D. 1977. Legislatures and oversight: A review article on a neglected area of research. *Legislative Studies Quarterly* (May 1977): 193–208.

Levi, Edward. 1948. *Legal reasoning*. Chicago: University of Chicago Press.

Lowi, Theodore. 1969. *The end of liberalism*. New York: Norton.

Matthews, Donald. 1960. *U.S. Senators and their world*. Chapel Hill: University of North Carolina Press.

Mayhew, David. 1974. *Congress: The electoral connection*. New Haven, Conn.: Yale University Press.

McConnell, Grant. 1966. *Private power and American democracy*. New York: Vintage Books.

McCubbins, Mathew. 1982a. Rational individual behavior and collective irrationality: The legislative choice of regulatory forms. Ph.D. dissertation, California Institute of Technology, Pasadena, Calif.

———. 1982b. On the form of regulatory intervention. Paper presented at the 1983 Annual Meeting of the Public Choice Society, Savannah, Ga., March 24–26, 1983.

McCubbins, Mathew, and Talbot Page. 1982. On the failure of environmental, health and safety regulation. Paper presented at the 1983 Annual Meeting of the Midwest Political Science Association, Chicago, Ill., April 20–23, 1983.

Mitnick, Barry. 1980. *The political economy of regulation*. New York: Columbia University Press.

Oakeshott, Michael. 1973. Political education. In *Rationalism in politics*, edited by Michael Oakeshott, pp. 110–36. New York: Basic Books, 1962. Reprinted in *Freedom and authority*, edited by Thomas Schwartz, 362–80. Encino, Calif.: Dickenson.

Ogul, Morris. 1976. *Congress oversees the bureaucracy*. Pittsburgh: University of Pittsburgh Press.

———. 1977. Congressional oversight: Structure and incentives. In *Congress reconsidered*, edited by Lawrence Dodd and Bruce Oppenheimer, pp. 207–221. New York: Praeger.

Ornstein, Norman, ed. 1975. *Congress in change*. New York: Praeger.

Parker, Glenn, and Roger Davidson. 1979. Why do Americans love their congressmen so much more than their Congress? *Legislative Studies Quarterly* 4 (February 1979): 53–62.

Pearson, James. 1975. Oversight: A vital yet neglected congressional function. *Kansas Law Review* 23: 277–88.

Plott, Charles. 1967. A notion of equilibrium and its possibility under majority rules. *American Economic Review* 57 (September 1967): 787–806.

Ripley, Randall 1969. *Power in the Senate*. New York: St. Martin's.

———. 1971. *The politics of economic and human resource development*. Indianapolis: Bobbs-Merrill.

———. 1978. *Congress: Process and policy*. 2nd ed. New York: Norton.

Ripley, Randall, and Grace Franklin. 1976. *Congress, the bureaucracy and public policy*. Homewood, Ill.: Dorsey.

Scher, Seymour. 1963. Conditions for legislative control. *Journal of Politics* 25 (August 1963): 526–51.

Schultze, Charles. 1977. *The public use of private interest*. Washington, D.C.: Brookings.

Schwartz, Thomas. 1970. On the possibility of rational policy evaluation. *Theory and Decision* 1 (October 1970): 89–106.

———. 1981. The universal-instability theorem. *Public Choice* 37 (3): 487–501.

———. 1982a. A really general impossibility theorem. *Quality and Quantity* 16 (December 1982): 493–505.

———. 1982b. The porkbarrel paradox. University of Texas, Austin, Tex. Mimeo.

Seidman, Harold. 1975. *Politics, position, and power: The dynamics of federal organization*. New York: Oxford.

U.S. Senate. Committee on Government Operations. 1977. *Study on federal regulation, vol. II, congressional oversight of regulatory agencies*. Washington, D.C.: Government Printing Office.

Weingast, Barry, and Mark Moran. 1981. Bureaucratic discretion of congressional control: Regulatory policymaking by the Federal Trade Commission. Washington University, St. Louis: Center of the Study of American Business. Mimeo.

Woll, Peter. 1977. *American bureaucracy*. New York: Norton.

7.3

DANIEL CARPENTER

From *The Forging of Bureaucratic Autonomy*

Bureaucrats in the executive branch need some autonomy from politicians in order to do their work. Regulators of food and drugs, for example, should not be influenced by political pressure. After all, many of these bureaucrats have technical expertise or are in jobs that require impartial decisions. Carpenter argues that it took a long time for many bureaucratic positions to gain the appropriate amount of autonomy. Bureaucrats in the early twentieth century had to play their own political games to earn this autonomy, namely by cultivating their own loyal constituencies within industry and among the population.

Bureaucratic autonomy occurs when bureaucrats take actions consistent with their own wishes, actions to which politicians and organized interests defer even though they would prefer that other actions (or no action at all) be taken. Bureaucratic autonomy so defined is a common feature, though far from a universal one, of American government in the twentieth century. Agencies have at times created and developed policy with few, if any, constraints from legislative and executive overseers, and they have frequently coordinated organized interests as much as responded to them. To suggest that bureaucracies have policymaking autonomy may strike some readers as a controversial if not outlandish claim. Surely agencies lack the ability to take any action they desire in our system of representative government and rule of law. Yet I contend here that bureaucratic autonomy lies less in *fiat* than in *leverage*. Autonomy prevails when agencies can establish political legitimacy—a reputation for expertise, efficiency, or moral protection and a uniquely diverse complex of ties to organized interests and the media—and induce politicians to defer to the wishes of the agency even when they prefer otherwise. Under these conditions, politicians grant agency officials free rein in program building. They stand by while agency officials do away with some of their cherished programs and services. They even welcome agencies in shaping legislation itself.

■　■　■

CONCLUSION

The Politics of Bureaucratic Autonomy

Bureaucrats are politicians, and bureaucracies are organizations of political actors. Autonomy arises when bureaucrats successfully practice a politics of legitimacy. It occurs when agency leaders build reputations for their organizations—reputations for efficacy, for uniqueness of service, for moral protection, and for expertise. It occurs, further, when they ground this reputation in a diverse coalition wrought from the multiple networks in which they are engaged. These coalitions, suspended in beliefs and in networks, and uncontrollable by politicians, are the stuff of autonomous bureaucratic policy innovation. This, I submit, is the basic lesson of the forging of bureaucratic autonomy in the United States. *Bureaucratic autonomy is politically forged.*

Contemporary political science—including an entire literature on bureaucracy that depends on "principal-agent" models of bureaucratic politics—assumes that the linkages between voters and policies occur through parties, elections, representatives, and the legislature. Yet the decisive steps in forging bureaucratic autonomy occurred when federal bureaucrats broke free from the traditional model of politics and established links directly to citizens and the new associations that increasingly claimed their allegiance. Long before the "iron triangles" of the New Deal Era, bureaucracies began to aggregate citizens and voters precisely when parties and politicians were having a difficult time doing so.

Because some agencies did this more successfully than others, the state-building achievement of the Progressive Era was concrete but limited. What emerged in the 1910s and 1920s was not a uniformly more powerful bureaucracy than existed three decades earlier. In pockets of the American state, relative autonomy conditioned upon political legitimacy materialized. Most other agencies lay dormant. Therein lies the puzzle of American state building. Why was the Department of Agriculture able to establish a foothold in writing significant legislation? Why was the Interior Department, with authority over public lands and ties to numerous western interests, unable to capitalize on the movements for conservation and western reclamation? Why were reformers in the Post Office Department able to eliminate systematically the positions of strong Republican identifiers in fourth-class offices at the very time when Republicans enjoyed hegemony in electoral politics? Why were postal officials able to grab all of the moral policing powers they wanted and resist political control of their use? Why was the USDA able to take its new-found authority in food and drug regulation and turn its fire on the very firms who most supported Republicans during the Progressive period?

The answer lies in the organizational properties of executive agencies at the turn of the century. Bureaucratic autonomy cannot exist apart from the organizational characteristics of the agencies that experience it. If it exists, bureaucratic autonomy *must* be premised not upon the popularity of a policy, not upon occasional administrative fiat, not upon a single well-heeled lobby, but upon the stable political legitimacy of the bureaucracy itself. To focus on organizational reputations is not, as I have emphasized, to divorce bureaucracies from politics. Instead, it is to reconceive politics as a process of coalition building and to acknowledge that in some circumstances bureaucrats can take the decisive initiative (at times, the *only* initiative) in building them. It is to these reputations—and the capacities and coalitions that supported them—that autonomous bureaucracies in America owe their origins.

■   ■   ■

The Poverty of Procedural Politics

The argument elaborated here poses several challenges to contemporary erudition on bureaucracies. Following the highly influential work of Mathew McCubbins, Roger Noll, and Barry Weingast, a generation of scholars has argued that an agency's "enacting coalition" of politicians can use administrative procedures to induce the agency to take exactly those actions that the coalition desires. These "procedural politics" theories suggest that most of the political action in bureaucratic politics occurs when the methods and processes for a given policy are set by politicians and the interests to which they respond. Hence bureaucratic politics does not really involve bureaucracies at all; "the administrative system is automatic."

The theory elaborated here suggests that procedural politics is unlikely to control agencies with stable political legitimacy. Agencies with esteemed officials who have publicly recognized capacity and expertise, and who have independent access to organized citizens, exercise power over the procedures of their agency. Autonomous agencies are powerful bargaining agents in procedural design. The more powerful constraint on administrative procedures is that legitimated agency officials can make it politically costly for politicians to constrain them. Partisans of the procedural-politics school of bureaucracy have discussed all sorts of mechanisms for controlling the bureaucracy without recognizing that these strategies have costs. In some respects, these amount to forfeiting the benefits of agency specialization. The argument here, however, is that when agencies have political legitimacy, the costs of control are *explicitly political and electoral.*

■   ■   ■

Congress, the Media, and Multiplicity

The role of general beliefs about agencies in bureaucratic reputations points to important changes in Congress and the media that enabled agencies to erect reputations. The building of bureaucratic reputations between Congress and executive departments found fertile soil in the Progressive period.

Not only were bureau chiefs serving longer tenures, but members of Congress were investing more and more time in committees. As a result, agency officials and their overseers in Congress began to develop a mutual familiarity. The institutional memory of Congress grew, the abilities and interests of bureaus became clearer and more consistent, and uncertainty over the bureaucracy declined. The stability of these relations gave bureau chiefs an incentive to cultivate the trust of committee chairs and congressional party leaders, and some Progressive-Era program leaders adopted this strategy to great advantage.[1]

Perhaps the most important venue of bureaucratic reputation lay in the rapidly expanding media. At a time when broadcast news remained only an imaginary possibility, Americans received their political information from a highly variegated print industry. In this market the critical split was between the larger urban newspapers and related syndicates and the rural farm weeklies. In the urban newspapers arose the "muckraking" of Progressive reformers, whereas farm editors remained committed to a mix of populist and pro-agrarian sentiments. In part because these papers depended increasingly on the USDA and the Post Office for information and rate classification, both agencies were treated with favor by urban and rural presses. Yet the network advantages of the two agencies transcended mere resource dependence. Numerous Agriculture Department officials were close acquaintances with one or more rural newspaper editors. And newspaper editors, urban and rural, interacted frequently with postal officials over matters of rate classification. As a result of these ties, Progressive-Era citizens were better (and more favorably) informed about the USDA and Post Office than any other agencies in American government.

Reputations for Neutrality and Moral Protection

Traditionally, political scientists have expected greater autonomy where agencies can lay claim to expertise—especially where agencies possess a monopoly on information in a given area. A more interesting case of "policy" in this book emerges from "moral politics" during the culturally conservative Progressive Era. A key component of both the USDA's and the Post Office's march to autonomy was their linkages to Victorian moral reformers and their anti-adulteration campaigns, both in the adulteration of food and the adulteration of morals (through pornography and gambling). The Interior Department lacked any such connection to anti-adulteration themes. These moral reputations, and the framing of policy campaigns in terms of "protection" from "the evils of adulteration," served to enhance the agencies' esteem for national service. A core component of strong agency reputations is the mien of neutrality, impartiality, or orientation toward the public good. Where an agency's innovations appear patently to serve its own interests or those of a selected group or region, the political legitimacy necessary for autonomy is less likely to emerge.

In the case of postal state building, coalition building combined moralist Progressives, media organizations, agrarians, and corporate business. Each of these interests sought something different from the Post Office. Progressive Victorians wanted moral policing in the form of Comstockery, agrarians wanted expanded services in rural America and an alternative to institutions dominated by corporate industry, and business interests and the media (for different reasons) wanted an efficient national communications infrastructure. Each saw their interests met in the same programs. Without all four (and more) of these organizational forces, programs such as rural free delivery, parcels post, and postal savings would not have marked Progressive change as they did. More critically, without Anthony Comstock, August Machen, John Wanamaker, and other postal officials to bridge these forces and to create a multifaceted coalition, the possibility of institutional change would have been trifling.

The logic of multifaceted coalitions was demonstrated nowhere more powerfully than in the Department of Agriculture. Republican presidents, women's organizations, conservationists, congressional committees, agrarian organizations—all of these interests converged to influence policy change in areas as diverse as pharmaceutical regulation, forest preservation, and agricultural extension. The central point, again, is that the coalitions were nursed and maintained not by elected politicians but by middle-level bureaucrats. Far more than in Herbert Hoover's Department of Commerce, the "associational state" in America was established in the early-twentieth-century USDA. Unlike Commerce, moreover, the USDA exerted an immense influence on the groups in its coalitions.

■   ■   ■

The organizational flourishing that was characteristic of Progressive society offers one reason that the patterns of bureaucratic autonomy witnessed in this book are less likely to be observed in contemporary politics. To be sure, modern America is rife with organizations in the formal sense. The day-by-day embedment of Americans in organizations has waned, not strengthened, over the last few decades. The challenge of contemporary American state building, in this view, may demand more than "reinventing" American government.

NOTE

1. Jonathan N. Katz and Brian R. Sala, "Careerism, Committee Assignments, and the Electoral Connection," *American Political Science Review* 90 (March 1996): 21.

8

THE JUDICIARY

8.1

ALEXANDER M. BICKEL

From *The Least Dangerous Branch: The Supreme Court at the Bar of Politics*

Bickel points out that judicial review, the right of courts to determine the constitutionality of government actions, was not part of the U.S. Constitution and was asserted later by the U.S. Supreme Court in Marbury v. Madison *(1803). While the legitimacy of judicial review has been questioned at times, it has largely held in place because political actors of all stripes have understood its importance in stabilizing the American system of government.*

1. ESTABLISHMENT AND GENERAL JUSTIFICATION OF JUDICIAL REVIEW

The least dangerous branch of the American government is the most extraordinarily powerful court of law the world has ever known. The power which distinguishes the Supreme Court of the United States is that of constitutional review of actions of the other branches of government, federal and state. Curiously enough, this power of judicial review, as it is called, does not derive from any explicit constitutional command. The authority to determine the meaning and application of a written constitution is nowhere defined or even mentioned in the document itself. This is not to say that the power of judicial review cannot be placed in the Constitution; merely that it cannot be found there.

Marbury v. Madison

Congress was created very nearly full blown by the Constitution itself. The vast possibilities of the presidency were relatively easy to perceive and soon, inevitably, materialized. But the institution of the judiciary needed to be summoned up out of the constitutional vapors, shaped, and maintained; and the Great Chief Justice, John Marshall—not singlehanded, but first and foremost—was there to do it and did. If any social process can be said to have been "done" at a given time and by a given act, it is Marshall's achievement. The time was 1803; the act was the decision in the case of *Marbury* v. *Madison*.

William Marbury's law suit against Secretary of State Madison was an incident in the peaceful but deep-cutting revolution signaled by Jefferson's accession to the presidency. The decision was both a reaction and an accommodation to the revolution. It was, indeed, as Professor Robert G. McCloskey has written, "a masterwork of indirection, a brilliant example of Marshall's capacity to sidestep danger while seeming to court it, to advance in one direction while his opponents are looking in another." The Court was "in the delightful position . . . of rejecting and assuming power in a single breath"; although Marshall's opinion "is justly celebrated," "not the least of its virtues is the fact that it is somewhat beside the point."[1]

■　　■　　■

William Marbury and some others sued Secretary Madison for delivery of their commissions as justices of the peace for the County of Washington in the District of Columbia, an office to which they had been appointed in the last moments of the administration of President John Adams. Marshall held that Marbury and the others were entitled to their commissions, but that the Supreme Court was without power to order Madison to deliver, because the section of the Judiciary Act of 1789 that purported to authorize the Court to act in such a case as this was itself unconstitutional. Thus did Marshall assume for his Court what is nowhere made explicit in the Constitution—the ultimate power to apply the Constitution, acts of Congress to the contrary notwithstanding.

"The question," Marshall's opinion begins, "whether an act repugnant to the Constitution, can become the law of the land, is a question deeply interesting to the United States; but, happily, not of an intricacy proportioned to its interest." Marshall's confidence that he could traverse the path ahead with ease is understandable, since he had already begged the question-in-chief, which was not whether an act repugnant to the Constitution could stand, but who should be empowered to decide that the act is repugnant. Marshall then posited the limited nature of the government established by the Constitution. It follows—and one may grant to Marshall that it follows as "a proposition too plain to be contested"—that the Constitution is a paramount law, and that ordinary legislative acts must conform to it. For Marshall it follows, further, that a legislative act contrary to the Constitution is not law and need not be given effect in court; else "written constitutions are absurd attempts, on the part of the people; to limit a power in its own nature illimitable." If two laws conflict, a court must obey the superior one. But Marshall knew (and, indeed, it was true in this very case) that a statute's repugnancy to the Constitution is in most instances not self-evident; it is, rather, an issue of policy that someone must decide. The problem is who: the courts, the legislature itself, the President, perhaps juries for purposes of criminal trials, or ultimately and finally the people through the electoral process?

This is the real question. Marshall addressed himself to it only partially and slightly. To leave the decision with the legislature, he said, is to allow those whose power is supposed to be limited themselves to set the limits—an absurd invitation to consistent abuse. Perhaps so, but the Constitution does not limit the power of the legislature alone. It limits that of the courts as well, and it may be equally absurd, therefore, to allow courts to set the limits. It is, indeed, more absurd, because courts are not subject to electoral control. (It may be argued that to leave the matter to the legislature is to leave it ultimately to the people at the polls. In this view the people as the principal would set the limits of the power that they have delegated to their agent.)

The case can be constructed where the conflict between a statute and the Constitution is self-evident in accordance with Marshall's general assumption. Even so, Marshall offers no real reason that the Court should have the power to nullify the statute. The function in such a case could as well be confided to the President, or ultimately to the electorate. Other controls over the legislature, which may be deemed equally important, are so confided. Courts do not pass on the validity of statutes by inquiring into election returns or into the qualifications of legislators. They will entertain no suggestion that a statute whose authenticity is attested by the signatures of the Speaker of the House and the President of the Senate, and which is approved by the President, may be at variance with the bill actually passed by both Houses.[2] Marshall himself, in *Fletcher* v. *Peck*,[3] the Yazoo Frauds case, declined to inquire into the "motives" of a legislature, having been invited to do so in order to upset a statute whose passage had been procured by fraud. Why must courts control self-corruption through power, a condition difficult of certain diagnosis, when they rely on other agencies to control corruption by money or like inducements, which is no less dangerous and can be objectively established?

So far Marshall's argument proceeded on the basis of a single textual reliance: namely, the fact itself of a written Constitution. But Marshall did go on to some more specific textual references. His first was to Article III of the Constitution, which establishes the judiciary and reads in relevant part as follows:

SECTION 1. The judicial Power of the United States, shall be vested in one supreme Court, and in such inferior Courts as the Congress may from time to time ordain and establish. The Judges, both of the supreme and inferior Courts, shall hold their Offices during good Behavior, and shall, at stated Times, receive for their Services a Compensation which shall not be diminished during their Continuance in Office.

SECTION 2. The judicial Power shall extend to all Cases, in Law and Equity, arising under this Constitution, the Laws of the United States, and Treaties made, or which shall be made, under their Authority;—to all Cases affecting Ambassadors, or other public Ministers and Consuls;—to all Cases of admiralty and maritime jurisdiction;—to Controversies to which the United States shall be a Party;—to Controversies between two or more States;—between a State and Citizens of another State;—between Citizens of different States;—between Citizens of the same State claiming. Lands under Grants of different States, and between a State, or the Citizens thereof, and foreign States, Citizens or Subjects.

In all Cases affecting Ambassadors, other public Ministers and Consuls, and those in which a State shall be a Party, the supreme Court shall have original Jurisdiction. In all the other Cases before mentioned, the supreme Court shall have appellate Jurisdiction, both as to Law and Fact, with such Exceptions, and under such Regulations as the Congress shall make.

Could it be, Marshall asked, that those who granted the judicial power and extended it to all cases arising under the Constitution, laws, and treaties meant that cases arising under the Constitution should be decided without examination and application of the document itself? This was for Marshall "too extravagant to be maintained." Note well, however, that what the Constitution extends to cases arising under it is "the judicial Power." Whether this power reaches as far as Marshall wanted it to go—namely, to reviewing acts of the legislature—is the question to be decided. What are the nature and extent of the function of the Court—the judicial power? Is the Court empowered, when it decides a case, to declare that a duly enacted statute violates the Constitution, and to invalidate the statute? Article III does not purport to describe the function of the Court; it subsumes whatever questions may exist as to that in the phrase "the judicial Power." It does not purport to tell the Court how to decide cases; it only specifies which kinds of case the Court shall have jurisdiction to deal with at all. Thus, in giving jurisdiction in cases "arising under . . . the Laws" or "under . . . Treaties," the clause is not read as prescribing the process of decision to be followed. The process varies. In cases "under . . . the Laws" courts often leave determination of issues of fact and even issues that may be thought to be "of law" to administrative agencies. And under both "the Laws . . . and Treaties," much of the decision concerning meaning and applicability may be received ready-made from the Congress and the President. In some cases of all three descriptions, judicial decision may be withheld altogether—and it is for this reason that it will not do to place reliance on the word "all" in the phrase "all cases . . . arising. . . ." To the extent that the Constitution speaks to such matters, it does so in the tightly packed phrase "judicial Power."

Nevertheless, if it were impossible to conceive a case "arising under the Constitution" which would not require the Court to pass on the constitutionality of congressional legislation, then the analysis of the text of Article III made above might be found unsatisfactory, for it would render this clause quite senseless. But there are such cases which may call into question the constitutional validity of judicial, administrative, or military actions without attacking legislative or even presidential acts as well, or which call upon the Court, under appropriate statutory authorization, to apply the Constitution to acts of the states. Any reading but his own was for Marshall "too extravagant to be maintained." His own, although out of line with the general scheme of Article III, may be possible; but it is optional. This is the strongest bit of textual evidence in support of Marshall's view, but it is merely a hint. And nothing more explicit will be found.

Marshall then listed one or two of the limitations imposed by the Constitution upon legislative power and asked whether no one should enforce them. This amounts to no more than a repetition of his previous main argument, based on the very fact of limited government established by a written Constitution. He then quoted the clause (significantly constituting Section 3 of Article III, the Judiciary Article) which provides that no person "shall be convicted of Treason unless on the Testimony of two Witnesses to the same overt Act, or on Confession in open Court." If the legislature were to change that rule, he asked, and declare that one witness or a confession out of court was sufficient for conviction, would the courts be required to enforce such a statute? In one aspect, this is but another restatement of the argument proceeding from the existence of limitations embodied in the written Constitution. But even if it were admitted that a court, in the treason case Marshall put, should apply the Constitution and not the contrary statute, this may mean only that it is the judiciary's duty to enforce the Constitution within its own sphere, when the Constitution addresses itself with fair specificity to the judiciary branch itself. The same might be true as well of other clauses prescribing procedures to be followed upon a trial in court and also of the provisions of Article III setting forth the jurisdiction of the courts. Such a provision was in question in *Marbury* v. *Madison* itself, and perhaps the result there might be supported in this fashion. The upshot would be that each branch of the government would construe the Constitution for itself as concerns its own functions, and that this construction would be final, not subject to revision by any of the other branches. Marshall himself, at this point in his argument, drew only the following conclusion: "From these, and many other selections from the Constitution which might be made, it is apparent that the Framers of the Constitution contemplated that instrument as a rule for the government of courts, as well as of the legislature." And of the legislature as well as of courts, so that when the Constitution addresses itself to the legislature, or to the President, or to the states, for that matter, each may be the final arbiter of the meaning of the constitutional commands addressed to it. The distinction would lie between such provisions as those empowering Congress "to regulate Commerce" or "to coin Money," on the one hand, and, on the other, such commands as that of the Sixth Amendment that, "In all criminal prosecutions, the accused shall enjoy the right to a speedy and public trial, by an impartial jury. . . ." To find such an arrangement textually permissible is not, of course, to advocate it or to vouch for its workability. I should make plain my disavowal of an analysis by Professor William Winslow Crosskey, which is in some respects similar but which is also quite different, having regard to its context and supports and to the purposes it is made to serve.[4]

But, Marshall continued, the judges, under Article VI of the Constitution, are "bound by Oath or Affirmation, to support this Constitution." Would it not be immoral to impose this oath upon them while at the same time expecting them, in upholding laws they deem repugnant to the Constitution, to violate what they are sworn to support? This same oath, however, is also required of "Senators and Representatives. . . . Members of the several State Legislatures, and all executive and judicial Officers, both of the United States and of the several States. . . ." Far from supporting Marshall, the oath is perhaps the strongest textual argument against him. For it would seem to obligate each of these officers, in the performance of his own function, to support the Constitution. On one reading, the consequence might be utter chaos—everyone at every juncture interprets and applies the Constitution for himself. Or, as we have seen, it may be deduced that everyone is to construe the Constitution with finality insofar as it addresses itself to the performance of his own peculiar function. Surely the language lends itself more readily to this interpretation than to Marshall's apparent conclusion, that everyone's oath to support the Constitution is qualified by the judiciary's oath to do the same, and that every official of government is sworn to support the Constitution as the judges, in pursuance of the same oath, have construed it, rather than as his own conscience may dictate.

Only in the end, and then very lightly, does Marshall come to rest on the Supremacy Clause of Article VI, which in later times has seemed to many the most persuasive textual support.[5] The Supremacy Clause is as follows:

> This Constitution and the Laws of the United States which shall be made in Pursuance thereof; and all Treaties made, or which shall be made, under the Authority of the United States, shall be the supreme Law of the Land; and the Judges in every State shall be bound thereby, any Thing in the Constitution or Laws of any State to the Contrary notwithstanding.

"It is also not entirely unworthy of observation," Marshall wrote—and this was all he had to say on the point—that in declaring what is to be the supreme law of the land, this clause mentions the Constitution first and then not the laws of the United States generally but only those which shall be made in pursuance of the Constitution. Marshall left it at that, and what is to be concluded from this remark? First, it must be noted that nothing here is addressed to federal courts. Any command to them will have to be inferred, if there is to be one at all. Only as a forensic amusement can the phrase "Judges in every State" be taken to include federal judges, on the ground that some of them sit in the states. After all, the Supreme Court does not. The clause speaks to the constituent states of the federation and tells them that federal law will supersede any contrary state law. Further, it goes over the heads of the state governments and speaks to state judges directly, telling them that it will be their duty to enforce the supreme federal law above any contrary state law. State judges need enforce, however, only such federal law as is made in pursuance of the Constitution. Conceivably the reference here might be to more than just the mechanical provisions that describe how a federal law is to be enacted—by the concurrence of both Houses and with the signature of the President. Conceivably state judges were to be authorized to measure federal law against the federal Constitution and uphold it or strike it down in accordance with their understanding of the relevant constitutional provision. But such an arrangement, standing alone, would have been extraordinary, and it would have been self-destructive.

It is perfectly evident that the purpose of the clause is to make federal authority supreme over state. It is also certain that if state judges were to have final power to strike down federal statutes, the opposite effect would have been achieved, even though the authority of the state judges was drawn from the federal Constitution. The result is possible on the language, and there have been those who have contended for it precisely because it is destructive. The argument, known as interposition, is grounded in the oath provision discussed above as well as in the Supremacy Clause. And it is easily met. There is no call thus to upend the plain purpose of the clause. State judges must apply supreme federal law, statutory and constitutional, and must do it faithfully on their oaths. So much is unavoidable. But it fully meets all else that is compelling in the language of the clause simply to conclude that the proviso that only those federal statutes are to be supreme which are made in pursuance of the Constitution means that the statutes must carry the outer indicia of validity lent them by enactment in accordance with the constitutional forms. If so enacted, a federal statute is constitutional. That is to be taken as a given fact by state courts, on the authority and responsibility of the federal Congress and President who enacted the statute. No obstacle is thus raised to the exercise of the state judicial function. A court can just as well uphold the Constitution, thus performing its duty under the Supremacy Clause, by taking the meaning of the Constitution to have been settled by another authority and going on from there as by going to the trouble of parsing out the meaning of the document for itself.

Different considerations, however, govern the function (with which the state courts are also charged under the Supremacy Clause) of applying, not the federal Constitution against other federal laws, but federal statute and treaty law itself. Here, when a question of meaning arises, there will be no ready answer emanating from the fact of enactment or ratification. If a federal statute is said to conflict with the Constitution, and the question thus raised is, what is the meaning of the Constitution, that question can be said to have been answered by Congress and the President in favor of the validity of the statute which they enacted. But if the question is, what is the meaning of a statute or of a treaty as applied to a given situation, then there can be no similar, complete prior answer. Partial solution of, or guides to, the problem of interpretation and applicability may exist ready-made. But, barring the intervention of some other agency, the state court will in some measure have to construe the statute or the treaty for itself. The Supremacy Clause does not tell it to do otherwise, and it refers it nowhere else. Yet there is an obvious interest, if for no other reason than uniformity of application, in having federal law construed as well as declared by an institution of the general government. No single state should be empowered to lay down a uniform interpretation; only the federal government represents and can bind all. And a court is, in the very nature of things, the only agency that can be used to perform, in behalf of the general government, the ultimate task of lending uniformity and national authority to the construction and application of federal law in specific cases.

The option was open to set up a lower federal court system and to withdraw into it cases arising in the state courts which involved issues of the construction of federal law; or perhaps to withdraw into it only those issues themselves and remand the cases back to the state system once the issues had been decided. Another option was to set up in one Supreme Court appellate jurisdiction over state courts, again for the purposes of such cases or such issues. Is there anything in the Supremacy Clause to prevent either solution? Its drift, if anything, is equally in favor of either, and certainly not against. Article III, in turn, is also open to either solution. And Congress has in fact adopted a bit of both, although the chief reliance in the early days was on the appellate jurisdiction of the Supreme Court.

So much is reasonably clear. But from this starting point, many modern commentators take the Supremacy Clause on a giant leap. It would be just as absurd and destructive, it is said, for state courts to be authorized to render final constructions of the federal Constitution, in cases of alleged conflict with a federal statute, as it would be for them to have the last word on the meaning of such a statute itself, or of a treaty; indeed, more absurd. State courts are subjected to the reviewing authority of federal courts in their construction of statutes and treaties. By the same token, they ought to be subjected to the reviewing authority of federal courts when they construe the Constitution. Moreover, it would be silly to empower state judges, as courts of first instance, to construe and apply the Constitution in passing on the validity of federal statutes without so empowering federal judges also, in cases coming directly to them. What sense is there in allowing federal judges to function as spokesmen of the Constitution in cases coming from state courts but not in cases originating in the federal system itself? It follows that the Supremacy Clause addresses itself specifically to state judges only, because as to them there might have been some doubt, whereas it was regarded as obvious that the federal Constitution would bind, and would be construed and applied by, federal judges.

But this is all quite circular. Why is the power to declare federal statutes unconstitutional conceded to state courts? In order to enable one to lodge it in the federal courts also, and for no other reason. We have seen the need for judicial authority to construe federal statutes and treaties, and the reasons for subjecting state courts to federal appellate jurisdiction when they do so. We have also seen, however, that there is no similar exigency dictating similar judicial authority and similar appellate jurisdiction when the validity of a federal statute under the Constitution is in question, because neither state nor federal courts need to decide that for themselves in the first instance; they can take it as settled for them by the federal legislature and President. The ends of uniformity and of the vindication of federal authority are served in this fashion, without recourse to any power in the federal judiciary to lay down the meaning of the Constitution.

"Thus," the opinion in *Marbury* v. *Madison* concludes, "the particular phraseology of the Constitution of the United States confirms and strengthens the principle supposed to be essential to all written constitutions, that a law repugnant to the constitution is void," and that it is for the federal courts to declare it so. I have attempted to show that the principle must indeed be "supposed," and that the "phraseology of the Constitution" itself neither supports nor disavows it. I have suggested that it is of value to be aware that this is so, both for the sake of the security of the principle against attack and, as we shall see, for the sake of a true understanding of the nature and reach of the principle. Of course, the document must be read as a whole, and any particular phraseology is informed by the purpose of the whole. But I have tried to show that the purpose around which Marshall organized his argument does not necessarily emerge from the text.

Our discussion has centered on the claim actually staked out in *Marbury* v. *Madison*—that is, that a federal court has the power to strike down a duly enacted federal statute on the ground that it is repugnant to the Constitution. Of necessity, I have dealt also with the power, if any, of state judges to do the same. Marshall elsewhere established as well the separate, though of course closely connected, power of the federal courts to strike down state statutes and other actions for repugnancy to the federal Constitution. The bare text of Article III and of the Supremacy Clause is again equivocal. The Supremacy Clause, addressing itself to state judges alone, does put them on a different plane than state legislators and other officials. Yet it says nothing of federal judges, and hence it would not foreclose a system in which the sole reliance for the integrity and supremacy of the federal Constitution as against contravening state enactments would be on the conscientious performance of duty by state judges, subject to no other control. There is surely, however, a strong interest, to which we have alluded in connection with federal statute and treaty law, in the uniform construction and application of the Constitution as against inconsistent state law throughout the country. This is an interest fairly to be imputed to states which formed a federal union, and it is an interest that can be vindicated only by a federal institution. Congress can and in fact does from time to time perform this function, both as to statute and as to constitutional law; but, if for no other reason than that the instances in which performance of this function is necessary are extremely numerous, it is obviously sensible to lodge the function as well, and indeed chiefly, in the federal judiciary. This is not compelled by the language of the Constitution; it is implied from desirable ends that are attributed to the entire scheme. But most assuredly there is nothing in the language that forbids it. And Congress has so provided—consistently, from the first Judiciary Act of the first Congress onward—and it has done so unambiguously.

Judiciary acts have, from the beginning, also given the Supreme Court jurisdiction to review state court cases in which is drawn in question the validity of a treaty or statute of the United States, presumably under the federal Constitution. If that was a grant to the Supreme Court of final authority to construe the Constitution as against acts of Congress, why, then, well and good. Nothing in the text prevents such a gesture of congressional abnegation, although in that event, what Congress can give away, Congress can, at least in theory, take back. But it is question-begging so to understand this provision of the first Judiciary Act. Reading no presuppositions into it, one may as easily conclude that the Supreme Court was meant only to enforce against state courts a rule that duly enacted federal statutes are constitutional by virtue of their due enactment. There is no similar ambiguity, however, in the first Judiciary Act's grant to the Supreme Court of jurisdiction to review cases which draw in question the validity of a statute of, or an authority exercised under, any state, on the ground of its being repugnant to the Constitution, treaties, or laws of the United States. This provision would be senseless unless it was intended to authorize the Court, in these circumstances, to construe and apply the federal Constitution as well as federal statute and treaty law. Only thus could this provision serve the interest of uniformity and of the superiority of federal power—and what other purpose could it have? As we have seen, the Supremacy Clause itself does not compel, although it permits and no doubt invites, this arrangement. This being so, Congress could change it all tomorrow. And perhaps it could, if textual considerations were all that governed the matter, just as it could change the course of the Mississippi River, if all we had to indicate the location of its bed were some general description by a traveler of a body of water traversing the middle of the country from north to south.

▪   ▪   ▪

The Counter-Majoritarian Difficulty

The root difficulty is that judicial review is a counter-majoritarian force in our system. There are various ways of sliding over this ineluctable reality. Marshall did so when he spoke of enforcing, in behalf of "the people," the limits that they have ordained for the institutions of a limited government. And it has been done ever since in much the same fashion by all too many commentators. Marshall himself followed Hamilton, who in the 78th *Federalist* denied that judicial review implied a superiority of the judicial over the legislative power—denied, in other words, that judicial review constituted control by an unrepresentative minority of an elected majority. "It only supposes," Hamilton went on, "that the power of the people is superior to both; and that where the will of the legislature, declared in its statutes, stands in opposition to that of the people, declared in the Constitution, the judges ought to be governed by the latter rather than the former." But the word "people" so used is an abstraction. Not necessarily a meaningless or a pernicious one by any means; always charged with emotion, but nonrepresentational—an abstraction obscuring the reality that when the Supreme Court declares unconstitutional a legislative act or the action of an elected executive, it thwarts the will of representatives of the actual people of the here and now; it exercises control, not in behalf of the prevailing majority, but against it. That, without mystic overtones, is what actually happens. It is an altogether different kettle of fish and it is the reason the charge can be made that judicial review is undemocratic.

Most assuredly, no democracy operates by taking continuous nose counts on the broad range of daily governmental activities. Representative democracies— that is to say, all working democracies—function by electing certain men for certain periods of time, then passing judgment periodically on their conduct of public office. It is a matter of a laying on of hands, followed in time by a process of holding to account—all through the exercise of the franchise. The elected officials, however, are expected to delegate some of their tasks to men of their own appointment, who are not directly accountable at the polls. The whole operates under public scrutiny and criticism—but not at all times or in all parts. What we mean by democracy, therefore, is much more sophisticated and complex than the making of decisions in town meeting by a show of hands. It is true also that even decisions that have been submitted to the electoral process in some fashion are not continually resubmitted, and they are certainly not continually unmade. Once run through the process, once rendered by "the people" (using the term now in its mystic sense, because the reference is to the people in the past), myriad decisions remain to govern the present and the future despite what may well be fluctuating majorities against them at any given time. A high value is put on stability, and that is also a counter-majoritarian factor. Nevertheless, although democracy does not mean constant reconsideration of decisions once made, it does mean that a representative majority has the power to accomplish a reversal. This power is of the essence, and no less so because it is often merely held in reserve.

I am aware that this timid assault on the complexities of the American democratic system has yet left us with a highly simplistic statement, and I shall briefly rehearse some of the reasons. But nothing in the further complexities and perplexities of the system, which modern political science has explored with admirable and ingenious industry, and some of which it has tended to multiply with a fertility that passes the mere zeal of the discoverer—nothing in these complexities can alter the essential reality that judicial review is a deviant institution in the American democracy.

It is true, of course, that the process of reflecting the will of a popular majority in the legislature is deflected by various inequalities of representation and by all sorts of institutional habits and characteristics, which perhaps tend most often in favor of inertia. Yet it must be remembered that statutes are the product of the legislature and the executive acting in concert, and that the executive represents a very different constituency and thus tends to cure inequities of over- and underrepresentation. Reflecting a balance of forces in society for purposes of stable and effective government is more intricate and less certain than merely assuring each citizen his equal vote. Moreover, impurities and imperfections, if such they be, in one part of the system are no argument for total departure from the desired norm in another part. A much more important complicating factor—first adumbrated by Madison in the 10th *Federalist* and lately emphasized by Professor David B. Truman and others[6]—is the proliferation and power of what Madison foresaw as "faction," what Mr. Truman calls "groups," and what in popular parlance has always been deprecated as the "interests" or the "pressure groups."

No doubt groups operate forcefully on the electoral process and no doubt they seek and gain access to and an effective share in the legislative and executive decisional process. Perhaps they constitute also, in some measure, an impurity or imperfection. But no one has claimed that they have been able to capture the governmental process except by combining in some fashion, and thus capturing or constituting (are not the two verbs synonymous?) a majority. They often tend themselves to be majoritarian in composition and to be subject to broader majoritarian influences. And the price of what they sell or buy in the legislature is determined in the biennial or quadrennial electoral marketplace. It may be, as Professor Robert A. Dahl has written, that elections themselves, and the political competition that renders them meaningful, "do not make for government by majorities in any very significant way," for they do not establish a great many policy preferences. However, "they are a crucial device for controlling leaders." And if the control is exercised by "groups of various types and sizes, all seeking in various ways to advance their goals," so that we have "minorities rule" rather than majority rule, it remains true nevertheless that only those minorities rule which can command the votes of a majority of individuals in the legislature who can command the votes of a majority of individuals in the electorate. In one fashion or another, both in the legislative process and at elections, the minorities must coalesce into a majority. Although, as Mr. Dahl says, "it is fashionable in some quarters to suggest that everything believed about democratic politics prior to World War I, and perhaps World War II, was nonsense," he makes no bones about his own belief that "the radical democrats who, unlike Madison, insist upon the decisive importance of the election process in the whole grand strategy of democracy are essentially correct."[7]

■   ■   ■

It has been suggested[8] that the Congress, the President, the states, and the people (in the sense of current majorities) have from the beginning and in each generation acquiesced in, and thus consented to, the exercise of judicial review by the Supreme Court. In the first place, it is said that the Amending Clause of the Constitution has been employed to reverse the work of the Court only twice, perhaps three times; and it has never been used to take away or diminish the Court's power. But the Amending Clause itself incorporates an extreme minority veto. The argument then proceeds to draw on the first Judiciary Act, whose provisions regarding the jurisdiction of the federal courts have been continued in effect to this day. Yet we have seen that the Judiciary Act can be read as a grant of the power to declare federal statutes unconstitutional only on the basis of a previously and independently reached conclusion that such a power must exist. And even if the Judiciary Act did grant this power, as it surely granted the power to declare state actions unconstitutional, it amounted to an expression of the opinion of the first Congress that the Constitution implies judicial review. It is, in fact, extremely likely that the first Congress thought so. That is important; but it merely adds to the historical evidence on the point, which, as we have seen, is in any event quite strong. Future Congresses and future generations can only be said to have acquiesced in the belief of the first Congress that the Constitution implies this power. And they can be said to have become resigned to what follows, which is that the power can be taken away only by constitutional amendment. That is a very far cry from consent to the power on its merits, as a power freely continued by the decision or acquiescence of a majority in each generation. The argument advances not a step toward justification of the power on other than historical grounds.

A further, crucial difficulty must also be faced. Besides being a countermajoritarian check on the legislature and the executive, judicial review may, in a larger sense, have a tendency over time seriously to weaken the democratic process. Judicial review expresses, of course, a form of distrust of the legislature. . . . To this day, in how many hundreds of occasions does Congress enact a measure that it deems expedient, having essayed consideration of its constitutionality (that is to say, of its acceptability on principle), only to abandon the attempt in the declared confidence that the Court will correct errors of principle, if any? It may well be, as has been suggested,[9] that any lowering of the level of legislative performance is attributable to many factors other than judicial review. Yet there is no doubt that what Thayer observed remains observable. It seemed rather a puzzle, for example, to a scholar who recently compared British and American practices of legislative investigation. . . .

Finally, another, though related, contention has been put forward. It is that judicial review runs so fundamentally counter to democratic theory that in a society which in all other respects rests on that theory, judicial review cannot ultimately be effective. We pay the price of a grave inner contradiction in the basic principle of our government, which is an inconvenience and a dangerous one; and in the end to no good purpose, for when the great test comes, judicial review will be unequal to it. The most arresting expression of this thought is in a famous passage from a speech of Judge Learned Hand, a passage, Dean Eugene V. Rostow has written, "of Browningesque passion and obscurity," voicing a "gloomy and apocalyptic view."[10] Absent the institution of judicial review, Judge Hand said:

> I do not think that anyone can say what will be left of those [fundamental principles of equity and fair play which our constitutions enshrine]; I do not know whether they will serve only as counsels; but this much I think I do know—that a society so riven that the spirit of moderation is gone, no court *can* save; that a society where that spirit flourishes, no court *need* save; that in a society which evades its responsibility by thrusting upon the courts the nurture of that spirit, that spirit in the end will perish.[11]

Over a century before Judge Hand spoke, Judge Gibson of Pennsylvania, in his day perhaps the ablest opponent of the establishment of judicial review, wrote: "Once let public opinion be so corrupt as to sanction every misconstruction of the Constitution and abuse of power which the temptation of the moment may dictate, and the party which may happen to be predominant will laugh at the puny efforts of a dependent power to arrest it in its course."[12] And Thayer also believed that "under no system can the power of courts go far to save a people from ruin; our chief protection lies elsewhere."[13]

■　　■　　■

The Mystic Function

This inquiry into a general justification of judicial review cannot end without taking account of a most suggestive and perceptive argument recently advanced by Professor Charles L. Black, Jr.[14] It begins by emphasizing that the Court performs not only a checking function but also a legitimating one, as Mr. Black well calls it. Judicial review means not only that the Court may strike down a legislative action as unconstitutional but also that it may validate it as within constitutionally granted powers and as not violating constitutional limitations. Mr. Black contends, further, that the legitimating function would be impossible of performance if the checking function did not exist as well: what is the good of a declaration of validity from an institution which is by hypothesis required to validate everything that is brought before it? This is plainly so, though it is oddly stated. The picture is accurate, but it is stood on its head. The truth is that the legitimating function is an inescapable, even if unintended, by-product of the checking power. But what follows? What is the nature of this legitimating function, and what the need for it?

■　　■　　■

Very probably, the stability of the American Republic is due in large part, as Professor Louis Hartz has eloquently argued, to the remarkable Lockeian consensus of a society that has never known a feudal regime; to a "moral unity" that was seriously broken only once, over the extension of slavery. This unity makes possible a society that accepts its principles from on high, without fighting about them. But the Lockeian consensus is also a limitation on the sort of principles that will be accepted. It is putting the cart before the horse to attribute the American sense of legitimacy to the institution of judicial review. The latter is more nearly the fruit of the former, although the "moral unity" must be made manifest, it must be renewed and sharpened and brought to bear—and this is an office that judicial review can discharge.[15]

No doubt it is in the interest of the majority to obtain the acquiescence of the minority as often and in as great a degree as possible. And no doubt the Court can help bring about acquiescence by assuring those who have lost a political fight that merely momentary interest, not fundamental principle, was in play. Yet is it reasonable to assume that the majority would wish to see itself checked from time to time just to have an institution which, when it chooses to go along with the majority's will, is capable of helping to assuage the defeated minority? That is too much of an indirection. The checking power must find its own justification, particularly in a system which, in a number of important ways, (e.g., the Senate's reflection of the federal structure, practices of legislative apportionment), offers prodigious political safeguards to the minority.

Thus the legitimating function of judicial review cannot be accepted as an independent justification for it. Yet it exists. Not only is the Supreme Court capable of generating consent for hotly controverted legislative or executive measures; it has the subtler power of adding a certain impetus to measures that the majority enacts rather tentatively. There are times when the majority might, because of strong minority feelings, be inclined in the end to deny itself, but when it comes to embrace a measure more firmly, and the minority comes to accept it, because the Court—intending perhaps no such consequence—has declared it consistent with constitutional principle. This tendency touches on Thayer's anxiety that judicial review will "dwarf the political capacity of the people" and "deaden its sense of moral responsibility." We shall return to it as a consideration that should cause the Court to stay its hand from time to time.

But the Supreme Court as a legitimating force in society also casts a less palpable yet larger spell. With us the symbol of nationhood, of continuity, of unity and common purpose, is, of course, the Constitution, without particular reference to what exactly it means in this or that application. The utility of such a symbol is a commonplace. Britain—the United Kingdom, and perhaps even the Commonwealth—is the most potent historical demonstration of the efficaciousness of a symbol, made concrete in the person of the Crown. The President in our system serves the function somewhat, but only very marginally, because the personification of unity must be above the political battle, and no President can fulfill his office while remaining above the battle. The effective Presidents have of necessity been men of power, and so it has in large part been left to the Supreme Court to concretize the symbol of the Constitution. Keeping in mind that this is offered as an observation, not as justification, it is surely true that the Court has been able to play the role partly—but only partly—by virtue of its power of judicial review.

The Court is seen as a continuum. It is never, like other institutions, renewed at a single stroke. No one or two changes on the Court, not even if they include the advent of a new Chief Justice, are apt to be as immediately momentous as a turnover in the presidency. To the extent that they are instruments of decisive change, Justices are time bombs, not warheads that explode on impact. There are exceptions, to be sure. In 1870, President Grant made two appointments that promptly resulted in the reversal of a quite crucial recent decision concerning the monetary powers of the federal government.[16] And it may seem that strong new doctrine became ascendant soon after the first of President Roosevelt's appointees, Mr. Justice Black, came on the Bench in 1937. But on the whole, the movements of the Court are not sudden and not suddenly affected by new appointments. Continuity is a chief concern of the Court, as it is the main reason for the Court's place in the hearts of its countrymen.

No doubt, the Court's symbolic—or, if you will, mystic—function would not have been possible, would not have reached the stage at which we now see it, if the Court did not exercise the power of judicial review. It could scarcely personify the Constitution unless it had the authority finally to speak of it. But as the symbol manifests itself today, it seems not always to depend on judicial review. It seems at times to have as much to do with the life tenure of the Court's members and with the fact of the long government service of some of them, not only on the Court; in short, with the total impression of continuity personified. Here the human chain goes back unbroken in a small, intimate group to the earliest beginnings.

▪   ▪   ▪

The foregoing discussion of the origin and justification of judicial review has dealt for the most part indiscriminately with the power of the federal courts to strike down federal legislation and the power of those courts to pass on actions of the states. There are, of course, differences. Many judges and commentators who have questioned the power of judicial review of federal legislation have freely conceded the same power when exercised with respect to state actions. It is vital, as we have seen, that some federal agency have power authoritatively to declare and apply federal law to the member states of the federation. Clearly, for the sake of full effectiveness, a substantial portion of this power must be exercised by a judicial body. Yet it remains true that when the Court invalidates the action of a state legislature, it is acting against the majority will within the given jurisdiction; what is more, it also promises to foreclose majority action on the matter in issue throughout the country. The Court represents the national will against local particularism; but it does not represent it, as the Congress does, through electoral responsibility. The need to effectuate the superiority of federal over state law is not a sufficient justification for judicial review of state actions in those instances in which the federal law in question is constitutional and hence judge-made. In this respect also, therefore, the function must be supported by the other reasons we have surveyed. This is not to say, however, that there will not be instances when it seems justifiable to exercise judicial review more vigorously against the states than against the federal legislature or executive, and instances calling for less vigor as well.

NOTES

1. R. G. McCloskey, *The American Supreme Court* (Chicago: University of Chicago Press, 1960), pp. 40, 42, 43. (Copyright 1960 by The University of Chicago.)

2. *Field* v. *Clark*, 143 U.S. 649 (1892).

3. 6 Cranch 87 (1810).

4. See W. W. Crosskey, *Politics and the Constitution in the History of the United States*, Vol. 2 (Chicago: University of Chicago Press, 1953), chs. XXVII–XXIX; cf. H. M. Hart, Jr., "Professor Crosskey and Judicial Review," 67 *Harvard Law Review* 1456 (1954).

5. See, e.g., C. L. Black, Jr., *The People and the Court* (New York: Macmillan, 1960), p. 6; H. Wechsler, *Principles, Politics and Fundamental Law* (Cambridge: Harvard University Press, 1961), p. 7; E. V. Rostow, "The Supreme Court and the People's Will," 33 *Notre Dame Lawyer* 573, 575–76 (1958); cf. L. H. Pollak, "Racial Discrimination and Judicial Integrity: A Reply to Professor Wechsler," 108 *University of Pennsylvania Law Review* 1, 3 (1959).

6. See D. B. Truman, *The Governmental Process* (New York: Knopf, 1951).

7. R. A. Dahl, *A Preface to Democratic Theory* (Chicago: University of Chicago Press, 1956), pp. 125, 132. (Copyright 1956 by the University of Chicago.)

8. See, *e.g.,* Black, *op. cit. supra* n. 6, at pp. 23 *et seq.,* 210 *et seq.*

9. See E. V. Rostow, "The Democratic Character of Judicial Review," 66 *Harvard Law Review* 193, 195 (1952) n. 15, at p. 201.

10. Rostow, *op. cit. supra* n. 15, at p. 205.

11. L. Hand, "The Contribution of an Independent Judiciary to Civilization," in I. Dilliard, ed., *The Spirit of Liberty* (New York: Knopf, 1953), pp. 155–65.

12. *Eakin* v. *Raub,* 12 S. & R. 330, 343, 355 (1825).

13. J. B. Thayer, "The Origin and Scope of the American Doctrine of Constitutional Law," in *Legal Essays* (Boston: The Boston Book Co., 1908), pp. 1, 39.

14. See Black, *op. cit. supra* n. 6, at pp. 34 *et seq.*

15. See L. Hartz, *The Liberal Tradition in America* (New York: Harcourt, Brace, 1955), pp. 9 *et seq.*; B. F. Wright, "Editor's Introduction," in *The Federalist,* John Harvard Edition (Cambridge: Harvard University Press, 1961), p. 41.

16. See C. Fairman, "Joseph P. Bradley," in A. Dunham and P. B. Kurland, eds., *Mr. Justice* (Chicago: University of Chicago Press, 1956), pp. 69, 80–82; C. Fairman, "Mr. Justice Bradley's Appointment to the Supreme Court and the Legal Tender Cases," 54 *Harvard Law Review* 977 (1941).

8.2

Bowers v. Hardwick (1986)

In 1986, the Supreme Court upheld a Georgia law that criminalizes homosexual sodomy even between consenting adults in private, reasoning that the right to privacy as construed in constitutional law did not extend to actions that are not widely accepted by the public as moral. The Court reversed this decision in Lawrence, 2003, which is next in this chapter.

Justice White delivered the opinion of the Court.

In August 1982, respondent Hardwick (hereafter respondent) was charged with violating the Georgia statute criminalizing sodomy[1] by committing that act with another adult male in the bedroom of respondent's home. After a preliminary hearing, the District Attorney decided not to present the matter to the grand jury unless further evidence developed.

Respondent then brought suit in the Federal District Court, challenging the constitutionality of the statute insofar as it criminalized consensual sodomy.[2] He asserted that he was a practicing homosexual, that the Georgia sodomy statute, as administered by the defendants, placed him in imminent danger of arrest, and that the statute for several reasons violates the Federal Constitution. The District Court granted the defendants' motion to dismiss for failure to state a claim, relying on *Doe v. Commonwealth's Attorney for the City of Richmond*, (ED Va. 1975), which this Court summarily affirmed.

A divided panel of the Court of Appeals for the Eleventh Circuit reversed. The court first held that, because *Doe* was distinguishable and in any event had been undermined by later decisions, our summary affirmance in that case did not require affirmance of the District Court. Relying on our decisions in *Griswold v. Connecticut*, (1965); *Eisenstadt v. Baird*, (1972); *Stanley v. Georgia*, (1969); and *Roe v. Wade*, (1973), the court went on to hold that the Georgia statute violated respondent's fundamental rights because his homosexual activity is a private and intimate association that is beyond the reach of state regulation by reason of the Ninth Amendment and the Due Process Clause of the Fourteenth Amendment. The case was remanded for trial, at which, to prevail, the State would have to prove that the statute is supported by a compelling interest and is the most narrowly drawn means of achieving that end.

Because other Courts of Appeals have arrived at judgments contrary to that of the Eleventh Circuit in this case, we granted the Attorney General's petition for certiorari questioning the holding that the sodomy statute violates the fundamental rights of homosexuals. We agree with petitioner that the Court of Appeals erred, and hence reverse its judgment.

This case does not require a judgment on whether laws against sodomy between consenting adults in general, or between homosexuals in particular, are wise or desirable. It raises no question about the right or propriety of state legislative decisions to repeal their laws that criminalize homosexual sodomy, or of state-court decisions invalidating those laws on state constitutional grounds. The issue presented is whether the Federal Constitution confers a fundamental right upon homosexuals to engage in sodomy and hence invalidates the laws of the many States that still make such conduct illegal and have done so for a very long time. The case also calls for some judgment about the limits of the Court's role in carrying out its constitutional mandate.

We first register our disagreement with the Court of Appeals and with respondent that the Court's prior cases have construed the Constitution to confer a right of privacy that extends to homosexual sodomy and for all intents and purposes have decided this case. The reach of this line of cases was sketched in *Carey v. Population Services International*, (1977). *Pierce v. Society of Sisters*, (1925), and *Meyer v. Nebraska*, (1923), were described as dealing with child rearing and education; *Prince v. Massachusetts*, (1944), with family relationships; *Skinner v. Oklahoma ex rel. Williamson*, (1942), with procreation; *Loving v. Virginia*, (1967), with marriage; *Griswold v. Connecticut*, and *Eisenstadt v. Baird*, with contraception, and *Roe v. Wade*, (1973), with abortion. The latter three cases were interpreted as construing the Due Process Clause of the Fourteenth Amendment to confer a fundamental individual right to decide whether or not to beget or bear a child.

Accepting the decisions in these cases and the above description of them, we think it evident that none of the rights announced in those cases bears any resemblance to the claimed constitutional right of homosexuals to engage in acts of sodomy that is asserted in this case. No connection between family, marriage, or procreation on the one hand and homosexual activity on the other has been demonstrated, either by the Court of Appeals or by respondent. Moreover, any claim that these cases nevertheless stand for the proposition that any kind of private sexual conduct between consenting adults is constitutionally insulated from state proscription is unsupportable. Indeed, the Court's opinion in *Carey* twice asserted that the privacy right, which the *Griswold* line of cases found to be one of the protections provided by the Due Process Clause, did not reach so far.

Precedent aside, however, respondent would have us announce, as the Court of Appeals did, a fundamental right to engage in homosexual sodomy. This we are quite unwilling to do. It is true that despite the language of the Due Process Clauses of the Fifth and Fourteenth Amendments, which appears to focus only on the processes by which life, liberty, or property is taken, the cases are legion in which those Clauses have been interpreted to have substantive content, subsuming rights that to a great extent are immune from federal or state regulation or proscription. Among such cases are those recognizing rights that have little or no textual support in the constitutional language. *Meyer, Prince*, and *Pierce* fall in this category, as do the privacy cases from *Griswold* to *Carey*.

Striving to assure itself and the public that announcing rights not readily identifiable in the Constitution's text involves much more than the imposition of the Justices' own choice of values on the States and the Federal Government, the Court has sought to identify the nature of the rights qualifying for heightened judicial protection. In *Palko v. Connecticut*, (1937), it was said that this category includes those fundamental liberties that are "implicit in the concept of ordered liberty," such that "neither liberty nor justice would exist if [they] were sacrificed." A different description of fundamental liberties appeared in *Moore v. East Cleveland*, (1977) (opinion of Powell, J.), where they are characterized as those liberties that are "deeply rooted in this Nation's history and tradition."

It is obvious to us that neither of these formulations would extend a fundamental right to homosexuals to engage in acts of consensual sodomy. Proscriptions against that conduct have ancient roots. Sodomy was a criminal offense at common law and was forbidden by the laws of the original 13 States when they ratified the Bill of Rights. In 1868, when the Fourteenth Amendment was ratified, all but 5 of the 37 States in the Union had criminal sodomy laws. In fact, until 1961, all 50 States outlawed sodomy, and today, 24 States and the District of Columbia continue to provide criminal penalties for sodomy performed in private and between consenting adults. Against this background, to claim that a right to engage in such conduct is "deeply rooted in this Nation's history and tradition" or "implicit in the concept of ordered liberty" is, at best, facetious.

Nor are we inclined to take a more expansive view of our authority to discover new fundamental rights imbedded in the Due Process Clause. The Court is most vulnerable and comes nearest to illegitimacy when it deals with judge-made constitutional law having little or no cognizable roots in the language or design of the Constitution. That this is so was painfully demonstrated by the face-off between the Executive and the Court in the 1930's, which resulted in the repudiation of much of the substantive gloss that the Court had placed on the Due Process Clauses of the Fifth and Fourteenth Amendments. There should be, therefore, great resistance to expand the substantive reach of those Clauses, particularly if it requires redefining the category of rights deemed to be fundamental. Otherwise, the Judiciary necessarily takes to itself further authority to govern the country without express constitutional authority. The claimed right pressed on us today falls for short of overcoming this resistance.

Respondent, however, asserts that the result should be different where the homosexual conduct occurs in the privacy of the home. He relies on *Stanley v. Georgia*, (1969), where the Court held that the First Amendment prevents conviction for possessing and reading obscene material in the privacy of one's home: "If the First Amendment means anything, it means that a State has no business telling a man, sitting alone in his house, what books he may read or what films he may watch."

Stanley did protect conduct that would not have been protected outside the home, and it partially prevented the enforcement of state obscenity laws; but the decision was firmly grounded in the First Amendment. The right pressed upon us here has no similar support in the text of the Constitution, and it does not qualify for recognition under the prevailing principles for construing the Fourteenth Amendment. Its limits are also difficult to discern. Plainly enough, otherwise illegal conduct is not always immunized whenever it occurs in the home. Victimless crimes, such as the possession and use of illegal drugs, do not escape the law where they are committed at home. Stanley itself recognized that its holding offered no protection for the possession in the home of drugs, firearms, or stolen goods. And if respondent's submission is limited to the voluntary sexual conduct between consenting adults, it would be difficult, except by fiat, to limit the claimed right to homosexual conduct while leaving exposed to prosecution adultery, incest, and other sexual crimes even though they are committed in the home. We are unwilling to start down that road.

Even if the conduct at issue here is not a fundamental right, respondent asserts that there must be a rational basis for the law and that there is none in this case other than the presumed belief of a majority of the electorate in Georgia that homosexual sodomy is immoral and unacceptable. This is said to be an inadequate rationale to support the law. The law, however, is constantly based on notions of morality, and if all laws representing essentially moral choices are to be invalidated under the Due Process Clause, the courts will be very busy indeed. Even respondent makes no such claim, but insists that majority sentiments about the morality of homosexuality should be declared inadequate. We do not agree, and are unpersuaded that the sodomy laws of some 25 States should be invalidated on this basis.

Accordingly, the judgment of the Court of Appeals is Reversed.

NOTES

1. Georgia Code Ann. 16-6-2 (1984) provides, in pertinent part, as follows: "(a) A person commits the offense of sodomy when he performs or submits to any sexual act involving the sex organs of one person and the mouth or anus of another. . . . "(b) A person convicted of the offense of sodomy shall be punished by imprisonment for not less than one nor more than 20 years. . . ."

2. John and Mary Doe were also plaintiffs in the action. They alleged that they wished to engage in sexual activity proscribed by 16-6-2 in the privacy of their home, App. 3, and that they had been "chilled and deterred" from engaging in such activity by both the existence of the statute and Hardwick's arrest. Id., at 5. The District Court held, however, that because they had neither sustained, nor were in immediate danger of sustaining, any direct injury from the enforcement of the statute, they did not have proper standing to maintain the action. Id., at 18. The Court of Appeals affirmed the District Court's judgment dismissing the Does' claim for lack of standing, 760 F.2d 1202, 1206-1207 (CA11 1985), and the Does do not challenge that holding in this Court. The only claim properly before the Court, therefore, is Hardwick's challenge to the Georgia statute as applied to consensual homosexual sodomy. We express no opinion on the constitutionality of the Georgia statute as applied to other acts of sodomy.

8.3

Lawrence v. Texas (2003)

In 2003, seventeen years after the Bowers *decision, the Supreme Court reversed itself and declared that a Texas law banning homosexual sodomy was unconstitutional. The majority decided that such state laws banning private sexual activity between consenting adults violated the constitutional right to privacy.*

Justice Kennedy delivered the opinion of the Court.

Liberty protects the person from unwarranted government intrusions into a dwelling or other private places. In our tradition the State is not omnipresent in the home. And there are other spheres of our lives and existence, outside the home, where the State should not be a dominant presence. Freedom extends beyond spatial bounds. Liberty presumes an autonomy of self that includes freedom of thought, belief, expression, and certain intimate conduct. The instant case involves liberty of the person both in its spatial and more transcendent dimensions.

I

The question before the Court is the validity of a Texas statute making it a crime for two persons of the same sex to engage in certain intimate sexual conduct.

In Houston, Texas, officers of the Harris County Police Department were dispatched to a private residence in response to a reported weapons disturbance. They entered an apartment where one of the petitioners, John Geddes Lawrence, resided. The right of the police to enter does not seem to have been questioned. The officers observed Lawrence and another man, Tyron Garner, engaging in a sexual act. The two petitioners were arrested, held in custody over night, and charged and convicted before a Justice of the Peace.

The complaints described their crime as "deviate sexual intercourse, namely anal sex, with a member of the same sex (man)." The applicable state law is Tex. Penal Code Ann. §21.06(a) (2003). It provides: "A person commits an offense if he engages in deviate sexual intercourse with another individual of the same sex." The statute defines "[d]eviate sexual intercourse" as follows:

"(A) any contact between any part of the genitals of one person and the mouth or anus of another person; or

"(B) the penetration of the genitals or the anus of another person with an object."

The petitioners exercised their right to a trial *de novo* in Harris County Criminal Court. They challenged the statute as a violation of the Equal Protection Clause of the Fourteenth Amendment and of a like provision of the Texas Constitution. Tex. Const., Art. 1, §3a. Those contentions were rejected. The petitioners, having entered a plea of *nolo contendere*, were each fined $200 and assessed court costs of $141.25.

The Court of Appeals for the Texas Fourteenth District considered the petitioners' federal constitutional arguments under both the Equal Protection and Due Process Clauses of the Fourteenth Amendment. After hearing the case en banc the court, in a divided opinion, rejected the constitutional arguments and affirmed the convictions. The majority opinion indicates that the Court of Appeals considered our decision in *Bowers v. Hardwick*, (1986), to be controlling on the federal due process aspect of the case. *Bowers* then being authoritative, this was proper.

We granted certiorari, to consider three questions:

1. Whether Petitioners' criminal convictions under the Texas "Homosexual Conduct" law—which criminalizes sexual intimacy by same-sex couples, but not identical behavior by different-sex couples—violate the Fourteenth Amendment guarantee of equal protection of laws?
2. Whether Petitioners' criminal convictions for adult consensual sexual intimacy in the home violate their vital interests in liberty and privacy protected by the Due Process Clause of the Fourteenth Amendment?
3. Whether *Bowers v. Hardwick*, should be overruled?

The petitioners were adults at the time of the alleged offense. Their conduct was in private and consensual.

II

We conclude the case should be resolved by determining whether the petitioners were free as adults to engage in the private conduct in the exercise of their liberty under the Due Process Clause of the Fourteenth Amendment to the Constitution. For this inquiry we deem it necessary to reconsider the Court's holding in *Bowers*.

There are broad statements of the substantive reach of liberty under the Due Process Clause in earlier cases, including *Pierce v. Society of Sisters*,

(1925), and *Meyer v. Nebraska,* (1923); but the most pertinent beginning point is our decision in *Griswold v. Connecticut,* (1965).

In *Griswold* the Court invalidated a state law prohibiting the use of drugs or devices of contraception and counseling or aiding and abetting the use of contraceptives. The Court described the protected interest as a right to privacy and placed emphasis on the marriage relation and the protected space of the marital bedroom.

After *Griswold* it was established that the right to make certain decisions regarding sexual conduct extends beyond the marital relationship. In *Eisenstadt v. Baird,* (1972), the Court invalidated a law prohibiting the distribution of contraceptives to unmarried persons. The case was decided under the Equal Protection Clause; but with respect to unmarried persons, the Court went on to state the fundamental proposition that the law impaired the exercise of their personal rights. It quoted from the statement of the Court of Appeals finding the law to be in conflict with fundamental human rights, and it followed with this statement of its own:

> It is true that in *Griswold* the right of privacy in question inhered in the marital relationship. . . . If the right of privacy means anything, it is the right of the *individual,* married or single, to be free from unwarranted governmental intrusion into matters so fundamentally affecting a person as the decision whether to bear or beget a child.

The opinions in *Griswold* and *Eisenstadt* were part of the background for the decision in *Roe v. Wade,* (1973). As is well known, the case involved a challenge to the Texas law prohibiting abortions, but the laws of other States were affected as well. Although the Court held the woman's rights were not absolute, her right to elect an abortion did have real and substantial protection as an exercise of her liberty under the Due Process Clause. The Court cited cases that protect spatial freedom and cases that go well beyond it. *Roe* recognized the right of a woman to make certain fundamental decisions affecting her destiny and confirmed once more that the protection of liberty under the Due Process Clause has a substantive dimension of fundamental significance in defining the rights of the person.

In *Carey v. Population Services Int'l,* (1977), the Court confronted a New York law forbidding sale or distribution of contraceptive devices to persons under 16 years of age. Although there was no single opinion for the Court, the law was invalidated. Both *Eisenstadt* and *Carey,* as well as the holding and rationale in *Roe,* confirmed that the reasoning of *Griswold* could not be confined to the protection of rights of married adults. This was the state of the law with respect to some of the most relevant cases when the Court considered *Bowers v. Hardwick.*

The facts in *Bowers* had some similarities to the instant case. A police officer, whose right to enter seems not to have been in question, observed Hardwick, in his own bedroom, engaging in intimate sexual conduct with another adult male. The conduct was in violation of a Georgia statute making it a criminal offense to engage in sodomy. One difference between the two cases is that the Georgia statute prohibited the conduct whether or not the participants were of the same sex, while the Texas statute, as we have seen, applies only to participants of the same sex. Hardwick was not prosecuted, but he brought an action in federal court to declare the state statute invalid. He alleged he was a practicing homosexual and that the criminal prohibition violated rights guaranteed to him by the Constitution. The Court, in an opinion by Justice White, sustained the Georgia law. Chief Justice Burger and Justice Powell joined the opinion of the Court and filed separate, concurring opinions. Four Justices dissented. (opinion of Blackmun, J., joined by Brennan, Marshall, and Stevens, JJ.); (opinion of Stevens, J., joined by Brennan and Marshall, JJ.).

The Court began its substantive discussion in *Bowers* as follows: "The issue presented is whether the Federal Constitution confers a fundamental right upon homosexuals to engage in sodomy and hence invalidates the laws of the many States that still make such conduct illegal and have done so for a very long time." That statement, we now conclude, discloses the Court's own failure to appreciate the extent of the liberty at stake. To say that the issue in *Bowers* was simply the right to engage in certain sexual conduct demeans the claim the individual put forward, just as it would demean a married couple were it to be said marriage is simply about the right to have sexual intercourse. The laws involved in *Bowers* and here are, to be sure, statutes that purport to do no more than prohibit a particular sexual act. Their penalties and purposes, though, have more far-reaching consequences, touching upon the most private human conduct, sexual behavior, and in the most private of places, the home. The statutes do seek to control a personal relationship that, whether or not entitled to formal recognition in the law, is within the liberty of persons to choose without being punished as criminals.

This, as a general rule, should counsel against attempts by the State, or a court, to define the meaning of the relationship or to set its boundaries absent injury to a person or abuse of an institution the law protects. It suffices for us to acknowledge that adults may choose to enter upon this relationship in the confines of their homes and their own private lives and still retain their dignity as free persons. When sexuality finds overt expression in intimate conduct with another person, the conduct can be but one element in a personal bond that is more enduring. The liberty protected by the Constitution allows homosexual persons the right to make this choice.

Having misapprehended the claim of liberty there presented to it, and thus stating the claim to be whether there is a fundamental right to engage in consensual sodomy, the *Bowers* Court said: "Proscriptions against that conduct have ancient roots." In academic writings, and in many of the scholarly *amicus* briefs filed to assist the Court in this case, there are fundamental criticisms of the historical premises relied upon by the majority and concurring opinions in *Bowers*. We need not enter this debate in the attempt to reach a definitive historical judgment, but the following considerations counsel against adopting the definitive conclusions upon which *Bowers* placed such reliance.

At the outset it should be noted that there is no longstanding history in this country of laws directed at homosexual conduct as a distinct matter. Beginning in colonial times there were prohibitions of sodomy derived from the English criminal laws passed in the first instance by the Reformation Parliament of 1533. The English prohibition was understood to include relations between men and women as well as relations between men and men. Nineteenth-century commentators similarly read American sodomy, buggery, and crime-against-nature statutes as criminalizing certain relations between men and women and between men and men. The absence of legal prohibitions focusing on homosexual conduct may be explained in part by noting that according to some scholars the concept of the homosexual as a distinct category of person did not emerge until the late 19th century. Thus early American sodomy laws were not directed at homosexuals as such but instead sought to prohibit nonprocreative sexual activity more generally. This does not suggest approval of homosexual conduct. It does tend to show that this particular form of conduct was not thought of as a separate category from like conduct between heterosexual persons.

Laws prohibiting sodomy do not seem to have been enforced against consenting adults acting in private. A substantial number of sodomy prosecutions and convictions for which there are surviving records were for predatory acts against those who could not or did not consent, as in the case of a minor or the victim of an assault. As to these, one purpose for the prohibitions was to ensure there would be no lack of coverage if a predator committed a sexual assault that did not constitute rape as defined by the criminal law. Thus the model sodomy indictments presented in a 19th-century treatise, addressed the predatory acts of an adult man against a minor girl or minor boy. Instead of targeting relations between consenting adults in private, 19th-century sodomy prosecutions typically involved relations between men and minor girls or minor boys, relations between adults involving force, relations between adults implicating disparity in status, or relations between men and animals.

To the extent that there were any prosecutions for the acts in question, 19th-century evidence rules imposed a burden that would make a conviction more difficult to obtain even taking into account the problems always inherent in prosecuting consensual acts committed in private. Under then-prevailing standards, a man could not be convicted of sodomy based upon testimony of a consenting partner, because the partner was considered an accomplice. A partner's testimony, however, was admissible if he or she had not consented to the act or was a minor, and therefore incapable of consent. The rule may explain in part the infrequency of these prosecutions. In all events that infrequency makes it difficult to say that society approved of a rigorous and systematic punishment of the consensual acts committed in private and by adults. The longstanding criminal prohibition of homosexual sodomy upon which the *Bowers* decision placed such reliance is as consistent with a general condemnation of nonprocreative sex as it is with an established tradition of prosecuting acts because of their homosexual character.

The policy of punishing consenting adults for private acts was not much discussed in the early legal literature. We can infer that one reason for this was the very private nature of the conduct. Despite the absence of prosecutions, there may have been periods in which there was public criticism of homosexuals as such and an insistence that the criminal laws be enforced to discourage their practices. But far from possessing "ancient roots," American laws targeting same-sex couples did not develop until the last third of the 20th century. The reported decisions concerning the prosecution of consensual, homosexual sodomy between adults for the years 1880–1995 are not always clear in the details, but a significant number involved conduct in a public place.

It was not until the 1970's that any State singled out same-sex relations for criminal prosecution, and only nine States have done so. Post-*Bowers* even some of these States did not adhere to the policy of suppressing homosexual conduct. Over the course of the last decades, States with same-sex prohibitions have moved toward abolishing them.

In summary, the historical grounds relied upon in *Bowers* are more complex than the majority opinion and the concurring opinion by Chief Justice Burger indicate. Their historical premises are not without doubt and, at the very least, are overstated.

It must be acknowledged, of course, that the Court in *Bowers* was making the broader point that for centuries there have been powerful voices to condemn homosexual conduct as immoral. The condemnation has been shaped by religious beliefs, conceptions of right and acceptable behavior, and respect for the traditional family. For many persons these are not trivial concerns but profound and deep convictions accepted as ethical and moral principles to which they aspire and which thus determine the course of their lives. These considerations do not answer the question before us, however. The issue is whether the majority may use the power of the State to enforce these views on the whole society through operation of the criminal law. "Our obligation is to define the liberty of all, not to mandate our own moral code." *Planned Parenthood of Southeastern Pa. v. Casey,* (1992).

Chief Justice Burger joined the opinion for the Court in *Bowers* and further explained his views as follows: "Decisions of individuals relating to homosexual conduct have been subject to state intervention throughout the history of Western civilization. Condemnation of those practices is firmly rooted in Judeao-Christian moral and ethical standards." 478 U.S., at 196. As with Justice White's assumptions about history, scholarship casts some doubt on the sweeping nature of the statement by Chief Justice Burger as it pertains to private homosexual conduct between consenting adults. In all events we think that our laws and traditions in the past half century are of most relevance here. These references show an emerging awareness that liberty gives substantial protection to adult persons in deciding how to conduct their private lives in matters pertaining to sex. "[H]istory and tradition are the starting point but not in all cases the ending point of the substantive due process inquiry." *County of Sacramento v. Lewis*, (1998) (Kennedy, J., concurring).

This emerging recognition should have been apparent when *Bowers* was decided. In 1955 the American Law Institute promulgated the Model Penal Code and made clear that it did not recommend or provide for "criminal penalties for consensual sexual relations conducted in private." It justified its decision on three grounds: (1) The prohibitions undermined respect for the law by penalizing conduct many people engaged in; (2) the statutes regulated private conduct not harmful to others; and (3) the laws were arbitrarily enforced and thus invited the danger of blackmail. In 1961 Illinois changed its laws to conform to the Model Penal Code. Other States soon followed.

In *Bowers* the Court referred to the fact that before 1961 all 50 States had outlawed sodomy, and that at the time of the Court's decision 24 States and the District of Columbia had sodomy laws. Justice Powell pointed out that these prohibitions often were being ignored, however. Georgia, for instance, had not sought to enforce its law for decades.

The sweeping references by Chief Justice Burger to the history of Western civilization and to Judeo-Christian moral and ethical standards did not take account of other authorities pointing in an opposite direction. A committee advising the British Parliament recommended in 1957 repeal of laws punishing homosexual conduct. Parliament enacted the substance of those recommendations 10 years later.

Of even more importance, almost five years before *Bowers* was decided the European Court of Human Rights considered a case with parallels to *Bowers* and to today's case. An adult male resident in Northern Ireland alleged he was a practicing homosexual who desired to engage in consensual homosexual conduct. The laws of Northern Ireland forbade him that right. He alleged that he had been questioned, his home had been searched, and he feared criminal prosecution. The court held that the laws proscribing the conduct were invalid under the European Convention on Human Rights. Authoritative in all countries that are members of the Council of Europe (21 nations then, 45 nations now), the decision is at odds with the premise in *Bowers* that the claim put forward was insubstantial in our Western civilization.

In our own constitutional system the deficiencies in *Bowers* became even more apparent in the years following its announcement. The 25 States with laws prohibiting the relevant conduct referenced in the *Bowers* decision are reduced now to 13, of which 4 enforce their laws only against homosexual conduct. In those States where sodomy is still proscribed, whether for same-sex or heterosexual conduct, there is a pattern of nonenforcement with respect to consenting adults acting in private. The State of Texas admitted in 1994 that as of that date it had not prosecuted anyone under those circumstances.

Two principal cases decided after *Bowers* cast its holding into even more doubt. In *Planned Parenthood of Southeastern Pa. v. Casey,* the Court reaffirmed the substantive force of the liberty protected by the Due Process Clause. The *Casey* decision again confirmed that our laws and tradition afford constitutional protection to personal decisions relating to marriage, procreation, contraception, family relationships, child rearing, and education. In explaining the respect the Constitution demands for the autonomy of the person in making these choices, we stated as follows:

> These matters, involving the most intimate and personal choices a person may make in a lifetime, choices central to personal dignity and autonomy, are central to the liberty protected by the Fourteenth Amendment. At the heart of liberty is the right to define one's own concept of existence, of meaning, of the universe, and of the mystery of human life. Beliefs about these matters could not define the attributes of personhood were they formed under compulsion of the State. (Ibid.)

Persons in a homosexual relationship may seek autonomy for these purposes, just as heterosexual persons do. The decision in *Bowers* would deny them this right.

The second post-*Bowers* case of principal relevance is *Romer v. Evans,* (1996). There the Court struck down class-based legislation directed at homosexuals as a violation of the Equal Protection Clause. *Romer* invalidated an amendment to Colorado's constitution which named as a solitary class persons who were homosexuals, lesbians, or bisexual either by "orientation, conduct, practices or relationships," and deprived them of protection under state antidiscrimination laws. We concluded that the provision was "born of animosity toward the class of persons affected" and further that it had no rational relation to a legitimate governmental purpose.

As an alternative argument in this case, counsel for the petitioners and some *amici* contend that *Romer* provides the basis for declaring the Texas statute invalid under the Equal Protection Clause. That is a tenable argument, but we conclude the instant case requires us to address whether *Bowers* itself has continuing validity. Were we to hold the statute invalid under the Equal Protection Clause some might question whether a prohibition would be valid if drawn differently, say, to prohibit the conduct both between same-sex and different-sex participants.

Equality of treatment and the due process right to demand respect for conduct protected by the substantive guarantee of liberty are linked in important respects, and a decision on the latter point advances both interests. If protected conduct is made criminal and the law which does so remains unexamined for its substantive validity, its stigma might remain even if it were not enforceable as drawn for equal protection reasons. When homosexual conduct is made criminal by the law of the State, that declaration in and of itself is an invitation to subject homosexual persons to discrimination both in the public and in the private spheres. The central holding of *Bowers* has been brought in question by this case, and it should be addressed. Its continuance as precedent demeans the lives of homosexual persons.

The stigma this criminal statute imposes, moreover, is not trivial. The offense, to be sure, is but a class C misdemeanor, a minor offense in the Texas legal system. Still, it remains a criminal offense with all that imports for the dignity of the persons charged. The petitioners will bear on their record the history of their criminal convictions. Just this Term we rejected various challenges to state laws requiring the registration of sex offenders. We are advised that if Texas convicted an adult for private, consensual homosexual conduct under the statute here in question the convicted person would come within the registration laws of at least four States were he or she to be subject to their jurisdiction. This underscores the consequential nature of the punishment and the state-sponsored condemnation attendant to the criminal prohibition. Furthermore, the Texas criminal conviction carries with it the other collateral consequences always following a conviction, such as notations on job application forms, to mention but one example.

The foundations of *Bowers* have sustained serious erosion from our recent decisions in *Casey* and *Romer*. When our precedent has been thus weakened, criticism from other sources is of greater significance. In the United States criticism of *Bowers* has been substantial and continuing, disapproving of its reasoning in all respects, not just as to its historical assumptions. The courts of five different States have declined to follow it in interpreting provisions in their own state constitutions parallel to the Due Process Clause of the Fourteenth Amendment.

To the extent *Bowers* relied on values we share with a wider civilization, it should be noted that the reasoning and holding in *Bowers* have been rejected elsewhere. The European Court of Human Rights has followed not *Bowers* but its own decision in *Dudgeon v. United Kingdom*. Other nations, too, have taken action consistent with an affirmation of the protected right of homosexual adults to engage in intimate, consensual conduct. The right the petitioners seek in this case has been accepted as an integral part of human freedom in many other countries. There has been no showing that in this country the governmental interest in circumscribing personal choice is somehow more legitimate or urgent.

The doctrine of *stare decisis* is essential to the respect accorded to the judgments of the Court and to the stability of the law. It is not, however, an inexorable command. In *Casey* we noted that when a Court is asked to overrule a precedent recognizing a constitutional liberty interest, individual or societal reliance on the existence of that liberty cautions with particular strength against reversing course. The holding in *Bowers*, however, has not induced detrimental reliance comparable to some instances where recognized individual rights are involved. Indeed, there has been no individual or societal reliance on *Bowers* of the sort that could counsel against overturning its holding once there are compelling reasons to do so. *Bowers* itself causes uncertainty, for the precedents before and after its issuance contradict its central holding.

The rationale of *Bowers* does not withstand careful analysis. In his dissenting opinion in *Bowers* Justice Stevens came to these conclusions:

> Our prior cases make two propositions abundantly clear. First, the fact that the governing majority in a State has traditionally viewed a particular practice as immoral is not a sufficient reason for upholding a law prohibiting the practice; neither history nor tradition could save a law prohibiting miscegenation from constitutional attack. Second, individual decisions by married persons, concerning the intimacies of their physical relationship, even when not intended to produce offspring, are a form of "liberty" protected by the Due Process Clause of the Fourteenth Amendment. Moreover, this protection extends to intimate choices by unmarried as well as married persons. (footnotes and citations omitted)

Justice Stevens' analysis, in our view, should have been controlling in *Bowers* and should control here.

Bowers was not correct when it was decided, and it is not correct today. It ought not to remain binding precedent. *Bowers v. Hardwick* should be and now is overruled.

The present case does not involve minors. It does not involve persons who might be injured or coerced or who are situated in relationships where consent might not easily be refused. It does not involve public conduct or prostitution. It does not involve whether the government must give formal recognition to any relationship that homosexual persons seek to enter. The case does involve two adults who, with full and mutual consent from each other, engaged in sexual practices common to a homosexual lifestyle. The petitioners are entitled to respect for their private lives. The State cannot demean their existence or control their destiny by making their private sexual conduct a crime. Their right to liberty under the Due Process Clause gives them the full right to engage in their conduct without intervention of the government. "It is a promise of the Constitution that there is a realm of personal liberty which the government may not enter." The Texas statute furthers no legitimate state interest which can justify its intrusion into the personal and private life of the individual.

Had those who drew and ratified the Due Process Clauses of the Fifth Amendment or the Fourteenth Amendment known the components of liberty in its manifold possibilities, they might have been more specific. They did not presume to have this insight. They knew times can blind us to certain truths and later generations can see that laws once thought necessary and proper in fact serve only to oppress. As the Constitution endures, persons in every generation can invoke its principles in their own search for greater freedom.

The judgment of the Court of Appeals for the Texas Fourteenth District is reversed, and the case is remanded for further proceedings not inconsistent with this opinion.

It is so ordered.

8.4

Bush v. Gore (2000)

The Supreme Court decided, in a narrow ruling, that the State of Florida had to stop its recount of votes in the 2000 presidential election. The majority of the Court reasoned that there was no way that the state could count those votes in a manner consistent with existing interpretation of the Equal Protection Clause of the Fourteenth Amendment that all votes when possible need to be treated equally under the law. The decision effectively handed the election to George W. Bush.

In a scathing dissenting opinion, which is included here at the end of the majority opinion below, Justice Ruth Bader Ginsburg argued that the case was actually about federalism and not about the Fourteenth Amendment, and that the majority's decision trampled on Florida's right to run its own elections as guaranteed in the U.S. Constitution.

CERTIORARI TO THE FLORIDA SUPREME COURT

I

On December 8, 2000, the Supreme Court of Florida ordered that the Circuit Court of Leon County tabulate by hand 9,000 ballots in Miami-Dade County. It also ordered the inclusion in the certified vote totals of 215 votes identified in Palm Beach County and 168 votes identified in Miami-Dade County for Vice President Albert Gore, Jr., and Senator Joseph Lieberman, Democratic Candidates for President and Vice President. The Supreme Court noted that petitioner, Governor George W. Bush asserted that the net gain for Vice President Gore in Palm Beach County was 176 votes, and directed the Circuit Court to resolve that dispute on remand. . . . The court further held that relief would require manual recounts in all Florida counties where so-called "undervotes" had not been subject to manual tabulation. The court ordered all manual recounts to begin at once. Governor Bush and Richard Cheney, Republican Candidates for the Presidency and Vice Presidency, filed an emergency application for a stay of this mandate. On December 9, we granted the application, treated the application as a petition for a writ of certiorari, and granted certiorari.

The proceedings leading to the present controversy are discussed in some detail in our opinion in *Bush* v. *Palm Beach County Canvassing Bd. . . . (Bush I).* On November 8, 2000, the day following the Presidential election, the Florida Division of Elections reported that petitioner, Governor Bush, had received 2,909,135 votes, and respondent, Vice President Gore, had received 2,907,351 votes, a margin of 1,784 for Governor Bush. Because Governor Bush's margin of victory was less than "one-half of a percent . . . of the votes cast," an automatic machine recount was conducted under §102.141(4) of the election code, the results of which showed Governor Bush still winning the race but by a diminished margin. Vice President Gore then sought manual recounts in Volusia, Palm Beach, Broward, and Miami-Dade Counties, pursuant to Florida's election protest provisions. Fla. Stat. §102.166 (2000). A dispute arose concerning the deadline for local county canvassing boards to submit their returns to the Secretary of State (Secretary). The Secretary declined to waive the November 14 deadline imposed by statute. §§102.111, 102.112. The Florida Supreme Court, however, set the deadline at November 26. We granted certiorari and vacated the Florida Supreme Court's decision, finding considerable uncertainty as to the grounds on which it was based. . . . On December 11, the Florida Supreme Court issued a decision on remand reinstating that date.

On November 26, the Florida Elections Canvassing Commission certified the results of the election and declared Governor Bush the winner of Florida's 25 electoral votes. On November 27, Vice President Gore, pursuant to Florida's contest provisions, filed a complaint in Leon County Circuit Court contesting the certification. Fla. Stat. §102.168 (2000). He sought relief pursuant to §102.168(3)(c), which provides that "[r]eceipt of a number of illegal votes or rejection of a number of legal votes sufficient to change or place in doubt the result of the election" shall be grounds for a contest. The Circuit Court denied relief, stating that Vice President Gore failed to meet his burden of proof. He appealed to the First District Court of Appeal, which certified the matter to the Florida Supreme Court.

Accepting jurisdiction, the Florida Supreme Court affirmed in part and reversed in part. The court held that the Circuit Court had been correct to reject Vice President Gore's challenge to the results certified in Nassau County and his challenge to the Palm Beach County Canvassing Board's determination that 3,300 ballots cast in that county were not, in the statutory phrase, "legal votes."

The Supreme Court held that Vice President Gore had satisfied his burden of proof under §102.168(3)(c) with respect to his challenge to Miami-Dade County's failure to tabulate, by manual count, 9,000 ballots on which the machines had failed to detect a vote for President ("undervotes"). Noting the closeness of the election, the Court explained that "[o]n this record, there can be no question that there are legal votes within the 9,000 uncounted votes sufficient to place the results of this election in doubt." A "legal vote," as determined by the Supreme Court, is "one in which there is a 'clear indication of the intent of the voter.'" The court therefore ordered a hand recount of the 9,000 ballots in Miami-Dade County. Observing that the contest provisions vest broad discretion in the circuit judge to "provide any relief appropriate under such circumstances," Fla. Stat. §102.168(8) (2000), the Supreme Court further held that the Circuit Court could order "the Supervisor of Elections and the Canvassing Boards, as well as the necessary public officials, in all counties that have not conducted a manual recount or tabulation of the undervotes . . . to do so forthwith, said tabulation to take place in the individual counties where the ballots are located."

The Supreme Court also determined that both Palm Beach County and Miami-Dade County, in their earlier manual recounts, had identified a net gain of 215 and 168 legal votes for Vice President Gore. Rejecting the Circuit Court's conclusion that Palm Beach County lacked the authority to include the 215 net votes submitted past the November 26 deadline, the Supreme Court explained that the deadline was not intended to exclude votes identified after that date through ongoing manual recounts. As to Miami-Dade County, the Court concluded that although the 168 votes identified were the result of a partial recount, they were "legal votes [that] could change the outcome of the election." The Supreme Court therefore directed the Circuit Court to include those totals in the certified results, subject to resolution of the actual vote total from the Miami-Dade partial recount.

The petition presents the following questions: whether the Florida Supreme Court established new standards for resolving Presidential election contests, thereby violating Art. II, §1, cl. 2, of the United States Constitution and failing to comply with *3 U.S.C. § 5* and whether the use of standardless manual recounts violates the Equal Protection and Due Process Clauses. With respect to the equal protection question, we find a violation of the Equal Protection Clause.

II

A

The closeness of this election, and the multitude of legal challenges which have followed in its wake, have brought into sharp focus a common, if heretofore unnoticed, phenomenon. Nationwide statistics reveal that an estimated 2% of ballots cast do not register a vote for President for whatever reason, including deliberately choosing no candidate at all or some voter error, such as voting for two candidates or insufficiently marking a ballot. In certifying election results, the votes eligible for inclusion in the certification are the votes meeting the properly established legal requirements.

This case has shown that punch card balloting machines can produce an unfortunate number of ballots which are not punched in a clean, complete way by the voter. After the current counting, it is likely legislative bodies nationwide will examine ways to improve the mechanisms and machinery for voting.

B

The individual citizen has no federal constitutional right to vote for electors for the President of the United States unless and until the state legislature chooses a statewide election as the means to implement its power to appoint members of the Electoral College. U.S. Const., Art. II, §1. This is the source for the statement in *McPherson v. Blacker*, (1892), that the State legislature's power to select the manner for appointing electors is plenary; it may, if it so chooses, select the electors itself, which indeed was the manner used by State legislatures in several States for many years after the Framing of our Constitution. History has now favored the voter, and in each of the several States the citizens themselves vote for Presidential electors. When the state legislature vests the right to vote for President in its people, the right to vote as the legislature has prescribed is fundamental; and one source of its fundamental nature lies in the equal weight accorded to each vote and the equal dignity owed to each voter. The State, of course, after granting the franchise in the special context of Article II, can take back the power to appoint electors.

The right to vote is protected in more than the initial allocation of the franchise. Equal protection applies as well to the manner of its exercise. Having once granted the right to vote on equal terms, the State may not, by later arbitrary and disparate treatment, value one person's vote over that of another. It must be remembered that "the right of suffrage can be denied by a debasement or dilution of the weight of a citizen's vote just as effectively as by wholly prohibiting the free exercise of the franchise." *Reynolds v. Sims*, (1964).

There is no difference between the two sides of the present controversy on these basic propositions. Respondents say that the very purpose of vindicating the right to vote justifies the recount procedures now at issue. The question before us, however, is whether the recount procedures the Florida Supreme Court has adopted are consistent with its obligation to avoid arbitrary and disparate treatment of the members of its electorate.

Much of the controversy seems to revolve around ballot cards designed to be perforated by a stylus but which, either through error or deliberate omission, have not been perforated with sufficient precision for a machine to count them. In some cases a piece of the card-a chad-is hanging, say by two corners. In other cases there is no separation at all, just an indentation.

The Florida Supreme Court has ordered that the intent of the voter be discerned from such ballots. For purposes of resolving the equal protection challenge, it is not necessary to decide whether the Florida Supreme Court had the authority under the legislative scheme for resolving election disputes to define what a legal vote is and to mandate a manual recount implementing that definition. The recount mechanisms implemented in response to the decisions of the Florida Supreme Court do not satisfy the minimum requirement for nonarbitrary treatment of voters necessary to secure the fundamental right. Florida's basic command for the count of legally cast votes is to consider the "intent of the voter." This is unobjectionable as an abstract proposition and a starting principle. The problem inheres in the absence of specific standards to ensure its equal application. The formulation of uniform rules to determine intent based on these recurring circumstances is practicable and, we conclude, necessary.

The law does not refrain from searching for the intent of the actor in a multitude of circumstances; and in some cases the general command to ascertain intent is not susceptible to much further refinement. In this instance, however, the question is not whether to believe a witness but how to interpret the marks or holes or scratches on an inanimate object, a piece of cardboard or paper which, it is said, might not have registered as a vote during the machine count. The factfinder confronts a thing, not a person. The search for intent can be confined by specific rules designed to ensure uniform treatment.

The want of those rules here has led to unequal evaluation of ballots in various respects. As seems to have been acknowledged at oral argument, the standards for accepting or rejecting contested ballots might vary not only from county to county but indeed within a single county from one recount team to another.

The record provides some examples. A monitor in Miami-Dade County testified at trial that he observed that three members of the county canvassing board applied different standards in defining a legal vote. 3 Tr. 497, 499 (Dec. 3, 2000). And testimony at trial also revealed that at least one county changed its evaluative standards during the counting process. Palm Beach County, for example, began the process with a 1990 guideline which precluded counting completely attached chads, switched to a rule that considered a vote to be legal if any light could be seen through a chad, changed back to the 1990 rule, and then abandoned any pretense of a *per se* rule, only to have a court order that the county consider dimpled chads legal. This is not a process with sufficient guarantees of equal treatment.

An early case in our one person, one vote jurisprudence arose when a State accorded arbitrary and disparate treatment to voters in its different counties. The Court found a constitutional violation. We relied on these principles in the context of the Presidential selection process in *Moore v. Ogilvie*, (1969), where we invalidated a county-based procedure that diluted the influence of citizens in larger counties in the nominating process. There we observed that "[t]he idea that one group can be granted greater voting strength than another is hostile to the one man, one vote basis of our representative government."

The State Supreme Court ratified this uneven treatment. It mandated that the recount totals from two counties, Miami-Dade and Palm Beach, be included in the certified total. The court also appeared to hold *sub silentio* that the recount totals from Broward County, which were not completed until after the original November 14 certification by the Secretary of State, were to be considered part of the new certified vote totals even though the county certification was not contested by Vice President Gore. Yet each of the counties used varying standards to determine what was a legal vote. Broward County used a more forgiving standard than Palm Beach County, and uncovered almost three times as many new votes, a result markedly disproportionate to the difference in population between the counties.

In addition, the recounts in these three counties were not limited to so-called undervotes but extended to all of the ballots. The distinction has real consequences. A manual recount of all ballots identifies not only those ballots which show no vote but also those which contain more than one, the so-called overvotes. Neither category will be counted by the machine. This is not a trivial concern. At oral argument, respondents estimated there are as many as 110,000 overvotes statewide. As a result, the citizen whose ballot was not read by a machine because he failed to vote for a candidate in a way readable by a machine may still have his vote counted in a manual recount; on the other hand, the citizen who marks two candidates in a way discernable by the machine will not have the same opportunity to have his vote count, even if a manual examination of the ballot would reveal the requisite indicia of intent. Furthermore, the citizen who marks two candidates, only one of which is discernable by the machine, will have his vote counted even though it should have been read as an invalid ballot. The State Supreme Court's inclusion of vote counts based on these variant standards exemplifies concerns with the remedial processes that were under way.

That brings the analysis to yet a further equal protection problem. The votes certified by the court included a partial total from one county, Miami-Dade. The Florida Supreme Court's decision thus gives no assurance that the recounts included in a final certification must be complete. Indeed, it is respondent's submission that it would be consistent with the rules of the recount procedures to include whatever partial counts are done by the time of final certification, and we interpret the Florida Supreme Court's decision to permit this. This accommodation no doubt results from the truncated contest period established by the Florida Supreme Court in *Bush I*, at respondents' own urging. The press of time does not diminish the constitutional concern. A desire for speed is not a general excuse for ignoring equal protection guarantees.

In addition to these difficulties the actual process by which the votes were to be counted under the Florida Supreme Court's decision raises further concerns. That order did not specify who would recount the ballots. The county canvassing boards were forced to pull together ad hoc teams comprised of judges from various Circuits who had no previous training in handling and interpreting ballots. Furthermore, while others were permitted to observe, they were prohibited from objecting during the recount.

The recount process, in its features here described, is inconsistent with the minimum procedures necessary to protect the fundamental right of each voter in the special instance of a statewide recount under the authority of a single state judicial officer. Our consideration is limited to the present circumstances, for the problem of equal protection in election processes generally presents many complexities.

The question before the Court is not whether local entities, in the exercise of their expertise, may develop different systems for implementing elections. Instead, we are presented with a situation where a state court with the power to assure uniformity has ordered a statewide recount with minimal procedural safeguards. When a court orders a statewide remedy, there must be at least some assurance that the rudimentary requirements of equal treatment and fundamental fairness are satisfied.

Given the Court's assessment that the recount process underway was probably being conducted in an unconstitutional manner, the Court stayed the order directing the recount so it could hear this case and render an expedited decision. The contest provision, as it was mandated by the State Supreme Court, is not well calculated to sustain the confidence that all citizens must have in the outcome of elections. The State has not shown that its procedures include the necessary safeguards. The problem, for instance, of the estimated 110,000 overvotes has not been addressed, although Chief Justice Wells called attention to the concern in his dissenting opinion.

Upon due consideration of the difficulties identified to this point, it is obvious that the recount cannot be conducted in compliance with the requirements of equal protection and due process without substantial additional work. It would require not only the adoption (after opportunity for argument) of adequate statewide standards for determining what is a legal vote, and practicable procedures to implement them, but also orderly judicial review of any disputed matters that might arise. In addition, the Secretary of State has advised that the recount of only a portion of the ballots requires that the vote tabulation equipment be used to screen out undervotes, a function for which the machines were not designed. If a recount of overvotes were also required, perhaps even a second screening would be necessary. Use of the equipment for this purpose, and any new software developed for it, would have to be evaluated for accuracy by the Secretary of State, as required by Fla. Stat. §101.015 (2000).

The Supreme Court of Florida has said that the legislature intended the State's electors to "participat[e] fully in the federal electoral process," as provided in *3 U.S.C. § 5.*___ That statute, in turn, requires that any controversy or contest that is designed to lead to a conclusive selection of electors be completed by December 12. That date is upon us, and there is no recount procedure in place under the State Supreme Court's order that comports with minimal constitutional standards. Because it is evident that any recount seeking to meet the December 12 date will be unconstitutional for the reasons we have discussed, we reverse the judgment of the Supreme Court of Florida ordering a recount to proceed.

Seven Justices of the Court agree that there are constitutional problems with the recount ordered by the Florida Supreme Court that demand a remedy. The only disagreement is as to the remedy. Because the Florida Supreme Court has said that the Florida Legislature intended to obtain the safe-harbor benefits of *3 U.S.C. § 5* Justice Breyer's proposed remedy-remanding to the Florida Supreme Court for its ordering of a constitutionally proper contest until December 18-contemplates action in violation of the Florida election code, and hence could not be part of an "appropriate" order authorized by Fla. Stat. §102.168(8) (2000).

None are more conscious of the vital limits on judicial authority than are the members of this Court, and none stand more in admiration of the Constitution's design to leave the selection of the President to the people, through their legislatures, and to the political sphere. When contending parties invoke the process of the courts, however, it becomes our unsought responsibility to resolve the federal and constitutional issues the judicial system has been forced to confront.

The judgment of the Supreme Court of Florida is reversed, and the case is remanded for further proceedings not inconsistent with this opinion.

Pursuant to this Court's Rule 45.2, the Clerk is directed to issue the mandate in this case forthwith.

It is so ordered.

Justice Ginsburg, with whom Justice Stevens joins, and with whom Justice Souter and Justice Breyer join as to Part I, dissenting.

I

The Chief Justice acknowledges that provisions of Florida's Election Code "may well admit of more than one interpretation." *Ante*, at 3. But instead of respecting the state high court's province to say what the State's Election Code means, The Chief Justice maintains that Florida's Supreme Court has veered so far from the ordinary practice of judicial review that what it did cannot properly be called judging. My colleagues have offered a reasonable construction of Florida's law. Their construction coincides with the view of one of Florida's seven Supreme Court justices. I might join The Chief Justice were it my commission to interpret Florida law. But disagreement with the Florida court's interpretation of its own State's law does not warrant the conclusion that the justices of that court have legislated. There is no cause here to believe that the members of Florida's high court have done less than "their mortal best to discharge their oath of office," *Sumner v. Mata*, (1981), and no cause to upset their reasoned interpretation of Florida law.

This Court more than occasionally affirms statutory, and even constitutional, interpretations with which it disagrees. For example, when reviewing challenges to administrative agencies' interpretations of laws they implement, we defer to the agencies unless their interpretation violates "the unambiguously expressed intent of Congress." *Chevron U.S. A. Inc. v. Natural Resources Defense Council, Inc.*, (1984). We do so in the face of the declaration in Article I of the United States Constitution that "All legislative Powers herein granted shall be vested in a Congress of the United States." Surely the Constitution does not call upon us to pay more respect to a federal administrative agency's construction of federal law than to a state high court's interpretation of its own state's law. And not uncommonly, we let stand state-court interpretations of *federal* law with which we might disagree. Notably, in the habeas context, the Court adheres to the view that "there is 'no intrinsic reason why the fact that a man is a federal judge should make him more competent, or conscientious, or learned with respect to [federal law] than his neighbor in the state courthouse.'" *Stone v. Powell*, 35 (1976) (quoting Bator, Finality in Criminal Law and Federal Habeas Corpus For State (1963)). . . .

No doubt there are cases in which the proper application of federal law may hinge on interpretations of state law. Unavoidably, this Court must sometimes examine state law in order to protect federal rights. But we have dealt with such cases ever mindful of the full measure of respect we owe to interpretations of state law by a State's highest court. In the Contract Clause case, *General Motors Corp. v. Romein*, (1992), for example, we said that although "ultimately we are bound to decide for ourselves whether a contract was made," the Court "accord[s] respectful consideration and great weight to the views of the State's highest court." And in *Central Union Telephone Co. v. Edwardsville*, (1925), we upheld the Illinois Supreme Court's interpretation of a state waiver rule, even though that interpretation resulted in the forfeiture of federal constitutional rights. Refusing to supplant Illinois law with a federal definition of waiver, we explained that the state court's declaration "should bind us unless so unfair or unreasonable in its application to those asserting a federal right as to obstruct it."

In deferring to state courts on matters of state law, we appropriately recognize that this Court acts as an "'outside[r]' lacking the common exposure to local law which comes from sitting in the jurisdiction." *Lehman Brothers v. Schein*, (1974). That recognition has sometimes prompted us to resolve doubts about the meaning of state law by certifying issues to a State's highest court, even when federal rights are at stake. Notwithstanding our authority to decide issues of state law underlying federal claims, we have used the certification devise to afford state high courts an opportunity to inform us on matters of their own State's law because such restraint "helps build a cooperative judicial federalism."

Just last Term, in *Fiore v. White* (1999), we took advantage of Pennsylvania's certification procedure. In that case, a state prisoner brought a federal habeas action claiming that the State had failed to prove an essential element of his charged offense in violation of the Due Process Clause. Instead of resolving the state-law question on which the federal claim depended, we certified the question to the Pennsylvania Supreme Court for that court to "help determine the proper state-law predicate for our determination of the federal constitutional questions raised." The Chief Justice's willingness to *reverse* the Florida Supreme Court's interpretation of Florida law in this case is at least in tension with our reluctance in *Fiore* even to interpret Pennsylvania law before seeking instruction from the Pennsylvania Supreme Court. I would have thought the "cautious approach" we counsel when federal courts address matters of state law, *Arizonans*, and our commitment to "build[ing] cooperative judicial federalism," *Lehman Brothers*, demanded greater restraint.

Rarely has this Court rejected outright an interpretation of state law by a state high court. *Fairfax's Devisee v. Hunter's Lessee*, (1813), *NAACP* v. *Alabama ex rel. Patterson*, (1958), and *Bouie v. City of Columbia*, (1964), cited by The Chief Justice, are three such rare instances. But those cases are embedded in historical contexts hardly comparable to the situation here. *Fairfax's Devisee*, which held that the Virginia Court of Appeals had misconstrued its own forfeiture laws to deprive a British subject of lands secured to him by federal treaties, occurred amidst vociferous States' rights attacks on the Marshall Court. The Virginia court refused to obey this Court's *Fairfax's Devisee* mandate to enter judgment for the British subject's successor in interest. That refusal led to the Court's pathmarking decision in *Martin v. Hunter's Lessee*, (1816). *Patterson*, a case decided three months after *Cooper v. Aaron*, (1958), in the face of Southern resistance to the civil rights movement, held that the Alabama Supreme Court had irregularly applied its own procedural rules to deny review of a contempt order against the NAACP arising from its refusal to disclose membership lists. We said that "our jurisdiction is not defeated if the nonfederal ground relied on by the state court is without any fair or substantial support." *Bouie*, stemming from a lunch counter "sit-in" at the height of the civil rights movement, held that the South Carolina Supreme Court's construction of its trespass laws—criminalizing conduct not covered by the text of an otherwise clear statute—was "unforeseeable" and thus violated due process when applied retroactively to the petitioners.

The Chief Justice's casual citation of these cases might lead one to believe they are part of a larger collection of cases in which we said that the Constitution impelled us to train a skeptical eye on a state court's portrayal of state law. But one would be hard pressed, I think, to find additional cases that fit the mold. As Justice Breyer convincingly explains, this case involves nothing close to the kind of recalcitrance by a state high court that warrants extraordinary action by this Court. The Florida Supreme Court concluded that counting every legal vote was the overriding concern of the Florida Legislature when it enacted the State's Election Code. The court surely should not be bracketed with state high courts of the Jim Crow South.

The Chief Justice says that Article II, by providing that state legislatures shall direct the manner of appointing electors, authorizes federal superintendence over the relationship between state courts and state legislatures, and licenses a departure from the usual deference we give to state court interpretations of state law. . . . The Framers of our Constitution, however, understood that in a republican government, the judiciary would construe the legislature's enactments. In light of the constitutional guarantee to States of a "Republican Form of Government," U.S. Const., Art. IV, §4, Article II can hardly be read to invite this Court to disrupt a State's republican regime. Yet The Chief Justice today would reach out to do just that. By holding that Article II requires our revision of a state court's construction of state laws in order to protect one organ of the State from another, The Chief Justice contradicts the basic principle that a State may organize itself as it sees fit. Article II does not call for the scrutiny undertaken by this Court.

The extraordinary setting of this case has obscured the ordinary principle that dictates its proper resolution: Federal courts defer to state high courts' interpretations of their state's own law. This principle reflects the core of federalism, on which all agree. "The Framers split the atom of sovereignty. It was the genius of their idea that our citizens would have two political capacities, one state and one federal, each protected from incursion by the other." *Saenz v. Roe*, (1999). The Chief Justice's solicitude for the Florida Legislature comes at the expense of the more fundamental solicitude we owe to the legislature's sovereign. U.S. Const., Art. II, §1, cl. 2 ("Each *State* shall appoint, in such Manner as the Legislature *thereof* may direct," the electors for President and Vice President) (emphasis added).[1] Were the other members of this Court as mindful as they generally are of our system of dual sovereignty, they would affirm the judgment of the Florida Supreme Court.

II

I agree with Justice Stevens that petitioners have not presented a substantial equal protection claim. Ideally, perfection would be the appropriate standard for judging the recount. But we live in an imperfect world, one in which thousands of votes have not been counted. I cannot agree that the recount adopted by the Florida court, flawed as it may be, would yield a result any less fair or precise than the certification that preceded that recount.

Even if there were an equal protection violation, I would agree with Justice Stevens, Justice Souter, and Justice Breyer that the Court's concern about "the December 12 deadline," is misplaced. Time is short in part because of the Court's entry of a stay on December 9, several hours after an able circuit judge in Leon County had begun to superintend the recount process. More fundamentally, the Court's reluctance to let the recount go forward-despite its suggestion that "[t]he search for intent can be confined by specific rules designed to ensure uniform treatment," *ante*, at 8–ultimately turns on its own judgment about the practical realities of implementing a recount, not the judgment of those much closer to the process.

Equally important, as Justice Breyer explains, the December 12 "deadline" for bringing Florida's electoral votes into *3 U.S.C. § 5*'s safe harbor lacks the significance the Court assigns it. Were that date to pass, Florida would still be entitled to deliver electoral votes Congress *must* count unless both Houses find that the votes "ha[d] not been . . . regularly given." *3 U.S.C. § 15*. The statute identifies other significant dates. But none of these dates has ultimate significance in light of Congress' detailed provisions for determining, on "the sixth day of January," the validity of electoral votes. §15.

The Court assumes that time will not permit "orderly judicial review of any disputed matters that might arise." But no one has doubted the good faith and diligence with which Florida election officials, attorneys for all sides of this controversy, and the courts of law have performed their duties. Notably, the Florida Supreme Court has produced two substantial opinions within 29 hours of oral argument. In sum, the Court's conclusion that a constitutionally adequate recount is impractical is a prophecy the Court's own judgment will not allow to be tested. Such an untested prophecy should not decide the Presidency of the United States.

I dissent.

NOTES

1. "[B]ecause the Framers recognized that state power and identity were essential parts of the federal balance, see The Federalist No. 39, the Constitution is solicitous of the prerogatives of the States, even in an otherwise sovereign federal province. The Constitution . . . grants States certain powers over the times, places, and manner of federal elections (subject to congressional revision), Art. I, §4, cl. 1 . . . , and allows States to appoint electors for the President, Art. II, §1, cl. 2." *U.S. Term Limits, Inc. v. Thornton, 514 U.S. 779*, 841–842 (1995) (Kennedy, J., concurring).

8.5

LAWRENCE BAUM

From *Judges and Their Audiences*

*Judges, like everyone else, seek the approval of others they respect. To under-
stand a given judge's behavior, Baum argues, we need to pay attention to the
legal audiences the judge chooses to play to. If a judge runs in conservative legal
circles and wants to be nominated to a higher court by a conservative president,
he or she will want to be consistent in pursuing approval from that audience.
Vice versa for liberal judges. In a judge's career, the early choice of legal and
intellectual audiences is key.*

2. JUDGING AS SELF-PRESENTATION

In their essence, the premises of my inquiry into judges and their audiences
are simple:

1. People want to be liked and respected by others who are important to
   them.
2. The desire to be liked and respected affects people's behavior.
3. In these respects, judges are people.

■   ■   ■

General implications of an audience-based perspective

. . . As with other public officials, the selection processes that determine
which people become judges tend to favor those with an especially strong
interest in the esteem of other people. Lawyers who become judges often give
up substantial income to do so. To varying degrees they accept constraints on
their activities as well. The prestige of being a judge is one of the benefits that
outweigh these costs for those who pursue or accept judicial positions. Further, gregarious people who are effective in social settings have an advantage
in securing judgeships.

This recruitment pattern should be especially pronounced at higher levels
of the judiciary. On average, the sacrifice of income for enhanced prestige is
greatest for federal appellate judges. Undoubtedly, the power to shape legal
policy is an important attraction for many judges on higher courts. But the
opportunity to win deference and admiration may be even more important.

If the people who become judges care more about the esteem of others than do most other people, that difference will affect their behavior on the bench. The same traits that make judgeships especially attractive to certain people give them a strong interest in how their actions as judges are evaluated. If those evaluations are positive, they provide an individualized recognition that goes beyond the diffuse prestige attached to judgeships.

The psychological scholarship has a second implication that diverges sharply from the dominant models of judicial behavior. These models typically allow for variation among judges in the bases for their choices, but that variation exists only because courts vary in institutional characteristics that affect judges' instrumental motives. For instance, judges who hold life terms and those who regularly face the electorate are expected to give different weights to public opinion in reaching decisions. In these models, however, it is assumed that judges in the same institutional situations—judges on a particular court or at the same court level—respond to the same mixes of influences.

This assumption is questionable if judges have personal motives to seek approval from people outside their courts.[1] The audiences that judges care most about depend on their social identities, identities that inevitably differ from judge to judge. Thus two judges whose objective situations are identical may have different sets of personal audiences, so that they act on different mixes of influences.

■   ■   ■

Motives for judicial self-presentation

The ways that judges choose to present themselves could reflect a wide array of motives. Of the possible instrumental motives, the most powerful is probably judges' interest in advancing their career goals. When elected judges publicize popular decisions or seek to justify unpopular rulings, they usually have their eye on the electorate. In one of the episodes described at the beginning, . . . a federal judge may have used his opinions to enhance his prospects for promotion to the Supreme Court. Some appearances in public forums are intended to serve the same purposes.

A second instrumental motive that can underlie self-presentation is an effort to advance a judge's legal or policy goals, an effort that fits into strategic models of judicial behavior. Inherent in the writing of opinions for a court is an effort to win support for a decision. Effective opinions might enhance the prospects for compliance with a decision or reduce the chances of reversal by a higher court. Opinion writers may have the additional aim of underlining a court's adherence to legal norms in order to maintain support for the court as an institution. Writers of minority opinions may seek to garner support for their positions outside of their court and, in the long run, within it.

Expressions outside court can also be used to win support for judges' conceptions of good judicial policy. That is one purpose of extracurricular expressions by Supreme Court justices. One noteworthy example is the law review article in which Justice William Brennan (1977) advocated that state supreme courts use their own constitutions to broaden legal support for civil liberties.

These instrumental motives undoubtedly account for much of what judges do in presenting themselves to their audiences. This is especially true of elected judges who have a strong stake in keeping their offices. But an explanation of judicial self-presentation based on these motives would be highly incomplete. The limits of an instrumental explanation can be identified by thinking about judges as opinion writers.

Consider, for example, the career goals of Samuel Kent and Alex Kozinski. Almost certainly, each would welcome promotion to a higher federal court. "Kozinski used to joke about being a member of OOPPSSCA, the Organization of People Patiently Seeking Supreme Court Appointments" (Bazelon 2004, 32). Their flamboyant expressions in opinions enhance their visibility, and visibility can help in winning promotion. Even so, their opinions probably work against their promotion. Like other judges who employ humor at the expense of litigants or lawyers, Judge Kent risks annoying both the targets of his words and others who disapprove of their tone. Judge Kozinski's free expression of his views in opinions and out of court makes him controversial and probably rules him out as a candidate for the Supreme Court. He is aware of that effect, explaining,

> I decided a long time ago that it ain't worth it. If I don't live the job for all it's worth, I cheat myself and the public. So I write my opinions and I try to say something. (Bazelon 2004, 32)

Justice Scalia's opinions illustrate the limits of a policy-based explanation of self-presentation. Scalia's strongly worded dissents might advance his conception of good legal policy by winning over his colleagues and legal audiences outside the Court. In this way his opinions could be part of a strategy for shaping the law. Judge Kozinski, who knows Scalia personally, argued early in Scalia's Supreme Court tenure that he was creating the conditions for long-term influence over legal doctrine (Kozinski 1991, 1586–91).

Yet Scalia could write forceful opinions without the vitriolic language that he frequently includes in them. It is difficult to see how that language enhances his influence. Indeed, it carries the risk of alienating the colleagues at whom it is directed as well as other judges who find it unseemly. Scalia himself surely recognizes that reality. A justice who was concerned solely with advancing policy goals would write opinions in ways that minimized this risk.

If these judges do not advance their instrumental goals through the ways they present themselves in opinions, what do they gain? Several Supreme Court justices have provided a sense of the benefits when they discuss dissenting opinions. Oliver Wendell Holmes wrote that "one of the advantages of a dissent is that one can say what one thinks without having to blunt the edges and cut off the corners to suit someone else" (Howe 1953, 646–67). Similarly, Justice Blackmun said that it was "fun to dissent. . . . You have all the enjoyment without the responsibility" (Barbash and Kamen 1984, A42; see also Murphy 2003, 402). Justice Scalia (1994, 42; emphasis in original) was especially eloquent on this point:

> To be able to write an opinion solely for oneself, without the need to accommodate, to any degree whatever, the more-or-less differing views of one's colleagues; to address precisely the points of law that one considers important and *no others*; to express precisely the degree of quibble, or foreboding, or disbelief, or indignation that one believes the majority's disposition should engender—that is indeed an unparalleled pleasure.[2]

If he chose, Scalia could write such opinions and then file them for his own future reference rather than disseminating them through the *United States Reports*. Clearly, part of his pleasure derives from the knowledge that other people will read what he writes. Indeed, Scalia's style of opinion writing has won him an admiring audience,[3] an audience that he clearly enjoys (see Tushnet 2005, 147).

The same can be said of the other judges whose opinions I excerpted. Judge Kent undoubtedly enjoys injecting humor into his opinions, regardless of any audience, but his writing style has also attracted attention in the legal community—attention that, undoubtedly, he also enjoys (e.g., Cox 2001). In combination with his off-the-court expressions, Judge Kozinski's opinions have given him an unusual degree of celebrity for a lower-court judge and the kind of reputation that he seeks.[4]

Justice Frankfurter used opinions as a means to reinforce the image of a self-denying judge devoted to principle over personal preferences (Hirsch 1981). This self-concept was linked with his social identity, in that Frankfurter expected it to win approval from those whose approval he most valued. That self-concept also strengthened his identification with the judges, living and dead, whom he admired and treated as his peer group: Learned Hand, Louis Brandeis, and Oliver Wendell Holmes (Hirsch 1981, 129, 181–82).

Nor can instrumental motives fully explain judges' self-presentation off the bench. This is especially true of judges whose positions are secure, so that they need not campaign to maintain those positions. It is true that judges sometimes can advance their policy goals through their off-the-court speaking or writing. Justice Brennan's advocacy of action by state courts to expand civil liberties probably helped to stimulate that action. But on the whole, judges' off-the-court expressions do not have much impact on public policy. Occasionally they even work against judges' chances to achieve their policy goals. Justice Scalia had to recuse himself from *Elk Grove v. Newdow*, the pledge of allegiance case. Judge Jackson's interviews during the Microsoft case resulted in his removal from the case by the court of appeals (*United States v. Microsoft Corporation*, 2001). Commitments to off-the-bench activities have another cost that is more prosaic but more pervasive: judges who spend substantial time on nonjudicial pursuits have less time to advance their policy positions through their court work.

On the whole, then, judges' willingness to expend this time is better understood in personal rather than instrumental terms. Judges seek approval, and at a deeper level they seek to establish self-concepts that they find pleasing. In their activities off the bench, as in their judicial work, they present themselves to audiences they care about in an effort to achieve those fundamental ends.

Audiences and Judicial Behavior

If judges seek the regard of their personal audiences, it is certainly plausible that this goal influences their behavior as decision makers. Indeed, . . . this is the view of some scholars and observers of the courts. Sheldon Goldman and Austin Sarat (1977, 336) argued that judges are moved by their sense of "what will be acceptable to . . . those people whom the judge respects and looks to for approval." Frank Askin, a litigating attorney, made the same point in stronger form:

> Even lifetime-appointed Supreme Court justices have a constituency to answer to: the bar from which they come, the social and cultural elite with whom they mix; and the general public, whose acclaim they desire. Nobody likes to be a pariah. Faced with disapproval from close associates and disdain from others, only the hardiest ideologue remains true to the faith. (1997, 202)

The dominant models of judicial behavior implicitly disagree with this view, in that they give no consideration to judges' interest in esteem for its own sake. In research based on these models, the existence of this influence on judges' choices is not refuted; it simply is not considered. Thus it is necessary to anticipate possible arguments against a linkage between an interest in approval and judicial behavior.

Two arguments stand out. The first rests on a distinction between judges' self-presentation and the positions they take in decisions. The second rests on the premise that judges can choose the audiences they seek to impress, so that their audiences are endogenous to their preferences. Addressing these arguments provides a way to probe the links between personal audiences and judicial behavior.

Self-presentation and decision making

Even those who agree that judges seek the approval of their personal audiences could argue that this interest in approval has no impact on their choices as decision makers. According to this argument, judges act on the basis of other goals when they adopt their positions in cases. In the dominant models of judicial behavior, the primary (or only) goal is to make good policy or some combination of good law and good policy. Only after judges have chosen their positions do they present those positions and themselves in ways intended to appeal to their personal audiences.

Thus the judge who reaches a decision that will disappoint important audiences could use an opinion to reduce that disappointment. Anthony Kennedy joined in the Supreme Court's decision to strike down the Texas statute prohibiting flag burning in *Texas v. Johnson* (1989). He then wrote a short concurring opinion that declared his unhappiness about helping to let Gregory Johnson go free: "The hard fact is that sometimes we must make decisions we do not like" (420). Presumably, Kennedy's vote reflected his conception of good legal policy in this case. His opinion can be interpreted as an effort to limit the negative reactions to his vote among audiences that he cared about, ranging from personal friends to the segment of the public that became aware of his position.

From the same perspective, Felix Frankfurter might be considered someone who used opinions and other forms of communication to shore up his image among his old associates in the legal and political communities. Perhaps Frankfurter became a conservative on judicial protection of civil liberties early in his Supreme Court tenure, a stance reflected in his votes on case outcomes. Yet he wanted to be perceived as someone who held his liberal beliefs in check because of his commitment to judicial restraint. Thus he explained his votes in that way in his opinions and other communications. Among students of judicial behavior, this is a widely accepted interpretation of Frankfurter's behavior.

These interpretations of the two justices' behavior may well be accurate. Undoubtedly, some judges in some situations take personal audiences into account only after they reach decisions based on other motives. But this does not mean that there is usually such a clear separation between decision making and self-presentation. To the contrary, there are reasons to doubt that such a clear separation exists.

One reason is the limited strength of good legal policy as a goal. It should be kept in mind that judges seldom gain anything concrete by trying to achieve good legal policy. For this reason it seems doubtful that their concern with the content of legal policy is sufficiently powerful to exclude other considerations from the decision-making process.

Like good legal policy, the esteem of personal audiences in itself is not a source of concrete benefits. But to be liked and respected is of fundamental importance to people. In light of this reality, there is no reason to think that judges invariably give precedence to legal policy over the approval of others. When there is a direct trade-off between the two kinds of goals, judges could be expected to depart from their most preferred policies on some occasions in order to appeal to audiences they care about.[5]

For students of judicial behavior, this should not be all that strange an idea. Within the framework of strategic models it seems natural—even inevitable—that judges depart from their most preferred policy positions when doing so would advance their careers or their policy goals. It is at least equally natural for judges to modify their positions when their motives are personal rather than instrumental.

■ ■ ■

But judges' choices are expressive in their own way, because votes and opinions link judges to particular values and to other people who hold those values. The ultimate impact of a decision is uncertain and contingent; in contrast, a judge's choice between alternative positions is direct. Moreover, by taking positions, judges align themselves implicitly with groups whose positions are consistent with theirs. Kuran's (1995, 30–31) concept of reputational utility is a reminder that the very publicness of judges' choices enhances this function: unlike citizens' votes in mass elections, judges' votes and opinions in cases are known to their audiences.

In the discussion thus far, I have depicted judges who make deliberate trade-offs between the approval of personal audiences and other considerations. The reality is more complicated than that image in at least two ways. First, the desire for esteem is not fully parallel with judges' legal and policy goals or entirely separate from those goals. For instance, judges' social identities may underlie their interest in making good legal policy or condition the impact of that interest on their choices. Of course, judges' preferences themselves are shaped by their reference groups; attitudes develop within a social context.

Second, the impact of judges' social identities on their choices generally does not result from a fully conscious process. When judges try to appeal to audiences for instrumental reasons, that response is usually deliberate: they decide to take a particular position in a case in order to avoid retaliation from Congress or the disapproval of voters. But personal motives for responses to audiences typically operate more subtly and at deeper levels. In general, judges who take certain positions to solidify their ties with a social group are not fully aware of that motive and its effects on their behavior.

These complications suggest why there could not be a sharp line between judges' self-presentation to their personal audiences and their choices in cases. If judges' interest in approval is intertwined with other motives, and if it is not fully conscious, this interest inevitably affects what judges decide and not just how they depict what they decide.

Choosing audiences

Even if it is clear that judges' interest in esteem affects their choices, the strength of this effect can be debated. A second possible argument against a linkage between personal audiences and judicial behavior is that these audiences typically want the same things that judges themselves want. According to this argument, judges choose to link their social identities with individuals and groups whose preferences are similar to their own. As a result, judicial behavior that is consistent with judges' own preferences also enhances regard for them among their most important audiences, so judges' social identities exert little independent impact on their choices.

This line of analysis clearly has some validity. People with strong views about policy, especially people who are politically active, tend to gravitate toward reference groups whose members have similar views. During their tenure on the bench judges can continue to form ties with like-minded audiences. And no matter what positions a judge takes, the judge will find people and groups who applaud those positions. If Clarence Thomas is unlikely to win accolades from the American Civil Liberties Union, he can expect an enthusiastic welcome from the Federalist Society.

But the validity of this argument is limited by two realities. First, people do not have complete freedom to choose the audiences that are important to them, to select a particular social identity. People who become judges may be strongly oriented toward a local community or a segment of the legal profession for reasons that have little to do with their self-interest or their policy preferences. Those kinds of identifications can be difficult to shed, even when they create cross-pressures that complicate decision making.

Further, judges sometimes have limited choices among audiences when they seek a particular kind of approval. The federal judge who wants to be well regarded by legal scholars must take legal academia as it is. The same is true of the Supreme Court justice who seeks favorable coverage from the reporters who cover the Court. If legal scholars or Supreme Court reporters lean toward certain positions on the issues the Court addresses, that leaning does not necessarily coincide with a justices' own preferences.

The second reality is that reference groups can influence a judge even when their preferences are similar. A judge and a legal audience may share an inclination toward decisions that adhere to certain standards of legal interpretation. Similarly, a judge and a policy-oriented audience may share a commitment to conservative legal policies. On the surface, audiences of this type would seem to have no independent impact on a judge's choices; judges who seek to please them need do only what they wanted to do anyway.

But such audiences still exert influence by reinforcing tendencies in judges' behavior. Awareness of a legal audience can strengthen a judge's commitment to good legal interpretation as a goal and thereby reduce the weight of policy considerations that might compete with this goal. Judges who identify with a politically liberal audience may feel subtle pressures from that audience against deviation from liberal positions in particular cases. Not surprisingly, consistency between an individual's attitudes and behavior is enhanced by support for those attitudes from important reference groups (Terry, Hogg, and Duck 1999). For this reason even a judge whose audiences perfectly mirror the judge's preferences could be influenced by an interest in maintaining the approval of those audiences.

An audience that accords with a judge's preferences can have more fundamental effects on that judge's behavior. Most important, judges' interest in the approval of their personal audiences helps to solve the motivational problem: judges gain nothing concrete by trying to achieve good legal policy, so why should they devote themselves to this goal? At least part of the answer is that such devotion can serve judges' interest in establishing a desired image with their audiences and ultimately with themselves. Achieving a desired self-image is not a tangible self-interest, but few things are so important to people. It follows that judges may be willing to work to achieve what they see as good law or good policy, even to undertake some of the difficult labor required by strategic models, if they think those efforts foster the image they want.

Further, judges' links with their audiences help to determine their choices between good law and good policy and between sincere and strategic behavior in the pursuit of those goals. For that matter, personal audiences may encourage judges to pursue goals other than advancing good legal policy. And all these effects can occur even if judges and their reference groups agree fully about what constitutes good law or good policy.

Taking an audience-based perspective

If judges' interest in the esteem of their audiences affects their choices as decision makers, then much can be gained from thinking about judicial behavior from the perspective of judges' audiences. One way to frame that inquiry is in terms of two questions.

First, for a single judge or a set of judges in a particular situation, what audiences are likely to be salient? The answer to this question depends on the attributes of both judges and the situations in which they make decisions. Inferences about the answer can be made on the basis of what we know about human motivation in general, about the experiences and expressions of individual judges and broader groups of judges, and about the opportunities and constraints created by the contexts in which they work. For example, a judge whose career has been entirely within the legal community is likely to identify with that community. On a different level, the requirement that most judges win elections to retain their positions orients judges toward the voting public.

Second, how is a judge's concern with approval from those audiences likely to affect the judge's behavior? The answer rests in part on what is valued by the people who constitute an audience and thus what kinds of behavior would win their approval. It also depends on the salience of a particular audience, both in absolute terms and relative to other audiences. Winning the esteem of audiences is a matter of fundamental importance to human beings; even so, it is not the only thing people want. Further, audiences are not equal in importance. I have emphasized the distinction between instrumental and personal audiences. Those audiences whose esteem is important to judges chiefly for personal reasons are typically more salient and thus have greater potential impact on judicial behavior.

■   ■   ■

The final and most fundamental point is on a different level. Whether or not it is possible to ascertain the impact of judges' personal audiences on their choices, it is useful to consider judicial behavior from the perspective of the relationships between judges and their audiences. That perspective offers new ways to think about the forces that shape judges' choices and about what we have learned from scholarship on judicial behavior. Indeed, that is the most important benefit of taking this perspective.

NOTES

1. This is not the only ground on which that assumption can be questioned. So long as judges differ in their goals or the ways they seek to achieve those goals, no matter what form these differences take, the mix of considerations that shape their decisions can be expected to differ as well.

2. The same may be true of Scalia's oral announcements of his dissents. William Suter, the head of the Court clerk's office, disputed press reports that Scalia read his "angry dissent" in one case. "'He didn't look angry,' said Suter. . . . 'He looked happy'" (Ringel 2003).

3. One example is the "Cult of Scalia" website, now out of date, whose text begins: "Overcome by unadulterated awe . . ." (members.aol.com/schwenkler/scalia/, accessed July 20, 2004). A wide-ranging blog by a law school professor at Regent University is entitled "Ninomania" in honor of Justice Scalia, using his nickname (ninomania .blogspot.com/, accessed February 22, 2005). See also Ring 2004.

4. Judge Kozinski is also the subject of a website, "The Unofficial Judge Alex Kozinski Site," albeit one that is not as effusive in its praise as the one honoring Justice Scalia (see note 3). (notabug.com/kozinski, accessed July 30, 2004.)

5. "In Timur Kuran's terms (1995, 30–31), judges are willing to sacrifice some "expressive utility" that they gain from expressing their own views to gain "reputational utility" from expressing views that important audiences approve. Kuran uses the term "expressive" differently from Alexander Schuessler (2000), whose perspective is discussed shortly.

REFERENCES

Askin, Frank. 1997. *Defending Rights: A Life in Law and Politics.* Atlantic Highlands, N.J.: Humanities Press.

Barbash, Fred, and Al Kamen. 1984. "Third Justice Speaks Out." *Washington Post,* September 20, A1, A42.

Bazelon, Emily. 2004. "The Big Kozinski." *Legal Affairs,* January–February, 22–32.

Brennan, William J., Jr. 1977. "State Constitutions and the Protection of Individual Rights." *Harvard Law Review* 90:489–504.

Cox, Gail Diane. 2001. "Thar He Blows—Again and Again." *National Law Journal,* August 6, A26.

Hirsch, H. N. 1981. *The Enigma of Felix Frankfurter.* New York: Basic Books.

Howe, Mark De Wolfe, ed. 1953. *Holmes-Laski Letters: The Correspondence of Mr. Justice Holmes and Harold J. Laski, 1916–1935.* Cambridge, Mass.: Harvard University Press.

Kozinski, Alex. 1991. "My Pizza with Nino." *Cardozo Law Review* 12:1583–91.

Kuran, Timur. 1995. *Private Truths, Public Lies: The Social Consequences of Preference Falsification.* Cambridge, Mass.: Harvard University Press.

Murphy, Bruce Allen. 2003. *Wild Bill: The Legend and Life of William O. Douglas.* New York: Random House.

Ring, Kevin A., ed. 2004. *Scalia Dissents: Writings of the Supreme Court's Wittiest, Most Outspoken Justice.* Washington, D.C.: Regnery Publishing.

Ringel, Jonathan. 2003. "Supreme Court Clerk Speaks His Mind." *Legal Times*, September 15, 11.

Sarat, Austin. 1977. "Judging in Trial Courts: An Exploratory Study." *Journal of Politics* 39:368–98.

Scalia, Antonin. 1994. "The Dissenting Opinion." *Journal of Supreme Court History* 1994:33–44.

Schuessler, Alexander A. 2000. *A Logic of Expressive Choice.* Princeton, N.J.: Princeton University Press.

Terry, Deborah J., Michael A. Hogg, and Julie M. Duck. 1999. "Group Membership, Social Identity, and Attitudes." In *Social Identity and Social Cognition*, ed. Dominic Abrams and Michael A. Hogg, 280–314. Oxford: Blackwell Publishers.

Tushnet, Mark. 1994. "Style and the Supreme Court's Educational Role in Government." *Constitutional Commentary* 11:215–25.

Court Decisions

Texas v. Johnson. 1989. 491 U.S. 397.

United States v. Microsoft Corporation. 2001. 253 F.2d 34 (D.C. Cir.).

9

PUBLIC OPINION

9.1

ARTHUR LUPIA AND MATHEW D. McCUBBINS

From *The Democratic Dilemma: Can Citizens Learn What They Need to Know?*

Some observers have concluded that Americans do not know enough about politics and government to make wise choices in voting and other political decisions. The "dilemma" in the title is that citizens are quite uninformed but are being asked to make weighty decisions, like who should be president. Lupia and McCubbins argue that most of the time, under normal conditions, citizens get enough information to make reasonable decisions.

> Knowledge will forever govern ignorance: And a people who mean to be their own Governors, must arm themselves with the power which knowledge gives. A popular Government, without popular information, or the means of acquiring it, is but a Prologue to a Farce or a Tragedy; or, perhaps both.
>
> —James Madison[1]

The founders of the American republic, and many of their contemporaries around the world, believed that democracy requires citizens to make reasoned choices. Reasoned choice, in turn, requires that people know the consequences of their actions.

Can voters, legislators, and jurors make reasoned choices? Many observers conclude that they cannot. The evidence for this conclusion is substantial—study after study documents the breadth and depth of citizen ignorance. Making matters worse is the fact that many people acquire what little information they have from thirty-minute news summaries, thirty-second political advertisements, or eight-second sound bites. From this evidence, it seems very likely that "Men of factious tempers, of local prejudices, or of sinister designs, may, by intrigue, by corruption, or by any other means, first obtain the suffrages, and then betray the interests, of the people" (Madison, *Federalist* 10).

It is widely believed that there is a mismatch between the requirements of democracy and most people's ability to meet these requirements. If this mismatch is too prevalent, then effective self-governance is impossible. The *democratic dilemma* is that the people who are called upon to make reasoned choices may not be capable of doing so.

[W]e concede that people lack political information. We also concede that this ignorance can allow people "of sinister designs" to deceive and betray the underinformed. We do not concede, however, that democracy *must* succumb to these threats. Rather, we conclude that:

- Reasoned choice does not require full information; rather, it requires the ability to predict the consequences of actions. We define this ability as knowledge.[2]
- People *choose* to disregard most of the information they could acquire and base virtually all of their decisions on remarkably little information.
- People often *substitute* the advice of others for the information they lack. This substitution can give people the capacity for reasoned choice.
- Relying on the advice of others involves tradeoffs. Although it decreases the costs of acquiring knowledge, it also introduces the possibility of deception.
- A person who wants to gain knowledge from the advice of others must choose to follow some advice while ignoring other advice. People make these choices in systematic and predictable ways.
- Political institutions can help people choose which advice to follow and which advice to ignore. Institutions do this when they *clarify* the incentives of advice givers.
- Understanding how people learn not only helps us better identify when presumed democratic dilemmas are real but also shows us how we might begin to resolve these dilemmas. . . .

DEMOCRACY, DELEGATION, AND REASONED CHOICE

Democracy is a method of government based upon the choices of the people. In all modern democracies, the people elect or appoint others to represent them. Legislative assemblies, executives, commissions, judges, and juries are empowered by the people to make collective decisions on their behalf. These delegations form the foundation of democracy.

But there are dangers. As Dahl (1967: 21) warns, the principal danger is that uninformed decision makers, by failing to delegate well, will transform democracy into a *tyranny of experts:* "there are decisions that require me to *delegate* authority to others . . . but if I delegate, may I not, in practice, end up with a kind of aristocracy of experts, or even false experts?"

Must democracy become a tyranny of experts? Many observers answer yes, because those who delegate seem uninformed when compared with those to whom they delegate.

The principal democratic delegation, that of the people electing their governors, seems most susceptible to tyranny. Cicero's observation that "in the common people there is no wisdom, no penetration, no power of judgment" is an apt summary of modern voting studies (see Berelson 1952, Campbell et al. 1960, Converse 1964, Kinder and Sears 1985, Lane and Sears 1964, Luskin 1987, McClosky 1964, Neuman 1986, Schattschneider 1960, Schumpeter 1942, Zaller 1992, Zaller and Feldman 1992; for a survey, see Delli Carpini and Keeter 1996). Many scholars argue that voters, because of their obstinance or their inability to educate themselves, become the unwitting puppets of campaign and media puppet-masters (Bennett 1992, Sabato 1991). Iyengar (1987: 816) summarizes the literature on voting and elections: "the low level of political knowledge and the absence of ideological reasoning has lent credence to the charges that popular control of government is illusory." These studies suggest that voters who lack information cannot use elections to control their governors.

Other observers make similar arguments about elected representatives. Weber, for example, argues that legislators cannot control bureaucrats:

> Under normal conditions, the power position of a fully developed bureaucracy is always overtowering. The "political master" finds himself in the position of the "dilettante" who stands opposite the "expert," facing the trained official who stands within the management of administration. This holds whether the "master" whom the bureaucracy serves is a "people," equipped with the weapons of "legislative initiative," the "referendum," and the right to remove officials, or a parliament, elected on a more aristocratic or more "democratic" basis and equipped with the right to vote a lack of confidence, or with the actual authority to vote it. (Weber quoted in Gerth and Mills 1946: 232)

Niskanen (1971) continues that public officials' inability to contend with the complexities of modern legislation places them at the mercy of self-serving special interests and bureaucrats. Lowi (1979: xii) concludes, "actual policy-making will not come from voter preferences or congressional enactments but from a process of tripartite bargaining between the specialized administrators, relevant members of Congress, and the representatives of self-selected organized interests."

Jurors also seem to lack the information they need. Posner (1995: 52), for example, argues, "As American law and society become ever more complex, the jury's cognitive limitations will become ever more palpable and socially costly." Other observers characterize the legal system, not as a forum where citizens make reasoned choices, but as a stage for emotional appeals where style and deception overwhelm knowledge. As Abramson (1994: 3) laments,

> The gap between the complexity of modern litigation and the qualifications of jurors has widened to frightening proportions. The average jury rarely understands the expert testimony in an anti-trust suit, a medical malpractice case, or an insanity defense. Nor do most jurors know the law or comprehend the judge's crash course of instructions on it. Trial by jury has thus become trial by ignorance.

Although the critiques of democracy's delegations are myriad and diverse, all have a common conclusion—*reasoned choice does not govern delegation.* As Schumpeter (1942: 262) argues, "the typical citizen drops down to a lower level of mental performance as soon as he enters the political field. He argues and analyzes in a way which he would readily recognize as infantile within the sphere of his real interests. He becomes a primitive again. His thinking is associative and affective. . . . [T]his may prove fatal to the nation."

If voters, legislators, and jurors lack the capability to delegate effectively, then democracy may be "but a prologue to a farce or a tragedy." Like the scholars just quoted, we find this possibility alarming. Unlike these scholars, however, we argue that the capabilities of the people and the requirements of democracy are not as mismatched as many critics would have us believe. In what follows, we will identify the conditions under which this mismatch does and does not exist.

A PREVIEW OF OUR THEORY

We argue that *limited information need not prevent people from making reasoned choices.* Of course, we are not the first analysts to make this type of argument. In the 1950s, for example, Berelson, Lazarfeld, and McPhee (1954) and Downs (1957) argued that voters rely on opinion leaders and political parties to overcome their information shortfalls. More recently, a generation of scholars has further countered the view that the "democratic citizen is expected to be well informed about political affairs" (Berelson, Lazarsfeld, and McPhee 1954: 308). Collectively, these scholars have demonstrated that voters can use a wide range of simple cues as substitutes for complex information. We concur with the basic insight of each of these studies—people can use substitutes for encyclopedic information.

However, we want to do more than argue that limited information need not prevent people from making reasoned choices. We want to argue that *there are specific conditions under which people who have limited information can make reasoned choices.* Therefore, in addition to showing that people *can* use cues, we want to answer questions about *when and how* people use cues, *when* cues are effective substitutes for detailed information, and *when* cues are detrimental. To understand who is (and who is not) capable of reasoned choice, we must be able to answer questions such as:

- When do people use simple cues?
- When do people ignore simple cues and seek more detailed information instead?
- When are simple cues sufficient for reasoned choice?
- When can people who offer simple cues manipulate or deceive those who use them?
- What factors determine why a person relies on some simple cues while ignoring many others?
- How do political institutions affect the use and effectiveness of simple cues?

To answer these questions, we construct theories of attention, persuasion, and delegation. . . . [O]ur theory has the rare advantage of being relevant to the usually separate debates on learning, communication, and choice held in cognitive science, economics, political science, and psychology. Next, we describe our theory and preview the answers it gives to the questions listed previously.

Knowledge and Information

We begin by developing a theory of attention. The purpose of our theory is to explain how humans cope with complexity and scarcity. As Simon (1979: 3) argues, "human thinking powers are very modest when compared with the complexities of the environments in which human beings live." Making matters worse is the fact that many of the resources people need to survive are scarce.

Ironically, for many political issues, information is not scarce; rather it is the cognitive resources that a person can use to process information that are scarce. For example, political information appears in the newspapers, in the mail, on community bulletin boards, and on television and radio and is relayed to us in person by friends and family. People often lack the time and energy needed to make sense of all this information. As a consequence, people often have only incomplete information. Fortunately, reasoned choice does not require complete information. Instead, it requires *knowledge: the ability to predict the consequences of actions.*[3]

Implicit in many critiques of democracy is the claim that people who lack *information* are incapable of reasoned choice. By contrast, we argue that people who lack information solve enormously complex problems every day. They do so by making effective use of the information available to them, sorting that which is useful from that which is not.

Information is useful only if it helps people avoid costly mistakes. By contrast, if more information does not lead people to change their decisions, then it provides no instrumental benefit and they should ignore it. Indeed, ignoring useless information is necessary for humans and other species to survive and prosper (Churchland and Sejnowski 1992).

Those who find such statements surprising should consider the almost boundless range of actions, both mundane and grand, for which people ignore available information. For example, people take medication without knowing all of the conditions under which it might be harmful. They also buy houses based on limited information about the neighborhoods around them and with little or no information about the neighbors. People make choices in this way not because the information is unavailable but because the costs of paying attention to it exceed the value of its use.[4]

Although reasoned choice does not require complete information, it does require the ability to predict the consequences of actions. In many cases, simple pieces of information can provide the knowledge people need. For example, to navigate a busy intersection successfully, you must *know* where all of the other cars are going to be sure that you can avoid crashing into them. Advocates of complete information might argue that successful automotive navigation requires as much information as you can gather about the intentions of other drivers and the speed, acceleration, direction, and mass of their cars. At many intersections, however, there is a simple substitute for *all* of this information—a traffic signal. At these intersections, traffic signals are substitutes for more complex information and reduce the amount of information required to make a reasoned choice. At intersections without working traffic signals or other simple cues, reasoned choices require more information. Using similar logic, it follows that limited information precludes reasoned choice only if people are stuck at complex political intersections and lack access to effective political traffic signals.

Persuasion, Enlightenment, and Deception

People who want to make reasoned choices need knowledge. There are two ways to acquire knowledge. The first way is to draw from personal experience. People who exercise this option use their own observations of the past to derive predictions about the future consequences of their actions. The second way is to learn from others. People who exercise this option substitute other people's observations of the past for the personal experience they lack.

In many political settings, only the second option is available. This is true because politics is often abstract and its consequences are remote. In these settings, personal experience does not provide sufficient knowledge for reasoned choice. For many political decisions, reasoned choice requires learning from others.

There are many explanations of how people learn from others. Indeed, a generation of scholars, starting with Knight, Simon, Berelson et al. and

Downs, suggest numerous heuristics—simple means for generating information substitutes.[5] . . .

Individually, each of these explanations of how we learn from others is valuable and enlightening. Each reveals a source of the judgmental shortcuts that people undoubtedly use. However, as Sniderman, Brody, and Tetlock (1991: 70) argue, "The most serious risk is that . . . every correlation between independent and dependent variables [is] taken as evidence of a new judgmental shortcut." We agree. We need a theory that explains when or how people choose among the shortcuts listed in the preceding paragraph. To understand how people learn from others, we must be able to explain *how people choose whom to believe.*

■　　■　　■

[N]otice that any attempt to learn from others leads to one of three possible outcomes.

- The first outcome is *enlightenment.* When someone furnishes us with knowledge, we become enlightened. Enlightenment, then, is the process of becoming enlightened. If we initially lack knowledge sufficient for reasoned choice and can obtain such knowledge only from others, then we can make reasoned decisions only if others enlighten us.
- The second outcome is *deception.* Deception is the process by which the testimony we hear reduces our ability to predict accurately the consequences of our actions. For example, we are deceived when someone lies to us *and* we believe that individual.
- The third outcome is that we *learn nothing.* When we learn nothing, our beliefs go unchanged and we gain no knowledge.

Both enlightenment and deception, in turn, require *persuasion: a successful attempt to change the beliefs of another.* The key to understanding whether people become enlightened or deceived by the testimony of others is to understand the conditions under which they can persuade one another.

Most scholars of communication and politics, dating back to Aristotle, focus on a speaker's *internal character* (e.g., honesty, ideology, or reputation) as a necessary condition for persuasion. If a speaker lacks the right character, then these scholars conclude that the speaker will not be persuasive. [W]e present a different set of necessary and sufficient conditions for persuasion. We argue that persuasion need not be contingent upon personal character; rather, *persuasion requires that a listener perceive a speaker to be both knowledgeable and trustworthy.* Although a perception of trust can arise from a positive evaluation of a speaker's character, we show that *external forces can substitute for character* and can thus generate persuasion in contexts where it would not otherwise occur.

An example of an external force that generates trust and persuasion is a listener's observation of a speaker's costly effort. From this observation, the listener can learn about the intensity of a speaker's preferences. This particular condition is also very much like the adage that actions speak louder than words. When speaker costs have this effect, they can provide a basis for trust by providing listeners with a window to speaker incentives.

To see how costly effort affects persuasion, consider the following situation. First, suppose that a listener knows a speaker to have one of three possible motivations—he is a conservative with intense preferences, a conservative with non-intense preferences, or a liberal with non-intense preferences. Second, suppose that the listener does not know which of the three motivations the speaker actually has. Third, suppose that the listener can make a reasoned choice only if he or she knows whether the speaker is liberal or conservative. Fourth, suppose that if the listener observes that the speaker paid a quarter of his or her income to affect a policy outcome, then the listener can conclude that the speaker has intense preferences. If all four suppositions are true, then the speaker's costly effort persuades the listener. As a result, the listener can make a reasoned choice because she can infer that the speaker is a conservative.

Another example of a trust-inducing external force is a penalty for lying. Penalties for lying, whether explicit, such as fines for perjury, or implicit, such as the loss of a valued reputation, can also generate trust by revealing a speaker's incentives. That is, although a listener may believe that a speaker has an interest in deception, the presence of a penalty for lying may lead the listener to believe that certain types of lies are prohibitively costly, rendering certain types of statements very likely to be true.

Our conditions for persuasion show when forces such as costly effort and penalties for lying are, and are not, effective substitutes for a speaker's character.[6] These conditions reveal that you do not necessarily learn more from people who are like you, nor do you learn more from people you like. This is why most people turn to financial advisors, instead of their mothers, when dealing with mutual funds, and back to Mom when seeking advice about child rearing.

Unlike most well-known theories of persuasion and strategic communication, our conditions for persuasion also clarify how and when people suffer as a result of substituting simple cues for complex information. For example, our theory allows us to identify conditions under which a speaker can deceive a listener (i.e., conditions under which a speaker lies *and* a listener believes the lie). These conditions are important because many critics of democracy claim that uninformed citizens are ripe for manipulation at the hands of slick political salesmen.

▪   ▪   ▪

More generally, our conditions for persuasion show why some statements are persuasive and others are not. The obvious reason for these differences is that statements vary in content. The less obvious reason is that the context under which a speaker makes a statement also affects persuasion considerably. Two people making precisely the same statement may not be equally persuasive if only one is subject to penalties for lying.

Our conditions for persuasion further imply that not everyone can persuade. People listen to some speakers and not others. They read some books and not others. They buy some products even though the manufacturers spend very little money on advertising while refusing to buy others supported by celebrity endorsements. Similarly, people respond to the advice of some experts or interest groups and not that of others. Our conditions for persuasion explain how people make these choices.

Our results also reveal the bounds on the effectiveness of the heuristics mentioned earlier. Consider, for example, the use of ideology as a heuristic. When there is a high correlation between a speaker's ideology and that speaker's knowledge and trustworthiness, then people are likely to find ideological cues useful. By contrast, when there is no clear correlation, ideology is useless. Similar arguments can be made about other heuristics, such as party, reputation, and likability. In sum, *concepts such as reputation, party, or ideology are useful heuristics only if they convey information about knowledge and trust. The converse of this statement is not true*—knowledge and trust are the fundamental factors that make cues persuasive; the other factors are not.

▪   ▪   ▪

Successful Delegation and the Institutions of Knowledge

. . . Two reasons are commonly cited for the failure of delegation: principals and agents have *conflicting interests* over the outcome of delegation, and agents have *expertise* regarding the consequences of the delegation that principals do not. When delegation occurs under these conditions, agents are free to take any action that suits them, irrespective of the consequences for the principal, and the principal cannot cause them to do otherwise.

We find that delegation succeeds if two conditions are satisfied: the knowledge condition and the incentive condition. The knowledge condition is satisfied in one of two ways. First, it is satisfied when the principal's personal experience allows her to distinguish beneficial from detrimental agent actions. Second, it is satisfied when the principal can obtain this knowledge from others. Therefore, the knowledge condition does not require the principal to know everything the agent knows; it requires only that the principal know enough to distinguish welfare-enhancing from welfare-decreasing agent actions.

The incentive condition is satisfied when the agent and the principal have at least some goals in common. In many cases, satisfaction of the knowledge condition is sufficient for satisfaction of the incentive condition: A principal who becomes enlightened with respect to the consequences of delegation either can motivate the agent to take actions that enhance her welfare or can reject the agent's actions that do not enhance her welfare.

We find that the outcome of delegation is not determined by whether or not the principal can match the agent's technical expertise. Instead, it is determined by the principal's ability to use the testimony of others effectively. If the principal has this ability, then delegation can succeed despite the information she lacks. If the principal lacks information about the agent and lacks the ability to learn from others, then delegation is doomed.

Moreover, we argue that, if democratic principals can create the context in which knowledgeable and persuasive speakers can inform them of the consequences of their agent's actions, then they can facilitate successful delegation. We argue that institutions, such as administrative procedure, rules of evidence, and statutory law, provide the context in which principals can learn about their agent's actions. Institutions can, if properly structured, offer principals a way to better judge their agent's actions. When institutions are poorly designed, or the incentives they induce are opaque, then the political consequence of limited information is likely to be failed delegation. By contrast, when these institutions properly and clearly structure incentives, then they facilitate enlightenment, reasoned choice, and successful delegation even in complex circumstances.

Conclusion

The mismatch between what delegation demands and citizens' capabilities constitutes the democratic dilemma. If people are not capable of reasoned political choices, then effective self-governance is an illusion. After observing that voters, legislators, and jurors are ignorant of many of the details of the decisions they face, many scholars and political commentators conclude that the illusion is real and argue for some type of reform. If their conclusion is correct, then effective self-governance may indeed require political reform. If their conclusion is incorrect, their reforms may restrain the truly competent and do more harm than good.

Other scholars have argued that people are quite capable of making complex decisions with very little information. They point to instances in which people use heuristics and conclude that such heuristics are sufficient for reasoned choice. If these conclusions are correct, then successful delegation does not require reform and the critics mentioned previously are akin to democracy's Chicken Littles. If, however, these latter conclusions are incorrect, then the optimistic scholars are akin to democracy's Pollyannas, advocating the perpetuation of ineffective and harmful systems of governance.

Both sides of this debate recognize that people are often ignorant about the details of the choices they make. They also both recognize the existence of information shortcuts, cues, and heuristics. What is missing from this debate is an understanding of when ignorance of details prevents reasoned choice, how people choose among potential heuristics, and when these heuristics provide effective substitutes for the detailed information people lack. Only when we have these understandings will we be able to make constructive use of the common observation that people lack information. At that point, we can separate the Chicken Littles from the Pollyannas and build effective solutions to the democratic dilemma.

NOTES

1. From Hunt (1910: 103). Madison expressed similar beliefs in *Federalist 57* and in a speech before the Virginia Ratifying Convention, where he argued that it is necessary that the people possess the "virtue and intelligence to select men of virtue and wisdom" (Riemer 1986: 40).

2. There exists a centuries-old debate about what democracy *should* do. This debate has involved many great minds, is wide ranging, and is totally unresolved. We do not believe ourselves capable of resolving this debate. However, we strongly believe that we can make the debate more constructive. We can do so by clarifying the relationship between what information people have and what types of decisions they can make. Our reading is firmly about determining the capabilities of people who lack political information. It is designed to resolve debates about how much information voters, jurors, and legislators need in order to perform certain tasks. So, although our reading may help to clarify debates about what democracy should do, it will not resolve these debates.

We mention this because our relationship to the debate about what democracy should do motivates our definition of reasoned choice. Our definition of reasoned choice allows the reader to define an amount of knowledge that is required for reasoned choice. Some readers may argue that a reasoned choice requires knowledge of very technical matters, whereas others may argue that a reasoned choice requires less knowledge. Note that the difference between these viewpoints reduces to different views on what democracy should do. Therefore, our definition of reasoned choice is purposefully precise with respect to the relationship between information, knowledge, and choice and is purposefully vague with respect to most normative debates about what democracies *should* do.

3. For example, knowing which of two products is "better" than the other is often sufficient for us to make the same choice we would have made had we been completely informed about each product.

4. Furthermore, beyond being useless, some types of information cause people to make the wrong (i.e., welfare-reducing) choices when they would have otherwise made the right (i.e., welfare-increasing) ones with less information. For example, a person who votes for Jones instead of Smith because a newspaper endorses Jones may regret having attended to this additional information when Jones later opposes a policy that both she and Smith support.

5. Also, see Key (1966) and Tversky and Kahneman (1974).

6. A third external force that can induce a listener to trust a speaker arises when the speaker's statements are subject to some chance of being externally verified.

REFERENCES

Abramson, Jeffrey. 1994. *We, the Jury: The Jury System and the Ideal of Democracy.* New York: Basic Books.

Bennett, W. Lance. 1992. *The Governing Crisis: Media, Money, and Marketing in American Elections.* New York: St. Martin's Press.

Berelson, Bernard. 1952. "Democratic Theory and Public Opinion." *Public Opinion Quarterly* XVI: 313–30.

Berelson, Bernard, Paul F. Lazarfeld, and William N. McPhee. 1954. *Voting: A Study of Opinion Formation in a Presidential Campaign.* Chicago: University of Chicago Press.

Campbell, Angus, Philip E. Converse, Warren E. Miller, and Donald E. Stokes. 1960. *The American Voter.* New York: Wiley.

Churchland, Patricia S., and Terrence J. Sejnowski. 1992. *The Computational Brain.* Cambridge, Mass.: MIT Press.

Converse, Philip E. 1964. "The Nature of Belief Systems in Mass Publics." In David E. Apter, ed., *Ideology and Discontent.* New York: Free Press.

Dahl, Robert A. 1967. *Pluralist Democracy in the United States: Conflict and Consent.* Chicago: Rand McNally.

Delli Carpini, Michael X., and Scott Keeter. 1991. "Stability and Change in the United States Public's Knowledge of Politics." *Public Opinion Quarterly* 55: 583–612.

Downs, Anthony. 1957. *An Economic Theory of Democracy.* New York: Harper.

Gerth, H. H., and C. Wright Mills, eds. 1946. *From Max Weber: Essays in Sociology.* New York: Oxford University Press.

Hunt, Gaillard, ed. 1910. *The Writings of James Madison.* New York: Putnam.

Iyengar, Shanto. 1987. "Television News and Citizens' Explanations of National Affairs." *American Political Science Review* 81: 815–32.

Key, V. O. 1966. *The Responsible Electorate: Rationality in Presidential Voting, 1936–1960.* Cambridge, Mass.: Belknap Press of Harvard University Press.

Kinder, Donald R., and David O. Sears. 1985. "Public Opinion and Political Participation." In G. Lindzey and E. Aronson, eds., *Handbook of Social Psychology.* Reading, Mass.: Addison-Wesley.

Lane, Robert E., and David O. Sears. 1964. *Public Opinion.* Englewood Cliffs, N.J.: Prentice-Hall.

Lowi, Theodore J. 1979. *The End of Liberalism: The Second Republic of the United States.* 2nd ed. New York: Norton.

Luskin, Robert C. 1987. "Measuring Political Sophistication." *American Journal of Political Science* 31: 856–99.

Madison, James. *Federalist.* In Clinton Rossiter, ed., *The Federalist Papers.* New York: Penguin.

McClosky, Herbert. 1964. "Consensus and Ideology in American Politics." *American Political Science Review* 58: 361–82.

Neuman, W. Russell. 1986. *The Paradox of Mass Politics: Knowledge and Opinion in the American Electorate.* Cambridge, Mass.: Harvard University Press.

Niskanen, William A. 1971. *Bureaucracy and Representative Government.* Chicago: Aldine-Atherton.

Posner, Richard. 1995. "Juries on Trial." *Commentary* 99: 49–52.

Riemer, Neal. 1986. *James Madison: Creating the American Constitution.* Washington, D.C.: Congressional Quarterly.

Sabato, Larry J. 1991. *Feeding Frenzy.* New York: Free Press.

Schattschneider, Elmer Eric. 1960. *The Semisovereign People: A Realist's View of Democracy in America.* New York: Holt, Rinehart and Winston.

Schumpeter, Joseph Alois. 1942. *Capitalism, Socialism, and Democracy.* New York: Harper.

Simon, Herbert A. 1979. *Models of Thought.* New Haven, Conn.: Yale University Press.

Sniderman, Paul M., Richard A. Brody, and Philip E. Tetlock. 1991. *Reasoning and Choice: Explorations in Political Psychology.* Cambridge: Cambridge University Press.

Tversky, Amos, and Daniel Kahneman. 1974. "Judgment under Uncertainty: Heuristics and Biases." *Science* 185: 1124–131.

Zaller, John. 1992. *The Nature and Origins of Mass Opinion.* Cambridge: Cambridge University Press.

Zaller, John, and Stanley Feldman. 1992. "A Simple Theory of the Survey Response: Answering Questions Versus Revealing Preferences." *American Journal of Political Science* 36: 579–616.

9.2

KRISTIN LUKER

From *Abortion and the Politics of Motherhood*

In this excerpt from Luker's powerful book, she argues that the differences among people over abortion stem from deeply held beliefs about women and motherhood. She offers a valuable peek into the origins of public opinion on this controversial issue.

[W]hen pro-life and pro-choice activists think about abortion, abortion itself is merely "the tip of the iceberg." Different beliefs about the roles of the sexes, about the meaning of parenthood, and about human nature are all called into play when the issue is abortion. Abortion, therefore, gives us a rare opportunity to examine closely a set of values that are almost never directly discussed. Because these values apply to spheres of life that are very private (sex) or very diffuse (morality), most people never look at the patterns they form. For this reason the abortion debate has become something that illuminates our deepest, and sometimes our dearest, beliefs.

At the same time, precisely because these values are so rarely discussed overtly, when they are called into question, as they are by the abortion debate, individuals feel that an entire *world view* is under assault. An interesting characteristic of a world view, however, is that the values located within it are so deep and so dear to us that we find it hard to imagine that we even have a "world view"—to us it is just reality—or that anyone else could not share it. By definition, those areas covered by a "world view" are those parts of life we take for granted, never imagine questioning, and cannot envision decent, moral people not sharing.

When an event such as the abortion controversy occurs, which makes it clear that one's world view is not the only one, it is immediately apparent why surprise, outrage, and vindictiveness are the order of the day. Individuals are surprised because for most of them this is the first time their deepest values have been brought to explicit consciousness, much less challenged. They are outraged because these values are so taken for granted that people have no vocabulary with which to discuss the fact that what is at odds is a fundamental view of reality. And they are vindictive because denying that one's opponents are decent, honorable people is one way of distancing oneself from the unsettling thought that there could be legitimate differences of opinion on one's most cherished beliefs.

In the course of our interviews, it became apparent that each side of the abortion debate has an internally coherent and mutually shared view of the world that is tacit, never fully articulated, and, most importantly, completely at odds with the world view held by their opponents. [We] will examine in turn the world views of first the pro-life activists, then the pro-choice activists to demonstrate the truth of what many of the activists we interviewed asserted: that abortion is just "the tip of the iceberg." To be sure, not every single one of those interrelated values that I have called a "world view" characterized each and every pro-life or pro-choice person interviewed. It is well within the realm of possibility that an activist might find some individual areas where he or she would feel more akin to the values expressed by their opponents than by those on their own side. But taken as a whole, there was enough consistency in the way people on each side talked about the world to warrant the conclusion that each side has its own particular "world view," that these world views tend to be isolated from competing world views, and that forced to choose, most activists would find far more in common with the world view of their side than that of their opponents.

PRO-LIFE VIEWS OF THE WORLD

To begin with, pro-life activists believe that men and women are intrinsically different, and this is both a cause and a product of the fact that they have different roles in life. Here are some representative comments from the interviews:

> The question is, what is natural for human life and what will make people happy? Now I deplore the oppression of any people, and so I would ipso facto deplore the oppression of women but a lot of things are being interpreted as oppression simply [out of] restless agitation against a natural order that should really be allowed to prevail. The feminist movement has wanted to, as it were, really turn women into men or to kind of de-sex them, and they [feminists] pretend that there are no important differences between men and women. Now when it comes to a woman doing a job, a woman being paid the same rate that a man gets for the same job, I'm very much in favor of all that. [What] I find so disturbing [about] the whole abortion mentality is the idea that family duties—rearing children, managing a home, loving and caring for a husband—are somehow degrading to women. And that's an idea which is very current in our society—that women are not going to find fulfillment until they get out there and start competing for a livelihood with men and talking like men, cursing and whatever, although not all men curse. I don't mean that to sound . . . maybe that's beginning to have an emotional overtone that I didn't want it to have.

The women's lib thing comes in, too. They've got a lot of good ideas, but their whole thing ran off so far on it. How can they not see that men and women are different? I don't know, they're different, period, that's truth.

[Men and women] were created differently and we're meant to comple-ment each other, and when you get away from our [proper] roles as such, you start obscuring them. That's another part of the confusion that's going on now, people don't know where they stand, they don't know how to act, they don't know where they're coming from, so your psychiatrists' couches are filled with lost souls, with lost people that for a long time now have been gradually led into confusion and don't even know it.

I believe that there's a natural mother's instinct. And I'm kind of chau-vinist this way, but I don't believe men and women are equal. I believe men and women are very different, and beautifully different, and that they're complementary in their nature to one another.

Pro-life activists agree that men and women, as a result of these intrinsic differences, have different roles to play: men are best suited to the public world of work, and women are best suited to rear children, manage homes, and love and care for husbands. Most pro-life activists believe that motherhood—the raising of children and families—is the most fulfilling role that women can have. To be sure, they live in a country where over half of all women work, and they do acknowledge that some women are employed. But when they say (as almost all of them do) that women who work should get equal pay for equal work, they do not mean that women *should* work. On the contrary, they sub-scribe quite strongly to the traditional belief that women should be wives and mothers *first*. Mothering, in their view, is so demanding that it is a full-time job, and any woman who cannot commit herself fully to it should avoid it entirely.

■   ■   ■

Because pro-life activists see having a family as an emotionally demand-ing, labor-intensive project, they find it hard to imagine that a woman could put forty hours a week into an outside job and still have time for her husband and children. Equally important, they feel that different kinds of emotional "sets" are called for in the work world and in the home. . . . For a woman to shift gears from her emotional role in the home to a competitive role in the office is not only difficult, they argue, but damaging to both men and women, and to their children.

These views on the different nature of men and women and the roles appropriate to each combine to make abortion look wrong three times over. First, it is intrinsically wrong because it takes a human life and what makes women special is their ability to nourish life. Second, it is wrong because *by giving women control over their fertility*, it breaks up an intricate set of social relationships between men and women that has traditionally surrounded (and in the ideal case protected) women and children. Third and finally, abortion is wrong because it fosters and supports a world view that deemphasizes (and therefore *downgrades*) the traditional roles of men and women. Because these roles have been satisfying ones for pro-life people and because they believe this emotional and social division of labor is both "appropriate and natural," the act of abortion is wrong because it plays havoc with this arrangement of the world. For example, because abortion formally diminishes male decision-making power, it also diminishes male responsibility. Thus, far from liberating women, pro-life people argue, abortion oppresses them.

■　　■　　■

Because pro-life people see the world as inherently divided both emotionally and socially into a male sphere and a female sphere, they see the loss of the female sphere as a very deep one indeed. They see tenderness, morality, caring, emotionality, and self-sacrifice as the exclusive province of women; and if women cease to be traditional women, who will do the caring, who will offer the tenderness? A pro-life doctor argued that although women may have suffered from the softening influence they provided for men and for the society as a whole, they had much to gain as well.

■　　■　　■

In this view, everyone loses when traditional roles are lost. Men lose the nurturing that women offer, the nurturing that gently encourages them to give up their potentially destructive and aggressive urges. Women lose the protection and cherishing that men offer. And children lose full-time loving by at least one parent, as well as clear models for their own futures.

These different views about the intrinsic nature of men and women also shape pro-life views about sex. The nineteenth century introduced new terms to describe the two faces of sexual activity, distinguishing between "procreative love," whose goal is reproduction, and "amative love," whose goal is sensual pleasure and mutual enjoyment. (Although these two aspects of sexuality have undoubtedly existed for millennia, the Victorian era in the West democratized amative love so that it was no longer restricted to an elite who enjoyed the pleasures of lovers and courtesans.)[1]

For the pro-life people we talked with, the relative worth of procreative sex and amative sex was clear. In part this is because many of them, being Catholic, accept a natural law doctrine of sex, which holds that a body part is destined to be used for its physiological function. As one man put it: "You're not just given arms and legs for no purpose. . . . There must be some cause [for sex] and you begin to think, well, it must be for procreation ultimately, and certainly procreation in addition to fostering a loving relationship with your spouse."

In terms of this view, the meaning of sexual experiences is distorted whenever procreation is not intended. Contraception, premarital sex, and infidelity are wrong not only because of their social consequences but also because they strip sexual experience of its meaning . . .. One woman, a Catholic social worker, reiterated this connection between sex, procreation, and the sacred:

> At my father's funeral my aunt was telling me that she was the younger sister in a large family, and so as the older girls were having babies she would go from home to home and stay with them and help them out when the baby was born, and eventually there were enough sisters having babies that she had a little circuit. And she was telling me that my father never treated her with anything but respect—I guess she was about a fifteen-year-old at the time. I realized then that my father was a very literal Catholic, like he would never miss mass on Sunday, but he never really understood much about his religion. I think maybe his genuine respect for sex is the only thing that kind of filtered down [to me].

Because many pro-life people see sex as literally sacred, they are disturbed by values that seem to secularize and profane it. The whole constellation of values that supports amative (or "recreational") sex is seen by them as doing just that. Values that define sexuality as a wholesome physical activity, as healthy as volleyball but somewhat more fun, call into question everything that pro-life people believe in. Sex is sacred because in their world view it has the capacity to be something transcendent—to bring into existence another human life. To routinely eradicate that capacity through premarital sex (in which very few people seek to bring a new life into existence) or through contraception or abortion is to turn the world upside down.

As implied by our discussion so far, the attitudes of pro-life people toward contraception are rooted in their views about the inherent differences between men and women and about the nature and purpose of sexuality. Although the activists we interviewed often pointed out that the pro-life movement is officially neutral on the topic of contraception, this statement does not fully capture the complexity of their views and feelings. Virtually all of them felt very strongly that the pill and the IUD are abortifacients (they may cause the death of a very young embryo) and that passage of a human life law against abortion would also ban the pill and the IUD. Most of them, furthermore, refused to use traditional contraceptives on moral grounds.

■   ■   ■

Their stance toward other people's use of contraception is therefore ambivalent. They disapprove of "artificial" contraception, by which they mean use of the condom, the diaphragm, and vaginal spermicides. Many of them feel that the only acceptable "natural" method of birth control is natural family planning (NFP), the modern version of the rhythm method.

■   ■   ■

Again, several factors interact to reinforce the belief that "artificial" contraception is wrong. To begin with, if the goal of sex is pro-creation, then contraceptives are by nature wrong, and this is the starting point for many pro-life people. But it is important to remember that this is a personal choice for them, not a matter of unquestioning obedience to doctrine. Many will say that they do not use contraception because their church does not approve; but, in fact, Catholics are increasingly using contraception in patterns similar to those of non-Catholics, and their families (and family ideals) are becoming increasingly hard to distinguish from those of the population at large.[2] Moreover, some data suggest that the most direct representative of the church, the parish priest, is also likely to be tacitly in favor of birth control.[3] Most pro-life people are therefore part of an institution that proclaims a value that most of its members and some of its officials ignore.

■   ■   ■

Thus the one thing we commonly assume that everyone wants from a contraceptive—that it be 100 percent reliable and effective—is precisely what pro-life people do *not* want from their method of fertility control.

Pro-life values on the issue of abortion—and by extension on motherhood—are intimately tied to the values we have just illustrated. But they also draw more directly on notions of motherhood (and fatherhood) that are not shared by pro-choice people. This might seem obvious from the fact that pro-life people often account for their own activism by referring to the notion that babies are being murdered in their mothers' wombs. But pro-life feelings about the nature of parenthood draw on other more subtle beliefs as well.

Pro-life people believe that one becomes a parent by *being* a parent; parenthood is for them a "natural" rather than a social role. One is a parent by virtue of having a child, and the values implied by the invogue term *parenting* (as in *parenting classes*) are alien to them. The financial and educational preparations for parenthood that pro-choice people see as necessary are seen by pro-life people as a serious distortion of values. Pro-life people fear that when one focuses on job achievement, home owning, and getting money in the bank *before* one has children, children will be seen as barriers to these things.

■   ■   ■

Pro-life people tacitly assume that the way to upgrade motherhood is to make it an *inclusive* category, that all married people should be (or be willing to be) parents. In particular, women who choose to be in the public world of work should eschew the role of wife and mother, or, if they marry, should be prepared to put the public world of work second to their role as wife and mother. If a man or woman is to be sexually active, they feel, he or she should be married. And if married, one should be prepared to welcome a child whenever it arrives, however inopportune it may seem at the time. In their view, to try to balance a number of competing commitments—especially when parenthood gets shuffled into second or fourth place—is both morally wrong and personally threatening.

Pro-life people also feel very strongly that there is an anti-child sentiment abroad in our society and that this is expressed in the strong cultural norm that families should have only two children.

■   ■   ■

Since one out of every five pro-life activists in this study had six or more children, it is easy to see how these values can seem threatening. In the course of our interviews, a surprising number of activists said they did not feel discriminated against because of their pro-life activities, including their opposition to abortion, but that they did feel socially stigmatized because they had large families. As one woman with several children said: "[My husband,] being a scientist, gets a lot [of questions]. You know, having a large family, it's just for the poor uneducated person, but if you have a doctor's degree and you have a large family, what's wrong with you?" The pro-choice argument that parents must plan their families in order to give their children the best emotional and financial resources therefore sounds like an attack on people with large families. "[People think] children can't possibly make it and be successful if they come from a large family . . . because you can't give them all the time and energy that they need. Well, first of all, I'm here [at home], I'm not out working, which adds to the amount of time that I can give."

Pro-life values on children therefore represent an intersection of several values we have already discussed. Because pro-life people believe that the purpose of sexuality is to have children, they also believe that one should not plan the exact number and timing of children too carefully, for it is both wrong and foolish to make detailed life plans that depend upon exact control of fertility. Because children will influence life plans more than life plans will influence the number of children, it is also wrong to value one's planned accomplishments—primarily the acquisition of the things money can buy—over the intangible benefits that children can bring. Thus, reasoning backwards, pro-life people object to every step of the pro-choice logic. If one values material things too highly, one will be tempted to try to make detailed plans for acquiring them. If one tries to plan too thoroughly, one will be tempted to use highly effective contraception, which removes the potential of childbearing from a marriage. Once the potential for children is eliminated, the sexual act is distorted (and for religious people, morally wrong), and husbands and wives lose an important bond between them. Finally, when marriage partners who have accepted the logic of these previous steps find that contraception has failed, they are ready and willing to resort to abortion in order to achieve their goals.

This is not to say that pro-life people do not approve of planning. They do. But because of their world view (and their religious faith) they see human planning as having very concrete limits. To them it is a matter of priorities: if individuals want fame, money, and worldly success, then they have every right to pursue them. But if they are sexually active (and married, as they should be if they are sexually active), they have an obligation to subordinate other parts of life to the responsibilities they have taken on by virtue of that activity.

▪   ▪   ▪

Thus, abortion offends the deepest moral convictions of pro-life people in several ways. To begin with, it breaks a divine law. The Commandment says "Thou shalt not kill." The embryo is human (it is not a member of another species) and alive (it is not dead). Thus, according to the reasoning by syllogism they learned in childhood religion classes, the embryo is a "human life," and taking it clearly breaks one of the Commandments.

Moreover, the logic used by pro-choice advocates (and the Supreme Court) to justify abortion affronts the moral reasoning of pro-life people. For them, either the embryo is a human life or it is not; the concept of an intermediate category—a *potential* human life—seems simply inadmissible. Further, the argument that individuals should arrive at a *personal* decision about the moral status of this intermediate category is as strange to most of them as arguing that individual soldiers in wartime should act according to their own judgment of the wisdom of the army's battle plan.

A professed unwillingness to deviate from a strict moral code naturally has its repercussions in private life. Pro-life people, their rhetoric notwithstanding, do have abortions. Among pro-choice people who were associated with organizations that arrange abortions, it was something of a cliché that pro-life people were believers only until they found themselves with an unwanted pregnancy, which made them more than willing to seek an abortion. When pressed for proof, however, these pro-choice activists retreated behind medical ethics, claiming they could not invade a patient's privacy by actually naming names. Later in the study, however, more persuasive evidence was offered by pro-life people active in Life Centers. These centers, staffed and funded by the pro-life movement, are located in hospitals or other medical settings and offer free pregnancy tests and pregnancy counseling should the pregnancy test prove positive. Although counselors in Life Centers actively encourage women to continue their pregnancies, they do not openly advertise their pro-life stand; they explain only that they provide free pregnancy tests and counseling. But since most places that offer free tests and counseling are also abortion referral centers, many women come to Life Centers in order to get such a referral. Life Center counselors estimate that as many as a third of the women they see go on to have an abortion, even after having had pro-life counseling. Since Life Centers are by definition pro-life, when people who work in them say that pro-life members (and in particular the children of pro-life members) have come into their centers seeking abortions, we can probably believe them. After all, they have nothing to gain by admitting that their own members (and their own children), like the rest of us, sometimes have trouble living up to their ideals.

Thus, pro-life people, like the pro-choice people we will examine shortly, have a consistent, coherent view of the world, notwithstanding the fact that like anyone else, they cannot always bring their behavior in line with their highest ideals. The very coherence of their world view, however, makes clear that abortion, and all it represents, is profoundly unsettling to them. By the same token, the values that pro-life people bring to bear on the abortion issue are deeply threatening to those people active in the pro-choice movement.

PRO-CHOICE VIEWS OF THE WORLD

On almost all the dimensions just considered, the values and beliefs of pro-choice diametrically oppose those of pro-life people, as does the logic whereby they arrive at their values. For example, whereas pro-life people believe that men and women are inherently different and therefore have different "natural" roles in life, pro-choice people believe that men and women are substantially equal, by which they mean substantially similar. As a result, they see women's reproductive and family roles not as a "natural" niche but as potential barriers to full equality. The organization of society, they argue, means that motherhood, so long as it is involuntary, is potentially always a low-status, unrewarding role to which women can be banished at any time. Thus, from their point of view, *control* over reproduction is essential for women to be able to live up to their full human potential. Here is how one woman put it:

> I just feel that one of the main reasons women have been in a secondary position culturally is because of the natural way things happen. Women would bear children because they had no way to prevent it, except by having no sexual involvement. And that was not practical down through the years, so without knowing what to do to prevent it, women would continually have children. And then if they were the ones bearing the child, nursing the child, it just made sense [for them to be] the ones to rear the child. I think that was the natural order. When we advanced and found that we could control our reproduction, we could choose the size of our families or whether we wanted families. But that changed the whole role of women in our society. Or it opened it up to change the role. It allowed us to be more than just the bearers of children, the home-makers. That's not to say that we shouldn't continue in that role. It's a good role, but it's not the *only* role for women.

Pro-choice people agree that women (and men) find children and families a satisfying part of life, but they also think it is foolhardy for women to believe that this is the only life role they will ever have. They argue, in essence, that pro-life women who do not work outside the home are only "one man away from disaster." A death, a divorce, a desertion, or a disability can push a woman with no career skills or experience perilously close to the edge of penury—as shown by the ever-increasing numbers of "displaced homemakers"—widows and divorcées left with virtually no financial or employment resources.

At the same time, pro-choice people value what I have called "amative" sex, that is, sex whose primary purpose is not reproduction. The idea that sexual activity is valuable and indeed sacred because of its inherent reproductive capacity strikes many pro-choice people as absurd. From their point of view, if the purpose of sex were limited to reproduction, no rational Creator would have arranged things so that an individual can have hundreds or even thousands of acts of intercourse in a lifetime, with millions of sex cells—egg and sperm—always at the ready. More to the point, they argue that belief in the basically procreative nature of sex leads to an oppressive degree of *social regulation of sexual behavior, particularly the behavior of women*, who must be protected (in their viewpoint, repressed) because free expression of sexual wishes will get them "in trouble" and lead the species into overpopulation. In the pro-choice value system, both the "double standard" and "purdah"—the ancient custom of veiling women and keeping them entirely out of the public eye, lest they be too sexually arousing to men—are logical outcomes of a preoccupation with protecting and controlling women's reproductive capacities.

Significantly, many of the pro-choice activists described themselves as having grown up in families with traditional, "sex-negative" values that focused on the dangers of uncontrolled sexual feelings. They now see themselves as seeking a set of "sex-positive" values, for themselves and for the society as a whole, that emphasize the pleasure, beauty, and joy of sex rather than the dangers. When pro-choice people speak of being raised under "sex-negative" values, they mean that sex was not openly talked about, that it was certainly not portrayed as something to be enjoyed for its own sake, and that budding childish sexuality—masturbation and adolescent flirting—was often treated harshly. Premarital sexuality leading to pregnancy was a "fate worse than death." The following anecdote, though more vivid and unusual than some that pro-choice people recounted, indicates the kind of thing they had in mind when they spoke about "sex-negative" attitudes:

> The custom in my youth was that if a woman became pregnant and she was unmarried . . . the penalty was in effect to be excommunicated. Not literally, because she was still somewhat in touch, but she was removed from the roll of [church] members and became a "listener" as they said, an auditor. She could attend [church] but she would not be a member. And [she was] ostracized in that little community. . . . I'm thinking of one woman in particular, Kitty. Before she was known to be pregnant, people would talk to her after the evening service was over, when everybody was outside socializing; but once this happened they wouldn't talk

to her. None of the [church] elders would, except one—my father. . . . He
was the one who eventually made the motion that she should be read-
mitted to membership.

Such harsh treatment makes sense if it is presumed that sexuality inevitably finds genital expression and that pregnancy is a thing that can (and
indeed *should*) occur as a result. But for people who plan anyway to have
small families, who have no moral opposition to contraceptives, who value
rational planning in all realms including pregnancy, and whose other values
focus on the present and other people rather than on the future and God, putting a taboo on sexual expression seems irrelevant at best and potentially
damaging at worst.

Pro-choice people believe that sexual activity is good as an end in itself. For
much of a lifetime at least, its main purpose is not to produce children (or to
remind them of that possibility) but to afford pleasure, human contact, and,
perhaps most important, intimacy. Whereas for pro-life people sex is *inherently* transcendent—because a new life may be created at any time—for pro-
choice people, it is *potentially* transcendent, and its spiritual meaning is a
goal to be pursued rather than a fact to be faced. Despite the claims of some
pro-life people, pro-choice people *do* believe that sex can be sacred, but it is a
different kind of sacredness that they have in mind. For them, sex is sacred
when it is mystical, when it dissolves the boundaries between self and other,
when it brings one closer to one's partner, and when it gives one a sense of the
infinite. Transcendent sex, for them, grows out of feelings experienced in
the present rather than beliefs about what may happen in the future. It can be
achieved only when people feel secure, when they feel trusting, and when
they feel love for themselves and for the other. And because mobilizing such
delicate social and emotional resources as trust, caring, and intimacy
requires *practice*, pro-choice people do not denigrate sexual experiences that
fall short of achieving transcendence. They judge individual cases of premarital sex, contraception, and infidelity according to the ways in which they
enhance or detract from conditions of trust and caring. In their value scheme,
something that gives people opportunities for intimacy simply cannot be seen
as wrong.

These general attitudes about the nature and meaning of sex influence pro-
choice views on contraception. To be sure, the significance of contraception
in itself is not a very salient issue for most pro-choice people. They see using
contraceptives as something like taking good care of one's teeth—a matter
of sensible routine, a good health habit. (Indeed, they find pro-life objections
to contraception mysterious and dismiss them as "medieval" or "religious.")
They do have some pragmatic concerns about contraceptive methods—how
unpleasant or how safe they are—but contraception in the abstract has no
moral connotations for them. Since the primary moral value they see in sexuality is its potential for creating intimacy with the self and another, a good

contraceptive (and a moral one, to stretch the term) is one that is safe, undistracting, and not unpleasant to use. And since they *do* use contraception to postpone childbearing for long periods of time, their ideal contraceptive is easy to use, *highly effective*, and not a risk to their health.

The few pro-choice people who have heard of Natural Family Planning, which so many pro-life people advocate so enthusiastically, tend to dismiss it as irrelevant or irresponsible. NFP can require abstinence for as many as ten or twelve days a month, and some studies suggest that one-fourth of the couples who use it may get pregnant.[4] Since pro-choice people place a high value on the intimacy offered by sexual activity, abstaining from it for ten or twelve days a month is a high price to pay, and NFP's high pregnancy rate (and what they see as a corresponding need for abortions) is an unacceptable cost. Thus, pro-choice people reject NFP for precisely the reasons that pro-life people find it attractive: it calls for abstinence and keeps pregnancy a lively possibility.

Pro-choice people do have one clearly moral concern about sexuality, however: most of them oppose the use of abortion, instead of traditional methods of contraception, as a routine method of birth control.

▪   ▪   ▪

As this comment suggests, opposition to abortion as a routine form of birth control is based on a complex and subtle moral reasoning. For most pro-choice people, the personhood of the embryo does not exist at conception, but it does develop at some later time. The pro-choice view of personhood is thus a *gradualist* one. An embryo may not be a full person until it is viable (capable of sustaining its own life if born prematurely), but it has the rights of a potential person at all times, and those rights increase in moral weight as the pregnancy continues. (Wearing an IUD is morally acceptable to pro-choice people because they consider very early embryos to be little more than fertilized eggs.) Pro-choice people accept that sometimes the potential rights of the embryo have to be sacrificed to the actual rights of the mother. But a woman who arbitrarily or capriciously brings an embryo into existence, *when she had an alternative*, is seen as usurping even the potential rights of the embryo by trivializing them, and this offends the moral sense of pro-choice activists.

This explains an otherwise baffling feature of pro-choice morality. A great many pro-choice activists in this study, particularly those active in helping women have abortions, find multiple abortions morally troubling. Some of them even volunteered the fact that they felt like personal failures when a woman came back to them for a second, third, or higher-order abortion. At first glance, this would appear to be illogical: if it is morally acceptable for a woman to end one pregnancy with an abortion, why is it wrong for her to end subsequent pregnancies by abortion? For pro-choice people, the answer is simple and draws on both the gradualist and contextualist moral reasoning outlined above. The first abortion presumably represents the lesser of several evils, where the abortion of an embryo is seen as less morally wrong than bringing a child one cannot effectively parent into the world.* But since most women are given contraceptive services after an abortion, every abortion after the first represents a case where a woman had the option of avoiding pregnancy and did not. Except in extraordinary cases, pro-choice people see this bringing of an embryo into existence when it could have been avoided as morally wrong.

It is in the context of the relative rights of babies and embryos that pro-choice values about parenting—about the kind of life the baby-to-be might be reasonably expected to have—play such an important role. Pro-choice people have very clear standards about what parenting entails: it means giving a child the best set of emotional, psychological, social, and financial resources that one can arrange as a preparation for future life. Pro-choice people believe that it is the duty of a parent to prepare the child for the future, and good parents are seen as arranging life (and childbearing) so that this can be done most effectively.

These values about what constitutes a good parent therefore support and shape pro-choice attitudes toward children and the timing of their arrival. Since children demand financial sacrifices, for example, couples should not have them until they have acquired the financial position to give their children the best. Otherwise, under pressure, parents will come to resent a child, and this will limit their ability to be caring, attentive, and nurturing to their children. As a corollary, pro-choice people want children who feel loved, who have self-esteem, and who "feel good about themselves"; they believe that parents should postpone childbearing until they have the proper emotional resources needed to do the intense one-to-one psychological caring that good parenting requires. (It is these two factors that they have in mind when they make the statement, which pro-life people find unfathomable, that they are not "ready" for childbearing.)

Because pro-choice people see the optional raising of children as requiring financial resources, interpersonal and social skills, and emotional maturity, they often worry about how easy it is to have children. In their view, too many people stumble into parenthood without really appreciating what it takes.

■   ■   ■

Since pro-choice activists think that in the long run abortion will enhance the quality of parenting by making it optional, they see themselves as being on the side of children when they advocate abortion. In contrast to pro-life

---

* Keeping in mind the pro-choice distinction between an embryo and a baby, the values expressed here account for why having a baby and giving it up for adoption, as pro-life people advocate, is not seen by most pro-choice people as a moral solution to the abortion problem. To transform an embryo into a baby and then send that baby out into a world where the parents can have no assurance that it will be well loved and cared for is, for pro-choice people, the height of moral irresponsibility.

people, who believe that parenthood will be enhanced by making it *inclusive*, that is, making it a mandatory part of the package of being a sexually active person, pro-choice people feel that the way to improve the quality of parenthood is to make it more *exclusive*.

▪　▪　▪

In part, this attitude stems from the value placed on planning. A planned child is a wanted child, and a child who is wanted starts out on a much better basis than one who is not. But the pro-choice activists did not necessarily accept a narrow view of "being wanted."

▪　▪　▪

Connected to this value is an acceptance of teen-aged sex. Pro-choice people are concerned about teen-aged *parenthood* because young people and the unwed are in no position to become good parents, but they have no basic objection to sexual activity among young people *if they are "responsible,"* that is, if they do not take the risk of becoming parents. Because pro-choice people view the goal of sex as being the creation of intimacy, caring, and trust, they also believe that people need to practice those skills before making a long-term commitment to someone. They may practice them with a number of people or with the person they intend to marry. In either case, premarital sex is not only likely to occur but desirable. Because pro-choice people see premarital sex as reasonable and because their values give them no intrinsic reason to be against it, any concerns they may have about premarital and teen-aged sex are almost exclusively pragmatic. In some respects, pro-choice people agree with the pro-life conclusion: teenagers are not ready to be parents. But whereas pro-life people see the answer as chastity, pro-choice people are skeptical. In part because of the experiences of their own lives, they do not believe that individuals choose not to have sex merely because someone tells them that they shouldn't. Taboos, from their point of view, merely inhibit planning for sex, not sex itself.

▪　▪　▪

Naturally enough, the values that pro-choice people attach to sex, contraception, and abortion are rooted in certain basic convictions about the nature of morality, and to some extent their opponents recognize this. Several pro-life activists spoke disparagingly of pro-choice morality as "situation ethics," and a few of the more sophisticated mentioned Joseph Fletcher by name.[5] Although this is hardly sympathetic, it does imply that pro-life people are aware that pro-choice people use a different basis for their moral reasoning. In fact, pro-choice people *do* believe in what might be called "situation ethics." Partly because they are pluralists, they seriously doubt whether a single moral code can serve everyone. Partly because they are secularists, they do not accept the traditional Judeo-Christian codes as absolute moral standards;

they see them as ethical guidelines that emerged in one historical period and may or may not be relevant to the present. Perhaps most centrally, they see morality not as obedience to a set of inflexible rules, such as the Ten Commandments, but rather as the application of a few general ethical principles to a vast array of cases. All of these factors, combined with a staunch belief in the rights of the individual, lead them to believe that only individuals, not governments or churches, can ultimately make ethical decisions—which makes it tempting to describe their moral position as quintessentially protestant, in a secular rather than a religious sense. Hence pro-choice people emphasize that abortion is an *individual, private* choice.

■　■　■

First, there is a distinction between an embryo and a child, which all pro-choice people take for granted. Second, there is the idea that the embryo, though not a baby or a full human being, is nonetheless "alive" and therefore has some implicit moral rights. Finally, there is a pluralist bias: if a person has a different moral view of abortion, she should follow her own conscience, "even if it means some other sacrifice." Morality thus consists of weighing a number of competing situations and rights and trying to reconcile them under general moral principles rather than specific moral rules. This view is not confined to laypeople in the pro-choice movement; it is embraced by men and women of the clergy as well. One minister said: "Throughout [an earlier] period, my theological thinking [was still] an amorphous thing, but I felt okay. The bottom line on it was that if there be a God, then God could hardly object to people asking questions. And I looked at life, as I guess I still do to some extent, as a kind of laboratory where you test things and what's okay [you keep] and what isn't you junk it."

To use another religious metaphor, pro-choice activists seem to have a New Testament approach to morality. Although relatively few of them mention either the New Testament or Joseph Fletcher's ethics by name, they do call on the moral principles associated with these two sources. That is, when trying to decide what is the moral thing to do, pro-choice people ask what is the *loving* thing to do. The choice of the word *loving* emphasizes the fact that moral judgment relies upon a subjectively reasoned application of moral principles rather than upon an externally existing moral code.

As a result, pro-choice activists often find themselves debating moral dilemmas with themselves. Because they do not see certain activities as intrinsically right or wrong, they find that they must decide how individual moral conflicts are to be resolved in the light of moral principles. (To be sure, pro-choice people, like pro-life people, do find certain behaviors intrinsically wrong and justify their rejection of such behaviors in terms not far afield from those of the pro-life people.) However, because they believe in and can afford a moral world that has many shades of gray, they often, as in the case of the embryo, find themselves drawing fine distinctions that their opponents dismiss as "hair-splitting."

The moral conflict about abortion for pro-choice people is in some way the mirror image of the pro-life conflict. If pro-life people have trouble accommodating complex real-life situations, such as their own need for an abortion, with a strict moral code, then pro-choice people face the dilemmas inherent in having a code so flexible that what is right and wrong is not immediately apparent but is discovered only as the product of immense amounts of intellectual effort. Because the morality of the pro-choice people rests on a delicate balancing of a range of competing rights, they are always slightly insecure as to whether they have covered all of the relevant data. Moreover, they are aware that the average person in the street is not as morally nuanced as they are, and they worry that what is for them the product of careful moral thought will just be taken for granted. Given these two very different methods of moral assessment, therefore, it might fairly be said that the demon of pro-life people is guilt, and the demon of pro-choice people is anxiety.

WORLD VIEWS

All these different issues that divide pro-life and pro-choice activists from one another—their views on men and women, sexuality, contraception, and morality—in turn reflect the fact that the two sides have two very different orientations to the world and that these orientations in turn revolve around two very different moral centers. The pro-life world view, notwithstanding the occasional atheist or agnostic attracted to it, is at the core one that centers around God: pro-life activists are on the whole deeply committed to their religious faith and deeply involved with it. A number of important consequences follow.

Because most pro-life people have a deep faith in God, they also believe in the rightness of His plan for the world. They are therefore skeptical about the ability of individual humans to understand, much less control, events that unfold according to a divine, rather than human, blueprint. From their point of view, human attempts at control are simply arrogance, an unwillingness to admit that larger forces than human will determine human fate. One woman made the point clearly: "God is the Creator of life, and I think all sexual activity should be open to that [creation]. That does not mean that you have to have a certain number of children or anything, but it should be open to Him and His will. The contraceptive mentality denies his will, 'It's my will, not your will.' And here again, the selfishness comes in."

This comment grew out of a discussion on contraception, but it also reveals values about human efficacy and its role in a larger world. While individuals can and should control their lives, pro-life people believe they should do so with a humility that understands that a force greater than themselves exists and, furthermore, that unpredicted things can be valuable. A woman who lost two children early in life to a rare genetic defect makes the point: "I didn't plan my son, my third child, and only because I was rather frightened that I might have a problem with another child. But I was certainly delighted when I became pregnant and had him. That's what I mean, I guess I feel that you can't plan everything in life. Some of the nicest things that have happened to me have certainly been the unplanned." Another woman went further: "I think people are foolish to worry about things in the future. The future takes care of itself."

Consequently, from the pro-life point of view, the contemporary movement away from the religious stand, what they see as the "secularization" of society, is at least one part of the troubles of contemporary society. By this they mean at least two things. First, there is the decline in religious commitment, which they feel keenly. But, second, they are also talking about a decline of a common community, a collective sense of what is right and wrong. From their viewpoint, once morality is no longer codified in some central set of rules that all accept and that finds its ultimate justification in the belief in a Supreme Being, then morality becomes a variation of "do your own thing."

For pro-life people, once the belief in a Supreme Being (and by definition a common sense of culture) is lost, a set of consequences emerge that not only creates abortion per se but creates a climate where phenomena such as abortion can flourish. For example, once one no longer believes in an afterlife, then one becomes more this-worldly. As a consequence, one becomes more interested in material goods and develops a world view that evaluates things (and, more importantly, people) in terms of what Marxists would call their "use value." Further, people come to live in the "here-and-now" rather than thinking of this life—and in particular the pain and disappointments of this life—as spiritual training for the next life. When the belief in God (and in an afterlife) are lost, pro-life people feel that human life becomes selfish, unbearably painful, and meaningless.

■   ■   ■

One of the harshest criticisms pro-life people make about pro-choice people, therefore, which encapsulates their feeling that pro-choice people are too focused on a short-term pragmatic view of the present world rather than on the long-term view of a transcendent world, is that pro-choice people are "utilitarian."

In part, pro-life people are right: the pro-choice world view is not centered around a Divine Being, but rather around a belief in the highest abilities of human beings. For them, reason—the human capacity to use intelligence, rather than faith, to understand and alter the environment—is at the core of their world; for many of them, therefore, religious or spiritual beliefs are restricted only to those areas over which humans have not yet established either knowledge or control: the origin of the universe, the meaning of life, etc. As one pro-choice activist, speaking of her own spiritual beliefs, noted: "What should I call it? Destiny? A Supreme Being? I don't know. I don't worship anything, I don't go anyplace and do anything about it, it's just an awareness that there's a whole area that might be arranging something for me, that I am not arranging myself—though every day I do more about arranging things myself."

Whatever religious values pro-choice people have are subordinated to a belief that individuals live in the here and now and must therefore make decisions in the present about the present. Few pro-choice people expressed clear beliefs in an afterlife so that their time frame includes only the worldly dimension of life. Thus, the entire articulation of their world view focuses them once again on human—rather than divine—capacities and, in particular, on the capacity for reason.

There are important implications to the fact that reason is the centerpiece of the pro-choice universe. First, they are, as their opponents claim, "utilitarian." Without explicitly claiming the heritage of the Scottish moralists, utilitarianism is consonant with many of the pro-choice side's vaguely Protestant beliefs and, more to the point, with their value of rationality and its extensions: control, planning, and fairness. Second, as this heritage implies, they are interventionists. From their point of view, the fact of being the only animal gifted with intellect means that humans should use that intellect to solve the problems of human existence. What the pro-life people see as a humility in the face of a God whose ways are unknowable to mere humans, pro-choice people see as a fatalistic reliance upon a Creator whom humans wishfully endow with magical powers. These same values lead pro-choice people to be skeptical of the claim that certain areas are, or should be, sacrosanct, beyond the reach of human intervention. *Sacred* to them is too close to *sacred cow*, and religion can merge imperceptibly into dogma, where the church could persecute Galileo because science was too threatening both to an old way of thinking of things and an established power structure. Truth, for pro-choice people, must always take precedence over faith.

Because of their faith in the human ability to discover truth, pro-choice people are on the whole optimistic about "human nature." While in their more despairing moments they can agree with the pro-life diagnosis of malaise in contemporary American life—that "things fall apart and the center does not hold" in Yeats' terms—they emphatically disagree upon the solution. Rather than advocate what they see as a retreat from the present, an attempt to re-create idealized images of the past, they would argue that "the Lord helps those who help themselves" and that people should rally to the task of applying human ingenuity to the problems that surround us.

In consequence, pro-choice people do not see suffering as either ennobling or as spiritual discipline. In fact, they see it as stupid, as a waste, and as a failure, particularly when technology exists to eliminate it. While some problems are not at present amenable to human control, pro-choice people will admit, they are sure to fall to the march of human progress. Thus, not only can humans "play God," it is, in an ironic sort of way, what they owe their Creator, if they have one: given the ability to alter Nature, it is immoral not to do so, especially when those activities will diminish human pain.

All of these values come home for pro-choice people when they talk about the *quality of life*. By this term they mean a number of things. In part they use this phrase as a short-hand way of indicating that they think of *life* as consisting of social as well as biological dimensions. The embryo, for example, is only a potential person to them in large part because it has not yet begun to have a social dimension to its life, only a physical one. In corollary, a pregnant woman's rights, being both social and physical, transcend those of the embryo. This view is rooted in their values about reason: biological life is physical and of the body. Humans share physical life with all other living beings, but reason is the gift of humans alone. Thus social life, which exists only by virtue of the human capacity for reason, is the more valuable dimension of life for pro-choice people. (This viewpoint explains in part why many pro-choice people find unfathomable the question of "when does life begin?" For them it is obvious: physical life began only once, most probably when the "cosmic soup" yielded its first complex amino acids, the forerunners of DNA; social life begins at "viability" when the embryo can live—and begin to form social relationships—outside of the womb.)

But for pro-life people, this line of reasoning is ominous. If social life is more important than physical life, it then follows that people may be ranked by the value of their social contributions, thus making invidious distinctions among individuals. In contrast, if physical life is valued because it is a gift from the Creator, then no mere human can make claim to evaluate among the gifts with which various individuals are born. A view that the physical or genetic dimension of life is paramount—that all who are born genetically human are, a priori, persons—means that at some level all are equal. A hopelessly damaged newborn is, on this level, as equally deserving of social resources as anyone else. What pro-life people fear is that if the pro-choice view of the world is adopted, then those who are less socially *productive* may be deemed less socially *valuable*. For pro-life people, many of whom have situational reasons to fear how pro-choice people would assign them a social price tag, such a prospect is a nightmare.

The phrase *quality of life* evokes for pro-choice people a pleasing vista of the human intellect directed to resolving the complicated problems of life—the urge for knowledge used to tame sickness, poverty, inequality, and other ills of humankind. To pro-life people, in contrast, precisely because it is focused on the here and now and actively rejects the sacred and the transcendent, it evokes the image of Nazi Germany where the "devalued" weak are sacrificed to enlarge the comfort of the powerful.

Thus, in similar ways, both pro-life and pro-choice world views founder on the same rock, that of assuming that others do (or must or should) share the same values. Pro-life people assume that all good people should follow God's teachings, and moreover they assume that most good-minded people would agree in the main as to what God's teachings actually are. (This conveniently overlooks such things as wars of religion, which are usually caused by differences of opinion on just such matters.) Pro-choice people, in their turn, because they value reason, assume that most reasonable people will come to similar solutions when confronted with similar problems. The paradox of utilitarianism, that one person's good may be another person's evil, as in the case of the pro-life belief that a too-effective contraceptive is a bad thing, is not something they can easily envisage, much less confront.[6]

NOTES

1. The classic study is Denis de Rougement, *Love in the Western World*.

2. Charles Westoff and Larry Bumpass, "The Revolution in Birth Control Practices of U.S. Roman Catholics," pp. 41–44.

3. Maurice Moore, *Death of a Dogma?*

4. See J. Marshall, "Cervical Mucus and Basal Body Temperature Methods of Regulating Births: A Field Trial," p. 282; M. E. Wade et al., "A Randomized Prospective Study of the Use-Effectiveness of Two Methods of Natural Family Planning," *American Journal of Obstetrics and Gynecology* 141 (1981):368–76.

5. Joseph Fletcher is considered the "father" of situation ethics. See Joseph Fletcher, *Medicine and Morals*.

6. For a thoughtful exposition of this and other dilemmas associated with the philosophy of utilitarianism, see Amartya Sen and Bernard Williams, eds., *Utilitarianism and Beyond*.

BIBLIOGRAPHY

De Rougement, Denis. *Love in the Western World*. New York: Harcourt Brace, 1940.

Fletcher, Joseph. *Medicine and Morals*. Princeton, NJ: Princeton University Press, 1954.

Marshall, J. "Cervical Mucus and Basal Body Temperature Methods of Regulating Births: A Field Trial." *Lancet* 2 (Aug. 1976):282.

Moore, Maurice. *Death of a Dogma? The American Catholic Clergy's View of Contraception*. Chicago: Community and Family Study Center, University of Chicago, 1973.

Sen, Amartya, and Bernard Williams, eds. *Utilitarianism and Beyond*. Cambridge: Cambridge University Press, 1982.

Westoff, Charles, and Larry Bumpass. "The Revolution in Birth Control Practices of U.S. Roman Catholics." *Science* 174 (June 1973):41–44.

9.3

GARY JACOBSON

From *A Divider, Not a Uniter*

Jacobson argues that George W. Bush's presidency (2001–2008) led to the deepest partisan divides in public opinion since the 1950s. Bush's decision to invade Iraq divided Democrats and Republicans over his presidency, and more generally over foreign policy and national security policy. Issues of national security have remained highly salient in public discourse over politics.

I. INTRODUCTION

In his convention speech accepting the Republican presidential nomination in August 2000, George W. Bush pledged to be "a uniter, not a divider," offering himself as an outsider with "no stake in the bitter arguments of the last few years" who could "change the tone of Washington to one of civility and respect."[1] Bush has instead become the most divisive and polarizing president in the more than 50 years that public opinion polls have regularly measured citizens' assessments of presidents. My purpose [here] is to explain how and why.

Bush's pledge of reconciliation was well gauged to appeal to a public weary of the fierce partisanship characteristic of the previous administration, epitomized by the congressional Republicans' attempt to impeach and remove Democratic president Bill Clinton less than two years earlier. Moreover, coming from a candidate who, as governor of Texas, had worked effectively with a Democratic legislature, it was credible. And indeed for a time during his first term, in the aftermath of the attacks on New York and Washington, D.C. by al Qaeda terrorists, Bush did rally virtually the entire nation, politicians and public alike, behind his leadership. But in the months before the events of September 11, 2001, had radically altered the political context, Bush had inspired the widest partisan differences in evaluations of·a newly elected president ever recorded. And by the time he sought reelection in 2004, he had become by a wide margin the most polarizing president on record.

The overall trends in public evaluations of George Bush are displayed in Figure 1.[2] . . . Summarized briefly—I will have much more to say about these patterns later—Bush's overall approval ratings drifted in the mid-50 percent range until the September 11 terrorist attacks, and the president's resolute response to them, provoked the greatest "rally"[3] in presidential approval ever

398

FIGURE 1 Approval of George W. Bush's Job Performance, 2001–2005

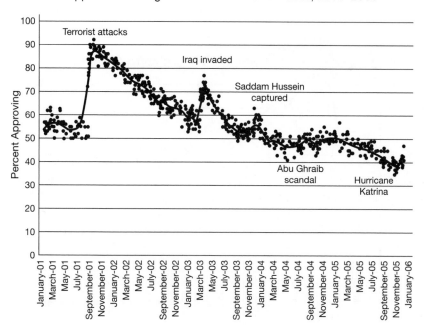

observed. Over the following fifteen months, his ratings returned gradually to where they had been before 9/11. The effects of another, more modest rally following the invasion of Iraq in March of 2003 eroded more quickly, as did the even smaller spike in approval later that year inspired by the capture of Saddam Hussein in December. Bush's low point for 2004 coincided with the Abu Ghraib prison scandal in the spring. His ratings recovered a bit around his reelection but continued on a downward trajectory thereafter, reaching the lowest point of his presidency to date in November 2005 in the face of rising gas prices, the federal government's inept response to the devastation wrought by Hurricane Katrina, the indictment of the vice president's top aide for perjury, and continuing difficulties in Iraq. A small up tick in early December, attributed to good economic numbers and a concentrated campaign to stem the decline in support for the Iraq War, still left his approval ratings hovering a little above 40 percent.

These trends reflect, then, the signal events of Bush's presidency to date more or less as the standard literature on presidential approval would predict.[4] Far less standard is their partisan composition. When the data are disaggregated by the respondent's party identification (Figure 2),[5] it is apparent that independents and Democrats account for nearly all of the temporal variance in the president's job approval. Republicans' approval rates have been very high from the start and have moved comparatively little in response to changing circumstances and events. Even at his low point in the fall of 2005,

FIGURE 2 Approval of George W. Bush's Job Performance, 2001–2005, by Party Identification

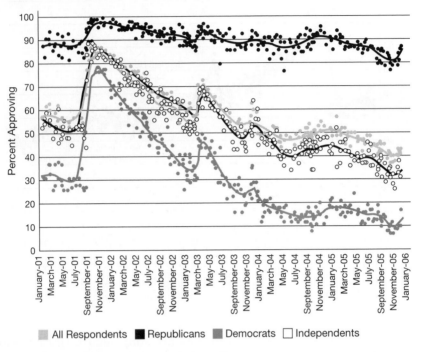

Legend: ■ All Respondents ■ Republicans ■ Democrats □ Independents

Source: 279 CBS News/New York Times polls.

about 80 percent of Republicans continued to approve of Bush's performance. He received relatively low marks from Democrats until the terrorist attacks, after which they rallied to deliver the highest approval ratings ever given to a president by rival-party identifiers, reaching a record 84 percent in one October 2001 Gallup Poll. Thereafter, the steady downward trend in approval among Democrats was interrupted only temporarily by the onset of the Iraq War and later capture of Saddam Hussein and, by the beginning of 2004, had dipped below 20 percent. Democrats' approval fell further during the campaign, hitting a low of 8 percent in one October 2004 Gallup Poll. It rose a bit after the election, but a year later had fallen to the lowest levels ever recorded by Gallup among rival party identifiers, reaching 7 percent in one late October 2005 survey.[6] To put this figure in perspective, it is 4 percentage points lower than Richard Nixon's worst showing among Democrats just before he resigned in disgrace in 1974.

In the course of his first term, then, partisan differences in George W. Bush's approval ratings went from the widest for any newly elected president, to the narrowest ever recorded after 9/11, and then to the widest for any president at any time by the end of his first term in office. . . .

Before Bush and going back to Eisenhower, the partisan difference in approval ratings had never exceeded 70 percentage points in any Gallup Poll (Figure 3). In the 18 Gallup Polls taken during the final two quarters of 2004, the gap never fell *below* 70, averaged 78 and peaked at 83 (94-11). The gap decreased somewhat after the election (averaging 72 points during 2005) but still remained in previously uncharted territory. The partisan divisions were deep as well as wide; in the sixteen ABC News/*Washington Post* surveys taken from the beginning of 2004 through August 2005 that asked respondents how strongly they approved or disapproved of the president, an average of 66 percent of Republicans approved strongly (comprising 75 percent of all Republican approvers), while 62 percent of Democrats disapproved strongly (comprising 78 percent of all Democratic disapprovers).[7]

Several other things are noteworthy in this historical comparison. In previous administrations, approval ratings offered by both parties' identifiers tended to move together and by similar amounts. When, for example, the president's party's approval rating is regressed on the opposing party's approval rating approval for each administration from Eisenhower through Clinton, the regression coefficient ranges from .33 to .92, with an average of .56. That is, on average in previous administrations, a 10 point shift in approval among the opposing partisans is accompanied by a 5.6 point shift among the president's partisans. For the George W. Bush administration,

FIGURE 3 Partisan Differences in Presidential Approval, Eisenhower through G.W. Bush (Quarterly Averages)

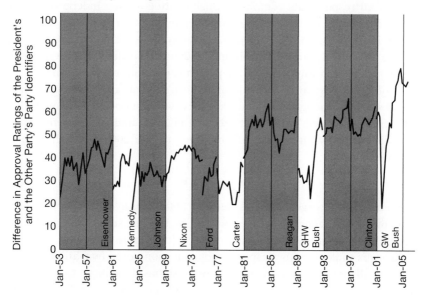

SOURCE: Gallup Polls.

the coefficient is .16; a 10 point shift among Democrats would be accompanied by a 1.6 point shift among Republicans. Among Bush's own partisans, approval is not only highest on average for any president, but it is also the least volatile, with a standard deviation of only 4.1 percentage points. Among Democrats, it is the most volatile, with the standard deviation at 19.6 percentage points.[8]

The data in Figure 3 also indicate that partisan differences in presidential approval have grown since the 1970s. From Eisenhower through Carter, the partisan gap averaged 34 percentage points. Under Reagan the average gap rose to 52 points. The partisan gap for the senior Bush was similar to that for pre-Reagan presidents, 36 points, but by the end of his presidency it was as wide as for Reagan. The average difference for Clinton was 55 points, and for G.W. Bush so far it is 59 points, the highest of any president despite the extraordinarily high level of approval he received from Democrats in the year following 9/11. I will have more to say about this upward trend in the next chapter.

Finally, returning to Figure 2, notice that Bush's approval level among self-identified independents has been considerably closer to that of Democrats than of Republicans. This is unusual. Although independents are usually a bit closer to opposition partisans than to the president's partisans on this measure, the difference has always been much smaller than for Bush. For example, Bill Clinton's average approval rating among independents was 27 points higher than among Republicans, 28 points lower than among Democrats. Independents were thus only about 1 point closer to one set of partisans than the other, and the average ratings of independents were virtually identical to those of all respondents combined. Bush's rating among independents has averaged 35 points lower than among Republicans, 21 points higher than among Democrats, and thus 14 point closer to the latter. If analysis is confined to polls taken since the beginning of 2004, the difference is even larger, 18 points, and his rating among independents is 6 points lower than his average among all respondents. Thus only Bush's sustained, remarkably high level of support among Republicans kept his overall support level from falling well below 50 percent after the beginning of 2004, and without continuing Republican loyalty, the president's numbers in late 2005 would have been even more dismal.

■　　■　　■

In retrospect, George W. Bush's pledge in 2000 to be a "uniter, not a divider" turns out to be deeply ironic, as he has, by the measures examined here, become the most divisive occupant of the White House in at least 50 years. The irony is underlined by responses to a question posed by Gallup in October 2004, displayed in Figure 4. Asked if Bush has done more to unite or to divide the country, Americans as a whole divided precisely in half, 48 percent choosing each alternative; 87 percent of Republicans said that he had done

FIGURE 4 "Has George W. Bush done more to unite the country, or has he done more to divide the country?"

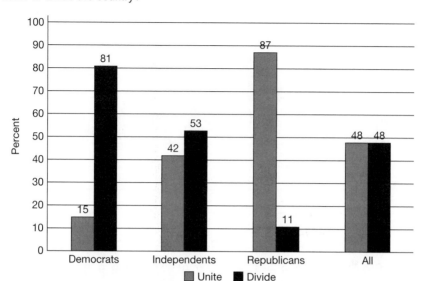

more to unite the country, while 81 percent of Democrats said he had done more to divide it. This is the rare survey question that, in the distribution of responses, effectively answered itself.

. . . Why has the public become so thoroughly divided along party lines about this president? There is, I shall argue, no single answer, but rather a complex set of converging political forces, events, and decisions that brought public opinion on this president to its present state. Responses to Bush had been shaped by both deep, enduring historical currents and random historical accidents; they have been affected by the president's own character, policy choices, and strategies, as well as by conditions entirely beyond his (or anyone else's) control. . . .

6. ILLUSION, DISILLUSION, AND FAITH IN THE PRESIDENT AFTER "MISSION ACCOMPLISHED"

■ ■ ■

The Iraq Rally

. . . [T]he onset of war in Iraq inspired a substantial rally in President Bush's overall job approval ratings (Figures 1 and 2) and in evaluations of his handling of the situation in Iraq. The rally was joined by partisans across the board but was naturally smaller among Republicans than among other citizens because their ratings of the president were already so high. The war was

FIGURE 5 Popular Support for War in Iraq (All Question Wordings)

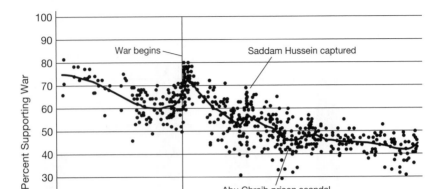

SOURCE: See note 9.

also the subject of its own rally, visible in Figure 5. Assessing support for the war is complicated by the diversity of questions pollsters use to measure it; different questions elicit different levels of support, and the frequency with which each is asked has changed with evolving circumstances. . . . Figure 5 displays the most general picture by including data from multiple variants of 11 different questions, with a smoothing line summarizing the noisy trend.[9] [S]upport for invading Iraq was high right after September 11, when most Americans suspected Saddam Hussein was at least partly responsible. It declined as the focus turned to Osama bin Laden and Afghanistan, revived late in the administration's campaign to portray Iraq as a threat requiring immediate action, rose sharply after the onset of hostilities, and peaked in April just before the president's "Mission Accomplished" moment on the carrier.

■　　■　　■

It is likely that support for the war policy itself grew during March and April with the military successes of U.S. forces on the ground, the remarkably low American casualties,[10] and televised images of joyful Iraqis toppling Saddam's statue. Thereafter, however, the continuing chaos, insurgency, and loss of American and allied lives began to sap support for the war, particularly among Democrats and independents. Figure 6 displays the data and

FIGURE 6 Party Identification and Support for the Iraq War (All Question Wordings)

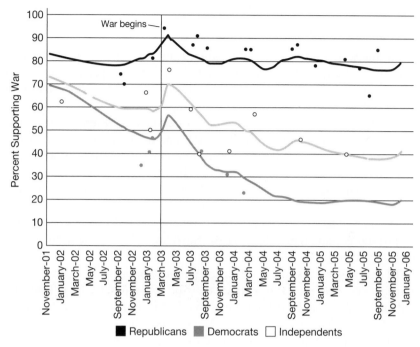

Lowess-smoothed trends in support for the Iraq War, disaggregated by party. The gap between Republicans and Democrats narrowed slightly in the first month of the war then grew steadily wider for the following 18 months. . . . It reaches an average of about 63 percentage points in the last quarter of 2004 before narrowing a bit to an average of about 58 percent during 2005. A *Los Angeles Times* Poll question asking whether Bush had made the right decision to go to war, in light of the CIA's report that Saddam had no WMD and no active program to produce them, generated the widest divergence of any survey, with 90 percent of Republicans but only 10 percent of Democrats answering "yes."[11]

▪   ▪   ▪

[P]artisan divisions on the Iraq War were already substantial before it began. These narrowed in the early weeks of the war but soon widened again when the war's principal premises could not be confirmed and partisans responded to that emerging story quite differently. Most Republicans either refused to recognize that neither WMD nor a 9/11 connection could be substantiated or accepted the substitute justifications offered by the administration after the fact, whereas Democrats, with no inclination to miss the message or adopt new reasons for support, grew increasingly opposed to the war—and increasingly disaffected with President Bush.

Belief in the War's Premises

Before the war, a large majority of Americans regardless of party believed Saddam was hiding WMD, and about half thought he was personally involved in 9/11. After the war, as time passed and the search for WMD and an al Qaeda connection continued to turn up nothing of substance, these beliefs became less common, but neither rapidly or completely. Right after the war, about a third of the public thought WMD had actually been found; a year later, nearly 20 percent still clung to this misconception. The proportion who believed Iraq possessed WMD (even if they had not been found) also declined, but more than a year after the war a majority held this view and continued to do so through March 2005 despite all the official reports to the contrary. The belief that Saddam had a hand in September 11 also declined, but not very steeply; more than 30 months after Baghdad had fallen, about a third of the public still thought he had been involved.

The data suggest that the main reason public opinion did not respond more sharply to postwar revelations is that they did surprisingly little to shake the faith of Republicans in Bush's original case for the war, even after the administration had officially abandoned it. Among Republicans, belief in Saddam's WMD peaked at 95 percent just before the war and has not fallen below 69 percent since; it actually increased a bit in the first quarter of 2005, averaging 81 percent and leaving a partisan gap on this question of about 46 points. In February 2003, 79 percent of Democrats had thought Saddam possessed WMD; within about 15 months, that figure had fallen to 33 percent. Belief in Saddam's involvement in 9/11 also declined less steeply among Republicans than among Democrats or independents. From a peak right after Baghdad fell in April 2003 through October 2005, it dropped from 65 to 44 percent among Republicans, from 51 to 32 percent among independents, and from 49 percent to 25 percent among Democrats in these surveys.

Rather more surprising than these partisan differences is the extent to which even Democrats continued to believe the allegations long after well-publicized official reports had found no evidence to support them and the president and his administration had ostensibly disavowed them. Evidently, Saddam's evil reputation continued to predispose Americans to think the worst and to ignore or forget exculpatory information. A March 2005 ABC News/*Washington Post* Poll documented its staying power; a majority of Americans continued to believe that solid evidence has been found proving that Iraq had directly supported al Qaeda (21 percent) or at least to suspect such a connection (39 percent).[12] One important source of these continuing misperceptions is no doubt the Bush administration's continued use of artfully insinuating rhetoric. On March 19, 2005, the second anniversary of the U.S. invasion, the president put it this way: "We knew of Saddam Hussein's record of aggression and support for terror. We knew of his long history of pursuing, even using, weapons of mass destruction, and we know that September 11 requires our country to think differently."[13] With rhetoric like this—lumping together in two sentences Saddam Hussein, September 11, terror, and WMD—no wonder most Americans thought the administration was still advancing claims unsubstantiated by its own investigations despite having officially abandoned them.

■ ■ ■

In sum, revelations that its main premises were faulty did little to undermine Republicans' support for the Iraq War because they were less likely than other Americans to get the message, less likely to withdraw support if they did, and more willing to adopt alternative rationales emphasized after the fact by the Bush administration. Among independents and Democrats, however, support for the war depended heavily on its original justifications and thus fell as these became increasingly untenable. As a consequence, on virtually every question concerning the premises, necessity, wisdom, and effect of going to war in Iraq, partisan differences grew very large.

NOTES

1. Speech to Republican National Convention, August 3, 2000, accepting the nomination.

2. Each point in the figure represents the proportion of respondents in a poll who responded "approve" when asked, "Do you approve or disapprove of the way George W. Bush is handling his job as president?" or some close variant. The Lowess smoothed trend (bandwidth=.05) is shown by the solid line. Data are from the CBS/*New York Times* Poll, the Gallup Poll, NBC News/*Wall Street Journal* Poll, Pew Research Center for the People and the Press Poll, *Newsweek* Poll, ABC News/*Washington Post* Poll, *Los Angeles Times* Poll, *Time* Poll, CNN/*Time* Poll, and Associated Press/IPSOS Poll reported at http://pollingreport.com/wh.htm, December 22, 2005. Only surveys that sample the entire adult population are included.

3. The term entered the literature with John E. Mueller's *War, Presidents, and Public Opinion* (New York: John Wiley and Sons, 1973), p. 53.

4. Cf. Richard A. Brody, *Assessing the President* (Stanford: Stanford University Press, 1991); Mueller, *Wars, Presidents, and Public Opinion*.

5. Unless otherwise specified, I do not include leaners in the partisan categories; I do so not on theoretical grounds (although some, notably Warren E. Miller and J. Merrill Shanks in *The New American Voter* [Cambridge: Harvard University Press, 1996], Ch. 6, would argue that I should), but because most of the polls I examine here treat leaners as independents. Typically in these polls, a little more than a third of the respondents identify themselves as Democrats, a little less than a third call themselves Republicans, and about a third say they are independents.

6. The 7 percent figure was matched in the November 10–13, 2005 Gallup survey.

7. On average in these polls, 66 percent of all respondents have expressed strong approval or disapproval of the president, compared to 31 percent who said they approved or disapproved "somewhat." They are accessible at http://www.washington post.com/wp-dyn/politics/polls.

8. The opposing partisans usually display greater volatility in approval ratings; the ratio of the standard deviation of approval ratings of the opposing party to that of the president's party ranges from .97 to 2.18:1, with an average of 1.53:1. For G.W. Bush, the ratio is 4.90:1.

9. These data are from national polls sampling all adults or registered or likely voters conducted by the CBS News/*New York Times*, ABC News/*Washington Post*, NBC News/*Wall Street Journal*, *Los Angeles Times*, *Gallup*, Pew Center for the People and Press, *Newsweek*, CNN/*Time*, Fox News, Quinnipiac College, National Annenberg Election Study, Knowledge Networks, and Democracy Corps polls reported at http://www.pollintreport.com or at the polling outfit's website. The various question wordings are shown in the Appendix.

10. American military deaths in Iraq in March and April 2003 numbered 139; there were also 33 British fatalities; the number of wounded is listed as 542. See http://icasualties.org/oif/ (accessed July 19, 2005).

11. *Los Angeles Times Poll Alert*, Study #510, October 25, 2004.

12. ABC News/*Washington Post* Poll, March 10–13, 2005, analyzed by author.

13. Richard Boudreaux, "Insurgent Attacks Continue 2 Years After the U.S. Invasion," *Los Angeles Times*, March 20, 2005, A4.

10

PARTICIPATION

10.1

STEVEN ROSENSTONE AND JOHN MARK HANSEN

From *Mobilization, Participation,*
and American Democracy

People participate in politics for a variety of reasons. Rosenstone and Hansen
emphasize several key factors in explaining why some types of people participate
more than others. Simply put, those people who are easily mobilized and who
tend to have similar preferences to the organizations that routinely mobilize are
the ones most likely to participate. Rosenstone and Hansen's arguments put
more emphasis on the attributes of mobilizing organizations than on the per-
sonal attributes of the people being mobilized.

Why do people get involved in politics? Why do some people participate in
politics while others do not? Why are citizens deeply committed to participation in politics at some times and wholly passive at other times?

We offer two answers, one personal, one political. Working from one side,
the personal, we trace participation to the individual characteristics of citizens. People participate in politics when they get valuable benefits that are
worth the costs of taking part. Working from the other side, the political, we
trace participation to the strategic choices of political leaders. People participate in politics when political leaders coax them into taking part in the game.
Both sides are necessary: Strategic mobilization without individual motivation is impossible, and individual motivation without strategic mobilization
is illogical.

The complex interaction of the personal and the political stems from the
nature of democratic politics. We view democratic politics as a struggle for

political power among competing political leaders. In such a system, citizen activism has *two* beneficiaries: It is a source of policy benefits for citizens and a source of political advantage for leaders. Accordingly, to understand political participation, we must appreciate how it is used, both by individual citizens and by their leaders.

In this [reading], we lay out the political logic of citizen activism in politics. First, working from the individual perspective, we lay out the benefits and costs of political participation and show how individual resources, interests, preferences, identifications, and beliefs determine the relative attractions of the benefits and the relative burdens of the costs. Next, we consider individuals in political society. We show how the social nature of political life affects the individual rewards of involvement. We show how the social nature of political life makes people accessible and amenable to the appeals of political leaders. And we show how the strategic choices of political leaders determine who participates and when.

Political participation, we conclude, cannot be explained entirely by the orientations and endowments of individual citizens. The competitive pressures of the democratic system encourage political leaders to mobilize their fellow citizens, and if we are to understand participation, we must also comprehend their choices.

INDIVIDUAL INFLUENCES ON POLITICAL PARTICIPATION

People participate in politics for a variety of personal reasons. Some people participate because it does not cost them much; some participate because they receive lots of benefits. As stated, this personal explanation of political activism is both obvious and tautological: It explains everything because it rules out nothing.

Even so, as political theorist Brian Barry noted, "it is still a quite potent tautology, because it can be combined with empirical assertions to produce significant implications." Our task in this section is to supply empirical linkages, to develop the implications of different resources for the relative costs of participation, and to develop the implications of different interests and attitudes for the relative benefits of participation.

Costs and Resources

Participation in politics puts demands on people's scarce resources. Working on a political campaign requires time; writing a letter requires verbal acuity; making a donation to a candidate requires money; signing a petition requires a sense of personal competence. Participation in politics, that is, has a price, a price that is some combination of money, time, skill, knowledge, and self-confidence.

Some people are better able to pay the price than others. In economic life people with greater resources can consume more of (almost) everything, from fancy meals to fast cars to flashy clothes. In social life people with greater resources can do more of (almost) everything, from entertaining friends to joining organizations to volunteering at schools, churches, and charities. So, too, in political life. People with abundant money, time, skill, knowledge, and self-confidence devote more resources to politics, not because politics gives them more in return (although it might) but because they can more easily afford it. Many of the most familiar empirical regularities in American politics follow from this simple observation.

First, the wealthy vote, write, campaign, and petition more than the poor. This should come as no surprise. Citizens with lots of income can simply afford to do more—of everything—than citizens with little money. The wealthy have discretionary income that they can contribute directly to political parties, candidates, political action committees, and other causes. Moreover, money is fungible—it can be freely converted into other political resources that make it easier for people to take part in politics. A car is not a necessary condition for political action, for example, but having one makes it much easier to get to a school board meeting, a political rally, or a candidate's campaign headquarters. Money can be used to hire someone to do the daily chores—to clean the house, buy the groceries, cook dinner, baby-sit the kids—and free up time for politics. Thus, if people want to participate in politics, money makes it easier for them to do so.

The costs of political activity can also be measured in opportunities forgone. Taking part in politics requires that people forfeit or postpone other activities, and these opportunity costs of participation are higher for some people than for others. Because the resources of the wealthy are more ample, they do not face the same hard tradeoffs that the poor face every day of their lives. As important and interesting as politics may be, its significance pales in comparison with paying the rent, maintaining the car, keeping the children in school, and putting food on the table. In short, for people whose resources are limited, politics is a luxury they often cannot afford, particularly when political outcomes may have only a modest impact on their own economic situations.

Second, the more educated are more likely to take part in politics than the less educated. Again, no surprise. In the United States, the educational experience fosters democratic values and nurtures a sense of citizen competence, both of which encourage participation. More important, however, education provides skills that facilitate participation in politics. As Wolfinger and Rosenstone argue, "education imparts information about politics and cognate fields and about a variety of skills, some of which facilitate political learning. . . . Schooling increases one's capacity for understanding and working with complex, abstract and intangible subjects, that is, subjects like politics. Skills in research, writing, and speaking, developed through education, help citizens to negotiate the maze of demands that participation places on them. To cast a ballot, citizens must figure out how to register to vote; they must make sense of the candidates and issues; they must locate polling places. To write a letter to a senator, citizens must compose a persuasive message once they have identified the senator and looked up her address. For the grade-school educated, these are daunting tasks; for the college educated, they are easy. The better educated have been better trained to participate in politics.

Finally, those with many years of formal schooling are substantially more likely to read newspapers, follow the news, and be politically informed, all of which makes them more aware of the opportunities to participate and more likely to possess information with which to do so.

This is not to say that politically useful knowledge and skills derive only from the classroom. Lessons picked up from the "school of hard knocks" can compensate for formal education, imparting equivalent knowledge, experience, and skills. With experience comes familiarity with the political process, familiarity with and increased attachment to the political parties and their candidates, and familiarity with the ins and outs of political action: what people need to do to take part and where people need to go to do it. Hence, older citizens vote, write, campaign, and petition more than young citizens who have had less experience in politics.

Finally, people with a sense of political efficacy are more likely to take a more active part in politics than those without this belief. By efficacy we mean both a sense of personal competence in one's ability to understand politics and to participate in politics (what political scientists call internal efficacy), as well as a sense that one's political activities can influence what the government actually does (external efficacy). Some people come to believe in their personal competence because they have been told again and again, by parents, teachers, and friends, that their efforts make a difference. Other people come to believe in their personal competence because they have acted and in fact found their actions consequential. As defined, it is already evident that efficacy is an important political resource. Working in a campaign or signing a petition involves some sense that the cause is not hopeless (even if the particular effort is). Participation is a waste of time if one does not believe that one's efforts make a material difference to political outcomes. Those who have confidence that their participation will make a difference are more likely to act than those who lack that basic confidence.

In summary, the costs of political activism affect different people in different ways, depending on their resources. For people with abundant money, time, knowledge, skills, and efficacy, involvement costs very little. Consequently, they participate more.

Rewards Interests, and Beliefs

People participate in politics because they get something out of it. The rewards take many forms. Participants sometimes enjoy *material benefits*, tangible rewards that are easily converted into money, like a government job or a tax break. Those active in politics can also receive *solidary benefits*, intangible rewards that stem from social interaction, like status, deference, and friend-ship. And participation can also yield *purposive benefits*, intrinsic rewards that derive from the act of participation itself, such as a sense of satisfaction from having contributed to a worthy cause.

This typology, suggested by James Q. Wilson, gives an idea of the great variety of possible benefits from participation, but for our purposes, the dis-tinction between collective and selective rewards is more important. *Collective rewards,* on the one hand, benefit every resident of a particular place or every member of a particular group, whether she took part in politics or not. Most, but not all, are material. A clean air bill, for example, benefits every resident of Los Angeles, New York, or Denver. A residential parking ordi-nance benefits every resident of the neighborhoods surrounding a hospital. A mortgage interest deduction for homeowners benefits every homeowner, homebuilder, and realtor. An end to the ban on interstate sales of firearms benefits every gun owner and gun dealer. People receive collective rewards regardless of whether they participate. *Selective rewards,* on the other hand, benefit only those people who take part in politics. Some selective rewards are material: Government jobs in Brooklyn, for instance, may go exclusively to campaign workers. Others are solidary: Recognition as a leader falls only to neighborhood activists. Many are purposive: A sense of having done one's duty accrues only to those who have done their duty. Unlike collective rewards, people receive selective rewards because they participate; by the same token, people forgo selective rewards because they do not.

Each form of citizen participation in politics offers a unique mix of collec-tive and selective benefits. Citizens find each combination of benefits more or less worthwhile depending on their interests, preferences, identifications, and beliefs. A man who works for the park district of the city of Chicago might view campaign work as a requirement of his job. A woman who lives on a farm in west Texas might see attendance at county commission meetings as a rare opportunity for visiting with friends and neighbors. A man who has been socialized with a deep sense of obligation to participate in the community might see voting as a way to live up to his duty. Depending on their needs, cer-tain kinds of participation make more sense for certain people than other kinds of participation.

These observations help to structure our ideas about the role that interests, preferences, identifications, and beliefs play in promoting participation in politics.

First, people who have a direct stake in political outcomes are obviously more likely to participate in politics than people who do not have such an immediate stake. Parents who have children in public schools, for instance, are much more likely to attend school board meetings than other people, sim-ply because the school board makes decisions that affect the welfare of their children directly, broadly, and consequentially. Although everybody in the community has an interest in the financial decisions that school boards make, only parents typically care very much about such matters as curricular requirements, athletics and activities, bus routes, crossing guards, and dress codes. People with direct interests anticipate greater material rewards, both collective and selective, from their actions.

Second, people who strongly prefer one political outcome to another are more likely to enter politics than people who have weaker preferences. Voters consistently complain that American elections offer no choices, only echoes. Their complaint, however, is not always on the mark. Some people see differences where others see none. For many Americans in 1948, Harry Truman and Thomas Dewey were Tweedledum and Tweedledee: Both supported the New Deal welfare state and both were anticommunist cold warriors. But for members of industrial labor unions the differences between them were clear: Truman was the defender of the National Labor Relations Act against the anti-union Republicans in Congress. Likewise, the system sometimes offers a real choice. Although voters might be forgiven for confusing Gerald Ford and Jimmy Carter in 1976, few could fail to discern the differences between Lyndon Johnson and Barry Goldwater in 1964 or Ronald Reagan and Walter Mondale in 1984.

The variations in preferences are important. Those who strongly prefer one candidate or one party or one policy to another anticipate greater policy benefits from the outcome than those whose preferences are weaker. Accordingly, they are more likely to get involved in politics.

Third, people who identify closely with political contenders are more likely to participate in politics than people whose psychological identifications are weaker. This may sound, on its face, like a restatement of the preceding point, but it is not. Before, we argued that strong preferences heighten the value of extrinsic rewards of participation, of material and solidary benefits that arise as a consequence of political action. Here, we argue that strong psychological attachments heighten the value of intrinsic rewards from participation, of the internal satisfactions that derive from taking part. Just as sports fans take pleasure in cheering on their favorite teams, so partisans take pleasure in acting on behalf of their favorite politicians, parties, or groups. The more committed the fans, the more lusty their cheers; the more committed the partisans, the more likely their participation.

Because of their psychological attachments, then, issue activists are more likely to write letters to their representatives in Congress. Because of their psychological attachments, likewise, strong Democrats and strong Republicans are more likely to be active in elections than independents or weak partisans. Political participation appeals more to the strongly than the weakly committed because the strongly committed derive greater personal satisfaction from it.

Finally, some people hold beliefs and preferences that motivate their participation internally. The most common is a sense of citizen duty. Because of their socialization by family, teachers, or friends, some people believe it is their responsibility to participate in politics—and in particular to vote—regardless of whether their participation has any effect on the outcome. Obviously, people who hold these beliefs are more likely to participate: Taking part makes them feel that they have discharged their obligations. The purposive rewards of participation are selective.

Thus, the benefits of political participation appeal to different people in different ways, depending on their interests, preferences, identifications, and beliefs. People who perceive more at stake in politics—because policies affect them more, identities beckon them more, options appeal to them more, or duty calls them more—participate more in politics.

People get involved in politics, then, in predictable ways: Because of their resources, some people can better afford politics than others; because of their interests, preferences, identifications, and beliefs, some people get more benefit from politics than others. Clearly, the two work together. No matter how valuable the benefits of participation, people cannot take part unless they have sufficient resources to do so. No matter how ample the resources, people will not take part unless they get more out of politics than other pursuits. Taken together, these considerations help to explain why some people take part in politics and others do not.

POLITICAL INFLUENCES ON PARTICIPATION: STRATEGIC MOBILIZATION

When applied to the question of *which* people participate in politics, the individual explanations of political activism that we have just discussed seem to satisfy. But when applied to the question of *when* people participate in politics, their inadequacies begin to show.

Suppose, for instance, that people participate in politics because of the solidary or the purposive benefits they receive—the approbations of their friends or the satisfactions from a duty performed. It stands to reason, then, that participation should not fluctuate very much from month to month or from year to year because fundamental social identifications and political beliefs change only slowly, if at all. The same people should turn out for politics time and time again.

Yet this prediction is wrong. . . . Both the level of political participation and the people who participate change significantly from month to month, year to year, and election to election. That being the case, we need to turn to the *political* circumstances that change over time and induce people to take part at one moment and not another: the personal qualities and policy stands of the candidates for office; the issues that appear and disappear on the political agenda; the actions of the politicians, parties, and interest groups that compete for political advantage. These considerations, in turn, lead to an explanation of political participation that emphasizes the collective benefits that people receive from political outcomes, such as military spending, abortion rights, tax breaks, and other public policies. But this line of thinking immediately runs up against two deadly logical conundrums.

Two Paradoxes: Participation and Rational Ignorance

The first difficulty is the famous "paradox of voting," or, more broadly, the "paradox of participation in politics.[1] If people are rational, the paradox holds, and if they receive only collective benefits, they will not turn out to vote, and for very good reason: The result of the election will be the same whether they participate or not. In any election, hundreds or thousands or millions of voters will cast ballots; the chance that a single ballot will determine the result is exceedingly small. In 1960, for example, the closest presidential election in the twentieth century, John F. Kennedy's victory over Richard M. Nixon hinged on 115,000 votes, only 0.2 percent of the total, but still a very large number. At the same time, casting a vote is costly. At a minimum, voters must spend time, energy, and money rousting themselves to polling places and marking their ballots. Thus, even if the outcome of the election really matters to people, trying to affect it does not make any sense. Rational people choose the most efficient means to achieve their goals; they do not knowingly waste their scarce resources. Voting, it follows, is irrational: It consumes resources but achieves no results that would not be achieved otherwise.

The same paradox holds with equal force for other forms of political activity. Objectively, the probability that any one person's one lonely act will determine a political outcome is vanishingly small. One more letter mailed to Congress, one more person attending a meeting, one more dollar sent to a campaign, one more person persuaded to vote will not make a bit of difference to the result, but it will cost the participant. If people receive only collective benefits from political outcomes, therefore, they will not participate in politics. Political action, if it occurs, is irrational.[2]

The second difficulty is "rational ignorance."[3] If political involvement is irrational, so, for much the same reason, is political learning. First, information about politics and government must be gathered, and its cost is far above zero. Washington is a distant place, government is a complicated business, and the press can be relied on to cover only a fraction of what the government is up to. Likewise, candidates for office are unfamiliar people, their records are voluminous, and the media are quite selective in their coverage of the campaigns. Second, the value of information, once obtained, is very small, precisely because of the paradox of participation in politics. Even if voters had lots of information about the issues debated in Washington and the issues contested in campaigns, what good would it do them? It makes no sense for them to act on it anyway: The outcome will be the same regardless. Thus, citizens have few incentives to inform themselves about politics. They stay "rationally ignorant."

Thus, the question of when people involve themselves in politics cannot be addressed solely within the context of individual motives and behaviors. One approach fails to provide an answer, and the other gets tangled in its own logic. Instead, the explanation of participation, to make any sense, must move beyond the worlds of individuals to include family, friends, neighbors, and co-workers, plus politicians, parties, activists, and interest groups.

The Social Nature of Political Life

With few exceptions, people are deeply embedded in a web of social relationships with family, friends, neighbors, and co-workers. Within these circles, people convey expectations to others about the kinds of behaviors, some political, that are appropriate and desirable. Sometimes they relate their expectations overtly: They ask acquaintances directly to do something. More often they relate their expectations subtly: They simply raise their concerns. What's more, people in these networks reward those who comply with expectations, and they sanction those who do not. They praise, esteem, and owe favors to those who do act, and reprove, shun, and take note of those who do not. Social networks, in short, create solidary rewards and bestow them, selectively, on those who act in the common interest.

For most people, the obligations and rewards of friendship, camaraderie, neighborliness, and family ties are very powerful. People want to be accepted, valued, and liked. As a consequence, social networks play a key role in overcoming the paradoxes of participation and rational ignorance.

Social networks address rational ignorance. They provide information. Participants in family, work, and friendship groups communicate, and in doing so they learn about politics from others in the group. They likewise reward contributions of information. Family, work, and friendship groups favor those who offer their knowledge to the collegium. Thus, because of social networks, each person bears the cost of collecting only a fraction of the political information she receives.

Too, social networks address the paradox of participation. People take part in family, work, and friendship groups on a regular and sustained basis. Consequently, members of social networks can identify readily those who comply with social expectations and those who do not, that is, those who vote and write and attend and otherwise participate in politics and those who do not. In turn, because members of social networks can distinguish participants from pikers, they can also selectively reward the one and sanction the other. Finally, because they can reward and sanction discerningly, they can also create and enforce expectations that many will act in concert. Although one letter to Congress is not likely to have any impact, one thousand letters is, and although one vote for governor is not likely to make a difference, one hundred thousand votes is. Social networks, the everyday groupings of friends, family, and associates, make effective, coordinated, political action possible.

They do not, however, make effective, coordinated, political action probable. Most citizens are not in positions to know what is occurring in politics, nor do they know anybody who is. Neither they nor their families, friends, and co-workers really know whether their interests are enough at stake at the moment to warrant political action—of whatever kind—being undertaken to advance or defend them.

Others in the system have such knowledge close at hand. Because they are in the thick of political battles, political leaders, be they candidates, party officials, interest groups, or activists, know exactly what is on the political agenda and exactly how it affects people. And because they are in the thick of political battles, they have a tangible incentive to convey such information to the people who can help them to win.

For politicians, political parties, interest groups, and activists, citizen involvement is an important political resource. In a democracy, the people's wants are supposed to matter. In elections, for example, candidates for office and their organized supporters need citizens' votes, money, and time. In national government, likewise, elected officials, interest groups, and activists want votes in Congress, favors from the White House, and rulings from the bureaucracy, and they can use citizens' letters, petitions, and protests to help get them. In local government, finally, neighborhoods want stop signs from city councils and parents want computer labs from school boards, and they can use citizens' contacts, presence, and pressures to try to get them. Citizen participation is a resource that political leaders use in their struggles for political advantage. We call their efforts to deploy it "mobilization."

Political Mobilization

Mobilization is the process by which candidates, parties, activists, and groups induce other people to participate. We say that one of these actors has *mobilized* somebody when it has done something to increase the likelihood of her participation.

We distinguish two types of mobilization. Leaders mobilize people *directly* when they contact citizens personally and encourage them to take action. Door-to-door canvasses by campaign organizations, direct mail solicitations by political agitators, televised appeals for aid by presidents, and grass-roots letter drives by interest groups are examples of direct mobilization. Leaders mobilize people *indirectly* when they contact citizens through mutual associates, whether family, friends, neighbors, or colleagues. When candidates solicit employers for campaign money and bosses in turn encourage their employees to give, when local activists push their friends to attend meetings and friends ask family to accompany them, when parties contact workers in a plant and the workers ask their co-workers to vote, that is indirect mobilization.

Direct mobilization

Through direct mobilization, political leaders provide opportunities for political action that citizens would not have otherwise. They build the organizations that give people the chance to contribute their time and money to political causes. They sponsor the meetings and rallies that give people the opportunity to attend. They circulate petitions that give people the chance to sign. They request contributions to causes that people may never have heard of until the moment of contact. The mobilization efforts of political leaders create the very opportunities for citizens to participate.

Through direct mobilization, likewise, political leaders subsidize political information. Because information is costly and because politics is far from the most pressing concern in most people's lives, few citizens know much about politics unless somebody tells them. People remain rationally ignorant. Through the mobilization efforts of political leaders, however, they are informed about the issues on the congressional agenda, alerted to the meetings of the school board, and reminded about the upcoming city council elections. In short, they are given information about the issues at stake and the opportunities to affect them. The mobilization efforts of political leaders help citizens to overcome their rational ignorance.

Through direct mobilization, finally, political leaders subsidize the costs of citizen activism. They distribute voter registration forms and absentee ballots. They drive people to the polls on election day. They provide child care to free parents to attend meetings and demonstrations. They supply people with the texts for letters to representatives and senators. By underwriting the costs of political participation, the mobilization efforts of political leaders help to overcome the paradox of participation.

Indirect mobilization

The impact of political mobilization, though, extends far beyond the effect it has on the limited number of people who are contacted directly. Membership in social networks makes people available to politicians, organizations, and activists. Membership in social networks makes people responsive to mobilization. Social networks, that is, convert direct mobilization into indirect mobilization. Political leaders mobilize citizens for political action through social networks.

For politicians, parties, interest groups, and activists, access to social networks reduces the costs of making contact. Leaders need not communicate with every person directly. Instead, leaders contact their associates, associates contact their colleagues and colleagues contact their friends, families, and co-workers. Through social networks, leaders get the word out, and citizens get the word. Social networks multiply the effect of mobilization: Direct mobilization reverberates through indirect mobilization.

Even more important, for politicians, parties, interest groups, and activists, access to social networks makes it possible to mobilize people to participate. Absent the involvement of social networks, leaders usually have only collective rewards to offer to potential participants: They hold out the prospect that favored candidates will win or that the government will formulate beneficial policies. Because rewards are collective, however, citizens receive them whether they act or not. Mobilization runs aground on the paradox of participation.

With the involvement of social networks, however, mobilization occasions the creation of selective rewards. When friends, neighbors, and co-workers present the opportunities to participate, they also convey social expectations about desirable courses of action. Citizens who comply and participate reap the rewards of social life. They enjoy the attentions and esteem of their friends and associates; they enjoy the instrinsic satisfactions of having helped their colleagues' cause. Citizens who fail to comply and refuse to participate receive no rewards; in fact, they may suffer social sanctions.

Indirect mobilization promotes participation, then, by allowing political leaders to exploit citizens' ongoing obligations to friends, neighbors, and social groups. Citizens feel an obligation to help people they like, people they identify with, people who are like them, and people who have helped them in the past—an obligation, that is, to help their friends, family, and daily associates. Likewise, citizens are more likely to contribute when they know that the people who expect them to help can tell whether or not they have done so. Political organizers have long thought personal, face-to-face contacts to be much more effective than impersonal mobilization through the mail or the media, and this is why.

Contact through social networks adds the power of social expectations to the message of mobilization.

Thus, by working through social networks, political leaders need not provide selective incentives themselves, need not coax, cajole, and persuade people to take part. Social networks do it for them. Family, friends, neighbors, and co-workers echo leaders' calls to action, and participants respond to please their neighbors and co-workers and to honor their obligations to friends. Working through social networks, politicians, parties, interest groups, and activists piggyback political action onto the everyday hum of social relationships.

The Strategy of Political Mobilization

Of course, mobilization is not a universal or a constant occurrence. Political leaders do not try to mobilize everybody, and they do not try to mobilize all of the time. Mobilization, after all, is not their real goal; they have little interest in citizen activism per se. Rather, they seek to use public involvement to achieve other ends: to win elections, to pass bills, to modify rulings, to influence policies. Mobilization is one strategy they may use, but it is neither the only one nor, always, the best one. Alternatively, politicians, parties, interest groups, and activists might (among other things) incite other politicians, ally with other interest groups, compile facts and figures, muster experts, or even (we hope rarely) pay bribes. Because each strategy is costly, and because resources are scarce, political leaders simply cannot use every tool in their toolkit on every job.

Consequently, citizen participation is a resource that political leaders use selectively in their fights for political advantage. For maximum effect, they *target* their efforts on particular people, and they *time* them for particular occasions.

Targeting mobilization

Once political leaders decide to pursue a mobilization strategy, they want to get the most effective number of people involved with the least amount of effort. This simple—indeed obvious—criterion suggests four kinds of citizens whom leaders are most eager to contact.

First, politicians, parties, and other activists are most likely to mobilize the people they already know. For one thing, they are close at hand, easy to contact, and responsive to requests—because they are friends or associates. For another thing, they are familiar. Political leaders, naturally, want their allies to participate, not their enemies. Democrats want Democrats to vote, not Republicans, and abortion rights advocates want pro-choice voters to write letters, not pro-life voters. When leaders mobilize people they know, they have a good idea of how they are going to act.

Second, politicians, groups, and other activists are more likely to mobilize people who are centrally positioned in social networks. They are easier to identify, simply because they are more visible and because they know more people. More important, because they are in the middle of things they are in a good position to mobilize others. They turn direct mobilization into indirect mobilization.

Third, politicians, parties, groups, and agitators are more likely to mobilize the people whose actions are most effective at producing political outcomes. Like it or not, some citizens are more influential in politics than others, and legislators, executives, or bureaucrats like, fear, respect, or depend on them more. Because political leaders are interested in outcomes, they concentrate their mobilization efforts on the powerful.

Finally, politicians and activists are more likely to mobilize people who are likely to respond by participating. As we already argued earlier in this chapter, some people, because of their resources, interests, preferences, or beliefs, are more likely to participate in politics than other people. Because political leaders cannot afford to mobilize everyone, they concentrate their efforts on people they have the greatest chance of mobilizing.

A number of simple predictions follow from these observations.

First, people who are employed, especially in large workplaces, are more likely to be mobilized than people who are not; they are more likely, consequently, to participate. Their jobs make them visible. Political leaders know where to find them—at work—and know what they care about—their jobs. Their jobs make them powerful. Workplaces represent concentrations of numbers, wealth, and power, the currencies to which politicians respond. Finally, their jobs incline them toward participation. They have powerful incentives to act in defense of their livelihoods, and they have powerful incentives to live up to the expectations of their employers and co-workers.

Second, people who belong to associations are more likely to be mobilized and more likely to participate than people who do not belong. Group members are more visible. Labor unions, service clubs, and churches meet daily, weekly, or monthly, and their purposes often reveal their politics. Group members are more influential. In politics, organizations have the power of numbers, attentiveness, and singular purpose. Finally, through their organizations, group members get greater encouragement to participate. They voluntarily associate with people who share their identities and their interests; accordingly, they find it difficult to resist the entreaties of other members. Indeed, their very involvement in organizations signals their susceptibility to social expectations.

Third, leaders of organizations, businesses, and local governments are more likely to be mobilized: They are better known to political leaders, more likely to be effective, and more likely to participate, for the reasons we have already discussed. In addition, their positions atop organizations and institutions give them the ability to reach other people. Business owners have access to employees, union stewards to rank-and-file, club presidents to members, and church deacons to the faithful. They occupy the center of social networks. They turn direct mobilization into indirect mobilization.

Finally, the wealthy, the educated, and the partisan are more likely to be targeted for mobilization than the poor, the uneducated, and the uncommitted, which is part of the reason for their greater potential for political action. The advantaged are better known to political leaders because they travel in the same social circles. Politicians and activists are usually wealthier, better educated, and more partisan than ordinary citizens, and so are their friends and associates. Likewise, their actions are more likely to produce favorable political outcomes. Because of their social positions, they often know legislators, executives, and bureaucrats personally. Moreover, because of their status and wealth, they stand as benefactors of many politicians and government officials: campaign contributors, information sources, former and future employers. Consequently, political elites know them, like them, respect them, and depend on them. They, in short, have power. Finally, they are more likely to respond to political leaders' requests. They have more resources. They have the money, the leisure, and the skills to meet the demands that participation places on them. Likewise, they receive more rewards. Because of their social status they have a greater stake in political decisions, and because of their socialization they have a bigger psychological investment in political affairs. Perhaps most important, they are part of social networks that esteem, expect, and reward activism in politics; hence, they receive greater selective and solidary rewards from their activism. The greater propensity of the advantaged toward participation, that is, stems not only from their individual characteristics but also from their placement in the political system.

Thus, the strategic calculations of political leaders determine a lot about who participates. Intent on creating the greatest effect with the least effort, politicians, parties, interest groups, and activists mobilize people who are known to them, who are well placed in social networks, whose actions are effective, and who are likely to act. Their efforts to move the organized, the employed, the elite, and the advantaged into politics exacerbate rather than reduce the class biases in political participation in America.

Timing mobilization

Political leaders likewise identify favorable times to move citizens into politics. Sometimes mobilization of public participation is a worthwhile enterprise—it is likely to accomplish its purpose—and sometimes it is not.

Clearly, for mobilization of citizen activism to be an effective strategy, two conditions must obtain. First, people must be ready to follow their leaders into politics. If people are not interested in the issues or are distracted by other concerns, mobilization is wasted effort. Second, citizen participation must have a consequential effect on political outcomes. If important decisions are not on the docket, if political outcomes are foregone conclusions, or if public officials are unmoved by citizens' pleas, mobilization is wasted effort. Unless citizens are likely to act and action is likely to yield outcomes, leaders' resources are better spent on strategies other than mobilization.

These observations provide some perspective on when people are likely to be mobilized, and when in turn people are likely to participate in politics.

First, people participate in politics more when salient issues top the agenda. Leaders can only lead, after all, when the public is willing to follow. Big pocketbook issues, such as pensions and jobs, and big moral issues, such as prohibition and abortion, draw greater public attention than more arcane issues, such as deregulation of natural gas pipelines and accounting rules for capital depreciation. Salient issues affect more people more directly. Knowing that, political leaders adopt mobilization strategies when the issues excite people and adopt other strategies when they bore people. Because of their strategic calculations, citizens receive more pressure to participate when the issues are salient than when they are not.

Second, people participate more in politics when other concerns do not demand their attentions. As important as politics is, for most people other things come first: making a living, spending time with the family, and so forth. Leaders understand this, and they hesitate to mobilize citizen activism when more pressing needs dominate. On campus, for instance, college politicos rarely schedule political events during midterms and finals. In real politics, likewise, activists curb their efforts during holidays, when people want only to spend time with family, and during hard spells, when people want only to get back to work or to pay their bills. Because political leaders accommodate the more pressing concerns of the public, people feel less encouragement and pressure to participate when more important events distract them.

Third, people participate more in politics when important decisions are pending. Politics moves to its own distinctive rhythms. Elections, for example, are cyclic: Presidential elections occur every four years, House elections every two years, Senate elections every six years, and state and local elections idiosyncratically, some in presidential years, some in midterm years, and some in off years. Legislation, on the other hand, is seasonal: The U.S. Congress and the larger state legislatures formulate proposals in committees in the spring and summer, debate policies on the floor in the summer and fall, and recess in the winter. Cyclic or seasonal, calendars regulate the activities of political leaders. For maximum effect, these leaders mobilize citizens at the moment when conflicts near resolution. Because leaders are more likely to contact them when decisions are imminent, citizens respond to the rhythms of the calendar as well.

Fourth, people participate more in politics when outcomes hang in the balance. Some elections are so close that a few votes can make a difference, whereas others are so lopsided that hundreds of thousands could not affect them. Similarly, some legislative battles are so evenly matched that a burst of public involvement could clinch them, whereas others are so settled that nothing could perturb them. Given scarce resources, political leaders focus their efforts on the tight contests and forget about the cakewalks. Because leaders are more likely to contact them when decisions come down to the wire, citizens respond to political competition.

Finally, people are more likely to be mobilized to participate in politics when issues come before legislatures than when they come before bureaucracies and courts. The institutions of American government expose legislators to popular pressures, but they insulate bureaucrats and judges. Representatives, senators, county commissioners, and members of city councils submit regularly to the discipline of the voters, but bureaucrats and judges do not. Accordingly, public participation potentially has more impact when elected officials make decisions than when civil servants and judges do. Accordingly, politicians and activists pursue mobilization strategies when issues are before legislatures, but they favor other strategies when decisions are before agencies and courts. Because leaders are more likely to contact them when the outcomes they seek are laws, people participate more in legislative politics than in bureaucratic and judicial battles.

Thus, the strategic choices of political leaders determine a lot about when people are mobilized, and hence about when they participate. Eager to time their efforts so that they will have the greatest effect, candidates, parties, interest groups, and activists mobilize people when their efforts are most likely to be effective: when issues are salient, when distractions are few, when resolutions are imminent, when decisions are closely contested, and when decision makers depend on the evaluations of the public.

CONCLUSION

Political participation arises from the interaction of citizens and political mobilizers. Few people participate spontaneously in politics. Participation, instead, results when groups, political parties, and activists persuade citizens to take part. Personal characteristics—resources, perceived rewards, interests, and benefits from taking part in politics—define every person's predisposition toward political activity. The strategic choices of political leaders—their determinations of who and when to mobilize—determine the shape of political participation in America.

In mobilizing citizens for political action, political leaders intend only their own advantage. Seeking only to win elections, pass bills, amend rulings, or influence policies, they target their appeals selectively and time them strategically. Nevertheless, in doing so, they extend public involvement in political decision making. They bring people into politics at crucial times in the process. Their strategic choices impart a distinctive *political* logic to political participation.

Through mobilization of both kinds—direct contact, and indirect contact through social networks—political leaders supply information about politics that many citizens otherwise would not have. Politics is remote from the experience of most people. Absent mobilization, rational ignorance would defeat much citizen involvement in politics. Through mobilization of both kinds, moreover, political leaders create selective, solidary inducements to participate that many citizens otherwise would not have. Politics is not a priority for most people; absent mobilization, the paradox of participation would defeat much citizen involvement in politics.

People participate in politics for a host of reasons, but mobilization makes citizen participation both more common and more consequential. As Rosenau summarized,

> Most citizens . . . are not autonomous actors who calculate what ought to be done in public affairs, devise a strategy for achieving it, establish their own resources, and then pursue the course of action most likely to achieve their goals. Their instrumental behavior is often suggested, if not solicited, by others, either directly in face-to-face interactions or indirectly through the mass media; either explicitly through calls for support by mobilizers or implicitly through the statements of leaders, journalists and acquaintances that situations might be altered (or preserved) if support were available. Thus, to conceive of the practices of citizenship as being largely sustained by independent action toward the political arena initiated by individuals is to minimize the relational context in which people participate in public affairs.[4]

NOTES

1. Downs, *An Economic Theory of Democracy*, chap. 14; Olson, *The Logic of Collective Action*, chap. 1; Barry *Sociologists, Economists and Democracy*, chap. 2.

2. On this more general point, see Olson, *The Logic of Collective Action*, chap. 1. See also Barry, *Sociologists, Economists and Democracy*, chap. 2.

3. Downs, *An Economic Theory of Democracy*, chaps. 12–13.

4. Rosenau, *Citizenship Between Elections*, p. 96.

REFERENCES

Barry, Brian. *Sociologists, Economists and Democracy*. London: Collier-Macmillan, 1970.

Downs, Anthony. *An Economic Theory of Democracy*. New York: Harper & Row, 1957.

Olson, Mancur, Jr. *The Logic of Collective Action*. Cambridge: Harvard University Press, 1965.

Rosenau, James N. *Citizenship Between Elections: An Inquiry into the Mobilizable American*. New York: Free Press, 1974.

10.2

NANCY BURNS, KAY SCHLOZMAN, AND SIDNEY VERBA

From *Private Roots of Public Action*

Burns, Schlozman, and Verba offer the most comprehensive findings so far on comparing men and women in their political participation and engagement. Surveys indicate that men tend to pay more attention to politics and to be more interested in certain political issues, like international affairs, than women. Women, however, bring deeper religious sensibilities and greater concern for children and the poor to politics.

4. THE POLITICAL WORLDS OF MEN AND WOMEN

Political activity is embedded in a larger set of orientations to the political world. Behind what individuals do in politics is how they think and feel about it: whether they know or care about politics, feel capable of having an impact, have a taste for political participation and the gratifications it can provide, or harbor policy preferences they wish to communicate to public officials. . . . [W]e investigate gender differences with respect to a diverse set of predispositions that shape the motivation and propensity to take part. We first consider gender differences in the set of orientations toward political life that foster activity, including political interest, efficacy, and knowledge, as well as other indicators of affect toward politics. Second, we consider gender differences in what is sought from political action: the gratifications attendant to participation and the policy issues behind it.

Psychological Involvement with Politics

Participation is closely linked to a variety of psychological orientations that would make someone *want* to take part in political life. [W]e observed a noticeable but moderate participation gap between women and men. In this one, we see a wider gap in psychological involvement with politics. Data from the Citizen Participation Study confirm the findings of various studies to the effect that, compared with men, women are less interested in and less knowledgeable about politics and less likely to feel politically efficacious. Not only have differences in political involvement persisted over time, but similar relationships—of varying degrees of strength—have been observed in a number of democratic countries, especially countries in which Catholicism is the

TABLE 1 Measures of Psychological Involvement with Politics

	Women		Men
POLITICAL INTEREST			
Very interested in politics (screener)	24%	⇔	29%
Very interested in national politics	29%	⇔	38%
Very interested in local politics	21%		22%
POLITICAL INFORMATION			
Mean number of correct answers (out of 10)	4.5	⇔	5.2
Correct answers to individual items			
Name of one U.S. senator	51%	⇔	67%
Name of second U.S. senator	30%	⇔	43%
Name of representative in Congress	32%	⇔	42%
Name of state representative	29%	⇔	34%
Name of head of the local public school system	40%	⇔	34%
Government spends more on NASA or Social Security	18%	⇔	40%
Meaning of Fifth Amendment	39%	⇔	52%
Origin of primaries—bosses or reformers	44%	⇔	49%
Meaning of civil liberties	77%	⇔	84%
Difference between democracy and dictatorship	85%	⇔	91%
Respondent above average in political information[a]	32%	⇔	42%
POLITICAL DISCUSSION			
Discuss national politics nearly every day	20%	⇔	31%
Discuss local politics nearly every day	16%	⇔	22%
Enjoy political discussion	26%	⇔	36%
SENSITIVITY TO POLITICAL CUES			
Say AARP takes stands in politics (AARP members)	79%		80%
Say clergy sometimes or frequently discuss political issues from pulpit (attenders)[b]	22%	⇔	28%
EXPOSURE TO THE MEDIA			
Watch news on television daily	57%		56%
Watch public affairs programs on television weekly	38%	⇔	45%
Read newspaper daily	55%	⇔	59%
Pay a great deal of attention to national politics	24%	⇔	40%
Pay a great deal of attention to local politics	36%		36%
POLITICAL EFFICACY			
Mean for efficacy scale	5.08	⇔	5.45
Government would pay some or a lot of attention			
National	40%		41%
Local	60%		64%

TABLE 1 *(continued)*

	Women		Men
Feeling of being able to influence some or a lot of governmental decisions (political voice)			
National	19%		17%
Local	46%	⇔	53%

SOURCES: Citizen Participation Study—Main Survey and Screener Survey.
a. Rating by interviewer.
b. Among those who attend religious services two or three times a month or more.
⇔ Difference between women and men is statistically significant at the .05 level.

dominant religion. Table 1 presents data about gender differences in a number of aspects of psychological involvement with politics. A majority of these measures show statistically significant gender differences; in all but one of these cases women are less politically involved than men.

First, with respect to *political interest*, the data show men to have been somewhat more likely than women to report being very interested in national politics or, in the larger Screener sample, in politics in general. In a pattern that is repeated elsewhere in the table, there is no gender difference with respect to being very interested in local politics.

Political information differs from other aspects of political involvement in being an objective rather than a subjective measure. Thus the gender disparity in political knowledge cannot be the result of a masculine willingness to claim credit—although it might reflect differential willingness to guess and, therefore, to inflate scores. We measure political information with a ten-item scale, five asking the names of public officials and five testing knowledge of government and politics. As shown in Table 1, for nine of the ten items, men are more likely to provide a correct answer. Compared with women, men answered, on average, almost one additional item correctly across the whole test—an information gain roughly equivalent to that acquired from an additional 2¾ years of schooling.

Women are more likely than men to know the name of the head of the local school system. This single reversal is consistent with both what is known about political knowledge and what is known about women's experiences in politics. The ability to acquire political information is often domain specific and selective, based on preexisting information and the ease of incorporating new information. According to Shanto Iyengar, "people acquire information in domains about which they are already relatively informed." School politics is the political realm that has traditionally been defined as an appropriate one for women and that has been most welcoming to them. Before the enfranchisement of women in 1920, a number of states and even more locales extended a partial suffrage to women for participation in local elections, especially school elections. Moreover, school boards have traditionally been, and continue to be, the elected councils on which women have achieved their greatest representation. Furthermore, women legislators have traditionally been overrepresented on education committees. It is fully consistent with these patterns that women would be more likely than men to know the name of the head of the school system.

Although taking part in *political discussion* constitutes an action rather than a psychological state, it seems reasonable to examine it in this context as an indicator of psychological involvement with politics. Men are more likely than women to report that they discuss local and, especially, national politics every day or nearly every day. What is perhaps even more germane to our concerns, they were more likely to indicate enjoying, rather than avoiding, political discussion.

The data show relatively little disparity when it comes to whether, among individuals similarly situated, there is a gender difference in *sensitivity to political cues,* that is, in the likelihood of perceiving the political content of messages in the environment. AARP members, whether male or female, are equally likely to know that the organization takes stands in politics. Some evidence in the opposite direction might be the fact that among regular church attenders, women are less likely to report that clergy in their church sometimes or frequently discuss political issues from the pulpit.

In terms of *exposure to the media,* the data replicate patterns we have already seen. There is no gender gap in terms of either watching news on television or paying attention to newspaper stories about local politics and community affairs. However, men are somewhat more likely to report watching public affairs programs on television, reading a newspaper daily, or, especially, paying attention to stories about national and world politics in the newspaper.

Gender differences in *political efficacy* are well known. Our data, which focus on the respondent's perception of being able to have an impact on politics, or what is sometimes called "external efficacy," show a relatively small gender disparity, with men having higher average efficacy scores. However, when the four items in the scale are considered separately, the differences are not especially consistent and, in contrast to what we have seen for other measures, are more pronounced for local rather than for national politics.

We can highlight these findings about political orientations by focusing briefly on religion, a domain that we use throughout this reading as a counterpoint to the arena of politics. Data about gender differences in religious attitudes and orientations contrast strikingly with the data just reviewed about gender differences in political orientations. As we have mentioned, Americans are more deeply committed religiously than are people in the democracies of Europe; in turn, American women are more deeply committed religiously than are American men. For a series of measures of religious attitudes and orientations, Table 2 presents findings that are consistent with the higher

TABLE 2 Religious Attitudes and Orientations

	Women		Men
Express a Religious Preference	96%	⇔	90%
Religious Attitudes (among those expressing a preference)			
Say religion is very important	67	⇔	49
Think Bible is God's word	56	⇔	42
Have had a "born again" experience (among Protestants and Catholics)	39	⇔	32
Support Prayer in Schools	60	⇔	50
Reasons for Church Activity (among those active)			
Civic reasons			
Make the nation better	67		68
Influence government	6		5
Charitable reasons			
Lend a hand to people in need	77		73
Religious reasons			
To affirm religious faith	80	⇔	69
Further goals of religion	56	⇔	50

SOURCE: Citizen Participation Study—Main Survey.

⇔ Difference between women and men is statistically significant at the .05 level.

level of religious practice—attendance at religious services and activity in religious institutions.

On each of several measures, women express greater depth of religious belief and concern about religious matters: they are more likely to report that religion is very important in their life, that the Bible is God's word, and, if Christian, that they have had a "born again" experience. In addition, they are more likely to support school prayer.

We also find an interesting pattern in the responses to a battery of questions posed to church activists about their reasons for being active in their churches. There was no significant difference between women and men with respect to civic reasons, such as making the nation a better place to live, or charitable reasons, such as lending a hand to those in need. However, women were more likely than men to mention religious reasons, affirming their faith or furthering the goals of their religion. The data reinforce our understanding that men and women direct their concerns in somewhat different directions.

Gender Consciousness and Experience of Gender Bias

With respect to politics, we have focused on general orientations—knowing and caring about politics, thinking that one could make a difference politically—that serve as a background to political participation. There is another set of political orientations, however, that deserves consideration. As members of a group that is disadvantaged in various ways, women may experience discrimination on the basis of sex. In addition, they may develop a sense of group consciousness. Either of these might be associated with political activity. These are not the easiest matters to probe in the context of a mass survey. Nevertheless, in the Citizen Participation Study we used a standard survey item in order to ask women and men whether they had ever experienced discrimination in jobs, school admissions, housing, or in other important things on the basis of their sex or gender. Because one individual might deem discriminatory an experience that another shrugs off, we consider this measure to be neither entirely objective nor entirely subjective. In addition, to measure gender consciousness for women, we asked them whether they felt closer to women than to men; whether they thought that there are problems of special concern to women that they need to work together to solve; and, if so, whether they thought that the government should be doing more about these problems. Analogous questions were posed to all respondents about discrimination on the basis of race or ethnicity. In addition, African-Americans and Latinos were asked questions about feeling close to other group members, thinking that they had joint problems, and the government's responsibility to assist in solving shared problems.

In Table 3 we present data about these group orientations. Because responses to these questions are difficult to interpret in isolation, for comparative purposes we include data about the parallel questions having to do with race or ethnicity. Not surprisingly, as shown in the top portion of Table 3, there are, overall, fewer reports of gender bias than of racial or ethnic bias from Blacks or Latinos respectively. Although women are more likely than men to have reported experiencing sex discrimination, only a small proportion of either group—11 percent of women and 6 percent of men—indicated experiencing this kind of discrimination. When it comes to racial or ethnic discrimination, as we would expect, compared with Anglo-Whites, minority group members are more likely to report having experienced bias, and African-Americans, especially African-American men, are more likely than Latinos to report having experienced racial or ethnic bias. In addition, Black women and Latina women each report at least twice as much racial or ethnic bias as gender bias.

In the bottom portion of Table 3, we report data on the three measures of group consciousness: whether respondents feel close to other group members; whether they think that there are problems of special concern to group members which they need to work together to solve; and, if so, whether the government should be doing more about these problems. In general, with respect to these measures, the similarities across groups are more striking than the differences. Only a modest proportion in each group report feeling particularly close to other group members.

TABLE 3 Group Orientations: Experiences of Discrimination and Group Consciousness

A. Percentage Who Say They Experienced Discrimination on the Basis of Sex and Race or Ethnicity

	On Basis of Sex	On Basis of Race or Ethnicity	On Basis of Either or Both
Women	11%	6%	14%
Anglo-White women	11	3	13
Black women	10	20	23
Latina women	7	19	21
Men	6	9	11
Anglo-White men	6	7	9
Black men	6	30	31
Latino men	5	16	19

B. Expressions of Group Consciousness by Gender and Race or Ethnicity

	Feel Close to Others in the Group	Believe They Have Problems in Common	Government Should Help
Feel about Women			
All women	10%	81%	78%
Anglo-White women	10	81	77
Black women	11	84	86
Latina women	13	77	82
Feel about Blacks			
All Blacks	16	87	88
Black women	15	86	89
Black men	17	88	88
Feel about Latinos			
All Latinos	14	80	82
Latina women	14	82	84
Latino men	14	78	78

SOURCE: Citizen Participation Study—Main Survey.

Only a small minority of women say they feel especially close to other women, but 81 percent indicate that they believe women have common problems and, of them, 78 percent believe that the government has some responsibility to help out. Similar proportions of African-Americans reported feeling especially close to other African-Americans and believing that African-Americans face joint problems. However, a somewhat higher proportion of

African-Americans, 88 percent, indicated that the government should be involved in solving these problems.

Gender Differences in Political Voice?

We have examined gender differences with respect to a number of predispositions that provide background for political participation. Our next task is to get closer to political activity in order to explore the values and preferences that give to political activity its raison d'être. In this section, we consider gender differences in the rewards that activists seek in taking part and in the issue concerns they bring to their participation. We ask whether women and men derive different gratifications from their activity and whether their activity is inspired by different sets of policy priorities.

Over the past two decades, political scientists have cast considerable light on the question of whether there are gender differences in political voice. A number of theoretical perspectives have been developed with respect to the issue of whether we should expect women and men to display different orientations to politics. In terms of empirical findings, at the level of the mass public, scholars have focused upon gender differences in partisan identification and vote choices as well as in political attitudes.

In the aftermath of the 1980 election—when men gave 53 percent, and women gave 49 percent, of their votes to Ronald Reagan—scholars as well as observers in the media discovered the gender gap. Since then, women have consistently been somewhat more Democratic than men in both their electoral choices and their party leanings. This circumstance is ordinarily interpreted as the result of women's distinctive preferences. Longitudinal data, however, make clear that it is men's, not women's, partisanship and vote choices that have changed. While men have moved toward the Republicans, thus creating the gender gap, women's preferences have, in the aggregate, remained largely unchanged.

When it comes to attitudes on issues, the results of public opinion surveys, in which members of the mass public are asked to respond to a series of issues pre-selected by the researcher, have long shown interesting, and perhaps unexpected, patterns of gender difference. With respect to "women's issues"— that is, issues like women's rights, abortion, or during the 1970s, the Equal Rights Amendment (ERA) that affect men and women differently—the gender differences in opinion are narrow and inconsistent. The disparities in opinion are somewhat more marked with respect to what are sometimes called "compassion issues," such as support for government welfare guarantees. The differences are wider still and more consistent when it comes to a series of issues—ranging from gun control to support for military intervention in international conflicts—that involve violence or coercion.

We have also learned a great deal about gender differences in the orientations and agendas of political elites. Recent studies of public officials— especially legislators in both the state houses and the U.S. Congress—concur in finding that it makes a difference when women hold office. Compared with their male fellow partisans, female representatives tend to have distinctive attitudes: they are more liberal with respect not only to the issues on which there has traditionally been a gender gap in public opinion among citizens but also to a much broader array of policy concerns, including the relatively abbreviated list of issues that might be deemed women's issues. Moreover, their attitudes are reflected in their behavior and legislative priorities. Most notably, women legislators are more likely to support and to champion measures concerning women, children, and families.

Although political scientists have made substantial progress in probing the differences between men and women in the attitudes and choices of voters or political elites, we know much less about whether men and women speak with distinctive political voices when they participate as citizens and communicate to public officials about their needs, preferences, and priorities. Both the nature of the sample and the interview schedule of the Citizen Participation Study make it particularly useful for examining what activists seek when they take part. In contrast to ordinary random samples of the public, which net very few cases of those who undertake rare activities—respondents who, for example, have attended a protest or worked in a campaign within the recent past—the Citizen Participation Study deliberately oversampled activists. In addition, whenever a respondent indicated having been active in a particular way, we asked a series of questions designed to measure the relative importance of a range of possible rewards in animating the activity. We also inquired whether there was any issue or problem, "ranging from public policy issues to community, family, and personal concerns," that led to the activity. We later coded the verbatim answers into categories of issue concerns. These data permit us to investigate the roots of citizen activity in terms of the gratifications attendant to their participation and the issue concerns behind it.

The Rewards of Participation

The fact of political participation, for women or for men, is often considered a paradox. From a rational choice perspective, joint activity on behalf of shared objectives is, under ordinary circumstances, irrational. The logic is as follows: since governmental policies are collective goods—affecting citizens whether or not they are active in promoting or opposing them—the rational, self-interested individual has no incentive to invest scarce resources in political participation. Because the efforts of any single individual are unlikely to have a significant effect on whether the desired policy outcome is achieved, the rational individual will hitch a free ride on the activity of others and thus reap the benefits of the preferred policy without expending resources on its attainment. The result is that rational, self-interested individuals will refrain from taking part.

Nonetheless, millions vote and take part in other ways. Many solutions have been given to this puzzle; most of them focus on the range of selective, usually self-interested, gratifications that political activity can provide. In the

Citizen Participation Study, we took a simple, somewhat novel, approach to this issue. We looked at it from the perspective of the activists by asking them how *they* interpret their participation; in particular, how they recall the reasons for their activity.

Although we might entertain contradictory hypotheses about differences between women and men in their retrospective understandings of the reasons that led to activity, inferences from a variety of studies suggest that women would be more likely than men to cite civic concerns and less likely than men to indicate seeking material rewards. For example, in her study of delegates to the 1972 presidential nominating conventions, Jeane Kirkpatrick found women delegates in both parties to be less ambitious for elective office than their male counterparts. In addition, the literature on social feminism and women's involvements in the period just before the granting of suffrage emphasizes the extent to which that work was charitably oriented and motivated by community-spirited value orientations. Furthermore, in her study of state legislators, Kirkpatrick found women in the state houses to be more comfortable with a conception of politics as an arena characterized by problem solving in search of the common good rather than by self-interested conflict. Raymond Bauer, Ithiel de Sola Pool, and Louis Anthony Dexter echo this understanding of a distinctively female approach to politics in their patronizing 1963 characterization of "The Ladies from the League."

We consider four kinds of motivations: selective benefits of three types—material benefits, social gratifications, and civic gratifications—as well as the desire to influence a collective policy. *Selective gratifications* may be material or intangible. *Material benefits*, such as jobs, career advancement, or help with a personal or family problem, were the lubricant of the classic urban machine. They continue to figure importantly in contemporary discussions of congressional constituency service and incentives for joining organizations. *Social gratifications*, such as the enjoyment of working with others or the excitement of politics, cannot be enjoyed apart from the activity itself. Without taking part, there is no way to partake of the fun, gain the recognition, or enjoy other social benefits. Similarly, *civic gratifications*, such as satisfying a sense of duty or a desire to contribute to the welfare of the community also derive from the act itself. In this case, however, we are concerned that social norms give respondents an incentive to emphasize the desire for these psychological rewards in order to please the interviewer. Although there is no reason to expect respondents to exaggerate the social gratifications attendant to voluntary activity, they might overstate the extent to which they were motivated by civic concerns. *Collective outcomes* are the enactment or implementation of desired public policies or the election of a favored candidate.

■   ■   ■

In discussing voting, respondents—whether male or female—referred frequently to civic rewards and only rarely to material ones. With respect to the gratifications attendant to working in a campaign, social gratifications assume greater prominence—again for both women and men. What this means is that it is the nature of the act rather than the sex of the participant that determines the rewards associated with it. Since men and women choose to engage in the same kinds of participatory acts, the consequent rewards accruing to them are necessarily similar.

The Issue Agenda of Participation

One of the striking features of the data in Table 4 is the large proportion of activists, both women and men, who mention the chance to influence government policy as a reason for their activity—despite the fact that theories of rational choice would argue that it is irrational for them to do so. As we might expect, for most of those who contact a government official directly, there is some policy issue at stake. However, we also find that about half of the voters and campaign workers also mention a policy concern associated with their activity. In short, activists do hope to further a public purpose through their activity.

Our principal concern, of course, is whether men and women differ systematically in the issues and problems they bring into political life. Earlier we mentioned the results of studies of the gender differences among legislators with respect to their discretionary activities—cosponsoring bills, attending committee meetings, making speeches, and so forth. In contrast to casting roll-call votes, these are activities that afford a legislator considerable control over the issue agenda. With respect to these discretionary activities, studies show that women are more likely than men to place a high priority on issues relating to children, to families, and to women. These results seem especially germane to our concerns here because—like legislators undertaking discretionary activities, but unlike legislators casting roll-call votes or respondents to a public opinion poll, who must decide about a pre-selected set of issues—citizen activists choose freely the issue baskets in which to place their participatory eggs. In one respect, however, we might expect differences between citizens and legislators when it comes to the content of their discretionary agendas. Women legislators self-consciously assume that part of their legislative responsibility is to represent women. Presumably, most women activists do not feel a similar responsibility.

The scope of the agenda

Given women's traditional role within the family as well as the particularistic orientation to politics that has been ascribed to them since the Greeks, we might expect women to bring to politics more personal or family concerns. We can investigate this surmise by considering the scope of the issues behind political activity. Each time a respondent indicated having engaged in a particular activity, we inquired whether there was any particular issue or problem—"ranging from public policy issues to community, family, and personal concerns"—that led to the activity. Across the totality of more than

3,600 political acts discussed by our respondents, in 63 percent of cases respondents provided a comprehensible, "codable" answer about the policy concerns that animated the activity. Analyzing the substantive concerns behind this "issue-based activity" allows us to characterize the participatory input from various groups—including men and women.

Since we wish to assess whether women and men differ in the likelihood of mentioning a concern limited to the individual and the family rather than issues with a broader referent, we focus, at the outset, on contacts with public officials, the only activity for which sizable numbers of respondents said that their concern was narrowly personal. (With regard to all other participatory acts, for the overwhelming majority of activists, the referent was broader.) It turns out that there is remarkable similarity between men and women who get in touch with public officials with respect to whether the matter raised is germane only to themselves or their families or a policy issue of more general concern. Discussing their most recent contact, 22 percent of the men and 21 percent of the women indicated that the subject was a matter of particularized concern. Thirty-five percent of the female contactors indicated that the issue affects the whole community and 25 percent that it affects the entire nation (or the whole world); the analogous figures for male contactors are 38 percent and 22 percent respectively.

■   ■   ■

Participatory agendas: a further probe

We can probe further by considering the participatory agendas of men and women who differ in terms of their class and their family circumstances. We begin with socioeconomic advantage, and the findings are complex. In Table 4 we compare men and women who are relatively advantaged (who have had at least a year of college education and whose family incomes were $50,000 or more) with those who are much less advantaged (who have no more than a high school education and whose family incomes were no more than $20,000). Educational concerns figure importantly in the issue-based activity of both advantaged and disadvantaged respondents. Once again, however, they occupy greater space in women's activity than in men's. Abortion weighs more heavily in the issue-based activity of the advantaged, for whom there is no gender gap, than in the activity of the disadvantaged, for whom there is a gender disparity in abortion-related activity.

Disadvantaged respondents, both female and male, are more concerned with issues of basic human need. Among the advantaged there is no difference between women and men in the extent to which these issues figure in issue-based activity. In contrast, among the disadvantaged issues of basic human need occupy much more space in the bundle of issue concerns for women than for men. A similar pattern obtains for issues associated with drugs and crime. Concern about crime and drugs figures much more importantly on the agenda

TABLE 4 Socioeconomic Advantage and the Issues That Animate Political Participation[a]

	Advantaged[b]		Disadvantaged[c]	
	Women	*Men*	*Women*	*Men*
Basic Human Needs	9%	9%	27%	12%
Taxes	8	16	13	15
Economic Issues (except taxes)	14	15	4	5
Abortion	13	12	6	0
Social Issues (except abortion)	1	1	6	0
Education	24	14	17	8
Children or Youth (except education)	5	3	9	5
Crime or Drugs	8	5	15	6
Environment	5	10	0	4
Foreign Policy	7	9	2	4
Women's Issues	2	d	0	0
Number of Respondents	197	228	297	182
Number of Issue-Based Acts	326	338	113	72

SOURCE: Citizen Participation Study—Main Survey.

a. Entries are the proportion of issue-based participation motivated by concern about particular issues.

b. Advantaged: At least one year of college and family income at least $50,000.

c. Disadvantaged: No college education and family income less than $20,000.

d. Less than 1 percent.

of issues that inspire activity among disadvantaged women than among disadvantaged men or among the advantaged of either sex.

A special concern with single mothers led us to investigate the participatory agendas of parents with children living at home. In light of what we have seen so far, the findings in Table 5 are not unexpected. Consistent with the results we have already reviewed, concerns about education or about crime or drugs weigh less heavily—and concerns about taxes more heavily—in the activity of married fathers than of mothers, whether single or married. Reflecting their economic circumstances, single mothers are much more likely than their married counterparts to mention matters of basic need in connection with their issue-based activity. However, the most striking finding in Table 5 is not that public officials hear about different issues from single mothers than from married parents of either sex but rather that public officials hear so little from single mothers. The rate of issue-based activity among married mothers and fathers is nearly twice that among single mothers. In short, what is distinctive about the participation of single mothers is not its issue content but its rarity.

TABLE 5 Parenthood and the Issues That Animate Political Participation[a]

| | Mothers | | Fathers |
	Single	Married	Married
Basic Human Needs	16%	6%	11%
Taxes	13	13	18
Economic Issues (except taxes)	12	6	11
Abortion	11	14	8
Social Issues (except abortion)	2	1	2
Education	22	25	13
Children or Youth (except education)	7	7	5
Crime or Drugs	16	10	5
Environment	4	6	8
Foreign Policy	7	3	7
Women's Issues	5	1	b
Number of Respondents	184	430	405
Number of Issue-based Acts	116	485	494

SOURCE: Citizen Participation Study—Main Survey.

a. Table lists the proportion of issue-based participation motivated by concern about particular issues.

b. Less than 1 percent.

Agendas for Women–Agendas for Men

Because we were struck at how little activity—pro or con, by women or by men—is animated by concern about women's issues, we decided to focus more explicitly on gender issues in the Follow-up study that we conducted in 1994. We asked two open-ended questions: one about whether there are any problems on which women need to work together in order to solve and an analogous one about problems men need to work together to solve. Because the question was open-ended, the issues mentioned came spontaneously from the respondents. However, the questions clearly directed the respondent to focus on gender. It is important to note that these data were collected a few years after those just reviewed, and the intervening years witnessed the Hill-Thomas hearings in the Senate, which brought attention to the issue of sexual harassment in the workplace, and the replacement of George H. W. Bush by Bill Clinton as president and, concomitantly, the replacement of Barbara Bush by Hillary Rodham Clinton as first lady.

The resulting data give us four possible sets of issues:

Issues that *women* believe require common action by *women;*
Issues that *men* believe require common action by *women;*
Issues that *women* believe require common action by *men;*
Issues that *men* believe require common action by *men.*

Not surprisingly, men and, especially, women see women as being more likely than men to have problems that they need to work together to solve: 64 percent of the men and 74 percent of the women mentioned an interpretable issue requiring joint action by women; in contrast, 49 percent of the men and 52 percent of the women mentioned an interpretable issue requiring joint action by men.

. . . Especially striking is the relative salience both to men and to women of matters pertaining to equality for women in the workplace—a category that includes reference to, for example, equal pay, sex discrimination on the job, unequal chances for advancement, and the glass ceiling. Thirty-five percent of the women and 26 percent of the men mentioned this issue as one on which women should work together—a quite high proportion for an open-ended question of so general a nature. No other issue draws this kind of spontaneous mention. In addition, a smaller, but still noticeable, number of both men and women referred to issues of sex discrimination and equal treatment for women without specifying a particular domain such as the workplace or the home.

Abortion was also mentioned frequently—by 14 percent of the women and 21 percent of the men—as a problem on which women should work together. Given the greater prominence of abortion on the participatory agendas of activists, it is notable that matters of workplace equality weigh more importantly in respondents' conceptions of what women need to work on together. A clue to the source of this seeming discrepancy may be in the extent to which the brief word bites describing concern about workplace equality are devoid of references to political solutions. Although the nature and implementation of civil rights laws have enormous potential consequences for the establishment of equal opportunity on the job, it may be that workplace discrimination—like child care and joblessness—are not fully politicized but are instead construed as problems that individuals can solve on their own. In contrast, both sides in the abortion controversy are only too aware of the political nature of the conflict.

Another subject that arose frequently is children and child care. In discussing problems of joint concern to women, women were especially likely to bring up child care and other issues concerning children: 15 percent of the women mentioned child care and 7 percent referred to other issues involving children as issues on which women should work together; 5 percent mentioned child care, and 1 percent brought up other children's issues, as concerns for men's joint action. Of the men, only 8 percent discussed child care and 1 percent referred to other child-related issues as something on which women ought to work together; 2 percent of the men mentioned child care, and 1 percent mentioned other children's issues, as matters on which men need to work together.

What is noteworthy is the extent to which these are deemed, by both men and women, as problems on which women, but not men, should work together. It is hardly surprising that abortion is considered a problem requiring joint action by women. After all, one side in the abiding political controversy frames the issue in terms of a "woman's right to choose." Similarly, with respect to equality for women, both men and women might reasonably assume that the burden for collective action in addressing inequality should be on the shoulders of the group that has the most to gain from it—the group seeking equality rather than the group that enjoys superior status. However, it is not clear why this principle should obtain for children, who are usually construed as being the joint responsibility of both parents.

The pattern continues when it comes to a final set of loosely related issues, various aspects of the relations between men and women. The issue of male violence or harassment of women—sexual harassment, spousal abuse, and other manifestations of violence against women, including rape—is, once again, more likely to be considered by both women and men as an issue on which women have to work together, even though it would seem that changing male behavior is the key to making progress. Only when it comes to men's "attitude problem"—the need for men to be more sensitive or less aggressive, to curb their egos, or to be less macho—is the problem construed as men's work. Thus to the extent that they think about these problems at all, men and women seem to view problems that men and women might be considered to share—issues surrounding children or relations between the sexes—as women's responsibility to solve.

Conclusion

We have found unmistakable gender differences in a variety of orientations toward politics. . . . We found that, in a variety of ways, men are more likely than women to register psychological involvement with politics, especially national politics: to be politically interested and informed; to feel that they can make a difference if they take part; to discuss politics on a regular basis; and to follow politics in the media. In contrast, women are more likely than men to manifest deep religious commitment and to consider religion to be important in their lives. . . .

With respect to matters more proximate to political activity—the rewards that derive from it and the issue concerns that animate it—we found much less evidence of a distinctive political voice. In terms of the gratifications attendant to participation, we found overall similarity between women and men. What was striking was not any systematic patterning by gender but rather the differences among political acts as well as the extent to which respondents cited civic and policy benefits in their retrospective understandings of their activity.

When we examined the issues that activists bring to their participation, we also found a great deal of similarity in the overall contours of men's and women's policy agendas. Both groups carry a diverse set of policy matters to their activity, and their relative priorities are quite similar. However, we also found evidence of subtle differences between women and men when it comes to the content of participation.

Where we found gender differences in the issue concerns that animate political activity, they come closer to replicating the distinctive policy priorities of men and women legislators than to mapping the issues on which there is the greatest gender disparity in the attitudes of the mass public. Educational issues, in particular, weigh more heavily in the concerns of women activists, a result that holds even when we consider groups defined by their socioeconomic and family circumstances. This finding mirrors that of the studies of the discretionary priorities of women in legislatures. Abortion also occupies greater space among the issue concerns of female than male activists. This is an issue that divides women—and men—resulting in polarized conflict between pro-life and pro-choice activists of both sexes, a pattern that differs from that among legislators, among whom men are distinctly more pro-life than women are.

REFERENCES

Jeane J. Kirkpatrick. 1974. *Political Woman*. New York: Basic Books.

Jeane J. Kirkpatrick. 1976. *The New Presidential Elite*. New York: Russell Sage.

Shanto Iyengar. 1990. "Shortcuts to political knowledge: selective attention and the accessibility bias," in John Ferejohn and James Kuklinski (eds.). *Information and Democratic Processes*. Champaign: University of Illinois Press.

11

INTEREST GROUPS

11.1

TERRY M. MOE

From *The Organization of Interests: Incentives and the Internal Dynamics of Political Interest Groups*

Moe builds on the work of Olson on the collective action problem (see Chapter 1). In this excerpt, Moe argues that interest group leaders use people's overestimation of their impact on group goals to persuade them to participate in group activities and lobbying.

2. THE DECISION TO JOIN

Because interest groups are comprised of members, it is only reasonable to begin an analysis of interest groups by asking why individuals choose to become members in the first place. What explains an individual's decision to join? Before *The Logic of Collective Action* first appeared, this question seemed to have a simple and obvious answer: people join groups because they agree with group goals. Indeed, the answer seemed so simple and so obvious that the question itself was not considered particularly interesting, and it was rarely the subject of inquiry. Olson changed all this. He did so by structuring his analysis of group membership around a theoretical concept that was essentially new to political scientists, but whose analytical value was recognized early on by writers in economics and public finance. This is the concept of a collective (or public) good.

For our purposes, this concept can be defined very simply. Any good can be viewed as a collective good for some set of individuals if, once it is supplied by one or more individuals in the set, it is automatically available for consumption by *all* individuals in the set.[1] A little reflection is enough to suggest that collective goods are widely sought and supplied in the political system. A public park is a collective good, for instance, because it can be enjoyed by everyone interested in using it, not just those persons who pay taxes and "supply" the park. Expenditures on national defense operate automatically to protect everyone in the nation, even though many individuals make no contributions at all.

These examples help to suggest why collective goods have such an intriguing theoretical role to play. In the first place, collective goods like public parks and national defense are often expensive to supply, while the average individual tends to gain an amount which, by comparison to the good's cost, is exceedingly small. If we think that an individual will typically be unwilling to contribute (pay) more than he stands to gain, then any contribution he could feasibly offer would constitute only a tiny portion of the total funds available to cover the necessary costs. It would appear to be a drop in the bucket, with little likelihood of making any noticeable difference in the good's supply. This should often serve as a major inhibitor of individual contributions. After all, if one persons fails to pay taxes, the national defense will not be impaired, nor will the public parks shut down. Moreover, this restraint on contributions is reinforced by a second factor that derives from the nature of the collective good itself: once it is supplied, the individual can enjoy the benefits even if he has shouldered none of the cost burden. As long as financial sources are found for public parks, national defense, and other collective goods, the individual can freely take advantage of them—without voluntarily throwing his money away on contributions that would, at any rate, have had no real impact in and of themselves.

This oversimplifies matters somewhat. But it should be clear that, when a collective good is at issue, the interesting question is why an individual would voluntarily want to pay something toward its supply. Olson's achievement is that he brought the analytical importance of collective goods to the full attention of political scientists. In effect, he shows how an "economic" concept can be transformed into a "political" concept, yielding a new and dramatically different perspective on the incentives for political action.

He does this by reconceptualizing the pluralist contention that individuals will act on the basis of common interests. He points out that, when individuals have a common interest in pursuing political goals—tax relief, civil rights legislation, farm subsidies, or minimum wage laws, to name only a few—these goals are typically collective goods for the "group" of individuals in question. If some of these people were willing to contribute toward the formation of a lobbying organization, and if this organization were successful in realizing the commonly held goals, all affected individuals would ultimately receive the benefits—noncontributors and contributors alike. This, along with the frequently high expense of political success, will clearly influence the willingness of individuals to contribute in the first place and thereby to "pursue their common interests." Thus, if we are to understand the conditions under which individuals will contribute toward interest group activity, the relationship between contributions and collective goods emerges as the fundamental consideration.

The Olson Theory

Olson's approach is straightforward. He proceeds by adopting a rational choice model and applying it to a group context which, from a pluralist standpoint, is ideally suited for the emergence of collective action: all individuals are taken to agree on the desirability of achieving a given political goal, viewed as a collective good. The question becomes: how much will rational individuals be willing to contribute toward the supply of a collective good that they have a common interest in obtaining?

Assumptions and basic conclusions

Olson is surprisingly vague about some of his assumptions, and a casual reading of his argument can easily lead to confusion about how conclusions are logically derived. This is particularly so with respect to individual values, since his intermittent reference to social pressure, ideology, and even altruism can leave the mistaken impression that a full range of values has been entered into the theory's premises. Because of such ambiguities, we will supplement Olson's explicit assumptions with others that are implicit in his analysis. The resulting set of assumptions, listed here, will be referred to as the Olson model. (*a*) Each individual is rational, perfectly informed, motivated by economic gain, and an independent decision maker. (*b*) The collective good is infinitely divisible.[2] (*c*) The marginal costs of providing the collective good are positive and increasing. (*d*) The marginal benefits of obtaining the good are positive and decreasing.

On the basis of assumptions corresponding to those presented here, Olson develops a mathematical analysis that justifies his conclusions about collective action. Given the task at hand, however, it is more instructive to forego a mathematical treatment and set out the elements of his argument diagrammatically.[3] Figure 1 consists of various marginal cost and marginal benefit curves expressed as a function of the level of collective good, X, supplied. For purposes of illustration, the "group" is assumed to have N "members," N minus two of whom derive equal benefits from increments of the collective good and have identical marginal benefit curves $MB_.$. The other two group members, j and k, are assumed to derive much greater benefit from the good, as shown by MB_j and MB_k. The group marginal benefit schedule, MB, is the sum of the curves of the N members. The MC curve expresses the marginal costs of supplying the collective good, and it is the same for everyone. It represents all the costs that are involved, organizational and otherwise, in achieving each additional increment.

Each individual, in deciding how much to contribute, must take into account how much it costs to supply each increment of the good, how much he stands to gain from each increment, and how much of the good has already been supplied (if any). Because he acts independently, he does not try to

FIGURE 1

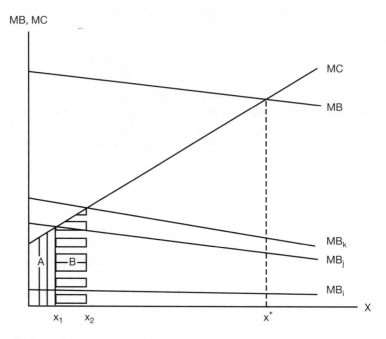

"game" his decision, nor does he enter into any cooperative agreements. This being so, he will contribute up to the point where the marginal costs of providing the good are equal to the marginal benefits he derives. At this level he is maximizing his net benefits. Assuming none of the good is as yet provided, it is to k's advantage to supply x_2, to j's advantage to supply x_1, and to everyone else's advantage to contribute nothing. Based on their incentives to contribute, we will refer to j and k as "Large Members" and to the rest as "Small Members," as does Olson.

What is the total contribution? Although j and k have an incentive to contribute amounts A and $A+B$, respectively,[4] the total contribution is not $2A+B$. This is where the "prevailing level of supply" factor comes into play. For if k contributes first—which he might do, since he is not gaming the situation—then the new level of supply becomes a fact which, by assumption, is immediately known by j. Acting rationally, j will then ask himself, How much should I contribute given that x_2 has already been provided? The answer is that he should contribute nothing: at x_2, the costs to j of providing more of the good are greater than any benefits he will derive. Hence, in this case only x_2 will be provided, and even though everyone gains when the good is made available, k will have paid the entire cost.

If, on the other hand, j contributes first, then x_1 of the good is provided for the group and k must ask himself: How much should I contribute given that x_1, is already supplied? His optimal solution is to contribute an amount B sufficient to move the group from x_1 to x_2. In this case, j and k split the cost of x_2 while again the other members pay nothing. But in either case, and thus regardless of who contributes first, only x_2 is provided, the Large Members pay for all of it, and the Small Members get a "free ride"—illustrating what Olson calls "the exploitation of the great by the small."

This outcome is suboptimal for the group. We can see this by viewing the group as a "superindividual" with marginal benefit curve *MB*. Such an individual would contribute beyond x_2 until x^* is reached. At each point between x_2 and x^*, the gains to the group as a whole outweigh the costs. Because there is an aggregate surplus, it is clear that our superindividual could distribute the costs and benefits among members so that each gains at least as much as he is required to pay. When the group moves from x_2 to x^*, then, everyone can be made at least as well off as before.

Such a move cannot occur within the model because it requires some sort of coordination, which violates the assumption of independence. As the situation stands, group members have no incentive to provide themselves with anything more than x_2. The group must remain at a level of provision that is "too low," with the cost load shared unevenly. Moreover, when individuals are added to the group (and k remains the largest member), the suboptimality increases. As N grows, the group's *MB* curve increases and pushes x^* farther out, thus widening the gap between x^* and x_2.

One final point: if all individuals in the group are Small Members, then no one will contribute and none of the collective good will be supplied. This conclusion is obvious enough, but it is especially important from Olson's perspective, because he makes the empirical argument that the Large Member phenomenon is very rare and thus many interest groups cannot turn to this source for any political support whatever.[5]

Bargaining and selective incentives

These aspects of the theory paint a bleak picture indeed. Yet interest groups are not necessarily doomed to failure or even to inadequate resources. This is because there are two basic mechanisms for circumventing, at least to some degree, the problem of contributions.[6]

The first is member cooperation through bargaining. This mechanism violates the assumption of independence, but it can be viewed as a "solution" of sorts if its relevance is allowed to turn on an empirical point—that the likelihood of effective bargaining varies with group size. In very large groups, the costs of communication and coordination tend to be prohibitive; each individual tends to see his own participation as unnecessary to a successful bargain; and, not least, each individual will get the benefits anyway if he lets the other members do the cooperating. As the group gets smaller—in particular, as it gets small enough to enable face-to-face interaction—members can become personally acquainted, aware of each other's interests, and in a position to predict and react to each other's behavior. It is more likely, then, that they will recognize their mutual dependence and calculate accordingly.

Small groups thus are different from large groups, in that they facilitate certain behavior—strategic behavior—that Olson's model assumes away. Even in very small groups, however, there remains a major obstacle to the success of bargaining agreements: as long as members are economically self-interested, and as long as they are bargaining over the supply of a collective good, the free-rider incentive is inherent in individual decision-making, including bargaining activities. Each member knows that if the *other* members (or some of them) do the cooperating and contributing, then he will get the benefits anyway. This makes bargaining agreements more difficult to arrange and constantly threatens the cohesion of any agreements that are actually arrived at. Additionally, the free-rider incentive should work to the disadvantage of Large Members, just as it does in the absence of bargaining, since they have an incentive to contribute even if the others do not, and they stand to lose a great deal if they hold back.

In sum, even for small groups in which bargaining occurs, the free-rider incentive continues to inhibit contributions and encourage the exploitation of the great by the small. The theoretical importance of bargaining is not that it solves the contributions problem, but that it holds out the possibility that small groups will be able to supply themselves with more of the collective good than independent behavior would lead us to expect. In view of this, Olson correctly suggests that his model is more usefully applied to large interest groups. It is here that individuals are most likely to make their decisions independently, and here that his theory's pessimistic conclusions are most likely to be borne out. Thus while bargaining is not actually incorporated into the model, its empirical relevance serves to qualify the model's range of applicability.[7]

There is another mechanism for increasing member contributions, however, that is entirely consistent with the original assumptions. This is what Olson calls a "selective incentive." Through the introduction of this crucial concept, he explains how large interest groups are able to attract financial support even when composed entirely of Small Members who calculate independently.

Selective incentives are private benefits which, precisely because they are private rather than collective in nature, can operate selectively on the membership as a whole: they can be conferred upon those who contribute and withheld from those who do not. For goods of this sort, there is no free-rider incentive. If a person wishes to obtain selective incentives, he cannot do so by waiting for others to shoulder the costs. He will have to "qualify" to receive them, which, in practice, ordinarily means paying dues and becoming a formal member.

This greatly expands the group's potential pool of inducements, for members will purchase anything of material value as long as they expect net benefits on the exchange. Information services, pension plans, group insurance— these are but a few of the most common selective incentives to be found in actual interest groups. Legal coercion is sometimes used as well; in these instances, the laws may be such that individuals are faced with fines, loss of employment, or loss of business if they do not join.

Herein lies the key to success for large groups. While the collective good itself is insufficient to induce member support, individuals who choose to pay for selective incentives are nonetheless contributing funds to group coffers, and leaders can use these funds to supply some of the collective good. Thus, even if no one has an incentive to supply any of the good at all, some of it may be provided as a by-product of the sale of selective incentives.

The Olson theory: Concluding comments

By recognizing that common interests typically take the form of collective goods and by making certain assumptions about individuals, Olson is able to arrive at basic conclusions about collective action. These he summarizes as follows:

> If the members of a large group rationally seek to maximize their personal welfare, they will *not* act to advance their common or group objectives unless there is coercion to force them to do so, or unless some separate incentive, distinct from the achievement of common or group interest, is offered to the members of the group individually on the condition that they help bear the costs or burdens involved in the achievement of the group objectives. . . .
>
> In small groups there may very well be some voluntary action in support of the common purposes of the individuals in the group, but in most cases this action will cease before it reaches the optimal level for the members of the group as a whole. In the sharing of the costs of efforts to achieve a common goal in small groups, there is however a surprising tendency for the "exploitation" of the *great* by the *small*.[8]

Olson's logic has quite a bit to say about politics. Above all, it subverts the traditional pluralist notion that common interests give rise to collective action, demonstrating that there are certain obstacles inherent in the situation that inhibit the average individual from "doing his part." Indeed, the irony is that the only way vast numbers of individuals can be induced to contribute their share is to offer them something different from, and perhaps entirely unrelated to, the group's goals.

This result has implications for a host of pluralist notions, because once the motivational connection between common interests and member support is undermined, a good part of the pluralist perspective on politics is called into question. For instance, Olson's analysis contradicts the notion that the effectiveness of a group, or at least its resource base, is a function of its degree of support in society. Widespread and enthusiastic agreement on a political goal may give rise to no contributions at all for its organizational sponsor—while other groups, enjoying far less support, may be better financed and more effective as a result of selective incentives, or perhaps the presence of a few Large Members. Thus, in terms of the impact on public policy, a political pluralism of groups may severely distort the underlying social pluralism of interests.

To take another example: we can see that a group's formal membership is not a valid indicator of its political support. This is particularly true of mass-based groups that successfully organize large numbers of average individuals. In such groups—like the Farm Bureau, the Chamber of Commerce, or Common Cause—Olson's theory points to selective incentives, not political goals, as the explanation of large size. Formal membership indicates that the group is successful at selling selective incentives, not that it is politically popular. Indeed, since selective incentives need have nothing whatever to do with the group's goals, there is no guarantee that any dues-payers even agree with those goals. What could be further from pluralist preconceptions?

A Revision: Imperfect Information

Olson's theory is a major contribution to the study of interest groups. It contradicts traditional ways of thinking about political groups, their connection to the social system, and their roles in politics. Moreover, it does this by employing new concepts—collective good, selective incentive—which, while previously accorded almost no systematic attention in political science, are clearly of the greatest relevance for political behavior and promise exciting new directions for theoretical inquiry.

Yet Olson's model is not the only way of constructing a rational theory of interest groups, nor are his dramatic conclusions the only ones implied by the assumption of rationality. What rationality "entails" depends upon the nature of the other assumptions operating in conjunction with it, and, when these are allowed to vary, different rational models are created along with different sets of conclusions. We have already shown this to be so for the assumption of independence. In this section, we will see that the same sort of thing happens when the assumption about perfect information is relaxed.

Olson assumes that individuals are perfectly informed about marginal costs, marginal benefits, and the amount supplied by others. We can now drop this restriction and assume instead that individuals are imperfectly informed, that they arrive at estimates of each curve, and that their rational choices derive from these estimates. The question becomes: under what perceptual conditions will they have an incentive to contribute?

The most general relationships between perceptions and incentives are apparent if we mentally allow the curves in Figure 2 to undergo basic shifts (and disregard any effects of attitudes toward risk). Consider individual i, who, given his present perceptions, is like Olson's Small Member in that he has no incentive to contribute. It is obvious from the figure that any upward shift in his estimated gains from the collective good, as well as any downward

FIGURE 2

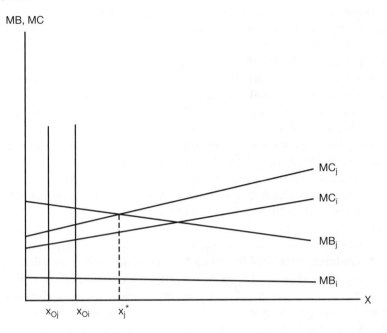

shift in the amount he thinks additional increments cost, enhances the likelihood that his marginal cost and benefit curves will intersect at some point to the right of x_{oi}, the amount of X he expects others to supply. When this occurs, he has every incentive to contribute—and the amount he wants to contribute will then vary inversely with any changes in his estimate x_{oi}. Now consider individual j, who, like Olson's Large Member, has an incentive to contribute as things stand. Because his marginal cost and benefit curves already intersect to the right of x_{oj}, even the slightest changes in his estimates will alter his rational choice. The amount of the collective good he chooses to supply, $x_j^* - x_{oj}$, will vary directly with his estimated marginal benefits, inversely with his estimated marginal costs, and inversely with the amount of X he expects others to supply. And his contribution will adjust accordingly.[9]

The actual estimates people rely on and the way their perceptions are determined are, of course, empirical questions. The point to be stressed here is a logical one: that behavioral expectations are contingent in specific ways upon perceptions. This yields a perspective on interest groups that is very different from Olson's. Above all, whereas Olson claims that the vast majority of individuals can have no incentive to contribute toward collective goods, the revised model implies that anyone can have an incentive to contribute, depending upon his subjective estimates of the relevant quantities. Generally speaking, an individual is more likely to contribute the higher his estimate of marginal benefits, the lower his estimate of marginal costs, and the lower his estimate of the total level of supply. These estimates in effect lead him to think that his contribution will make a difference in bringing about net personal gains. They lead him, in other words, to have a perception of personal efficacy. The efficacious individual can have a rational incentive to contribute whether or not his efficacy is justified by the objective context.

It follows that interest organizations, even in the complete absence of selective incentives, are better able to recruit members and amass contributions to the extent that these estimates are characteristic of individuals in their sectors. Individuals will then join and quit for political reasons and, accordingly, a group's size and resource base should tend to be more strongly linked to its underlying political support. Thus, perceptions of efficacy among members and potential members suggest an organizational setting that may be roughly consistent with pluralist expectations and is certainly more conducive to political action than Olson's theory would imply.

Additionally, we should recognize that a model in which information about costs, benefits, and the level of supply is assumed to be less than perfect intrinsically contains a new tool for group leaders: some of that information can purposely be manipulated in order to attract members and contributions. This is all the more potent a device given that leaders are in an ideal position to possess (or claim to possess) such information, while the average individual has very few facts on which to base his estimates, other than what the leaders say. Thus, leaders need not simply leave the estimation process to chance, but can play an active role in shaping how individuals arrive at their decisions.

The Role of Efficacy: An Empirical Aside

It might be claimed that Olson's model is the "central tendency," since individuals are as likely to underestimate as to overestimate their true efficacy, and that this modification of his theory is uncalled for. Two basic responses are in order. First, it is an empirical question whether individuals are as likely to underestimate as to overestimate, and there is some basis for believing that overestimation is actually more common. There is now a good deal of research, for example, to indicate that efficacy plays a role in explaining individual involvement in various types of political activity—even when, as in voting, the objective likelihood that the individual's contribution will affect the outcome is infinitesimally small. Why should membership in interest groups be any different? Empirical work also indicates that subjective efficacy is not entirely derived from factors intrinsic to the decisional context itself. In many Western democracies, and certainly in the United States, individuals tend to be socialized to political efficacy by their experiences (e.g., childhood schooling experiences) within the prevailing political culture. They thus come to specific political contexts with certain "efficacy predispositions"—which, in coloring perceptions of the objective context, enhance the likelihood that they will think that their contributions make a difference. In democratic nations, then, perceptual errors by potential members may not be anywhere near randomly distributed about the true cost, benefit, and level of supply curves. The vast majority of individuals may well tend to err in the direction of greater efficacy. This expectation is only reinforced by the informational roles that leaders doubtless play in shaping perceptions.[10]

Second, even if individual estimates are distributed randomly, those who sufficiently overestimate their efficacy will have an incentive to join for political reasons because of it. Depending upon the size of the sector, this could translate into large numbers of people who join in support of group goals; and, especially if selective incentives are not too valuable, it is perfectly possible that most of any given group's formal members (as opposed to those individuals who might have joined but did not) are attracted because of its goals. Thus, even if Olson's model is the central tendency (and it probably is not), informational variations are still basic to an understanding of group membership—and, as we will see . . . , they play major organizational roles as well.

Conclusion

In this reading, we began with Olson's model of the individual's decision to join, relaxed the assumption of perfect information, and arrived at a more general but still quite simple revised theory. From this perspective, the key to group membership does not rest solely with the congruence of member interests and group goals, as the pluralists contend; nor does it rest with the singular role of economic selective incentives, as Olson claims. Instead, we find that both group goals and selective incentives can serve as membership inducements for ordinary members, regardless of their economic size. . . .

These inducements come into play in different ways. Selective incentives are direct member inducements which the individual receives in exchange for his contribution; in deciding whether to buy, he is concerned with whether his gain from selective incentives exceeds their cost. If an individual is to be attracted purely on the basis of group goals, by contrast, he must perceive that his contribution makes a difference for the group's political success, resulting in net gains for himself. As a modification of Olson's analysis, this efficacy requirement opens the door for the inducement value of group goals; but it also represents a condition which many individuals may not satisfy even if they place very high value on the collective good itself. Thus, the introduction of imperfect information does not eliminate the "Olson problems" intrinsic to the individual's collective goods calculus. But it does imply a wider range of (perceptual) conditions under which these problems are overcome.

Selective incentives therefore retain their basic advantage over group goals as member inducements, but this advantage is now of less significance than Olson's original model contends. For any given group, the relative salience of the two types of inducements can vary depending upon the perceptual characteristics of potential members and upon the value of the selective incentives supplied. Some groups may be able to form by offering nothing more than political goals with which enough individuals agree. Other groups may have to supplement political goals with selective incentives in order to attract sufficient support. And still others may find that their goals have no inducement value at all, and that they can form only by relying entirely upon selective incentives. While we have a logical basis for highlighting the importance of selective incentives, then, both types of inducements play special roles in attracting members to the group—and both will take on distinctive organizational roles in the analysis that follows.

NOTES

1. For more technical definitions and discussions of the various dimensions and "degrees" of collective goods, see Paul A. Samuelson, "The Pure Theory of Public Expenditure," *Review of Economics and Statistics* 36 (November 1954): 387–90; "Diagrammatic Exposition of a Theory of Public Expenditure," Ibid., 37 (November 1955): 350–56; "Aspects of Public Expenditure Theories," Ibid., 40 (November 1958): 332–38; Richard Musgrave, *The Theory of Public Finance* (New York: McGraw-Hill, 1959); John G. Head, "Public Goods and Public Policy," *Public Finance* 17, no. 3 (1962): 197–219.

2. We are assuming, with Olson, that various levels or amounts of the collective good can be achieved, and that the provision of the good is not simply an all-or-nothing proposition. Were we to assume the latter, a slightly different analysis would be required.

3. Some of the more technically oriented readers would doubtless prefer a mathematical presentation and will consider this sort of diagrammatical exposition too primitive. An adequate mathematical analysis, however, would eventually become quite involved. One suitable method, given the kinds of substantive issues we are concerned with in this reading, would be to interpret the decisional problem as one of maximization subject to nonlinear constraints and to arrive at optimal solutions by applying the Kuhn-Tucker conditions. An analysis along these lines is set out in Terry M. Moe, "A Calculus of Group Membership," Working Paper No. 7, Public Policy and Political Studies Center, Michigan State University, November 1978. Because most readers would probably find such approaches too technical to be very enlightening, it seems preferable simply to illustrate diagrammatically how Olson's model can be employed and modified to generate conclusions about individual behavior. In this way, at least, it is quite apparent why we have certain expectations about the bases for membership, since it is actually possible to "see" the various theoretical components at work.

4. Solely for purposes of illustration, the implicit assumption here is that fixed costs are zero; were they nonzero, the area under the marginal cost curve would not represent the entire amount necessary for supplying any specified level of X. This simplification does not affect the general conclusions that follow.

5. For simplicity, income effects are assumed to be zero and multiple time periods are not considered. Were these two factors taken into account, the ceiling on provision would be somewhat greater than x_2 and the precise sharing of costs between j and k would be affected. But the basic conclusions outlined in the text would still hold. For a dynamic analysis of collective action that incorporates income effects, see, e.g., John Chamberlin, "Provision of Collective Goods as a Function of Group Size," *American Political Science Review* 68 (June 1974): 707–16. See also Mancur Olson and Richard

Zeckhauser, "An Economic Theory of Alliances," *Review of Economics and Statistics* 43 (August 1966): 66–79.

6. Olson develops these parts of his analysis with the aid of a three-fold typology of groups: privileged, intermediate, and latent. These categories are unnecessary and we will not rely upon them here.

7. Olson also seems to assume that Large Members will emerge only in small groups and that this, too, gives them advantages over large groups. What makes someone a Large Member, however, is the relationship between his marginal cost and benefit curves, and neither of these logically depends on the size of the group. Thus, it seems preferable to say that Large Members can be present in groups of any size and to stress that the advantages of small groups derive from strategic interaction.

8. Olson, *The Logic of Collective Action*, pp. 2–3.

9. Two general points about x_{om}, the amount that any individual m expects others to supply. First, the individual's estimate x_{om} is not necessarily altered when others contribute, since he may be entirely unaware of their behavior. Second, the relationship between x_{om} and contributions will be attenuated when income effects are taken into account: a decrease in x_{om} will have a less positive impact and an increase in x_{om} will have a less negative impact. (In effect, his marginal benefit curve becomes contingent upon x_{om} and shifts when the latter shifts.)

10. On political efficacy, see, e.g., Gabriel A. Almond and Sidney Verba, *The Civic Culture* (Princeton, N.J.: Princeton University Press, 1963); Sidney Verba and Norman H. Nie, *Participation in America: Political Democracy and Social Equality* (New York: Harper and Row, 1972); David Easton and Jack Dennis, "The Child's Acquisition of Regime Norms: Political Efficacy," *American Political Science Review* 61 (March 1967): 25–38; Robert Weissberg, "Political Efficacy and Political Illusion," *Journal of Politics* 37 (May 1975): 469–87; and, for a review of studies of efficacy, Paul R. Abramson, *The Political Socialization of Black Americans: A Critical Evaluation of Research on Efficacy and Trust* (New York: Free Press, 1977).

11.2

KEN KOLLMAN

From *Outside Lobbying: Public Opinion and Interest Group Strategies*

Kollman contrasts two types of lobbying, inside and outside. The inside game is more private and is played among people in Washington. The outside game is played by interest group leaders who bring people from outside Washington into the business of persuading members of Congress. Outside lobbying both signals existing public opinion to lawmakers and tries to shape that public opinion to an interest group's advantage.

1. INTRODUCTION

Outside lobbying is defined as attempts by interest group leaders to mobilize citizens outside the policymaking community to contact or pressure public officials inside the policymaking community. It represents a viable and effective strategy for many interest groups trying to influence representative government between elections. What better way is there to win favorable legislation in Congress, for example, than to mobilize a significant number of constituents to contact key legislators? Old-fashioned inside lobbying, the personal access and contact with legislators so necessary for maintaining good relations with government, may have only limited effectiveness today. Just as elected officials in Washington feel the need to monitor and assuage public opinion through polls and public relations, modern lobbying increasingly requires sophisticated methods of public mobilization. Lobbying in Washington is not just a game among well-paid lawyers, ideological activists, and legislators in the Capitol. The outside public is increasingly involved.

Mass expressions of public concern directed toward the federal government are rarely spontaneous. Behind most telephone calls, letters, faxes, and E-mails to members of Congress, behind marches down the Mall in Washington, D.C., and behind bus caravans to the Capitol, there are coordinating leaders, usually interest group leaders, mobilizing a select group of citizens to unite behind a common message. At the most basic level, an interest group leader seeks to persuade policymakers that what the members of the group want (as specified by the leader) is good public policy and/or good politics. And the leader uses outside lobbying to demonstrate first, that the members of the group are in fact united behind the leader, and second, that many other constituents agree with what the group leader wants. Faced with organized groups of constituents making noise about this or that policy issue, not many members of Congress could afford to ignore these efforts completely. Any leader who can organize thousands of citizens to write letters to their congressional representative, for example, can with some probability organize a good number of voters on election day to support or oppose the incumbent. For all the apparent benefits of outside lobbying to an interest group—sending a strong message to policymakers or reinforcing to voters that the group represents a credible source of political information—it is surprising nonetheless that outside lobbying is not undertaken more often by groups with an interest in controversial policy issues.

Outside lobbying, however, is in fact applied selectively, and lobbyists and interest group leaders spend precious hours and resources crafting careful public campaigns of persuasion. On some policy issues, groups on all sides use outside lobbying intensively. On other policy issues, only groups on one side of the issue use outside lobbying. There are many issues, even those considered extremely important to specific interest groups, where no groups use outside lobbying. And of course, groups try to time their public appeals for maximum effect. As every lobbyist (or salesperson, parent, or leader) knows, persuasion is a subtle business, and careless lobbying strategies can backfire. It is not always the case that outside lobbying, even when it generates a substantial public response, wins over the policymakers targeted.

The selective application and timing of outside lobbying strategies raises important questions. Obviously, outside lobbying is not always influential, even when interest group leaders on only one side of an issue use it. Who or what captures the attention of Washington policymakers? When are demonstrations of popular support effective in influencing policymakers? How do outside lobbying campaigns compare to financial donations or inside lobbying in influencing policymakers? V. O. Key raised similar questions nearly four decades ago, and he found answers difficult to come by. In the 1961 book *Public Opinion and American Democracy*, he expresses doubts about the influence of outside lobbying activities. "Their function in the political process," he writes in reference to "propagandizing campaigns" by interest groups, "is difficult to divine" (528). Outside lobbying activities are "rituals in obeisance to the doctrine that public opinion governs" and are "on the order of the dance of the rainmakers. . . . Sometimes these campaigns have their effects—just as rain sometimes follows the rainmakers' dance. Yet the data make it fairly clear that most of these campaigns do not affect the opinion of many people and even clearer that they have a small effect by way of punitive or approbative feedback in the vote" (528).

Why and when, Key is really asking, do policymakers pay attention to outside lobbying? Certainly many organizational leaders consider outside lobbying potentially influential; otherwise, they would not do it. The leaders of the major labor unions, peak business organizations, and civil rights and environmental groups use outside lobbying regularly enough to indicate that they believe outside lobbying is more than the dancing of rainmakers. Even corporate leaders use outside lobbying occasionally. And policymakers admit that organized groups of constituents influence their decisions. One congressional staff member justified his boss's vote to repeal catastrophic health insurance in 1990, little more than a year after voting for the insurance bill, by explaining, "It was a no-brainer. He got over five thousand letters for the repeal of the insurance, and literally eight letters in favor of the current insurance. He didn't have much choice really. He had to vote for repeal."

But beyond the relatively uninteresting claims that interest group leaders consider outside lobbying effective and that policymakers sometimes consider it influential, the topic deserves more attention than it receives. If, as most observers claim, interest groups wield considerable power in Washington, and if interest groups spend resources using outside lobbying fairly regularly, then outside lobbying should be an important part of the process by which these groups wield their power. Precisely when, why, or how outside lobbying operates to enhance group influence, however, is not well understood.

Our evaluations of the normative effects of outside lobbying are similarly imprecise. We know very little about whether outside lobbying serves to improve the correspondence between what constituents want and what their representatives do or whether it merely confuses representatives with meaningless information or reinforces inequalities in access to representatives that accrue from campaign contributions and other less edifying activities of interest groups. Surprisingly, many depictions of outside lobbying in the national press are as unfavorable as those of lobbying in general. The image of fat-cat lobbyists shoving money in the pockets of legislators has been supplemented by negative images of farmers, teachers, truckers, or public employees demonstrating at the Capitol or flooding Congress with telephone calls for a bigger slice of the budgetary pie, or of business lobbyists spending money to generate so-called astroturf (in contrast to real grass-roots support) to save a valuable tax provision. The press depiction of interest group activities has had either a large influence on Americans or has tapped into deeply negative sentiments among the general population. Recent polls show that a vast majority of Americans are cynical about the power of special interests. In the 1992 American National Election Study (ANES), when asked whether "the government is pretty much run by a few big interests looking out for themselves or [if] it is run for the benefit of all the people," 78 percent of those offering a response answered, "a few big interests." Common wisdom, it appears, holds that some interest groups have their way in Washington, and that outside lobbying either reinforces existing inequalities in access or is irrelevant to the real game of special interest lobbying.

The cynicism of the press and the general public toward interest groups is not shared by many political scientists. Studies have tended to describe a more sanguine climate of bargaining and information gathering between interest groups and policymakers in Washington. Descriptions of interest group activities and influence from the last four decades range from the near impotence of business lobbyists during legislative conflicts over free trade to subtle forms of persuasion and pressure that influence legislation marginally. Many studies of policymaking or interest groups have concluded that other pressures on policymakers besides interest group lobbying— colleagues in the House or Senate, public opinion in the district, the White House, party leaders—were more important in determining policy. Even those who ascribe considerable power to special interests suggest that that power is wielded subtly or silently, without the intense lobbying activity so common in Washington.

One reason the press and the general public may tend to exaggerate the influence of interest groups is that the news overemphasizes dramatic instances of graft, exploited campaign finance loopholes, or extraordinary pressure exerted on members of Congress by organizations like the National Rifle Association. Successful outside lobbying campaigns and increasingly large campaign contributions due to the reporting of the Federal Election Commission attract attention and are visible manifestations of group power. Inside lobbying in the form of interpersonal contacts, while an everyday occurrence for nearly all interest groups, is harder for the mass media to observe on a regular basis and has more of the flavor of relationship building and coordination among lobbyists and legislators than of outright pressure. Thus, the media fail to report adequately on the effects of inside strategies, and if they were to do so, it would probably bring the popular evaluation of interest group power more into balance.

In contrast, some of the conclusions of political scientists about the muted influence of interest groups may have something to do with the lack of research on outside lobbying. Researchers have tended to focus on inside lobbying, campaign contributions, and especially organizational formation. For each of these subjects, conclusions of researchers have highlighted the limitations of organized interests. Inside lobbying rarely changes legislators' positions on policy issues. Campaign contributions seem to correlate only weakly with legislative or electoral success. And groups are hard to form because of collective action problems. Given all the obstacles interest groups presumably face, one wonders why there are more than seven thousand registered organizations in Washington, and why so many of them spend precious resources trying to influence policymakers. Interest groups work hard to influence legislation, and it is difficult to believe that their money and efforts go to waste.

Part of the problem for political scientists may be that they fail to see the role that outside lobbying serves in enhancing the inside lobbying of interest groups. Interest groups choose lobbying strategies at the same time policymakers are trying to please constituents. Groups thus choose strategies intended to convince policymakers that group goals align with constituent goals. If successfully wielded, these strategies can enable interest group leaders to be quite influential in shaping public policies. While this seems apparent, outside lobbying does not get the attention it deserves in interest group research. Simply put, outside lobbying has rarely been studied systematically. The kinds of interest group activities the mass media tend to highlight are precisely those that political scientists tend to understudy, and the differences in coverage among the two affect conclusions about interest group power. This reading, in attempting to answer three questions—Why do groups use outside lobbying? When does outside lobbying work? Who benefits from outside lobbying?—is an effort to rectify the imbalance in interest group research.

Of course, interest group leaders are not the only ones who find it in their interests to mobilize citizens to pressure American policymakers. Political party leaders, politicians (especially the president), and even newspapers and mass media personalities actively encourage citizens to contact their elected representatives. The question of when it is advantageous in a democracy to mobilize citizens to pressure policymakers is considerably more general than the more specific question of when interest groups should do so. Many of the ideas in this reading about outside lobbying by interest groups should certainly apply to other actors in the political system.

Overview

Outside lobbying is important because it is a common means (perhaps the most common means except for elections) for elite policymakers to experience pressure in the form of popular participation. Were it not for outside lobbying from interest groups, many policy decisions would take place solely among a relatively insulated group of Washington insiders. Instead, interest group leaders call upon people outside of Washington to remind policymakers that a sizable portion of their constituents is paying attention. At least potentially, outside lobbying can pressure policymakers to adopt more popularly supported policies than they would in the absence of outside lobbying.

Outside lobbying accomplishes two tasks simultaneously. First, at the elite level it communicates aspects of public opinion to policymakers. The many forms of outside lobbying—publicizing issue positions, mobilizing constituents to contact Congress, protesting or demonstrating—have the common purpose of trying to show policymakers that the people the group claims to represent really do care about some relevant policy issue. These tactics say, in effect, "See, we told you constituents were angry about policy X, and now you can hear it from them."

I refer to this role for outside lobbying as *signaling* because it has many characteristics of basic signaling models in game theory. An interest group (the sender) tries to signal its popular support (its type) to a policymaker (the receiver). . . . When do the signals sent by interest group leaders actually influence policymakers' behavior?

The noteworthy characteristic of outside lobbying, however, is that it is not just an elite-level phenomenon. It is intended to influence members of the mass public as well. The second role for outside lobbying is to influence public opinion by changing how selected constituents consider and respond to policy issues. I shall call this its *conflict expansion* role in reference to the theoretical legacy of Schattschneider, who wrote in 1960 that the "most important strategy of politics is concerned with the scope of the conflict. . . . Conflicts are frequently won or lost by the success that the contestants have in getting the audience involved in the fight or in excluding it, as the case may be" (3–4). As Schattschneider emphasized, political elites, when faced with intransigent opposition, can bring attention to their cause, invite constituents to participate in the policy process, and hope to swing momentum to their side.

For both of these roles, the salience of policy issues to constituents, an often-overlooked characteristic of public opinion, lies at the center of interest group politics. It is not the popularity of policies that is mostly communicated or altered through outside lobbying. For one, the popularity of policies tends to stay relatively fixed over long periods of time, even given the outside lobbying activities of interest groups. But even more important, policymakers tend to have good information on the popularity of policies, primarily through opinion polls, but also because such popularity stays relatively constant and they can learn about it over time. Salience, however, defined as the relative importance people attach to policy issues, is an aspect of public opinion that policymakers perpetually running for reelection want to know but cannot learn about from ordinary opinion polls and experience. Policymakers want to know what proportion of constituents, when voting in the next election, will weigh the actions of their elected representatives on a particular policy issue. More salient policy issues will weigh more heavily on voting decisions than will less salient policy issues, and policymakers rely to a considerable extent on interest groups for current information on which issues rank high on salience. Because they can mobilize constituents to speak for themselves and can occasionally increase the salience of issues to those constituents, interest group leaders have a comparative advantage in sending credible signals on this precious information.

In sum, interest group leaders can turn their informational and leadership advantages into policy influence. They can try through inside lobbying to convince policymakers that voters care about an issue and are on the side of their group on the issue. But outside lobbying goes a step further in making a costly, public demonstration that, one, the issue is in fact salient to voters and, two, the interest group can make the issue even more salient.

The distinction between the two roles can be quite fuzzy, especially in practice. Consider two analogous situations. An opposition leader in an authoritarian regime wants to hold a large rally in the capital. The rally, if it successfully gathers hundreds of thousands of people as planned, accomplishes the two tasks just specified. It both communicates to the current regime the swelling sentiment among the population that the current regime is offensive *and* coordinates or mobilizes the opposing citizens on a particular course of action: support the opposition leader and work to topple the current government. To the government the rally signals the status of the opposition, and to the citizens in the rally it reinforces the notion that the effort to topple the regime is important and worthy of risky collective action.

Outside lobbying is also similar to the marketing behavior of business entrepreneurs promoting new product ideas to consumers and investors at the same time. Entrepreneurs do their own brand of inside lobbying among investors, hawking their product ideas and wooing support among a small group of people. At the same time, they gauge consumer demand for their products, communicate that level of demand to potential investors, and even try to stimulate more demand among consumers. Success among one audience (consumers) will likely lead to success among the other audience (investors). Just as investors try to assess potential consumer response to the entrepreneur's marketing efforts because future investments will succeed or fail based on consumer behavior, elected officials look to constituents' responses to outside lobbying because reelection efforts may hinge on the interest group success in mobilizing constituents. For interest groups, as with entrepreneurs, there are two audiences in mass marketing, but the overall goals converge because one audience relies very much on the other audience. . . .

The duality of purpose makes outside lobbying a powerful tool in the hands of interest groups. It can simultaneously fan the flames of constituent anger and bring the heat of those flames to the attention of representatives far away, whose job it is to put out or contain the fire. However, while the two roles can get mixed together in practice, there are important conceptual distinctions between them. In the signaling role, the salience of a policy issue must be considered *exogenous* in that there is something fixed and unknown to policymakers about salience that the group claims to be able to demonstrate through outside lobbying. Perhaps it is the potential salience of an issue that interest groups want to communicate. In this case, the "fixed" element of public opinion being communicated is the latent salience of an issue. The group is confident it can expand the conflict to a certain point, and it wants to communicate that confidence through outside lobbying. In the conflict expansion role, the salience of a policy issue is *endogenous*, in that the strategy is intended to influence the very characteristic of public opinion that is being communicated in the signaling role.

■　　■　　■

Communication costs in particular are relevant to the study of outside lobbying because the costs of successful outside lobbying are related systematically to the existing state of public salience on an issue. Precisely because outside lobbying is costly, and the strategies of interest groups conditional on those costs offer clues to the underlying public salience groups are trying to communicate, outside lobbying can influence policymakers. Policymakers learn about salience by making inferences from the revealed efforts of interest groups.

When group leaders are confident they can expand the conflict—raise public awareness of an issue or frame issues in different ways to their advantage—additional considerations besides the advantages of signaling to policymakers become important. What information should a group present to constituents to convince them the issue is worth costly collective action? When in the course of legislation should conflict expansion happen for maximum impact? How should a group frame the advantages of one policy over another policy? In general, when there are opportunities to expand the conflict, decision making over strategies turns on how potential increases in salience (or sometimes popularity) will benefit interest group goals, rather than on how the current level of popular support will play with policymakers.

As a first cut at understanding conflict expansion, we might think it benefits groups that do not have ready access to policymakers. Much of our understanding of this comes from Schattschneider. Schattschneider believed not only that outsider groups would want to outside lobby, but also that such groups tend to have advantages in the realm of public opinion. According to Schattschneider, "It is the weak who want to socialize conflict, i.e., to involve more and more people in the conflict until the balance of forces is changed" (1960, 40), the assumption being that groups with concentrated wealth or power would eschew politics involving broad popular participation and do not stand to gain from increased salience.

Schattschneider's ideas, however, do not completely square with contemporary interest group politics. In an age when all kinds of organizations, including large corporations, wealthy trade associations, and professional groups outside lobby on policy issues of great concern to millions of Americans, clearly there are times when the strong and those groups with considerable inside access want to expand the scope of the conflict as well. . . .

Two aspects of the policy context that influence outside lobbying are discussed in detail in that chapter: the stage of legislation and the policy alternatives confronting policymakers. The stage of legislation—whether a policy problem is just being introduced to the government or whether well-defined alternatives are being considered by legislators—will have a large effect on both signaling and conflict expansion decisions (Kingdon 1984). In decisions over lobbying strategies or tactics, groups facing policies in earlier stages, when they merely try to raise consciousness on a new policy issue, will be less concerned about popular support for their policy positions than will groups facing policies in later stages, when they fight to swing a few key votes in a congressional committee. The stage of legislation shapes the way public opinion constrains interest group strategies mostly by varying the benefits groups attain in signaling the current salience of an issue versus in trying to increase the salience of that issue or the popularity of specific policies.

Policy alternatives, or more specifically the relative popularity of policy alternatives, matter a great deal because they also determine whether increasing salience is a good idea for a group. What may not be overwhelmingly popular—say, needle exchange programs—may be more popular than the most prominent policy alternative, increased spending on drug rehabilitation programs. Thus, as for influencing outside lobbying decisions, the popularity of policies must be regarded as relative, not absolute, a consideration that carries implications about whether a group benefits from conflict expansion.

▪   ▪   ▪

Most us would presumably like to see outside lobbying coming from groups supporting popular policies on salient issues. Instead, the empirical conclusions of this study are mixed. I find that outside lobbying, contrary to the view that most of it produces phony grass-roots support, is far from artificial. It is actually a good way for policymakers to learn what their constituents care about. My data show that outside lobbying on average works as a policymaker might hope: it communicates fairly accurately the salience of policy issues to large numbers of constituents, and it often influences the salience of policy issues to benefit the more popular side of an issue. At the same time, however, and more often than we would like, outside lobbying springs forth from intense groups pursuing relatively unpopular policies (especially early in the legislative process), and in this regard, it falls somewhat short in reinforcing the majority's preferences. Outside lobbying, in sum, does not distort the policymaking process nearly as much as many people like to claim, but it does a better job in communicating salience information than in bolstering popular pressure for majoritarian policies.

▪   ▪   ▪

2. TACTICS AND STRATEGIES

The Story of the Hat Trick

One beautiful August morning in 1989, Leona Kozien took the bus from near her home in Chicago to the Copernicus Center for senior citizens on the city's northwest side. Kozien, who was sixty-nine years old, had no idea at the time that she was going to become a brief media star and a figure of political lore. All she knew was that she was angry with the politicians in Washington. In particular, she felt betrayed by her congressman, Dan Rostenkowski, chairman of the Ways and Means Committee of the House of Representatives. Kozien was upset by a new policy from Washington that caused her husband to pay a surtax for catastrophic health care insurance. In her mind, it was an unfair attempt by the federal government to make senior citizens pay unreasonably for health care.

Rostenkowski knew many seniors were angry, but he did not know the extent of the anger. Since the unveiling of the policy a year earlier, a policy that he and the largest seniors lobby, the American Association of Retired Persons (AARP), had sponsored and supported all through the legislative process, he had been reluctant to meet with smaller senior citizens' groups, even those from his own district. National groups separate from the AARP, especially the National Committee to Preserve Social Security and Medicare, run by James Roosevelt, son of President Franklin D. Roosevelt, had been mobilizing grass-roots opposition to the policy for more than a year. The AARP then decided to oppose the new policy. Partly as a concession and partly as a compromise, Rostenkowski had agreed to meet with a few of the leaders of local senior citizens groups. The meeting was held at the Copernicus Center, right in the heart of Rostenkowski's district.

After prodding by her husband (who could not attend), Kozien joined approximately one hundred seniors who waited in the main hall of the center for Rostenkowski to emerge from the meeting with the group leaders. She and other seniors had been given signs to wave at Rostenkowski. The signs indicated displeasure with the current policy: Congressman Rostenkowski, Don't Tax the Seniors and Read My Lips: Catastrophic Act Is a Seniors Tax.

While Rostenkowski met with group leaders, Kozien and her own group were holding a meeting of their own in the main hall. Participants were taking turns telling the rest of the group why the catastrophic health policy was bad for seniors. The group waiting for Rostenkowski agreed that the catastrophic "tax" had to go, but they also agreed on something else. They wanted Rostenkowski to speak to them in person.

"A lot of people felt they were owed something," one local interest group leader recalls. "They just wanted to see him. He was right there, and they felt this was their opportunity [to tell him what they thought of the policy]."

Rostenkowski emerged from his meeting and headed for the exit. The group waiting for him booed and hissed. Before the congressman could get to the door, a television crew stopped him to ask questions about events in Poland, a topic of keen interest to many of his constituents. This pause gave a small group of seniors enough time to run out of the building and surround Rostenkowski's car. Kozien led the charge.

Kozien shouted, "Where's his car parked? I'm going to make him talk to us!"

A small mob followed Kozien outside, and pretty soon there were fifteen to twenty seniors surrounding the congressman's car, while television crews stood nearby. Rostenkowski, meanwhile, fought through the crowd and got in the car.

"Coward!" "Shame!" "Impeach Rottenkowski!" The seniors stood in front of the car and waved placards. The congressman's driver honked the horn and moved the car a few inches. The front bumper brushed against Kozien's thigh, and she staggered a bit. Some man shouted, "You knocked her down!

You hurt her!" This same man then turned to Kozien and said quietly, "Lay down under the car."

"Are you crazy? No way, he'd run me over!" retorted Kozien, who was barely over five feet tall. The car moved again, and this time Kozien fell on the hood of the car. Her face was inches from Rostenkowski's, with glass separating them. She was still carrying her placard, and from inside the car, Rostenkowski saw her placard, her face, and her body sprawled across the windshield.

"Killer! Killer!" the crowd shouted.

Rostenkowski then got out of the car and ran through a parking lot while angry seniors chased after him. The driver maneuvered through the crowd, drove around the block, and caught up with Rostenkowski down the street from the center. Rostenkowski jumped in, and the car sped off.

"It was a funny picture," recalled one local politician present, "because it was a true chase. The seniors would move faster, and Rosty would move faster. He gets in the car, and they stand in front of the car."

The scene made for dramatic television. The Chicago film crews, delighted with the footage, distributed it immediately to the national networks. All three major television news shows carried the story prominently that evening, earning the interest group leaders what they call "a hat trick," in reference to a hockey player scoring three goals in one game.

Kozien, meanwhile, the activist and agitator for that day, was an unlikely hero. She had never before been active in politics. She knew little about the seniors groups at the Copernicus Center. Her relatives called that evening, expressing amazement at their "crazy Aunt Leona." Over the next several years politicians, prior to speaking at senior citizen events, would ask her to accompany them onstage. She always refused.

She likewise downplayed her heroism. "We just wanted answers. Had he answered our questions, there would have been no incident." Yet the incident was a bonanza for the leaders of the interest groups. The image of Kozien on the hood of Rostenkowski's car was used for years afterward on network news to symbolize the potency of the senior citizen lobby.

The catastrophic insurance program, which had passed the House in June 1988 by a vote of 328 to 72, was soon after repealed. The vote was not even close. The House voted 360 to 66 in favor of repeal in October 1989. Incidentally, Rostenkowski stood firm, voting to oppose repeal.

Many members of Congress had heard from people like Kozien, though presumably not from atop the hoods of their cars. Two Florida legislators reported getting more than seventy-five thousand pieces of mail, each opposing the policy. One staffer reported to me that his boss received more than two thousand mail pieces in favor of repeal, and eight mail pieces against repeal. The turn of events on catastrophic health insurance had people shaking their heads.

To some, the outside lobbying gave a large voice to a small number of people. "It was a case of the House of Representatives being stampeded by a small, vocal group of seniors," said Pete Stark, a Democratic congressman from California. "Ambushed is how a lot of people here feel now," Tim Penny, a Democrat from Minnesota, said at the time. "Every member of Congress was getting accosted at town meetings," said Senator John McCain, Republican from Arizona.

Others were more positive about the outcome, preferring to think that the outside lobbying tapped into a widespread sentiment. "We made a mistake last year [in 1988]," said Brian Donnelly, a Democratic congressman from Massachusetts. "This time, we listened to the voters."

Significance of the Story

The story of the Rostenkowski incident in north Chicago, while hardly typical of stories of outside lobbying, is useful for several reasons. For one, it shows in dramatic fashion how interest groups can instigate or facilitate collective action through outside lobbying. Contrary to what interest group leaders were claiming afterward, the mobbing of Rostenkowski was not all that spontaneous. The meeting between Rostenkowski and the interest group leaders was set up by the interest group leaders, and seniors from around the neighborhood were encouraged to attend by the interest group leaders. The interest groups leaders, not Rostenkowski's staff, had invited the networks to the meetings at the Copernicus Center. Rostenkowski's staff wanted to avoid media attention. And the interest group leaders made the placards and distributed them to Kozien and other seniors.

Interest group leaders also knew that the seniors attending were unusually angry about the new policy, and the leaders wanted to communicate that anger forcefully and make it seem less than fully staged. The seniors at the Copernicus Center were to represent the tip of the iceberg of constituent opinion. As for the seniors, their reactions could not have been better for the group leaders. The leaders provided a small, low-cost spark and let it turn into a conflagration. The behavior of Kozien and others was spontaneous and chaotic enough to indicate that the seniors were just plain mad. After all the preparations, events got out of control at the right time and at the right level. "Just barely out of control" might be the optimum level of behavioral response interest group leaders want from constituents in an outside lobbying campaign.

Therefore, what was communicated loudly and clearly to policymakers was the ease with which interest group leaders mobilized Kozien and her fellow seniors. The low costs involved for the interest groups to get hundreds of seniors to stampede the car of a powerful committee chairman counted for much more than the stampede itself. In trying to signal the "true" level of public salience over an issue, an interest group that succeeds with little effort can gain credibility. I shall discuss this important point in more detail in the next chapter.

Most of the conflict expansion on the issue had occurred well before that fateful day. National seniors organizations like the Gray Panthers and the

National Committee to Preserve Social Security and Medicare had been running advertisements for months, and they had successfully framed the issue as one of unfair taxation for all seniors as opposed to one of health care benefits for a vast majority of seniors. By one reasonable interpretation, through the summer of 1989 interest groups had increased the level of salience among seniors on the issue. Then, as the salience of the issue peaked in late summer, interest group leaders had only to signal to policymakers the salience of the issue among those seniors who opposed the new policy. The Rostenkowski incident was timed perfectly. The conflict had been expanded, and the time had come to let policymakers know about it.

The story also neatly illustrates the roles assumed by the main players described in the previous chapter. Interest group leaders, the ones who had invited people like Kozien in the first place, set the stage for the famous confrontation (though they got lucky when it succeeded beyond their expectations). A policymaker, in this case a powerful House committee chairman, found himself the target of outside lobbying efforts by interest group leaders and constituents. And the ordinary constituents like Kozien, who behaved in both an organized and disorganized manner, made the lives of policymakers more difficult through simple expressions of anger.

The story is useful as well for highlighting the potential influence of outside lobbying. The renegade senior citizens groups, those distinguishing themselves early on from the AARP on the catastrophic health care policy, appear to have had an effect on Rostenkowski's colleagues in the House. As Table 1 indicates, 240 members of the House switched their votes from supporting catastrophic coverage in June 1988 to supporting repeal of catastrophic coverage sixteen months later. This is a remarkable instance of collective reconsideration. Only 124 members, or approximately half of the number that switched votes, voted the "same" way for both bills—that is, 124 either voted against the original bill and for repeal, or they voted for the original bill and

TABLE 1 Reconsidering Catastrophic Health Insurance: Number of Members of the House of Representatives Voting For or Against Original Bill and Repeal

	Original Bill	
Repeal	*Yea*	*Nay*
Yea	240	64
Nay	60	1

NOTE: This takes into account turnover from the 100th to 101st Congress, in that only members who voted on both bills are included. One member, Larry Hopkins, a Republican from Kentucky, voted against the original proposal and against repeal. The original bill was HR 2470, Catastrophic Health Insurance/Rule. The repeal was HR 3299, Amendment to Budget Reconciliation, Repealing Catastrophic Health Insurance Surtax.

against repeal. The latter vote, on the amendment to repeal the Catastrophic Coverage Act, was the first time Congress had ever voted to repeal a major social benefit it had created.

"An event of about 150 elderly people changed the tide of the thing," recalled Jan Schakowsky, at the time a leader of the Illinois State Council of Senior Citizens, one of the groups that mobilized seniors on that day. "It was a pivotal event." It was pivotal not because it changed Rostenkowski's mind (which it did not), but because it had such an influence on his colleagues. As the story and its aftermath remind us, a well-publicized event among a small number of people can send very strong signals about, and enhance the reputation of, a group numbering many thousands or even millions of people. More than five years later, members of Congress referred to the Rostenkowski incident as cementing the reputation of the senior citizens lobby. This, according to people in Washington who are inclined to slight hyperbole, is one group in the population they do not want to cross.

Another revealing aspect of the story is that the Rostenkowski event happened because of a grave miscalculation on the part of the chairman and his colleagues. They enacted the original policy because they were led to believe that seniors were behind it, but they gambled and lost when interest groups tapped into a undiscovered level of antipathy among certain groups of seniors.[1] In general, legislators try to estimate the policy preferences and issue salience among their constituents, yet these estimates are shots in the dark on many controversial issues. They never know how some groups will respond, or which issues their next electoral opponent will use against them. They need to do the near impossible: anticipate how latent constituent opinion will manifest itself in the coming years. Rostenkowski was probably warned when he led his committee to recommend the original policy. Like anyone facing a difficult decision, however, he listened to the people who had previously established a credible reputation for electoral power, the AARP. Yet until Kozien and her fellow seniors let him know loudly and clearly their preferences, he could not have been certain about the consequences of his previous actions. The response among seniors led Rostenkowski and other policymakers to move toward repeal.

The Rostenkowski story is unusual, of course. Rarely are outside lobbying efforts as successful. Famous examples, such as this one, become lore around the Capitol. Another example from the early 1980s still generates discussion around Washington. During the successful outside lobbying efforts in 1982 by the American Bankers Association to repeal tax withholding from interest-bearing accounts, 22 million postcards from depositors flooded into Congress within days of the passage of the tax bill containing the provision. Every congressional district responded, according to the staff of Robert Dole, the chair of the Senate Finance Committee at the time. The marvel is that bankers, of all people, were able to make an issue more salient through conflict expansion, and at the same time were able to signal that salience to policymakers with a successful outside lobbying campaign. They did all of this without hiding their identities as bankers, indicating that latent salience among constituents is a great resource for all groups, not just for those with popular images or credibility as electoral powerhouses.

NOTE

1. In truth, even the AARP was caught off guard. Dissident elderly groups, those opposed to the policy all along, begun stirring opposition until the AARP changed its policy on the issue. Then, once the AARP was opposed to the policy, it galvanized further action by the dissident elderly groups.

BIBLIOGRAPHY

Key, V. O. 1961. *Public Opinion and American Democracy.* New York: Alfred Knopf.
Kingdon, John. 1984. *Agendas, Alternatives, and Public Policies.* Boston: Little, Brown.
Schattschneider, E. E. 1960. *The Semi-Sovereign People.* Hinsdale, Illinois: Dryden Press.

11.3

DARA STROLOVITCH

From *Affirmative Advocacy*

There are many organizations in the United States representing the interests of groups disadvantaged economically and politically, such as women, African Americans, Latinos, gays and lesbians, and welfare recipient families. Strolovitch finds in her research that these organizations do not do as well as they could in representing the most disadvantaged from within those groups. Advocacy organizations are highly responsive to the needs of the wealthier and more educated among their clientele groups.

1. INTRODUCTION

. . . Writers since Alexis de Tocqueville have recognized that American civic organizations are a key component of a healthy democratic society and citizenry (Tocqueville [1835] 1965). Tocqueville and his intellectual descendants argue that civil-society organizations, including everything from unions to bowling leagues, promote democratic values such as freedom of speech and association, social capital, civic participation, leadership skills, trust in government, and cross-class alliances.

One form of civic organization—national-level advocacy or social movement organizations—has historically been a crucial conduit for the articulation and representation of disadvantaged interests in U.S. politics, particularly for groups that are ill served by the two major political parties. Advocacy organizations have presented historically marginalized groups with an alternative mode of representation within an electoral system that provides insufficient means for transmitting the preferences and interests of those citizens. For many years, these organizations often were the sole political voice afforded groups such as southern blacks and women of all races, who were denied formal voting rights until well into the twentieth century. Long before women won the right to vote in 1920, for example, organizations such as the National American Woman Suffrage Association (formed in 1890) and the National Woman's Party (formed in 1913) mobilized women and lobbied legislators on their behalf, providing some insider access for the mass movements with which they were associated. Similarly, the National Association for the Advancement of Colored People (NAACP, formed in 1909) provided political and legal representation for

African Americans in the South who, after a brief period of voting following Reconstruction and the passage of the Fifteenth Amendment in 1870, were largely disenfranchised and denied formal representation until the passage and enforcement of the Voting Rights Act of 1965.

While advocacy organizations often were the only voice for these groups, they were nonetheless comparatively weak, greatly outnumbered and out-resourced by business, financial, and professional interest groups.[1] The 1960s and 1970s, however, witnessed an explosion in the number of movements and organizations speaking on behalf of disadvantaged populations. Mass mobilization and increased representation led to greater opportunity and mobility for many women, members of racial minority groups, and low-income people. Organizations advocating on their behalf pursued lawsuits, regulations, and legislation aimed at ending de jure racial and sex-based discrimination and increasing resources and opportunities for those groups, and many of their efforts bore fruit.

In 1963, for example, the Equal Pay Act prohibited sex-based wage discrimination. The following year saw the passage of the 1964 Civil Rights Act, which barred discrimination in public accommodations, in government, and in employment, and established the Equal Employment Opportunity Commission (EEOC) to investigate complaints of discrimination and impose penalties on offenders. That same year, the United States Congress passed the Economic Opportunity Act, the centerpiece of President Lyndon Johnson's War on Poverty, creating programs to attack poverty and unemployment through, for example, job training, education, legal services, and community health centers. In 1965, the Voting Rights Act prohibited racial discrimination in voting, amendments to the Immigration and Nationality Act liberalized national-origins quotas in immigration, and the Social Security Act established Medicare and Medicaid, providing health care for elderly and low-income people. That was also the year that President Johnson signed Executive Order 11246, calling on federal government contractors to "take affirmative action" against discrimination based on "race, creed, color, or national origin." Two years later, in 1967, this order was extended by Executive Order 11375 to include sex-based discrimination. Title IX of the Education Amendments of 1972 banned sex discrimination in schools. In 1973, the Supreme Court struck down the restrictive abortion laws that were on the books in most states at that time and upheld a 1968 EEOC ruling prohibiting sex-segregated "help wanted" ads in newspapers. Also in 1973, Congress passed the Equal Credit Opportunity Act, prohibiting discrimination on the basis of sex, race, marital status, religion, national origin, age, or receipt of public assistance in consumer credit practices.

With these developments came increased resources, newly fortified rights, more political power, and greater levels of mobilization than ever before for groups such as women, racial minorities, and low-income people. As a consequence, they became what Anne Larason Schneider and Helen Ingram call "emergent contenders" in American politics. Emergent contenders are groups that have gained some political, economic, and social power but have not yet completely shaken their powerlessness, stigmatized identities, or political and social marginalization (Schneider and Ingram 1997). Decades after advocacy groups helped government officials lay the legal and legislative groundwork that made possible these changes, however, important questions remain about how well these organizations represent their constituents. How much power and access do the organizations in the community of social and economic justice interest organizations have relative to that of organizations representing more-advantaged constituencies? How far-reaching is the impact of the policy issues that these organizations pursue? How effectively do advocacy organizations empower those members of marginalized groups who will be in the best position to uplift less-powerful members of their communities? How much access do these organizations have to elected officials, and how successfully do they pursue their policy goals? Are formal organizations and insider tactics the "enemies of protest" that lead to oligarchy, conservatism, moderated demands, and demobilization? How well do such organizations serve to build social capital, boost civic participation, or bring people together across class lines? Each of these questions focuses on a critical aspect of how successfully organizations represent their constituents.

■　　■　　■

Overview of Argument and Major Findings

Legal scholar and critical race theorist Kimberlé Crenshaw has termed the multiply disadvantaged subgroups of marginalized groups such as women, racial minorities, and low-income people "intersectionally marginalized" (Crenshaw 1989), an insight that has prompted considerable interest and attention on the part of political and social theorists. Recognizing that important inequalities persist *among* racial, gender, and economic groups, intersectional approaches highlight inequalities *within* marginalized groups. For example, the low-income women who are unlikely to manage to afford the membership fees at the Augusta National Golf Club constitute an *intersectionally disadvantaged subgroup* of women, as they face marginalization both economically and based on gender.

Despite widespread interest in the concept of intersectionality, it has proven difficult to assess empirically. To do so, I examine three key questions fundamental to evaluating the representation of marginalized groups in the United States: First, how active are advocacy organizations when it comes to policy issues that affect intersectionally marginalized subgroups of their constituencies? Second, when they are involved with such issues, in what ways are they active—in particular, at which political institutions do they target their advocacy, and what kind of coalitions do they form? Third, how do organizations define their mandates as representatives, and what are some of the steps that can be taken by organizations to strengthen representation for intersectionally marginalized groups?

To answer these questions, I collected new quantitative and qualitative data using a survey of 286 organizations as well as in-depth face-to-face interviews with officers and professional staff at 40 organizations. To collect the survey data, I designed the first quantitative study that focuses on the organizations that together make up the social and economic justice interest community, the 2000 Survey of National Economic and Social Justice Organizations (hereafter referred to as the SNESJO). Coupled with the information that I collected through the in-person interviews and analyzed in light of insights based in theories of intersectionality as well as theories of representation, these data allow for the first large-scale and in-depth examination of the extent to which these advocacy organizations represent disadvantaged subgroups of their constituents.

The data paint a complicated and nuanced portrait of social and economic justice advocacy organizations and the challenges that they face as they work to represent marginalized groups in the contemporary United States. First, the evidence reveals that it does not suffice to distinguish only between advantaged and disadvantaged groups. To understand the priorities and activities of advocacy organizations, we must distinguish among *four* types of issues affecting four differently situated constituencies: *universal issues*, which, at least in theory, affect the population as a whole, regardless of race, gender, sexual orientation, disability, class, or any other identity; *majority issues*, which affect an organization's members or constituents relatively equally; *disadvantaged-subgroup issues*, which affect an organization's constituents who are disadvantaged economically, socially, or politically compared to the broader constituency; and *advantaged-subgroup issues*, which also affect a subgroup of an organization's constituents but one that is relatively advantaged compared to the broader constituency.

Distinguishing among these four policy types reveals that advocacy organizations are much more active on policy issues affecting a majority of their constituents than they are on issues that affect subgroups within their constituencies. This finding might seem to suggest that these organizations conform to a traditional conception of majoritarian representation that is based on the idea that attention should be devoted to constituents in proportion to their numbers. Such an interpretation is challenged, however, by the more startling finding that shows that organizations apply a double standard when it comes to the levels of energy that they devote to issues affecting differently situated subgroups of their constituencies. Issues affecting advantaged subgroups are given disproportionately high levels of attention, whereas issues affecting disadvantaged subgroups are given disproportionately low levels. In fact, once we account for other effects, issues affecting advantaged subgroups receive more attention than majority issues. Moreover, although organizations are extremely active when it comes to issues affecting advantaged subgroups regardless of the breadth of impact of the issue, the level of activity on issues affecting disadvantaged subgroups depends on the proportion of constituents that is affected by these issues.

So, for example, the survey data show that women's organizations are only slightly more active on violence against women—a majority issue—than they are on affirmative action in higher education—an issue affecting a subgroup of relatively advantaged women. Organizations are much *less* active, however, when it comes to welfare reform, an issue affecting a sub-constituency of *intersectionally disadvantaged* women. Instead of working on issues affecting disadvantaged subgroups directly, officers at these organizations assume that representation for these subgroups will happen as a by-product of their efforts on other issues and that the benefits of other efforts will "trickle down" to disadvantaged constituents.

At the same time, I find that organizations that speak on behalf of marginalized groups do not lack interest in advocating on behalf of disadvantaged subgroups within their constituencies. To the contrary, concerns about representing disadvantaged subgroups weigh heavily on the minds of organization officers, and the majority of them are genuinely committed to the goal of advocacy for their multiply disadvantaged constituents. Indeed, most of the officers I interviewed view representation as far more than a process of interest aggregation or a duty to represent the majority will.[2] Rather, they conceive of representation as a form of advocacy, and they express principled commitments to using their roles as representatives as a means to achieve social justice. As a consequence, most of these officers feel a responsibility to advocate for and to "do right" by disadvantaged subgroups of their constituencies. However, while many demonstrate a commitment to incorporate such advocacy into their roles as representatives, fewer operate this way in practice. Instead, attention to the concerns of intersectionally disadvantaged constituents is superseded by the fact that most organizations do not regard the intersectionally-constituted inequalities and issues that affect these constituents as central to their agendas. Consequently, officers at these organizations marginalize and downplay the impact of such issues, framing them as narrow and particularistic in their effect, while constructing policy images of issues affecting advantaged subgroups as common interests that have a broad impact.

Because of these framings and constructions, organizations are far more willing to expend resources and political capital on behalf of advantaged subgroups than they are on behalf of disadvantaged ones. As a result, organizations are active not only at different *levels* when it comes to issues affecting intersectionally disadvantaged subgroups of their constituencies, they are also active in different *ways* when it comes to these issues. The differences between the tactics used for each subgroup exacerbate the lower levels of activity on behalf of intersectionally disadvantaged subgroups. In contrast to the popularly held stereotype that depicts profligate litigation by progressive organizations, I find that these organizations are actually quite hesitant to target the judiciary. However, while overall levels of court use by advocacy organizations are quite low, these organizations are substantially more likely to use the politically and financially expensive courts on behalf of advantaged subgroups of their constituencies than they are on behalf of disadvantaged subgroups. Finally, coalitions are ideally suited to pursuing issues affecting intersectionally disadvantaged groups and issues that cut across the constituencies of a range of organizations, and organizations do indeed pursue much of their work on issues affecting disadvantaged subgroups through coalitions with other groups. However, while organizations often work in alliances with other groups on disadvantaged-subgroup issues, they devote lower levels of energy to their coalitional efforts on these issues than they devote to coalitions dedicated to working on issues affecting advantaged subgroups.

Thus, although they constitute a critical source of representation for their intersectionally marginalized constituents, advocacy organizations are considerably *less* active, and active in *substantially different ways*, when it comes to issues affecting disadvantaged subgroups than they are when it comes to issues affecting more advantaged subgroups.

Affirmative Advocacy

Although the trends that I uncover are widespread, they are not ubiquitous, nor are they intentional. Indeed, the story of interest groups as representatives of intersectionally marginalized groups is more one of possibility than it is one of failure, and some organizations do speak extensively and effectively on behalf of intersectionally disadvantaged subgroups of their constituencies. Evidence from the survey and interviews demonstrates that what separates these organizations from those that fail to provide extensive representation for intersectionally disadvantaged groups is their commitment to a set of practices and principles that together constitute a framework of representational redistribution that I call *affirmative advocacy*.

Like affirmative action in education or employment, which is intended to redistribute resources and level the playing field for disadvantaged individuals in these arenas, the principle of affirmative advocacy recognizes that equitable representation for disadvantaged groups requires proactive efforts to overcome the entrenched but often subtle biases that persist against marginalized groups in American politics. This recognition compels those organizations that appreciate it to redistribute resources and attention to issues affecting intersectionally disadvantaged subgroups in order to level the playing field among groups. Among the practices they adopt to accomplish this redistribution are creating decision rules that elevate issues affecting disadvantaged minorities on organizational agendas; using internal processes and practices to improve the status of intersectionally disadvantaged groups within the organization; forging stronger ties to state and local advocacy groups; promoting "descriptive representation" by making sure that staff and boards include members of intersectionally marginalized subgroups of their constituencies; resisting the silencing effects of public and constituent opinion that are biased against disadvantaged subgroups; and cultivating among advantaged subgroups of their constituencies the understanding that their interests are inextricably linked to the well-being of intersectionally disadvantaged constituents. Through procedures and mores such as these, organizations engage in a form of redistributive representation that blurs the boundaries between advocacy and representation and that is itself a prefigurative form of social justice (Urbinati 2000, 2002). In these ways, organizations advance an innovative conception of representation that has great potential to equalize both representation and policy outcomes by offsetting the power of relatively advantaged subgroups.

I derive the substance and component measures encompassed within the affirmative advocacy framework inductively from empirical evidence about the practices of organizations found in the survey and interview data. Many of the principles and commitments that are embodied by the practices of affirmative advocacy, however, reflect ideas in political, social, and legal theories about interests, identities, representation, and redistribution. The framework draws on and brings into conversation a broad range of scholarship in these areas, including the contention of political theorist Iris Young (1992, 2000) that oppressed groups should receive extra representation, and legal scholar Lani Guinier's notion of "taking turns," which counters the dominance of purely majoritarian systems of voting and democratic governance. The framework also has a rough analogue in the "difference principle" articulated by political philosopher John Rawls in his classic book, *A Theory of Justice* (Rawls 1971). Rawls offered this principle to rebut utilitarian ideas that hold that distributive schemes should bring "the greatest good for the greatest number." Among Rawls's central arguments is that rather than following the majoritarian logic of utilitarianism, institutions should instead be designed to benefit the least well-off members of society and that inequalities are justifiable only to the extent that they meet this criterion.[3]

My examination of organizations that represent marginalized groups suggests that analogous principles animate the *representational* schemes of the organizations that most vigorously advocate for intersectionally disadvantaged subgroups. These organizations prioritize advocacy and representation that benefit their least well-off constituents, redistributing representational resources and energy to issues that affect intersectionally disadvantaged subgroups of their constituencies. As affirmative advocates, organizations harness a version of what Michael Dawson (1994) calls "linked fate" in order to better represent disadvantaged subgroups. That is, they engage in a form of what Nancy Schwartz (1988) labels "constitutive representation," cultivating among advantaged subgroups of their constituencies the understanding that their interests are bound up with the well-being of intersectionally disadvantaged constituents, nurturing a sense of what I call *intersectionally linked fate*.[4]

■   ■   ■

4. TRICKLE-DOWN REPRESENTATION?

■   ■   ■

Exacerbating the Bias?

It is clear that low levels of advocacy on disadvantaged-subgroup issues are strongly related to the power of those affected and to the tendency on the part of organizations to downplay the effects that these issues have on their constituent groups. Nevertheless, other factors also exacerbate the biases against disadvantaged subpopulations. Some of these factors manifest differently in membership organizations than they do in non-membership groups, but the net result is the same: disproportionately low levels of advocacy on behalf of intersectionally disadvantaged groups and disproportionately high levels of attention to the issues affecting their advantaged counterparts.

Constituent concern

First, in membership and nonmembership organizations alike, constituent concern about an issue leads to increased advocacy on that issue. The interviews support this finding and confirm that organizations conform to traditional notions of representation in this way. That is, they are more active on issues that they perceive as being important to their constituents, something that they gauge either by means of constituent surveys or by evaluating the number of constituents who call or write with opinions on a given issue. The executive director of an African American organization, for example, told me that his group took a proactive approach to trying to determine its constituents' attitudes and policy priorities, conducting regular polls to identify issues that are important to them. Several other respondents said, however, that they make the decision to mobilize around an issue when they begin "getting lots of phone calls" about it. The executive director of an Asian Pacific American organization explained that her group became involved in advocacy to change the regulations governing H-1B work visas (for skilled workers) because "our community wanted us to lead on [it] . . . that's kind of what sparked our interest to . . . get involved."[5] In contrast, the executive director of an economic justice organization told me that his organization has never done anything regarding public funding for abortion or reproductive health more generally because it is not an issue that they "particularly get a lot of pressure from our constituencies to work on and it's not high on our list."[6]

Pegging levels of activity to constituent concerns is understandable and congruent with traditional notions of representation and concerns about organizational maintenance. However, this practice has problematic implications for advocacy on disadvantaged-subgroup issues because concern about these issues is, on average, lower than it is for majority and advantaged-subgroup issues. For example, while 58 percent of respondents reported that "almost all" of their members are concerned about the majority issues about which they were asked, and 45 percent gave this answer regarding the advantaged-subgroup issues, only 30 percent believed that almost all of their members are concerned about their designated disadvantaged-subgroup issues. The effect of these uneven levels is further compounded by the fact that interest groups, like members of Congress, are more likely to address issues that are important to those "passionate minorities" of their constituencies who have the motivation and the resources to make themselves heard (Kollman 1998). Because advantaged subgroups are likely to have the resources necessary to make organizations aware of their concerns, organizations perceive more constituent interest in issues that are of concern to those subgroups (Verba, Schlozman, and Brady 1995). This perception, in turn, contributes to the disproportionately high levels of attention devoted to advantaged-subgroup issues.

Constituent agreement

Both membership and nonmembership organizations respond to constituent concerns about policy issues, but the former also pay particular attention to whether their constituents *support* the organization's positions on these issues. The higher the proportion of constituents in agreement with a membership organization's position on an issue, the more active the organization is likely to be on that issue. Constituent agreement does not, however, have a significant effect on the activity levels of nonmembership organizations. This discrepancy between membership and nonmembership organizations makes sense: organizations that depend on member support fear alienating their constituents, a concern that does not have the same urgency for nonmembership organizations.

In the interviews, many respondents from membership-based organizations affirmed this relationship and explained that they are unlikely to take action on an issue unless their constituents agree with the organization's position on it. For example, a policy analyst at a labor organization told me, "Anything that is going to be internally divisive for us tends to be something that we're less likely to take a strong position on." For this organization, the aversion to divisive issues manifests itself as a focus on "issues affecting working people and their families" and an avoidance of what the respondent called "social and civil rights issues."[7] Likewise, the executive director of an Asian Pacific American organization commented, "We have to be very careful. We don't want to turn off or upset our community. . . . What's the point of having an advocacy organization if you're turning them off?" In particular, she said, violence against women is an issue "that we steer away from" because, in her opinion, it is "not a topic that is openly discussed . . . in our community."[8]

It is part of an organization's mandate to reflect and respond to its constituents' attitudes and policy preferences, and, once again, such responsiveness is in keeping with traditional notions of representation and the exigencies of organizational maintenance. However, the foregoing examples suggest that constituents' dissent is more likely to prevent advocacy when it comes to issues affecting disadvantaged-subgroups—in the cases just mentioned, Asian Pacific American women within Asian Pacific American organizations and low-income women and people of color within labor organizations. Consequently, organizations' patterns of response and non-response to constituent preferences suggest that they pass up important opportunities to supplement their responsiveness with more active mediation on behalf of disadvantaged subgroups of their constituencies. Rather than nurturing the understanding among more-advantaged constituents that their fortunes and interests are linked to less-advantaged members of their communities, they reinforce the marginalization of intersectionally disadvantaged groups by validating the idea that these issues, and the people they affect, are not worthy of the organization's attention.

Although the foregoing statements reflect and reinforce the statistical finding that activity rises and falls with constituent support, these trends are by no means ubiquitous. Instead, the comments of several other officers remind us of the important findings regarding organization leaders' beliefs that their organizations should compensate for biases against marginalized groups by acting as mediators on their behalf. Many officers, for example, expressed a commitment to taking the lead on issues rather than following the leads of their constituents. For example, the executive director of an African American organization commented that in his view, leadership entails a responsibility "to promote [an] issue regardless of whether it's popular or not."[9] In a more specific example, the president of a large union explained that his organization decided to address affirmative action and gender discrimination in hiring, salaries, promotion, and job classification even though, at the time, "that wasn't always a popular issue with some of the male members" who dominated the union's membership. "Ultimately," he continued, these resistant members "came to understand that it was the right thing to do" because his organization "told the truth" about the issue. Now, he said, "we get participation and great acceptance from our members" about gender issues in the workplace. In his view, this kind of constituent education is an important part of his role. "You can't run from issues," he said. "A good union will never run from the issues."[10]

While the responses of many organizations to constituent opinion exacerbate biases against intersectionally disadvantaged subgroups, this example demonstrates that there are also important instances of leaders who work instead to resist and even reverse these attitudes by framing issues and educating advantaged constituents about the ways in which their interests are tied to those of disadvantaged subgroups. In the case of the aforementioned union leader, for example, he refused to defer to the unsympathetic attitudes of male members who were unreceptive to addressing gender-related workplace issues. By insisting that the union work on these issues and by educating his members about the issues in the process, this officer demarginalized women and the workplace issues that affect them. Framing these issues as central to the concerns of the organization as he did, he signaled to members that women are worthy of the organization's energy.

The political environment

Although constituents' opinions on an issue affect membership organizations' levels of policy advocacy, *public* opinion does not have a significant effect on either membership or nonmembership organizations (though the slope is positive in both cases). This finding suggests that low levels of activity on disadvantaged-subgroup issues are not a function of the fact that public support is, on average, lower when it comes to such issues than it is for majority and advantaged-subgroup issues. By refusing to curtail their activities in response to unsupportive public attitudes, organizations mediate on behalf of intersectionally disadvantaged groups within the broader polity.

In line with not bending to public opinion, another result of this analysis shows that heightened levels of controversy significantly augment levels of activity, at least in the case of nonmembership organizations (the effect is positive but insignificant for membership organizations). This unanticipated effect is likely the result of the double-edged nature of controversy, which can help create political opportunities that are simultaneously risky and potentially productive. On the one hand, advocacy on a controversial issue can risk arousing the public's ire about an issue to which it might otherwise pay little attention. On the other hand, the work of Mark Smith (2000) suggests that controversy can help increase the salience of an issue, opening up opportunities to address it by stimulating attention and debate.

The interviews echo these contrasting possibilities—disagreement and controversy seem to drive organizations to avoid some issues, while stimulating action on others. For example, asked whether concerns about controversy affect their organizations' involvement in public policy issues, many respondents made statements such as, "I would say that this is not an organization that shies away from controversy."[11] The executive director of an economic justice organization told me that his organization in fact is "looking for controversy, usually" so that the organization can arouse and harness public interest in an issue and "lead a debate on it."[12] While many respondents claimed that controversy was inevitable and often a boon, others expressed quite the opposite sentiment. "I doubt we'd ever take on something that controversial," the executive director of another economic justice organization confided.[13]

In general, however, the officers with whom I spoke seemed far less hesitant to take on controversial issues when such issues are understood to relate directly to their organizations' raisons d'être. For example, the chair of the board at an Asian Pacific American organization said that in a controversial case such as that of Wen Ho Lee (the Taiwanese-American Los Alamos physicist who was accused of espionage), it was "very controversial, [but] we felt like we had to be out in front [on it] . . . because . . . it's affecting an Asian American, has a disparate impact on Asian American scientists, and so it would be odd, almost, if we didn't have [a] voice in it." However, he said, other issues are "so controversial that we don't [even] take a position." "For example," he said, "we would never take a position on abortion. Two reasons—one is [that] it's politically very, very sensitive. Two, and more importantly, it doesn't have a special impact on the APA [Asian Pacific American] community."[14]

Although in general, respondents were not reluctant to take on controversial issues, as is the case with concerns about constituent agreement, the foregoing example demonstrates that controversy is more likely to depress activity on issues that affect an intersectionally disadvantaged subgroup—in this case, Asian Pacific American women. Moreover, as the foregoing statement from the chair of the board suggests, in order to justify a lack of involvement leaders often frame controversial issues affecting intersectionally disadvantaged subgroups as either having a very narrow impact or lacking a specific impact on the organization's primary constituency.

This particular case, however, underscores how subjective and malleable such criteria can be. The Wen Ho Lee racial-profiling case has a disparate impact on the Asian Pacific American population and is highly symbolic given the history of the ways in which allegations of disloyalty have been deployed to discriminate against Asian Pacific Americans. However, this particular form of racial profiling is primarily likely to affect relatively advantaged members of that community—defense industry employees, academics, and research scientists. In addition, this chair of the board's assertions notwithstanding, many Asian Pacific American feminists and women's health activists claim that the abortion issue *does* have a particular impact on women in the Asian Pacific American community because they face considerable constraints, structured by limited access and community norms against abortion (Nowrojee and Silliman 1997). Moreover, in spite of being framed as a special interest that affects fewer Asian Pacific Americans than the Wen Ho Lee case, reproductive rights arguably affect a *larger* portion of the community, as there are far more Asian Pacific American women than there are Asian Pacific American scientists and defense industry workers. Although the broader issue underlying the firing and investigation of Wen Ho Lee is racial discrimination in the workplace, the impact of this issue is universalized, while the impact of abortion is downplayed and particularized.

Once again, because the level of advocacy depends so heavily on the proportion of constituents perceived to be affected by a disadvantaged-subgroup issue, downplaying the effects of such issues further depresses levels of activity on such issues by exacerbating the biases against the affected subgroup that are already present in the broader political environment. Moreover, rather than taking the occasion to insist upon conveying an understanding that links the fate of Asian Pacific Americans women to the more general fate of the Asian American community, this officer passed up an opportunity to mediate on behalf of this intersectionally disadvantaged subgroup of his constituency.

In general, then, advocacy on behalf of disadvantaged subgroups is low, and strategic considerations such as attentiveness to constituent attitudes suppress it further. However, because membership and nonmembership organizations each respond to slightly different pressures, these biases offset each other and reduce, at least to some degree, the mobilization of bias among elites, among the mass public, and within the advocacy universe. Membership organizations are much more responsive to the attitudes of their constituents than are nonmembership organizations, while nonmembership organizations seem almost to thrive on controversy in ways that membership organizations do not. In addition, because levels of activity are not based on public agreement with their position on an issue, advocacy organizations mitigate the negative effects of public opinion on politically unpopular groups and issues. Together, these results illustrate some of the ways in which the practices of advocacy organizations defy majoritarian and rationalist incentives, providing a window into innovative conceptions of representation on behalf of marginalized groups.

NOTES

1. I use the terms *advocacy organization, interest group,* and *social movement organization* relatively interchangeably. For a comprehensive discussion of the many labels (and the implications of these labels) that are used to categorize organizations that are active in U.S. politics, see Frank Baumgartner and Beth Leech's book, *Basic Interests* (Baumgartner and Leech 1998). For a discussion and taxonomy of organizations that do not engage in politics, see Debra Minkoff's book *Organizing for Equality* (Minkoff 1995).

2. Political theorist Andrew Rehfeld calls the former view, associated with the tradition of social contract theorists such as Hobbes, Locke, and Rousseau, the "sociological view of legitimacy" (Rehfeld 2005, 16).

3. The notion that distributive schemes should be designed to benefit the least well-off members of society is not, of course, John Rawls's invention. Rather, it is a cornerstone of many calls for redistribution, such as Karl Marx's call for resources to be distributed "from each according to his ability, to each according to his needs" (Marx [1875] 1978). I invoke Rawls's difference principle mainly as a point of relatively common reference that provides a useful shorthand for engaging with and understanding the redistributive spirit of affirmative advocacy. I am not claiming that the organizations in the study endorse Rawls's particular brand of liberalism, nor that Rawls would necessarily endorse the precise kinds of redistributive representation implied by the framework that I sketch out in this reading.

This caveat is important because Rawls's difference principle (and, in fact, his entire *Theory of Justice*) has been subjected to a wide range of powerful and important critiques. Some critics argue that its redistributive goals are overly radical and that they entail unacceptable infringements on individual liberty (Nozick 1974). Others take the opposite view, contending that the difference principle does little more than justify a minimal neoliberal welfare state. Sill others argue that it is "a disingenuous defense of capitalism and huge inequalities" (Chambers 2006, 83). Simone Chambers reminds us, however, that Rawls made it clear that his intentions in *A Theory of Justice* are far more egalitarian than anything that could be accomplished by welfare-state capitalism (Chambers 2006, 83). In that light, while I am not advocating the difference principle as a guide for individual behavior, nor as a principle for economic policy, I invoke the difference principle because it captures something important about the motivations and spirit of many of the organizations in this study. As I will demonstrate in subsequent chapters, these organizations explicitly charge themselves with fighting for justice and equality for disadvantaged groups. Officers at such organizations are therefore far more likely than most individuals or political institutions to embrace the egalitarian goals embodied in Rawls's theory. These officers also are consequently likely to interpret a concept like the difference principle in its most redistributive light and are *un*likely to reject it based on its redistributive implications. In their hands, then, we might be more confident that a principle that dictates that inequalities should benefit the least well-off members will be applied in noncynical ways that are actually intended to help the "truly disadvantaged" (Wilson 1987).

4. Nancy Schwartz (1988) argues that representatives should engage in what she calls "constitutive representation," a process of citizen empowerment and community formation among constituents. In contrast to my invocation of this idea, Schwartz focuses on territorially based elected representation, arguing that constitutive representation works best when it is rooted in local constituencies, in particular in single-member electoral districts.

5. Interview with organization officer, April 2001. H-1B visas benefit relatively privileged immigrants to the United States because they are used to employ aliens who, as the Web site for U.S. Citizenship and Immigration Services explains, "will be employed temporarily in a specialty occupation or as a fashion model of distinguished merit and ability." To qualify as a specialty occupation, a job must require "theoretical and practical application of a body of specialized knowledge along with at least a bachelor's degree or its equivalent. For example, architecture, engineering, mathematics, physical sciences, social sciences, medicine and health, education, business specialties, accounting, law, theology, and the arts are specialty occupations" (http://uscis.gov/graphics/howdoi/hib.htm; accessed August 11, 2005).

6. Interview with organization officer, May 2001.

7. Interview with organization officer, July 2001.

8. Interview with organization officer, April 2001.

9. Interview with organization officer, April 2001.

10. Interview with organization officer, May 2001.

11. Interview with organization officer, April 2001.

12. Interview with organization officer, April 2001.

13. Interview with organization officer, April 2001.

14. Interview with organization officer, April 2001.

BIBLIOGRAPHY

Baumgartner, Frank R., and Beth L. Leech. 1998. *Basic Interests: The Importance of Groups in Politics and Political Science.* Princeton, NJ: Princeton University Press.

Chambers, Simone. 2006. "The Politics of Equality: Rawls on the Barricades." *Perspectives on Politics* 4 (1): 81–89.

Crenshaw, Kimberlé. 1989. "Demarginalizing the Intersection of Race and Sex." *University of Chicago Legal Forum* 39:139–67.

Dawson, Michael C. 1994. *Behind the Mule.* Princeton, NJ: Princeton University Press.

Kollman, Ken. 1998. *Outside Lobbying: Public Opinion and Interest Group Strategies.* Princeton, NJ: Princeton University Press.

Marx, Karl. [1875] 1978. "Critique of the Gotha Program." In *The Marx-Engels Reader,* edited by Robert Tucker, 525–41. New York: Norton.

Minkoff, Debra. 1995. *Organizing for Equality: The Evolution of Women's and Racial-Ethnic Organizations in America, 1955–1985.* New Brunswick, NJ: Rutgers University Press.

Nowrojee, Sia, and Jael Silliman. 1997. "Asian Women's Health: Organizing a Movement." In *Dragon Ladies: Asian American Feminists Breathe Fire,* edited by S. Shah, 73–89. Boston: South End Press.

Nozick, Robert. 1974. *Anarchy, State, and Utopia.* New York: Basic Books.

Rawls, John. 1971. *A Theory of Justice.* Cambridge, MA: Belknap Press.

Rehfeld, Andrew. 2005. *The Concept of Constituency: Political Representation, Democratic Legitimacy, and Institutional Design.* New York: Cambridge University Press.

Schneider, Anne Larason, and Helen Ingram. 1997. *Policy Design for Democracy.* Lawrence: University Press of Kansas.

Schwartz, Nancy L. 1988. *The Blue Guitar: Political Representation and Community.* Chicago: University of Chicago Press.

Smith, Mark. 2000. *American Business and Political Power: Public Opinion, Elections, and Democracy.* Chicago: University of Chicago Press.

Tocqueville, Alexis de. [1835] 1965. *Democracy in America.* New York: Harper and Row.

Urbinati, Nadia. 2000. "Representation as Advocacy: A Study of Democratic Deliberation." *Political Theory* 28:258–786.

———. 2002. *Mill on Democracy: From the Athenian Government to Representative Government.* Chicago: University of Chicago Press.

Verba, Sidney, Kay Lehman Schlozman, and Henry Brady. 1995. *Voice and Equality: Civic Voluntarism in American Politics.* Cambridge, MA: Harvard University Press.

Wilson, William Julius. 1987. *The Truly Disadvantaged: The Inner City, the Underclass, and Public Policy.* Chicago: University of Chicago Press.

Young, Iris M. 1992. "Social Groups in Associative Democracy." *Politics and Society* 20:529–34.

———. 2000. *Inclusion and Democracy.* New York: Oxford University Press.

12

POLITICAL PARTIES

12.1

JOHN H. ALDRICH

From *Why Parties? The Origin and Transformation of Party Politics in America*

Political parties are multifaceted organizations, and scholars have struggled to describe them and their functions in ways that make sense across eras and across countries. In this important piece Aldrich writes that, above all, parties are designed to serve the needs of ambitious politicians seeking public office. According to Aldrich, parties have to be understood as solutions to a variety of collective dilemmas. Parties help government officials coordinate their actions so they can make public policy, they help candidates coordinate their behavior to win office, and they help voters overcome their collective action problems during elections.

1. POLITICS AND PARTIES IN AMERICA

. . . My basic argument is that the major political party is the creature of the politicians, the ambitious office seeker and officeholder. They have created and maintained, used or abuse, reformed or ignored the political party when doing so has furthered their goals and ambitions. The political party is thus . . . an institution shaped by these political actors. Whatever its strength or weakness, whatever its form and role, it is the ambitious politicians' creation. These politicians do not have partisan goals per se. Rather, they have more fundamental goals, and the party is only the instrument for achieving them. Their goals are several and come in various combinations. Following Richard Fenno (1973), they include most basically the desire to have a long and successful career in political office, but they also encompass the desire to achieve policy ends and to attain power and prestige within the government. These goals are to be sought in government, not in parties, but they are goals that at times have best been realized *through* the parties.

Ambitious politicians turn to the political party to achieve such goals only when parties are useful vehicles for solving problems that cannot be solved as effectively, if at all, through other means. Thus I believe that the political party must be understood not only in relation to the goals of the actors most consequential for parties, but also only in relation to the electoral, legislative, and executive institutions of the government. Fiorina was correct: only given our institutions can we understand political parties.

The third major force shaping the political party is the historical setting. Technological changes, for instance, have made campaigning for office today vastly different than it was only a few decades ago, let alone in the nineteenth century. Such changes have had great consequences for political parties. In the nineteenth century, political parties were the only feasible means for organizing mass elections. Today television, air travel, and the computer allow an individual member of Congress to create a personal, continuing campaign organization, something that was technologically impossible a century ago. There is more to the historical context than technology, of course.

Normative understandings have changed greatly. Even Ronald Reagan, who claimed that "government is not the solution to our problems, government *is* the problem," also held to the value of a "social safety net" provided by the government that is far larger than even the most progressive politician of the nineteenth century could have imagined. Ideas, in short, matter a great deal. Founders had to overcome antipathy verging on disgust over the very idea of political parties in order to create them in the first place, and Martin Van Buren's ideas about the nature and value of the "modern mass party" greatly shaped the nature of Jacksonian democracy and political parties generally for at least a century.

History matters in yet another way, beyond the ideas, values, and technological possibilities available at any given historical moment. The path of development matters as well. Some call the partisan alignment—realignment path the fundamental dynamic of American political history (albeit perhaps in the past tense). Once a set of institutional arrangements is in place, the set of equilibrium possibilities is greatly reduced, and change from the existing equilibrium path to a new and possibly superior one may be difficult or impossible. In other words, that there are now two major parties induces incentives for ambitious politicians to affiliate with one party or the other, and some of these incentives emerge only because of the prior existence of these two parties.

The combination of these three forces means that the fundamental syllogism for the theory of political parties to be offered here is just what Rohde and Shepsle (1978) originally offered as the basis for the rational-choice-based new institutionalism: political outcomes—here political parties—result from actors' seeking to realize their goals, choosing within and possibly shaping a given set of institutional arrangements, and so choosing within a given historical context.

■   ■   ■

Previous Approaches to the Study of American Political Parties

Parties as diverse coalitions

There are three basic views or understandings of major political parties in America.[1] The first is most often associated with V. O. Key Jr. (e.g., 1964), Frank Sorauf (1964; now Beck and Sorauf 1991), Samuel Eldersveld (1964, 1982), and others. The major American party, to them, is a broad and encompassing organization, a coalition of many and diverse partners, that is commonly called umbrella-like. In seeking to appeal to a majority of the public, the two parties are based on similar values, roughly defining the "American creed." McClosky (1969) said of political (which is to say partisan) elites, "The evidence suggests that it is the [political elites] rather than the public who serve as the major repositories of the public conscience and as the carriers of the Creed. Responsibility for keeping the system going, hence, falls most heavily upon them" (p. 286). His basic finding was that such elites share most elements of this "creed."

On many policy issues, however, there are clear and sometimes sharply drawn lines between the two parties. What Benjamin I. Page (1978) referred to as "partisan cleavages" are possible, even likely.

■   ■   ■

Each party is a coalition of many and diverse groups. This is most evident in the New Deal coalition Roosevelt forged in creating a working Democratic majority in the 1930s. It consisted of the then solid South, cities, immigrants, blacks, ethnic and religious groups of many types, the working class and unions, and so on. Over half a century later this "coalition of minorities" has frayed considerably; some parts of it have exited from the coalition entirely, and the remnants are no longer capable of reaching majority size in presidential elections. Although some elements have left entirely or their loyalties have weakened, they have been replaced by others. For example, the Democratic coalition may no longer be home to as much of the South or as many blue-collar voters, but teachers' unions, women's groups, and organizations representing blacks, Hispanics, gays, environmentalists, and many others have been added since the 1960s to the panoply of voices seeking to be heard at their national convention. The Republican party may once have been defined more easily by what wasn't included in the New Deal coalition, but it too has attracted a range of groups and interests. At Republican conventions one can find both Wall Street and Main Street fiscal conservatives, westerners who seek to remove government interference in their lives (and lands), and social conservatives, such as pro-life groups, fundamentalist Christians, and so on, who seek active government intervention in behalf of their central concerns.

Although there are good reasons why these groups are allied with their particular party, there is still great diversity within each party. There are even apparent contradictions latent—and at critical moments active—within each party. Blacks and white southerners may have found alliance comfortable when both were so deeply affected by the depression; but when civil rights made it onto the agenda, the latent tensions in their respective views become active and divisive. Recent Republican conventions may have been noncontroversial, but "yuppies," fundamentalists, Main Street business leaders, or others may well find that latent disagreements will become just as divisive when circumstances and the political agenda change—as their 1992 convention perhaps foreshadows.

In this view James Madison was correct. There is no small set of fixed interests; there are, rather, many and diverse interests in this extended Republic. He argued that a fundamental advantage of the new Constitution in creating a stronger federation was that the most evident and serious concern about majority rule—that a cohesive majority could tyrannize any minority—would be alleviated because there could be no cohesive majority in an extended republic. So too could no political party, no matter how large, rule tyrannically, because it must also be too diverse.

In a truly diverse republic, the problem is the opposite of majority tyranny. The problem is how to form *any* majority capable of taking action to solve pressing problems. A major political party, then, aggregates these many and varied interests sufficiently to appeal to enough voters to form a majority in elections and to forge partisan-based, majority coalitions in government. In this view, parties are intermediaries that connect the public and the government. Parties also aggregate these diverse interests into a relatively cohesive, if typically compromise, platform,[2] and they articulate these varied interests by representing them in government. The result, in this view, is that parties parlay those compromise positions into policy outcomes, and so they—a ruling, if nonhomogeneous and shifting, government majority—can be held accountable to the public in subsequent elections.

■   ■   ■

The responsible party thesis

The second view of parties is tighter. Instead of a theory of what actually is, it is a doctrine—that of responsible parties—and is thus inherently normative. No one believes that American parties are consistent with the responsible party thesis, except on rare occasions. But the doctrine is more than a lament about what it would be nice to have; it is also an ideal type or standard by which to measure the adequacy and strength of the major political parties at any given time. Their thesis is most directly associated with E. E. Schattsch- neider (1942) and the Committee for a more Responsible Two-Party System, sponsored by the American Political Science Association, that he chaired (1950). But this view has deeper historical roots. Woodrow Wilson's *Congres- sional Government* (1881), for example, included a plea for parties more in the responsible party mold, and as Ranney (1975) and Epstein (1986) report, prom- inent political scientists at the turn of the century were much enamored of this doctrine.

Ranney (1975, p. 43) lists four criteria that define responsible parties. Such parties: (1) make policy commitments to the electorate; (2) are willing and able to carry them out when in office; (3) develop alternatives to government policies when out of office; and (4) differ sufficiently between themselves to "provide the electorate with a proper range of choice between alternative actions."[3] This doctrine derives from an idealized (and more closely realized) form of the British system, what Lijphart (1984) calls the "Westminster model." As a normative standard, it has several obvious defects. For example, it reduces choices for the public to exactly two. If the United States is a diverse and extended Madisonian republic, it is not obvious that the public would find its views as adequately articulated by exactly two options, no mat- ter how clear and distinct. A mélange of compromise proposals may be more suitable. Alternation of parties in office may also make policy trajectories shift dramatically back and forth. And if one party does capture a longtime working majority, majority tyranny could follow. This is a normative stan- dard that thus places great weight on the accountability of elected officials, through their party's control of office, and less weight on interest articula- tion. In more practical terms, it is an idealization that fits more readily with a unified, essentially unicameral assembly that combines the legislative and executive branches and that is elected all at once. It fits more poorly with a government designed around the principles of separated but intermingled powers, with officials elected at different times from differently defined con- stituencies for the Madisonian purpose of making ambition check ambition.

▪ ▪ ▪

When the parties' candidates do address issues, it is often felt, they are too similar. The parties are at times like Tweedledum and Tweedledee, or as George Wallace claimed in his third-party presidential campaign in 1968, "there ain't a dime's worth of difference" between them. It was not always so. In other eras parties were stronger, and they were stronger in the sense of responsible parties. At the very least they were sufficiently united in office to "be willing and able to carry out" whatever policy commitments the majority party chose. They may not have been truly responsible parties, consistent with that doctrine, but they once were stronger, more effective, and more easily held accountable. Perhaps they can be again.

■　　■　　■

Parties and electoral competition

The third view of parties focuses on the importance of this competition for office. Of course both earlier views also saw electoral competition as a central characteristic of partisan politics. But this third view sees competition for office as the singular, defining characteristic of the major American political party. The most rigorous advocates of this position are Anthony Downs (1957) and Joseph A. Schlesinger (1991; see also Demsetz 1990). Both are rational choice theorists, positing that actors are goal seekers and that their actions, and eventually the institutional arrangements they help shape, are the product of their attempts to realize their goals. At the center of their theory are the partisan elites, the aspiring office seekers and the successful officeholders. Their theories rest, moreover, on a simple assumption about the goal of each such partisan elite; office seeking and holding per se. That is, party leaders are motivated to win elections. As a result a party is, in the words of Downs (1957, p. 25), "a team seeking to control the governing apparatus by gaining office in a duly constituted election." The political party therefore is the organization that team uses to realize its goals. Electoral victory is paramount; other motives are at most secondary. Most important, as Downs puts it, parties formulate policies to win elections rather than winning elections to promulgate policies. In a two-party system, the "health" of the system is measured by how competitive the two parties are for a wide range of elective offices over a long period. As we will see below, Schlesinger (1991) argues strongly against the decline of parties thesis precisely because the two parties are capable of competing effectively for so many offices in every region. The hallmark of a party, in his view, is its ability to channel the competing career ambitions of its potential and actual officeholders, forming them into an effective electoral machine. More accurately, Schlesinger argues that each office and its partisan seeker serves as one "nucleus" of a party, and a strong party is one that has many strong organizational nuclei connected to each other in supporting its ambitious partisan office seekers.

The genius of democracy, in this view, is rather like the genius Adam Smith found in the free market. In Smith's case individuals acting in their own self-interest turn out to be guided, as if by some unseen hand, to act in the economic interests of the collective. In Schlesinger's case ambitious politicians, seeking to have a long and successful career, are all led by the necessity of winning broad support in the face of stiff competition to reflect the desires of those citizens who support them. Without competition for office—without strong political parties—career ambition is not necessarily harnessed to reflect the desires of the public. In elections, political parties serve the Madisonian principle of having ambition clash with, and thereby check, ambition.

Seeking popular support in the face of competition yields officeholders who find it in their self-interest to respond to the wishes of the public so that that public will continually reelect then, thereby satisfying their career ambition. All else about parties flows from this Schumpeterian view. Office seekers will try to create a strong electoral machine for mobilizing the electorate, but only if competition forces them to do so. Thus will the party-as-organization flow from competition for office. So too will the party-in-government flow naturally from electoral competition—but only so long as it is in the long-term career interests of office seekers and holders to do so. Only so long, that it, as there is a shared, collective interest in working together in office, and doing so to remain in office.[4] And that collective interest must come from a common electoral fate.

These, then, are the three major views or understandings of political parties. I will offer a fourth. . . . [I]t will be one that takes career ambitions of elective office seekers and holders as one of its central building blocks. It will differ, however, in seeing office seeking as only one of several goals held by those with political ambitions. To be sure, winning elections is an intermediary end in addition to being an end in itself. Motivations for policy ends and for power and prestige in office require electoral victory. But for many winning office per se is not the end of politics but the beginning. As we will see, this leads naturally and inevitably to drawing from the other views of parties, and it will be necessary to trace the historical . . . path of development.

■　　■　　■

A Theory of Political Parties

As diverse as are the conclusions reached by these and other astute observers, all agree that the political party is—or should be—central to the American political system. Parties are—or should be—integral parts of all political life, from structuring the reasoning and choice of the electorate, through all facets of campaigns and seemingly all facets of the government, to the very possibility of effective governance in a democracy.

How is it that such astute observers of American politics and parties, writing at virtually the same time and looking at much the same evidence, come to such diametrically opposed conclusions about the strength of parties? Eldersveld provided an obvious answer. He wrote that "political parties are complex institutions and processes, and as such they are difficult to understand and evaluate" (1982, p. 407). As proof, he went on to consider the decline of parties thesis. At one point he wrote, "The decline in our parties, therefore, is difficult to demonstrate, empirically or in terms of historical perspective" (p. 417). And yet he then turned to signs of party decline and concluded his book with the statement: "Despite their defects they continue today to be the major instruments for democratic government in this nation. With necessary reforms we can make them even more central to the governmental process and to the lives of American citizens. Eighty years ago, Lord

James Bryce, after studying our party system, said, 'In America the great moving forces are the parties. The government counts for less than in Europe, the parties count for more. . . .' If our citizens and their leaders wish it, American parties will still be the 'great moving forces' of our system" (Eldersveld, 1982, pp. 432–33).

The "fundamental equation" of the new institutionalism applied to parties

That parties are complex does not mean they are incomprehensible. Indeed complexity is, if not an intentional outcome, at least an anticipated result of those who shape the political parties. Moreover, they are so deeply woven into the fabric of American politics that they cannot be understood apart from either their own historical context and dynamics or those of the political system as a whole. Parties, that is, can be understood only in relation to the polity, to the government and its institutions, and to the historical context of the times.

The study of political parties, second, is necessarily a study of a major pair of political *institutions*. Indeed, the institutions that define the political party are unique, and as it happens they are unique in ways that make an institutional account especially useful. Their establishment and nature are fundamentally extralegal; they are nongovernmental political institutions. Instead of statute, their basis lies in the actions of ambitious politicians that created and maintain them. They are, in the parlance of the new institutionalism, *endogenous institutions*—in fact, the most highly endogenous institutions of any substantial and sustained political importance in American history.

By endogenous, I mean it was the actions of political actors that created political parties in the first place, and it is the actions of political actors that have shaped and altered them over time. And political actors have chosen to alter their parties dramatically at several times in our history, reformed them often, and tinkered with them constantly. Of all major political bodies in the United States, the political party is the most variable in its rules, regulations, and procedures—that is to say, in its formal organization—and in its informal methods and traditions. It is often the same set of actors who write the party's rules and then choose the party's outcomes, sometimes at nearly the same time and by the same method. Thus, for example, one night national party conventions debate, consider any proposed amendments, and then adopt their rules by a majority vote of credentialed delegates. The next night these same delegates debate, consider any proposed amendments, and then adopt their platform by majority vote, and they choose their presidential nominee by majority vote the following night.

Who, then, are these critical political actors? Many see the party-in-the-electorate as comprising major actors. To be sure, mobilizing the electorate to capture office is a central task of the political party. But America is a republican democracy. All power flows directly or indirectly from the great body of the people, to paraphrase Madison's definition. The public elects its political leaders, but it is that leadership that legislates, executes, and adjudicates policy. The parties are defined in relation to this republican democracy. Thus it is political leaders, those Schlesinger (1975) has called "office-seekers"—*those who seek and those who hold elective office*—who are the central actors in the party.[5]

Ambitious office seekers and holders are thus the first and most important actors in the political party. A second set of important figures in party politics comprises those who hold, or have access to, critical resources that office seekers need to realize their ambitions. It is expensive to build and maintain the party and campaign organizations necessary to compete effectively in the electoral arena. Thomas Ferguson, for example, has made an extended argument for the "primary and constitutive role large investors play in American politics" (1983, p. 3; see also Ferguson 1986, 1989, 1991). Much of his research emphasizes this primary and constitutive role in party politics in particular, such as in partisan realignments. The study of the role of money in congressional elections has also focused in part on concentrations of such sources of funding, such as from political action committees (e.g., Sorauf 1988) which political parties are coming to take advantage of (see Hernnson 1988; Kayden and Mayhe 1985). Elections are also fought over the flow of information to the public. The electoral arm of political parties in the eighteenth century was made up of "committees of correspondence," which were primarily lines of communication among political elites and between them and potential voters, and one of the first signs of organizing of the Jeffersonian Republican party was the hiring of a newspaper editor. . . . The press was first a partisan press, and editors and publishers from Thomas Ritchie . . . to Horace Greeley long were critical players in party politics. Today those with specialized knowledge relevant to communication, such as pollsters, media and advertising experts, and computerized fund-raising specialists, enjoy influence in party, campaign, and even government councils that greatly exceeds their mere technical expertise (see Aldrich 1992).

In more theoretical terms, this second set of party actors include those Schlesinger (1975) has called "benefit seekers," those for whom realization of their goals depends on the party's success in capturing office. Party activists shade from those powerful figures with concentrations, of, or access to, money and information described above to the legions of volunteer campaign activists who ring doorbells and stuff envelopes and are, individually and collectively, critical to the first level of the party—its office seekers. All are critical because they command the resources, whether money, expertise, and information or merely time and labor, that office seekers need to realize their ambitions. As a result, activists' motivations shape and constrain the behavior of office seekers, as their own roles are, in turn, shaped and constrained by the office seekers. . . . [T]he changed incentives of party activists have played a significant role in the fundamentally altered nature of the contemporary party, but the impact of benefit seekers will be seen scattered throughout this account.

Voters, however, are neither office seekers nor benefit seekers and thus are not a part of the political party at all, even if they identify strongly with a party and consistently support its candidates.[6] Voters are indeed critical, but they are critical as the targets of party activities. Parties "produce" candidates, platforms, and policies. Voters "consume" by exchanging their votes for the party's product (see Popkin et al. 1976). Some voters, of course, become partisans by becoming activists, whether as occasional volunteers, as sustained contributors, or even as candidates. But until they do so, they may be faithful consumers, "brand name" loyalists a it were, but they are still only the targets of partisans' efforts to sell their wares in the political marketplace.

Why, then, do politicians create and recreate the party, exploit its features, or ignore its dictates? The simple answer is that it has been in their interests to do so. That is, this is a *rational choice* account of the party, an account that presumes that rational, elective office seekers and holders use the party to achieve their ends.

I do not assume that politicians are invariably self-interested in a narrow sense. This is not a theory in which elective office seekers simply maximize their chances of election or reelection, at least not for its own sake. They may well have fundamental values and principles, and they may have preferences over policies as means to those ends. They also care about office, both for its own sake and for the opportunities to achieve other ends that election and reelection make possible. In chapters 3–5, I recount several historical cases in some detail. None of these make sense under the assumption of a single-minded office-seeking goal. All are understandable as the rational actions of goal-seeking politicians using the political party to help achieve their ends. Their ends are simply more numerous, interesting, and political than mere careerism. Just as winning elections is a means to other ends for politicians (whether career or policy ends), so too is the political party a means to these other ends.[7]

Why, then, do politicians turn to create or reform, to use or abuse, partisan institutions? The answer is that parties are designed as attempts to solve problems that current institutional arrangements do not solve and that politicians have come to believe they cannot solve. These problems fall into three general and recurring categories.[8]

The problem of ambition and elective office seeking

Elective office seekers, as that label says, want to win election to office. Parties regulate access to those offices. If elective office is indeed valuable, there will be more aspirants than offices, and the political party and the two-party system are means of regulating that competition and channeling those ambitions. Major party nomination is necessary for election, and partisan institutions have been developed—and have been reformed and re-reformed—for regulating competition. Intra-institutional leadership positions are also highly valued and therefore potentially competitive. There is, for example, a fairly well institutionalized path to the office of Speaker of the House. It is, however, a Democratic party institution. Elective politicians, of course, ordinarily desire election more than once. They are typically careerists who want a long and productive career in politics. Schlesinger's ambition theory (1966), developed and extended by others (see especially Rohde 1979), is precisely about this general problem. Underlying this theory, though typically not fully developed, is a problem. The problem is that if office is desirable, there will be more, usually many more, aspirants than there are offices to go around. When stated in rigorous form, it can be proved that in fact there is no permanent solution to this problem.[9] And it is a problem that can adversely affect the fortunes of a party. In 1912 the Republican vote was split between William Howard Taft and Theodore Roosevelt. This split enabled Woodrow Wilson to win with 42 percent of the popular vote. Not only was Wilson the only break in Republican hegemony of the White House in this period, but in that year Democrats increased their House majority by sixty-five additional seats and captured majority control of the Senate. Thus failure to regulate intraparty competition cost Republicans dearly.

For elective office seekers, regulating conflict over who holds those offices is clearly of major concern. It is ever present. And it is not just a problem of access to government offices but is also a problem internal to each party as soon as the party becomes an important gateway to office.

The problem of making decisions for the party and for the polity

Once in office, partisans determine outcomes for the polity. They propose alternatives, shape the agenda, pass (or reject) legislation, and implement what they enact. The policy formation and execution process, that is, is highly partisan. The parties-in-government are more than mere coalitions of like-minded individuals, however; they are enduring institutions. Very few incumbents change their partisan affiliations. Most retain their partisanship throughout their career, even though they often disagree (i.e., are not uniformly like-minded) with some of their partisan peers. When the rare incumbent does change parties, it is invariably to join the party more consonant with that switcher's policy interests. This implies that there are differences between the two parties at some fundamental and enduring level on policy positions, values, and beliefs. Thus, parties are institutions designed to promote the achievement of collective choices—choices on which the parties differ and choices reached by majority rule. As with access to office and ambition theory, there is a well-developed theory for this problem: *social choice theory*. Underlying this theory is the well-known problem that no method of choice can solve the elective officeholders' problem of combining the interests, concerns, or values of a polity that remains faithful to democratic values, as shown by the consequences flowing from Arrow's theorem (Arrow 1951). Thus, in a republican democracy politicians may turn to partisan institutions to solve the problem of collective choice. In the language of politics, parties may help achieve the goal of attaining policy majorities in the first place, as well as the often more difficult goal of maintaining such majorities.

The problem of collective action

The third problem is the most pervasive and thus the furthest-ranging in substantive content. The clearest example, however, is also the most important. To win office, candidates need more than a party's nomination. Election requires persuading members of the public to support that candidacy and mobilizing as many of those supporters as possible. This is a problem of collective action. How do candidates get supporters to vote for them—at least in greater numbers than vote for the opposition—as well as get them to provide the cadre of workers and contribute the resources needed to win election? The political party has long been the solution.

As important as wooing and mobilizing supporters are, collective action problems arise in a wide range of circumstances facing elective office seekers. Party action invariably requires the concerted action of many partisans to achieve collectively desirable outcomes. Jimmy Carter was the only president in the 1970s and 1980s to enjoy unified party control of government. Democrats in Congress, it might well be argued, shared an interest in achieving policy outcomes. And yet Carter was all too often unable to get them to act in their shared collective interests. In 1980 not only he but the Democratic congressional parties paid a heavy price for failed cooperation. The theory here, of course, is the *theory of public goods* and its consequence, the *theory of collective action*.

The elective office seekers' and holders' interests are to win

Why should this crucial set of actors, the elective office seekers and officeholders, care about these three classes of problems? The short answer is that these concerns become practical problems to politicians when they adversely affect their chances of winning. Put differently, politicians turn to their political party—that is, use its powers, resources, and institutional forms—when they believe doing so increases their prospects for winning desired outcomes, and they turn from it if it does not.[10]

Ambition theory is about winning per se. The breakdown of orderly access to office risks unfettered and unregulated competition. The inability of a party to develop effective means of nomination and support for election therefore directly influences the chances of victory for the candidates and thus for their parties. The standard example of the problem of social choice theory, the "paradox of voting," is paradoxical precisely because all are voting to win desired outcomes, and yet there is no majority-preferred outcome. Even if there happens to be a majority-preferred policy, the conditions under which it is truly a stable equilibrium are extremely fragile and thus all too amenable to defeat. In other words, majorities in Congress are hard to attain and at least as hard to maintain. And the only reason to employ scarce campaign resources to mobilize supporters is that such mobilization increases the odds of victory. Its opposite, the failure to act when there are broadly shared interests—the problem of collective action—reduces the prospects of victory, whether at the ballot box or in government. Scholars may recognize these as manifestations of theoretical problems and call them "impossibility results" to emphasize their generic importance. Politicians recognize the consequences of these impossibility results by their adverse effects on their chances of winning—of securing what it is in their interests to secure.

So why have politicians so often turned to political parties for solutions to these problems? Their existence creates incentives for their use. It is, for example, incredibly difficult to win election to major office without the backing of a major party. It is only a little less certain that legislators who seek to lead a policy proposal through the congressional labyrinth will first turn to their party for assistance. But such incentives tell us only that an ongoing political institution is used when it is useful. Why form political parties in the first place? . . . A brief statement of three points will give a first look at the argument.

First, parties are institutions. This means, among other things, that they have some durability. They may be endogenous institutions, yet party reforms are meant not as short-term fixes but as alterations to last for years, even decades. Thus, for example, legislators might create a party rather than a temporary majority coalition to increase their chances of winning not just today but into the future. Similarly, a long and successful political career means winning office today, but it also requires winning elections throughout that career. A standing, enduring organization makes that goal more likely.

Second, American democracy chooses by plurality or majority rule. Election to office therefore requires broad-based support wherever and from whomever it can be found. So strong are the resulting incentives for a two-party system to emerge that the effect is called Duverger's law (Duverger 1954). It is in part the need to win vast and diverse support that has led politicians to create political parties.

Third, parties may help officeholders win more, and more often, than alternatives. Consider the usual stylized model of pork barrel politics. All winners get a piece of the pork for their districts. All funded projects are paid for by tax revenues, so each district pays an equal share of the costs of each project adopted, whether or not that district receives a project. Several writers have argued that this kind of legislation leads to "universalism," that is, adoption of a "norm" that every such bill yields a project to every district and thus passes with a "universal" or unanimous coalition. Thus everyone "wins." Weingast proved the basic theorem (1979). His theorem yields the choice of the rule of universalism over the formation of a simple majority coalition, because in advance each legislator calculates the chances of any simple majority coalition's forming as equal to that of any other. As a result, expecting to win only a bit more than half the time and lose the rest of the time, all legislators prefer consistent use of the norm of universalism.[11] But consider an alternative. Suppose some majority agree to form a more permanent coalition, to control outcomes now and into the future, and develop institutional means to encourage fealty to this agreement. If they successfully accomplish this, they will win regularly. Members of this institutionalized coalition would prefer it to universalism, since they always win a project in either case, but they get their projects at lower cost under the institutionalized majority coalition, which passes fewer projects.[12] Thus, even in this case with no shared substantive interests at all, there are nonetheless incentives to form an enduring voting coalition—to form a political party. And those in the excluded minority have incentives to counterorganize. United, they may be more able to woo defectors to their side. If not, they can campaign to throw those rascals in the majority party out of office.

In sum, these theoretical problems affect elective office seekers and officeholders by reducing their chances of winning. Politicians therefore may turn to political parties as institutions designed to ameliorate them. In solving these theoretical problems, however, from the politicians' perspective parties are affecting who wins and loses and what is won or lost. And it is to parties that politicians often turn, because of their durability as institutionalized solutions, because of the need to orchestrate large and diverse groups of people to form winning majorities, and because often more can be won through parties. Note that this argument rests on the implicit assumption that winning and losing hang in the balance. Politicians may be expected to give up some of their personal autonomy only when they face an imminent threat of defeat without doing so or only when doing so can block opponents' ability to build the strength necessary to win.

This is, of course, the positive case for parties, for its specifies conditions under which politicians find them useful. Not all problems are best solved, perhaps even solved at all, by political parties. Other arrangements, perhaps interest groups, issue networks, or personal electoral coalitions, may be superior at different times and under different conditions (see Hansen 1991, for example). The party may even be part of the problem. In such cases politicians turn elsewhere to seek the means to win.[13] Thus this theory is at base a theory of ambitious politicians seeking to achieve their goals. Often they have done so through the agency of the party, but sometimes, this theory implies, they will seek to realize their goals in other ways.

The political party has regularly proved useful. Their permanence suggests that the appropriate question is not When parties? but How much parties and how much other means? That parties are endogenous implies that there is no single, consistent account of the political party—nor should we expect one. Instead, parties are but a (major) part of the institutional context in which current historical conditions—the problems—are set, and solutions are sought with permanence only by changing that web of institutional arrangements. Of these the political party is by design the most malleable, and thus it is intended to change in important ways and with relatively great frequency. But it changes in ways that have, for most of American history, retained major political parties and, indeed, retained two major parties.

NOTES

1. I resist calling these theories, largely because some of them (especially the first view) are collections of sometimes quite different perspectives of particular scholars. For example, if the first view sees parties as "umbrella-like" organizations, including within them many and diverse views, so too are the scholars and their theoretical understandings many and diverse in this category I have constructed. This is less true of the responsible party scholars, and the competitive-party category is more uniform, consisting primarily of rational choice theories.

2. I use the term "platform" figuratively, as a set of policies proposed to be enacted in office.

3. Ranney is quoting Polsby and Wildavsky (1971, p. 225).

4. That is, collective interests as partisans are necessary for there to be a strong party-in-government. Such interests are not a sufficient condition, however, owing to the collective action problem. . . .

5. The justification for partisan use of political power, then, is that it is consistent with the republican principle. All power flows directly or indirectly from the great body of the people through elective office seekers and into the hands of the party. To be sure, partisan powers are often highly indirect and not very democratic. Indeed, major reforms of the political party are often sought to make the party a more republican-democratic institution in its own right. Thus was the invention of the convention system justified in the 1820s as more representative than "King Caucus," and thus was the primary election method of nomination so justified (see Aldrich 1989). Today, the nearly exclusive reliance on primary elections is rooted in the belief that all power should flow into the party more directly from the great body of the people. Nonetheless, primary voters do not choose party rules, platforms, organizations, or virtually any other form of outcome. They choose the leaders, but it is the leaders who will then choose the outcomes.

6. Office seekers, in Schlesinger's account, seek the private good of holding office, whereas benefit seekers, in addition to any value they, like office seekers, might obtain from good public policy, seek private preferments that come from the capture of office per se. Note that this distinction makes the most sense when speaking of benefit seekers in terms of the high-level resource providers or of the political machine, which had many private goods to allocate to its activists. The distinction becomes much less clear when discussing volunteer activists in general and especially the (purely) policy-motivated activist. . . .

7. In chapter 4 I give a detailed account of Van Buren's idea of the importance of the political party, above and beyond that of any individual (himself included). Even here, though, the reason for desiring this form of political party (and those who subsequently subscribed to this view of the political party throughout the "party period," see McCormick 1979; Silbey 1985; and various places throughout this text) was not for the party above all, even if for a party above men, but for the desirable effects such as party would have for democracy.

8. The reason these problems are recurring will be developed in the next chapter.

9. The allocation of n+k aspirants to n offices, at least for pure office-seeking candidates, defines an n-person, zero-sum game that, as such, lacks a core.

10. Riker's pathbreaking study of coalition formation (1962) that introduced many to rational choice theory began with a strong argument for the importance of winning in politics. Clearly, Schlesinger's ambition theory (1966) and its many related studies, such as those that follow Mayhew's emphasis on the importance of reelection in understanding Congress (1974) or those that follow Downs's accounts of elections (1957), place winning just as centrally as Riker does.

11. This result does not seem to depend heavily on the assumption that the alternative to universalism is the formation of minimal winning majority coalitions. What does seem to be crucial is the assumption that all coalitions are equally likely a priori.

12. At least they prefer this majority coalition to universalism if the costs of forming and maintaining it are less than the savings from not giving the minority any projects.

13. Once parties have organized, the current institutional arrangements will include those current partisan arrangements. Thus it may be that partisan institutions are part, even much, of the problem. By definition, these current partisan arrangements are at least insufficient to solve that problem. These three recurring problems share at their base something like an impossibility result. That is, no institutional arrangements, partisan or otherwise, that are consistent with republican democracy can solve any of these problems in all circumstances. This logical consequence is the reason partisan institutions are always threatened by, or in a state of, crisis. The party is designed to solve what cannot be permanently solved. The solution is thus contingent. That is, it is the solution that works for the particular set of circumstances currently faced; the same arrangements may not work adequately under other conditions. And in a purely logical sense, any given set of partisan institutions will necessarily fail at some time, if these are indeed true impossibility results. It is in part for this reason that the historical context is so important for understanding political parties.

REFERENCES

Aldrich, John H. 1989. Power and order in Congress. In *Home style and Washington work: Studies in congressional politics,* ed. Morris P. Fiorina and David W. Rohde, pp. 219–52. Ann Arbor: University of Michigan Press.

———. 1992. Presidential campaigns in party- and candidate-centered eras. In *Under the watchful eye: Managing presidential campaigns in the television era,* ed. Mathew D. McCubbins, pp. 59–82. Washington, D.C.: CQ Press.

Aldrich, John H., and William T. Bianco. 1992. A game-theoretic model of party affiliation of candidates and office holders. *Mathematical and Computer Modelling* 16 (8–9): 103–16.

Arrow, Kenneth J. 1951. *Social choice and individual values.* New York: Wiley.

Beck, Paul Allen, and Frank J. Sorauf. 1991. *Party politics in America.* 7th ed. New York: HarperCollins.

Demsetz, Harold. 1990. Amenity potential, indivisibilities, and political competition. In *Perspectives on political economy,* ed. James E. Alt and Kenneth A. Shepsle, pp. 144–60. New York. Cambridge University Press.

Downs, Anthony. 1957. *An economic theory of democracy.* New York: Harper and Row.

Duverger, Maurice. 1954. *Political parties: Their organization and activities in the modern state.* New York: Wiley.

Eldersveld, Samuel J. 1964. *Political parties: A behavioral analysis.* Chicago: Rand McNally.

———. 1982. *Political parties in American society.* New York: Basic Books.

Epstein, Leon D. 1986. *Political parties in the American mold.* Madison: University of Wisconsin Press.

Fenno, Richard F. 1973. *Congressmen in committees.* Boston: Little, Brown.

Ferguson, Thomas. 1983. Party realignment and American industrial structures: The investment theory of political parties in historical perspective. In *Research in political economy,* vol. 6, ed. Paul Zarembka, pp. 1–82. Greenwich, Conn.: JAI Press.

———. 1986. Elites and elections, or: What have they done to you lately? In *Do elections matter?* ed. Benjamin Ginsberg and Alan Stone, pp. 164–88. Armonk, N.Y.: Sharpe.

———. 1989. Industrial conflict and the coming of the New Deal: The triumph of multinational liberalism in America. In *The rise and fall of the New Deal order, 1930–80,* ed. Steve Fraser and Gary Gerstle, pp. 3–31. Princeton, N.J.: Princeton University Press.

———. 1991. An unbearable lightness of being—party and industry in the 1988 Democratic primary. In *Do elections matter?* 2d ed., ed. Benjamin Ginsberg and Alan Stone, pp. 237–54. Armonk, N.J.: Sharpe.

Hansen, John Mark. 1991. *Gaining access: Congress and the farm lobby.* Chicago: University of Chicago Press.

Herrnson, Paul S. 1988. *Party campaigning in the 1980s.* Cambridge: Harvard University Press.

Kayden, Xandra, and Eddie Mayhe Jr. 1985. *The party goes on: The persistence of the two-party system in the United States.* New York: Basic Books.

Key, V. O., Jr. 1964. *Politics, parties, and pressure groups.* 5th ed. New York: Crowell.

Lijphart, Arend. 1984. *Democracies: Patterns of majoritarian and consensus government in twenty-one countries.* New Haven, Conn.: Yale University Press.

Mayhew, David R. 1974. *Congress: The electoral connection.* New Haven, Conn.: Yale University Press.

McClosky, Herbert. 1969. Consensus and ideology in American politics. In *Empirical democratic theory,* ed. Charles F. Cnudde and Deane E. Neubauer, pp. 268–302. Chicago: Markham, 1969. Originally published in *American Political Science Review* 58 (June 1964): 361–82.

McCormick, Richard L. 1979. The party period and public policy: An exploratory hypothesis. *Journal of American History* 66 (September): 279–98.

Page, Benjamin I. 1978. *Choices and echoes in presidential elections: Rational man and electoral democracy.* Chicago: University of Chicago Press.

Polsby, Nelson W., and Aaron B. Wildavsky. 1971. *Presidential elections: Strategies of American electoral politics.* 3d ed. New York: Scribner.

Popkin, Samuel, John W. Gorman, Charles Phillips, and Jeffrey A. Smith. 1976. Comment: What have you done for me lately? Toward an investment theory of voting. *American Political Science Review* 70 (September): 779–805.

Ranney, Austin. 1975. *Curing the mischiefs of faction: Party reform in America.* Berkeley and Los Angeles: University of California Press.

Riker, William H. 1962. *The theory of political coalitions.* New Haven, Conn.: Yale University Press.

Rohde, David W. 1979. Risk-bearing and progressive ambition: The case of the United States House of Representatives. *American Journal of Political Science* 23 (February): 1–26.

Rohde, David W., and Kenneth A. Shepsle. 1978. Thinking about legislative reform. In *Legislative reform: The policy impact,* ed. Leroy N. Rieselbach. Lexington, Mass.: Lexington Books.

Schattschneider, E. E. 1942. *Party government.* New York: Rinehart.

Schlesinger, Joseph A. 1966. *Ambition and politics: Political careers in the United States.* Chicago: Rand McNally.

———. 1975. The primary goals of political parties: A clarification of positive theory. *American Political Science Review* 69 (September): 840–49.

———. 1984. On the theory of party organization. *Journal of Politics* 46 (May): 369–400.

———. 1985. The new American political party. *American Political Science Review* 79 (December): 1152–69.

———. 1991. *Political parties and the winning of office.* Chicago: University of Chicago Press.

Silbey, Joel H. 1985. *The partisan imperative: The dynamics of American politics before the Civil War.* New York: Oxford University Press.

Sorauf, Frank J. 1964. *Party politics in America.* Boston: Little, Brown.

———. 1984. *Party politics in America.* 5th ed. Boston: Little, Brown.

———. 1988. *Money in American elections.* Glenview, Ill.: Scott, Foresman/Little, Brown.

Weingast, Barry R. 1979. A rational choice perspective on congressional norms. *American Journal of Political Science* 23 (May): 245–62.

Wilson, Woodrow. 1881. *Congressional government: A study in American society.* Baltimore: Johns Hopkins University Press.

12.2

ANGUS CAMPBELL, PHILIP E. CONVERSE, WARREN E. MILLER,
AND DONALD E. STOKES

From *The American Voter*

In this selection from the classic book, The American Voter, *the authors depict partisanship as a deep psychological attachment to one of the two major parties, an attachment that largely determines individual voting decisions and shapes the way individuals evaluate policies and politicians. The authors demonstrate a way to measure partisanship in the population using surveys. Even though the original book was published in 1960, this conceptualization of partisanship and the method of measuring it are still widely used by scholars all over the world.*

5. THE IMPACT OF PARTY IDENTIFICATION

A general observation about the political behavior of Americans is that their partisan preferences show great stability between elections. . . . Often a change of candidates and a broad alteration in the nature of the issues disturb very little the relative partisanship of a set of electoral units, which suggests that great numbers of voters have party attachments that persist through time.

The fact that attachments of this sort are widely held is confirmed by survey data on individual people. In a survey interview most of our citizens freely classify themselves as Republicans or Democrats and indicate that these loyalties have persisted through a number of elections. Few factors are of greater importance for our national elections than the lasting attachment of tens of millions of Americans to one of the parties. These loyalties establish a basic division of electoral strength within which the competition of particular campaigns takes place. And they are an important factor in assuring the stability of the party system itself.

The Concept and Measurement of Party Identification

Only in the exceptional case does the sense of individual attachment to party reflect a formal membership or an active connection with a party apparatus. Nor does it simply denote a voting record, although the influence of party allegiance on electoral behavior is strong. Generally this tie is a psychological identification, which can persist without legal recognition or evidence of formal membership and even without a consistent record of party support. Most Americans have this sense of attachment with one party or the other. And for the individual who does, the strength and direction of party identification are facts of central importance in accounting for attitude and behavior.

The importance of stable partisan loyalties has been universally recognized in electoral studies, but the manner in which they should be defined and measured has been a subject of some disagreement. In keeping with the conception of party identification as a psychological tie, these orientations have been measured in our research by asking individuals to describe their own partisan loyalties. Some studies, however, have chosen to measure stable partisan orientations in terms of an individual's past voting record or in terms of his attitude on a set of partisan issues. We have not measured party attachments in terms of the vote or the evaluation of partisan issues precisely because we are interested in exploring the *influence* of party identification on voting behavior and its immediate determinants. When an independent measure of party identification is used, it is clear that even strong party adherents at times may think and act in contradiction to their party allegiance. We could never establish the conditions under which this will occur if lasting partisan orientations were measured in terms of the behavior they are thought to affect.

Our measurement of party identification rests fundamentally on self-classification. Since 1952 we have asked repeated cross sections of the national population a sequence of questions inviting the individual to state the direction and strength of his partisan orientation.[1] The dimension presupposed by these questions appears to have psychological reality for virtually the entire electorate. The partisan self-image of all but the few individuals who disclaim any involvement in politics permits us to place each person in these samples on a continuum of partisanship extending from strongly Republican to strongly Democratic. The sequence of questions we have asked also allows us to distinguish the Independents who lean toward one of the parties from those who think of themselves as having no partisan coloration whatever.

The measure these methods yield has served our analysis of party identification in a versatile fashion. To assess both the direction and intensity of partisan attachments it can be used to array our samples across the seven categories shown in Table 1, which gives the distribution of party identification in the electorate during the years from 1952 to 1958.

In using these techniques of measurement we do not suppose that every person who describes himself as an Independent is indicating simply his lack of positive attraction to one of the parties. Some of these people undoubtedly are actually repelled by the parties or by partisanship itself and value their position as Independents. Certainly independence of party is an ideal of some currency in our society, and it seems likely that a portion of those who call themselves Independents are not merely reporting the absence of identification with one of the major parties.

Sometimes it is said that a good number of those who call themselves Independents have simply adopted a label that conceals a genuine psychological

TABLE 1   The Distribution of Party Identification

	Oct. 1952	Sept. 1953	Oct. 1954	Apr. 1956	Oct. 1956	Nov. 1957	Oct. 1958
Strong Republicans	13%	15%	13%	14%	15%	10%	13%
Weak Republicans	14	15	14	18	14	16	16
Independent Republicans	7	6	6	6	8	6	4
Independents	5	4	7	3	9	8	8
Independent Democrats	10	8	9	6	7	7	7
Weak Democrats	25	23	25	24	23	26	24
Strong Democrats	22	22	22	19	21	21	23
Apolitical, don't know	4	7	4	10	3	6	5
Total	100%	100%	100%	100%	100%	100%	100%
Number of cases	1614	1023	1139	1731	1772	1488	1269

commitment to one party or the other. Accordingly, it is argued that a person's voting record gives a more accurate statement of his party attachment than does his own self-description. Our samples doubtless include some of these undercover partisans, and we have incorporated in our measure of party identification a means of distinguishing Independents who say they lean toward one of the parties from Independents who say they do not. We do not think that the problem of measurement presented by the concealed partisan is large. Rather it seems to us much less troublesome than the problems that follow if psychological ties to party are measured in terms of the vote.

This question can be illuminated a good deal by an examination of the consistency of party voting among those of different degrees of party identification, as is done in Table 2. The proportion of persons consistently supporting one party varies by more than sixty percentage points between strong party identifiers and complete Independents. For the problem of the undercover partisan, the troublesome figure in Table 2 is the 16 per cent of full Independents who have voted for the candidates of one party only. The importance of this figure diminishes when we remember that some of these persons have voted in very few presidential elections and could have supported one party consistently because of the way their votes fell, free of the influence of a genuine party tie.

■   ■   ■

The measurement of party identification in the period of our research shows how different a picture of partisan allegiance voting behavior and

TABLE 2   Relation of Strength of Party Identification to Partisan Regularity in Voting for President, 1956[a]

	Strong Party Identifiers	Weak Party Identifiers	Independents Leaning to Party	Independents
Voted always or mostly for same party	82%	60%	36%	16%
Voted for different parties	18	40	64	84
Total	100%	100%	100%	100%
Number of cases	546	527	189	115

[a]The question used to establish party consistency of voting was this: "Have you always voted for the same party or have you voted for different parties for President?"

self-description can give. Despite the substantial Republican majorities in the elections of 1952 and 1956, the percentages of Table 1 make clear that the Democratic Party enjoyed a three-to-two advantage in the division of party identification within the electorate in these same years. Moreover, Table 1 documents the stability of this division of party loyalty in a period whose electoral history might suggest widespread change. Except for the shifting size of the group of respondents refusing to be assigned any position on the party scale, there is not a single variation between successive distributions of party identification that could not be laid to sampling error.

The great stability of partisan loyalties is supported, too, by what we can learn from recall data about the personal history of party identification. We have asked successive samples of the electorate a series of questions permitting us to reconstruct whether an individual who accepts a party designation has experienced a prior change in his party identification. The responses give impressive evidence of the constancy of party allegiance.

The fact that nearly everyone in our samples could be placed on a unitary dimension of party identification and that the idea of prior movements on this dimension was immediately understood are themselves important findings about the nature of party support within the electorate. In view of the loose, federated structure of American parties it was not obvious in advance that people could respond to party in these undifferentiated terms. Apparently the positive and negative feelings that millions of individuals have toward the parties are the result of orientations of a diffuse and generalized character that have a common psychological meaning even though there may be a good deal of variation in the way party is perceived.

Party Identification and Political Attitude

The psychological function of party identification undoubtedly varies among individuals. Our interest here centers primarily on the role of party as a supplier of cues by which the individual may evaluate the elements of politics. The fact that most elements of national politics are far removed from the world of the common citizen forces the individual to depend on sources of information from which he may learn indirectly what he cannot know as a matter of direct experience. Moreover, the complexities of politics and government increase the importance of having relatively simple cues to evaluate what cannot be matters of personal knowledge.

In the competition of voices reaching the individual the political party is an opinion-forming agency of great importance. This is not to say that party leaders are able as a matter of deliberate technique to transmit an elaborate defense of their position to those in the electorate who identify with the party. To the contrary, some of the most striking instances of party influence occur with only the simplest kind of information reaching the party's mass support. For example, a party undoubtedly furnishes a powerful set of cues about a political leader just by nominating him for President. Merely associating the party symbol with his name encourages those identifying with the party to develop a more favorable image of his record and experience, his abilities, and his other personal attributes. Likewise, this association encourages supporters of the opposite party to take a less favorable view of these same personal qualities. Partisans in each camp may incorporate into their view of the candidates whatever detailed information they can, and the highly-involved may develop an elaborate and carefully-drawn portrait. But the impact of the party symbol seems to be none the less strong on those who absorb little of politics and whose image of the candidates is extremely diffuse.

Apparently party has a profound influence across the full range of political objects to which the individual voter responds. The strength of relationship between party identification and the dimensions of partisan attitude suggests that responses to each element of national politics are deeply affected by the individual's enduring party attachments.

▪   ▪   ▪

In the period of our studies the influence of party identification on attitudes toward the perceived elements of politics has been far more important than the influence of these attitudes on party identification itself. We are convinced that the relationships in our data reflect primarily the role of enduring partisan commitments in shaping attitudes toward political objects. Our conviction on this point is rooted in what we know of the relative stability and priority in time of party identification and the attitudes it may affect. We know that persons who identify with one of the parties typically have held the same partisan tie for all or almost all of their adult lives. But within their experience since coming of voting age many of the elements of politics have changed.

■   ■   ■

What is more, even the elements of politics that carry over from one election to another may be evaluated anew in later campaigns by part of the electorate. The involvement of many Americans in politics is slight enough that they may respond *de novo* to issues and personalities that have been present in earlier elections but that are salient to them only at the height of a presidential campaign. For many voters the details of the political landscape may be quite blurred until they are brought more into focus during the campaign period. The formative influence of party identification on these re-evaluations would not be essentially different from its influence on responses to newer elements of politics.

Because the influence of party identification extends through time, its workings cannot be fully disclosed by the relationships seen at a particular moment. For this reason, our statement of causal priorities is in the end an inference, but one for which the evidence is strong. If the inference is correct, the differences in attitude between those of differing partisan loyalties enlarge considerably our understanding of the configuration of forces leading to behavior.

■   ■   ■

Our hypothesis that party identification influences the voting act by influencing attitudes toward the objects to which this act relates needs to be modified for the person who has only the faintest image of these objects. If someone has little perception of the candidates, of the record of the parties, of public issues or questions of group interest, his attitudes toward these things may play a less important intervening role between party identification and the vote. Like the automobile buyer who knows nothing of cars except that he prefers a given make, the voter who knows simply that he is a Republican or Democrat responds directly to his stable allegiance without the mediating influence of perceptions he has formed of the objects he must choose between.

Party Identification and Electoral Choice

The role of general partisan orientations in molding attitudes toward the elements of politics is thus very clear. As a consequence of this role, party identification has a profound impact on behavior. . . . From the strength and direction of attitudes toward the various elements of politics we could order the individuals in our samples according to the probability of their voting Republican. That is, we could form an array extending from those most likely to vote Democratic to those most likely to vote Republican. Let us now make explicit the impact party identification has on behavior through its influence on attitude, by showing a separate array for each of five groups defined by our party identification scale. For each of the distributions shown in Fig. 1 the

FIGURE 1 Probable Direction of Vote by Party Identification Groups, 1956

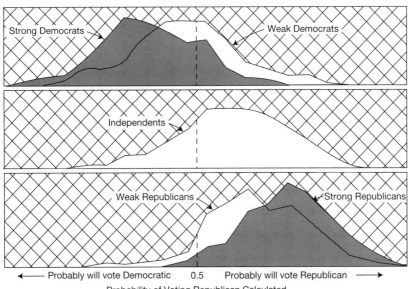

← Probably will vote Democratic   0.5   Probably will vote Republican →

Probability of Voting Republican Calculated
from Evaluations of Elements of National Politics

horizontal dimension is the probability an individual will vote Republican; to the left this probability is low (that is, the likelihood the individual will vote Democratic is high), and to the right the probability that the individual will vote Republican is high. The effect of party is seen at once in the changing location of the distributions along this probability dimension as we consider successively Strong Democrats, Weak Democrats, Independents, Weak Republicans, and Strong Republicans. The moving positions of these arrays show clearly the impact of party identification on the forces governing behavior.

NOTE

1. The initial question was this: "Generally speaking, do you think of yourself as a Republican, a Democrat, an Independent, or what?" Those who classified themselves as Republicans or Democrats were also asked, "Would you call yourself a strong (Republican, Democrat) or a not very strong (Republican, Democrat)?" Those who classified themselves as Independents were asked this additional question: "Do you think of yourself as closer to the Republican or Democratic Party?" The concept itself was first discussed in George Belknap and Angus Campbell, "Political Party Identification and Attitudes toward Foreign Policy," *Public Opinion Quarterly*, XV (Winter 1952), 601–623.

13

ELECTIONS

13.1

GWEN IFILL

From *The Breakthrough*

What role did race play in the 2008 election of Barack Obama to the presidency? Ifill argues that Barack Obama's run for the presidency was about much more than his being an African American. It was also about complicated ideological divisions within the African American community.

3. BARACK OBAMA

Two events in the course of Barack Obama's tumultuous twenty-one-month campaign for president stand as testament to the clashing impulses of race and politics. One occurred on a bitterly cold morning in Atlanta, Georgia, the other on a perfect balmy evening in Denver, Colorado.

■　■　■

Obama, who almost exactly one year later would be sworn in as the nation's first African American president, had an appointment that day in Dr. King's pulpit—or at least in the new version of it. The congregation at Ebenezer now worshiped in a soaring, modern sanctuary directly across the street from the old red brick church, which still stands. The future president laid a wreath on the graves of Martin and his wife, Coretta, who are buried next door.

Obama had come to Atlanta, a city where every other downtown street seems to be named after peaches or 1960s civil rights leaders, to pay his respects. Just the night before, Hillary Clinton had beaten him like a drum in the Nevada

Democratic caucuses, and he was in need of reassurance. The warm and welcoming Sunday morning crowd was eager to supply it.

Two thousand worshipers filled the sanctuary to the rafters. Hundreds more who could not get in braved the frigid weather outside to listen via loudspeakers. Here was the familiar: an African American candidate for office entering a sanctuary while a choir sang James Weldon Johnson's "Lift Every Voice and Sing," known as the Negro national anthem. (Bill Clinton famously knew every word of every verse.) Next the candidate and the ministers clasped hands as the congregation swayed and joined in the full-throated singing of "We Shall Overcome." The choir, surrounding the candidate on three sides and draped in kente cloth, broke into the rollicking gospel song "Victory Is Mine": *I told Satan, get thee behind; victory today is mine.*

"We don't take this pulpit lightly," the Reverend Raphael G. Warnock said as he introduced Obama. "We invited this brother because he's committed, he's brilliant. He has a spiritual foundation. And he is the embodiment of the American dream. Regardless of whether you are a Democrat, a Republican, or an independent, when you think about the long history of America, Barack Obama makes us proud."

Congregants, crammed into every seat on the floor and the balcony, all but willed the young senator to bring them to their feet. But the candidate had other things in mind. This sermon would not be about race. Not exactly.

"Unity is the great need of the hour," he told the worshipers. "It is the great need of this hour as well. Not because it sounds pleasant or because it makes us feel good, but because it's the only way we can overcome the essential deficit that exists in this country."

Then Obama slipped into what would become a running theme when he addressed black audiences: spreading the blame around. "All of us understand intimately the insidious role that race still sometimes plays—on the job, in the schools, in our health care system, and in our criminal justice system," he said. "And yet, if we are honest with ourselves, we must admit that none of our hands are entirely clean. If we're honest with ourselves, we'll acknowledge that our own community has not always been true to King's vision of a beloved community."

This was classic Obama. When given the chance to talk about race in the ways most expected to hear, he resisted. Race was worth talking about, he thought, but only in the context of broader issues. You would never catch this black man with his fist in the air.

Obama accepted the Democratic nomination for president at Invesco Field in Denver on the forty-fifth anniversary of King's "I Have a Dream" speech. Once again—this time in front of eighty thousand cheering supporters and thirty-eight million television viewers—he was presented with a tailor-made opportunity to talk about the nation's racial history. Again he sidestepped, although there was blackness all around him. Stevie Wonder, Jennifer Hudson, Will.i.am, and John Legend performed. Black politicians spoke. In the stands and on the field, black people danced, cried, and celebrated. But in the nearly ten-minute biographical video the campaign played on the stadium's gigantic screens, there was no acknowledgment that black history was about to turn a new page. Oscar-winning director Davis Guggenheim, who assembled the film, chose instead to emphasize Obama's Kansas roots, his white grandparents, and his white mother, alluding only briefly to his Kenyan father and his ties to the African nation where some of his relatives still live. Similarly, the film raced past his multicultural upbringing in Hawaii and Indonesia.

The nominee that night offered policy prescriptions and ritual attacks on the Republican nominee, but got to the final paragraphs of his speech before he alluded to the words of "a young preacher from Georgia," never mentioning King by name.

"The men and women who gathered there could've heard many things," he said, referring to the March on Washington. "They could've heard words of anger and discord. They could've been told to succumb to the fear and frustrations of so many dreams deferred. But what the people heard instead—people of every creed and color, from every walk of life—is that, in America, our destiny is inextricably linked, that together our dreams can be one."

This too was classic Obama. He did not deny his race, but he generally didn't bring it up either. You had to look in the pages of his acclaimed autobiography, *Dreams from My Father*, to learn about his admiration for Malcolm X and his collegiate flirtation with black activism. But the book also held these words: "My identity might begin with the fact of my race," he wrote. "But it didn't, couldn't end there."[1]

Obama and his advisers decided early that he was not going to win the presidency by playing up his race. Those who would be drawn to that aspect of his biography would vote for him in any case, they reasoned. The toughest votes to win would come from those who might overlook or distrust him because of something he could not control—the color of his skin.

"The thing is, a *black man* can't be president of America, given the racial aversion and history that's still out there," Cornell Belcher, an Obama pollster who is himself African American, told me after the election. "A *black man* can't be president of America. However, an extraordinary, gifted, and talented young man who happens to be black can be president."

So Obama was to become the world's most famous black man not by denying his biracial identity but by embracing parts of it selectively. On the podium at the Democratic National Convention, we saw his Indonesian half sister Maya Soetoro-Ng, but not his Kenyan half sister Auma Obama. And the omissions in his biography were not limited to race: There was just passing reference made to Michelle and Barack Obama's elite educations at Princeton and Harvard and to their law degrees.

▪   ▪   ▪

It was a fairly perilous tightrope Obama walked, and one that had never been managed at this level before. He had to integrate the tactical with the strategic, reaching out to some voters without alienating others, and change the face of black politics altogether. He did this in part by crafting his persona and his speeches to appeal to all listeners. On the night he won the Iowa caucuses, he was making history, but he allowed others to interpret his meaning when he bellowed, "They said this day would never come!" "I knew that it would have multiple meanings to multiple people," Obama's twenty-seven-year-old white speechwriter, Jon Favreau, acknowledged later.[2] Obama's caution continued even after he won the presidency. Steve Kroft of *60 Minutes* asked him after the election what he thought of his racial breakthrough, and Obama once again spoke of other people's reactions—the faces in the crowd, his mother-in-law—not his own.

But it became clear early on that this would be no color-blind campaign. During the heated and competitive primary season, an edgy and alarming debate took place between Hillary Clinton and Obama about race, gender, and even the legacy of Bill Clinton. The former president had famously deemed Obama's plan for Iraq a "fairy tale," and compared Obama's South Carolina victory to Jesse Jackson's twenty years before. Then Hillary Clinton credited Lyndon B. Johnson rather than King, it seemed to critics, with getting the Civil Rights Act passed. "It took a president to get it done," she said. "That dream became a reality, the power of that dream became real in people's lives, because we had a president who said we're going to do it and actually got it done."

Obama called her remarks "ill-advised." Senator John Edwards told a black church audience he was "troubled" by the comment.[3]

The Clintons were furious at being accused of playing the race card. There was "not one shred of truth" to suggestions that she was trying to exploit racial tension in the campaign, Hillary Clinton said indignantly on *Meet the Press*. "I don't think this campaign is about gender, and I certainly hope it is not about race."[4]

"She started this campaign saying that she wanted to make history, and lately she has been spending a lot of time rewriting it," Obama responded tartly.[5]

But most of the time, Obama left it to his surrogates to defend him when it came to race. In narrowing the differences between Obama and the majority-white nation he was appealing to, the campaign simply set out to erase race as a negative. This was no accident. The formula counted on white voters to be comforted by this approach, and for black voters to be willing to look the other way.

■   ■   ■

In some quarters, however, Obama came across as a scold for repeatedly calling on the black community to lift itself up rather than asking others to do it for them. "We need fathers to realize that responsibility doesn't just end at conception," he told a gathering at the Apostolic Church of God on Chicago's South Side. "That doesn't just make you a father. What makes you a man is not the ability to have a child. Any fool can have a child. It's the courage to raise a child that makes you a father."

Obama would point out that he liked hip-hop music but not its often misogynistic lyrics. He told MTV he thought it was a waste of time for jurisdictions to pass laws banning young men from wearing fashionably sagging pants, but added, "Having said that, brothers should pull up their pants. You are walking by your mother, your grandmother, your underwear is showing. . . . Come on."[6]

And in a widely noted address to the National Association for the Advancement of Colored People—the nation's oldest civil rights organization—Obama admitted he was aware of the sensitivity his comments stirred. "I know some say I've been too tough on folks, talking about responsibility," he said to the three thousand members gathered in Cincinnati. "At the NAACP, I'm here to report, I'm not going to stop talking about it."

Later in that speech he added, "When we are taking care of our own stuff, then a lot of other folks are going to be interested in joining up and working with us and taking care of America's stuff."[7]

Many conservative black churchgoers applauded this approach, rising to their feet in venue after venue to cheer him on. But some black leaders wondered if something wasn't missing. Why wasn't Obama speaking as a champion for black people instead of pointing out their shortcomings? Why wasn't he talking specifically about racial disparities when he discussed issues such as education, health care, and criminal justice? Or, as Jesse Jackson famously whispered into an open microphone, was Obama "talking down to black people"?

Obama was not in this to prove he could lead or speak only to black people. The goal here was to romance the entire country. When I asked Obama in the summer of 2007 about whether the prospect of electing a black president was affecting how people viewed him, he recounted a conversation he'd had with Jackson.

"He said something that's very accurate," Obama told me. "He said, 'Barack, we had to break the door down, which means sometimes you're not polite. You get bloodied up a little bit. You get some scars. You haven't had to go through that, and that's a good thing. That's part of what we went through. I don't expect you to have the same battle scars that I did.'"

Obama made his most overt attempt to acknowledge the racial debt in March 2007, when every living member of civil rights royalty gathered in Selma, Alabama, to observe and reenact the 1965 "Bloody Sunday" march across the city's Edmund Pettus Bridge. Georgia congressman John Lewis, who'd had his head bashed in with a brick during the original protest forty-two years before, spent part of the day attempting to get Obama and Hillary Clinton to link arms for the photographers. It did not work, but Obama was there with another goal in mind anyway. He needed to silence the naysayers within his own community, many of whom had known the Clintons long before they had ever heard Obama's name.

"I'm here because somebody marched," he said from the pulpit of Brown Chapel African Methodist Episcopal Church. "I'm here because you all sacrificed for me. I stand on the shoulders of giants. I thank the Moses generation; but we've got to remember, now, that Joshua still had a job to do. . . .

"The previous generation, the Moses generation, pointed the way. They took us 90 percent of the way there. We still got that 10 percent in order to cross over to the other side," he said. "So the question, I guess, that I have today is: What's called of us in this Joshua generation? What do we do in order to fulfill that legacy, to fulfill the obligations and the debt that we owe to those who allowed us to be here today?"[8]

In invoking the notion that the baton should now be handed to a new generation of Joshuas, Obama was speaking for a cohort of young, accomplished African Americans who were also battling doubters within their own communities. Weeks later, Michelle Obama expanded on the theme to me, remarking that nothing worth having was ever going to come easy. "You know, this is what we were taught by the Moses generation," she said. "Short-term sacrifice—suck it up. Isn't that what we went to all these schools for? I tell myself all the time, we're *supposed* to be the ones that take the risk. What do we have to lose? And I don't mean it lightly. But in the end, who can take these risks? Who can do it?"

The risks were many. Obama received Secret Service protection earlier than any other candidate in history. In the days after he won the November election, law enforcement agencies reported that threats directed at the newly elected president spiked dramatically. Such serious safety concerns made some of the racial gibes aimed at Obama during the campaign seem juvenile, but they acted as reminders that not all of America was buying into the notion of racial transcendence.

It's hard to pick a favorite outrage. There were the men who wore monkey shirts to Obama's rallies, and elected officials who called him "uppity." There was the Kentucky Republican, Representative Geoff Davis, who referred to Obama as "that boy" during a GOP dinner in Frankfort.[9] There was the GOP vendor in Texas who marketed buttons that read, "If Obama is president . . . will we still call it the White House?"[10] And there was the ten-dollar box of "Obama Waffles" sold at a conservative political convention, complete with a picture of a black man with pop eyes and big lips, smiling at a plate of waffles.[11] There was the newsletter distributed by a California Republican club that featured an Obama caricature surrounded by ribs, watermelon, and fried chicken—all on a fake food stamp.[12] I could go on.

The taunts did not come only from white Republicans. During the heated primary campaign, Robert Johnson, the founder of Black Entertainment Television and a prominent Clinton supporter, managed to allude to Obama's teenage drug use. "Obama was doing something in the neighborhood," he said, as if steering around a confidence. "I won't say what he was doing, but he said it in his book." He also suggested Obama was a sellout, comparing him to Sidney Poitier's character in the interracial romance drama *Guess Who's Coming to Dinner.* This earned a rebuke even from the conservative columnist George Will. "For the uninitiated," Will wrote, "that is how you call someone an Uncle Tom in an age that has not read 'Uncle Tom's Cabin.'"[13]

"We're letting other people pick our leaders," Johnson later complained to the *Washington Post.*[14]

"I think we looked like we were going to win, and I think that an element of overt race awareness kicked in," campaign manager David Plouffe told me in the spring. "Which is really, 'Should it be this easy for this guy? Is he getting a break because he's an African American political superstar?' Each time he's looked like he could secure this thing, there's been a backlash."

Most of the time, Obama refused to be drawn into the racial dramas. Whenever he did, as when he suggested mildly that he did not look like other presidents seen on U.S. dollar bills, he was accused—as John McCain's campaign manager once said—of playing "the race card . . . from the bottom of the deck."[15]

Axelrod and Plouffe had worked for black candidates before, notably Massachusetts governor Deval Patrick, and they were convinced talking about race was not going to get their candidate elected. Axelrod said it was a "function of math." "It was obvious that if you were going to play in a larger venue and not just a majority-black one, you needed a candidate who could appeal" to nonblack voters, he said.

This worked for Patrick when he was elected governor in 2006. "I don't care whether the next president is the first black president or the first woman president or the first whatever, to tell you the truth," the governor told a Boston Common crowd early in the Obama campaign. "I care that the next president has moral courage, a political backbone, the humility to admit what he doesn't know, and the wisdom to learn from others."

This approach, however, was thrown spectacularly off track in spring 2008, when Obama's pastor, the Reverend Jeremiah Wright Jr., almost derailed the Obama candidacy. The campaign had worried about Wright enough to yank him from the program at Obama's February 2007 announcement of his candidacy. But that was before snippets of videotape surfaced featuring Wright at his most incendiary.

It was a controversy, which we explore at greater length in Chapter 8, ultimately kept alive by the resentful and unhelpful Wright himself. The association with a church that characterized itself as "unashamedly black and unapologetically Christian" immediately undercut Obama's labored efforts to portray himself as race neutral. Even sympathetic Obama supporters asked how he could not have known about Wright.

The future president had little choice but to attempt to calm the waters his old friend had roiled. Only then did he finally decide to talk about race.

Obama, wearing an ice-blue tie on St. Patrick's Day, strode into an interview with me in the midst of the Wright storm. He was subdued, clearly troubled, and laboring under the weight of too little sleep and too much controversy.

I asked him if all this had been inevitable—this blowup about race, politics, and grievance. "It would have been naive for me to think that I could run and end up with quasi-front-runner status in a presidential election, as potentially the first African American president, and that issues of race wouldn't come up, any more than Senator Clinton could expect that gender issues might not come up," he mused. "But, ultimately, I don't think it's useful. I think we've got to talk about it. I think we've got to process it. But we've got to remind ourselves that what we have in common is far more important than what's different."

His pastor's comments, Obama said, lapsing into the harshest language he would use all week, were "stupid." "We benefit from that past," he told me. "We benefit from the difficult battles that were taking place. But I'm not sure that we benefit from continuing to perpetuate the anger and the bitterness that I think, at this point, serves to divide rather than bring us together."[16]

The next day, Obama channeled this thinking into a speech that decried the nation's "racial stalemate" and returned to his campaign's most uplifting themes—change and hope.

"The profound mistake of Reverend Wright's sermons is not that he spoke about racism in our society," Obama said. "It's that he spoke as if our society was static; as if no progress has been made; as if this country—a country that has made it possible for one of his own members to run for the highest office in the land and build a coalition of white and black, Latino and Asian, rich and poor, young and old—is still irrevocably bound to a tragic past."

Wright himself suggested that Obama was ducking a race debate: "I do what pastors do. He does what politicians do. I am not running for office."[17] But by then, Obama was not much listening to Wright anymore.

Plouffe told me the campaign and the candidate had hoped never to have to give a "race speech." "The Wright thing made it more than necessary, and he needed to put that in context," he said. "He's obviously running to do big things domestically and internationally. And if the campaign gets defined by 'Are we going to have racial reconciliation or not?' I think a lot of that gets crowded out.

"The issues he raised in that speech are not essential to his candidacy," Plouffe added. "They are essential, they're important problems we're dealing with in this country, but it's not like in August and September and October he's going to keep reprising his speech and offering his candidacy as a way to heal the country."

Indeed, just as Plouffe, Axelrod, and the candidate himself planned, Obama never gave a speech exclusively about race again. "Barack's candidacy, while he spoke to those issues, it was pitched in a much broader way," Axelrod said after Election Day. "He came to this not primarily as the black candidate, but as a candidate for president who happened to be black."

It is impossible to overstate how complicated a feat this was to pull off in a nation where the races worship and socialize separately, listen to different music, and watch different television shows. Somehow, instead of becoming a dominant feature of a historic campaign, the divisive issue of race—in Obama's words, "a part of our union that we have yet to perfect"—was ultimately reduced to the occasional eruption.

Part of the reason this happened is the temperament of the candidate himself. Obama was convinced that focusing the conversation on race in and of itself was a losing argument for a crossover black politician. "I'm sympathetic to efforts to have a racial conversation in this country," he told the National Association of Black Journalists at their summer 2007 convention. "But I find that generally there's a lot of breast-beating and hand-wringing and then not much follow-through. The kind of conversation I'm interested in having about race is very concrete. Do we have a criminal justice system that is color-blind? If we do not, how do we fix it? . . .

"My belief is that African Americans, like other racial minorities in this country, are much more interested in deeds than words," he continued. "And that's the kind of leadership that I want to show as president of the United States."

Obama campaigned in much the same way as he talked to us that day. On one occasion in South Carolina, a black woman stepped forward to tell him that her elderly father was not convinced a black man could win. "If I came to you and I had polka dots," he responded, "but you were convinced that I was going to put more money in your pockets, and help you pay for college and help keep America safe, you'd say, 'OK. You know, I wish you didn't have polka dots, but I'm still voting for him.'"[18]

This was sort of revolutionary in the defined world of black politics—appealing to black voters with the same arguments used to convince white ones. This meant setting aside certain articles of faith. For decades, speaking to black voters meant going to Harlem, South Central, the South Side, and Liberty City—touchstone black communities—climbing into black pulpits and speaking before black fraternal organizations, saying essentially the same thing over and over again. Obama went to these places, but not as often and with little fanfare.

▪   ▪   ▪

But under the radar, Obama was careful not to completely reject more traditional methods. He devoted a fair share of his time to courting black radio, dialing up influential deejays such as Tom Joyner, Steve Harvey, and Michael Baisden, who in turn filled the airwaves with unabashed Obama cheerleading. Most of this was invisible to larger white audiences and the larger white media. This was no accident. Before he gave a version of his tough-love speech to an African Methodist Episcopal church conference in St. Louis last July, he prayed with the denomination's leaders, but backstage. No media allowed.

"To think clearly about race . . . requires us to see the world on a split screen," Obama wrote after he was elected to the Senate. "To maintain in our sight the kind of America that we want while looking squarely at America as it is."[19]

"I would always get the question, 'What is Barack Obama's agenda for black America?'" Corey Ealons, who directed campaign outreach to African American media outlets, told me. "I would respond by saying, 'It's the same as Barack Obama's agenda for all America.'"

Obama's star turn at the 2004 Democratic National Convention arose out of the efforts of a trio of black Democrats—Brazile, Minyon Moore, and Alexis Herman—to lobby for black speakers in prime speaking spots. They called their plan the "Barbara Jordan Project," an homage to the Texas congresswoman who delivered a memorable convention keynote in 1976. Obama was just fifteen years old at the time, but Jordan's words sounded the themes he would utter from that podium twenty-eight years later. "Are we to be one people bound together by common spirit, sharing in a common endeavor, or will we become a divided nation?" she thundered. "For all of its uncertainty, we cannot flee the future."[20]

It was little noted how much Obama's words in 2004 echoed Jordan's. "There is not a liberal America and a conservative America," he said. "There is the United States of America. There is not a black America and white America and Latino America and Asian America—there's the United States of America."

The future, Obama was convinced, could not be painted in black and white. "I did not travel around this state over the last year and see a white South Carolina or a black South Carolina," he said in 2008 after trouncing Clinton in the Palmetto State's primary. "I saw crumbling schools that are stealing the future of black children and white children."[21]

Erasing race had another side benefit. Before he could be taken seriously as a national candidate, Obama had to get conventional wisdom on his side. Since white opinion leaders rarely engaged in race-specific conversations and largely found them uncomfortable, color blindness was considered a good thing. They were willing to embrace a black man who did not make them feel guilty about race.

This conventional wisdom about Barack Obama began forming, as it so often does about rising stars, in Washington—at Georgetown dinner parties and in fussy ballrooms all over the nation's capital, where the city's most self-referentially powerful lawmakers, government officials, and journalists meet to socialize.

Membership organizations such as Washington's Gridiron Club are almost entirely white. (Until 1974, the journalists' group was entirely male as well.)

How white? The first time I attended one of their annual spring dinners, in the mid-1990s, Donna Brazile and I were greeting each other amid the sea of white ties and white skin, happy to discover at least one other African American in the room. Suddenly, we felt our elbows encased in a firm grasp, and Vernon Jordan leaned in. He was grinning, his teeth very white against his very black skin. "This isn't what they expected at all," he chortled. We laughed too. When these clubs were created we were expected to be serving, not dining. Even now, I'd bet most people in that room possessed not a single black friend. And if they did, it was likely to be Vernon or Donna or me.

So it was that much more remarkable when Obama strode onto the dais at the annual dinner in March 2006. It could have been an intimidating evening. The room was filled with movers and shakers of the first order. But Obama, who had spent a lifetime challenging preconceptions about race, politics, and political timing, seemed entirely at home. He made fun of himself, poked light fun at President Bush and Vice President Cheney, and even sang a little. He was a hit.

At some basic, well-concealed level, most politicians and the people who cover politics are idealists, so for that crowd, the idea of Obama was deeply appealing. To white people who considered themselves to be forward-thinking, he was a black man (but not too black). To black people, he was a source of pride—like Tiger Woods, only with a less murky racial identity.

Washington, a town that appreciates a good straddle, ate him up with a spoon. That was the night the whispering officially began that he might one day be president. Two years later, when he was indeed running, Obama made a return visit, this time in absentia, portrayed in one of the evening's mocking skits by an actor dressed like a knight in shining armor.

This racial straddle set the stage for what Obama would later accomplish as he hopscotched from the covers of *Ebony, Jet, Essence,* and *Vibe* to *GQ, Men's Vogue,* and *Fast Company* (cover line: "The Brand Called Obama"). The key, Michael Eric Dyson said, was for Obama to figure out "how to wink at black America while speaking to white America."

That is tougher than it sounds. Obama may have won over many liberal whites—at least those not already aligned with Hillary Clinton—but black voters remained skeptical for months, in part because Obama refused to demand support based solely on his breakthrough potential.

Roger Wilkins found Obama's racial straddle to be shrewd politics "that effectively calls on Americans to get serious about their nation's founding ideals, including we don't torture people, we don't get involved in wars of choice, we don't get wildly into debt as if the future doesn't count, and we don't ignore global warming because we think scientists are stupid. The racial issue gets subsumed in what he's doing—and that's a good thing. It's very sophisticated and it's very complex and sensitive; but right now he is pulling it off."[22]

But Obama was not naive. He was well aware there were voters who would never support him—the ones who bought the waffles and laughed. "I don't believe it is possible to transcend race in this country," Obama told me one day while he was on the campaign trail in New Hampshire. "The notion that if we just ignore race, somehow our racial problems are solved, is the kind of unfortunate thinking the Supreme Court recently engaged in on the Seattle schools case." Obama was referring to a Supreme Court decision that limited the Seattle school district's ability to use race as a factor in promoting integration.

"Race is a factor in this society," he said. "The legacy of Jim Crow and slavery has not gone away. It is not an accident that African Americans experience high crime rates, are poor, and have less wealth. It is a direct result of our racial history. We have never fully come to grips with that history."

"You just don't walk away from the past," Michelle Obama told me separately. "You bring it along with you. It is always a part of the tradition. You don't move to the next phase without understanding what happened in the civil rights movement."

Like many people of their generation, the Obamas operate at something of a remove from that movement—speaking of it with respect but not with the passion expressed by their elders. Michelle did more of this than her husband did, and even then much was under the conventional political radar. While campaigning in South Carolina, where the black vote was crucial, she would invoke the names of Coretta Scott King, Harriet Tubman, and Rosa Parks. "These were all women who cast aside the voices of doubt and fear that said, 'Wait, you can't do that. It's not your turn. The timing's not right. The country's not ready,'" she told an Orangeburg audience in a speech the campaign circulated to black voters online and on DVDs. "That gnawing sense of self-doubt that is so common in all of us, is a lie—it's a lie," she said, breaking into a preacher's cadence that belied her Princeton and Harvard education. "It's just in our heads. See, nine times out of ten, we are *more* ready. We are more prepared than we could ever know."

Obama saw himself as the bridge between those fears and the possibilities his candidacy represented. "Part of what happened in the sixties after the initial civil rights era was we lost some balance and we started thinking in terms of either-or," Obama told me during the campaign. "Either you were picking yourself up by your own bootstraps, you were an integrationist, you were Sidney Poitier, or you were burning down the house."

▪ ▪ ▪

Obama's fiercest critics often came from the left. Princeton's Glaude, who early on was one of Obama's most prominent black skeptics, said he was frustrated with the way the nation's first black presidential nominee was handling race.

"He's supposed to be a transformative figure," Glaude told me. "Why is it the case that he can't simply say, when we talk about health care, we know it disproportionately affects poor people and black people? Why can't he begin to talk about these issues in ways that identify black communities, without trying to sound like Reverend Jesse Jackson and Reverend Al Sharpton? The thing is, the very way that Jesse and Al have exploited the theater of racial politics, he's doing it from a different vantage point. We haven't changed the game. That's what makes me so angry. He hasn't stepped outside of the game."

Perhaps he hadn't. But an NBC News/*Wall Street Journal* poll taken one month before Election Day pointed to the reason. Forty percent of whites, and an equal percentage of self-described swing voters, declared themselves bothered that "Barack Obama has been supported by African American leaders such as Reverend Jeremiah Wright and Al Sharpton."[23] This was the backlash risk the Obama campaign had been worried about.

In the end, nothing succeeds like success, and most of Obama's black critics were muted, some because they believed political sacrifice was a necessary ingredient for victory. "We inherently believe that what he's doing he has to do," Kevin Wardally, a New York political consultant, said. "He has to not be in Harlem to get those white votes."[24]

Others, however, are playing wait-and-see. Will the nation's first African American president deliver? And what does delivering mean anymore if the normal corridors to power are not more readily available to African Americans by virtue of the fact that the man in the Oval Office is black?

There is every chance the Moses generation, in ceding the next round to the Joshua generation, may have to adapt to a new definition of success. There is also every evidence that Barack Obama has not transcended race. But his election has provided new proof that he has redefined what racial politics is.

NOTES

1. Barack Obama, *Dreams from My Father* (New York: Three Rivers Press, 1995).

2. Ashley Parker, "What Would Obama Say," *New York Times,* January 20, 2008.

3. Audie Cornish, "Race Matters Emerge Ahead of South Carolina Primary," National Public Radio, January 14, 2008.

4. *Meet the Press,* NBC, January 13, 2008.

5. Obama conference call with reporters, January 13, 2008.

6. *Barack Obama Answers Your Questions,* MTV, November 2, 2008.

7. Glen Johnson and Dan Sewell, "Obama Tells NAACP Blacks Must Take Responsibility," Associated Press, July 14, 2008.

8. Obama speech in Selma, Alabama, text as delivered, *Chicago Sun-Times,* March 4, 2007.

9. "GOP Lawmaker Apologized for Referring to Obama as 'Boy,'" Associated Press, April 14, 2008.

10. Charles Babington, "Obama Braces for Race-Based Ads," Associated Press, June 23, 2008.

11. Joan Lowy, "Forum Sells 'Obama Waffles' with Racial Stereotype," Associated Press, September 13, 2008.

12. "Club President Who Sent Image of Obama Quits Post," Associated Press, October 23, 2008.

13. George Will, "Misstep in a Liberal Minefield," *Washington Post*, January 17, 2008.

14. Frank Ahrens, "BET Founder Johnson Defends His Recent Criticisms of Obama," *Washington Post*, January 15, 2008.

15. Alexandra Berzon and Michael Mishak, "Tackling Race to Negate It," *Las Vegas Sun*, September 10, 2008.

16. Barack Obama interview on *The NewsHour with Jim Lehrer*, March 17, 2008.

17. Transcript of Rev. Jeremiah Wright speech to National Press Club, *Los Angeles Times*, April 28, 2008.

18. Lynn Sweet, "Obama Woos Black—and White—Voters on Basis of What He Can Get Done," *Chicago Sun-Times*, January 24, 2008.

19. Barack Obama, *The Audacity of Hope: Thoughts on Reclaiming the American Dream* (New York: Crown), p. 233.

20. Barbara Jordan, Democratic National Convention keynote address, July 12, 1976.

21. Barack Obama, victory speech after South Carolina primary, *New York Times*, January 26, 2008.

22. Charles Kaiser, "Full Court Press," Radar.com, February 13, 2008.

23. NBC News/*Wall Street Journal* poll, October 2008.

24. Ben Smith, "How Obama Quietly Targets Blacks," *Politico*, October 7, 2008.

13.2

Wesberry v. Sanders (1964)

The Supreme Court in this 1964 case decided that the Equal Protection Clause of the Fourteenth Amendment mandates that congressional districts for House elections should be of roughly equal population size. This case builds on a previous decision the year earlier involving state electoral districts, Baker v. Carr.

Justice Black delivered the opinion of the Court.

Appellants are citizens and qualified voters of Fulton County, Georgia, and as such are entitled to vote in congressional elections in Georgia's Fifth Congressional District. That district, one of ten created by a 1931 Georgia statute, includes Fulton, Dekalb, and Rockdale Counties and has a population according to the 1960 census of 823,680. The average population of the ten districts is 394,312, less than half that of the Fifth. One district, the Ninth, has only 272,154 people, less than one-third as many as the Fifth. Since there is only one Congressman for each district, this inequality of population means that the Fifth District's Congressman has to represent from two to three times as many people as do Congressmen from some of the other Georgia districts.

Claiming that these population disparities deprived them and voters similarly situated of a right under the Federal Constitution to have their votes for Congressmen given the same weight as the votes of other Georgians, the appellants brought this action under 42 U.S.C. 1983 and 1988 and 28 U.S.C. 1343 (3) asking that the Georgia statute be declared invalid and that the appellees, the Governor and Secretary of State of Georgia, be enjoined from conducting elections under it. The complaint alleged that appellants were deprived of the full benefit of their right to vote, in violation of (1) Art. I, 2, of the Constitution of the United States, which provides that "The House of Representatives shall be composed of Members chosen every second Year by the People of the several States . . ."; (2) the Due Process, Equal Protection, and Privileges and Immunities Clauses of the Fourteenth Amendment; and (3) that part of Section 2 of the Fourteenth Amendment which provides that "Representatives shall be apportioned among the several States according to their respective numbers. . . ."

The case was heard by a three-judge District Court, which found unanimously, from facts not disputed, that:

> It is clear by any standard . . . that the population of the Fifth District is grossly out of balance with that of the other nine congressional districts of Georgia and in fact, so much so that the removal of Dekalb and Rockdale Counties from the District, leaving only Fulton with a population of 556, 326, would leave it exceeding the average by slightly more than forty per cent.

Notwithstanding these findings, a majority of the court dismissed the complaint, citing as their guide Mr. Justice Frankfurter's minority opinion in *Colegrove v. Green*, an opinion stating that challenges to apportionment of congressional districts raised only "political" questions, which were not justiciable. Although the majority below said that the dismissal here was based on "want of equity" and not on nonjusticiability, they relied on no circumstances which were peculiar to the present case; instead, they adopted the language and reasoning of Mr. Justice Frankfurter's *Colegrove* opinion in concluding that the appellants had presented a wholly "political" question. Judge Tuttle, disagreeing with the court's reliance on that opinion, dissented from the dismissal, though he would have denied an injunction at that time in order to give the Georgia Legislature ample opportunity to correct the "abuses" in the apportionment. He relied on *Baker v. Carr*, which, after full discussion of *Colegrove* and all the opinions in it, held that allegations of disparities of population in state legislative districts raise justiciable claims on which courts may grant relief. We noted probable jurisdiction. We agree with Judge Tuttle that in debasing the weight of appellants' votes the State has abridged the right to vote for members of Congress guaranteed them by the United States Constitution, that the District Court should have entered a declaratory judgment to that effect, and that it was therefore error to dismiss this suit. The question of what relief should be given we leave for further consideration and decision by the District Court in light of existing circumstances.

I

Baker v. Carr considered a challenge to a 1901 Tennessee statute providing for apportionment of State Representatives and Senators under the State's constitution, which called for apportionment among counties or districts "according to the number of qualified voters in each." The complaint there charged that the State's constitutional command to apportion on the basis of the number of qualified voters had not been followed in the 1901 statute and that the districts were so discriminatorily disparate in number of qualified voters that the plaintiffs and persons similarly situated were, "by virtue of the debasement of their votes," denied the equal protection of the laws guaranteed them by the Fourteenth Amendment. The cause there of the alleged "debasement" of votes for state legislators—districts containing widely varying numbers of people—was precisely that which was alleged to debase votes for Congressmen in *Colegrove v. Green*, supra, and in the present case. The Court in *Baker* pointed out that the opinion of Mr. Justice Frankfurter in *Colegrove*, upon the reasoning of which the majority below leaned heavily in dismissing "for want of equity," was approved by only three of the seven Justices sitting. After full consideration of *Colegrove*, the Court in *Baker* held (1) that the District Court had jurisdiction of the subject matter; (2) that the qualified Tennessee voters there had standing to sue; and (3) that the plaintiffs had stated a justiciable cause of action on which relief could be granted.

The reasons which led to these conclusions in *Baker* are equally persuasive here. Indeed, as one of the grounds there relied on to support our holding that state apportionment controversies are justiciable we said:

> . . . *Smiley v. Holm*, *Koenig v. Flynn*, and *Carroll v. Becker*, concerned the choice of Representatives in the Federal Congress. Smiley, Koenig and Carroll settled the issue in favor of justiciability of questions of congressional redistricting. The Court followed these precedents in *Colegrove* although over the dissent of three of the seven Justices who participated in that decision.

This statement in Baker, which referred to our past decisions holding congressional apportionment cases to be justiciable, we believe was wholly correct and we adhere to it. Mr. Justice Frankfurter's *Colegrove* opinion contended that Art. I, 4, of the Constitution[1] had given Congress "exclusive authority" to protect the right of citizens to vote for Congressmen, but we made it clear in Baker that nothing in the language of that article gives support to a construction that would immunize state congressional apportionment laws which debase a citizen's right to vote from the power of courts to protect the constitutional rights of individuals from legislative destruction, a power recognized at least since our decision in *Marbury v. Madison* in 1803. The right to vote is too important in our free society to be stripped of judicial protection by such an interpretation of Article I. This dismissal can no more be justified on the ground of "want of equity" than on the ground of "nonjusticiability." We therefore hold that the District Court erred in dismissing the complaint.

II

This brings us to the merits. We agree with the District Court that the 1931 Georgia apportionment grossly discriminates against voters in the Fifth Congressional District. A single Congressman represents from two to three times as many Fifth District voters as are represented by each of the Congressmen from the other Georgia congressional districts. The apportionment statute thus contracts the value of some votes and expands that of others. If the Federal Constitution intends that when qualified voters elect members of Congress each vote be given as much weight as any other vote, then this statute cannot stand.

We hold that, construed in its historical context, the command of Art. I, 2, that Representatives be chosen "by the People of the several States"[2] means that as nearly as is practicable one man's vote in a congressional election is to be worth as much as another's. This rule is followed automatically, of course, when Representatives are chosen as a group on a statewide basis, as was a widespread practice in the first 50 years of our Nation's history. It would be extraordinary to suggest that in such statewide elections the votes of inhabitants of some parts of a State, for example, Georgia's thinly populated Ninth District, could be weighted at two or three times the value of the votes of people living in more populous parts of the State, for example, the Fifth District around Atlanta. We do not believe that the Framers of the Constitution intended to permit the same vote-diluting discrimination to be accomplished through the device of districts containing widely varied numbers of inhabitants. To say that a vote is worth more in one district than in another would not only run counter to our fundamental ideas of democratic government, it would cast aside the principle of a House of Representatives elected "by the People," a principle tenaciously fought for and established at the Constitutional Convention. The history of the Constitution, particularly that part of it relating to the adoption of Art. I, 2, reveals that those who framed the Constitution meant that, no matter what the mechanics of an election, whether statewide or by districts, it was population which was to be the basis of the House of Representatives.

During the Revolutionary War the rebelling colonies were loosely allied in the Continental Congress, a body with authority to do little more than pass resolutions and issue requests for men and supplies. Before the war ended the Congress had proposed and secured the ratification by the States of a somewhat closer association under the Articles of Confederation. Though the Articles established a central government for the United States, as the former colonies were even then called, the States retained most of their sovereignty, like independent nations bound together only by treaties. There were no separate judicial or executive branches: only a Congress consisting of a single house. Like the members of an ancient Greek league, each State, without regard to size or population, was given only one vote in that house. It soon became clear that the Confederation was without adequate power to collect needed revenues or to enforce the rules its Congress adopted. Farsighted men felt that a closer union was necessary if the States were to be saved from foreign and domestic dangers.

The result was the Constitutional Convention of 1787, called for "the sole and express purpose of revising the Articles of Confederation. . . ." When the Convention met in May, this modest purpose was soon abandoned for the greater challenge of creating a new and closer form of government than was possible under the Confederation. Soon after the Convention assembled, Edmund Randolph of Virginia presented a plan not merely to amend the Articles of Confederation but to create an entirely new National Government with a National Executive, National Judiciary, and a National Legislature of two Houses, one house to be elected by "the people," the second house to be elected by the first.

The question of how the legislature should be constituted precipitated the most bitter controversy of the Convention. One principle was uppermost in the minds of many delegates: that, no matter where he lived, each voter should have a voice equal to that of every other in electing members of Congress. In support of this principle, George Mason of Virginia

> argued strongly for an election of the larger branch by the people. It was to be the grand depository of the democratic principle of the Govt.

James Madison agreed, saying "If the power is not immediately derived from the people, in proportion to their numbers, we may make a paper confederacy, but that will be all." Repeatedly, delegates rose to make the same point: that it would be unfair, unjust, and contrary to common sense to give a small number of people as many Senators or Representatives as were allowed to much larger groups—in short, as James Wilson of Pennsylvania put it, "equal numbers of people ought to have an equal no. of representatives . . ." and representatives "of different districts ought clearly to hold the same proportion to each other, as their respective constituents hold to each other."

Some delegates opposed election by the people. The sharpest objection arose out of the fear on the part of small States like Delaware that if population were to be the only basis of representation the populous States like Virginia would elect a large enough number of representatives to wield overwhelming power in the National Government. Arguing that the Convention had no authority to depart from the plan of the Articles of Confederation which gave each State an equal vote in the National Congress, William Paterson of New Jersey said, "If the sovereignty of the States is to be maintained, the Representatives must be drawn immediately from the States, not from the people: and we have no power to vary the idea of equal sovereignty." To this end he proposed a single legislative chamber in which each State, as in the Confederation, was to have an equal vote. A number of delegates supported this plan.

The delegates who wanted every man's vote to count alike were sharp in their criticism of giving each State, regardless of population, the same voice in the National Legislature. Madison entreated the Convention "to renounce a principle wch. was confessedly unjust," and Rufus King of Massachusetts "was prepared for every event, rather than sit down under a Govt. founded in a vicious principle of representation and which must be as shortlived as it would be unjust."

The dispute came near ending the Convention without a Constitution. Both sides seemed for a time to be hopelessly obstinate. Some delegations threatened to withdraw from the Convention if they did not get their way. Seeing the controversy growing sharper and emotions rising, the wise and highly respected Benjamin Franklin arose and pleaded with the delegates on both sides to "part with some of their demands, in order that they may join in some accommodating proposition." At last those who supported representation of the people in both houses and those who supported it in neither were brought together, some expressing the fear that if they did not reconcile their differences, "some foreign sword will probably do the work for us." The deadlock was finally broken when a majority of the States agreed to what has been called the Great Compromise, based on a proposal which had been repeatedly advanced by Roger Sherman and other delegates from Connecticut. It provided on the one hand that each State, including little Delaware and Rhode Island, was to have two Senators. As a further guarantee that these Senators would be considered state emissaries, they were to be elected by the state legislatures, Art. I, 3, and it was specially provided in Article V that no State should ever be deprived of its equal representation in the Senate. The other side of the compromise was that, as provided in Art. I, 2, members of the House of Representatives should be chosen "by the People of the several States" and should be "apportioned among the several States . . . according to their respective Numbers." While those who wanted both houses to represent the people had yielded on the Senate, they had not yielded on the House of Representatives. William Samuel Johnson of Connecticut had summed it up well: "in one branch the people, ought to be represented; in the other, the States."

The debates at the Convention make at least one fact abundantly clear: that when the delegates agreed that the House should represent "people" they intended that in allocating Congressmen the number assigned to each State should be determined solely by the number of the State's inhabitants. The Constitution embodied Edmund Randolph's proposal for a periodic census to ensure "fair representation of the people," an idea endorsed by Mason as assuring that "numbers of inhabitants" should always be the measure of representation in the House of Representatives. The Convention also overwhelmingly agreed to a resolution offered by Randolph to base future apportionment squarely on numbers and to delete any reference to wealth. And the delegates defeated a motion made by Elbridge Gerry to limit the number of Representatives from newer Western States so that it would never exceed the number from the original States.

It would defeat the principle solemnly embodied in the Great Compromise—equal representation in the House for equal numbers of people—for us to hold that, within the States, legislatures may draw the lines of congressional districts in such a way as to give some voters a greater voice in choosing a Congressman than others. The House of Representatives, the Convention agreed, was to represent the people as individuals, and on a basis of complete equality for each voter. The delegates were quite aware of what Madison called the "vicious representation" in Great Britain whereby "rotten boroughs" with few inhabitants were represented in Parliament on or almost on a par with cities of greater population. Wilson urged that people must be represented as individuals, so that America would escape the evils of the English system under which one man could send two members to Parliament to represent the borough of Old Sarum while London's million people sent but four. The delegates referred to rotten borough apportionments in some of the state legislatures as the kind of objectionable governmental action that the Constitution should not tolerate in the election of congressional representatives.

Madison in *The Federalist* described the system of division of States into congressional districts, the method which he and others assumed States probably would adopt: "The city of Philadelphia is supposed to contain between fifty and sixty thousand souls. It will therefore form nearly two districts for the choice of Federal Representatives." "[N]umbers," he said, not only are a suitable way to represent wealth but in any event "are the only proper scale of representation." In the state conventions, speakers urging ratification of the Constitution emphasized the theme of equal representation in the House which had permeated the debates in Philadelphia. Charles Cotesworth Pinckney told the South Carolina Convention, "the House of Representatives will be elected immediately by the people, and represent them and their personal rights individually. . . ." Speakers at the ratifying conventions emphasized that the House of Representatives was meant to be free of the malapportionment then existing in some of the state legislatures—such as those of Connecticut, Rhode Island, and South Carolina—and argued that the power given Congress in Art. I, 4,[3] was meant to be used to vindicate the people's right to equality of representation in the House. Congress' power, said John Steele at the North Carolina convention, was not to be used to allow Congress to create rotten boroughs; in answer to another delegate's suggestion that Congress might use its power to favor people living near the seacoast, Steele said that Congress "most probably" would "lay the state off into districts," and if it made laws "inconsistent with the Constitution, independent judges will not uphold them, nor will the people obey them."

Soon after the Constitution was adopted, James Wilson of Pennsylvania, by then an Associate Justice of this Court, gave a series of lectures at Philadelphia in which, drawing on his experience as one of the most active members of the Constitutional Convention, he said:

> [A]ll elections ought to be equal. Elections are equal, when a given number of citizens, in one part of the state, choose as many representatives, as are chosen by the same number of citizens, in any other part of the state. In this manner, the proportion of the representatives and of the constituents will remain invariably the same.

It is in the light of such history that we must construe Art. I, 2, of the Constitution, which, carrying out the ideas of Madison and those of like views, provides that Representatives shall be chosen "by the People of the several States" and shall be "apportioned among the several States . . . according to their respective Numbers." It is not surprising that our Court has held that this Article gives persons qualified to vote a constitutional right to vote and to have their votes counted. Not only can this right to vote not be denied outright, it cannot, consistently with Article I, be destroyed by alteration of ballots, or diluted by stuffing of the ballot box. No right is more precious in a free country than that of having a voice in the election of those who make the laws under which, as good citizens, we must live. Other rights, even the most basic, are illusory if the right to vote is undermined. Our Constitution leaves no room for classification of people in a way that unnecessarily abridges this right. In urging the people to adopt the Constitution, Madison said in No. 57 of *The Federalist*:

> Who are to be the electors of the Federal Representatives? Not the rich more than the poor; not the learned more than the ignorant; not the haughty heirs of distinguished names, more than the humble sons of obscure and unpropitious fortune. The electors are to be the great body of the people of the United States. . . .

Readers surely could have fairly taken this to mean, "one person, one vote." While it may not be possible to draw congressional districts with mathematical precision, that is no excuse for ignoring our Constitution's plain objective of making equal representation for equal numbers of people the fundamental goal for the House of Representatives. That is the high standard of justice and common sense which the Founders set for us.

Reversed and remanded.

NOTES

1. "The Times, Places and Manner of holding Elections for Senators and Representatives, shall be prescribed in each State by the Legislature thereof; but the Congress may at any time by Law make or alter such Regulations, except as to the Places of chusing Senators. . . ." U.S. Const., Art. I, 4.

2. "The House of Representatives shall be composed of Members chosen every second Year by the People of the several States, and the Electors in each State shall have the Qualifications requisite for Electors of the most numerous Branch of the State Legislature. . . . "Representatives and direct Taxes shall be apportioned among the several States which may be included within this Union, according to their respective Numbers, which shall be determined by adding to the whole Number of free Persons, including those bound to Service for a Term of Years, and excluding Indians not taxed, three fifths of all other Persons. The actual Enumeration shall be made within three Years after the first Meeting of the Congress of the United States, and within every

subsequent Term of ten Years, in such Manner [376 U.S. 1, 8] as they shall by Law direct. The Number of Representatives shall not exceed one for every thirty Thousand, but each State shall have at Least one Representative. . . ." U.S. Const., Art. I, 2. The provisions for apportioning Representatives and direct taxes have been amended by the Fourteenth and Sixteenth Amendments, respectively.

3. "The Times, Places and Manner of holding Elections for Senators and Representatives, shall be prescribed in each State by the Legislature thereof; but the Congress may at any time by Law make or alter such Regulations, except as to the Places of chusing Senators. . . ." U.S. Const., Art. I, 4.

13.3

McConnell v. Federal Election Commission (2003)

In this complicated decision, the Supreme Court upheld most aspects of the McCain-Feingold campaign finance law passed in 2002 (also known as the Bipartisan Campaign Reform Act, or BCRA). The court allowed as constitutional the limits on campaign spending by political parties (so-called soft money), and some of the limits on campaign advertising by interest groups within specified time periods prior to an election.

Justice Stevens and Justice O'Connor delivered the opinion of the Court with respect to BCRA Titles I and II.

■ ■ ■

I

More than a century ago the "sober-minded Elihu Root" advocated legislation that would prohibit political contributions by corporations in order to prevent "'the great aggregations of wealth, from using their corporate funds, directly or indirectly,'" to elect legislators who would "'vote for their protection and the advancement of their interests as against those of the public.'" *United States v. Automobile Workers*, (1957). In Root's opinion, such legislation would "'strik[e] at a constantly growing evil which has done more to shake the confidence of the plain people of small means of this country in our political institutions than any other practice which has ever obtained since the foundation of our Government.'" The Congress of the United States has repeatedly enacted legislation endorsing Root's judgment.

BCRA is the most recent federal enactment designed "to purge national politics of what was conceived to be the pernicious influence of 'big money' campaign contributions."

■ ■ ■

Three important developments in the years after our decision in *Buckley* persuaded Congress that further legislation was necessary to regulate the role that corporations, unions, and wealthy contributors play in the electoral process. As a preface to our discussion of the specific provisions of BCRA, we

comment briefly on the increased importance of "soft money," the proliferation of "issue ads," and the disturbing findings of a Senate investigation into
campaign practices related to the 1996 federal elections.

▪   ▪   ▪

In 1995 the FEC concluded that the parties could also use soft money to defray
the costs of "legislative advocacy media advertisements," even if the ads mentioned the name of a federal candidate, so long as they did not expressly advocate the candidate's election or defeat.

As the permissible uses of soft money expanded, the amount of soft money
raised and spent by the national political parties increased exponentially. Of
the two major parties' total spending, soft money accounted for 5% ($21.6
million) in 1984, 11% ($45 million) in 1988, 16% ($80 million) in 1992, 30%
($272 million) in 1996, and 42% ($498 million) in 2000. The national parties
transferred large amounts of their soft money to the state parties, which were
allowed to use a larger percentage of soft money to finance mixed-purpose
activities under FEC rules. . . .

Many contributions of soft money were dramatically larger than the contributions of hard money permitted by FECA. For example, in 1996 the top
five corporate soft-money donors gave, in total, more than $9 million in non-
federal funds to the two national party committees. In the most recent election cycle the political parties raised almost $300 million—60% of their total
soft-money fundraising—from just 800 donors, each of which contributed a
minimum of $120,000. Moreover, the largest corporate donors often made
substantial contributions to both parties. Such practices corroborate evidence indicating that many corporate contributions were motivated by a
desire for access to candidates and a fear of being placed at a disadvantage in
the legislative process relative to other contributors, rather than by ideological support for the candidates and parties.

Not only were such soft-money contributions often designed to gain access
to federal candidates, but they were in many cases solicited by the candidates
themselves. Candidates often directed potential donors to party committees
and tax-exempt organizations that could legally accept soft money. . . . The
solicitation, transfer, and use of soft money thus enabled parties and candidates to circumvent FECA's limitations on the source and amount of contributions in connection with federal elections.

In *Buckley* we construed FECA's disclosure and reporting requirements, as
well as its expenditure limitations, "to reach only funds used for communications that expressly advocate the election or defeat of a clearly identified candidate." As a result of that strict reading of the statute, the use or omission of
"magic words" such as "Elect John Smith" or "Vote Against Jane Doe" marked
a bright statutory line separating "express advocacy" from "issue advocacy."
Express advocacy was subject to FECA's limitations and could be financed
only using hard money. The political parties, in other words, could not use

soft money to sponsor ads that used any magic words, and corporations and unions could not fund such ads out of their general treasuries. So-called issue ads, on the other hand, not only could be financed with soft money, but could be aired without disclosing the identity of, or any other information about, their sponsors.

While the distinction between "issue" and express advocacy seemed neat in theory, the two categories of advertisements proved functionally identical in important respects. Both were used to advocate the election or defeat of clearly identified federal candidates, even though the so-called issue ads eschewed the use of magic words. Little difference existed, for example, between an ad that urged viewers to "vote against Jane Doe" and one that condemned Jane Doe's record on a particular issue before exhorting viewers to "call Jane Doe and tell her what you think." Indeed, campaign professionals testified that the most effective campaign ads, like the most effective commercials for products such as Coca-Cola, should, and did, avoid the use of the magic words. Moreover, the conclusion that such ads were specifically intended to affect election results was confirmed by the fact that almost all of them aired in the 60 days immediately preceding a federal election. Corporations and unions spent hundreds of millions of dollars of their general funds to pay for these ads, and those expenditures, like soft-money donations to the political parties, were unregulated under FECA. Indeed, the ads were attractive to organizations and candidates precisely because they were beyond FECA's reach, enabling candidates and their parties to work closely with friendly interest groups to sponsor so-called issue ads when the candidates themselves were running out of money.

Because FECA's disclosure requirements did not apply to so-called issue ads, sponsors of such ads often used misleading names to conceal their identity. "Citizens for Better Medicare," for instance, was not a grassroots organization of citizens, as its name might suggest, but was instead a platform for an association of drug manufacturers. And "Republicans for Clean Air," which ran ads in the 2000 Republican Presidential primary, was actually an organization consisting of just two individuals—brothers who together spent $25 million on ads supporting their favored candidate.

While the public may not have been fully informed about the sponsorship of so-called issue ads, the record indicates that candidates and officeholders often were. A former Senator confirmed that candidates and officials knew who their friends were and "sometimes suggest[ed] that corporations or individuals make donations to interest groups that run 'issue ads.'" As with soft-money contributions, political parties and candidates used the availability of so-called issue ads to circumvent FECA's limitations, asking donors who contributed their permitted quota of hard money to give money to nonprofit corporations to spend on "issue" advocacy. . . .

In 1998 the Senate Committee on Governmental Affairs issued a six-volume report summarizing the results of an extensive investigation into the campaign practices in the 1996 federal elections. The report gave particular attention to the effect of soft money on the American political system, including elected officials' practice of granting special access in return for political contributions.

The committee's principal findings relating to Democratic Party fundraising were set forth in the majority's report, while the minority report primarily described Republican practices. The two reports reached consensus, however, on certain central propositions. They agreed that the "soft money loophole" had led to a "meltdown" of the campaign finance system that had been intended "to keep corporate, union and large individual contributions from influencing the electoral process." One Senator stated that "the hearings provided overwhelming evidence that the twin loopholes of soft money and bogus issue advertising have virtually destroyed our campaign finance laws, leaving us with little more than a pile of legal rubble."

The report was critical of both parties' methods of raising soft money, as well as their use of those funds. It concluded that both parties promised and provided special access to candidates and senior Government officials in exchange for large soft-money contributions. . . .

In 1996 both parties began to use large amounts of soft money to pay for issue advertising designed to influence federal elections. The Committee found such ads highly problematic for two reasons. Since they accomplished the same purposes as express advocacy (which could lawfully be funded only with hard money), the ads enabled unions, corporations, and wealthy contributors to circumvent protections that FECA was intended to provide. Moreover, though ostensibly independent of the candidates, the ads were often actually coordinated with, and controlled by, the campaigns. The ads thus provided a means for evading FECA's candidate contribution limits.

▪ ▪ ▪

The report discussed potential reforms, including a ban on soft money at the national and state party levels and restrictions on sham issue advocacy by nonparty groups. The majority expressed the view that a ban on the raising of soft money by national party committees would effectively address the use of union and corporate general treasury funds in the federal political process only if it required that candidate-specific ads be funded with hard money. The minority similarly recommended the elimination of soft-money contributions to political parties from individuals, corporations, and unions, as well as "reforms addressing candidate advertisements masquerading as issue ads." . . .

In BCRA, Congress enacted many of the committee's proposed reforms. BCRA's central provisions are designed to address Congress' concerns about the increasing use of soft money and issue advertising to influence federal elections. Title I regulates the use of soft money by political parties, officeholders, and candidates. Title II primarily prohibits corporations and labor unions from using general treasury funds for communications that are intended to, or have the effect of, influencing the outcome of federal elections.

▪ ▪ ▪

Title I is Congress' effort to plug the soft-money loophole. The cornerstone of Title I is new FECA §323(a), which prohibits national party committees and their agents from soliciting, receiving, directing, or spending any soft money. In short, §323(a) takes national parties out of the soft-money business.

The remaining provisions of new FECA §323 largely reinforce the restrictions in §323(a). New FECA §323(b) prevents the wholesale shift of soft-money influence from national to state party committees by prohibiting state and local party committees from using such funds for activities that affect federal elections. . . . New FECA §323(d) reinforces these soft-money restrictions by prohibiting political parties from soliciting and donating funds to tax-exempt organizations that engage in electioneering activities. New FECA §323(e) restricts federal candidates and officeholders from receiving, spending, or soliciting soft money in connection with federal elections and limits their ability to do so in connection with state and local elections. Finally, new FECA §323(f) prevents circumvention of the restrictions on national, state, and local party committees by prohibiting state and local candidates from raising and spending soft money to fund advertisements and other public communications that promote or attack federal candidates.

Plaintiffs mount a facial First Amendment challenge to new FECA §323, as well as challenges based on the Elections Clause, U.S. Const., Art. I, §4, principles of federalism, and the equal protection component of the Due Process Clause. We address these challenges in turn.

A

In *Buckley* and subsequent cases, we have subjected restrictions on campaign expenditures to closer scrutiny than limits on campaign contributions. In [other] cases we have recognized that contribution limits, unlike limits on expenditures, "entai[l] only a marginal restriction upon the contributor's ability to engage in free communication." In *Buckley* we said that:

"A contribution serves as a general expression of support for the candidate and his views, but does not communicate the underlying basis for the support. The quantity of communication by the contributor does not increase perceptibly with the size of the contribution, since the expression rests solely on the undifferentiated, symbolic act of contributing. At most, the size of the contribution provides a very rough index of the intensity of the contributor's support for the candidate. A limitation on the amount of money a person may give to a candidate or campaign organization thus involves little direct restraint on his political communication, for it permits the symbolic expression of support evidenced by a contribution but does not in any way infringe the contributor's freedom to discuss candidates and issues. While contributions may result in political expression if spent by a candidate or an association to present views to the voters, the transformation of contributions into political debate involves speech by someone other than the contributor."

Because the communicative value of large contributions inheres mainly in their ability to facilitate the speech of their recipients, we have said that contribution limits impose serious burdens on free speech only if they are so low as to "preven[t] candidates and political committees from amassing the resources necessary for effective advocacy."

We have recognized that contribution limits may bear "more heavily on the associational right than on freedom to speak," *Shrink Missouri*, since contributions serve "to affiliate a person with a candidate" and "enabl[e] like-minded persons to pool their resources," *Buckley*. Unlike expenditure limits, however, which "preclud[e] most associations from effectively amplifying the voice of their adherents," contribution limits both "leave the contributor free to become a member of any political association and to assist personally in the association's efforts on behalf of candidates," and allow associations "to aggregate large sums of money to promote effective advocacy." The "overall effect" of dollar limits on contributions is "merely to require candidates and political committees to raise funds from a greater number of persons." Thus, a contribution limit involving even "'significant interference'" with associational rights is nevertheless valid if it satisfies the "lesser demand" of being "'closely drawn'" to match a "'sufficiently important interest.'"

Our treatment of contribution restrictions reflects more than the limited burdens they impose on First Amendment freedoms. It also reflects the importance of the interests that underlie contribution limits—interests in preventing "both the actual corruption threatened by large financial contributions and the eroding of public confidence in the electoral process through the appearance of corruption." We have said that these interests directly implicate "'the integrity of our electoral process, and, not less, the responsibility of the individual citizen for the successful functioning of that process.'" Because the electoral process is the very "means through which a free society democratically translates political speech into concrete governmental action," contribution limits, like other measures aimed at protecting the integrity of the process, tangibly benefit public participation in political debate. For that reason, when reviewing Congress' decision to enact contribution limits, "there is no place for a strong presumption against constitutionality, of the sort often thought to accompany the words 'strict scrutiny.'" The less rigorous standard of review we have applied to contribution limits (*Buckley*'s "closely drawn" scrutiny) shows proper deference to Congress' ability to weigh competing constitutional interests in an area in which it enjoys particular expertise. It also provides Congress with sufficient room to anticipate and respond to concerns about circumvention of regulations designed to protect the integrity of the political process.

Our application of this less rigorous degree of scrutiny has given rise to significant criticism in the past from our dissenting colleagues. We have rejected such criticism in previous cases for the reasons identified above. We are also mindful of the fact that in its lengthy deliberations leading to the enactment of BCRA, Congress properly relied on the recognition of its authority contained in *Buckley* and its progeny. Considerations of *stare decisis*, buttressed by the respect that the Legislative and Judicial Branches owe to one another, provide additional powerful reasons for adhering to the analysis of contribution limits that the Court has consistently followed since *Buckley* was decided.

Like the contribution limits we upheld in *Buckley*, §323's restrictions have only a marginal impact on the ability of contributors, candidates, officeholders, and parties to engage in effective political speech. Complex as its provisions may be, §323, in the main, does little more than regulate the ability of wealthy individuals, corporations, and unions to contribute large sums of money to influence federal elections, federal candidates, and federal officeholders.

■ ■ ■

Section 323 thus shows "due regard for the reality that solicitation is characteristically intertwined with informative and perhaps persuasive speech seeking support for particular causes or for particular views." *Schaumburg v. Citizens for a Better Environment*, (1980). The fact that party committees and federal candidates and officeholders must now ask only for limited dollar amounts or request that a corporation or union contribute money through its PAC in no way alters or impairs the political message "intertwined" with the solicitation. And rather than chill such solicitations the restriction here tends to increase the dissemination of information by forcing parties, candidates, and officeholders to solicit from a wider array of potential donors. As with direct limits on contributions, therefore, §323's spending and solicitation restrictions have only a marginal impact on political speech.

■ ■ ■

With these principles in mind, we apply the less rigorous scrutiny applicable to contribution limits to evaluate the constitutionality of new FECA §323. Because the five challenged provisions of §323 implicate different *First Amendment* concerns, we discuss them separately. We are mindful, however, that Congress enacted §323 as an integrated whole to vindicate the Government's important interest in preventing corruption and the appearance of corruption.

■ ■ ■

The question for present purposes is whether large *soft-money* contributions to national party committees have a corrupting influence or give rise to the appearance of corruption. Both common sense and the ample record in these cases confirm Congress' belief that they do. [T]he FEC's allocation regime has invited widespread circumvention of FECA's limits on contributions to parties for the purpose of influencing federal elections. Under this system, corporate, union, and wealthy individual donors have been free to contribute substantial sums of soft money to the national parties, which the parties can spend for the specific purpose of influencing a particular candidate's federal election. It is not only plausible, but likely, that candidates would feel grateful for such donations and that donors would seek to exploit that gratitude.

The evidence in the record shows that candidates and donors alike have in fact exploited the soft-money loophole, the former to increase their prospects of election and the latter to create debt on the part of officeholders, with the national parties serving as willing intermediaries. Thus, despite FECA's hard-money limits on direct contributions to candidates, federal officeholders have commonly asked donors to make soft-money donations to national and state committees "solely in order to assist federal campaigns," including the office-holder's own. Parties kept tallies of the amounts of soft money raised by each officeholder, and "the amount of money a Member of Congress raise[d] for the national political committees often affect[ed] the amount the committees g[a]ve to assist the Member's campaign." . . . Donors often asked that their contributions be credited to particular candidates, and the parties obliged, irrespective of whether the funds were hard or soft. National party committees often teamed with individual candidates' campaign committees to create joint fundraising committees, which enabled the candidates to take advantage of the party's higher contribution limits while still allowing donors to give to their preferred candidate. Even when not participating directly in the fundraising, federal officeholders were well aware of the identities of the donors: National party committees would distribute lists of potential or actual donors, or donors themselves would report their generosity to officeholders.

For their part, lobbyists, CEOs, and wealthy individuals alike all have candidly admitted donating substantial sums of soft money to national committees not on ideological grounds, but for the express purpose of securing influence over federal officials. For example, a former lobbyist and partner at a lobbying firm in Washington, D. C., stated in his declaration:

"'You are doing a favor for somebody by making a large [soft-money] donation and they appreciate it. Ordinarily, people feel inclined to reciprocate favors. Do a bigger favor for someone-that is, write a larger check-and they feel even more compelled to reciprocate. In my experience, overt words are rarely exchanged about contributions, but people do have understandings.'"

Particularly telling is the fact that, in 1996 and 2000, more than half of the top 50 soft-money donors gave substantial sums to *both* major national parties, leaving room for no other conclusion but that these donors were seeking influence, or avoiding retaliation, rather than promoting any particular ideology.

The evidence from the federal officeholders' perspective is similar. For example, one former Senator described the influence purchased by nonfederal donations as follows:

"'Too often, Members' first thought is not what is right or what they believe, but how it will affect fundraising. Who, after all, can seriously contend that a $100,000 donation does not alter the way one thinks about—and quite possibly votes on—an issue? . . . When you don't pay the piper that finances your campaigns, you will never get any more money from that piper. Since money is the mother's milk of politics, you never want to be in that situation.'"

By bringing soft-money donors and federal candidates and officeholders together, "[p]arties are thus necessarily the instruments of some contributors whose object is not to support the party's message or to elect party candidates across the board, but rather to support a specific candidate for the sake of a position on one narrow issue, or even to support any candidate who will be obliged to the contributors."

Plaintiffs argue that without concrete evidence of an instance in which a federal officeholder has actually switched a vote (or, presumably, evidence of a specific instance where the public believes a vote was switched), Congress has not shown that there exists real or apparent corruption. But the record is to the contrary. The evidence connects soft money to manipulations of the legislative calendar, leading to Congress' failure to enact, among other things, generic drug legislation, tort reform, and tobacco legislation. To claim that such actions do not change legislative outcomes surely misunderstands the legislative process.

More importantly, plaintiffs conceive of corruption too narrowly. Our cases have firmly established that Congress' legitimate interest extends beyond preventing simple cash-for-votes corruption to curbing "undue influence on an officeholder's judgment, and the appearance of such influence." . . .

The record in the present case is replete with similar examples of national party committees peddling access to federal candidates and officeholders in exchange for large soft-money donations. As one former Senator put it:

"'Special interests who give large amounts of soft money to political parties do in fact achieve their objectives. They do get special access. Sitting Senators and House Members have limited amounts of time, but they make time available in their schedules to meet with representatives of business and unions and wealthy individuals who gave large sums to their parties. These are not idle chit-chats about the philosophy of democracy. . . . Senators are pressed by their benefactors to introduce legislation, to amend legislation, to block legislation, and to vote on legislation in a certain way.'"

So pervasive is this practice that the six national party committees actually furnish their own menus of opportunities for access to would-be soft-money donors, with increased prices reflecting an increased level of access. . . .

Despite this evidence and the close ties that candidates and officeholders have with their parties, *Justice Kennedy* would limit Congress' regulatory interest *only* to the prevention of the actual or apparent *quid pro quo* corruption "inherent in" contributions made directly to, contributions made at the express behest of, and expenditures made in coordination with, a federal officeholder or candidate. Regulation of any other donation or expenditure—regardless of its size, the recipient's relationship to the candidate or officeholder, its potential impact on a candidate's election, its value to the candidate, or its unabashed and explicit intent to purchase influence—would, according to *Justice Kennedy,* simply be out of bounds. This crabbed view of corruption, and particularly of the appearance of corruption, ignores precedent, common sense, and the realities of political fundraising exposed by the record in this litigation.

■　■　■

In sum, there is substantial evidence to support Congress' determination that large soft-money contributions to national political parties give rise to corruption and the appearance of corruption.

■　■　■

We begin by noting that, in addressing the problem of soft-money contributions to state committees, Congress both drew a conclusion and made a prediction. Its conclusion, based on the evidence before it, was that the corrupting influence of soft money does not insinuate itself into the political process solely through national party committees. Rather, state committees function as an alternate avenue for precisely the same corrupting forces. Indeed, both candidates and parties already ask donors who have reached the limit on their direct contributions to donate to state committees. There is at least as much evidence as there was in *Buckley* that such donations have been made with the intent—and in at least some cases the effect—of gaining influence over federal officeholders. Section 323(b) thus promotes an important governmental interest by confronting the corrupting influence that soft-money donations to political parties already have.

Congress also made a prediction. Having been taught the hard lesson of circumvention by the entire history of campaign finance regulation, Congress knew that soft-money donors would react to §323(a) by scrambling to find another way to purchase influence. It was "neither novel nor implausible," for Congress to conclude that political parties would react to §323(a) by directing soft-money contributors to the state committees, and that federal candidates would be just as indebted to these contributors as they had been to those who had formerly contributed to the national parties. We "must accord substantial deference to the predictive judgments of Congress," particularly when, as here, those predictions are so firmly rooted in relevant history and common sense. Preventing corrupting activity from shifting wholesale to state committees and thereby eviscerating FECA clearly qualifies as an important governmental interest.

■　■　■

[P]laintiffs contend that §323(b) is unconstitutional because its restrictions on soft-money contributions to state and local party committees will prevent them from engaging in effective advocacy. . . . [T]he political parties' evidence regarding the impact of BCRA on their revenues is "speculative and not based on any analysis." If the history of campaign finance regulation discussed above proves anything, it is that political parties are extraordinarily flexible in adapting to new restrictions on their fundraising abilities. Moreover, the mere fact that §323(b) may reduce the relative amount of money available to state and local parties to fund federal election activities is largely inconsequential. The question is not whether §323(b) reduces the amount of funds available over previous election cycles, but whether it is "so radical in effect as to . . . drive the sound of [the recipient's] voice below the level of notice." If indeed state or local parties can make such a showing, as-applied challenges remain available.

■　　■　　■

We must examine the degree to which BCRA burdens First Amendment expression and evaluate whether a compelling governmental interest justifies that burden. The latter question—whether the state interest is compelling—is easily answered by our prior decisions regarding campaign finance regulation, which "represent respect for the 'legislative judgment that the special characteristics of the corporate structure require particularly careful regulation.'" We have repeatedly sustained legislation aimed at "the corrosive and distorting effects of immense aggregations of wealth that are accumulated with the help of the corporate form and that have little or no correlation to the public's support for the corporation's political ideas." Moreover, recent cases have recognized that certain restrictions on corporate electoral involvement permissibly hedge against "'circumvention of [valid] contribution limits.'"

In light of our precedents, plaintiffs do not contest that the Government has a compelling interest in regulating advertisements that expressly advocate the election or defeat of a candidate for federal office. Nor do they contend that the speech involved in so-called issue advocacy is any more core political speech than are words of express advocacy. After all, "the constitutional guarantee has its fullest and most urgent application precisely to the conduct of campaigns for political office," *Monitor Patriot Co. v. Roy* (1971), and "[a]dvocacy of the election or defeat of candidates for federal office is no less entitled to protection under the First Amendment than the discussion of political policy generally or advocacy of the passage or defeat of legislation." *Buckley.* Rather, plaintiffs argue that the justifications that adequately support the regulation of express advocacy do not apply to significant quantities of speech encompassed by the definition of electioneering communications.

This argument fails to the extent that the issue ads broadcast during the 30- and 60-day periods preceding federal primary and general elections are the functional equivalent of express advocacy. The justifications for the regulation of express advocacy apply equally to ads aired during those periods if the ads are intended to influence the voters' decisions and have that effect. The precise percentage of issue ads that clearly identified a candidate and were aired during those relatively brief preelection time spans but had no electioneering purpose is a matter of dispute between the parties and among the judges on the District Court. Nevertheless, the vast majority of ads clearly had such a purpose. Moreover, whatever the precise percentage may have been in the past, in the future corporations and unions may finance genuine issue ads during those time frames by simply avoiding any specific reference to federal candidates, or in doubtful cases by paying for the ad from a segregated fund.

We are therefore not persuaded that plaintiffs have carried their heavy burden of proving that amended FECA §316(b)(2) is overbroad. Even if we assumed that BCRA will inhibit some constitutionally protected corporate and union speech, that assumption would not "justify prohibiting all enforcement" of the law unless its application to protected speech is substantial, "not only in an absolute sense, but also relative to the scope of the law's plainly legitimate applications." Far from establishing that BCRA's application to pure issue ads is substantial, either in an absolute sense or relative to its application to election-related advertising, the record strongly supports the contrary conclusion.

Plaintiffs also argue that FECA §316(b)(2)'s segregated-fund requirement for electioneering communications is underinclusive because it does not apply to advertising in the print media or on the Internet. The records developed in this litigation and by the Senate Committee adequately explain the reasons for this legislative choice. Congress found that corporations and unions used soft money to finance a virtual torrent of televised election-related ads during the periods immediately preceding federal elections, and that remedial legislation was needed to stanch that flow of money. As we held in *Buckley*, "reform may take one step at a time, addressing itself to the phase of the problem which seems most acute to the legislative mind." One might just as well argue that the electioneering communication definition is underinclusive because it leaves advertising 61 days in advance of an election entirely unregulated. The record amply justifies Congress' line drawing.

In addition to arguing that §316(b)(2)'s segregated-fund requirement is underinclusive, some plaintiffs contend that it unconstitutionally discriminates in favor of media companies. FECA §304(f)(3)(B)(i) excludes from the definition of electioneering communications any "communication appearing in a news story, commentary, or editorial distributed through the facilities of any broadcasting station, unless such facilities are owned or controlled by any political party, political committee, or candidate." Plaintiffs argue this provision gives free rein to media companies to engage in speech without resort to PAC money. Section 304(f)(3)(B)(i)'s effect, however, is much narrower than plaintiffs suggest. The provision excepts news items and commentary only; it does not afford *carte blanche* to media companies generally to ignore FECA's provisions. The statute's narrow exception is wholly consistent with First Amendment principles. "A valid distinction . . . exists between corporations that are part of the media industry and other corporations that are not involved in the regular business of imparting news to the public." Numerous federal statutes have drawn this distinction to ensure that the law "does not hinder or prevent the institutional press from reporting on, and publishing editorials about, newsworthy events."

■   ■   ■

Many years ago we observed that "[t]o say that Congress is without power to pass appropriate legislation to safeguard . . . an election from the improper use of money to influence the result is to deny to the nation in a vital particular the power of self protection." *Burroughs v. United States.* We abide by that conviction in considering Congress' most recent effort to confine the ill effects of aggregated wealth on our political system. We are under no illusion that BCRA will be the last congressional statement on the matter. Money, like water, will always find an outlet. What problems will arise, and how Congress will respond, are concerns for another day. In the main we uphold BCRA's two principal, complementary features: the control of soft money and the regulation of electioneering communications. Accordingly, we affirm in part and reverse in part the District Court's judgment with respect to Titles I and II.

It is so ordered.

13.4

BARACK OBAMA

Inaugural Address, January 2009

Barack Obama was sworn in as president in January 2009. As the first African American president, his ascension to the presidency took on deep historical significance. While his inaugural address expressed hope and optimism, he confronted many knotty problems upon taking office.

My fellow citizens I stand here today humbled by the task before us, grateful for the trust you've bestowed, mindful of the sacrifices borne by our ancestors.

I thank President Bush for his service to our nation—(applause)—as well as the generosity and cooperation he has shown throughout this transition.

Forty-four Americans have now taken the presidential oath. The words have been spoken during rising tides of prosperity and the still waters of peace. Yet, every so often, the oath is taken amidst gathering clouds and raging storms. At these moments, America has carried on not simply because of the skill or vision of those in high office, but because we, the people, have remained faithful to the ideals of our forebears and true to our founding documents.

So it has been; so it must be with this generation of Americans.

That we are in the midst of crisis is now well understood. Our nation is at war against a far-reaching network of violence and hatred. Our economy is badly weakened, a consequence of greed and irresponsibility on the part of some, but also our collective failure to make hard choices and prepare the nation for a new age. Homes have been lost, jobs shed, businesses shuttered. Our health care is too costly, our schools fail too many—and each day brings further evidence that the ways we use energy strengthen our adversaries and threaten our planet.

These are the indicators of crisis, subject to data and statistics. Less measurable, but no less profound, is a sapping of confidence across our land; a nagging fear that America's decline is inevitable, that the next generation must lower its sights.

Today I say to you that the challenges we face are real. They are serious and they are many. They will not be met easily or in a short span of time. But know this America: They will be met. (Applause.)

On this day, we gather because we have chosen hope over fear, unity of purpose over conflict and discord. On this day, we come to proclaim an end to the petty grievances and false promises, the recriminations and worn-out dogmas that for far too long have strangled our politics. We remain a young nation. But in the words of Scripture, the time has come to set aside childish things. The time has come to reaffirm our enduring spirit; to choose our better history; to carry forward that precious gift, that noble idea passed on from generation to generation: the God-given promise that all are equal, all are free, and all deserve a chance to pursue their full measure of happiness. (Applause.)

In reaffirming the greatness of our nation we understand that greatness is never a given. It must be earned. Our journey has never been one of short-cuts or settling for less. It has not been the path for the faint-hearted, for those that prefer leisure over work, or seek only the pleasures of riches and fame. Rather, it has been the risk-takers, the doers, the makers of things—some celebrated, but more often men and women obscure in their labor—who have carried us up the long rugged path towards prosperity and freedom.

For us, they packed up their few worldly possessions and traveled across oceans in search of a new life. For us, they toiled in sweatshops, and settled the West, endured the lash of the whip, and plowed the hard earth. For us, they fought and died in places like Concord and Gettysburg, Normandy and Khe Sahn.

Time and again these men and women struggled and sacrificed and worked till their hands were raw so that we might live a better life. They saw America as bigger than the sum of our individual ambitions, greater than all the differences of birth or wealth or faction.

This is the journey we continue today. We remain the most prosperous, powerful nation on Earth. Our workers are no less productive than when this crisis began. Our minds are no less inventive, our goods and services no less needed than they were last week, or last month, or last year. Our capacity remains undiminished. But our time of standing pat, of protecting narrow interests and putting off unpleasant decisions—that time has surely passed. Starting today, we must pick ourselves up, dust ourselves off, and begin again the work of remaking America. (Applause.)

For everywhere we look, there is work to be done. The state of our economy calls for action, bold and swift. And we will act, not only to create new jobs, but to lay a new foundation for growth. We will build the roads and bridges, the electric grids and digital lines that feed our commerce and bind us together. We'll restore science to its rightful place, and wield technology's wonders to raise health care's quality and lower its cost. We will harness the sun and the winds and the soil to fuel our cars and run our factories. And we will transform our schools and colleges and universities to meet the demands of a new age. All this we can do. All this we will do.

Now, there are some who question the scale of our ambitions, who suggest that our system cannot tolerate too many big plans. Their memories are short, for they have forgotten what this country has already done, what free

men and women can achieve when imagination is joined to common purpose, and necessity to courage. What the cynics fail to understand is that the
ground has shifted beneath them, that the stale political arguments that have
consumed us for so long no longer apply.

The question we ask today is not whether our government is too big or too
small, but whether it works—whether it helps families find jobs at a decent
wage, care they can afford, a retirement that is dignified. Where the answer
is yes, we intend to move forward. Where the answer is no, programs will
end. And those of us who manage the public's dollars will be held to account,
to spend wisely, reform bad habits, and do our business in the light of day,
because only then can we restore the vital trust between a people and their
government.

Nor is the question before us whether the market is a force for good or ill.
Its power to generate wealth and expand freedom is unmatched. But this crisis has reminded us that without a watchful eye, the market can spin out of
control. The nation cannot prosper long when it favors only the prosperous.
The success of our economy has always depended not just on the size of our
gross domestic product, but on the reach of our prosperity, on the ability to
extend opportunity to every willing heart—not out of charity, but because it
is the surest route to our common good. (Applause.)

As for our common defense, we reject as false the choice between our
safety and our ideals. Our Founding Fathers—(applause)—our Founding
Fathers, faced with perils that we can scarcely imagine, drafted a charter to
assure the rule of law and the rights of man—a charter expanded by the
blood of generations. Those ideals still light the world, and we will not give
them up for expedience sake. (Applause.)

And so, to all the other peoples and governments who are watching today,
from the grandest capitals to the small village where my father was born,
know that America is a friend of each nation, and every man, woman and
child who seeks a future of peace and dignity. And we are ready to lead once
more. (Applause.)

Recall that earlier generations faced down fascism and communism not
just with missiles and tanks, but with the sturdy alliances and enduring
convictions. They understood that our power alone cannot protect us, nor
does it entitle us to do as we please. Instead they knew that our power grows
through its prudent use; our security emanates from the justness of our
cause, the force of our example, the tempering qualities of humility and
restraint.

We are the keepers of this legacy. Guided by these principles once more we
can meet those new threats that demand even greater effort, even greater
cooperation and understanding between nations. We will begin to responsibly leave Iraq to its people and forge a hard-earned peace in Afghanistan.
With old friends and former foes, we'll work tirelessly to lessen the nuclear
threat, and roll back the specter of a warming planet.

We will not apologize for our way of life, nor will we waver in its defense. And for those who seek to advance their aims by inducing terror and slaughtering innocents, we say to you now that our spirit is stronger and cannot be broken—you cannot outlast us, and we will defeat you. (Applause.)

For we know that our patchwork heritage is a strength, not a weakness. We are a nation of Christians and Muslims, Jews and Hindus, and non-believers. We are shaped by every language and culture, drawn from every end of this Earth; and because we have tasted the bitter swill of civil war and segregation, and emerged from that dark chapter stronger and more united, we cannot help but believe that the old hatreds shall someday pass; that the lines of tribe shall soon dissolve; that as the world grows smaller, our common humanity shall reveal itself; and that America must play its role in ushering in a new era of peace.

To the Muslim world, we seek a new way forward, based on mutual interest and mutual respect. To those leaders around the globe who seek to sow conflict, or blame their society's ills on the West, know that your people will judge you on what you can build, not what you destroy. (Applause.)

To those who cling to power through corruption and deceit and the silencing of dissent, know that you are on the wrong side of history, but that we will extend a hand if you are willing to unclench your fist. (Applause.)

To the people of poor nations, we pledge to work alongside you to make your farms flourish and let clean waters flow; to nourish starved bodies and feed hungry minds. And to those nations like ours that enjoy relative plenty, we say we can no longer afford indifference to the suffering outside our borders, nor can we consume the world's resources without regard to effect. For the world has changed, and we must change with it.

As we consider the role that unfolds before us, we remember with humble gratitude those brave Americans who at this very hour patrol far-off deserts and distant mountains. They have something to tell us, just as the fallen heroes who lie in Arlington whisper through the ages.

We honor them not only because they are the guardians of our liberty, but because they embody the spirit of service—a willingness to find meaning in something greater than themselves.

And yet at this moment, a moment that will define a generation, it is precisely this spirit that must inhabit us all. For as much as government can do, and must do, it is ultimately the faith and determination of the American people upon which this nation relies. It is the kindness to take in a stranger when the levees break, the selflessness of workers who would rather cut their hours than see a friend lose their job which sees us through our darkest hours. It is the firefighter's courage to storm a stairway filled with smoke, but also a parent's willingness to nurture a child that finally decides our fate.

Our challenges may be new. The instruments with which we meet them may be new. But those values upon which our success depends—honesty and hard work, courage and fair play, tolerance and curiosity, loyalty and patriotism—these things are old. These things are true. They have been the quiet force of progress throughout our history.

What is demanded, then, is a return to these truths. What is required of us now is a new era of responsibility—a recognition on the part of every American that we have duties to ourselves, our nation and the world; duties that we do not grudgingly accept, but rather seize gladly, firm in the knowledge that there is nothing so satisfying to the spirit, so defining of our character than giving our all to a difficult task.

This is the price and the promise of citizenship. This is the source of our confidence—the knowledge that God calls on us to shape an uncertain destiny. This is the meaning of our liberty and our creed, why men and women and children of every race and every faith can join in celebration across this magnificent mall; and why a man whose father less than 60 years ago might not have been served in a local restaurant can now stand before you to take a most sacred oath. (Applause.)

So let us mark this day with remembrance of who we are and how far we have traveled. In the year of America's birth, in the coldest of months, a small band of patriots huddled by dying campfires on the shores of an icy river. The capital was abandoned. The enemy was advancing. The snow was stained with blood. At the moment when the outcome of our revolution was most in doubt, the father of our nation ordered these words to be read to the people:

"Let it be told to the future world . . . that in the depth of winter, when nothing but hope and virtue could survive . . . that the city and the country, alarmed at one common danger, came forth to meet [it]."

America: In the face of our common dangers, in this winter of our hardship, let us remember these timeless words. With hope and virtue, let us brave once more the icy currents, and endure what storms may come. Let it be said by our children's children that when we were tested we refused to let this journey end, that we did not turn back nor did we falter; and with eyes fixed on the horizon and God's grace upon us, we carried forth that great gift of freedom and delivered it safely to future generations.

Thank you. God bless you. And God bless the United States of America.

14

THE MEDIA

14.1

TIMOTHY GROSECLOSE AND JEFFREY MILYO

"A Measure of Media Bias"

Using an innovative research strategy, Groseclose and Milyo obtain measures of the ideological biases of major media outlets that cover political news, like newspapers, magazines, websites, and television programs. The researchers compare the media outlets according to the ideologies of the politicians who cite the outlets. They find a persistent liberal slant among the major media with the average media outlet more liberal than the average member of Congress. But overall the media outlets are (with certain exceptions) generally moderate or moderately liberal.

Do the major media outlets in the U.S. have a liberal bias? Few questions evoke stronger opinions, but so far, the debate has largely been one of anecdotes ("How can *CBS News* be balanced when it calls Steve Forbes' tax plan 'wacky'?") and untested theories ("if the news industry is a competitive market, then how can media outlets be systematically biased?").

Few studies provide an objective measure of the slant of news, and none has provided a way to link such a measure to ideological measures of other political actors. That is, none of the existing measures can say, for example, whether the *New York Times* is more liberal than Senator Edward Kennedy or whether *Fox News* is more conservative than Senator Bill Frist. We provide such a measure. Namely, we compute an adjusted Americans for Democratic Action (ADA) score for various news outlets, including the *New York Times*, the *Washington Post, USA Today,* the *Drudge Report, Fox News' Special Report,* and all three networks' nightly news shows.

Our results show a strong liberal bias. All of the news outlets except *Fox News'* *Special Report* and the *Washington Times* received a score to the left of the average member of Congress. And a few outlets, including the *New York Times* and *CBS Evening News*, were closer to the average Democrat in Congress than the center. These findings refer strictly to the *news* stories of the outlets. That is, we omitted editorials, book reviews, and letters to the editor from our sample.

To compute our measure, we count the times that a media outlet cites various think tanks and other policy groups.[1] We compare this with the times that members of Congress cite the same think tanks in their speeches on the floor of the House and Senate. By comparing the citation patterns, we can construct an ADA score for each media outlet.

As a simplified example, imagine that there were only two think tanks, and suppose that the *New York Times* cited the first think tank twice as often as the second. Our method asks: what is the estimated ADA score of a member of Congress who exhibits the same frequency (2:1) in his or her speeches? This is the score that our method would assign the *New York Times*.

A feature of our method is that it does not require us to make a subjective assessment of how liberal or conservative a think tank is. That is, for instance, we do not need to read policy reports of the think tank or analyze its position on various issues to determine its ideology. Instead, we simply observe the ADA scores of the members of Congress who cite it. This feature is important, since an active controversy exists whether, e.g., the Brookings Institution or the RAND Corporation is moderate, left-wing, or right-wing.

SOME PREVIOUS STUDIES OF MEDIA BIAS

Survey research has shown that an almost overwhelming fraction of journalists are liberal. For instance, Povich [1996] reports that only 7 percent of all Washington correspondents voted for George H. W. Bush in 1992, compared with 37 percent of the American public.[2] Lichter, Rothman, and Lichter [1986] and Weaver and Wilhoit [1996] report similar findings for earlier elections. More recently, the *New York Times* reported that only 8 percent of Washington correspondents thought George W. Bush would be a better president than John Kerry.[3] This compares with 51 percent of all American voters. David Brooks notes that for every journalist who contributed to George W. Bush's campaign, another 93 contributed to Kerry's campaign.[4]

These statistics suggest that Washington correspondents, as a group, are more liberal than almost any congressional district in the country. For instance, in the Ninth California district, which includes Berkeley, 12 percent voted for Bush in 1992, nearly double the rate of the correspondents. In the Eighth Massachusetts district, which includes Cambridge, 19 percent voted for Bush, approximately triple the rate of the correspondents.[5]

Of course, however, just because a journalist has liberal or conservative views, this does not mean that his or her reporting will be slanted. For instance, as Jamieson [2000, p. 188] notes: "One might hypothesize instead that reporters respond to the cues of those who pay their salaries and mask their own ideological dispositions. Another explanation would hold that norms of journalism, including 'objectivity' and 'balance' blunt whatever biases exist." Or, as Crouse [1973] explains:

> It is an unwritten law of current political journalism that conservative Republican Presidential candidates usually receive gentler treatment from the press than do liberal Democrats. Since most reporters are moderate or liberal Democrats themselves, they try to offset their natural biases by going out of their way to be fair to conservatives. No candidate ever had a more considerate press corps than Barry Goldwater in 1964, and four years later the campaign press gave every possible break to Richard Nixon. Reporters sense a social barrier between themselves and most conservative candidates; their relations are formal and meticulously polite. But reporters tend to loosen up around liberal candidates and campaign staffs; since they share the same ideology, they can joke with the staffers, even needle them, without being branded the "enemy." If a reporter has been trained in the traditional, "objective" school of journalism, this ideological and social closeness to the candidate and the staff makes him feel guilty; he begins to compensate; the more he likes and agrees with the candidate *personally*, the harder he judges him *professionally*. Like a coach sizing up his own son in spring tryouts, the reporter becomes doubly severe. [pp. 355–356]

However, a strong form of the view that reporters offset or blunt their own ideological biases leads to a counterfactual implication. Suppose that it is true that all reporters report objectively, and their ideological views do not color their reporting. If so, then all news would have the *same* slant. Moreover, if one believes Crouse's claim that reporters overcompensate in relation to their own ideology, then a news outlet filled with conservatives, such as *Fox News*, should have a more liberal slant than a news outlet filled with liberals, such as the *New York Times*.

■   ■   ■

In Table 1 we list the 50 groups from our list that were most commonly cited by the media. The first column lists the average ADA score of the legislator citing the think tank. These averages closely correspond to conventional wisdom about the ideological positions of the groups. For instance, the Heritage Foundation and Christian Coalition, with average scores of 20.0 and 22.6, are near the conservative end; the Economic Policy Institute and the Children's Defense Fund (80.3 and 82.0) are near the liberal end; and the Brookings Institution and the World Wildlife Fund (53.3 and 50.4) are in the middle of our mix of think tanks.

While most of these averages closely agree with the conventional wisdom, two cases are somewhat anomalous. The first is the ACLU. The average score

TABLE 1 The 50 Most-Cited Think Tanks and Policy Groups by the Media in Our Sample

Think Tank/Policy Group	Average Score of Legislators Who Cite the Group	Number of Citations by Legislators	Number of Citations by Media Outlets
1 Brookings Institution	53.3	320	1392
2 American Civil Liberties Union	49.8	273	1073
3 NAACP	75.4	134	559
4 Center for Strategic and International Studies	46.3	79	432
5 Amnesty International	57.4	394	419
6 Council on Foreign Relations	60.2	45	403
7 Sierra Club	68.7	376	393
8 American Enterprise Institute	36.6	154	382
9 RAND Corporation	60.4	352	350
10 National Rifle Association	45.9	143	336
11 American Association of Retired Persons	66.0	411	333
12 Carnegie Endowment for International Peace	51.9	26	328
13 Heritage Foundation	20.0	369	288
14 Common Cause	69.0	222	287
15 Center for Responsive Politics	66.9	75	264
16 Consumer Federation of America	81.7	224	256
17 Christian Coalition	22.6	141	220
18 Cato Institute	36.3	224	196
19 National Organization for Women	78.9	62	195
20 Institute for International Economics	48.8	61	194
21 Urban Institute	73.8	186	187
22 Family Research Council	20.3	133	160
23 Federation of American Scientists	67.5	36	139
24 Economic Policy Institute	80.3	130	138
25 Center on Budget and Policy Priorities	88.3	224	115
26 National Right to Life Committee	21.6	81	109
27 Electronic Privacy Information Center	57.4	19	107
28 International Institute for Strategic Studies	41.2	16	104

TABLE 1   (*continued*)

Think Tank/Policy Group	Average Score of Legislators Who Cite the Group	Number of Citations by Legislators	Number of Citations by Media Outlets
29 World Wildlife Fund	50.4	130	101
30 Cent. for Strategic and Budgetary Assessments	33.9	7	89
31 National Abortion and Reproductive Rights Action League	71.9	30	88
32 Children's Defense Fund	82.0	231	78
33 Employee Benefit Research Institute	49.1	41	78
34 Citizens Against Government Waste	36.3	367	76
35 People for the American Way	76.1	63	76
36 Environmental Defense Fund	66.9	137	74
37 Economic Strategy Institute	71.9	26	71
38 People for the Ethical Treatment of Animals	73.4	5	70
39 Americans for Tax Reform	18.7	211	67
40 Citizens for Tax Justice	87.8	92	67
41 National Federation of Independent Businesses	26.8	293	66
42 Hudson Institute	25.3	73	64
43 National Taxpayers Union	34.3	566	63
44 Stimson Center	63.6	26	63
45 Center for Defense Information	79.0	28	61
46 Handgun Control, Inc.	77.2	58	61
47 Hoover Institution	36.5	35	61
48 Nixon Center	21.7	6	61
49 American Conservative Union	16.1	43	56
50 Manhattan Institute	32.0	18	54

of legislators citing it was 49.8. Later, we shall provide reasons why it makes sense to define the political center at 50.1. This suggests that the ACLU, if anything, is a *right*-leaning organization. The reason the ACLU has such a low score is that it opposed the McCain-Feingold Campaign Finance bill, and conservatives in Congress cited this often. In fact, slightly more than one-eighth of all ACLU citations in Congress were due to one person alone, Mitch McConnell

(R.-KY), perhaps the chief critic of McCain-Feingold. If we omit McConnell's citations, the ACLU's average score increases to 55.9. Because of this anomaly, in the Appendix we report the results when we repeat all of our analyses but omit the ACLU data.

The second apparent anomaly is the RAND Corporation, which has a fairly liberal average score, 60.4. We mentioned this finding to some employees of RAND, who told us they were not surprised. While RAND strives to be middle-of-the-road ideologically, the more conservative scholars at RAND tend to work on military studies, while the more liberal scholars tend to work on domestic studies. Because the military studies are sometimes classified and often more technocratic than the domestic studies, the media and members of Congress tend to cite the domestic studies disproportionately. As a consequence, RAND appears liberal when judged by these citations. It is important to note that this fact—that the research at RAND is more conservative than the numbers in Table 1 suggest—will not bias our results. To see this, think of RAND as two think tanks: RAND I, the left-leaning think tank which produces the research that the media and members of Congress tend to cite, and RAND II, the conservative think tank which produces the research that they tend not to cite. Our results exclude RAND II from the analysis. This causes no more bias than excluding any other think tank that is rarely cited in Congress or the media.

The second and third columns, respectively, report the number of congressional and media citations in our data. These columns give some preliminary evidence that the media is liberal, relative to Congress. To see this, define as *right-wing* a think tank that has an average score below 40. Next, consider the ten most-cited think tanks by the media. Only one right-wing think tank makes this list: the American Enterprise Institute. In contrast, consider the ten most-cited think tanks by *Congress*. (These are the National Taxpayers Union, AARP, Amnesty International, Sierra Club, Heritage Foundation, Citizens Against Government Waste, RAND, Brookings, NFIB, and ACLU.) Four of these are right-wing.

■ ■ ■

OUR DEFINITION OF BIAS

Before proceeding, it is useful to clarify our definition of bias. Most important, the definition has nothing to do with the honesty or accuracy of the news outlet. Instead, our notion is more like a taste or preference. For instance, we estimate that the centrist United States voter during the late 1990s had a left-right ideology approximately equal to that of Arlen Specter (R-PA) or Sam Nunn (D-GA). Meanwhile, we estimate that the average *New York Times* article is ideologically very similar to the average speech by Joe Lieberman (D-CT). Next, since vote scores show Lieberman to be more liberal than Specter or Nunn, our method concludes that the *New York Times* has a liberal bias. However, in no way does this imply that the *New York Times* is inaccurate or dishonest—just as the vote scores do not imply that Joe Lieberman is any less honest than Sam Nunn or Arlen Specter.

In contrast, other writers, at least at times, *do* define bias as a matter of accuracy or honesty. We emphasize that our differences with such writers are ones of semantics, not substance. If, say, a reader insists that *bias* should refer to accuracy or honesty, then we urge him or her simply to substitute another word wherever we write "bias." Perhaps "slant" is a good alternative.

However, at the same time, we argue that our notion of bias is meaningful and relevant, and perhaps more meaningful and relevant than the alternative notion. The main reason, we believe, is that only seldom do journalists make dishonest statements. Cases such as Jayson Blair, Stephen Glass, or the falsified memo at *CBS* are rare; they make headlines when they do occur; and much of the time they are orthogonal to any political bias.

Instead, for every sin of commission, such as those by Glass or Blair, we believe that there are hundreds, and maybe thousands, of sins of omission—cases where a journalist chose facts or stories that only one side of the political spectrum is likely to mention. For instance, in a story printed on March 1, 2002, the *New York Times* reported that (i) the IRS increased its audit rate on the "working poor" (a phrase that the article defines as any taxpayer who claimed an earned income tax credit); while (ii) the agency decreased its audit rate on taxpayers who earn more than $100,000; and (iii) more than half of all IRS audits involve the working poor. The article also notes that (iv) "The roughly 5 percent of taxpayers who make more than $100,000 . . . have the greatest opportunities to shortchange the government because they receive most of the nonwage income."

Most would agree that the article contains only true and accurate statements; however, most would also agree that the statements are more likely to be made by a liberal than a conservative. Indeed, the centrist and right-leaning news outlets by our measure (the *Washington Times, Fox News' Special Report*, the *Newshour with Jim Lehrer, ABC's Good Morning America*, and *CNN's Newsnight with Aaron Brown*) failed to mention any of these facts. Meanwhile, three of the outlets on the left side of our spectrum (*CBS Evening News, USA Today*, and the [news pages of the] *Wall Street Journal*) did mention at least one of the facts.

Likewise, on the opposite side of the political spectrum there are true and accurate facts that conservatives are more likely to state than liberals. For instance, on March 28, 2002, the *Washington Times*, the most conservative outlet by our measure, reported that Congress earmarked $304,000 to restore opera houses in Connecticut, Michigan, and Washington.[6] Meanwhile, none of the other outlets in our sample mentioned this fact. Moreover, the *Washington Times* article failed to mention facts that a liberal would be more likely to note. For instance, it did not mention that the $304,000 comprises a very tiny portion of the federal budget.

■ ■ ■

Similar to the facts and stories that journalists report, the citations that they gather from experts are also very rarely dishonest or inaccurate. Many, and perhaps most, simply indicate the side of an issue that the expert or his or her organization favors. For instance, on April 27, 2002, the *New York Times* reported that Congress passed a $100 billion farm subsidies bill that also gave vouchers to the elderly to buy fresh fruits and vegetables. "This is a terrific outcome—one of the most important pieces of social welfare legislation this year," said Stacy Dean of the Center on Budget and Policy Priorities, her only quote in the article. In another instance, on May 19, 2001, *CBS Evening News* described President Bush's call for expanding nuclear power. It quoted the Sierra Club's Daniel Becker: "[S]witching from coal to nuclear power is like giving up smoking and taking up crack." Most would agree that these statements are more normative than positive; that is, they are more an indication of the author's preferences than a fact or prediction.

Similarly, another large fraction of cases involve the organization's views of *politicians*. For instance, on March 29, 2002, the *Washington Times* reported that the National Taxpayers' Union (NTU) gave Hillary Clinton a score of 3 percent on its annual rating of Congress. The story noted that the score, according to the NTU, was "the worst score for a Senate freshman in their first year in office that the NTU has ever recorded."

Finally, many other citations refer to facts that are generally beyond dispute. However, like the facts that reporters themselves note, these facts are ones that conservatives and liberals are not equally likely to state. For instance, on March 5, 1992, *CBS Evening News* reported a fact that liberals are more likely to note than conservatives: "The United States now has greater disparities of income than virtually any Western European country," said Robert Greenstein of the Center on Budget and Policy Priorities. Meanwhile, on May 30, 2003, *CNN's Newsnight with Aaron Brown* noted a fact that conservatives are more likely to state than liberals. In a story about the FCC's decision to weaken regulations about media ownership, it quoted Adam Thierer of the Cato Institute, "[L]et's start by stepping back and taking a look at . . . the landscape of today versus, say, 10, 15, 25, 30 years ago. And by almost every measure that you can go by, you can see that there is more diversity, more competition, more choice for consumers and citizens in these marketplaces."[7]

■ ■ ■

DISCUSSION: IMPLICATIONS FOR THE INDUSTRIAL ORGANIZATION OF THE NEWS INDUSTRY

At least four broad empirical regularities emerge from our results. In this section we document these regularities and analyze their significance for some theories about the industrial organization of the news industry.

First, we find a systematic tendency for the United States media outlets to slant the news to the left.

▪ ▪ ▪

For instance, Hamilton [2004] notes that news producers may prefer to cater to some consumers more than others. In particular, Hamilton notes that young females tend to be one of the most marginal groups of news consumers (i.e., they are the most willing to switch to activities besides reading or watching the news). Further, this group often makes the consumption decisions for the household. For these two reasons, advertisers are willing to pay more to outlets that reach this group. Since young females tend to be more liberal on average, a news outlet may want to slant its coverage to the left. Thus, according to Hamilton's theory, United States news outlets slant their coverage leftward, not *in spite of* consumer demand, but *because* of it.[8]

A more compelling explanation for the liberal slant of news outlets, in our view, involves production factors, not demand factors. As Sutter [2001] has noted, journalists might systematically have a taste to slant their stories to the left. Indeed, this is consistent with the survey evidence that we noted earlier. As a consequence, "If the majority of journalists have left-of-center views, liberal news might cost less to supply than unbiased news [p. 444]." Baron [2005] constructs a rigorous mathematical model along these lines. In his model journalists are driven, not just by money, but also a desire to influence their readers or viewers. Baron shows that profit-maximizing firms may *choose* to allow reporters to slant their stories, and consequently in equilibrium the media will have a systematic bias.[9]

A second empirical regularity is that the media outlets that we examine are fairly centrist relative to members of Congress. . . .

Moreover, when we add price competition to the basic spatial model, then, as Mullainathan and Shleifer [2003] show, even fewer media outlets should be centrist. Specifically, their two-firm model predicts that both media firms should choose slants that are outside the preferred slants of *all* consumers. The intuition is that in the first round, when firms choose locations, they want to differentiate their products significantly, so in the next round they will have less incentive to compete on price. Given this theoretical result, it is puzzling that media outlets in the United States are not more heterogeneous. We suspect that, once again, the reason may lie with production factors. For instance, one possibility may involve the sources for news stories—what one could consider as the raw materials of the news industry. If a news outlet is too extreme, many of the newsmakers may refuse to grant interviews to the reporters.

A third empirical regularity involves the question whether reporters will be faithful agents of the owners of the firms for which they work. That is, will the slant of their news stories reflect their own ideological preferences or the firm's owners? The conventional wisdom, at least among left-wing commentators, is that the latter is true. For instance, Alterman [2003] titles a chapter of his book "You're Only as Liberal as the Man Who Owns You." A weaker assertion is that the particular news *outlet* will be a faithful agent of the firm that owns it. However, our results provide some weak evidence that this is not true. For instance, although *Time* magazine and *CNN*'s *Newsnight* are owned by the same firm (Time Warner), their ADA scores differ substantially, by 9.4 points.[10] Further, almost half of the other outlets have scores between those of *Newsnight* and *Time*.

A fourth regularity concerns the question whether one should expect a government-funded news outlet to be more liberal than a privately funded outlet. "Radical democratic" media scholars McChesney and Scott [2004] claim that it will. For instance, they note "[Commercial journalism] has more often served the minority interests of dominant political, military, and business concerns than it has the majority interests of disadvantaged social classes [2004, p. 4]." And conservatives, who frequently complain that *NPR* is far left, also seem to agree. However, our results do not support such claims. If anything, the government-funded outlets in our sample (*NPR*'s *Morning Edition* and *Newshour with Jim Lehrer*) have a slightly *lower* average ADA score (61.0), than the private outlets in our sample (62.8).[11] Related, some claim that a free-market system of news will produce less diversity of news than a government-run system. However, again, our results do not support such a claim. The variance of the ADA scores of the privately run outlets is substantially higher (131.3) than the variance of the two government-funded outlets that we examine (55.1).

In interpreting some of the above regularities, especially perhaps the latter two, we advise caution. For instance, with regard to our comparisons of government-funded versus privately funded news outlets, we should emphasize that our sample of government-funded outlets is small (only two), and our total sample of news outlets might not be representative of all news outlets.

■　■　■

NOTES

1. Our sample includes policy groups that are not usually called think tanks, such as the NAACP, NRA, and Sierra Club. To avoid using the more unwieldy phrase "think tanks and other policy groups" we often use a shorthand version, "think tanks." When we use the latter phrase, we mean to include the other groups, such as the NAACP, etc.

2. Eighty-nine percent of the Washington correspondents voted for Bill Clinton, and two percent voted for Ross Perot.

3. "Finding Biases on the Bus," John Tierney, *New York Times*, August 1, 2004. The article noted that journalists outside Washington were not as liberal. Twenty-five percent of these journalists favored Bush over Kerry.

4. "Ruling Class War," *New York Times*, September 11, 2004.

5. Cambridge and Berkeley's preferences for Republican presidential candidates have remained fairly constant since 1992. In the House district that contains Cam-

bridge, Bob Dole received 17 percent of the two-party vote in 1996, and George W. Bush received 19 percent in 2000. In the House district that contains Berkeley, Bob Dole received 14 percent of the two-party vote, and George W. Bush received 13 percent.

6. We assert that this statement is more likely to be made by a conservative because it suggests that government spending is filled with wasteful projects. This, conservatives often argue, is a reason that government should lower taxes.

7. Like us, Mullainathan and Shleifer [2003] define bias as an instance where a journalist fails to report a relevant fact, rather than chooses to report a false fact. However, unlike us, Mullainathan and Shleifer define bias as a question of accuracy, not a taste or preference. More specifically, their model assumes that with any potential news story, there are a finite number of facts that apply to the story. By their definition, a journalist is unbiased only if he or she reports all these facts. (However, given that there may be an unwieldy number of facts that the journalist could mention, it also seems consistent with the spirit of their definition that if the journalist merely selects facts randomly from this set or if he or she chooses a representative sample, then this would also qualify as unbiased.) As an example, suppose that, out of the entire universe of facts about free trade, most of the facts imply that free trade is good. However, suppose that liberals and moderates in Congress are convinced that it is bad, and hence in their speeches they state more facts about its problems. Under Mullainathan and Shleifer's definition, to be unbiased a journalist must state more facts about the *advantages* of free trade—whereas, under our definition a journalist must state more facts about the *disadvantages* of free trade. Again, we emphasize that our differences on this point are ones of semantics. Each notion of bias is meaningful and relevant. And if a reader insists that "bias" should refer to one notion instead of the other, we suggest that he or she substitute a different word for the other notion, such as "slant." Further, we suggest that Mullainathan and Shleifer's notion is an ideal that a journalist perhaps *should* pursue before our notion. Nevertheless, we suggest a weakness of Mullainathan and Shleifer's notion: it is very inconvenient for empirical work, and perhaps completely infeasible. Namely, it would be nearly impossible—and at best a very subjective exercise—for a researcher to try to determine all the facts that are relevant for a given news story. Likewise, it would be very difficult, and maybe impossible, for a *journalist* to determine this set of facts. To see this, consider just a portion of the facts that may be relevant to a news story, the citations from experts. There are hundreds, and maybe thousands, of think tanks, not to mention hundreds of academic departments. At what point does the journalist decide that a think tank or academic department is so obscure that it does not need to be contacted for a citation? Further, most think tanks and academic departments house dozens of members. This means that an unbiased journalist would have to speak to a huge number of potential experts. Moreover, even if the journalist could contact all of these experts, a further problem is how long to talk to them. At what point does the journalist stop gathering information from one particular expert before he or she is considered unbiased? Even if a journalist only needs to contact a representative sample of these experts, a problem still exists over defining the relevant universe of experts. Again, when is an expert so obscure that he or she should not be included in the universe? A similar problem involves the journalist's choice of stories to pursue. A news outlet can choose from a huge—and possibly infinite—number of news stories. Although Mullainathan and Shleifer's model focuses only on the bias for a *given* story, a relevant source of bias is the journalist's choice of stories to cover. It would be very difficult for a researcher to construct a universe of stories from which journalists choose to cover. For instance, within this universe,

what proportion should involve the problems of dual-career parents? What proportion should involve corporate fraud?

8. Sutter [2001] similarly notes that demand factors may be the source of liberal bias in the newspaper industry. Specifically, he notes that liberals may have a higher demand for newspapers than conservatives, and he cites some suggestive evidence by Goff and Tollison [1990], which shows that as the voters in a state become more liberal, newspaper circulation in the state increases.

9. Perhaps even more interesting, in Baron's (2005) model news consumers, in equilibrium, can be influenced in the direction of the bias of the news outlet, despite the fact that they understand the equilibrium of the game and the potential incentives of journalists to slant the news.

10. This difference, however, is *not* statistically significant at the 95 percent confidence level. A likelihood ratio test, constraining *Time* and *Newsnight* to have the same score gives a log-likelihood function that is 1.1 units greater than the unconstrained function. This value, multiplied by two, follows a Chi-Square distribution with one degree of freedom. The result, 2.2, is almost significant at the 90 percent confidence level, but not quite. (The latter has a criterion of 2.71.) We obtained similar results when we tested, the joint hypothesis that (i) *Newsnight* and *Time* have identical scores and that (ii) all three network morning news shows have scores identical to their respective evening news shows. A likelihood ratio test gives a value of 8.04, which follows a Chi-Square distribution with four degrees of freedom. The value is significant at the 90 percent confidence level (criterion=7.78), but not at the 95 percent confidence level (criterion=9.49). Our hunch is that with more data we could show conclusively that at least sometimes different news outlets at the same firm produce significantly different slants. We suspect that, consistent with Baron's [2005] model, editors and producers, like reporters, are given considerable slack, and that they are willing to sacrifice salary in order to be given such slack.

11. This result is broadly consistent with Djankov, McLiesh, Nenova, and Shleifer's [2003] notion of the *public choice theory of media ownership*. This theory asserts that a government-owned media will slant news in such a way to aid incumbent politicians. If so, some reasonable theories (e.g., Black [1958]) suggest that the slant should conform to the median view of the incumbent politicians. We indeed find that the slant of the government-funded outlets in the United States on average is fairly close to the median politicians' view. In fact, it is closer to the median view than the average of the privately funded outlets that we examine. See Lott [1999] for an examination of a similar public-choice theory applied to the media *and* the education system in a country.

REFERENCES

Alterman, Eric, *What Liberal Media? The Truth about Bias and the News* (New York: Basic Books, 2003).

Baron, David, "Persistent Media Bias," *Journal of Public Economics*, LXXXIX (2005).

Black, Duncan, *The Theory of Committees and Elections* (London: Cambridge University Press, 1958).

Crouse, Timothy, *Boys on the Bus* (New York: Ballentine Books, 1973).

Djankov, Simeon, Caralee McLiesh, Tatiana Nenova, and Andrei Shleifer, "Who Owns the Media?" *Journal of Law and Economics*, XLVI (2003), 341–381.

Goff, Brian, and Robert Tollison, "Why Is the Media so Liberal?" *Journal of Public Finance and Public Choice*, I (1990), 13–21.

Hamilton, James, *All the News That's Fit to Sell: How the Market Transforms Information into News* (Princeton, NJ: Princeton University Press, 2004).

Jamieson, Kathleen Hall, *Everything You Think You Know About Politics . . . and Why You're Wrong* (New York: Basic Books, 2000).

Lichter, S.R., S. Rothman, and L.S. Lichter, *The Media Elite* (Bethesda, MD: Adler and Adler, 1986).

Lott, John R., Jr., "Public Schooling, Indoctrination, and Totalitarianism," *Journal of Political Economy*, CVII (1999), S127–S157.

McChesney, Robert, and Ben Scott, *Our Unfree Press: 100 Years of Radical Media Criticism* (New York: The New Press, 2004).

Mullainathan, Sendhil, and Andrei Shleifer, "The Market for News," manuscript, Harvard University, 2003.

Povich, Elaine, *Partners and Adversaries: The Contentious Connection Between Congress and the Media* (Arlington, VA: Freedom Forum, 1996).

Sutter, Daniel, "Can the Media Be So Liberal? The Economics of Media Bias," *The Cato Journal*, XX (2001), 431–451.

14.2

SHANTO IYENGAR AND JENNIFER McGRADY

From *Media Politics: A Citizen's Guide*

In this selection, Iyengar and McGrady discuss how new forms of media, such as the Internet and cell phones, are changing American politics. They evaluate three types of theories about how these new media influence politics. Partisan theories suggest that the new media only highlight and enhance partisan differences among people. Issue-public theories focus on how new media lead to the creation of small groups of people intensely interested in isolated topics. And attentive-public theories emphasize that the new media perpetuate inequalities among people in how much they pay attention to politics. The authors contend that research is still inconclusive on which of these kinds of theories is supported by data.

5. THE RISE OF NEW MEDIA

The revolution in information technology has altered not only the shape of the media landscape, but also the very concept of communication. The traditional forms of communication were either *point-to-point* (between a single sender and recipient) or *broadcast* (between a single sender and multiple recipients). Most senders did not have ready access to broadcast forms of communication and could not reach a significant audience. Traditional media were also limited to a single form (print, audio, or video).

The development of the Internet permitted simultaneous point-to-point and broadcast forms of communication for the first time, and it provided individual users with easy access to an unlimited audience. Every individual on the network of computers making up the World Wide Web is both a sender and a receiver. Any user of the Internet can direct e-mail messages to individual recipients and at the same time communicate with a worldwide audience by hosting a Web site, posting a message on a message board, or participating in an online chat room. Moreover, unlike conventional media, Internet-based communication is multichannel, allowing the free transmission of text, voice, still images, and video.

■ ■ ■

Effects of New Media on News Consumers

There are two schools of thought concerning the potential impact of new media on the end user. *Optimists* see technology as a means of revitalizing the public sphere. By providing direct and immediate access to diverging political perspectives, the Internet should enhance the ability of ordinary people to follow events and to participate in the political process. The hope is that even modest levels of online news consumption will build civic awareness and engagement. . . .

Skeptics, on the other hand, warn that information technology is no panacea for the limitations of conventional news programming and the weak demand for political information. If "serious" news coverage cannot attract television viewers, why should it draw people online? If Americans are not used to reading or watching foreign media, is there any reason to suppose that they will suddenly access the BBC or the Press Trust of India just because it's possible to do so? Pessimists think not. They believe that the Internet will actually discourage consumers from devoting time to news programming (whether Internet or conventional) in favor of more engaging pursuits, such as online shopping, dating, or keeping in touch. As people become more fluent in the ways of the Web, they may become more personally isolated, preferring "surfing alone" over community involvement or social interaction. Quite possibly, the net effect of technology could be to weaken community and civic engagement.

Quite apart from the question of whether Internet technology will increase or decrease the average time devoted to public affairs content is the question of whether the Internet will, in practice, be used to broaden users' political horizons. Although an infinite variety of information is available, individuals may well sample selectively, limiting their exposure to news or sources that they expect to find agreeable. There is no doubt that the Internet makes available an ample supply of "news" that is not screened for accuracy or objectivity. . . .

A third debate over the potential impact of technology on individuals' civic empowerment concerns inequalities of access. Pessimists argue that the costs of going online, in terms of both money and skills, create striking disparities in access to information. Technology use is significantly correlated with social class and, interestingly, age; the on-ramp to the "information superhighway" is closed to the poor and the technologically less educated, making it less likely that they will be informed on the same level as most Americans.

■ ■ ■

Biased Exposure to Online News?

For obvious reasons, candidates, political parties, and interest groups have all taken to the Internet to get out their messages, solicit money and other forms of support, and mobilize their members. The increased volume of online political communication has two immediate consequences. First, conventional news organizations have lost some of their near-monopolistic control over the delivery of public affairs information. Republicans dissatisfied with the *New York Times* coverage of President Bush can turn to the *Drudge Report* or the Republican National Committee Web site for an alternative slant on daily events. In fact, the Pew Research Center's surveys of Internet use show that gathering news is a relevant objective for many Internet users. . . . But at the same time, the largest segment of online Americans has only limited interest in news. . . .

The second consequence of the increased flow of information is overload. In a world dominated by conventional news sources, the supply of campaign information hardly burdens the typical voter's attention span. The average candidate sound bite in the networks' evening newscasts, for instance, runs for less than ten seconds. New forms of communication not only deliver much larger chunks of campaign information, but they also facilitate consumers' ability to attend to the information selectively. The audience for conventional news programs is hard-pressed to avoid coverage of the candidate they dislike, because news reports typically assign equal coverage to each. When browsing a Web site, on the other hand, users can filter or search through masses of text more easily than in conventional media. . . .

In short, as candidates, interest groups, and voters all converge on the Internet, the possibility of selective exposure to political information increases. Given the availability of so much information and so many news providers, the audience must make choices or be overwhelmed. Exactly how do Internet users decide whether the information they're getting is worth considering or should be passed over?

There are three main possibilities. First, people may prefer to encounter information that they find supportive or consistent with their beliefs (the *partisan polarization hypothesis*). For example, Republicans may tune in to Fox News, Democrats to the *New York Times*. Second, people may pay attention not on the basis of their anticipated agreement with the message, but because of their interest in particular issues (the *issue public hypothesis*). For example, the elderly seek out information bearing on Social Security or Medicare legislation simply because these policies have an immediate impact on their welfare. Third, exposure to political information online may be simply a matter of generic political interest (the *attentive public hypothesis*). Political junkies sample widely while the apolitical majority simply tunes out, except when major events generate a torrent of coverage that is impossible to ignore. From this perspective, multiplying the number of information sources only widens the information gap between the more and the less interested.

■   ■   ■

Impact of the Internet on Campaign Organizations

. . . In principle, campaigns can harness the immense networking power of the Internet to accomplish multiple campaign objectives, including fundraising, increasing the candidate's visibility and likability, and most critically, recruiting and mobilizing a cadre of activists. To date, the impact of new media has been greatest on the goal of mobilization. Other facets of the campaign remain grounded in conventional (especially broadcast) media because there are still more voters to be reached in front of their television sets than at their computers. Nonetheless, the networking advantages of the Internet have already transformed the conduct of campaigns.

Before the Internet, candidates recruited volunteers and raised money by making phone calls, sending mass mailings, or going door to door. These old-fashioned forms of mobilization and fund-raising were both capital- and time-intensive; successful campaigns had an existing organization, professional (paid) staff, and access to phone banks or mailing lists of prospective supporters. Candidates themselves might spend long hours on the phone with prospective donors. The amount of time between the initial contact and receipt of a financial contribution might take weeks or even months. These infrastructure costs made it nearly impossible for lesser-known and cash-strapped candidates to develop and manage a hard-core group of activists.

By lowering the cost of communication, the Internet has transformed the political arena by enabling any campaign, no matter how large its electoral constituency, to assemble a network of supporters. Any candidate with the ability to mount a basic Web site can instantly sign up volunteers and send them assignments for upcoming events, thus developing the nucleus of a viable field organization. Once formed, these groups become "smart mobs"— capable of acting in a coordinated manner, despite the absence of any face-to-face contact (for examples of smart mobs in action, see Rheingold, 2002). In effect, the Internet lowered the eligibility requirements for groups to engage in collective action.[1] For large and small campaigns alike, the Internet is a public good that can be exploited with minimal marginal costs.

The first campaign to take advantage of the Internet to organize its supporters was the 1998 Jesse Ventura campaign for governor of Minnesota. Running as the Reform Party candidate, Ventura was heavily outspent by his Republican and Democratic opponents (Norm Coleman and Hubert H. Humphrey III, respectively). But Ventura's campaign launched a Web site in early 1998 (at a monthly cost of under thirty dollars) and began to develop a statewide e-mail list of volunteers. The list was used to publicize information about local organizational meetings; one such meeting drew a standing-room-only crowd of more than 250 people.

Taking further advantage of its statewide network, the Ventura campaign scheduled a seventy-two-hour "Drive to Victory" caravan tour of the state.

Because supporters had been informed in advance of the candidate's appearance in their area, the tour attracted large, enthusiastic crowds, thus raising the candidate's media profile. Simultaneously, the campaign used its online network to raise much-needed funds. Online contributions to the Ventura campaign amounted to a third of its total fund-raising.

Despite being outspent and outstaffed by his opponents (the campaign had only one paid staff member, the campaign manager), Ventura was elected governor. It is difficult to say precisely how much difference Ventura's use of technology made to the upset victory. After all, his unusual persona and career as a professional wrestler combined to make him a highly visible candidate, and his antigovernment, populist platform resonated well in a state with a long history of supporting progressive reformers. In one respect, however, the payoff of using technology was clear: young people, who are most likely to be reached online, turned out to vote in large numbers. Over half of them voted for Ventura—more than enough to account for the margin of his victory.

The success of the Ventura campaign made it clear to campaign operatives that the Internet could and should be exploited for political action. By 2000, all reputable candidates had elaborate, interactive Web sites and e-mail lists of prospective supporters. Among the presidential contenders, it was John McCain who became the poster boy for use of the Internet. Capitalizing on McCain's special appeal to the young, his campaign went online to recruit some fifteen hundred volunteers in advance of the New Hampshire primary. The campaign scheduled regular online "chat" encounters with the candidate. In one such session, five hundred people each paid a hundred dollars for the privilege of submitting an e-mail question to McCain. Overall, the McCain campaign set a new record (four million dollars) for electronic fund-raising.

Despite McCain's stunning victory in the New Hampshire primary, his candidacy proved short-lived. George W. Bush rebounded from New Hampshire and soundly defeated McCain in South Carolina. Shortly thereafter, McCain withdrew from the race. But once again, an "insurgent" candidate had demonstrated competitiveness with the help of a relatively modest investment in new media.

It was during the 2004 campaign that Internet campaigning came into its own. Governor Howard Dean tied his presidential candidacy inextricably to the Internet. Although Dean was eventually forced to withdraw from the campaign for lack of support, his campaign's innovative use of technology contributed to his meteoric rise from the relatively unknown governor of a small state to the front-running contender for the Democratic nomination.

The Dean campaign hired a full-time Internet consultant. The first step was to use the networking portal Meetup.com to recruit Dean supporters from across the nation. Meetup is designed to create local groups for people with common interests, whether that interest is witches, cricket, or Howard Dean for president. The Dean campaign used Meetup to schedule face-to-face meetings across the nation, several of which were attended by the candidate himself. For the campaign, mailing out campaign materials was the only cost of maintaining this network of activists.

By July, the Dean Meetup group had grown to over 60,000 members, and membership peaked at 189,000 shortly before Dean withdrew in February 2004.[2] The Dean Web site served as the hub for the online campaign. Visitors were urged to "stay connected" and were informed about local Meetup groups and upcoming campaign events (in addition to the standard position papers, press releases, and televised advertisements). The Dean campaign also initiated the popular Weblog "Blog for America" (which is still active but is now known as Democracy for America[3]). By December 2003, with twenty-nine hundred entries and over thirty thousand spontaneous comments, the blog had become required required reading for the national press corps.

While organizing "Deaniacs" nationwide, the Dean campaign also demonstrated considerable prowess at online fund-raising. In one instance, the campaign responded to a Bush–Cheney two-thousand-dollar-a-plate dinner (which raised $250,000) by hosting an online "eat in" challenge featuring a Web page with an image of Dean eating a turkey sandwich and a "contribute now" button. In response, ninety-seven hundred people visited the page, and the campaign netted over $500,000. In the second quarter of 2003 alone, the campaign took in more than seven million dollars.

The Dean campaign also relied on online polling to take the pulse of supporters. In one case, the campaign even scheduled an online referendum on whether Dean should opt out of the public financing provisions of the campaign (thus enabling him to raise and spend unlimited amounts of money). A majority of his supporters voted for opting out, and no sooner had the campaign announced the results than it began to solicit contributions from those who voted. Another widely publicized online poll was sponsored by the liberal-leaning issue advocacy group MoveOn.org. MoveOn held a "virtual primary" in June 2003. More than three hundred thousand people voted. Given the ideological leanings of the group, it was not surprising that the two most liberal candidates in the Democratic field finished first (Dean) and second (Kucinich), respectively. Despite the wholly nonrepresentative nature of the result, the MoveOn primary attracted considerable media coverage, thus further cementing Dean's stature as the leading Democratic contender.

Given the Dean campaign's effective use of the Internet to mobilize supporters, why did he fail to win even one primary?[4] Dean's extensive network of online volunteers did not translate into an outpouring of primary votes. In the language of social scientists, the Dean campaign was doomed by a "self-selection bias." The American techno-literati, most of whom were eager to drive Bush from the White House and who seized the opportunity to volunteer for Dean, were much too small a group to swing even a small-state primary. In other words, the Deaniacs were not representative of Democratic primary voters. A Pew Research Center survey of Dean activists found that 54 percent had attended graduate school (for all Democratic activists, the comparable figure was 11 percent) and that they were significantly more lib-eral and anti-Bush than mainstream Democrats were. Dean's candidacy itself was clearly faithful to his supporters, but it also made Dean less appealing to most Democratic voters.

Thus the main lesson of 2004 was that, although the Internet provides a cost-efficient means of developing a network of campaign workers and donors, it is not yet the best platform for candidates to appeal for votes. It is one thing to develop an electronic network of enthusiastic supporters; it is quite another to attract enough votes to win a primary election. As of 2004, the Internet was not yet competitive with television as a way of communicating with rank-and-file voters.

Conclusion

The scholarly evidence concerning the emerging role of the Internet in Amer-ican public life does not support the dire forecasts that the Internet will cre-ate virtual "gated communities" of polarized groups. The research shows instead that what people see or read in news presentations—both conven-tional and online—is not motivated solely, or even primarily, by the desire to track sources with which they are likely to agree. Some people (conservatives in particular) do tend to gravitate to a "preferred" provider, but others con-sume news because they are generally interested in politics, or select content on the basis of its relative interest or utility.

■   ■   ■

Quite apart from the ambiguous verdict of the scholarly literature, there is another reason to be optimistic about the potential impact of the technological revolution on the political process. We have already documented that media-based campaigns fail to deliver substantive information. In place of the candi-dates' positions and past performance on the issues, news coverage gravitates inevitably toward the more "entertaining" facets of the campaign: the horse race, the strategy, and whenever possible, instances of scandalous or unethical behavior. Against this backdrop, technology at least makes it possible for voters to bypass or supplement media treatment of the campaign and access informa-tion about the issues that affect them.

Rather than waiting (typically in vain) for news organizations to report on the issues they care about, voters can take matters into their own hands and seek out information about the candidates' positions on these issues. This form of motivated exposure is hardly an impediment to deliberation: paying atten-tion to what the candidates have to say on the issues facilitates issue-oriented voting; paying attention to the media circus does not. Thus, there is some reason to hope that the spread of new forms of unmediated communication will provide a better way to inform and engage voters.

Finally, the brief case studies of candidates who have successfully orga-nized campaigns on the Internet make it clear that technology, in this respect at least, has leveled the campaign playing field. Even the poorest candidate has the capacity to publicize a candidacy and solicit support online. As the examples of Ventura, McCain, and Dean suggest, an Internet presence can, virtually overnight, help candidates establish a viable campaign organization. As technology spreads even further, and the next generation of software makes possible even closer contact and cooperation among like-minded individuals, we may expect the Internet to play a pivotal role in American campaigns. But for the moment at least, to campaign for votes, candidates still use relatively old-fashioned approaches, relying on conventional media.

NOTES

1. The Internet does not necessarily reduce the inequality in organizational capacity. Larger groups that invest more heavily in customized technology, for instance, may reap even larger benefits than those using cruder and more publicly available electronic tools.

2. Dean was not the only candidate to network online. John Kerry was quick to follow Dean as a client of Meetup.com, and the Wesley Clark campaign formed the "Clark Community Network." Not to be outdone by the Democrats, the Bush–Cheney campaign also developed a proprietary electronic networking system. Their Web site included an online invitation system, downloadable flyers, and a searchable zip code directory that allowed users to locate other supporters in their area. For a more detailed description of the various campaigns' online efforts, see Samuel, 2004.

3. www.democracyforamerica.com.

4. After withdrawing from the race, Dean did win his home-state primary.

REFERENCE

Samuel, A. (2004, October 18). Web plays U.S. election wild card. *The Toronto Star*, p. D1.

15

ECONOMIC POLICY

15.1

JOSEPH STIGLITZ

From *Making Globalization Work*

Stiglitz argues that it is impossible to reverse or slow globalization. The challenge, and imperative, is to manage it and make it work better for more people. Fundamental changes are necessary, especially in how the United States engages with international organizations and in how economic policies are set.

10. DEMOCRATIZING GLOBALIZATION

Globalization was supposed to bring unprecedented benefits to all. Yet, curiously, it has come to be vilified both in the developed and the developing world. America and Europe see the threat of outsourcing; the developing countries see the advanced industrial countries tilting the global economic regime against them. Those in both see corporate interests being advanced at the expense of other values. [T]here is much merit in these criticisms—but that they are criticisms of globalization as it has been managed.

■ ■ ■

[T]he problems have much to do with economic globalization outpacing political globalization, and with the economic consequences of globalization outpacing our ability to understand and shape globalization and to cope with these consequences through political processes. Reforming globalization is a matter of politics. In this reading, I want to deal with some of the key political issues. Among them are the prospects for unskilled workers and the impact of globalization on inequality; the democratic deficit in our global economic institutions, which weakens even democracy within our own countries; and

579

the human tendency to think locally even while we live in an increasingly global economy.

Growing Inequality and the Threat of Outsourcing

When in February 2004 President Bush's chief economic adviser, N. Gregory Mankiw, praised the opportunity that outsourcing, with its lower costs and hence higher profits, provided for U.S. companies, he was widely criticized. Americans were worried about jobs, in manufacturing—in which some 2.8 million jobs were lost from 2001 to 2004—and even in the high-tech and service sectors.[1] In some sense, outsourcing is not new: U.S. companies have been sending jobs overseas for decades. The number of manufacturing jobs in the United States has been shrinking since 1979, and the fraction of Americans working in manufacturing has been declining since the 1940s. (In 1945, 37 percent of working Americans were employed in manufacturing, while today the figure is less than 11 percent.)[2]

A dynamic economy is, of course, characterized by job loss and job creation—the loss of less-productive jobs and the shift of workers to areas of higher productivity. The production of horse carriages declined with the arrival of the automobile. During the debate over the North American Free Trade Agreement, 1992 presidential candidate Ross Perot warned that there would be a "giant sucking sound" as jobs were pulled out of the United States. The response from the Clinton administration was that America didn't want those low-wage, low-skill jobs, and that the market would create better-paid, higher-skill jobs. And during the first few years of NAFTA unemployment in the United States actually declined, from 6.8 percent, at the beginning of NAFTA, down to a low of 3.8 percent.

Just as the United States and European countries made the transition from agriculture to manufacturing more than a hundred years ago, more recently they have made the move from manufacturing to services. The share of manufacturing in employment and output has fallen not just in the United States but also in Europe and Japan (to 20 percent).[3] As America and Europe lost jobs in manufacturing, they gained jobs in the service sector, a sector that includes not only low-skill jobs flipping hamburgers but high-paid jobs in the financial services sector. It was thought that America, with its high level of skills and its service-sector dominated economy would be protected from competition from abroad. What made outsourcing so scary was that even highly skilled jobs began to go abroad. The strategy of "upskilling" and education, though clearly valuable and important, does not provide a full answer for how to respond to global competition.

The scale and pace of the competitive threat, of the job loss in a relatively short time, is beyond anything that has happened before. This is the flip side of another unprecedented change: two countries, China and India, that were once desperately poor and economically isolated are now part of the global economy. Never before have the incomes of so many people risen so fast.[4]

Standard economic theory, which underlies the call for trade liberalization, has a scenario for what should happen with full liberalization—a scenario that its advocates seldom mention, but which we noted briefly. . . . With full global economic integration, the world will become like a single country, and the wages of unskilled workers will be the same everywhere in the world, no matter where they live. Whether in America or in India or in China, unskilled workers of comparable skills performing comparable work will be paid the same. In theory, the actual wage will be *somewhere* between that received today by the Indian or Chinese unskilled worker and that received by his American or European counterpart; in practice, given the relative size of the populations, the likelihood is that the single wage to which they will converge will be closer to that of China and India than to that of the United States or Europe.

Of course, taking down all tariff and trade barriers will not lead instantly to full integration or to the equalization of wages. There will still be transportation costs, and in the case of very poor and remote countries, these remain important. In the past, at least two factors played a part in enabling wage differences to persist. The first is the scarcity of capital in developing countries. This matters because with less capital (such as new machines and technology) workers are less productive. Handlooms are less productive than machine looms—and because they are less productive, workers' wages will be lower. The second is the gap in knowledge between the developed and the less developed countries. Skills and technology have lagged in the developing world, and that has lowered productivity and depressed wages.

However, these impediments to wage equalization are disappearing. International capital markets have improved enormously. Today, while China is saving 42 percent of its GDP, it is also receiving more than $50 billion every year in foreign direct investment, an amount close to 4 percent of its GDP.[5] And in recent years, the flow of knowledge from the developed to the undeveloped countries has accelerated.

It will take decades to fully overcome the knowledge gap and the capital shortage in the developing world. The good news is that there will be a strong force pulling up wages in China and India. The downside is that there will be a strong force pushing down wages for unskilled workers in the West. So, while Americans and Europeans can rejoice in the rising living standards of unskilled workers in the developing world, they will be worrying about what is happening at home. The issue is not just the total number of jobs that will be outsourced—lost—to China or India. The real problem is that even a relatively small gap between the demand for and the supply of labor can create large problems, leading to wage stagnation and decline, and creating high levels of anxiety among the many workers who feel their jobs are at risk. That is what appears to be happening.

Of course, as we have seen, globalization and trade liberalization will increase overall incomes (if the country can manage to maintain full employment, a big "if"). But it follows that with incomes on average increasing, and wages, especially at the bottom, stagnating or falling, inequality will increase. Those in the industries who find themselves outcompeted especially will suffer; they may find their "human capital," the investments made in particular skills, no longer of much value. For the past five years, real wages in America have been basically stagnant; for those at the bottom, real wages have stagnated for more than a quarter of a century.[6] Whole communities may find themselves in difficult straits. As businesses shut down and jobs are lost, real estate prices will fall, which will hurt most people in those areas, since their main asset is their home.

Responding to the Challenges of Globalization

There are three ways in which the advanced industrial countries can respond to these challenges. One is to ignore the problem and accept the growing inequality. Those who take this position (many of them proponents of the now-discredited theory of trickle-down economics, which holds that so long as there is growth, *all* will benefit) emphasize the underlying strengths of a market economy and its ability to respond to change: we may not know where the new jobs will be created, they say, but so long as we allow markets to work their magic, new jobs will be created. It is only when, as in Europe, a government interferes with market processes by protecting jobs, that there are problems with unemployment.

But in both Europe and America, this approach is not working. While there are winners from globalization, there are numerous losers. Globalization is, of course, only one of the many forces affecting our societies and our economies. Even without it, there would be increasing inequality. Changes in technology have increased the premium the market places on certain skills, so that the winners in today's economy are those who have or can acquire those skills. These changes in technology may in the end be more important than globalization in determining the increase in inequality, and even the decline in unskilled wages. Voters can do little about the march of technology; but they can—through their elected representatives—do something about globalization. Protectionist sentiment has been increasing almost everywhere. In the United States, even a small trade bill, free trade with Central America, attracted enormous opposition, barely passing the House of Representatives by a 217 to 215 vote in July 2005. I do not believe it is tenable to pretend that everything will be fine if we just leave the markets alone. Nor is it tenable to ask workers to have faith that, with enough patience, globalization will make them all better off, even though now they must accept lower wages and decreased job security. Even if they were to accept on faith the proposition that globalization will lead to faster GDP growth, why should they believe that it would lead to faster growth in *their* incomes or an overall increase in *their* well-being? While politicians may refer obliquely to lessons of economics to reassure their constituents, both standard economic theory and a wealth of data is consistent with workers' own intuitions: without strong government redistributive policies, unskilled workers may well be worse off.

Similar issues arise with migration. I have explained . . . how migration may lead to an increase in global efficiency, and how it may be of particular benefit to those in the developing world. But migration of unskilled labor leads to lower wages for unskilled workers in the developed world. With both trade liberalization and migration, the country as a whole may benefit, but those at the bottom are likely to be made worse off.

The second tack is to resist fair globalization. In this view, now is the time for America and Europe to use their economic power to make sure that the rules of the game favor them permanently—or at least for as long as possible. Power begets power; and by using their current combined economic power, they can at least protect their position, and perhaps even enhance it. This is a view based not on what is right or fair but on realpolitik.

In this logic, the United States, while continuing to pay lip service to fair trade, should protect itself from the onslaught of foreign goods and from outsourcing, while at the same time doing what it can to get access to foreign markets. America's seeming brazenness in doubling its agricultural subsidies while preaching the rhetoric of free trade is an example. As a sop to those who insist on fairness, some effort is put into finding "legal" ways of providing these subsidies, such as devising concepts like "non-trade distorting subsidies," getting other countries to agree that such subsidies are allowed, and then claiming that one's subsidies are of that sort. The presumption seems to be that because something is legal, it is morally right.

I believe that this approach is both morally wrong and economically and politically unviable. America's standing in the world has long been based not just on its economic and military power but on its moral leadership, on doing what is right and fair. But for those who believe in realpolitik, this is of little concern. More to the point, this option is not really possible, given how far we already are down the path of globalization. While the Uruguay Round trade agreement may not be fair to the developing countries, it created the beginnings of a semblance of an international rule of law in trade, which the United States has to obey.

Moreover, one of the successes of the last three decades has been the creation of strong democracies in many parts of the developing world. Their citizens know what is going on, and they know when a proposed trade agreement is fundamentally unfair. American citizens may not care about the hypocrisy of its leaders in talking about free trade and maintaining agricultural subsidies, but Brazil's and Argentina's citizens do.

Too much is at stake—and there are too many who have already benefited from globalization—to allow America and Europe to pull back from globalization, to walk away from it. There are too many losers from globalization in the developing world to allow the developed world to try to shape globalization unfairly in its favor.

That leaves but one course—coping with globalization and reshaping it. For America, coping means recognizing that globalization will mean downward pressure on unskilled wages. The advanced industrial countries have to continue upskilling their labor forces, but they also have to strengthen their safety nets and increase the progressivity of their income tax systems; it is the people at the bottom who have been hurt by globalization (and, probably, by other forces, like changing technology); it seems the right thing to do, to lower taxes on them and to increase taxes on those who have been so well served by globalization. Regrettably, in America and elsewhere, policies have been moving in precisely the opposite direction. Investments in research, which will increase the productivity of the economy, are also important. These investments yield high returns. Increased productivity is likely to lead to increased wages and incomes; and if even a portion of the higher income that results is spent on a social agenda of education and health, the well-being of all citizens will be enhanced.

The critics of globalization are right: as it has been managed, there are too many losers. And I think the optimists among these critics—those who, at meetings like the World Social Forum at Mumbai with which I began this reading, claimed that "another world is possible"—are also right. This reading has laid out a number of reforms that would enable globalization more nearly to live up to its potential of benefiting those in both the developed and less developed countries: a reformed globalization that could receive the support of those in both.

▪   ▪   ▪

Over the past two centuries, democracies have learned how to temper the excesses of capitalism: to channel the power of the market, to ensure that there are more winners and fewer losers. The benefits of this process have been staggering, and have given many in the First World wonderfully high standards of living, much higher than were conceivable in 1800.

At the international level, however, we have failed to develop the democratic political institutions that are required if we are to make globalization work—to ensure that the power of the global market economy leads to the improvement of the lives of most of the people of the world, not just the richest in the richest countries. Because of the democratic deficit in the way globalization is managed, its excesses have not been tempered; indeed, as we noted in earlier chapters, globalization has sometimes circumscribed the ability of national democracies to temper the market economy.

The need for global institutions has never been greater, but confidence in them, and their legitimacy, has been eroding. The IMF's repeated failures in managing the crises of the past decade was the coup de grâce, following years of dissatisfaction with its programs in Africa and elsewhere, including the excessive austerity it forced upon these countries. The failure of the countries that followed the IMF–World Bank ideologically driven Washington Consensus policies and the contrast with the ongoing success of the East Asian countries . . . has not helped to restore confidence in these institutions. Neither did the arrogance with which the IMF demanded that it be allowed to force developing countries to open up their markets to speculative capital flows, followed a few years later by a quiet recognition that capital market liberalization might lead to instability but not growth. And while they pushed an agenda that led to financial market instability, they did nothing about one of the root causes of global instability, the global reserve system. At the WTO, in the trade front, matters are no better. After admitting at Doha, in November 2001, that the previous round of trade negotiations was unfair, the advanced industrial countries eventually effectively reneged on their promise of a development round.

The institutions themselves are, in some sense, not to blame: they are run by the United States and the other advanced industrial countries. Their failures represent failure of policy by those countries. The end of the Cold War gave the United States, the one remaining superpower, the opportunity to reshape the global economic and political system based on principles of fairness and concern for the poor; but the absence of competition from communist ideology also gave the United States the opportunity to reshape the global system based on its own self-interest and that of its multinational corporations. Regrettably, in the economic sphere, it chose the latter course.

Just as the international institutions cannot be fully blamed—the responsibility must lie partly with the governments that govern them—the governments themselves cannot be fully blamed. The responsibility lies partly with their voters. We may increasingly be part of a global economy, but almost all of us live in local communities, and continue to think, to an extraordinary degree, locally. It is natural for us to value a job lost at home far more than two jobs gained abroad (or in the context of war, a life lost at home far more than those lost abroad). Part of the mindset of thinking locally is that we don't often think of how policies that we advocate affect others and the global economy. We focus our attention on the direct effect on our *own* well-being. Cotton growers in the United States think of how they gain from their subsidies, not how millions in the rest of the world lose.

To make globalization work there will have to be a change of mind-set: we will have to think and act more globally. Today, too few have this sense of global identity. There is an old aphorism about all politics being local, and, with most people living "locally," it is not surprising that globalization is approached within the very narrow framework of local politics. Local thinking persists even as the world grows more economically interdependent. It is this disjunction between local politics and global problems that is the source of so much of the dissatisfaction with globalization.

The contrast between analysis and advocacy for policies at the national and global level is stark. Within each country, we are aware that laws and regulations affect different people differently. Economists carefully calculate, for each tax, rule, or regulation, the extent to which different income groups are affected. We argue for and against different policies on the basis of whether they are just, whether they hurt the poor, whether their burden falls dispro-portionately on those less well off.

In the international arena, not only do we fail to do the analysis, we almost never argue for a policy on the basis of its fairness. Trade negotiators are told to get the best agreement they can, from the perspective of their country's own interests. They are not sent off to Geneva (where the trade negotiations gener-ally occur) with the mandate to craft an agreement that is fair to all. Special attention is not given, as it should be, to the poorest, but to the strongest—such as the special interests that are the largest contributors to the campaigns of the American president and the party in power. In fact, often the special interests are elevated to be national interests: doing what is best for America's drug companies, for Microsoft and for ExxonMobil, is viewed as equivalent to doing what is best for the country in general. This is encapsulated in the famous quote of Charles Wilson, the head of GM, in 1953 that "what was good for our country was good for General Motors, and vice versa."[7] In the era of globalization, this is no longer true—if it ever was.

Even within the international institutions, seldom is global policy dis-cussed in terms of social justice. There is a pretense that there are no trade-offs, and that, accordingly, decision making can be delegated to technocrats, who are assigned the complex task of finding and managing the best eco-nomic system, and who are thought to be better equipped than politicians to make objective decisions. There are, of course, some problems which should be delegated to technocrats—like choosing the best computer system for run-ning the social security system. But delegating the writing of the rules of the economic game to technocrats can be justified only if there is a single best set of rules, one that makes everyone better off than any other set of rules. This is simply not the case; this view is not only wrong, but dangerous. With a few exceptions, there are always trade-offs. The existence of trade-offs means that there are choices to be made. It is only through the political system that those choices can be properly made, which is why it is so important to rem-edy the global democratic deficit.

Depoliticizing the decision-making process paves the way for decisions that are not representative of broader social interests. By removing deci-sions about the right trade regime or the right intellectual property regime from the *overt* political process, the door is opened to *covert* shaping of those decisions by particular interests. The drug companies can shape intel-lectual property agreements; producers, not consumers, can shape trade pol-icy. Monetary policy provides another example. No economic issue affects people more than the macroeconomic performance of the economy. Increas-ing the unemployment rate makes workers worse off, but the resulting lower inflation makes bondholders happy. Balancing these interests is a quintessentially political activity, but there has been an attempt by those in financial markets to depoliticize the decision, to turn it over to technocrats, with a mandate to pursue the policies that are in the interests of financial markets. The IMF has been encouraging, sometimes even forcing (as a condition of assistance), countries to have their central banks focus *only* on inflation.

Europe succumbed to these doctrines. Today, throughout Euroland, there is unhappiness as the European Central Bank pursues a monetary policy that, while it may do wonders for bond markets by keeping inflation low and bond prices high, has left Europe's growth and employment in shambles.

Responding to the Democratic Deficit

There are two responses to the problem of the democratic deficit in the international institutions. The first is to reform the institutional arrangements, along the lines suggested earlier. . . . But this will not happen overnight. The second is to think more carefully about what decisions are made at the international level.

Globalization means that events in one part of the world have ripple effects elsewhere, as ideas and knowledge, goods and services, and capital and people move more easily across borders. Epidemics never respected borders, but with greater global travel diseases spread more quickly. Greenhouse gases produced in the advanced industrial countries lead to global warming everywhere in the world. Terrorism, too, has become global. As the countries of the world become more closely integrated, they become more interdependent. Greater interdependence gives rise to a greater need for collective action to solve common problems.

The agenda for collective action should focus on those items that represent the most essential areas for benefiting the entire global community. Other items should not be on the agenda.[8] . . . Earlier I argued that there is no need for a uniform set of intellectual property rights rules; excessive standardization not only takes away important degrees of political sovereignty but is actually counterproductive. A focused agenda is especially important because the expansiveness of the agenda itself puts developing countries, which cannot afford large staffs, at a disadvantage in negotiations. Global collective action should focus upon the need to halt negative externalities—actions by one party that adversely affect others—and on the opportunity to promote, by acting together, the well-being of all through the provision of global public goods, the benefits of which are enjoyed around the world.

As the world becomes more globalized, more integrated, there will be more and more areas in which there are opportunities for cooperative action, and in which such collective action is not only desirable but necessary. There is an array of global public goods—from global peace to global health, to preserving the global environment, to global knowledge. If these are not provided *collectively* by the international community, there is a risk—indeed, a likelihood—that they will be underprovided.[9]

Providing global public goods requires some system of finance. . . . An earlier idea described how a reform of the global reserve system can provide a large source of finance, in the order of magnitude of $200 billion to $400 billion a year. A second idea is to use revenues from the management of global resources—auctioning off fishing rights, or the right to extract natural resources beneath the sea, or carbon emissions permits—for providing global public goods. Finally, there are some instances in which taxation can actually contribute to economic efficiency. Such taxes, levied to overcome problems of negative externalities, are called corrective taxes. Taxation on global negative externalities, such as arms sales to developing countries, pollution, and destabilizing cross-border financial flows, can provide a third source of revenues for financing global public goods.

In the long run, the most important changes required to make globalization work are reforms to reduce the democratic deficit. Without such changes, there is a real danger that any reforms will be subverted. . . . For instance, we saw how as tariffs have come down, nontariff barriers have been erected. This is not the place to provide a detailed description of how each of the international institutions needs to be changed. Instead, I list the major elements of any reform package:

- *Changes in voting structure* at the IMF and the World Bank, giving more weight to the developing countries. At the IMF, the United States remains the single country with an effective veto. At both institutions, votes are largely on the basis of economic power—and too often, not economic power today but, to a too large extent, economic power as it existed at the time these institutions were created more than a half century ago.[10]
- *Changes in representation*—who represents each country. So long as trade ministers determine trade policy and finance ministers determine financial policy, other related concerns, like the environment or employment, will be given short shrift. One possible change is to insist that when there are areas of overlapping concerns, all the relevant ministries be represented. When intellectual property provisions are being discussed, surely the science and technology ministries—who may not only have a more balanced position but will even know something about the matter—should be at the table.
- *Adopting principles of representation.* It is difficult to make decisions, or to engage in negotiations, when 100 or more countries are involved. But the way, for instance, that trade negotiators have responded to this problem in the past should be viewed as totally unacceptable. No matter what is done, there will be an imbalance of economic power, and there is little that can be done to stop the powerful from exercising that power; but at the very least, the formal processes should be

more in accord with democratic principles. The major countries should be joined in negotiations by representatives of each of the various major groups: the least developed countries, the small agricultural exporters, and so on. In fact, some progress in this direction is already taking place.

Given that it will be difficult to make these changes, it is all the more important to make the following reforms in the way international institutions operate:

- *Increased transparency.* Because there is no direct democratic accountability for these institutions (we do not vote for our representatives to these institutions or for their leadership), transparency, enforced through strong freedom of information acts, is vital. Ironically, these institutions are *less* transparent than the more democratic of their member governments.
- *Improvements in conflict-of-interest rules* will not only increase confidence in, and the legitimacy of, international governance but (if economists are correct and incentives do matter) might actually lead to policies that are more in the general interest.
- *More openness, including improvements in procedures* to ensure not only more transparency but that more voices are heard. NGOs have taken on increased importance in ensuring that voices other than those of the multinational corporations get heard in the process of global economic decision making. In democracies like the United States, when regulatory agencies propose rules, interested parties are given an opportunity to comment, and the regulatory agency must respond. It should be the same for global institutions and regulatory agencies.
- *Enhancing the ability of developing countries to participate meaningfully in decision making,* by providing them with assistance in assessing the impact on them of proposed changes. The U.S. Treasury and the finance ministries of some of the other advanced industrial countries can make their own assessments, but developing countries typically do not have the resources to do so. The deliberative discussions of the WTO and other international economic organizations would also be helped if there were an independent body to evaluate alternative proposals and their impact on developing countries.
- *Improved accountability.* Even if there is not direct electoral accountability, there can be more independent evaluations of the performance of the international economic institutions. While the World Bank and the IMF presently do this—and, indeed, spend a considerable amount of money on such evaluations—the evaluation units have typically relied heavily on temporary staff supplied by the Fund or the Bank.

Though this has an advantage in that they are well informed about what is going on, it is hard for them to provide a fully independent evaluation. The task of evaluation should be moved—to the UN, for instance. Assessments must be made of the disparity between predicted consequences and what actually happens: Why, for instance, did the IMF bail-out packages not work in the way predicted during the crises? Why was there money available to bail-out international banks, but not money to pay for food subsidies to the poor? Why were the benefits received by many of the poorest countries from the last round of trade negotiations so much less than had been promised?

▪ *Better judicial procedures.* The need for this was highlighted by our earlier discussion . . . of the process by which dumping duties are imposed by the United States, where it is simultaneously the prosecutor, judge, and jury in assessing dumping duties. Such a judicial procedure is obviously flawed. There needs to be an independent global judicial body to determine, for instance, whether dumping has occurred, and if so, what the dumping duties should be.

▪ *Better enforcement of the international rule of law.* I have repeatedly commented on the great achievement of the Uruguay Round in creating the beginning of a semblance of international law. It means that principles, not just power, can govern trade relations. The law may be imperfect, but it is better than no law at all. There are, however, still many areas where the law would make for a better globalization *if it were enforced.* One important instance was noted in the last chapter: America's refusal to do anything about global warming can be considered a major and unwarranted trade subsidy. The enforcement of regulations against such subsidies could be an important instrument both in creating a fairer trading system and in addressing one of today's most important global problems.

We have an imperfect system of global governance without global government; and one imperfection is the limitations on our ability to enforce international agreements and stop negative externalities. We must use what instruments we have—including trade sanctions.[11]

. . . I noted another major problem: the fragmentation of the global trading system into a series of bilateral and regional trade agreements. The great achievement of the multilateral trading system over the past sixty years, the most favored nation principle under which each country gave to every other country the same terms, is now being undermined by the United States, followed by others. Such agreements are legal under WTO rules only when they create more trade than they divert; almost surely, some bilateral agreements would fail this test. There should be an international tribunal to determine whether, as each agreement is proposed, it is legal, with the burden of proof lying with the countries trying to fragment the global trading system. The tribunal would determine, for instance, whether Mexico's gains under NAFTA, to the extent that they exist, arose largely from diversion of the trade in textiles that the United States might have bought from Latin American countries other than Mexico. This might slow down, or even put a stop to, the rash of bilateral agreements that threatens to undermine the multilateral trade system.

Finding a New Balance

What is needed, if we are to make globalization work, is an international economic regime in which the well-being of the developed and developing countries are better balanced: a new *global social contract* between developed and less developed countries. Among the central ingredients are:

- A commitment by developed countries to a fairer trade regime, one that would actually promote development. . . .
- A new approach to intellectual property and the promoting of research, which, while continuing to provide incentives and resources for innovation, would recognize the importance of developing countries' access to knowledge, the necessity of the availability of lifesaving medicines at affordable prices, and the rights of developing countries to have their traditional knowledge protected.
- An agreement by the developed countries to compensate developing countries for their environmental services, both in preservation of biodiversity and contribution to global warming through carbon sequestration.
- A recognition that we—developed and less developed countries alike— share one planet, and that global warming represents a real threat to that planet—one whose effects may be particularly disastrous for some of the developing countries; accordingly, we all need to limit carbon emissions—we need to put aside our squabbling about who's to blame and get down to the serious business of doing something; America, the richest country on the earth, and the most energy profligate, has a special obligation—and one of its states, California—has already shown that there can be enormous emission reductions without eroding standards of living.
- A commitment by the developed countries to pay the developing countries fairly for their natural resources—and to extract them in ways that do not leave behind a legacy of environmental degradation.
- A renewal of the commitments already made by the developed countries to provide financial assistance to the poorer countries of 0.7 percent of GDP—a renewal accompanied this time by actions to fulfill that commitment. If America can afford a trillion dollars to fight a war in Iraq, surely it can afford less than $100 billion a year to fight a global war against poverty.
- An extension of the agreement for debt forgiveness made in July 2005 to more countries: too many countries' aspirations of development are being thwarted by the huge amounts they spend on servicing

their debt—so large, in fact, that, as we noted, net flows of money in some recent years have been going from developing countries to the developed.

- Reforms of the global financial architecture that would reduce its instability—which has had such a crushing effect on so many developing countries—and shift more of the burden of the risk to the developed countries, which are in such a better position to bear these risks. Among the key reforms is a reform in the global reserve system, . . . which, I believe, would not only lead to enhanced stability, from which all would benefit, but could also help finance the global public goods that are so important if we are to make globalization work.

- A host of institutional (legal) reforms—to ensure, for instance, that new global monopolies do not emerge, to handle fairly the complexities of cross-border bankruptcies both of sovereigns and companies, and to force multinational corporations to confront their liabilities, from, for instance, their damage to the environment.

- If the developed countries have been sending too little money to the developing world, they have also been sending too many arms; they have been part and partner in much of the corruption; and in a variety of other ways, they have undermined the fledgling democracies. The global social compact would entail not just lip service on the importance of democracy but the developed countries actually curtailing practices that undermine democracy and doing things to support it—and especially doing more to curtail arms shipments, bank secrecy, and bribery.

For globalization to work, of course, developing countries must do their part. The international community can help create an environment in which development is possible; it can help provide resources and opportunity. But in the end, responsibility for successful, sustainable development—with the fruits of that development widely shared—will have to rest on the shoulders of the developing countries themselves. Not all will succeed; but I believe strongly that with the global social contract described above, far more will succeed than in the past.

Elements of this new global social contract are already in place. At the international meeting on finance for development convened by the UN in Monterrey, Mexico, in March 2002, the advanced industrial countries made a commitment to increase their aid to 0.7 percent of GDP, but the meeting was also important because it recognized—at last—that development is too important and too complex to be left to finance ministers. Finance ministers and central bank governors bring a particular perspective to the discussion—an important perspective, but not the only one. Consider, for instance, the issue of sovereign debt restructuring. No government would entrust legislation setting forth the framework for bankruptcy to a committee dominated by creditor and creditor interests; however, putting the IMF in charge of the bankruptcy proceeding, as the IMF argued should happen, would have created an equivalent situation. Such decisions have to be approached with greater balance.

One way of achieving greater balance is to strengthen the Economic and Social Council at the UN. The Council could play an important role in defining the global economic agenda, in ensuring that attention gets focused not just on issues that are of interest to the advanced industrial countries but on those that are essential to the well-being of the entire world. It could encourage discussions of global financial reform which address the problems of the developing countries—the fact, for instance, that they are left to bear the brunt of exchange rate and interest rate risk. It could push for a reform of the global reserve system, or for new ways of handling sovereign debt restructuring—in which the bankruptcy process is not controlled by creditor countries. It could have a particularly important role in the many issues that cross the "silos" in which so much of international decision making is confined. It could push for the rainforest initiative, . . . which would simultaneously provide developing countries with incentives to maintain their rainforests (with enormous world-wide benefits for reducing global warming and maintaining biodiversity) and with money to promote their development. It could push an intellectual property regime that advances science and pays due respect to other values, like life and access to knowledge. It could make sure that any international oversight of a country's economic policies ("surveillance," as it is often called) focuses not just on inflation, which is of such concern to financial markets, but also on unemployment, which exerts such a toll on workers.

Discontent with globalization as it has been managed has partly reflected the discontent with outcomes, and partly the discontent with the lack of democratic process. Reducing the democratic deficit would be a major step forward in making globalization work on both counts. I have faith that policies and programs that have been subject to democratic scrutiny are likely to be more effective and more sensitive to the concerns of the citizenry.

NOTES

1. In January 2001, there were 17.1 million manufacturing jobs; by December 2004 this was down to 14.3 million. See Bureau of Labor Statistics (at www.bls.gov/), Employment, Hours, and Earnings from the Current Employment Statistics survey (National), Manufacturing employees (seasonally adjusted).

2. See Bureau of Labor Statistics (at www.bls.gov/), Employment, Hours, and Earnings from the Current Employment Statistics survey (National), Manufacturing employees and total nonfarm employees (seasonally adjusted). Probably more important than "outsourcing," however has been the tremendous increases in productivity in manufacturing. Given this productivity increase, there would have been large job losses in manufacturing in any case.

3. World Bank, World Development Indicators, Manufacturing, Value Added (percent of GDP). World Bank, Development Data and Statistics; available by subscription at www.worldbank.org/data/onlinedatabases/onlinedatabases.html.

4. [G]rowth rates in India and China have been two to three times that of the Industrial Revolution, or of the golden age in America in the 1950s and 1960s. See Nicholas Crafts, "Productivity Growth in the Industrial Revolution: A New Growth Accounting Perspective," *Journal of Economic History*, vol. 64, no. 2 (June 2004), pp. 521–35.

5. OECD Observer, "China Ahead in Foreign Direct Investment," August 2003; available at www.oecdobserver.org/news/fullstory.php/aid/1037/China_ahead_in_foreign_direct_investment.html.

6. Economic Policy Institute, "Hourly Wage Decile Cutoffs for All Workers, 1973–2003 (2003 Dollars)," at www.epinet.org/datazone/05/wagecuts_all.pdf.

7. Wilson himself seems to have been more qualified in seeing the two interests as identical. He actually said, in his congressional testimony, "I used to think that what was good for our country was good for General Motors, and vice versa." See James G. Cobb, "G.M. Removes Itself from Industrial Pedestal," *New York Times*, May 30, 1999, sect. 3, p. 4.

8. This is an example of what is sometimes called the principle of subsidiarity—issues should be addressed at the lowest level at which effective action can be undertaken.

9. Just as, without national governments, there will be underprovision of national public goods. Economists refer to this as the "free rider problem"—since everybody benefits (and it may be impossible or costly to exclude anyone from the benefits), there is a tendency for each to free ride on the efforts of others.

10. In its spring 2006 meeting, the IMF's managing director proposed modest changes in voting rights in this direction, but, not surprisingly, such proposals encountered resistance from some of those whose relative voting rights would be reduced.

11. [T]he current system of trade sanctions is far more effective in inducing responses by developing countries to violations in WTO rules against developed countries than the converse.

15.2

Kelo v. New London (2005)

In this controversial 2005 decision, the Supreme Court upheld the right of a local government to take land from private property owners (with just compensation) so that the land could be used for development deemed beneficial to the community. Forcing the sale of private property to the government is permitted in some circumstances, such as in building new highways or airports, under the doctrine of eminent domain from the Fifth Amendment. What was new here was extending eminent domain to include economic development projects by governments.

Justice Stevens delivered the opinion of the Court

In 2000, the city of New London approved a development plan that, in the words of the Supreme Court of Connecticut, was "projected to create in excess of 1,000 jobs, to increase tax and other revenues, and to revitalize an economically distressed city, including its downtown and waterfront areas." In assembling the land needed for this project, the city's development agent has purchased property from willing sellers and proposes to use the power of eminent domain to acquire the remainder of the property from unwilling owners in exchange for just compensation. The question presented is whether the city's proposed disposition of this property qualifies as a "public use" within the meaning of the Takings Clause of the Fifth Amendment to the Constitution.

I

The city of New London (hereinafter City) sits at the junction of the Thames River and the Long Island Sound in southeastern Connecticut. Decades of economic decline led a state agency in 1990 to designate the City a "distressed municipality." In 1996, the Federal Government closed the Naval Undersea Warfare Center, which had been located in the Fort Trumbull area of the City and had employed over 1,500 people. In 1998, the City's unemployment rate was nearly double that of the State, and its population of just under 24,000 residents was at its lowest since 1920.

These conditions prompted state and local officials to target New London, and particularly its Fort Trumbull area, for economic revitalization. To this end, respondent New London Development Corporation (NLDC), a private nonprofit entity established some years earlier to assist the City in planning economic development, was reactivated. In January 1998, the State authorized a $5.35 million bond issue to support the NLDC's planning activities and a $10 million bond issue toward the creation of a Fort Trumbull State Park. In February, the pharmaceutical company Pfizer Inc. announced that it would build a $300 million research facility on a site immediately adjacent to Fort Trumbull; local planners hoped that Pfizer would draw new business to the area, thereby serving as a catalyst to the area's rejuvenation. After receiving initial approval from the city council, the NLDC continued its planning activities and held a series of neighborhood meetings to educate the public about the process. In May, the city council authorized the NLDC to formally submit its plans to the relevant state agencies for review. Upon obtaining state-level approval, the NLDC finalized an integrated development plan focused on 90 acres of the Fort Trumbull area.

The Fort Trumbull area is situated on a peninsula that juts into the Thames River. The area comprises approximately 115 privately owned properties, as well as the 32 acres of land formerly occupied by the naval facility (Trumbull State Park now occupies 18 of those 32 acres). The development plan encompasses seven parcels. Parcel 1 is designated for a waterfront conference hotel at the center of a "small urban village" that will include restaurants and shopping. This parcel will also have marinas for both recreational and commercial uses. A pedestrian "riverwalk" will originate here and continue down the coast, connecting the waterfront areas of the development. Parcel 2 will be the site of approximately 80 new residences organized into an urban neighborhood and linked by public walkway to the remainder of the development, including the state park. This parcel also includes space reserved for a new U.S. Coast Guard Museum. Parcel 3, which is located immediately north of the Pfizer facility, will contain at least 90,000 square feet of research and development office space. Parcel 4A is a 2.4-acre site that will be used either to support the adjacent state park, by providing parking or retail services for visitors, or to support the nearby marina. Parcel 4B will include a renovated marina, as well as the final stretch of the riverwalk. Parcels 5, 6, and 7 will provide land for office and retail space, parking, and water-dependent commercial uses.

The NLDC intended the development plan to capitalize on the arrival of the Pfizer facility and the new commerce it was expected to attract. In addition to creating jobs, generating tax revenue, and helping to "build momentum for the revitalization of downtown New London," the plan was also designed to make the City more attractive and to create leisure and recreational opportunities on the waterfront and in the park.

The city council approved the plan in January 2000, and designated the NLDC as its development agent in charge of implementation. The city council also authorized the NLDC to purchase property or to acquire property by exercising eminent domain in the City's name. §8–193. The NLDC successfully negotiated the purchase of most of the real estate in the 90-acre area, but its negotiations with petitioners failed. As a consequence, in November 2000, the NLDC initiated the condemnation proceedings that gave rise to this case.

II

Petitioner Susette Kelo has lived in the Fort Trumbull area since 1997. She has made extensive improvements to her house, which she prizes for its water view. Petitioner Wilhelmina Dery was born in her Fort Trumbull house in 1918 and has lived there her entire life. Her husband Charles (also a petitioner) has lived in the house since they married some 60 years ago. In all, the nine petitioners own 15 properties in Fort Trumbull-4 in parcel 3 of the development plan and 11 in parcel 4A. Ten of the parcels are occupied by the owner or a family member; the other five are held as investment properties. There is no allegation that any of these properties is blighted or otherwise in poor condition; rather, they were condemned only because they happen to be located in the development area.

In December 2000, petitioners brought this action in the New London Superior Court. They claimed, among other things, that the taking of their properties would violate the "public use" restriction in the Fifth Amendment. After a 7-day bench trial, the Superior Court granted a permanent restraining order prohibiting the taking of the properties located in parcel 4A (park or marina support). It, however, denied petitioners relief as to the properties located in parcel 3 (office space).

After the Superior Court ruled, both sides took appeals to the Supreme Court of Connecticut. That court held, over a dissent, that all of the City's proposed takings were valid. It began by upholding the lower court's determination that the takings were authorized by chapter 132, the State's municipal development statute. That statute expresses a legislative determination that the taking of land, even developed land, as part of an economic development project is a "public use" and in the "public interest." Next, relying on cases such as *Hawaii Housing Authority v. Midkiff,* (1984), and *Berman v. Parker,* (1954), the court held that such economic development qualified as a valid public use under both the Federal and State Constitutions.

Finally, adhering to its precedents, the court went on to determine, first, whether the takings of the particular properties at issue were "reasonably necessary" to achieving the City's intended public use, and, second, whether the takings were for "reasonably foreseeable needs." The court upheld the trial court's factual findings as to parcel 3, but reversed the trial court as to parcel 4A, agreeing with the City that the intended use of this land was sufficiently definite and had been given "reasonable attention" during the planning process.

The three dissenting justices would have imposed a "heightened" standard of judicial review for takings justified by economic development. Although they agreed that the plan was intended to serve a valid public use, they would have found all the takings unconstitutional because the City had failed to adduce "clear and convincing evidence" that the economic benefits of the plan would in fact come to pass.

We granted certiorari to determine whether a city's decision to take property for the purpose of economic development satisfies the "public use" requirement of the Fifth Amendment.

III

Two polar propositions are perfectly clear. On the one hand, it has long been accepted that the sovereign may not take the property of *A* for the sole purpose of transferring it to another private party *B*, even though *A* is paid just compensation. On the other hand, it is equally clear that a State may transfer property from one private party to another if future "use by the public" is the purpose of the taking; the condemnation of land for a railroad with common-carrier duties is a familiar example. Neither of these propositions, however, determines the disposition of this case.

As for the first proposition, the City would no doubt be forbidden from taking petitioners' land for the purpose of conferring a private benefit on a particular private party. Nor would the City be allowed to take property under the mere pretext of a public purpose, when its actual purpose was to bestow a private benefit. The takings before us, however, would be executed pursuant to a "carefully considered" development plan. The trial judge and all the members of the Supreme Court of Connecticut agreed that there was no evidence of an illegitimate purpose in this case. Therefore, as was true of the statute challenged in *Midkiff*, the City's development plan was not adopted "to benefit a particular class of identifiable individuals."

On the other hand, this is not a case in which the City is planning to open the condemned land—at least not in its entirety—to use by the general public. Nor will the private lessees of the land in any sense be required to operate like common carriers, making their services available to all comers. But although such a projected use would be sufficient to satisfy the public use requirement, this "Court long ago rejected any literal requirement that condemned property be put into use for the general public." Indeed, while many state courts in the mid-19th century endorsed "use by the public" as the proper definition of public use, that narrow view steadily eroded over time. Not only was the "use by the public" test difficult to administer (*e.g.*, what proportion of the public need have access to the property? at what price?), but it proved to be impractical given the diverse and always evolving needs of society. Accordingly, when this Court began applying the Fifth Amendment to the States at the close of the 19th century, it embraced the broader and more natural interpretation of public use as "public purpose." Thus, in a case upholding a mining company's use of an aerial bucket line to transport ore over property it did not own, Justice Holmes' opinion for the Court stressed "the inadequacy of use by the general public as a universal test." *Strickley v. Highland Boy Gold Mining Co.,* (1906). We have repeatedly and consistently rejected that narrow test ever since.

The disposition of this case therefore turns on the question whether the City's development plan serves a "public purpose." Without exception, our cases have defined that concept broadly, reflecting our longstanding policy of deference to legislative judgments in this field.

In *Berman v. Parker,* (1954), this Court upheld a redevelopment plan targeting a blighted area of Washington, D.C., in which most of the housing for the area's 5,000 inhabitants was beyond repair. Under the plan, the area would be condemned and part of it utilized for the construction of streets, schools, and other public facilities. The remainder of the land would be leased or sold to private parties for the purpose of redevelopment, including the construction of low-cost housing.

The owner of a department store located in the area challenged the condemnation, pointing out that his store was not itself blighted and arguing that the creation of a "better balanced, more attractive community" was not a valid public use. Writing for a unanimous Court, Justice Douglas refused to evaluate this claim in isolation, deferring instead to the legislative and agency judgment that the area "must be planned as a whole" for the plan to be successful. The Court explained that "community redevelopment programs need not, by force of the Constitution, be on a piecemeal basis—lot by lot, building by building." The public use underlying the taking was unequivocally affirmed:

"We do not sit to determine whether a particular housing project is or is not desirable. The concept of the public welfare is broad and inclusive. . . . The values it represents are spiritual as well as physical, aesthetic as well as monetary. It is within the power of the legislature to determine that the community should be beautiful as well as healthy, spacious as well as clean, well-balanced as well as carefully patrolled. In the present case, the Congress and its authorized agencies have made determinations that take into account a wide variety of values. It is not for us to reappraise them. If those who govern the District of Columbia decide that the Nation's Capital should be beautiful as well as sanitary, there is nothing in the Fifth Amendment that stands in the way."

In *Hawaii Housing Authority v. Midkiff,* (1984), the Court considered a Hawaii statute whereby fee title was taken from lessors and transferred to lessees (for just compensation) in order to reduce the concentration of land ownership. We unanimously upheld the statute and rejected the Ninth Circuit's view that it was "a naked attempt on the part of the state of Hawaii to take the property of A and transfer it to B solely for B's private use and benefit." Reaffirming *Berman*'s deferential approach to legislative judgments in this field, we concluded that the State's purpose of eliminating the "social and economic evils of a land oligopoly" qualified as a valid public use. Our opinion also rejected the contention that the mere fact that the State immediately transferred the properties to private individuals upon condemnation somehow diminished the public character of the taking. "[I]t is only the taking's purpose, and not its mechanics," we explained, that matters in determining public use.

In that same Term we decided another public use case that arose in a purely economic context. In *Ruckelshaus v. Monsanto, Co.*, (1984), the Court dealt with provisions of the Federal Insecticide, Fungicide, and Rodenticide Act under which the Environmental Protection Agency could consider the data (including trade secrets) submitted by a prior pesticide applicant in evaluating a subsequent application, so long as the second applicant paid just compensation for the data. We acknowledged that the "most direct beneficiaries" of these provisions were the subsequent applicants, but we nevertheless upheld the statute under *Berman* and *Midkiff.* We found sufficient Congress' belief that sparing applicants the cost of time-consuming research eliminated a significant barrier to entry in the pesticide market and thereby enhanced competition.

Viewed as a whole, our jurisprudence has recognized that the needs of society have varied between different parts of the Nation, just as they have evolved over time in response to changed circumstances. Our earliest cases in particular embodied a strong theme of federalism, emphasizing the "great respect" that we owe to state legislatures and state courts in discerning local public needs. For more than a century, our public use jurisprudence has wisely eschewed rigid formulas and intrusive scrutiny in favor of affording legislatures broad latitude in determining what public needs justify the use of the takings power.

IV

Those who govern the City were not confronted with the need to remove blight in the Fort Trumbull area, but their determination that the area was sufficiently distressed to justify a program of economic rejuvenation is entitled to our deference. The City has carefully formulated an economic development plan that it believes will provide appreciable benefits to the community, including—but by no means limited to—new jobs and increased tax revenue. As with other exercises in urban planning and development, the City is endeavoring to coordinate a variety of commercial, residential, and recreational uses of land, with the hope that they will form a whole greater than the sum of its parts. To effectuate this plan, the City has invoked a state statute that specifically authorizes the use of eminent domain to promote economic development. Given the comprehensive character of the plan, the thorough deliberation that preceded its adoption, and the limited scope of our review, it is appropriate for us, as it was in *Berman*, to resolve the challenges of the individual owners, not on a piece-meal basis, but rather in light of the entire plan. Because that plan unquestionably serves a public purpose, the takings challenged here satisfy the public use requirement of the Fifth Amendment.

To avoid this result, petitioners urge us to adopt a new bright-line rule that economic development does not qualify as a public use. Putting aside the unpersuasive suggestion that the City's plan will provide only purely economic benefits, neither precedent nor logic supports petitioners' proposal. Promoting economic development is a traditional and long accepted function of government. There is, moreover, no principled way of distinguishing economic development from the other public purposes that we have recognized. In our cases upholding takings that facilitated agriculture and mining, for example, we emphasized the importance of those industries to the welfare of the States in question, see, *e.g., Strickley*; in *Berman*, we endorsed the purpose of transforming a blighted area into a "well-balanced" community through redevelopment, in *Midkiff*, we upheld the interest in breaking up a land oligopoly that "created artificial deterrents to the normal functioning of the State's residential land market," and in *Monsanto*, we accepted Congress' purpose of eliminating a "significant barrier to entry in the pesticide market." It would be incongruous to hold that the City's interest in the economic benefits to be derived from the development of the Fort Trumbull area has less of a public character than any of those other interests. Clearly, there is no basis for exempting economic development from our traditionally broad understanding of public purpose.

Petitioners contend that using eminent domain for economic development impermissibly blurs the boundary between public and private takings. Again, our cases foreclose this objection. Quite simply, the government's pursuit of a public purpose will often benefit individual private parties. For example, in *Midkiff*, the forced transfer of property conferred a direct and significant benefit on those lessees who were previously unable to purchase their homes. In *Monsanto*, we recognized that the "most direct beneficiaries" of the data-sharing provisions were the subsequent pesticide applicants, but benefiting them in this way was necessary to promoting competition in the pesticide market. The owner of the department store in *Berman* objected to "taking from one businessman for the benefit of another businessman," referring to the fact that under the redevelopment plan land would be leased or sold to private developers for redevelopment. Our rejection of that contention has particular relevance to the instant case: "The public end may be as well or better served through an agency of private enterprise than through a department of government—or so the Congress might conclude. We cannot say that public ownership is the sole method of promoting the public purposes of community redevelopment projects."

It is further argued that without a bright-line rule nothing would stop a city from transferring citizen *A*'s property to citizen *B* for the sole reason that citizen *B* will put the property to a more productive use and thus pay more taxes. Such a one-to-one transfer of property, executed outside the confines of an integrated development plan, is not presented in this case. While such an unusual exercise of government power would certainly raise a suspicion that a private purpose was afoot, the hypothetical cases posited by petitioners can be confronted if and when they arise. They do not warrant the crafting of an artificial restriction on the concept of public use.

Alternatively, petitioners maintain that for takings of this kind we should require a "reasonable certainty" that the expected public benefits will actually accrue. Such a rule, however, would represent an even greater departure from our precedent. "When the legislature's purpose is legitimate and its means are not irrational, our cases make clear that empirical debates over the wisdom of takings—no less than debates over the wisdom of other kinds of socioeconomic legislation—are not to be carried out in the federal courts." *Midkiff.* Indeed, earlier this Term we explained why similar practical concerns (among others) undermined the use of the "substantially advances" formula in our regulatory takings doctrine. The disadvantages of a heightened form of review are especially pronounced in this type of case. Orderly implementation of a comprehensive redevelopment plan obviously requires that the legal rights of all interested parties be established before new construction can be commenced. A constitutional rule that required postponement of the judicial approval of every condemnation until the likelihood of success of the plan had been assured would unquestionably impose a significant impediment to the successful consummation of many such plans.

Just as we decline to second-guess the City's considered judgments about the efficacy of its development plan, we also decline to second-guess the City's determinations as to what lands it needs to acquire in order to effectuate the project. "It is not for the courts to oversee the choice of the boundary line nor to sit in review on the size of a particular project area. Once the question of the public purpose has been decided, the amount and character of land to be taken for the project and the need for a particular tract to complete the integrated plan rests in the discretion of the legislative branch." *Berman.*

In affirming the City's authority to take petitioners' properties, we do not minimize the hardship that condemnations may entail, notwithstanding the payment of just compensation. We emphasize that nothing in our opinion precludes any State from placing further restrictions on its exercise of the takings power. Indeed, many States already impose "public use" requirements that are stricter than the federal baseline. Some of these requirements have been established as a matter of state constitutional law, while others are expressed in state eminent domain statutes that carefully limit the grounds upon which takings may be exercised. As the submissions of the parties and their *amici* make clear, the necessity and wisdom of using eminent domain to promote economic development are certainly matters of legitimate public debate. This Court's authority, however, extends only to determining whether the City's proposed condemnations are for a "public use" within the meaning of the Fifth Amendment to the Federal Constitution. Because over a century of our case law interpreting that provision dictates an affirmative answer to that question, we may not grant petitioners the relief that they seek.

The judgment of the Supreme Court of Connecticut is affirmed.

It is so ordered.

16

SOCIAL POLICY

16.1

FRANK R. BAUMGARTNER AND BRYAN D. JONES

From *Agendas and Instability in American Politics*

Why do certain social problems arise on the agenda of the national government, leading to demands by the public for new social policies? Baumgartner and Jones compare two theories. One predicts that issues like pesticides or smoking burst onto the scene due to negative media publicity, but then slowly fade from the government's agenda as the public loses attention. The other predicts that, once an issue is on the agenda, interest groups push for a government response, usually a set of regulations or agency actions, that forever transform the issue. A new set of interest groups need to keep that issue on the agenda. The authors find support for the latter theory.

5. TWO MODELS OF ISSUE EXPANSION

The Dual Mobilization Theories of Downs and Schattschneider

In his classic article "Up and Down with Ecology," Anthony Downs (1972) argues that public attention to political issues typically follows a cyclical pattern. In Downs's approach, a preproblem stage is characterized by low attention. Then a state of alarmed discovery and euphoria generates much attention, followed by a realization of the costs of solving the problem and a gradual decline in public interest. This is a decidedly pessimistic view of the agenda-setting process. According to Downs, hitting the agenda is of little policy relevance, for the public and the national political leaders are likely soon to reach the conclusion that action is futile, that the costs of solving the problem are too high, or that some other problem requires their attention even more urgently. Taken to its logical conclusion, this view of agenda-setting implies a never-ending series of "alarmed discoveries" during which the public suddenly focuses on an issue, but after which serious action may never take place. Attention simply fades as the difficulties of action become clear or as some new crisis pushes the old one out of the limelight.

Certainly some issues have followed the pattern described by Downs, but on the other hand, some issues remain on the agenda for quite some time. Now twenty years after his discussion of "ecology," environmental issues remain much higher on the national political agenda than they were at any time before Downs wrote about them, for example. So the cyclical pattern described by Downs is not the only possible outcome of the agenda-setting process. Agenda dynamics have important policy consequences; they are not simple exercises in futility. Some issues remain high on the public agenda for considerable periods of time, and some problems really do get solved, surprising as this might sound.

▪ ▪ ▪

When public attention focuses on some new problem in the way described by Downs, feelings of optimism lead policymakers to fund the research or to implement the programs of specialists who claim to have a solution. Specialists with potential solutions of course waste no time in asking for programs to be implemented, and, as John Kingdon (1984) describes, policies then result from the combinations of the problems that interest political leaders and the solutions proposed by the bureaucratic and other experts. The institution of new programs, policies, and agencies is thus strongly associated with the agenda-setting process.

Down's theory of cycles may be approximately correct when dealing with public attention to problems that lack a feasible solution. Attention surges, declines, as the futility of action becomes clear. Where solutions are present in the form of existing governmental programs, initiatives, and institutions, however, a surge in public attention to a problem may lead to the enactment of new programs and to the growth of new institutions. . . .

Consider the development and breakup of the civilian nuclear power subsystem in the United States. That issue went through at least two distinct periods of emergence on the national political agenda, each associated with opposite results for the industry. A period of enthusiasm for the potentials of nuclear power led government leaders to create an extremely favorable set of institutions in order to support and develop the industry. In the pages to come we call such a mobilization of enthusiasm a Downsian mobilization. In such mobilizations, government is called on to solve problems or take advantage of new technologies.

Public attention to nuclear power then faded, as the plants took years to build, as cost overruns multiplied, and as other issues came to the forefront of the nation's political agenda. But the institutional subsystem remained, and it worked quietly for about two decades implementing the new policy of encouraging greater use of nuclear power, building and ordering more nuclear plants in the United States than in any other country in the world. So the period of optimism and positive mobilization did not last for long, but it left a tremendous institutional legacy.

Nuclear power of course is no longer associated with the positive image it enjoyed in the early postwar years. Neither has it receded permanently from the agenda. Its reemergence on the political agenda in the 1970s was certainly not associated with enthusiasm, but with fear, mistrust, complaints, and criticism. We call this a Schattschneider mobilization since it often stems from the efforts of opponents of the status quo to expand the scope of conflict (Schattschneider 1960). Here the government is already involved in the solution, and some have begun to see the solution as the problem. Hence the issue must be expanded beyond the confines of the existing policymaking system.

■   ■   ■

Just as the Downsian mobilization led to the creation of the favorable institutional structure that the industry enjoyed for decades, the Schattschneider mobilization led to the destruction of these favorable structures. Two waves of mobilization, one positive for the industry, one negative, led to the emergence of the issue on the public agenda twice during the postwar period, each time with important institutional and policy changes. In between these periods of emergence, changes in nuclear power policy were mostly incremental. The system appeared to be near equilibrium during each period of low public attention, but this apparent equilibrium was punctuated by the emergence of the issue on the public agenda, when dramatic policy changes occurred.

■   ■   ■

Smoking and Tobacco Policies in the Twentieth Century

The tobacco industry in the United States benefits from a series of favorable institutional arrangements centering on agricultural subsidies to farmers. At the same time, the government is active in antismoking campaigns. When we look at the history of public attention and government action toward smoking since the turn of the century, we develop a better understanding of how these diverse governmental reactions came to be. Tobacco once generated almost no coverage in the media, and government actions were almost entirely supportive of the agricultural subsidy program. Tobacco, like wheat or corn, was seen as an important crop that generated export earnings, supported millions of farmers, and on which whole communities and even some state economies were dependent. With tobacco seen as an economic issue, the role of political leaders was clear: they should defer to experts and allow the agricultural subsystem to run its course. This is precisely what happened during the entire first half of the century.

FIGURE 1 Annual Coverage of Smoking in the *Readers' Guide* and Tobacco Consumption, 1900–1986

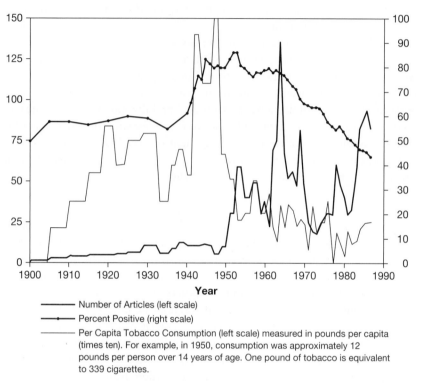

Year

——— Number of Articles (left scale)

——•— Percent Positive (right scale)

——— Per Capita Tobacco Consumption (left scale) measured in pounds per capita (times ten). For example, in 1950, consumption was approximately 12 pounds per person over 14 years of age. One pound of tobacco is equivalent to 339 cigarettes.

SOURCE: *Statistical Abstract of the United States.*

As can be seen in figure 1, media attention to smoking and tobacco questions has varied widely during the century. A total of 2,020 articles has appeared in the *Readers' Guide*, but these have been distributed very unevenly across the years. Coverage during the pre- 1950 period averaged only about 6 articles per year, but annual articles on smoking averaged 38 in the 1950s, 62 in the 1960s, 31 in the 1970s, and 58 from 1980 to 1987. In 1964 alone, the year of the surgeon general's report on smoking, there were 136 articles listed in the *Readers' Guide*, more than twenty times the prewar average.

Smoking received scant press coverage prior to the 1950s, and what coverage it received was decidedly mixed in tone. Press attention to cigarettes and smoking during World War Two was overwhelmingly positive, focusing on the use of cigarettes as barter by GIs in Europe, on shortages and rationing, on the size of the tobacco crop, and on other items that could not be considered bad for industry. Essentially, figure 1 shows that smoking has never been seen with great enthusiasm in the national media, but it was mostly a nonissue for the first fifty years of this century. A few negative articles might have appeared each year, but so did a few positive ones.

Figure 1 also shows how media attention to smoking and tobacco questions seems to have been related to the behavior itself. During the postwar years, the industry and the habit were glamorized in popular culture. Per capita consumption of tobacco in the United States increased from about eight pounds per person during the 1930s to eleven or twelve pounds during the 1950s (figures are from the *Statistical Abstract* [Bureau of the Census 1991]). Smoking was not a new industry to be built from scratch after World War Two. Rather, a powerful subsystem was already in place before the war, centering on agricultural subsidies for tobacco farmers (Fritschler 1989; Ripley and Franklin 1991, 88–90). The buildup of the tobacco subsystem appears to have its roots before the turn of the century, so we cannot discuss it as we did for nuclear power. We can see its continued operation and expansion during the first half of the century, however, and we can certainly observe its demise.

The dramatic increases in levels of coverage of smoking issues in the media that occurred in the years following World War Two were driven almost exclusively by negatives. Health warnings had always been a part of the media's coverage of this issue, but these suddenly became the dominant force during the 1960s. As more people began to smoke, health officials mobilized in an extremely effective manner. The number of articles we have coded as negative grew from an average of only 2 per year before 1950 to 20 during the 1950s, to 41 during the 1960s, 19 during the 1970s, and 44 during the 1980s. (There was also a slight increase in the number of positive stories on smoking, from 2 per year before 1950 to an average of 6 in the years from 1950 to 1987, but growth in the negatives far outstripped growth in the positives.) Following this explosion of emphasis on the health risks of smoking, per capita consumption of tobacco began its remarkable decline, which has continued unabated for three decades.

In the case of smoking, a Schattschneider mobilization was clearly evident: opponents of the industry were able to generate lots of bad news. This increase in public awareness led to a dramatic change in public behavior. Industry leaders had benefited from a long period of low public attention to the public health and public policy consequences of smoking policy during the prewar years and had benefited from a true glorification of smoking immediately after the war. This period of positive attention did not last, however, and the industry was not able to control the expansion of conflict once public attention shifted to public health questions.

■   ■   ■

While smoking became part of the systemic agenda during the 1960s, and even to some extent during the 1950s, it was not until the mid-1970s that the issue burst onto the congressional agenda. When it did, however, it followed a pattern remarkably similar to the one we observed for nuclear power. As the total number of hearings increased, the hearings were held before an increasing number of different congressional bodies. During the period when there was little congressional attention to smoking and tobacco questions, a large

FIGURE 2 Congressional Hearings on Smoking

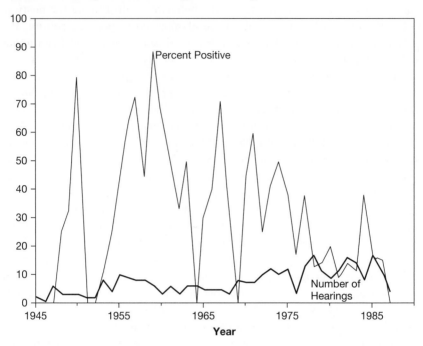

proportion of congressional hearings were relatively positive toward the industry; however, as participation expanded, this expansion was associated almost exclusively with criticism. Criticism did not come from previous allies changing their minds; rather it stemmed from conflict expansion, as previously uninvolved persons began to assert themselves.

The percentage of topics that our coders coded as proindustry in the congressional hearings declined steadily as the number of hearings increased, as the bottom part of figure 2 shows. This is precisely the pattern we expect to be associated with a Schattschneider mobilization. Opponents of the industry are able to appeal to congressional allies to hold hearings and generate adverse publicity. The more they are successful in generating adverse publicity and consideration on the systemic agenda, the more they are likely to be heard on the formal agenda. The more they are heard on the formal agenda, the more adverse publicity is likely to be generated in the media. So the Schattschneider mobilization process is a self-reinforcing mechanism, leading to dramatic, not only incremental, change.

Pesticides

Beginning in the early part of the twentieth century, demand for pesticides began to increase dramatically as the size and variety of farms changed from family producers to large-scale commercial ventures (Bosso 1987). Compared to modern chemicals, of course, the first pesticides were extremely mild and ineffectual, but they did increase crop yields significantly, and their use spread rapidly. As the chemicals became popular, a great number of manufacturers entered the market, and farmers were presented with a confusing variety of products. The first problems associated with the pesticides industry stemmed mostly from farmers not knowing the harmful effects of combining two pesticides, or not knowing the toxicity to skin or from ingestion of the chemicals. By the first decade of this century there was considerable fraud in the industry, with poor labeling of products one of the main sources of problems. Congress first regulated the pesticides industry when it passed the Insecticide Act of 1910, mostly a truth-in-labeling act (Bosso 1987; Dunlap 1981). Enforcement was entrusted to the Bureau of Chemistry in the Department of Agriculture. Agriculture officials saw their mission as one of protecting the farmer from unsafe products even while encouraging the increased use of chemical pesticide. One small voice within the USDA, the Food and Drug Administration, was concerned with the residue levels of toxic agents left on food, but the FDA did not have jurisdiction over pesticide questions, and its studies were generally ignored by USDA officials.

Research during World War Two yielded a new generation of pesticides—synthetic organics such as DDT. These chemicals were stronger and more persistent than their predecessors, and were thought to be nontoxic to humans. Proponents made optimistic claims for the new generation of pesticides, claiming that they would end malaria, increase food production to the point of ending world hunger, and even completely eradicate those persistent pests, the housefly and the mosquito. These arguments should sound familiar to our readers by now. They had the same effect as those arguments in favor of nuclear power. They were also responsible for a later backlash against the industry. Just as in the case of nuclear power, the postwar years saw a great American enthusiasm for the progress of science, this time as represented in the pesticides industry. American science and industry would turn its efforts from the war in Europe and Japan to another war, this one with the purpose of eradicating world hunger and disease through increased use of pesticides.

The strength of this wave of enthusiasm for progress through chemistry is graphically depicted in figure 3. Like smoking, pesticides were mostly a nonissue throughout the beginning of the century, and what little attention they did receive in the popular press came mostly from farm magazines, where their virtues were almost uniformily extolled. Popular coverage of the issue shot up dramatically in the late war years and has remained higher ever since.

The wave of popular attention to the pesticides industry in the late war years was overwhelmingly positive in tone. In this environment Congress passed its second major piece of legislation concerning the industry. The Federal Insecticide, Fungicide, and Rodenticide Act of 1947 (FIFRA) passed with the strong support of both agricultural and chemical industry interests. Christopher Bosso writes that "the shared assumptions about pesticides as a

FIGURE 3   Annual Coverage of Pesticides in the *Readers' Guide*

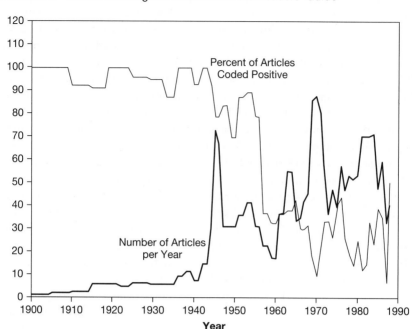

panacea, and the imperatives motivating their widespread use, provided the parameters for policy debate" (1987, 59). A cozy triangle governing pesticides (the Department of Agriculture; farm interests and chemical companies; and the congressional agriculture and appropriations committees) quickly controlled the regulation and use of these powerful new chemicals. Consumer interests, represented by the FDA, and environmental interests, basically unorganized, were excluded from participation. In other words, a Downsian mobilization took place in the late 1940s for pesticides. Great popular and official enthusiasm about the potentials of the industry to do good led government officials in Congress and the executive branch to facilitate the growth of the industry. They set up an institutional structure, based in the Agriculture Department, that promoted the industry for decades to come.

During the 1950s, the "golden age" of pesticides, widespread campaigns were developed to promote the use of pesticides, and local extension agents fanned out across the country encouraging and teaching farmers to increase their use of the chemicals. The degree of official optimism about the glories of pesticides is dramatically illustrated by two major policy disasters of the late 1950s. In 1957 the USDA launched two huge pest eradication campaigns, one in the Northeast, directed at the gypsy moth, and one in the South, aimed at the fire ant. Both involved massive aerial spraying; both resulted in huge fish kills, enormous crop damage, and the devastation of wildlife. Neither campaign was successful in eradicating the pest (see Bosso 1987). Figure 3 shows the decline in the positive tone of pesticide coverage in the press, coinciding exactly with the eradication programs—a decline in public image from which the industry never recovered. Another blow to the pesticides industry occurred in late 1959 when the FDA for the first time banned the sale of a crop because of pesticide residues. The cranberry scare, coming just before the holiday season, devastated annual sales of an entire crop, but more importantly it solidified the public's newly negative view of pesticides.

One simple example gives an idea of how small beginnings of criticism can be compounded through the interaction of image and venue. In reaction to the negative attention associated with the failed eradication campaigns in the late 1950s, of course a number of congressmen began to pay attention to pesticide issues where they had ignored them in the past. One of these was Rep. James Delaney, who became interested in the possible contamination of food through residues. The Delaney hearings in 1958, which led to the Food Additive Amendment, were home to a fierce battle among agricultural interests, health officials, and the food industry. The substantive legislative outcome of the hearings was a single important new rule: "no additive shall be deemed safe if it is found to induce cancer when ingested by man or animal" (Bosso 1987, 97). The institutional outcome of these debates was that the Food and Drug Administration, long the bureaucratic loser in its conflicts with Agriculture officials, was given expanded authority to restrict toxic residues in food. The cranberry scare, coming in 1959, could be seen as an adept piece of bureaucratic expansionism from a group that understood that increasing public attention to a problem in an especially dramatic way is one way to shift the issue from the bureaucratic institutions, where they continually lose, to the front pages of the papers and to congressional hearings, where their side might stand a better chance. From one change in levels of attention, new participants are called into a debate, then their participation leads to changes in the rules, leading to further changes in participation and public understanding of the issue: a pattern of self-reinforcement that we see again and again.

The golden age of pesticides in the United States was relatively short. The wave of popular enthusiasm about the benefits of the new industry lasted only from about 1945 until about 1956. After that, popular attention to the pesticide question was much more likely to focus on the problems than on the promises of the industry. However, our Downsian mobilization hypothesis implies that a powerful set of institutions may be set up during the initial period of popular enthusiasm, and this group of industry boosters may be powerful for years to come. This is exactly what occurred in the case of pesticides. It was several years before the Schattschneider mobilization of public outcry against the industry was able to make a significant difference.

The Schattschneider mobilization followed the abrupt reversal in the public image of pesticides that was associated with the three disasters of the late

1950s: the gypsy moth and fire ant campaigns and the cranberry scare. Attention did not reach its peak until the late 1960s, however. Rachel Carson's 1962 book, *Silent Spring* (parts of which were published in the 16, 23, and 30 June 1962 issues of *The New Yorker*), did not really change ideas about pesticides—the news was already bad for the industry, as can be seen in figure 3. Rather, it solidified a movement that had already gathered considerable steam. A rancorous debate between environmentalists and industry scientists ensued, a debate that went to the heart of the issue of scientific objectivity. Peak attention occurred in 1969, coinciding with the announcement of the banning of DDT, while the tone of media attention reached its all-time low of about 90 percent negative. Environmental groups pressed Congress, the courts, executive agencies, and state agencies during this time, with increased success, on air and water pollution, nuclear power, industrial wastes, and pesticides. In consequence, numerous major laws, regulations, and court decisions were issued during the late 1960s and early 1970s. Major revisions of pesticide regulation occurred in the National Environmental Policy Act (1969) and the Federal Environmental Pesticides Control Act (1972). Although the law was a result of compromises between the old agriculture-pesticides subsystem and environmentalists, it provided a new regulatory environment. The pesticides-Agriculture Department link was certainly not destroyed, but the Schattschneider mobilization of the late 1960s led to the breakup of much of the legacy of the Downsian mobilization of twenty years before.

For most of the history of pesticide policy, congressional attention has been low, and most hearings have been aimed at regulating and limiting the industry rather than promoting it. Unlike nuclear power or tobacco, the pesticides industry is not itself the center of a large body of government action. Rather, it is part of a large variety of agriculture policies centering on monoculture and price supports for a variety of crops. One example among many of how pesticide are heavily affected by government agriculture programs is the limitation of acreage in farm price-support programs. These limits encourage farmers to use more pesticides and fertilizers in order to maximize the yields from the land remaining under cultivation.

Because pesticides as such are rarely the exclusive focus of Congress in the normal process of administering programs, most hearings focusing specifically on pesticide issues are directed at problems in the industry. Figure 4 shows the levels and tone of congressional attention to pesticides during the twentieth century. Congress paid virtually no attention to pesticides until there were significant public worries about the industry in the 1960s. Despite passage of two major laws concerning the industry, in 1910 and 1947, there were almost no hearings before 1960. Congressional hearings seem to play an important role in the expansion of conflict, but Congress in its role of supporter or booster of an industry is not Congress in committees. Supportive laws seem to be passed with relatively limited discussion, while critical legislation tends to follow extensive hearings and debates.

FIGURE 4 Congressional Hearings on Pesticides

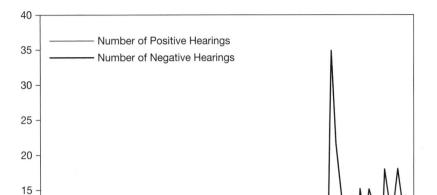

Between 1960 and 1975, no hearings could be classified as supportive of the pesticides industry. This is the period of *Silent Spring*, the DDT bans, and major environmental legislation. Congress acted as a venue of appeal for those interests not represented within the pesticide subsystem established after the 1947 legislation. Eventually, rules were changed to allow greater openness within that system of policymaking, and the result is considerably more conflict even within the pesticide policy community. Since 1975, Congress has held some hearings supportive of the industry, as actors on both sides now appeal to allies in the different committees and subcommittees. From a one-sided mobilization of interests centering on promoting the use of pesticides, Congress played a key role in expanding the opportunities for criticism. The once-powerful subsystem regulating and promoting the industry now is home to much more internal debate than was once the case.

The case of pesticides shows remarkable similarities to that of nuclear power. Both cases show tremendous growth of positive attention during the postwar period. Attention, as measured by press coverage, increased by factors of 10 to 20, as the industries were established and began to grow. The Downsian mobilization process worked almost identically in both cases. Attention dropped off after this initial surge, as the pesticides and nuclear power subsystems became firmly established. Later, the Schattschneider mobilization occurred. In both cases, we can note a second period of increased attention beginning in the 1960s and 1970s (slightly later for nuclear power than for pesticides), dominated by negative images. Pesticides and nuclear power emerged on the public agenda twice during the postwar period. The first time was the result of one-sided mobilization by proponents of the industry, as they sought and gained favorable government actions and institutionalized their control over these new industries. In the second phase of agenda access, however, the Schattschneider mobilization process led to major alterations in the proindustry subsystems.

■　　■　　■

Both Schattschneider and Downs are right, but only half right. There are clearly two types of agenda access, and the same issue studied over a relatively long period of time may show both. The remarkable element of each of these mobilizations, besides the tremendous policy implications that can follow from them, is their rapidity once they begin. Policymaking in many areas of American polities may not always be ruled by incrementalism, decreasing marginal returns, and slow changes (although these features remain important); rather, there are critical periods of mobilization of antagonists during which dramatic changes are put into effect. At any one time, there-may be little change, but periods of relative stability may be punctuated by fitful bursts of mobilization that change the structure of bias for decades to come. Institutions are the legacies of short periods of attention by the public to a given issue. They remain intact until attention increases at some later date to cause more institutional changes. Periods between agenda access may be characterized by stability, but this is not indicative of any equilibrium of values, tastes, or preferences. Rather, it is induced by the institutions that purposive entrepreneurs push through when they are able to take advantage of favorable conditions.

REFERENCES

Bosso, Christopher J. 1987. *Pesticides and Politics: The Life Cycle of a Public Issue.* Pittsburgh, Penn.: University of Pittsburgh Press.

Bureau of the Census. 1991. *Statistical Abstract of the United States.* Washington, D.C.: Department of Commerce.

Carson, Rachel. 1962. *Silent Spring.* Boston: Houghton Mifflin.

Downs, Anthony. 1972. Up and Down with Ecology: The Issue Attention Cycle. *Public Interest* 28: 38–50.

Dunlap, Thomas. 1981. *DDT: Scientists, Citizens, and Public Policy.* Princeton, N.J.: Princeton University Press.

Fritschler, A. Lee. 1989. *Smoking and Politics.* 4th ed. Englewood Cliffs, N.J.: Prentice-Hall.

Kingdon, John W. 1984. *Agendas, Alternatives, and Public Policies.* Boston: Little, Brown.

Ripley, Randall B., and Grace A. Franklin. 1991. *Congress, the Bureaucracy, and Public Policy.* 5th ed. Pacific Grove, Calif.: Brooks-Cole.

16.2

NOLAN McCARTY, KEITH POOLE, AND HOWARD ROSENTHAL

From *Polarized America*

McCarty, Poole, and Rosenthal show evidence that the two major political par-
ties have polarized and that this has been mostly driven by the increasing
income gap between voters supporting each party. Furthermore, nonvoting by
the poorest citizens (especially immigrants who cannot vote) has diminished
pressures on both parties (but especially the Democrats) to propose redistribu-
tive policies that would benefit the poor.

1. THE CHOREOGRAPHY OF AMERICAN POLITICS

In the middle of the twentieth century, the Democrats and the Republicans
danced almost cheek to cheek in their courtship of the political middle. Over
the past thirty years, the parties have deserted the center of the floor in favor
of the wings. In the parlance of punditry and campaign rhetoric circa 2004,
American politics have "polarized." Scarcely a day went by without headlines
such as the *San Francisco Chronicle*'s "Where did the middle go? How polarized politics and a radical GOP have put a chill on measured debate."[1] Story
after story attempted to explain the seemingly unbridgeable divide between
red and blue states. Was the country divided on moral issues, national security, or NASCAR? Even the First Lady offered her diagnosis, as the Associated
Press reported: "First Lady Laura Bush thinks the news media is increasingly
filled with opinions instead of facts, and suggested . . . that journalists are
contributing to the polarization of the country."[2]

What public commentators missed, however, was that polarization was not
a solo performer but part of a tight ensemble. Polarization's partners were
other fundamental changes in the American society and economy. Most
important, just as American politics became increasingly divisive, economic
fortunes diverged. Middle- and high-income Americans have continued to
benefit from the massive economic growth experienced since the Second
World War. But material well-being for the lower-income classes has stagnated. For each story about successful people like Bill Gates and Sam Walton,
there are contrasting stories about low-wage, no-benefit workers.

That Wal-Mart is the center of both the good news and the bad underscores
how unequally America's economic growth has been allocated. To put some
hard numbers on the disparities, in 1967 a household in the 95th percentile of

the income distribution had six times the income of someone in the 25th percentile. By 2003 the disparity had increased to 8.6 times.[3]

It is important to note that inequality rose in a period of increasing prosperity, with the added riches going much more to the haves than to the have-nots. Households with an annual income of over $100,000 (year 2000 dollars) increased from under 3 percent in 1967 to over 12 percent in 2000. Even the middle of the income distribution was more prosperous. In year 2000 dollars, median income increased from $31,400 in 1967 to $42,200 in 2000. Inequality probably had a real (versus perceived) bite on consumption only at the very bottom of the income distribution. This increase in riches, albeit unequal, is likely to have contributed to polarization.

Economists, sociologists, and others have identified a number of factors behind the shift to greater inequality. Returns to education have increased, labor union coverage has declined, trade exposure has increased, corporate executives have benefited from sharp increases in compensation and stock options, and family structure has changed through rising rates of divorce, late marriage, and two-income households. An additional factor helping tie our ensemble together is the massive wave of immigration, legal and illegal, since the 1960s.

The new immigrants are predominantly unskilled. They have contributed greatly to the economy by providing low-wage labor, especially in jobs that American citizens no longer find desirable. They also provide the domestic services that facilitate labor market participation by highly skilled people. On the other hand, immigrants have also increased inequality both directly, by occupying the lowest rungs of the economic ladder, and indirectly, through competition with citizens for low-wage jobs. Yet as noncitizens they lack the civic opportunities to secure the protections of the welfare state. Because these poor people cannot vote, there is less political support for policies that would lower inequality by redistribution.

[W]e trace out how these major economic and social changes are related to the increased polarization of the U.S. party system. We characterize the relationships as a "dance"—that is, relationships with give and take and back and forth, where causality can run both ways. On the one hand, economic inequality might feed directly into political polarization. People at the top might devote time and resources to supporting a political party strongly opposed to redistribution. People at the bottom would have an opposite response. Polarized parties, on the other hand, might generate policies that increase inequality through at least two channels. If the Republicans move sharply to the right, they can use their majority (as has been argued for the tax bills of the first administrations of Ronald Reagan and George W. Bush) to reduce redistribution. If they are not the majority, they can use the power of the minority in American politics to block changes to the status quo. In other words, polarization in the context of American political institutions now means that the political process cannot be used to redress inequality that may arise from nonpolitical changes in technology, lifestyle, and compensation practices.

Measuring Political Polarization

Before laying the groundwork for our argument that political polarization is related to economic inequality, we need to discuss how we conceptualize and measure political polarization. What do we mean by "polarization"? Polarization is, for short, a separation of politics into liberal and conservative camps. We all recognize that members of Congress can be thought of as occupying a position on a liberal-conservative spectrum. Ted Kennedy is a liberal, Dianne Feinstein a more moderate Democrat, Joe Lieberman even more so; Olympia Snowe is a moderate Republican and Rick Santorum a conservative Republican. The perception of conservativeness is commonly shared. There is a common perception because a politician's behavior is predictable. If we know that Olympia Snowe will fight a large tax cut, we can be fairly certain that all or almost all the Democrats will support her position.

There are two complementary facets to the polarization story. First, at the level of individual members of Congress, moderates are vanishing. Second, the two parties have pulled apart. *Conservative* and *liberal* have become almost perfect synonyms for *Republican* and *Democrat*.

Because we are social scientists and not journalists or politicians, we need to nail these shared impressions with precise operational definitions. When two of us (the two not in high school at the time) published "The Polarization of American Politics" in 1984, we measured polarization with interest group ratings. Each year, a number of interest groups publish ratings of members of Congress. Among the many groups are the United Auto Workers (UAW), the Americans for Democratic Action (ADA), the National Taxpayers Union (NTU), the American Conservative Union (ACU), and the League of Conservation Voters (LCV). Each interest group selects a fairly small number of roll call votes, typically twenty to forty, from the hundreds taken each year. A senator or representative who always votes to support the interest group's position is rewarded with a score of 100. Those always on the "wrong" side get a score of 0. Those who support the group half the time get a score of 50, and so on.

To see that moderates had vanished by 2003, consider the ratings of the Americans for Democratic Action for that year. The possible ADA ratings rose in five-point steps from 0 to 100. Of the twenty-one possible ratings, nine were in the range 30 through 70. Yet only eleven of the hundred senators (McCain, AZ; Campbell, CO; Lieberman, CT; Breaux, LA; Landrieu, LA; Collins, ME; Snowe, ME; Nelson, NE; Reid, NV; Edwards, NC; and Chafee, RI) fell in one of the nine middle categories. In contrast, ten Democrats got high marks of 95 or 100 and fourteen Republicans got 5 or 0. That is, more than twice as many senators (24) fell in the four very extreme categories as fell in the nine middle categories (11).

Our 1984 article documented two findings about the scores of the ADA and other interest groups. First, the interest groups gave out basically the same set of ratings or the mirror image of that set. If a general-purpose liberal interest group like the ADA gave a rating of 100 to a representative, the representative would nearly always get a very high rating from another liberal interest group, such as the LCV, even when the interest group focused on a single policy area, like the environment. Similarly, a 100 ADA rating made a very low rating from a conservative group like ACU or NTU a foregone conclusion. This agreement across interest groups meant that interest groups were evaluating members of Congress along a single, liberal-conservative dimension. Individual issue areas, such as race, no longer had a distinctive existence. Second, the interest groups were giving out fewer and fewer scores in the moderate range in the 40s, 50s, and 60s. Moderates were giving way to more extreme liberals and conservatives. Put simply, the interest groups had little difficulty placing Ted Kennedy and Jesse Helms as ideological opposites, and they were finding fewer and fewer Jacob Javitses and Sam Nunns to put in the middle. The change we noted occurred in the last half of the 1970s; indeed, our data went only through 1980.

We summarized our findings by combining all the ratings to give a single liberal-conservative score to each member.[4] We then measured polarization in a variety of technical ways, which we explain more fully in chapter 2. One measure was simply how much the scores for members of the two political parties overlapped. If moderates were abundant in both parties, there would be substantial overlap, or low polarization. If the Democrats had only liberals and the Republicans only conservatives, there would be no overlap, or high polarization. We found that the overlap had shrunk.

Using interest group ratings only, however, has two limitations. First, interest groups select only a small number of roll call votes. The ADA, for example, uses just twenty per year. But each house of Congress conducts hundreds of roll calls each year. ADA's selections might be a biased sample of this richer universe.[5] Second, interest group ratings became common only in the second half of the twentieth century. We cannot do a long-run study of polarization, inequality, and immigration just on the basis of interest group ratings. So we developed NOMINATE, a quantitative procedure that would score politicians directly from their roll call voting records, using all of the recorded votes. To locate the politicians' positions, these techniques use information on who votes with whom and how often. For example, if Arlen Specter votes with both Hillary Clinton and Bill Frist much more frequently than Clinton and Frist vote together, then these techniques position Specter as moderate, in between those more extreme senators. Using this algorithm over millions of individual choices made by thousands of legislators on tens of thousands of roll calls allows us to develop quite precise measures of each member's position on the liberal-conservative spectrum. . . .

The Common Trajectory of Polarization and Inequality

Our measure of political polarization closely parallels measures of economic inequality and of immigration for much of the twentieth century. We show this correlation with three plots of time series.

One measure of income inequality is the Gini coefficient of family income calculated by the Bureau of the Census. The Gini coefficient shows how the entire distribution of income deviates from equality. When every family has the same income, the Gini is zero. When one family has all the income, the Gini is one. In figure 1, we show the Gini and polarization in the post-World War II period.[6] Income inequality falls from 1947 through 1957 and then bounces up and down until 1969. After 1969, income inequality increases every two years, with a couple of slight interruptions. Polarization bounces at a low level until 1977, and thereafter follows an unbroken upward trajectory.

We stress an important aspect of the timing of the reversal in inequality and polarization. In some circles, both of these phenomena are viewed as the

FIGURE 1 Income Inequality and House Polarization

SOURCE: Gini index from the U.S. Census Bureau (2005).

NOTE: Polarization is measured as the difference between the Democratic and Republican Party mean NOMINATE scores in the U.S. House. The Gini and polarization measures correspond to the first year of each biennial congressional term.

consequence of Ronald Reagan's victory in the 1980 elections. Both reversals, however, clearly predate Reagan and Reaganomics. Reagan conservatism was a product sitting on a shelf in the political supermarket. In 1980, customers switched brands, arguably the result of a preference shift marked by rising inequality and party polarization.[7]

■ ■ ■

Piketty and Saez used income tax returns to compute the percentage share of income going to the richest of the rich. In figure 2, we plot the share going to the top one percent of the income distribution. This longer series matches up nicely with our polarization measure over the entire twentieth century.

The decline in polarization throughout the first seventy years of the twentieth century is echoed by much of the literature written toward the end of the decline or just after. During this period, Americans were seen as having grown closer together politically. In 1960, the sociologist Daniel Bell published *The End of Ideology: On the Exhaustion of Political Ideas in the Fifties.* A year later, the political scientist Robert Dahl pointed to a nation moving from oligarchy to pluralism (Dahl 1961). Similarly, the new "rational choice" school in political science emphasized Tweedle-dee/Tweedle-dum parties focused on

FIGURE 2 Top One Percent Income Share and House Polarization

SOURCE: Income shares from Piketty and Saez (2003), table II.

the median voter (Downs 1957), members of Congress largely concerned with constituency service (Fiorina 1978), and universalism in pork-barrel politics (Weingast, Shepsle, and Johnsen 1981). What these authors were pointing to was echoed in analyses of roll call voting patterns in the House and Senate. Put simply, the fraction of moderates grew and the fraction of extreme liberals and extreme conservatives fell from 1900 to about 1975 (Poole and Rosenthal 1997; McCarty, Poole, and Rosenthal 1997). By the beginning of the twenty-first century, the extremes had come back.

The corresponding story for immigration is told by figure 3. Immigration is captured by looking at the percentage of the population that is foreign-born. (This is the only measure available before the Census Bureau began biennial collection of data on citizenship in 1972. From 1972 on, we will look, in chapter 4, at the percentage of the population represented by those who claim to be noncitizens.) For comparison, we have taken the polarization period back to 1880, the first census after the modern Democrat-Republican two-party system formed upon the end of Reconstruction following the elections of 1876.

FIGURE 3 Percent Foreign-Born and House Polarization

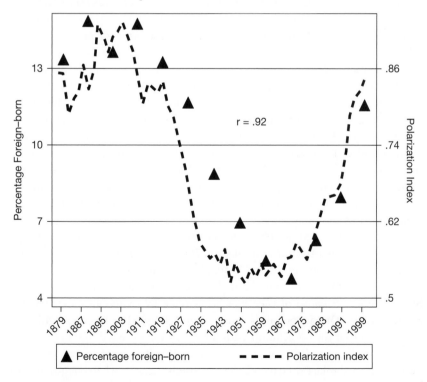

NOTE: Each observation of foreign-born population corresponds to a U.S. decennial census.

Until World War I, the percentage of foreign-born living in the United States was very high, hovering in the 13–15 percent range. With the curtailing of immigration, first by the war and then by the restrictive immigration acts of the 1920s, the percentage of foreign-born falls continuously until the 1970 census, just after immigration was liberalized by the 1965 reforms. The percentage of foreign-born thereafter increases sharply, exceeding 11 percent in the census of 2000. In 1970, a majority of the foreign-born had become naturalized citizens. By 2000, a substantial majority of the foreign-born was formed by noncitizens. Parallel to the track of immigration, polarization hovers at a high level until 1912 and then declines until 1967, with the exception of the uptick in the 1940s. The immigration series, like the income series, largely parallels our polarization measure.[8]

When we ourselves first saw figures 1, 2, and 3, we realized that major indicators of the politics, the economics, and the demographics of the United States had followed very similar trajectories over many decades. . . .

A Focus on Income

[W]e look at income and other components of economic well-being as an important variable in defining political ideology and voter preferences. We do not, however, discount the importance of such other factors as race and "moral values." We chose to emphasize economics partly because we seek to redress an imbalance in political science: income has been largely ignored, and race-ethnicity and class (as measured by occupation rather than income) receive more attention. We chose economics also because many public policies are defined largely in terms of income. Certainly the tax bills of 1993, 2001, and 2003 were among the most important domestic policy changes of the Clinton and George W. Bush administrations. Indeed, the overwhelming majority of congressional roll calls are over taxes, budgets, and economic policies, especially after the issue of *de jure* political rights for African-Americans left the congressional agenda at the end of the 1960s. Most importantly, income is closely related to how people vote, to whether they participate in politics by either voting or making campaign contributions, and to whether they are eligible to vote as United States citizens.

Race does appear to be related to the current absence of redistribution in the United States (Alesina and Glaeser 2004) and to the absence of public spending in local communities (Alesina, Baqir, and Easterly 1999; Alesina and La Ferrara 2000, 2002). The claim that welfare expenditures in the United States are low because of race has been made by many authors, including Myrdal (1960), Quadagno (1994), and Gilens (1999). The basic claim of this literature is that the correlation with poverty lowers the willingness of voters to favor public spending for redistribution. But it is hard to see racism as hardening in the last quarter of the twentieth century when inequality was increasing. Racism and racial tension seem to have been rife when inequality was falling: recall the lynchings and race riots in the first half of the century and the urban riots of the 1960s. (Similarly, with regard to occupation or class, unionization has been declining since the 1950s.) We do explicitly consider race when treating ideological polarization in Congress and income polarization in the mass public, but it does, in historical perspective, appear appropriate to make income and economics our primary focus.

The Dance Card

. . . Polarization has increased for two reasons. First, Republicans in the North and South have moved sharply to the right. Second, moderate Democrats in the South have been replaced by Republicans. The remaining, largely northern, Democrats are somewhat more liberal than the Democratic Party of the 1960s.

The movements we observe tell us only about the relative positioning of politicians. We say that Republicans have moved to the right because newly elected Republicans have, on the whole, voted in a more conservative manner than the Republicans who remain in Congress. Northern Democrats, in contrast, don't look sharply different from the Democrats of old.

At the same time, however, how policy issues map onto liberal-conservative preferences may have changed. The Republicans have moved sharply away from redistributive policies that would reduce economic inequality. The Democrats as analyzed by John Gerring (1998), a political scientist at Boston University, have moved their platforms away from general welfare issues to issues based on ascriptive characteristics (race, gender, and sexual preference) of individuals. For example, figure 4, drawn from Gerring, shows that the Democrats increased emphasis on general welfare through the 1960s but then deemphasized it in the 1970s. The turn in platforms thus matches the reversals in economic inequality and polarization. Parallel to Gerring's results, we show that race as an issue has been absorbed into the main redistributive dimension of liberal-conservative politics. Taxes, minimum wages, and other traditional redistributive policy areas continue to be liberal-conservative issues; they have been joined by issues related to ascription.

4. IMMIGRATION, INCOME, AND THE VOTERS' INCENTIVE TO REDISTRIBUTE

Economic inequality in the United States has increased sharply. At the same time, income differences have become more important in determining where a congressional district's representative is likely to fall on the liberal-conservative dimension and how voters identify with parties and make voting decisions in presidential elections. Why has the increased importance of income not translated into policies that would curtail the sharp growth in inequality? At least in part, noncitizens who are ineligible to vote are concentrated at the bottom of the income distribution, so politicians feel little pressure to respond to their interests. Although economic inequality has increased, the relative income of the vast majority of *voters* has not markedly deteriorated.

■   ■   ■

In 1972, noncitizens were a small fraction of the United States population. They were also relatively well-to-do. In fact, the median income of a noncitizen was actually higher than that of citizens reporting themselves as having not voted in the presidential race between Nixon and McGovern. Noncitizens today are growing in number, and they tend to be at the bottom of the income distribution. In contrast, the relative economic position of voters and nonvoters shows little change since 1972.

The changing economic position of noncitizens is politically relevant. It is likely to contribute to the failure of the political process in the United States to generate redistribution that would eliminate growing disparities in wage and income inequality. As we said, the income of the median voter has *not* declined relatively over the past thirty years. How has the median voter's economic position been sustained, while that of the median family has declined? Part of the answer, as we show, is that lower-income people are increasingly likely to be noncitizens. The median income of noncitizens has shifted sharply downward, and the fraction of the population that is noncitizen has increased dramatically. From 1972 to 2000, the median family income of noncitizens fell from 78 percent of the median income of voters to 59 percent, while the fraction of the population that is noncitizen rose from 2.6 percent to 7.8 percent.[9]

One of the main reasons for the dramatic change in the number and poverty of noncitizens is federal legislation that has opened the doors to increased legal immigration while doing little to control illegal immigration. During the late nineteenth and early twentieth centuries, immigration was made more difficult for Europeans, and the Chinese and Japanese were excluded entirely. The immigration acts of 1921, 1924, and 1929 set up permanent quotas by national origin that both restricted total immigration and favored the relatively wealthy people of northwestern Europe. The barriers of the 1920s were only broken down by the 1965 amendments to the Immigration and Nationality Act of 1952. The amendments largely ended discrimination on the basis of national origin. Annual immigration quotas were greatly increased by the Immigration Act of 1990.

Economists have recognized that immigration, through low wage competition, has had an effect on inequality. But how big is the effect? . . .

We stress that the direct economic effects must be combined with the indirect political effects. Changes in such public policies as minimum wages, income taxation, and estate taxation have, on balance, held the median voter's relative position in place. More redistributive policies would have occurred, we conjecture, had there been a sharp deterioration in the position of voters in the middle of the income distribution.

There is a large literature, including the references above, that focuses on immigration. In contrast, this chapter emphasizes citizenship because many immigrants eventually become naturalized citizens and are then eligible to vote. Our results suggest that naturalized immigrants are likely to look, in terms of income, much like native citizens. At least, it is clear that the relative income of the median voter has not greatly declined during the wave of poor, naturalized immigrants. In contrast, as some immigrants have become naturalized, they have more than been replaced by the continuing surge of poor immigrant noncitizens.

The analysis is all in terms of relative incomes. Only these, and not the real levels, matter in the economic model of redistribution. [O]ver the period of our study real median income has in fact increased. To the extent that redistribution accomplished by the political process is social insurance (such things as unemployment benefits, old-age benefits, and medical benefits), the increase in real income should diminish support for redistribution, complementing the results of this chapter.[10] The effects of income inequality, however, are all on relative incomes.

We explore the relationship between income and voting in a way that differs from the standard approach taken by political scientists. The usual approach is to see if the rich in fact vote more than the poor. We take a different approach, comparing characteristics of the income distribution of voters to the same characteristics for nonvoters and noncitizens. We ask how the income characteristics have changed over time. In the standard approach, one is also concerned with verifying that income has an effect when one controls for other demographics. We are less concerned with this issue because public policy depends less on covariates than on income. A person's taxes are not lower because he or she is a college graduate, an African American, or an evangelical. (One's labor market experience may differ, however.) Taxes may be slightly less if a person is over 65, but the monthly social security check still depends on lifetime earnings and not race, education, or gender. So if we want to study redistribution, we should start with income, at least as a first cut.

In most political economy models, the income inequality that has arisen since the 1970s would have self-equilibrated. As inequality increased, there would be more pressure to redistribute. . . . As inequality, defined as a decrease in the ratio of median voter income to mean income, went up, more redistribution should have occurred. In the United States, however, public policy veered in the opposite direction. . . .

Other industrial nations have been exposed to the same technological change or opportunities as the United States. Although economic inequality might be driven by technological change, the responses elsewhere have not been the same. For example, Piketty and Saez (2003) show that during the last three decades of the twentieth century, the share of national income going to the top 0.1 percent of the population remained unchanged in France but sharply increased in the United States. We also note, in keeping with the theme of this chapter, that France has had a dramatically different experience with noncitizenship. From 1975 to 1999, roughly the period of our study, French government statistics show that the percentage of noncitizens decreased, falling from 6.5 percent of the population to 5.6 percent.[11] France and the United States, thus, have had contrasting trends in income inequality and in citizenship. How might these trends have been reflected in political processes?

To answer this question, we return to the Bolton and Roland (1997) model and focus on median/mean ratios. From the perspective of that model, noncitizenship has both a *disenfranchisement* effect and a *sharing* effect.[12]

The *disenfranchisement effect* can be viewed as a change in the numerator of the median/mean ratio. The median income of voters is higher than that of all families. This fact reflects not just that voters have higher incomes than eligible nonvoters, but also that voters have higher incomes than noncitizens. The effect of disenfranchising non-citizens will increase either if noncitizens become more numerous or if they become poorer.

If all citizens voted, the appropriate ratio would be median citizen income/ mean family income. If all those over 18 voted, the appropriate ratio would be median family income/mean family income. By comparing these ratios to median voter income/mean family income, we can study how much "disenfranchisement" is due to nonvoting by citizens and how much to the ineligibility of noncitizens.

The presence of noncitizens in the population not only affects the numerator of the median/mean ratio, it also changes the denominator. Because noncitizens are poorer than citizens, mean family income is less than mean citizen income. Noncitizens thus increase the ratio, making redistribution less attractive to the median voter. Noncitizens shrink the per capita pie that has to be shared equally with all residents. The sharing of benefits with noncitizens has, of course, become a political hot potato. To assess the *sharing effect*, we will compare redistribution when mean family income for citizens is substituted for mean family income in the ratio. This counterfactual presumes that mean citizen income is unaffected by the presence of noncitizens. Although citizen income may well be affected by immigration, it is hard to argue that it would fall below realized mean family income. Some sharing effect must be present.

The sharing effect will drive all citizens to be less favorable to redistribution. The disenfranchisement effect decreases the political influence of relatively low-income families and increases the influence of higher-income families. We focus, for convenience, on median incomes, but our findings can be viewed as indicative of the incentives to redistribute that face a large segment of the electorate with incomes not very distant from the median. The main point of this chapter is that the relative income of the median income *voter* in the United States is in fact not worse today than it was thirty years ago. The disenfranchisement effect and the sharing effect have contributed to lessening voter support for redistribution despite increasing income inequality.

Although the ratio of family income of the median *individual* to mean family income has indeed fallen in the United States over the past thirty years, the ratio of the family income of the median *voter* to mean family income has been remarkably constant. The political process does appear to have equilibrated in the sense that the median voter is not worse off compared to the mean.

How has this distinction between the median voter and the median individual arisen?

First, not every eligible individual votes. United States citizens who do not vote have lower incomes than those who do. This income difference has always been the case, and it does not appear to have shifted much over the past thirty years.[13] An argument that it may have shifted originates in the observation that many states bar voting by convicted felons and that convictions and incarcerations have trended sharply upwards. Convicted felons—Bernie Ebbers, Michael Milken, and Martha Stewart aside—tend to be poor. Making felons ineligible might make nonvoters disproportionately poor. But we don't see such effects in our data. It is possible that the Census Bureau undersamples convicted felons and therefore consistently overestimates the incomes of nonvoters. But it is also possible that people susceptible to felony convictions always had very low turnout, so changing conviction rates and eligibility would have minimal impact on the income distribution of nonvoters. In any event, the impact of ineligible felons has to be small relative to that of noncitizens. McDonald and Popkin (2001), for example, estimate that, in 2000, noncitizens outnumbered ineligible felons by over five to one. Uggen and Manza (2002) estimate that 2.3 percent of the adult population was ineligible felons in 2000, in contrast to the 7.8 percent of the CPS sample that is noncitizen.

Second, and more important, the percentage of residents who are noncitizens has risen sharply, tripling between 1972 and 2000. Moreover, as emphasized by Bean and Bell-Rose (1999) and Borjas (1999), noncitizens are increasingly low-wage and poor. Our most striking observation is the rapid decline of the median income of noncitizens relative to the median income of voters. In a nutshell, continuing immigration has created a large population of noncitizens. These noncitizens appear to be a leading cause of the fall of median family income relative to mean income. Voters are doing as well as they have ever done.

We have a second interesting finding. There is a midterm cycle in the income of nonvoters. The median income of nonvoters increases in off years and declines in presidential years. In other words, marginal voters who vote in presidential elections but not in off years have higher incomes than persistent nonvoters. The smaller set of citizens who vote in neither presidential nor off-year elections have particularly low incomes. In presidential elections, then, the median family income of a voter is sharply higher than that of the median income of a nonvoter and much, much higher than that of a noncitizen.

■ ■ ■

Conclusion

The median income *voter's* incentive to redistribute has not increased as over-all economic inequality has risen in the United States. The reason is partly that the rise in inequality has been offset by immigration, which has changed the location of citizens in the income distribution. Those ineligible to vote are substantially poorer than the eligible. Moreover, poorer citizens have not become increasingly apathetic, at least as measured by the tendency to vote. Most citizens, and voters in particular, have been "bumped up" by the disen-franchisement of poorer noncitizens. At the same time, a voter of a given income is less eager to redistribute if that redistribution has to be shared with the noncitizen poor.

In any event, immigration cannot have been a driving force in the onset of the increase in income inequality and political polarization. In the early 1970s, noncitizens were quite a small share of the population of the United States, and their income profiles were close to those of citizens. Increas-ingly, however, noncitizens became a larger, poorer share of the population. From 1990 on, this change placed a number of ineligibles at the bottom of the income distribution, sufficient to make a substantial impact on the redistributive preferences of the median income voter. Even if immigration occurred too late to have produced the increases in inequality and polariza-tion, it may well be contributing to the blocking of efforts to redress these trends.

Our results argue against the claim of Lijphart (1997) in his American Political Science Association presidential address that low voter participation is responsible for the much greater inequality in the United States than in Europe. Lijphart's claim may make sense in terms of contemporary cross-national comparisons, but it does not hold up in the time series. Piketty and Saez (2003) present evidence that inequality fell in the United States just as much as in France and Britain from the First World War until 1970. During this period, there was considerably lower turnout in the United States than in France. Since 1970, the three nations have diverged in inequality, but turnout of eligible citizens in the United States has not fallen. Turnout in France fell, but inequality has remained in check. It is true that turnout of *residents* of the United States over 18 has fallen, but few would be prepared to extend the right to vote to noncitizens. Compulsory voting for citizens, proposed by Lijphart, might indeed lead to more redistribution, but the absence of com-pulsory voting cannot by itself explain the rise in inequality in the United States in the past thirty years. The explanation is likely to be more closely related to the rise in noncitizenship. The increase reflects two political out-comes. First, immigration reforms in the 1960s and 1990s permitted a large increase in legal immigration. Second, the United States did little to contain illegal immigration. The two outcomes have changed the relationship of income to voting.

NOTES

1. October 24, 2004. Quoted at http://www.sfgate.com/cgi-bin/article.cgi?file=/chronicle/archive/2004/10/10/RVG1T9289T1.DTL.

2. Story of August 24, 2004, found at http://www.editorandpublisher.com/eandp/news/article_display.jsp?vnu_content_id=1000592440.

3. Computed from http://www.census.gov/hhes/income/histinc/h01ar.html.

4. We used the least squares unfolding procedure of Poole (1984).

5. On this point, see Snyder (1992).

6. The Census Bureau series does not cover earlier years.

7. A number of commentators date the conservative Republican movement from organizational initiatives, including the formation of think tanks that arose in the early 1970s following the Goldwater candidacy in the 1964 election. See Perlstein (2001) and a *New York Times* opinion article by former New Jersey senator Bill Bradley. See http://www.nytimes.com/2005/03/30/opinion/30bradley.html. Downloaded April 3, 2005.

8. It is difficult to pinpoint the switch from a decline in polarization to a surge. The turning point occurred somewhere between the late 1960s (following the passage of the Great Society program of the Johnson administration and the immigration amendments of 1965) and the mid to late 1970s. The statistical correlations between polarization, income inequality, and immigration are all slightly sensitive to measurement. The polarization measure will change if the sample period used for DW-NOMINATE changes (end the series in 2000 or 2004), if Senate rather than House polarization is used, if a two-dimensional rather than one-dimensional measure is used, etc. Similarly, income inequality will change if one switches from a Gini to various income shares, etc., and the immigration measure will change if one uses percentage noncitizens (chapter 4) rather than percentage foreign born. The substantive tenor of our results is quite robust to these variations.

9. Our computations are from the November Current Population Survey. The November CPS family income series includes single adult households but does not combine the incomes of unmarried individuals with the same residence.

10. Welch (1999) finds that inequality has increased much less when one looks within the population that remains in the labor force in two periods or within age cohorts. This also reinforces the main claim of this chapter—that the median voter's incentive to redistribute has not increased. Voters may take into account where they stand in the life cycle when making voting decisions.

11. See http://www.insee.fr/fr/ffc/chifcle_fiche.asp?ref_id=NATTEF02131&tab_id=339, viewed on December 7, 2004. We equate *"étrangers"* to noncitizens. Immigrants, comprising both noncitizens and naturalized (*"acquisition"*) citizens rose slightly from 9.1% to 9.6%. We should point out that France counts citizens of other EU nations as noncitizens even though there is free mobility of labor within the EU. The EU "noncitizens" would have had, until the recent admission of former Soviet bloc nations, a very different skill mix from that of the largely unskilled Latin American, Caribbean, and Asian immigrants who have come to the United States.

12. We thank Patrick Bolton for suggesting this decomposition.

13. Brady (2004, p. 692) presents evidence, like ours drawn from the CPS, that there has been little change in voter turnout by income quintile over the past thirty years. Summarizing the data in terms of the ratio of turnout in the top quintile to the bottom quintile, he finds no trend in midterm elections and an increasing trend in presidential elections. Some of the trend may reflect inaccuracies engendered by how Brady formed

quintiles from the categorical data. Brady does not indicate whether he excluded non-citizens in forming the quintiles.

REFERENCES

Alesina, Alberto, Reza Baqir, and William Easterly. 1999. "Public Goods and Ethnic Divisions." *Quarterly Journal of Economics* 114(4): 1243–1284.

Alesina, Alberto, and Edward L. Glaeser. 2004. *Fighting Poverty in the U.S. and Europe.* New York: Oxford University Press.

Alesina, Alberto, and Eliana La Ferrara. 2000. "Participation in Heterogeneous Communities." *Quarterly Journal of Economics* 115(3): 847–904.

Alesina, Alberto, and Eliana La Ferrara. 2002. "Who Trusts Others?" *Journal of Public Economics* 85(2): 207–234.

Bean, Frank D., and Stephanie Bell-Rose. 1999. "Introduction" in Frank Bean and Stephanie Bell-Rose, eds. *Immigration and Opportunity: Race, Ethnicity, and Employment in the United States.* New York: Russell Sage Foundation, 1–28.

Bolton, Patrick, and Gerard Roland. 1997. "The Breakup of Nations." *Quarterly Journal of Economics* 112(4): 1057–1090.

Borjas, George J. 1999. *Heaven's Door: Immigration Policy and the American Economy.* Princeton, NJ: Princeton University Press.

Brady, Henry. 2004. "An Analytical Perspective on Participatory Inequality and Income Inequality." In Kathy Neckerman, ed. *Social Inequality.* New York: Russell Sage Foundation.

Dahl, Robert A. 1961. *Who Governs: Democracy and Power in an American City.* New Haven, CT: Yale University Press.

Downs, Anthony. 1957. *An Economic Theory of Democracy.* New York: Harper and Row.

Fiorina, Morris. 1978. *Congress: Keystone of the Washington Establishment.* New Haven, CT: Yale University Press.

Gerring, John. 1998. *Party Ideologies in America, 1828–1996.* New York: Cambridge University Press.

Gilens, Martin. 1999. *Why Americans Hate Welfare: Race, Media, and the Politics of Antipoverty Policy.* Chicago: University of Chicago Press.

Lijphart, Arend. 1997. "Unequal Participation: Democracy's Unresolved Dilemma." *American Political Science Review* 91(1): 1–14.

McCarty, Nolan, Keith T. Poole, and Howard Rosenthal. 1997. *Income Redistribution and the Realignment of American Politics.* Washington, DC: American Enterprise Institute.

McDonald, Michael P., and Samuel Popkin. 2001. "The Myth of the Vanishing Voter." *American Political Science Review* 95(4): 963–974.

Myrdal, Gunnar. 1960. *Beyond the Welfare State: Economic Planning and its International Implications.* New Haven, CT: Yale University Press.

Perlstein, Rick. 2001. *Before the Storm: Barry Goldwater and the Unmaking of the American Consensus.* New York: Hill and Wang.

Piketty, Thomas, and Emmanuel Saez. 2003. "Income Inequality in the United States, 1913–1998." *Quarterly Journal of Economics* 118(1): 1–39.

Poole, Keith T. 1984. "Least Squares Metric, Unidimensional Unfolding." *Psychometrica* 49: 311–323.

Poole, Keith T., and Howard Rosenthal. 1997. *Congress: A Political-Economic History of Roll Call Voting.* New York: Oxford University Press.

Quadagno, Jill S. 1994. *The Color of Welfare: How Racism Undermined the War on Poverty.* Oxford: Oxford University Press.

Snyder, James. 1992. "Artificial Extremism in Interest Group Ratings." *Legislative Studies Quarterly* 17(3): 319–345.

Uggen, Christopher, and Jeff Manza. 2002. "Democratic Contraction? Political Consequences of Felon Disenfranchisement in the United States." *American Sociological Review* 67(6): 777–803.

U.S. Census Bureau. 2005. "Table F–4. Gini Ratios for Families, by Race and Hispanic Origin of Householder: 1947 to 2003." Accessed at http://www.census.gov/hhes/income/histinc/f04.html.

Weingast, Barry R., Kenneth A. Shepsle, and Christopher Johnsen. 1981. "The Political Economy of Benefits and Costs: A Neoclassical Approach to Distributive Politics." *Journal of Political Economy* 89(4): 642–664.

Welch, Finnis. 1999. "In Defense of Inequality." *American Economic Review: Papers and Proceedings* 89(2): 1–17.

From *The Powers of War and Peace: The Constitution
and Foreign Affairs after 9/11*

*Yoo reacts to those who claim that the president has garnered too much power
in foreign and military policy. It may be true, he says, that Congress is weaker
than the president in these areas of policy, but this subordination of Congress
was explicit in the Constitution. Powers of presidential initiative have been
forged through experience. Congress has repeatedly shown the lack of political
will to challenge presidential authority.*

5. WAR POWERS FOR A NEW WORLD

. . . The Framers believed that separating the president's executive and
commander-in-chief powers from Congress's powers over declaring war and
funding would create a political system in which in each branch could use its
own constitutional powers to develop foreign policy. A close reading of the
constitutional text and structure shows that the original understanding of
the war power is fully reflected in the Constitution. The Constitution's flexible
warmaking system is especially pronounced when compared to other constitutional texts, and to the more formalistic processes established for other
forms of government action.

   This approach finds that the practice of the political branches in making
war since the end of World War II has fallen within the constitutional design.
While Congress never declared war in Korea or Vietnam, among many other
places, it had every opportunity to control those conflicts through its funding

powers. That it did not was a reflection of a lack of political will rather than a defect in the constitutional design. A more flexible approach also allows us to understand America's newest military interventions. Recent wars in Iraq, Afghanistan, and Kosovo were constitutional, even though in none of them was there a declaration of war and Kosovo received no statutory authorization, because Congress has had the full opportunity to participate in decisionmaking elsewhere.

■ ■ ■

War and the Constitutional Text

. . . Important and long-overlooked insights about the nature of the war power come to light through close examination of the text. First, it is apparent that Congress's power to "declare war" is not synonymous with the power to begin military hostilities. Professor Ramsey's article in the *University of Chicago Law Review* best expresses the opposite view. He argues that the Framers understood the power to "declare war" as the giving Congress the sole power to decide on whether to commence military hostilities against other nations. Under international and domestic law at the time of the ratification, therefore, "declare war" must have been shorthand for "begin war" or "commence war" or "authorize war."[1] Only once Congress had issued this authorization could the president trigger his commander-in-chief authority and fight the war to its conclusion. At best, the president has a limited authority to use force without congressional consent only when the United States has suffered an attack. Thus, the Declare War Clause both expands Congress's war powers and restricts those of the president. As Glennon has written, the clause not only "empowers Congress to declare war," but also "serves as a limitation on executive war-making power, placing certain acts off limits for the President."[2]

The constitutional text, however, simply does not support such an expansive reading. First, the Constitution uses the word "declare" war, rather than "make," "begin," "authorize," or "wage" war. At the time of the Constitution's ratification, "declare" carried a distinct and separate meaning from "levy," "engage," "make," or "commence." Samuel Johnson's English dictionary (perhaps the definitive dictionary at the time of the framing) defined "declare" as "to clear, to free from obscurity"; "to make known, to tell evidently and openly": "to publish; to proclaim"; "to shew in open view"; or "to make a declaration, to proclaim some resolution or opinion, some favour or opposition."[3] This definition suggests that declaring war recognized a state of affairs—clarifying the legal status of the nation's relationship with another country—rather than authorized the creation of that state of affairs.

Second, if this view were correct, we would expect the Framers to have repeated the phrase "declare war" elsewhere in the Constitution when addressing the same subject. They did not. When discussing war in other contexts, the Constitution's phrasing indicates that declaring war referred to something less than the sole power to send the nation into hostilities. As we have seen, Article I, Section 10 declares that states may not "engage" in war. If "declare war" meant the same thing as initiate hostilities, Article I, Section 10 should have forbidden states from declaring war. Granting Congress the sole authority to "engage" the nation in war would have been a much clearer, direct method for vesting in Congress the power to control the actual conduct of war.

To take another example, Article III of the Constitution defines the crime of treason, in part, as consisting of "levying War" against the United States. Again, "levying" appears to be broader in meaning than merely declaring. If the Framers had used "levy War" in Article I, Section 8, they certainly would have made far clearer their alleged intention to grant Congress the sole power to decide on war. Conversely, if the step of declaring war were as serious as some believe, Article III ought to have defined treason to occur when a citizen "declares war" against the United States. To be sure, as Adrian Vermeule and Ernest Young have argued, while there may be serious doubts about demanding a consistency in meaning between constitutional provisions, which have been added to the Constitution during different periods of time by different groups of legislators and delegates, this is not true of the original 1787 Constitution.[4] The unamended Constitution was drafted at one time and ratified at one time, and so it is not unreasonable to expect words used on the same subject to convey a common meaning throughout.

The structure of Article I, Section 10 deals an even heavier blow to the pro-Congress reading. It states:

> No State shall, without the Consent of Congress, lay any Duty of Tonnage, keep Troops or Ships of War in time of Peace, enter into any Agreement or Compact with another State, or with a foreign power, or *engage in War, unless actually invaded or in such imminent Danger as will not admit of delay.* (emphasis added)[5]

This provision creates the *exact* war powers process between Congress and the states that scholars critical of the presidency want to create between Congress and the president. It makes resort to force conditional on the "Consent of Congress," and it even includes an exception for defending against sudden attacks. Pro-Congress scholars have argued that the Framers understood the Declare War Clause to contain an unexpressed exception that permits the executive to use force in response to an attack without having to seek a declaration of war from Congress. Otherwise their strict interpretation would prevent the president from engaging in even defensive uses of force without congressional approval and have proven utterly unworkable in the real world. Article I, Section 10, however, shows the faults of this approach, because it requires us to believe that the Framers did not know how to express themselves in one part of the Constitution but did in another part of the Constitution on exactly the same subject.

Pro-Congress scholars have never attempted to account for the difference in language between Article I, Section 8 and Article I, Section 10.[6] If they assume that specific texts have specific meanings, they also must believe that different texts should be interpreted to have different meanings. If the pro-Congress reading were correct, the Framers naturally should have written a provision stating that "the President may not, without the Consent of Congress, engage in War, unless the United States are actually invaded, or in such imminent Danger as will not admit of delay." Or, Article I, Section 10 should have said that "no state shall, without the consent of Congress, declare war." Instead, the Constitution only allocates to Congress the declare war power and to the president the commander-in-chief power, without specifically stating—as it does in Article I, Section 10 with regard to the states—how those powers are to interact. The Constitution's creation of a specific, detailed war powers process at the state level, but its silence at the federal level, shows that the Constitution does not establish any specific procedure for going to war.

Two additional clues suggest that "declare war" served as a recognition of the legal status of hostile acts, rather than as a necessary authorization for hostilities. Congress's power to declare war does not stand alone, but instead is part of a clause that includes the power to "grant Letters of Marque and Reprisal" and to "make Rules concerning Captures on Land and Water."[7] Placement of the power to declare war alongside these other two is significant, because they clearly involve the power of Congress to recognize or declare the legal status and consequences of certain wartime actions, and not the power to authorize those actions. Ironically, the Marque and Reprisal Clause serves as the linchpin for some defenders of an expansive reading of Congress's war powers. Jules Lobel and Jane Stromseth, for example, who rely on the work of Charles Lofgren, argue that letters of marque and reprisal had come "to signify any intermediate or low-intensity hostility short of declared war."[8] In part, they respond to the history of the 1980s, in which presidents conducted "police actions," smaller conflicts, and convert activity that fall well short of World Wars I and II. When combined with Congress's control over declaring war, Stromseth, Lobel, and Lofgren argue, the Marque and Reprisal Clause provides Congress with full control over the initiation of all military hostilities, whether they be total war or covert actions.

Such interpretive moves, however, rip the constitutional text from its historical context. By the time of the framing, letters of marque and reprisal had come to refer to a fairly technical form of international reprisal, in which a government gave its permission to an injured private party to recover, via military operations, compensation from the citizens of a foreign nation. Without a letter of marque and reprisal, such actions—usually conducted on the high seas—would constitute piracy; with a letter, they were legitimate forms of privateering condoned by sovereign consent. While marque and reprisal certainly are one category of what we today might call "low-level conflict," it does not follow that marque and reprisal must refer to *all* forms of conflict short of war. Recent work suggests that, during the American Revolution, letters of marque and reprisal authorized a rather narrow form of commercial warfare that was conducted for profit and regulated by prize courts, in contrast to military actions by regular armed forces.[9] What seems fairly clear is that marque and reprisal did not refer to all forms of undeclared war, especially those with purely military and political goals, but rather with the legal implications of one species of commercial warfare.[10]

Other foundational documents of the period demonstrate that the Framers thought of the power to begin hostilities as different from the power to declare war. Under the Articles of Confederation, the nation's framework of government until the ratification. Congress operated as the executive branch of the United States.[11] As we have seen, Article IX vested Congress with "the sole and exclusive right and power of determining on peace and war."[12] Here the Framers (several of whom had served in the Continental Congress) had at hand a text that clearly and explicitly allocated to Congress the "sole and exclusive" authority to decide whether to fight a war. If the Framers had intended to grant Congress the power to commence military hostilities, they could easily have imported the phrase from the Articles of Confederation into the Constitution, as they did with other, related powers.[13] Instead, they changed Congress's power to "declare war" from "determining on peace and war." For the pro-Congress position to be correct, the Framers would have had to be clumsy draftsmen indeed.

Presidential critics also fail to take into account the next most important founding-era documents: the state constitutions. Most of the state constitutions did not explicitly transfer to their assemblies the power to initiate hostilities, but rather sought to control executive power by disrupting the structural unity of the executive branch.[14] One state, however chose to create exactly the type of arrangement contemplated by pro-Congress scholars. In its first 1776 constitution, South Carolina vested in its chief executive the power of commander in chief, but then declared that "the president and commander-in-chief shall have no power to make war or peace . . . without the consent of the general assembly and legislative council."[15] In its 1778 constitution. South Carolina reaffirmed its decision that the legislature first must authorize war by stating that "the governor and commander-in-chief shall have no power to commence war, or conclude peace" without legislative approval. South Carolina's 1776 and 1778 constitutions bear two important lessons. First, they show that the Framers did not understand the phrase "declare war" to amount to the power to "make war" or "commence war"— phrases the South Carolina constitution used to refer specifically to initiating war. Second, the South Carolina constitutions provide an example of constitutional language that clearly and explicitly created a legislature-dominated warmaking system—one that the Framers did not adopt.

Usage of these words during the late eighteenth century further supports the distinction between "declare" and "begin" or "commence." Recall that

Article I. Section 10 uses the phrase "engage in War," and Article III uses "levying War." Johnson's dictionary, for example, defined "engage" as "to embark in an affair; to enter in an undertaking," or "to conflict; to fight." Johnson defined "levy" as "to raise, applied to war."[16] Other dictionaries of the period drew a similar distinction between "declare" and "engage" or "levy." Nathan Bailey's English dictionary defined "declare" as "to make known, to manifest, publish, or shew," while "engage" meant "to encounter or fight," and "levy" to "raise."[17] Thomas Sheridan's dictionary defined "declare" as "to make known," "engage" as "to conflict, to fight," and levy as "to raise, to bring together men."[18] All three defined "commence," as used by the South Carolina constitution, as "to begin." Even today, we commonly think of the statutes that establish public programs and mandates as "authorization" statutes (to be followed by appropriations), not "declaring" statutes. A declaration does not authorize or make, it recognizes and proclaims.

When the Framers employed "declare" in a constitutional context, they usually used it in a juridical manner, in the sense that courts "declare" the state of the law or the legal status of a certain event or situation. An example from early American political history—the Declaration of independence—illustrates this narrower meaning. The Declaration did not "authorize" military resistance to Great Britain. At the time that the Continental Congress met to draft the Declaration, hostilities had existed for more than a year, and Congress had been exercising sovereign powers—negotiating with Britain, sending representatives abroad, seeking aid—for at least two years.[19] Rather than authorize hostilities, the Declaration announced the legal relationship between the mother country and its former colonies. Thus, the Declaration of Independence appears in the form almost of a complaint, in which the revolutionaries recount their grievances (taxation without representation, suspension of the laws, use of bench trials), the remedy sought (independence), and the applicable law ("the Laws of Nature and of Nature's God"). The Declaration's importance was not in authorizing combat, but in transforming the legal status of the hostilities between Great Britain and her colonies from an insurrection to a war between equals. As historian David Armitage has observed, "in order to turn a civil war into a war between states, and thus to create legitimate corporate combatants out of individual rebels and traitors, it was essential to declare war and to obtain recognition of the legitimacy of such a declaration."[20] The Declaration of Independence was the nation's first declaration of war.

■   ■   ■

Declarations of war serve a purpose, albeit one that does not amount to the sole authority to initiate hostilities. Declarations do simply what they say they do: they declare. To use the eighteenth-century understanding, they make public, show openly, and make known the state of international legal relations between the United States and another nation. This is a different concept than whether the laws of war apply to the hostilities; two nations could technically not be at war, even though their forces might be engaged in limited combat (which would be governed by the laws of war). During the eighteenth century, declarations often took the form of a legal complaint in which a nation identified the grounds for waging war, explained the new rules that would apply to interaction between the two nations, and outlined the remedy. Declarations are also important for domestic constitutional purposes. Textually, a declaration of war places the nation in a state of total war, which triggers enhanced powers on the part of the federal government. The Fifth Amendment, for example, says that "[n]o person shall be held to answer for a capital, or otherwise infamous crime, unless on a presentment or indictment of a Grand Jury, except in cases arising in the land or naval forces, or in the Militia, when in actual service in time of War or public danger."

Congress has recognized the distinction between declared total wars and nondeclared hostilities by providing the executive branch with expanded domestic powers—such as seizing foreign property, conducting warrantless surveillance, arresting enemy aliens, and taking control of transportation systems, to name a few—only when war is declared.[21] Even the Supreme Court has suggested that in times of declared war, certain actions by the federal government would survive strict scrutiny but would certainly fail if attempted in peacetime. Thus, the terrible internment of Japanese Americans during World War II was justified only because the United States was in the midst of a war declared by Congress.[22] One doubts whether the courts would have allowed the wholesale internment of Panamanian Americans during the 1989 Panama War, or of Yugoslavs during the Kosovo conflict, or of all Iraqis Americans during the recent invasion and occupation of Iraq. Only a declaration of war from Congress could trigger and permit such extreme measures reserved only for total war.

▪   ▪   ▪

Practice and the Constitution

A more flexible approach to the allocation of war powers shows that, rather than violating the Constitution, the American way of war during the last decade has complied with the constitutional design. It is worth taking a closer look at recent conflicts to show that Congress has had an ample opportunity to consider and to check presidential initiatives in warmaking. In 2001 Afghanistan and 2003–4 Iraq, no declaration of war issued, that Congress did enact statutes "authorizing" the president to engage in armed combat. In response to the September 11, 2001 attacks, for example, Congress quickly enacted Senate Joint Resolution 23 "to authorize the use of the United States Armed Forces against those responsible for the recent attacks launched against the United States.[23] It found not only that the September 11 attacks constituted an "unusual and extraordinary threat to the national security and foreign policy of the United States" but also declared that "the President has authority under the Constitution to take action to deter and prevent acts of international terrorism against the United States," an admission, it seems of the president's inherent authority to use force without congressional permission. Congress then authorized the president to use military force against "those nations, organizations, or persons he determines planned, authorized, committed, or aided the terrorist attacks" of September 11, or "harbored such organizations or persons." In the course of enacting this legislation, Congress had a full opportunity to debate the merits of using military force abroad, particularly in Afghanistan.

Even if such legislation had never been considered, Congress had several other moments to block presidential efforts to wage war against al Qaeda. Military operations in Afghanistan have required additional funds, which President Bush initially requested as part of a $20 billion emergency appropriations bill in October of 2001, which was granted by Congress. The expense of modern war has required ongoing demands for appropriations, with another bill enacted on July 23, 2002 that appropriated more than $4 billion for continuing operations in Afghanistan. Even before the war in Iraq, military operations in Afghanistan and around the world generated approximately $2.5 billion in additional costs per month that require periodic supplemental appropriations to refill the Pentagon's coffers. In the fall of 2001, Congress also enacted a Defense Department authorization bill that determines the military's size, force structure, and weapons systems. If Congress had wanted to prevent the war in Afghanistan, or if it had disagreed with the continuing role of American troops there, it could have refused to provide the funds needed to pay for the personnel, material, and operational expenses of waging the war. War went ahead without a declaration, and Congress had every chance to consider the merits of the conflict and to prevent it.

Congress similarly had ample opportunity to prevent President Bush from ordering the invasion of Iraq.

■   ■   ■

One might respond that it is unreasonable to expect Congress to use its appropriations powers to cut off troops in the field. . . . We should not, however, mistake a failure of political will for a violation of the constitution.

NOTES

1. Michael D. Ramsey, *Textualism and War Powers,* 69 U. Chi. L. Rev. 1590–1609 (2002).
2. Michael J. Glennon, Constitutional Diplomacy 17 (1990).
3. I Samuel Johnson, A Dictionary of the English Language (W. Strahan ed., 1755).
4. Adrian Vermeule and Ernest Young, *Hercules, Herbert, and Amar: The Trouble with Intratextualism,* 113 Harv. L. Rev. 730 (2000). But see Akhil Reed Amar, *Intratextualism,* 112 Harv. L. Rev. 747 (1999).
5. U.S. Const. art. I, § 10.

6. I have had the pleasure of engaging (not declaring) in several direct, published exchanges with pro-Congress scholars on war powers. See, e.g., Ramsey, *supra* note 1; Louis Fisher, Presidential War Power 11 (1995). None of them has ever explained the difference in language between Article I, Section 8 and Article I, Section 10 other than to say that there is nothing wrong with using different language in different parts of the Constitution.

7. U.S. Const. art. I, § 8, cl. 11

8. Jane E. Stromseth, *Understanding Constitutional War Powers Today: Why Methodology Matters,* 106 Yale L.J. 845, 854 (1996) (quoting Jules Lobel, *Covert War and Congressional Authority: Hidden War and Forgotten Power,* 134 U. Pa. L. Rev. 1035, 1045 [1986]). See also Charles A. Lofgren, *War-Making under the Constitution: The Original Understanding,* 81 Yale L.J. 672 (1972).

9. Privateers sought to capture enemy merchant vessels with the object of selling their cargoes back home. As individualistic commercial entrepreneurs, they failed miserably at actual fighting and did not coordinate their efforts with the American navy. See C. Kevin Marshall, Comment, *Putting Privateers in Their Place: The Applicability of the Marque and Reprisal Clause to Undeclared Wars,* 64 U. Chi. L. Rev. 953, 974–81 (1997); John C. Yoo, *The Continuation of Politics by Other Means: The Original Understanding of War Powers,* 84 Cal. L. Rev. 167, 250–52 (1996).

10. The Declare War Clause also comes immediately after another provision that is directly about legal effect and consequence. The immediate clause before gives Congress the authority "To define and punish Piracies and Felonies committed on the high Seas, and Offenses against the Law of Nations." Like the declare war power, this clause vests Congress with the authority to "define" the legal status of certain actions that, in its mind, constitute piracy, felonies, or violations of international law. It may then enact legislation criminalizing those actions. Similarly, the Declare War Clause gives Congress the power to "declare" whether the a certain state of affairs legally constitutes a war, which then gives it the authority to enact wartime regulations of individual persons and property both within and outside the United States.

11. Jerrilyn Greene Marston, King and Congress: The Transfer of Political Legitimacy, 1774–1776, at 303 (1987) (arguing that "the executive and administrative responsibilities that had been exercised by or under the aegis of the king's authority were confided to the successor to his authority, the Congress").

12. Articles of Confederation art. IX (1777).

13. Article IX also gave Congress the power to "establish[ ] rules for deciding, in all cases, what captures on land or water shall be legal," and "of granting letters of marque and reprisal in times of peace." Articles of Confederation art. IX. Both provisions remained substantially unchanged in the Constitution, and, in fact, they appear in the same clause as the power to declare war. The Framers' alteration of Congress's authority from determining on peace and war to declaring war, while leaving the other provisions unchanged, indicates an intention to alter Congress's war power.

14. See Yoo, *supra* note 9, at 222–23; Willi Paul Adams, The First American Constitutions: Republican Ideology and the Making of the State Constitution in the Revolutionary Era 271 (Rita and Robert Kimber trans., 1980).

15. S.C. Const. art XXVI (1776), reprinted in The Federal and State Constitutions, Colonial Charters, and Other Organic Laws 3247 (Francis N. Thorpe ed., 1909).

16. Johnson, *supra* note 3.

17. Nathan Bailey, An Universal Etymological English Dictionary (Neill ed., 24th ed. 1782).

18. Thomas Sheridan, A General Dictionary of the English Language (Dodsley ed., 1780).

19. See David Armitage, *The Declaration of Independence and International Law*, 59 Wm. & Mary Q. 39 (2002).

20. Id. at 39.

21. See, e.g., 50 U.S.C. § 5(b)(I)(1994 & Supp. 1999) (seizure of foreign property); 50 U.S.C. § 1811 (1994) (electronic surveillance); 50 U.S.C. § 1829 (1994) (physical searches); 50 U.S.C. § 1844 (Supp. 1999) (trap and trace devices); 50 U.S.C. § 21 (1994) (seizure of aliens); 10 U.S.C. § 2644 (1994 & Supp. 1996) (seizure of transportation systems).

22. *Korematsu v. United States*, 323 U.S. 214, 216 (1944) (upholding racial classifications during World War II and noting that "legal restrictions which curtail the civil rights of a single racial group" may be justified by "[p]ressing public necessity").

23. Joint Resolution to Authorize the Use of United States Armed Forces against Those Responsible for the Recent Attacks against the United States, Pub. L. No. 107–40, 115 Stat. 224 (2001).

17.2

BARACK OBAMA

Speech to the United Nations General Assembly, September 23, 2009

In this speech, President Obama discussed many of the foreign policy and security issues facing the United States and the rest of the world. It is notable for its change of tone from the previous George W. Bush administration. The speech highlights how Obama is more interested in collaborating with other countries and in using the tools of diplomacy than was his predecessor. His warm remarks toward the UN itself signal a change in approach in comparison with Bush, from one of skepticism and direct confrontation to one of finding common ground and working through international institutions.

Good morning. Mr. President, Mr. Secretary-General, fellow delegates, ladies and gentlemen, it is my honor to address you for the first time as the 44th president of the United States.

I come before you humbled by the responsibility that the American people have placed upon me, mindful of the enormous challenges of our moment in history, and determined to act boldly and collectively on behalf of justice and prosperity at home and abroad. I have been in office for just nine months, though some days it seems a lot longer.

I am well aware of the expectations that accompany my presidency around the world. These expectations are not about me. Rather, they are rooted, I believe, in the discontent with the status quo that has allowed us to be increasingly defined by our differences and outpaced by our problems.

But they are also rooted in hope. The hope that real change is possible and the hope that America will be a leader in bringing about such change.

I took office at a time when many around the world had come to view America with skepticism and distrust. A part of this was due to misperceptions and misinformation about my country. Part of this was due to opposition to specific policies and a belief on, on certain critical issues, America had acted unilaterally without regard for the interests of others.

And this is has fed an almost reflexive anti-Americanism which, too often, has served as an excuse for collective inaction.

Now, like all of you, my responsibility is to act in the interests of my nation and my people. And I will never apologize for defending those interests. But it is my deeply held belief that, in the year 2009, more than at any point in human history, the interests of nations and peoples are shared. The religious convictions that we hold in our hearts can forge new bonds among people or they can tear us apart.

The technology we harness could light the path to peace or forever darken it. The energy we use can sustain our planet or destroy it. What happens to the hope of a single child anywhere can enrich our world or impoverish it.

In this hall, we come from many places, but we share a common future. No longer do we have the luxury of indulging our differences to the exclusion of the work that we must do together. I have carried this message from London to Ankara, from Port of Spain to Moscow, from Accra to Cairo, and it is what I will speak about today.

Because the time has come for the world to move in a new direction, we must embrace a new era of engagement based on mutual interest and mutual respect. And our work must begin now.

We know the future will be forged by deeds and not simply words. Speeches alone will not solve our problem. It will take persistent action. For those who question the character and cause of my nation, I ask you to look at the concrete actions we have taken in just nine months.

On my first day in office, I prohibited without expectation or equivocation the use of torture by the United States of America.

I ordered the prison at Guantanamo Bay closed. And we are doing the hard work of forging a framework to combat extremism within the rule of law.

Every nation must know America will live its values, and we will lead by example. We have set a clear and focused goal to work with all members of this body to disrupt, dismantle and defeat Al Qaeda and its extremist allies, a network that has killed thousands of people of many faiths and nations and that plotted to blow up this very building.

In Afghanistan and Pakistan, we and many nations here are helping these governments develop the capacity to take the lead in this effort, while working to advance opportunity and security for their people.

In Iraq, we are responsibly ending a war. We have removed American combat brigades from Iraqi cities and set a deadline of next August to remove all our combat brigades from Iraqi territory. And I have made clear that we will help Iraqis transition to full responsibility for their future and keep our commitment to remove all American troops by the end of 2011.

I have outlined a comprehensive agenda to seek the goal of a world without nuclear weapons. In Moscow, the United States and Russia announced that we would pursue substantial reductions in our strategic warheads and launchers. At the Conference on Disarmament, we agreed on a work plan to negotiate an end to the production of fissile materials for nuclear weapons. And this week, my secretary of state will become the first senior American representative to the annual members conference of the Comprehensive Test Ban Treaty.

Upon taking office, I appointed a special envoy for Middle East peace. And America has worked steadily and aggressively to advance the cause of two states, Israel and Palestine, in which peace and security take root and the rights of both Israelis and Palestinians are respected.

To confront climate change, we have invested $80 billion in clean energy. We have substantially increased our fuel-efficiency standards. We have provided new incentives for conservation, launched an energy partnership across the Americas, and moved from a bystander to a leader in international climate negotiations.

To overcome an economic crisis that touches every corner of the world, we worked with the G-20 nations to forge a coordinated international response of over $2 trillion in stimulus to bring the global economy back from the brink. We mobilized resources that helped prevent the crisis from spreading further to developing countries, and we joined with others to launch a $20 billion global food security initiative that will lend a hand to those who need it most and help them build their own capacity.

We have also re-engaged the United Nations. We have paid our bills. We have joined the Human Rights Council.

We have signed the Convention on the Rights of Persons with Disabilities. We have fully embraced the Millennium Development Goals, and we address our priorities here in this institution, for instance, through the Security Council meeting that I will chair tomorrow on nuclear nonproliferation and disarmament and through the issues that I will discuss today.

This is what we have already done, but this is just a beginning. Some of our actions have yielded progress. Some have laid the groundwork for progress in the future. But make no mistake: This cannot solely be America's endeavor.

Those who used to chastise America for acting alone in the world cannot now stand by and wait for America to solve the world's problems alone. We have sought in word and deed a new era of engagement with the world, and now is the time for all of us to take our share of responsibility for a global response to global challenges.

If we are honest with ourselves, we need to admit that we are not living up to that responsibility. Consider the course that we're on if we fail to confront the status quo: extremists sowing terror in pockets of the world, protracted conflicts that grind on and on, genocide, mass atrocities, more nations with nuclear weapons, melting ice caps and ravaged populations, persistent poverty and pandemic disease.

I say this not to sow fear but to state a fact. The magnitude of our challenges has yet to be met by the measure of our actions.

This body was founded on the belief that the nations of the world could solve their problems together. Franklin Roosevelt died before he could see his vision for this institution become a reality. He put it this way, and I quote, "The structure of world peace should not be the work of one man or one party or one nation. It cannot be a peace of large nations or of small nations. It must be a peace which rests on the cooperative effort of the whole world."

Cooperative effort of the whole world—those words ring even more true today, but it is not simply peace but our very health and prosperity that we hold in common. Yet we also know that this body is made up of sovereign states and, sadly but not surprisingly, this body has often become a forum for sowing discord instead of forging common ground, a venue for playing politics and exploiting grievances rather than solving problems.

After all, it is easy to walk up to this podium and point fingers and stoke divisions. Nothing is easier than blaming others for our troubles and absolving ourselves of responsibility for our choices and our actions. Anybody can do that.

Responsibility and leadership in the 21st century demand more. In an era when our destiny is shared, power is no longer a zero-sum game. No one nation can or should try to dominate other nation. No world order that elevates one nation or group of people over another will succeed.

No balance of power among nations will hold. The traditional divisions between nations of the south and the north make no sense in an interconnected world nor do alignments of nations rooted in the cleavages of a long-gone Cold War.

The time has come to realize that the old habits, the old arguments are irrelevant to the challenges faced by our people. They lead nations to act in opposition to the very goals that they claim to pursue and to vote, often in this body, against the interests of their own people.

They build up walls between us and the future that our people seek. And the time has come for those walls to come down. Together, we must build new coalitions that bridge old divides, coalitions of different faiths and creeds, of northern and south, east, west, black, white, and brown.

The choice is ours. We can be remembered as a generation that chose to drag the arguments of 20th century into the 21st, that put off hard choices, refused to look ahead, failed to keep pace because we defined ourselves by what we were against instead of what we were for. Or we can be a generation that chooses to see the shoreline beyond the rough waters ahead; that comes together to serve the common interests of human beings and finally gives meaning to the promise embedded in the nation given to this institution, the United Nations.

That is the future America wants; a future of peace and prosperity that we can only reach if we recognize that all nations have rights but all nations have responsibilities as well. That is the bargain that makes this work. That must be the guiding principle of international cooperation.

Today, let me put forward four pillars that I believe are fundamental to the future that we want for our children. Nonproliferation and disbarment, the promotion of peace and security, the preservation of our planet, and a global economy that advances opportunity for all people.

First, we must stop the spread of nuclear weapons and seek the goal of a world without them. This institution was founded at the dawn of the atomic age, in part, because man's capacity to kill had to be contained. For decades, we averted disaster even under the shadow of a superpower standoff. But today the threat of proliferation is growing in scope and complexity.

If we fail to act, we will invite nuclear arms races in every region and the prospect of wars and acts of terror on a scale that we can hardly imagine.

A fragile consensus stands in the way of this frightening outcome, and that is the basic bargain that shapes the Nuclear Non-Proliferation Treaty. It says that all nations have the right to peaceful nuclear energy, that nations with nuclear weapons have a responsibility to move toward disarmament, and those without them have the responsibility to forsake them. The next 12 months could be pivotal in determining whether this compact will be strengthened or will slowly dissolve.

America intends to keep our end of the bargain. We will pursue a new agreement with Russia to substantially reduce our strategic warheads and launchers. We will move forward with ratification of the test ban treaty and work with others to bring the treaty into force so that nuclear testing is permanently prohibited.

We will complete a Nuclear Posture Review that opens the door to deeper cuts and reduces the role of nuclear weapons. And we will call upon countries to begin negotiations in January on a treaty to end the production of fissile material for weapons.

I will also host a summit next April that reaffirms each nation's responsibility to secure nuclear material on its territory and to help those who can't, because we must never allow a single nuclear device to fall into the hands of a violent extremist. And we will work to strengthen the institutions and initiatives that combat nuclear smuggling and theft.

All of this must support efforts to strengthen the NPT. Those nations that refuse to live up to their obligations must face consequences. Let me be clear: This is not about singling out individual nations. It is about standing up for the rights of all nations that do live up to their responsibilities, because a world in which IAEA inspections are avoided and the United Nations' demands are ignored will leave all people less safe and all nations less secure.

In their actions to date, the governments of North Korea and Iran threaten to take us down this dangerous slope. We respect their rights as members of the community of nations. I have said before and I will repeat: I am committed to diplomacy that opens a path to greater prosperity and more secure peace for both nations if they live up to their obligations.

But if the governments of Iran and North Korea choose to ignore international standards, if they put the pursuit of nuclear weapons ahead of regional stability and the security and opportunity of their own people, if they are oblivious to the dangers of escalating nuclear arms races in both East Asia and the Middle East, then they must be held accountable.

The world must stand together to demonstrate that international law is not an empty promise and that treaties will be enforced. We must insist that the future does not belong to fear.

That brings me to the second pillar for our future: the pursuit of peace.

The United Nations was born of the belief that the people of the world can live their lives, raise their families and resolve their differences peacefully. And yet we know that in too many parts of the world this ideal remains an abstraction, a distant dream.

We can either accept that outcome as inevitable and tolerate constant and crippling conflict or we can recognize that the yearning for peace is universal and reassert our resolve to end conflicts around the world.

That effort must begin with an unshakable determination that the murder of innocent men, women and children will never be tolerated. On this, no one can be—there can be no dispute.

The violent extremists who promote conflict by distorting faith have discredited and isolated themselves. They offer nothing but hatred and destruction. In confronting them, America will forge lasting partnerships to target terrorists, share intelligence, and coordinate law enforcement, and protect our people.

We will permit no safe haven for al Qaeda to launch attacks from Afghanistan or any other nation. We will stand by our friends on the front lines, as we and many nations will do in pledging support for the Pakistani people tomorrow. And we will pursue positive engagement that builds bridges among faiths and new partnerships for opportunity.

Our efforts to promote peace, however, cannot be limited to defeating violent extremists for the most powerful weapon in our arsenal is the hope of human beings, the belief that the future belongs to those who would build and not destroy, the confidence that conflicts can end and a new day can begin.

And that is why we will support—we will strengthen our support for effective peacekeeping while energizing our efforts to prevent conflicts before they take hold. We will pursue a lasting peace in Sudan through support for the people of Darfur and the implementation of the comprehensive peace agreement so that we secure the peace that the Sudanese people deserve.

And in countries ravaged by violence from Haiti to Congo to East Timor, we will work with the U.N. and other partners to support an enduring peace. I will also continue to seek a just and lasting peace [in] Israel, Palestine and the Arab world.

We will continue to work on that issue. . . .

Yesterday, I had a constructive meeting with Prime Minister [Benjamin] Netanyahu and President [Mahmoud] Abbas. We have made some progress. Palestinians have strengthened their efforts on security. Israelis have facilitated greater freedom of movement for the Palestinians. As a result of these efforts on both sides, the economy in the West Bank has begun to grow, but more progress is needed.

We continue to call on Palestinians to end incitement against Israel. And we continue to emphasize that America does not accept the legitimacy of continued Israeli settlements.

The time has come—the time has come to relaunch negotiations without preconditions that address the permanent status issues, security for Israelis and Palestinians, borders, refugees and Jerusalem. The goal is clear: Two states living side by side in peace and security; a Jewish state of Israel with true security for all Israelis and a viable, independent Palestinian state with contiguous territory that ends the occupation that began in 1967 and realizes the potential of the Palestinian people.

Now, as we pursue this goal, we will also pursue peace between Israel and Lebanon, Israel and Syria, and a broader peace between Israel and its many neighbors. In pursuit of that goal, we will develop regional initiatives with multilateral participation alongside bilateral negotiations.

Now, I am not naive. I know this will be difficult. But all of us—not just the Israelis and the Palestinians—but all of us must decide whether we are serious about peace or whether we will only lend it lip service. To break the old patterns, to break the cycle of insecurity and despair, all of us must say publicly what we would acknowledge in private.

The United States does Israel no favors when we fail to couple an unwavering commitment to its security with an insistence that Israel respect the legitimate claims and rights of the Palestinians.

And nations within this body do the Palestinians no favors when they choose vitriolic attacks against Israel over constructive willingness to recognize Israel's legitimacy and its right to exist in peace and security.

We must remember that the greatest price of this conflict is not paid by us. It's not paid by politicians. It's paid by the Israeli girl in Sderot who closes her eyes in fear that a rocket will take her life in the middle of the night. It's paid for by the Palestinian boy in Gaza who has no clean water and no country to call his own.

These are all God's children. And, after all the politics and all the posturing, this is about the right of every human being to live with dignity and security. That is a lesson embedded in the three great faiths that call one small slice of Earth the Holy Land. And that is why—even though there will be setbacks, and false starts, and tough days—I will not waiver in my pursuit of peace.

Third, we must recognize that in the 21st century there will be no peace unless we take responsibility for the preservation of our planet.

And I thank the secretary-general for hosting the subject of climate change yesterday.

The danger posed by climate change cannot be denied. Our responsibility to meet it must not be deferred. If we continue down our current course, every member of this assembly will see irreversible changes within their borders.

Our efforts to end conflicts will be eclipsed by wars over refugees and resources. Development will be devastated by drought and famine. Land that human beings have lived on for millennia will disappear. Future generations will look back and wonder why we refused to act, why we failed to pass on—why we failed to pass on an environment that was worthy of our inheritance.

And that is why the days when America dragged its feet on this issue are over. We will move forward with investments to transform our energy economy, while providing incentives to make clean energy the profitable kind of energy.

We will press ahead with deep cuts in emissions to reach the goals that we set for 2020 and eventually 2050.

We will continue to promote renewable energy and efficiency and share new technologies with countries around the world. And we will seize every opportunity for progress to address this threat in a cooperative effort with the entire world.

Now, those wealthy nations that did so much damage to the environment in the 20th century must accept our obligation to lead, but responsibility does not end there. While we must acknowledge the need for differentiated responses, any effort to curb carbon emissions must include the fast-growing carbon emitters who can do more to reduce their air pollution without inhibiting growth.

And any effort that fails to help the poorest nations both adapt to the problems that climate change have already wrought and help them travel a path of clean development simply will not work.

It's hard to change something as fundamental as how we use energy. I know that. It's even harder to do so in the midst of a global recession. Certainly, it will be tempting to sit back and wait for others to move first.

But we cannot make this journey unless we all move forward together. As we head into Copenhagen, let us resolve to focus on what each of us can do for the sake of our common future.

This leads me to the final pillar that must fortify our future: a global economy that advances opportunity for all people.

The world is still recovering from the worst economic crisis since the Great Depression. In America, we see the engine of growth beginning to churn, and yet many still struggle to find a job or pay their bills. Across the globe, we find promising signs, but little certainty about what lies ahead.

And far too many people in far too many places live through the daily crises that challenge our humanity: the despair of an empty stomach; the thirst brought on by dwindling water supplies; the injustice of a child dying from a treatable disease; or a mother losing her life as she gives birth.

In Pittsburgh, we will work with the world's largest economies to chart a course for growth that is balanced and sustained. That means vigilance to ensure that we do not let up until our people are back to work. That means taking steps to rekindle demand so that a global recovery can be sustained. And that means setting new rules of the road and strengthening regulation for all financial centers, so that we put an end to the greed and the excess and the abuse that led us into this disaster and prevent a crisis like this from ever happening again.

At a time of such interdependence, we have a moral and pragmatic interests, however, in broader questions of development, the questions of development that existed even before this crisis happened.

And so America will continue our historic effort to help people feed themselves. We have set aside $63 billion to carry forward the fight against HIV/AIDS, to end deaths from tuberculosis and malaria, to eradicate polio and to strengthen public health systems.

We are joining with other countries to contribute H1N1 vaccines to the World Health Organization. We will integrate more economies into a system of global trade. We will support the Millennium Development Goals and approach next year's summit with a global plan to make them a reality. And we will set our sights on the eradication of extreme poverty in our time.

Now is the time for all of us to do our part. Growth will not be sustained or shared unless all nations embrace their responsibilities. And that means that wealthy nations must open their markets to more goods and extend a hand to those with less, while reforming international institutions to give more nations a greater voice.

And developing nations must root out the corruption that is an obstacle to progress, for opportunity cannot thrive where individuals are oppressed and business have to pay bribes. That is why we support honest police and independent judges, civil society and a vibrant private sector. Our goal is simple: a global economy in which growth is sustained and opportunity is available to all.

Now, the changes that I've spoken about today will not be easy to make, and they will not be realized simply by leaders like us coming together in forums like this, as useful as that may be.

For as in any assembly of members, real change can only come through the people we represent. That is why we must do the hard work to lay the groundwork for progress in our own capitals. That's where we will build the consensus to end conflicts and to harness technology for peaceful purposes, to change the way we use energy and to promote growth that can be sustained and shared.

I believe that the people of the world want this future for their children. And that is why we must champion those principles which ensure that governments reflect the will of the people. These principles cannot be afterthoughts; democracy and human rights are essential to achieving each of the goals that I've discussed today, because governments of the people and by the people are more likely to act in the broader interests of their own people, rather than narrow interests of those in power.

The test of our leadership will not be the degree to which we feed the fears and old hatreds of our people. True leadership will not be measured by the ability to muzzle dissent or to intimidate and harass political opponents at home.

The people of the world want change. They will not long tolerate those who are on the wrong side of history.

This assembly's charter commits each of us—and I quote—"to reaffirm faith in fundamental human rights, in the dignity and worth of the human person, in the equal rights of men and women." Among those rights is the freedom to speak your mind and worship as you please, the promise of equality of the races, and the opportunity for women and girls to pursue their own potential, the ability of citizens to have a say in how you are governed, and to have confidence in the administration of justice.

For just as no nation should be forced to accept the tyranny of another nation, no individual should be forced to accept the tyranny of their own people.

As—as an African-American, I will never forget that I would not be here today without the steady pursuit of a more perfect union in my country. That guides my belief that no matter how dark the day may seem, transformative change can be forged by those who choose to side with justice.

And I pledge that America will always stand with those who stand up for their dignity and their rights, for the student who seeks to learn, the voter who demands to be heard, the innocent who longs to be free, the oppressed who yearns to be equal.

Democracy cannot be imposed on any nation from the outside. Each society must search for its own path, and no path is perfect. Each country will pursue a path rooted in the culture of its people and in its past traditions, and I admit that America has, too often, been selective in its promotion of democracy.

But that does not weaken our commitment. It only reinforces it. There are basic principles that are universal. There are certain truths which are self-evident, and the United States of America will never waiver in our efforts to stand up for the right of people everywhere to determine their own destiny.

Sixty-five years ago, a weary Franklin Roosevelt spoke to the American people in his fourth and final inaugural address. After years of war, he sought to sum up the lessons that could be drawn from the terrible suffering, the enormous sacrifice that had taken place. We have learned, he said, to be citizens of the world, members of the human community.

The United Nations was built by men and women like Roosevelt from every corner of the world, from Africa and Asia, Europe to the Americas. These architects of international cooperation had an idealism that was anything but naive. It was rooted in the hard-earned lessons of war, rooted in the wisdom that nations could advance their interests by acting together instead of splitting apart.

Now, it falls to us. Where this institution will be what we make of it, the United Nations does extraordinary good around the world feeding the hungry, caring for the sick, mending place that have been broken. But it also struggles to enforce its will and to live up to the ideals of its founding.

I believe that those imperfections are not a reason to walk away from this institution. They are a calling to redouble our efforts. The United Nations can either with a place where we bicker about outdated grievances or forge common ground, a place where we focus on what drives us apart or what brings us together, a place where we indulge tyranny or a source of moral authority.

In short, the United Nations can be an institution that is disconnected from what matters in the lives of our citizens or it can be an indispensable factor in advancing the interests of the people we serve.

We have reached a pivotal moment. The United States stands ready to begin a new chapter of international cooperation, one that recognizes the rights and responsibilities of all nations. So with confidence in our cause and with a commitment to our values, we call on all nations to join us in building the future that our people so richly deserve.

Thank you very much, everyone.

ACKNOWLEDGMENTS

Aldrich, John H.: From *Why Parties* by John H. Aldrich. Reprinted with the permission of the University of Chicago Press.

Arnold, R. Douglas: From *The Logic of Congressional Action* by R. Douglas Arnold. Reprinted with the permission of Yale University Press.

Baum, Lawrence: Baum, Lawrence, *Judges and Their Audiences.* © 2006 by Princeton University Press. Reprinted by permission of Princeton University Press.

Baumgartner, Frank R., and Bryan D. Jones: "Two Models of Issue Expansion" from *Agendas and Instability in American Politics.* Copyright © 1993, 2009 by The University of Chicago. Reprinted with the permission of the University of Chicago Press.

Bednar, Jenna: *James Madison: The Theory and Practice of Republican Government* edited by Samuel Kernell. Copyright © 2003 by the Board of Trustees of the Leland Stanford Jr. University.

Bickel, Alexander M.: Bickel, *Least Dangerous Branch,* 1st edition, © 1962. Adapted by permission of Pearson Education, Inc., Upper Saddle River, NJ.

Burns, Nancy, Kay Schlozman, and Sidney Verba: "The Political Worlds of Men and Women" reprinted by permission of the publisher from *The Private Roots of Public Action: Gender, Equality and Political Participation* by Nancy Burns, Kay Lehman Schlozman and Sidney Verba, pp. 99–133, Cambridge, Mass.: Harvard University Press. Copyright © 2001 by the President and Fellows of Harvard College.

Cameron, Charles: From *Presidential Power* by Charles Cameron. Copyright © 2000 by Columbia University Press. Reprinted with permission of the publisher.

Campbell, Angus, Philip E. Converse, Warren Edward Miller, and Donald E.

Stokes: "The Impact of Party Identification" from *The American Voter: An Abridgement* by Angus Campbell, Philip E. Converse, Warren Edward Miller, Donald E. Stokes. Copyright © 1960 by John Wiley & Sons, Inc.

Carpenter, Daniel: Carpenter, Daniel, *The Forging of Bureaucratic Autonomy.* Princeton University Press. Reprinted by permission of Princeton University Press.

Cox, Gary W., and Mathew D. McCubbins: "Procedural Cartel Theory" from *Setting the Agenda: Responsible Party Government in the U.S. House of Representatives,* Gary W. Cox and Matthew D. McCubbins. Reprinted with the permission of Cambridge University Press.

Cranes-Wrone, Brandice: From *Who Leads Whom?* by Brandice Canes-Wrone. Reprinted with the permission of the University of Chicago Press.

Dawson, Michael: Dawson, Michael C., *Behind the Mule.* © 1994 Princeton University Press, 1995 paperback edition. Reprinted by permission of Princeton University Press.

Groseclose, Timothy, and Jeffrey Milyo: Tim Groseclose and Jeffrey Milyo, "A Measure of Media Bias" 120:4 (November, 2005) pp. 1191–1237 © 2005 by the President and Fellows of Harvard College and the Massachusetts Institute of Technology.

Hardin, Garrett: "The Tragedy of the Commons" from *Science,* Vol. 152, pp. 1243–1248 (1968). Reprinted with permission from AAAS.

Howell, William G.: Howell, William G., *Power without Persuasion.* Princeton University Press. Reprinted by permission of Princeton University Press.

Ifill, Gwen: From *The Break-through: Politics and Race in the Age of Obama* by Gwen Ifill, copyright © 2009 by Gwen Ifill. Used by permission of Doubleday, a division of Random House, Inc.

Iyengar, Shanto, and Jennifer McGrady: From *Media Politics: A Citizen's Guide* by Shanto Iyengar and Jennifer A. McGrady. Copyright © 2007 by W. W. Norton & Company, Inc.

Jacobson, Gary: Excerpts pp. 1–15 and 119–147 from *A Divider, Not a Uniter: George W. Bush and the American People* by Gary C. Jacobson. Copyright © 2008 by Pearson Education, Inc. Reprinted by permission.

Kiewiet, D. Roderick, and Mathew McCubbins: From *Logic of Delegation* by D. Roderick Kiewiet and Mathew McCubbins. Reprinted by permission of the University of Chicago Press.

Kollman, Ken: From *Outside Lobbying: Public Opinion and Interest Group Strategies* by Ken Kollman. Copyright © 1998 by Princeton University Press. Reprinted by permission of Princeton University Press.

Luker, Kristin: "World Views of the Activists" from *Abortion and the Politics of Motherhood* by Kristin Luker. Copyright © 1984 by The Regents of the University of California. Reprinted by permission of University of California Press.

Lupia, Arthur, and Mathew D. McCubbins: Chapter 1 "Knowledge Democratic and the Foundation of Democracy" from *The Democratic Dilemma: Can Citizens Learn What They Need to Know?* by Arthur Lupia and Mathew D. McCubbins. Reprinted with the permission of Cambridge University Press.

Mayhew, David: From *Congress: The Electoral Connection* by David Mayhew. Reprinted with the permission of Yale University Press.

McCarty, Nolan, Keith T. Poole, and Howard Rosenthal: McCarty, Nolan, Keith T. Poole, and Howard Rosenthal, *Polarized America: The Dance of Ideology and Unequal Riches*, pp. 1–11, 115–138, plus associated Notes © 2006 Massachusetts Institute of Technology, by permission of The MIT Press.

McCubbins, Mathew D., and Thomas Schwartz: "Congressional Oversight Overlooked: Police Patrol vs. Fire Alarms," *American Journal of Political Science*, Vol. 28, No. 12, pp. 165–179.

Moe, Terry M.: From *The Organization of Interests* by Terry Moe. Reprinted with the permission of the University of Chicago Press.

Neustadt, Richard E.: Reprinted with the permission of The Free Press, a Division of Simon and Schuster, Inc., from *Presidential Power and the Modern Presidents: The Politics of Leadership from Roosevelt to Reagan* by Richard E. Neustadt. Copyright © 1990 by Richard E. Neustadt. All rights reserved.

Olson Jr., Mancur: "A Theory of Groups and Organizations," reprinted by permission of the publisher from *The Logic of Collective Action: Public Goods and the Theory of Groups* by Mancur Olson, pp. 5–50, Cambridge, Mass.: Harvard University Press. Copyright © 1965, 1971 by the President and Fellows of Harvard College.

Riker, William: "Chapter 6: Is the Federal Bargain Worth Keeping?" from *Federalism: Origin, Operation, Significance*. Reprinted by permission of the Estate of William Riker.

Rosenstone, Steven, and John Mark Hansen: Excerpts pp. 10–37 from *Mobilization, Participation, and Democracy in America* by Steven J. Rosenstone and John Mark Hansen. Copyright © 2003 by Pearson Education Inc. Reprinted by permission.

Stiglitz, Joseph: From *Making Globalization Work* by Joseph E. Stiglitz. Copyright © 2006 by Joseph E. Stiglitz. Used by permission of W. W. Norton & Company, Inc.

Strolovitch, Dara: From *Affirmative Advocacy* by Dara Strolovitch. Reprinted with the permission of the University of Chicago Press.

Strom, Gerald: Strom, Gerald. *The Logic of Lawmaking: A Spatial Theory Approach*. Pp. 8–33 © 1990 The Johns Hopkins University Press. Reprinted with permission of The Johns Hopkins University Press.

Wilson, James Q.: From *Bureaucracy* by James Wilson. Reprinted by permission of Basic Books, a member of the Perseus Books Group.

Yoo, John: "Chapter 5: War Powers for a New World" from *Powers of War and Peace*, pp. 143–181. Reprinted by permission of the University of Chicago Press.